Victimology

Victimology

Seventh edition

William G. Doerner
Steven P. Lab

ELSEVIER

Amsterdam • Boston • Heidelberg • London
New York • Oxford • Paris • San Diego
San Francisco • Singapore • Sydney • Tokyo

Anderson Publishing is an imprint of Elsevier

Acquiring Editor: Shirley Decker-Lucke
Development Editor: Ellen S. Boyne
Project Manager: Julia Haynes
Designer: Tin Box Studio, Inc.

Anderson Publishing is an imprint of Elsevier
225 Wyman Street, Waltham, MA 02451, USA

Library of Congress Cataloging-in-Publication Data
A catalogue record for this book is available from the Library of Congress

British Library Cataloguing-in-Publication Data
A catalogue record for this book is available from the British Library

ISBN: 978-0-323-28765-4

For information on all Anderson publications
visit our website at http://store.elsevier.com

Typeset by TNQ Books and Journals
www.tnq.co.in

Printed in the United States of America

14 15 16 17 18   10 9 8 7 6 5 4 3 2 1

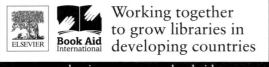

Working together
to grow libraries in
developing countries

www.elsevier.com • www.bookaid.org

Dedication

Thanks to my best friend and buddy—my wife Judy.

Bill Doerner

To Suz.

Steve P. Lab.

Contents

Online Resources

Thank you for selecting Anderson Publishing's *Victimology*, 7th edition. To complement the learning experience, we have provided online tools to accompany this edition.

Please consult your local sales representative with any additional questions. You may also e-mail the Academic Sales Team at textbook@elsevier.com

Qualified adopters and instructors can access valuable material for free by registering at: http://textbooks.elsevier.com/web/manuals.aspx?isbn=9780323287654

Students and other readers can access additional resources at: http://store.elsevier.com/product.jsp?&isbn=9780323287654

SECTION 1

Definition and Scope

The Scope of Victimology

INTRODUCTION

Something not very funny happened on the way to a formal system of justice. The victim was left out. As strange as it may sound, the bulk of history has seen crime victims become further removed from being an integral part of dealing with criminals. Fortunately, this trend is beginning to reverse itself. Recent years have seen an increased interest in the plight of crime victims and a movement toward reintegrating the victim into the criminal justice system. This chapter will look at the role of the victim throughout history and will trace the elimination of the victim from the social processing of criminal acts.

3

We will see how victimology emerged and we will investigate the resurgence of interest in the victim.

THE VICTIM THROUGHOUT HISTORY

Most people take the existence of the formal criminal justice system for granted. They do not realize that this method of handling deviant activity has not been the norm throughout history. Indeed, the modern version of criminal justice is a relatively new phenomenon. In days gone by, responsibility for dealing with offenders fell to the victim and the victim's kin. There were no "authorities" to turn to for help in "enforcing the law." Victims were expected to fend for themselves, and society acceded to this arrangement.

This state of affairs was not outlined in any set of laws or legal code. With rare exceptions, written laws did not exist. Codes of behavior reflected prevailing social norms. Society recognized murder and other serious affronts as *mala in se* (totally unacceptable behavior). However, it was up to victims or their survivors to decide what action to take against the offender. Victims who wished to respond to offenses could not turn to judges for assistance or to jails for punishment. These institutions did not exist yet. Instead, victims had to take matters into their own hands.

This depiction does not imply there were no provisions for victims to follow. Society recognized a basic system of retribution and restitution for offenders. In simplest terms, *retribution* meant the offender would suffer in proportion to the degree of harm caused by his or her actions. Oftentimes, retribution took the form of *restitution*, or making payment in an amount sufficient to render the victim whole again. If the offender was unable to make restitution, his or her kin were forced to assume the liability.

This response system emphasized the principle known as *lex talionis*—an eye for an eye, a tooth for a tooth. Punishment was commensurate with the harm inflicted upon the victim. Perhaps the most important feature of this system was that victims and their relatives handled the problem and were the beneficiaries of any payments. This arrangement was truly a "victim justice system."

This basic system of dealing with offensive behavior found its way into early codified laws. The Law of Moses, the Code of Hammurabi (2200 B.C.E.), and Roman law all entailed strong elements of individual responsibility for harms committed against others. Restitution and retribution were specific ingredients in many of these early codes. Part of the rationale behind this response was to deter such behavior in the future.

The major goal of *deterrence* is to prevent future transgressions. The thinking is that the lack of any enrichment or gain from criminal activity would make transgressive acts unattractive. Retribution and restitution attempt to reestablish the status quo that existed before the initial action of the offender. Thus, removing financial incentives would make it not profitable to commit crimes.

This basic system of dealing with offensive behavior remained intact throughout the Middle Ages. Eventually, though, it fell into disuse. Two factors signaled the end of this victim justice system. The first change was the move by feudal barons to lay a claim to any compensation offenders paid their victims (Schafer, 1968). These rulers saw this money as a lucrative way to increase their own riches. The barons accomplished this goal by redefining criminal acts as violations against the state, instead of the victim. This strategy recast the state (the barons being the heads of the state) as the aggrieved party. The victim diminished in stature and was relegated to the status of witness for the state. Now the state could step in and reap the benefits of restitution.

A second factor that reduced the victim's position was the enormous upheaval that was transforming society. Up until this time, society was predominantly rural and agrarian. People lived in small groups, eking out an existence from daily labor in the fields. Life was a rustic struggle to meet day-to-day needs.

People, for the most part, were self-sufficient and relied heavily upon their families for assistance. Families often lived in relative isolation from other people. Whenever a crime took place, it brought physical and economic harm not only to the individual victim, but also to the entire family network. This simple *gemeinschaft* society (Toennies, 1957) could rely on the individual to handle his or her own problems.

As the Middle Ages drew to a close, the Industrial Revolution created a demand for larger urbanized communities. People took jobs in the new industries, leaving the rural areas and relocating to the cities. They settled into cramped quarters, surrounded by strangers. Neighbors no longer knew the people living next door. As faces blended into crowds, relationships grew more depersonalized. The interpersonal ties that once bound people together had vanished.

As this *gesellschaft* type of society continued to grow, the old victim justice practices crumbled even further. Crime began to threaten the delicate social fabric that now linked people together. At the same time, concern shifted away from making the victim whole to dealing with the criminal. Gradually, the *victim* justice system withered and the *criminal* justice system became its replacement. In fact, some observers would contend that the victim *injustice* system would be a more apt description.

Today, crime victims remain nothing more than witnesses for the state. Victims no longer take matters into their own hands to extract retribution and restitution from their offenders. The victim must call upon society to act. The development of formal law enforcement, courts, and correctional systems in the past few centuries has reflected an interest in protecting the state. For the most part, the criminal justice system simply forgot about victims and their best interests. Instead, the focus shifted to protecting the rights of the accused.

THE RE-EMERGENCE OF THE VICTIM

The criminal justice system spends the bulk of its time and energy trying to control criminals. It was within this preoccupation of understanding criminal activity and identifying the causes of criminal behavior that the victim was "rediscovered" in the 1940s. Interestingly, the victim emerged not as an individual worthy of sympathy or compassion but as a possible partner or contributor to his or her own demise. Students of criminal behavior began to look at the relationship between the victim and the offender in the hopes of better understanding the genesis of the criminal act.

As interest in victims began to sprout and attract more scholarly attention, writers began to grapple with a very basic issue. What exactly was victimology? Some people believed that victimology was a specialty area or a subfield within criminology. After all, every criminal event had to include a criminal and a victim by definition. Others countered that because victimology was so broad and encompassing, it deserved to stand as a separate field or discipline in its own right. They foresaw the day when college catalogs would list victimology as a major area of study along with such pursuits as biology, criminology, psychology, mathematics, and political science.

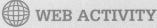 **WEB ACTIVITY**

The concept of *victim* and the growth of interest in victims can be examined through a range of materials available through the Office for Victims of Crime (**http://www.ovc.gov**) and the documents in the OVC archive (**http://ovc.gov/archive/index.html**).

Early scholarly work in victimology focused considerable energy upon creating victim typologies. A *typology* is an effort to categorize observations into logical groupings to reach a better understanding of our social world (McKinney, 1950, 1969). As we shall see in the following sections, these early theoretical reflections pushed the field in a direction that eventually created an explosive and haunting reaction, nearly crippling this fledgling enterprise.

The Work of Hans von Hentig: *The Criminal and His Victim*

An early pioneer in victimology was a German scholar, Hans von Hentig. As a criminologist, von Hentig spent much time trying to discover what made a criminal predisposed to being a criminal. As he focused on crime victims, von Hentig began to wonder what it was that made the victim a victim. The key ingredient, according to von Hentig, was the *criminal–victim dyad.*

In an early publication, von Hentig (1941) claimed the victim was often a contributing cause to the criminal act. One example would be an incident in which the ultimate victim began as the aggressor. However, for some reason, this person wound up becoming the loser in the confrontation. Von Hentig's message was clear. Simply examining the outcome of a criminal event sometimes presents a distorted image of who the real victim is and who the real offender is. A closer inspection of the dynamics underlying the situation might reveal that the victim was a major contributor to his or her own victimization.

Von Hentig expanded upon the notion of the victim as an *agent provocateur* in a later book called *The Criminal and His Victim.* He explained that "increased attention should be paid to the crime-provocative function of the victim. … With a thorough knowledge of the interrelations between doer and sufferer new approaches to the detection of crime will be opened" (1948: 450).

Von Hentig was not naive enough to believe that all victim contribution to crime was active. Much victim contribution results from characteristics or social positions beyond the control of the individual. As a result, von Hentig classified victims into 13 categories depending upon their propensity for victimization (Table 1.1).

Many of von Hentig's victim types reflect the inability to resist a perpetrator due to physical, social, or psychological disadvantages. For example, very young people, females, and elderly persons are more likely to lack the physical power to resist offenders. Immigrants and minorities, because of cultural differences, may feel they are outside the mainstream of society. This lack of familiarity may lead them into situations in which criminals prey upon them. Individuals who are mentally defective or deranged, "dull normal," depressed, lonesome, or blocked may not understand what is occurring around them or may be unable to resist. The acquisitive person and the tormentor are individuals who, due to their own desires, are either directly involved in the criminal act or place themselves in situations in which there is a clear potential for victimization.

The typology that von Hentig created does not imply that the victim is always the primary cause of the criminal act. What he does suggest is that victim characteristics may contribute to the victimization episode. According to von Hentig (1948: iii), we must realize "the victim is taken as one of the determinants, and that a nefarious symbiosis is often established between doer and sufferer…"

Table 1.1 Hans von Hentig's Victim Typology	
Type	**Example**
1. The Young	Children and infants
2. The Female	All women
3. The Old	Elderly persons
4. The Mentally Defective and Deranged	The feeble-minded, the insane, drug addicts, alcoholics
5. Immigrants	Foreigners unfamiliar with the culture
6. Minorities	Racially disadvantaged persons
7. Dull Normals	Simple-minded persons
8. The Depressed	Persons with various psychological maladies
9. The Acquisitive	The greedy, those looking for quick gains
10. The Wanton	Promiscuous persons
11. The Lonesome and the Heartbroken	Widows, widowers, and those in mourning
12. The Tormentor	An abusive parent
13. The Blocked, Exempted, or Fighting	Victims of blackmail, extortion, confidence games

Source: Adapted from von Hentig, H. (1948). The Criminal and His Victim: Studies in the Sociobiology of Crime. *New Haven: Yale University Press, pp. 404–438.*

The Work of Beniamin Mendelsohn: Further Reflections

Some observers credit Beniamin Mendelsohn, a practicing attorney, with being the "father" of victimology. Indeed, he coined the term *victimology*. Mendelsohn, like von Hentig, was intrigued by the dynamics that take place between victims and offenders. Before preparing a case, he would ask victims, witnesses, and bystanders in the situation to complete a detailed and probing questionnaire. After examining these responses, Mendelsohn discovered that usually there was a strong interpersonal relationship between victims and offenders. Using these data, Mendelsohn (1956) outlined a six-step classification of victims based on legal considerations of the degree of the victim's blame (see Table 1.2).

Mendelsohn's types range from the *completely innocent victim*, who exhibited no provocative or facilitating behavior prior to the offender's attack, to the victim who is *more guilty than offender*, because the victim instigates or provokes the criminal act. The person who comes out on the losing end of a punch after making an abusive remark or goading the other party would fit here. The *most guilty victim* is one who entered the situation as the offender and, because of circumstances beyond his or her control, ended up as the victim. Mendelsohn's classification is useful primarily for identifying the relative culpability of the victim in the criminal act.

Table 1.2 Mendelsohn's Victim Types	
Completely Innocent Victim	No provocation or facilitating behavior
Victim with Minor Guilt	Victim inadvertently places him- or herself in a compromising situation
Victim as Guilty as Offender	Victim was engaging in vice crimes and was hurt; suicide victim
Victim More Guilty Than Offender	Victim provokes or instigates the causal act
Most Guilty Victim	Started off as the offender and was hurt in turn
Imaginary Victim	Those who pretend to be a victim

Source: Mendelsohn, B. (1956). The Victimology. Etudes Internationale de Psycho-Sociologie Criminelle, *July, 23–26.*

The Work of Stephen Schafer: *The Victim and His Criminal*

Scholarly interest in victims and the role they played in their own demise evoked little interest throughout the 1950s and 1960s. Stephen Schafer, in a playful twist on Hans von Hentig's seminal work, revisited the victim's role in his book *The Victim and His Criminal*. The key concept that undergirded Schafer's thinking was what he termed *functional responsibility*. Once again, the victim–offender relationship came under scrutiny.

As Table 1.3 shows, Schafer (1968) provided a typology that builds upon victim responsibility for the crime. In many respects, Schafer's groupings are a variation of those proposed by von Hentig (1948). The difference between the two schemes is primarily one of emphasis on the culpability of the victim. Where von Hentig's listing identifies varying risk factors, Schafer explicitly sets forth the responsibility of different victims.

Other Scholarly Efforts

Von Hentig, Mendelsohn, and Schafer were not the only persons to produce significant analyses regarding victims during this time. Most assuredly, some other scholars began recognizing the importance of a victim-based orientation. These early attempts to probe the victim–offender relationship signaled the beginning of a renewed academic interest in the victim.

This concern, however, was lopsided. The early victimologists generally failed to look at the damage offenders inflicted upon their victims, ignored victim recuperative or rehabilitative efforts, and bypassed a host of other concerns. In an attempt to understand the causes of crime, they concentrated on how the victim contributed to his or her demise. Eventually, the idea of victim

Table 1.3 Schafer's Victim Precipitation Typology

1. Unrelated Victims (no victim responsibility)	Instances in which the victim is simply the unfortunate target of the offender
2. Provocative Victims (victim shares responsibility)	The offender is reacting to some action or behavior of the victim
3. Precipitative Victims (some degree of victim responsibility)	Victims leave themselves open for victimization by placing themselves in dangerous places or times, dressing inappropriately, acting, or saying the wrong things, etc.
4. Biologically Weak Victims (no victim responsibility)	The aged, young, infirm, and others who, due to their physical conditions, are appealing targets for offenders
5. Socially Weak Victims (no victim responsibility)	Immigrants, minorities, and others who are not adequately integrated into society and are seen as easy targets by offenders
6. Self-Victimizing (total victim responsibility)	Individuals who are involved in such crimes as drug use, prostitution, gambling, and other activities in which the victim and the criminal act in concert with one another
7. Political Victims (no victim responsibility)	Individuals who are victimized because they oppose those in power or are made victims in order to be kept in a subservient social position

Source: Adapted from Schafer, S. (1968). The Victim and His Criminal: A Study in Functional Responsibility. *New York: Random House.*

precipitation emerged from this preoccupation with "blaming the victim." As we shall see later in this chapter, the assumption that somehow the victim shared responsibility for or instigated the criminal episode would spark a major ideological confrontation.

EMPIRICAL STUDIES OF VICTIM PRECIPITATION

Victim precipitation deals with the degree to which the victim is responsible for his or her own victimization. That involvement can be either passive (as much of von Hentig's typology suggests) or active (as seen in Mendelsohn's classification). Each typology presented in this chapter implicates victim contribution as a causative factor in the commission of a crime. However, the first systematic attempt to provide empirical support of this argument was Wolfgang's (1958) analysis of police homicide records. A few years later, one of Wolfgang's students, Menachem Amir, applied this framework to forcible rape cases. His formulation and interpretation quickly met with a barrage of stinging criticism.

The Work of Marvin E. Wolfgang: *Patterns in Criminal Homicide*

Using homicide data from the city of Philadelphia, Wolfgang reported that 26% of the homicides that occurred from 1948 through 1952 resulted from victim precipitation. Wolfgang (1958: 252) defined victim-precipitated homicide as those instances in which the ultimate victim was

> the first in the homicide drama to use physical force directed against his subsequent slayer. The victim-precipitated cases are those in which the victim was the first to show and use a deadly weapon, to strike a blow in an altercation—in short, the first to commence the interplay of resort to physical violence.

Wolfgang identified several factors as typical of victim-precipitated homicides. First, the victim and the offender usually had some prior interpersonal relationship. Typical examples include relationships of spouses, boyfriends–girlfriends, family members, and close friends or acquaintances. In other words, victims were more likely to die at the hands of someone they knew rather than from the actions of a complete stranger.

Second, the homicide act is often the product of a small disagreement that escalates until the situation bursts out of control. That change in degree could be either short-term or the result of a longer, drawn-out confrontation. For instance:

> A husband had beaten his wife on several previous occasions. In the present instance, she insisted that he take her to the hospital. He refused, and a violent quarrel followed, during which he slapped her several times, and she concluded by stabbing him (Wolfgang, 1958: 253).

Third, alcohol consumed by the victim is a common ingredient in many victim-precipitated homicides. Several possibilities surface here. It may be that as intoxicated persons lose their inhibitions, they vocalize their feelings more readily. Eventually, these inebriated parties grow more obnoxious and belligerent, and unwittingly provoke their assailants into a deadly confrontation. Another alternative is that alcohol consumption renders these people so impaired that they lose the physical ability to defend themselves in a skirmish. In any event, Wolfgang (1958: 265) points out that "connotations of a victim as a weak and passive individual, seeking to withdraw from an assaultive situation, and of an offender as a brutal, strong, and overly aggressive person seeking out his victim, are not always correct."

The Work of Menachem Amir: *Patterns in Forcible Rape*

Several years later, Menachem Amir undertook what perhaps became the most controversial empirical analysis of rape. Amir (1971) gathered information from police records on rape incidents that took place in Philadelphia between 1958 and 1960. Based on details contained in the files, he claimed that 19% of all forcible rapes were victim-precipitated.

According to Amir (1971: 266), victim-precipitated rape referred to those situations in which:

> the victim actually, or so it was deemed, agreed to sexual relations but retracted before the actual act or did not react strongly enough when the suggestion was made by the offender. The term applies also to cases in risky situations marred with sexuality, especially when she uses what could be interpreted as indecency in language and gestures, or constitutes what could be taken as an invitation to sexual relations.

Amir proceeded to list a variety of factors that helped precipitate the criminal act. Similar to Wolfgang's homicide findings, alcohol use—particularly by the victim—was a major factor in a precipitated rape. The risk of sexual victimization intensified if both parties had been drinking.

Other important factors include seductive actions by the victim, wearing revealing clothing, using risqué language, having a "bad" reputation, and being in the wrong place at the wrong time. According to Amir, such behaviors could tantalize the offender to the point that he simply "misreads" the victim's overtures. At one point, Amir (1971) even suggested that some victims may have an unconscious need to be sexually controlled through rape.

In the concluding remarks of the section on victim precipitation, Amir (1971: 275–276) commented:

> These results point to the fact that the offender should not be viewed as the sole "cause" and reason for the offense, and that the "virtuous" victim is not always the innocent and passive party. Thus, the role played by the victim and its contribution to the perpetration of the offense becomes one of the main interests of the emerging discipline of victimology.

Criticisms and Reactions

The notion of victim precipitation, particularly regarding Amir's claims about rape, came under swift attack. Weis and Borges (1973; Weis, 1976), for example, attributed Amir's conclusions to faults implicit in relying upon police accounts, to a host of procedural errors, as well as to ill-conceived theoretical notions. For example, Amir suggested that victims may *psychologically* prompt or desire the rape as a means of rebelling against accepted standards of behavior. In contrast, though, the male is simply responding to *social* cues from the female. Interestingly, Amir does not provide any justification for why female behavior stems from psychological factors while male actions derive from social variables. Amir's study attracted blistering rebuttals from academic quarters, along with enraged reactions from women's groups and victim advocates. This reception made many victimologists very uncomfortable with the precipitation argument as it had developed to that point.

Cooler heads soon prevailed. Rather than abandoning the idea of victim precipitation, some scholars began a more sensitive probing. Curtis (1974), for one, suggested that what was needed was a more accurate definition of victim precipitation. For example, one set of researchers might define hitchhiking as a precipitating factor. Other studies may not make such a blanket assumption or may view hitchhiking as substantively different from other precipitating actions.

A more productive approach came from a critical examination of the underpinnings of the victim-precipitation argument. Franklin and Franklin (1976) exposed four major assumptions behind this victimological approach (see Table 1.4). First, victim precipitation assumes that the behavior of the victim can explain the criminal act. However, some factors often identified as precipitous also appear in instances where no criminal act takes place. For example, many people go to bars at night. Sometimes they drink excessively and then stagger home alone without becoming victimized. Thus, supposedly precipitating acts are not enough, in and of themselves, to cause criminal behavior.

Second, victim precipitation assumes the offender becomes activated only when the victim emits certain signals. This belief ignores the fact that many offenders plan their offenses ahead of time and do not simply react to another person's behavior. For these criminals, crime is a rational, planned enterprise.

Third, Franklin and Franklin (1976) disagree with the assumption that a victim's behavior is necessary and sufficient to trigger the commission of a criminal act. In fact, the opposite is probably closer to the truth. Many offenders commit crimes despite any specific action by the victim. Others will not seize the opportunity to commit a crime, for whatever reason, although a potential victim presents him- or herself.

Table 1.4 Problematic Assumptions of Victim Precipitation

- The behavior of the victim can explain the criminal act.
- The offender becomes activated only when a victim emits certain signals.
- A victim's behavior is necessary and sufficient to cause a criminal act.
- The intent of the victim can be gauged by the victimization incident.

Source: Compiled by authors from Franklin II, C. W., & Franklin, A. P. (1976). Victimology Revisited: A Critique and Suggestions for Future Direction. Criminology, 14, 177–214.

Finally, victim precipitation arguments assume that the intent of the victim can be gauged by the victimization incident. Unfortunately, if intent is equivalent to action, there would be no need for criminal court proceedings beyond the infallible identification of the person who perpetrated the crime. Our criminal justice system, however, explicitly assumes possible variation in intent, regardless of the action.

Although each of these assumptions shows how the victim precipitation argument falters, there is a much larger issue requiring attention. Studies of victim involvement tend to be myopic. That is, they do not address the offender. Instead, they imply all offenders are equal in their drive and desire to engage in deviant activity. This assumption, however, is untenable. Some offenders may actively hunt for the right situation, while others display little or no prior intent. What was needed was an integrated approach that would take both the victim and the offender into account.

Curtis (1974) attempted to do just this when he sketched a simple grid that allows the degree of victim precipitation to vary. As Table 1.5 shows, Curtis merged victim provocation with offender intent. This strategy results in recognizing five degrees of precipitation, ranging from pure victim precipitation to total offender responsibility. This presentation shows that even in the position of clear outright provocation by the victim, the offender may still be an equally responsible partner in the final outcome. What is important to remember here is that, at best, one should conceive of victim precipitation as a contributing factor and, certainly, not as the predominant force.

A NEW APPROACH: GENERAL VICTIMOLOGY

The preoccupation with victim precipitation, along with its divisiveness and ensuing fragmentation, threatened to stagnate this fledgling area of interest. The lack of theoretical advances brought genuine worries from some quarters that victimology was bogging down in an academic quagmire

Table 1.5 The Precipitation Grid Outlining the Relative Responsibility of Both Victim and Offender

Degree of Offender Intent	Degree of Victim Involvement		
	Clear Provocation	**Some Involvement**	**Little or No Involvement**
Deliberate premeditation	Equal	More offender	Total offender responsibility
Some intent	More victim	Equal	More offender
Little or no intent	Pure victim precipitation	More victim	Equal

Source: Adapted from Curtis, L. A. (1974). Criminal Violence: National Patterns and Behavior, p. 35. Jossey-Bass Inc., Publishers.

(Bruinsma & Fiselier, 1982; Levine, 1978). In response to this situation, Beniamin Mendelsohn called for victimology to move out of the provincial backwaters of criminology and into its own rightful domain. Mendelsohn attempted to assure victimology of its independence from criminology by devising the term *general victimology*.

According to Mendelsohn (1982: 59), victimologists aim to "investigate the causes of victimization in search of effective remedies." Because human beings suffer from many causal factors, focusing on criminal victimization is too narrow a perspective. A more global term, like *general victimology*, is needed to convey the true meaning of the field.

According to Mendelsohn (1976), *general victimology* subsumes five types of victims. They include victims of:

- a criminal
- one's self
- the social environment
- technology
- the natural environment.

The first category (crime victims) is self-explanatory. It refers to the traditional subject matter that victimologists have grown accustomed to studying. Self-victimization would include suicide, as well as any other suffering induced by victims themselves. The term *victims of the social environment* incorporates individual, class, or group oppression. Some common examples would include racial discrimination, caste relations, genocide, and war atrocities. Technological victims are people who fall prey to society's reliance upon scientific innovations. Nuclear accidents, improperly tested medicines, industrial pollution, and transportation mishaps provide fodder for this category. Finally, victims of the natural environment would embrace those persons affected by such events as floods, earthquakes, hurricanes, and famine.

In line with Mendelsohn's formulations, Smith and Weis (1976) proposed a broad overview of the areas encompassed by general victimology. As Figure 1.1 illustrates, there are four major areas of concern. They include the creation of definitions of victims, the application of these definitions, victim reactions during the post-victimization period, and societal reactions to victims.

When viewed in this context, general victimology becomes a very broad enterprise with extensive implications. As Mendelsohn (1976: 21) explains:

> Just as medicine treats all patients and all diseases, just as criminology concerns itself with all criminals and all forms of crime, so victimology must concern itself with all victims and all aspects of victimity in which society takes an interest.

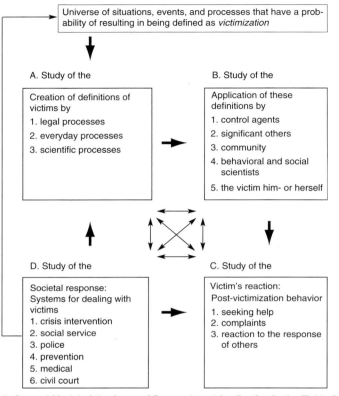

FIGURE 1.1 General Model of the Areas of Research and Application in the Field of Victimology.

Source: Smith, D. L., & Weis, K. (1976). Toward an Open-System Approach to Sudies in the Field of Victimology. In E. C. Viano (Ed.), Victims & Society. *Washington, DC: Visage Press Inc.*

CRITICAL VICTIMOLOGY

One trend in victimology since the 1990s is the call to shift focus from the more general approach outlined in the preceding section to what some people call *critical victimology.* Proponents of this move maintain that victimology fails to question the basic foundations of what crime is, overlooks the question of why certain acts are sanctioned, and, consequently, has developed in the wrong direction. Mawby and Walklate (1994: 21) define *critical victimology* as:

> an attempt to examine the wider social context in which some versions of victimology have become more dominant than others and also to understand how those versions of victimology are interwoven with questions of policy response and service delivery to victims of crime.

Central to critical victimology, therefore, is the issue of how and why certain actions are defined as criminal and, as a result, how the entire field of victimology becomes focused on one set of actions instead of another. This notion is not entirely different from Mendelsohn's category of *victim of the social environment*. Mawby and Walklate (1994) point out that many crimes committed by the powerful in society are not subjected to the criminal code. Some writers point to the neglect of criminological attention to genocide (Day & Vandiver, 2000; Friedrichs, 2000; Yacoubian, 2000), war crimes (Hoffman, 2000), political campaign law violations (Levine, 1997; Liddick, 2000; Taylor, 2000), clandestine arms sales and weapons of mass destruction (Berryman, 2000; Phythian, 2000; Whitby, 2001), smuggling (Beare, 2002; Bruinsma & Bernasco, 2004; Naylor, 2004; van Duyne, 2003), the human slave trade (Mameli, 2002; Schloenhardt, 1999; Shelley, 2003; Taylor & Jamieson, 1999), deportation (Chan, 2005), and investment and consumer fraud (Holtfreter, 2004; Holtfreter, van Slyke, & Blomberg, 2005; Naylor, 2007; Pontell, 2005) as evidence of the overly conservative nature of the field. Consequently, the victims of those crimes do not enter into the typical discussion of victimological concerns.

Under critical victimology, most victim-oriented initiatives tend to perpetuate the existing definitions of crime by failing to question the supportive social factors that give rise to the action and the response (Elias, 1990). The reason for this failure is multifaceted. One contributing factor is the reliance on official definitions and data in most analyses of victim issues. This inevitably leads to solutions that do not question the underlying social setting. Another factor is the ability of existing agencies to co-opt and incorporate emerging movements (such as children's rights) into existing social control systems. A more radical argument posits that the control of criminal justice and victimology rests in the hands of a powerful few who would view a critical approach as a threat to the status quo.

While critical victimology offers an interesting viewpoint and carries much potential for victimology, debating its merits is beyond the scope of this text. Various points throughout this book, however, will raise issues that are relevant to a critical approach. Examples of this include sociocultural discussions of why violence occurs and investigations of impediments to victim programs. A deeper and more intense examination of critical victimology will be left for other forums.

THE VICTIM MOVEMENT

While academicians were debating the victim-precipitation argument, practitioners had pinpointed the victim as someone who deserved assistance from society and the criminal justice system. To some extent, this grassroots concern for the victim's well-being was a reaction to the charges of victim complicity in the offense. Several different movements occurred simultaneously and contributed to the renewed interest in the plight of the victim. Among them were: (1) the women's movement; (2) efforts to establish children's rights; (3) concerns over the growing crime problem; (4) the advocacy of victim compensation; (5) legal reforms; and (6) some other factors.

The Women's Movement

The women's movement, especially in the mid- to late 1960s, included a large component dealing with victims. Victim-blaming arguments often dealt with rape and sexual assault. The female victim found herself and her lifestyle on trial whenever an offender was apprehended. Reformers complained that the system dealt with sexual assault victims as if they themselves were the offenders. Advocates pushed for equal treatment. They found the actions of the criminal justice system to be strong ammunition for their arguments. Beyond simply calling for changes in the formal system of justice, the women's movement made many gains. A short list would include the development of rape crisis centers, shelters for battered women, counseling for abused women and their children, and other forms of assistance. As women demanded an equal place in society, they worked to overcome the disadvantages of the criminal justice system.

Children's Rights

A growing concern over the needs and rights of youths blossomed during the 1960s. Many writers point to the mid-1960s as the time when child abuse was "discovered." It was around this time that society decided to define abuse against children as a social problem. However, that does not mean that child abuse was a new phenomenon. Child abuse is an age-old practice and, by many accounts, may have been much worse in the past than today. The difference in the 1960s, however, was that many physical and psychological actions used with children began to be questioned and labeled as abuse. States enacted legislation outlining the limits to which a child could be physically "disciplined." Specific children's bureaus within criminal justice agencies were either established or expanded to deal with the growing recognition of child maltreatment. Shelters were created to house children from abusive situations.

Runaways also gained publicity as a serious problem in the late 1960s. The general rebellion of youths in the United States enticed many juveniles to seek freedom from authority. Consequently, runaway shelters appeared in most large cities for the purpose of assisting the youths rather than returning them to their homes. Children were emerging as a new class of victims—both of abuse at home and of society in general.

The Growing Crime Problem

The level of crime in the United States began to register giant strides in the 1960s and throughout the 1970s. According to Uniform Crime Reports

(UCR) data, crime in the United States more than doubled from 1960 to 1980. Along with concern over the Vietnam War, crime was the most important issue of the day. Presidential and local elections targeted the problem of law and order as a major concern. In an attempt to identify the causes of the growing problem and possible solutions, President Johnson appointed a commission to examine crime and the criminal justice system. Victim issues were a major focus of the 1967 President's Commission on Law Enforcement and the Administration of Justice. Among the victim components of the commission report (1967) were the beginnings of systematic victimization surveys, suggestions for the means of alleviating the pain and loss of victims, ideas for community programs aimed at providing victim services, and calls for involving victims further in the criminal justice system.

Some 15 years after this report was aired, another national task force concluded that victims still had substantial needs that were going unfilled. Many of the identified problems were similar to those noted by the earlier commission.

Victim Compensation

One suggestion made by the President's Commission (1967) was the establishment of methods for compensating crime victims for their losses. Among these techniques were restitution and *victim compensation*. Neither of these ideas, however, originated with the commission. As was mentioned earlier in this chapter, restitution was the common method for dealing with crime throughout most of history. Victim compensation (state payments made to crime victims) was first introduced in Great Britain by Margery Fry in 1957. Although that early attempt failed, victim compensation quickly became a major issue around the world.

New Zealand passed the first compensation legislation in 1963, closely followed by England in 1964. In the United States, California established victim compensation in 1965, New York in 1966, Hawaii in 1967, and Massachusetts in 1968. The federal government enacted legislation in 1984 that outlined compensation in instances in which federal crimes were committed. The statute also provided for monetary assistance to states with compensation programs. By 1989, 45 states had enacted compensation statutes. Other countries, such as Australia and Finland, also have established compensation programs. While each program may differ in its particulars, the basic premise of assisting crime victims remains the same.

WEB ACTIVITY

While we will look at victim compensation in depth later in the book, you can take a look at this approach and investigate its impact on victimology at the National Association of Crime Victim Compensation Boards (**http://www.nacvcb.org**); the Office for Victims of Crime (**http://ovc.ncjrs.gov/topic.aspx?topicid=58**).

Legal Reforms

In addition to the establishment of compensation legislation, a variety of legal reforms aimed at protecting and helping crime victims have appeared since the 1960s. Among the changes that have emerged are statutes that protect the rape victim's background and character in court proceedings. New laws were designed to protect battered spouses and their children. Legislation mandating that doctors and teachers report suspected cases of child abuse represented a bold initiative. Guidelines for informing victims about court proceedings and the legal system, as well as provisions that allow victim impact statements in sentencing and parole decisions, began to surface. In some instances, states passed a "Victims' Bill of Rights." These provisions outline the rights of the victim in a manner similar to those appearing in the U.S. Bill of Rights, which focuses on protections for the accused (see Table 1.6 and Figure 1.2).

Other Factors

Other factors have played either a direct or an indirect role in emphasizing victim issues. One such source of influence has been the mass media. Rarely a week goes by in which a "crime of the week" does not appear in a special movie or as part of an ongoing series. Shows such as "America's Most Wanted" portray not only the offender but also the harm to the victim, often relying on interviews with the victim or victim's family. Such media attention and interest in the victim naturally influence viewers in the audience.

Another factor not to be overlooked is the increasing interest in victims among academics. Four decades ago, there were virtually no books specifically focusing on victims. The publication of Schafer's (1968) *The Victim and His Criminal* signaled an era of increasing interest in victimology. Many texts have appeared since then. They range from general victim topics to specific discussions of compensation, intimate partner violence, child abuse, victim services, and other areas of interest. The first International Symposium on Victimology was held in Jerusalem in 1973. Since then, there have been several more worldwide gatherings and an uncounted number of national, state, and local meetings of academics and professionals working with crime victims. These efforts culminated in the establishment of the American Society of Victimology in 2003.

The spurt in college courses devoted to victimology or topical victim issues is encouraging. Some campuses (e.g., California State University–Fresno, Sam Houston State University, University of New Haven) now offer specialized programs in victim services. As Table 1.7 shows, a variety of specialty journals devoted to victim issues now exist. In short, the victim movement has made strides over a relatively short period and continues to gain momentum.

🌐 WEB ACTIVITY

John Dussich offers a good discussion and overview of the development of victimology and key concepts in the field. Look over his comments at www.unafei.or.jp/english/pdf/RS_No70/No70_12VE_Dussich.pdf.

Table 1.6 Examples of Landmark Federal Victims' Rights Legislation Enacted During the Twenty-First Century

2001   *Air Transportation Safety and System Stabilization Act*

Created a new federal victim compensation program specifically for the victims of September 11. The program includes many types of damages normally available only through civil actions, such as payment for pain and suffering, lifetime lost earnings, and loss of enjoyment of life.

2003   *PROTECT Act ("Amber Alert" Law)*

Created a national AMBER network to facilitate rapid law enforcement and community response to kidnapped or abducted children.

2003   *Fair and Accurate Credit Transactions Act*

Provided new protections against identity theft and helped victims of identity theft recover their financial losses.

2004   *Justice for All Act*

Provided mechanisms at the federal level to enforce the rights of crime victims, giving victims and prosecutors legal standing to assert victims' rights, authorizing the filing of writs of mandamus to assert a victim's right, and requiring the Attorney General to establish a victims' rights compliance program within the Department of Justice.

2006   *Adam Walsh Child Protection and Safety Act*

Increased supervision of sex offenders; also extended the federal Crime Victims' Rights Act to federal habeas corpus proceedings arising out of state convictions, eliminated the statute of limitations for federal prosecution of sexual offenses or child abduction, and extended the civil remedy for child sex crime victims to persons victimized as children, even if their injuries did not surface until the person became an adult.

2008   *Protect Our Children Act*

Improved the ability of law enforcement to prosecute child predators.

2008   *Identity Theft Enhancement and Restitution Act*

Permits courts to order restitution to cybercrime victims.

2009   *Matthew Shepard and James Byrd, Jr. Hate Crimes Prevention Act*

Changes the federal definition of hate crimes to include crimes based on sexual orientation, gender identity, or disability.

2012   Uniform Crime Reports Changes Definition of Rape

Victim or perpetrator can be any gender, and defines instances in which the victim is incapable of giving consent because of temporary or permanent mental or physical incapacity

Source: Compiled from Department of Justice (2013). National Crime Victims' Rights Week Resource Guide: New Challenges, New Solutions. *Washington, DC: National Center for Victims of Crime. Retrieved on July 4, 2013, from http://ovr.ncjrs.gov/ncvrw2013/index.html; and B. S. Fisher & S. P. Lab (Eds).* Encyclopedia of Victimology and Crime Prevention. *Los Angeles: Sage.*

SUMMARY AND OVERVIEW OF THIS BOOK

As you have read, Mendelsohn (1976) saw general victimology as addressing five distinct types of victims. In addition to crime victims, he saw self-victimization, social victims, technological victims, and victims of the natural environment as legitimate focal concerns. All these victims suffer some degree of social or physical pain or loss. Each deserves assistance to offset the devastating effects of the victimization episode.

While Mendelsohn's vision of general victimology is quite impressive, it does cover a huge territory. Because Mendelsohn's approach is such a large undertaking, we will confine ourselves to a more manageable task. For that reason, this text must restrict itself to only the first category—crime victims. By the time you finish this book, we think you will agree with us. Victimology is so broad and complex that it makes sense to look at it in slices.

A glimpse of what lies ahead reveals an ambitious range of topics. The book is divided into three sections. The first section addresses the definition and scope of victimology. This first chapter has laid the foundation for a host of issues and ideas that we will take up in greater detail in later chapters. Many topics will appear in the context of more than one discussion. Chapter 2 examines methods for measuring victimization, particularly the development of victimization surveys. Victim surveys have become a key measure of crime and contribute a great deal of information to the study of victimization. Chapter 3 provides an overview of explanations for victimization.

FIGURE 1.2 California Governor Arnold Schwarzenegger, right, with newly appointed Crime Victim Advocate Susan Fisher during a news conference in 2006 at which Schwarzenegger proposed a new Crime Victims' Bill of Rights. In 2008, the state passed the California Victims' Bill of Rights Act of 2008, also known as *Marsy's Law* an Amendment to the state's Constitution and certain Penal Code sections that protects and expands the legal rights of crime victims. *Credit: AP Photo/Ben Margot.*

Section 2 of the book addresses the impact of victimization. Chapter 4 looks at the costs associated with being a crime victim and the additional burdens that result from becoming involved with the criminal justice system. As you will see, many people wrongly assume that victims do not cooperate with the authorities because of apathy. This chapter will demonstrate that the real reason reflects a very sensible cost–benefit analysis. Sometimes it is just too costly and too painful to be a "model citizen." Chapter 5 examines financial remedies for victimization. Included here are discussions of restitution, civil court, and victim compensation. Chapter 6 focuses on addressing the non-financial impact of victimization. The chapter addresses the emergence of restorative justice as well as the development of victim-witness projects in the criminal justice system. Chapter 7 focuses on the development of victims' rights and discusses the growth of legislation that mandates a role for victims in the system that is not limited to them being just a witness for the state.

The third and final section of the book investigates different types of victimization. After examining traditional crimes handled by the criminal justice system in Chapter 8, the book moves on to topics that include sexual battery, intimate partner violence, child maltreatment, elderly abuse, and hate crimes. Victimization that takes place on school campuses and in the workplace is discussed in the final chapter. Each of these specific victim groupings has developed its own literature about causes and possible remedies.

WEB ACTIVITY

You can examine and explore the national and international interest in victimology at the following websites: the International Victimology Institute (**http://www.tilburguniversity.edu/research/institutes-and-research-groups/intervict**); the World Society of Victimology (**http://www.worldsocietyofvictimology.org**); the American Society of Victimology (**http://american-society-victimology.us**); and others. Look over these sites and others you can find and make a list of the topics and issues that you think are most interesting.

Table 1.7 Selected Journals Devoted to Victim Issues

Child Abuse & Neglect
Child Maltreatment
Homicide Studies
International Review of Victimology
Journal of Child Sexual Abuse
Journal of Elder Abuse & Neglect
Journal of Family Violence
Journal of Interpersonal Violence
Trauma, Violence, & Abuse
Violence Against Women
Violence & Abuse Abstracts
Violence and Victims

KEY TERMS

agent provocateur	*lex talionis*
criminal–victim dyad	*mala in se*
critical victimology	restitution
deterrence	retribution
gemeinschaft	typology
general victimology	victim compensation
gesellschaft	victim precipitation

Measuring Criminal Victimization

LEARNING OBJECTIVES

After reading Chapter 2, you should be able to:

- Describe three major data sources for measuring crime.
- Explain what the UCR does.
- Outline three advantages of the UCR.
- Explain three disadvantages of the UCR.
- List the contents of the Index Offenses.
- Differentiate personal from property offenses.
- Give a definition of the dark figure of crime.
- Discuss NIBRS.
- Give advantages NIBRS provides beyond the UCR.
- Specify what a victimization survey is.
- Outline the four generations of victimization surveys.
- Summarize and criticize the findings from the 1967 NORC survey.
- Give an example of telescoping.
- Explain how memory decay affects victim surveys.
- Compare and contrast reverse and forward record checks.
- Identify three assumptions behind the record check strategy.
- Define the term *panel design*.
- Reveal why bounding is important for victim surveys.
- Distinguish a self-respondent from a household respondent.
- Outline the contributions of second-generation victim surveys.
- Explain why the development of the NCS was so important.
- Address the mover-stayer problem in the NCS.
- Relay a prime difficulty with business victimization surveys.
- Discuss redesign efforts behind fourth-generation victim surveys.
- Provide an example of a screen question in victim surveys.
- Know what the initials NCVS represent.
- Convey the goals and objectives behind the NCVS.
- Discuss victimization surveys from other countries (the BCS and ICVS).

INTRODUCTION

Measuring the extent of criminal victimization has long been a goal of the criminal justice system and those who study crime. Researchers and policy-makers typically rely upon three major data sources for measuring the level of crime (O'Brien, 1985). The first source, official records of police departments, is the traditional depository for crime information. However, dissatisfaction with police records prompted researchers to look elsewhere. Surveys that ask people about offenses they have committed became a popular alternative. Unfortunately, these surveys are not conducted on an annual or national basis, and they tell very little about the victims of crime. A third tactic is to question individuals about instances in which they were victimized. As we shall see in this chapter, this is perhaps the most cited data source today. Despite the common goal of measuring crime, none of these strategies alone yields a definitive answer to the question of how much victimization occurs in society. Each scheme provides a slightly different angle from which to view the crime problem. Each one of these methods has its own distinct advantages and inherent flaws.

This chapter examines some issues involved in measuring victimization, paying particular attention to the development and use of victimization surveys. We will also examine the level of crime and victimization presented by official police reports of crime and the *National Crime Victimization Survey*. As you will see, victim surveys provide a wealth of data that are quite useful for studying victims and related issues.

OFFICIAL POLICE REPORTS

The most widely cited measure of crime is the Uniform Crime Reports (UCR) produced by the Federal Bureau of Investigation. The UCR was initially developed by the International Association of Chiefs of Police before being taken over by the FBI in 1931 (Chilton, 2010). The UCR was envisioned as a mechanism by which police departments in different jurisdictions could exchange relevant information about crime. Police administrators around the country were very supportive of this effort. They felt that such knowledge could help identify the magnitude of the crime problem, map changes over time, and guide actions to combat the criminal element. This reporting system was meant to be a tool for the law enforcement community throughout the United States.

The UCR is characterized by a number of interesting and advantageous features. First, crime data are compiled annually from jurisdictions throughout the country. Such consistency and broad geographical coverage allow crime comparisons from year to year and from place to place. The fact that the UCR has been in operation since 1931 means that it is one of the longest-running systematic data collection efforts in the social sciences.

Second, the UCR has been influential in providing standardized crime definitions. Common definitions make it possible to draw comparisons across different times and jurisdictions. To achieve this goal, the FBI introduced what it calls the *Index*, or *Part I, Offenses*. The FBI divides these serious crimes into two groups. *Personal offenses* include murder, forcible rape, robbery, and aggravated assault. *Property offenses* consist of burglary, larceny-theft, motor vehicle theft, and arson. While state statutes and local codes are not bound to these definitions, the UCR does introduce a common metric among the 50 states.

> ### 🌐 WEB ACTIVITY
>
> You can read a great deal about the UCR and the data that are available on the FBI website at **http://www.fbi.gov/about -us/cjis/ucr**

Third, the UCR gathers a large amount of information and details about the Index crimes. These data are especially useful when attempting to identify patterns and trends about crime and criminals. In addition, the UCR collects data on reported crimes and arrests for an additional 21 categories of offenses, known as the *Part II* Offenses Included in this category are sex offenses (besides rape), offenses against the family, and vandalism. The same level of detail as found in the Part I Offenses, however, is not collected for these crimes.

The UCR is not immune from problems or disadvantages. Perhaps the greatest concern is that the UCR overlooks the *dark figure of crime*. In other words, these tabulations reflect only offenses that are known to the police. Any incidents in which victims or witnesses opt not to call the police are excluded from UCR figures. This drawback prompts critics to argue that the UCR grossly underreports the true level of crime in society. The UCR reflects police—and not necessarily criminal—activity.

A second limitation with the UCR is its reliance on the "hierarchy rule." The *hierarchy rule* dictates that only one offense (typically the most serious offense) is recorded when multiple offenses occur at the same time (Chilton, 2010). For example, when an offender robs a bank with a weapon and simultaneously detains customers and takes their wallets, he or she is committing multiple robberies, theft, assault, and kidnapping—but only a single count of robbery is recorded. Under this rule, the number of crimes recorded falls short of the actual number of offenses.

Another major concern, particularly for our discussion, is the fact that the UCR offers little information on victims and offenders. The UCR gathers detailed data primarily on the more serious personal offenses (murder, forcible rape, robbery, and aggravated assault). Even then, most of the data deal only with persons who are arrested. There is very little information about the victim, the victim's circumstances, the context of the offense, and other potentially valuable information. This fact should not be surprising because law enforcement is oriented more toward dealing with offenders than with crime victims.

Interest in victims and the need to know more about individual criminal events has led to changes in the UCR system over the years. The *Supplemental Homicide Reports* (SHR) was initiated in 1976 and provides data on victim characteristics, location, offender characteristics, relationship between the victim and offender, the use of weapons, and the circumstances surrounding the homicide event. As such, the SHR offers information about the homicide victim and victimization not typically found in the balance of the UCR data. Based on the SHR, we know that homicides rarely occur in commercial settings, occur more often on weekends, involve acquaintances or intimates, and typically occur with little planning (Schwartz & Gertseva, 2010). Despite the value of the SHR, problems with missing data and a lack of knowledge about the offender place limitations on its use (Schwartz & Gertseva, 2010).

The most recent set of changes in the UCR has been the introduction of the *National Incident-Based Reporting System* (NIBRS). The NIBRS grew out of a report completed in the mid-1980s that examined the changing needs for data collection and analysis that could assist law enforcement in combating crime. The NIBRS data have several major advantages over the traditional UCR data. First, NIBRS collects detailed information on 22 categories of offenses (see Table 2.1) rather than just the eight Index Offenses. There are an additional 24 subcategories for which data are recorded (Chilton, 2010). Second, rather than abiding by the hierarchy rule and counting only the most serious Index Offense, NIBRS reports on all of the offenses that occur during a criminal incident. Third, NIBRS collects 53 data elements, most of which are not found in the traditional UCR data, for each crime incident

 WEB ACTIVITY

The Supplemental Homicide Reports provide great detail and information useful in understanding homicide victimization. You can read more about this at **http://www.fbi.gov/about-us/cjis/ucr/crime-in-the-u.s/2010/crime-in-the-u.s.-2010/violent-crime/murdermain**

Table 2.1 NIBRS Offense Categories

Arson	Homicide Offenses
Assault Offenses	Kidnapping/Abduction
Bribery	Larceny/Theft Offenses
Burglary/Breaking and Entering	Motor Vehicle Theft
Counterfeiting/Forgery	Pornography/Obscene Material
Destruction/Damage/Vandalism	Prostitution Offenses
Drug/Narcotic Offenses	Robbery
Embezzlement	Sex Offenses, Forcible
Extortion/Blackmail	Sex Offenses, Non-Forcible
Fraud Offenses	Stolen Property Offenses
Gambling Offenses	Weapon Law Violations

Source: Compiled from Federal Bureau of Investigation (2010b). http://www.fbi.gov/about-us/cjis/ucr/nibrs/nibrscategories.pdf.

(Addington, 2010). Among the information included in this expanded data collection process is detailed information on the victim, the victim–offender relationship, injuries, and property loss (see Table 2.2). Other information collected includes the location of the offenses, the presence of weapons, property lost, number of victims and offenders, and arrestee information (Addington, 2010).

The great advantage of the NIBRS data is the ability of law enforcement and researchers to gain a more in-depth picture of the crime problem and to use that information to decide on appropriate courses of action. Unfortunately, participation in NIBRS requires increased data entry requirements and data-processing abilities on the part of local law enforcement. The agencies must also meet stringent guidelines for participation. Because of these requirements, NIBRS has not been implemented nationally and no nationally representative data are available for study. Local agencies using NIBRS, however, are able to undertake more sophisticated analyses of their crime problems.

WEB ACTIVITY

The NIBRS system offers a great deal to understanding crime. The NIBRS User Manual can be found on this textbook's companion website at **http://booksite.elsevier.com/9780323287654**

Despite the problems with the UCR, the data have a long history and are helpful in answering a variety of questions. Increased involvement in the NIBRS system will enhance the value of official police crime data. Indeed, NIBRS data have been used to examine childhood victimization, intimate partner violence, and hate crimes (Addington, 2010).

Table 2.2 Information Collected by NIBRS

Offense Information:
  Incident date/hour
  Location type
  Number of premises entered
  Method of entry
  Type of criminal activity/Gang information
  Type of weapon/Force involved
Property Segment:
  Type of property loss, etc.
  Property description
  Value of property
  Date recovered
  Number of stolen motor vehicles
  Number of recovered motor vehicles
  Suspected drug type
  Estimated drug quantity
  Type of drug measurement
Offender Segment:
  Age (of offender)
  Sex (of offender)
  Race (of offender)

Arrestee Segment:
  Arrest date
  Type of arrest
  Multiple arrestee segments indicator
  Arrestee was armed with
  Age (of arrestee)
  Sex (of arrestee)
  Race (of arrestee)
  Ethnicity (of arrestee)
  Resident status (of arrestee)
  Disposition of arrestee under 18
Victim Segment:
  Type of victim
  Age (of victim)
  Sex (of victim)
  Race (of victim)
  Ethnicity (of victim)
  Resident status (of victim)
  Aggravated assault/Homicide circumstances
  Additional justifiable homicide circumstances
  Type of injury
  Relationship(s) of victim to offender(s)

Source: Federal Bureau of Investigation (2000). National Incident-Based Reporting System, Volume 1: Data collection guidelines. Washington, DC: FBI.

VICTIMIZATION SURVEYS

While the UCR has a long history, victimization surveys are only about 50 years old. Victim surveys got their start with the work of the President's Commission in the mid-1960s. The Commission came about because of problems with increasing crime and civil unrest during that era. From its inception, the President's Commission (1967) recognized that an accurate description of the crime problem was lacking. As a result, it authorized a number of independent projects to gather information about crime victims.

From that modest starting point, victimization surveys have grown into an invaluable data source. A *victimization survey*, instead of relying upon police reports or other official information, entails contacting people and asking them if they have been crime victims. In looking at the development of victimization surveys, one can divide them into various stages, or "generations" (Hindelang, 1976). Each successive generation is marked by the way it grappled

Table 2.3 The Development of Victimization Surveys

First-Generation Surveys

- Mid-1960s
- Carried out for the 1967 President's Commission
- Pilot studies of the feasibility of victimization surveys
- Showed much greater victimization than police data

Second-Generation Surveys

- Late 1960s and early 1970s
- Probed methods to address problems found in first-generation surveys
- City-specific surveys

Third-Generation Surveys

- Early 1970s to late 1980s
- National Crime Survey (NCS) initiated in 1972
- Business victimization surveys—1972 to 1977
- City surveys—26 cities from 1972 to 1975

Fourth-Generation Surveys

- 1988 to present
- NCS renamed the National Crime Victimization Survey—initiated in 1992

with several methodological problems raised in earlier phases. Table 2.3 summarizes the four generations of victimization surveys since their inception in the mid-1960s.

First-Generation Victim Surveys

The initial victim surveys, undertaken at the behest of the President's Commission (1967), represented little more than a set of extensive feasibility studies. These efforts tested whether such an approach could elicit sensitive information from the public. The researchers also wanted to determine how the criminal justice system could use these victim-based findings.

The NORC Survey

Perhaps the best known of all the initial pilot studies was the poll sponsored by the National Opinion Research Center (NORC) and reported by Ennis (1967). This effort was the first national victim survey and targeted 10,000 households throughout the United States. Interviewers initially asked participants to report on incidents that happened to them during the preceding 12-month period. Then the interviewer sought more detailed information on the two most recent and most serious offenses.

What made this survey so well known was the subsequent claim that the UCR underreported by roughly 50% the crime rate indicated by the *NORC survey*.

Table 2.4 contains a comparison of crime rates based upon the NORC data and the UCR figures. The NORC survey uncovered almost four times as many rapes and more than three times as many burglaries as did the UCR. The lone exception to reporting discrepancies was motor vehicle theft, for which the data sources produced comparable rates. This similarity was probably due to the fact that most auto insurance companies will not issue a reimbursement check unless the victim files a police report. Combining the offenses into broader categories gave a much clearer picture. The NORC survey unearthed 1.9 times as many violent episodes and 2.2 times more property offenses than official crime statistics had logged. Critics quickly pointed to the NORC findings as definitive proof that official crime records were inaccurate and unreliable because they neglected the "dark figure of crime" (Biderman & Reiss, 1967).

Some Methodological Considerations

While the NORC results were dramatic, there were enough problems to compromise their usefulness. First, the claim that there was twice as much crime than what the police acknowledged was based on a very small number of victim accounts. Under normal conditions, someone conducting a victim survey might anticipate uncovering only a handful of rape and robbery incidents. Deriving estimates from a few observations can yield some questionable figures.

Second, the crime instances that victims reported were submitted to a panel of experts to assess whether these events were really crimes. Ultimately, the panel excluded more than one-third of the victim reports. An example of misclassification would be a person who returns home, finds all the furniture gone, and exclaims, "Help—I've been robbed!" The real crime here is a burglary, not a robbery. Employing a panel to check victim reports may

Table 2.4 Comparison of NORC Victimization Rates with UCR Rates

Crime Category	NORC	UCR	Ratio of NORC to UCR
Homicide	3.0	5.1	0.6
Rape	42.5	11.6	3.7
Robbery	94.0	61.4	1.5
Aggravated Assault	218.3	106.6	2.0
Burglary	949.1	299.6	3.2
Larceny $50+	606.5	267.4	2.3
Auto Theft	206.2	226.0	0.9
Violent Crimes	357.8	184.7	1.9
Property Crimes	1761.8	793.0	2.2

Source: The President's Commission on Law Enforcement and Administration of Justice (1967). Task Force Report: Crime and its Impact—An Assessment. *Washington, DC: U.S. Government Printing Office.*

help validate the results and impart a greater sense of confidence, but it also alerts us to the fact that the survey design had some major flaws in terms of question wording.

A third set of problems dealt with subject recall. Some participants experienced difficulties with telescoping. *Telescoping* takes place when respondents mistakenly bring criminal events that occurred outside the time frame into the survey period. For example, suppose that you are taking part in a victimization survey. The interviewer asks whether you had a car stolen during the past 12 months. In actuality, your automobile was taken 14 months ago. However, because you cannot remember exactly when the incident took place, you advise the interviewer that you were the victim of such a crime.

A related hindrance is faulty memory. *Memory decay* is evidenced when respondents were victimized during the survey time frame, but forgot the event and did not provide the correct answer to the question. Researchers also found that respondent fatigue could influence the results. For example, the level of crime reporting decreased as the length of the survey increased. Because of these considerations, victimization estimates derived from these efforts contained an unknown margin of error. Unless telescoping and memory decay "exactly offset one another, the survey estimate of the amount of crime that occurred is inaccurate" (Schneider et al., 1978: 18–19).

Another major concern emerged from the selection of respondents. The study did not randomly select respondents from households, and individuals under the age of 18 were excluded unless they were married. Additionally, all household offenses were counted as crimes against the head of the household. Each of these facts could add more bias to the results.

Besides the preceding concerns, a host of other imperfections contaminated the findings. There were definitional problems in the survey questions, an inability to locate where the crime actually took place, a problem in having a count of victims rather than offenses, and other nagging obstacles that plagued first-generation efforts. Despite these weaknesses, an important contribution had emerged. Criminologists and victimologists learned that the public was willing to answer questions about their victimization experiences. These early pilot studies clearly established the need for more refined victimization surveys and the avenues they should travel.

Second-Generation Victim Surveys

Preparations for the second generation of victim surveys began with several exploratory projects conducted during 1970 and 1971. These preliminary studies investigated a variety of methods for addressing the problems noted earlier with the first-generation surveys. Once these concerns received treatment, then it would be time to move on to running the surveys themselves.

Recall Problems

To test the accuracy of respondent recall, researchers in two different locations (Washington, DC, and Baltimore) conducted their own record checks. Their strategy was to compare information derived from police records with victimization survey data. Two types of record checks were involved: reverse record checks and forward record checks.

A *reverse record check* starts by locating crime victim names in police files. The next step is to contact these people and administer a victim survey to them. Therefore, survey responses are checked against the police records to assess the degree to which a respondent confirms offense characteristics that appear in the official files.

The reverse record check comparisons revealed that memory decay grew more problematic as the time period increased. The best recall usually occurred within three months of the incident. After that point, victims became more forgetful about the incident and its details. The results also showed that recall was better for some offenses than others and that there was a noticeable degree of telescoping. In other words, victims erroneously moved up events that occurred outside the time frame and placed them inside the targeted interval. In addition, the wording of some questions and their order of presentation also affected the responses (Hindelang, 1976: 46–53).

Schneider and her associates (1978) approached the very same issues with the exact opposite methodology. They opted to conduct a *forward record check*. After asking respondents in a victim survey whether they had contacted the police about the incident, the researchers combed police records for a written case report. Police reports could not be found for about one-third of the victims who said they had filed such a report. When case records were located, police reports and victim accounts showed a great deal of similarity. However, there was evidence that telescoping could produce some major distortions unless specific steps were taken to counteract this tendency.

Despite the gains that these record check studies provided, there was still a need for caution. Skogan (1981: 13–14) warned of three assumptions imbedded within this strategy. First, there is an assumption that police incident records are the appropriate benchmark against which to assess victim accounts. Just because an officer responds to a call does not mean that an official report will be filed by the officer. Second, record check studies can deal only with situations that have come to the attention of the record-keeper. Third, crime victims are a very mobile group whose frequent address changes make recontact difficult. Checking reports at a later time, therefore, becomes problematic.

The problem of telescoping received further consideration in a panel study of households undertaken by the Bureau of the Census in 1971. A *panel design* surveys the same group of households or respondents at regular intervals over a period of time. The repeated interviews or surveys allow for *bounding*. In other words, the first survey serves as the calendar reference point for the second, the second for the third, and so on. The earlier interview gives the respondent a solid referent for separating one time period from the next. It also permits the researcher to check on whether the same victimization instance is reported in more than one time period. This provision can eliminate any obvious repetition in the events that victims report. This panel study found more accurate recall and less telescoping in a six-month time frame than over a 12-month format (Hindelang, 1976).

Respondent Concerns

Incorporating recommendations from earlier exploratory pretests, surveys in San Jose, CA, and Dayton, OH, sought to compare information gathered from self-respondents with household respondents. A *self-respondent* is a person who reports victimization incidents for him- or herself. On the other hand, a *household respondent* relays information about crimes committed against all members of his or her household. The San Jose and Dayton surveys revealed that self-respondents reported more personal crimes and experienced fewer recall problems than did household respondents (Hindelang, 1976: 57–68).

In addition to interviewing victims from the general population, surveys of businesses and commercial establishments were also being developed at this time. Problems with such things as telescoping, memory decay, question wording, and bounding also existed in these evaluations. Sometimes, particular problems loomed even larger. For example, most reports of a business burglary or robbery would come from an employee who knew about the incident first-hand. Quite often, subsequent efforts to recontact the original informant were hampered by personnel turnover. The contact person, as well as anyone familiar with the episode, sometimes was no longer an employee of the business at the time of the second interview. Thus, the quality of record checks suffered from a lack of continuity among respondents.

The second-generation surveys were useful in identifying several factors that were incorporated into later survey instruments. First, it was found that more specific questions elicited more accurate information and better recall than did very general questions about prior victimization. Second, shorter recall periods (six months or less) significantly limited the problems of telescoping and memory decay. Third, bounding the time period by some concrete event (such as the last interview in a panel design) helped to limit the problem of telescoping. Fourth, interviewing individuals themselves about their victimization experiences was preferable to asking a proxy (a household respondent) about the experiences of others. Finally, through careful wording of questions, it was possible to approximate UCR offense definitions in order to enable comparisons across the two data sources.

Third-Generation Victim Surveys

The third generation witnessed an ambitious schedule of activity. The federal government launched a national victimization survey, a survey of commercial businesses, and a special victimization survey in 26 American cities. The following subsections outline each of these endeavors.

The National Crime Survey

The *National Crime Survey* (NCS) was launched in 1972 with a probability sample of 72,000 households set up in a panel format. The plan was to interview each member of these households. This strategy would produce a study group of approximately 100,000 people after eliminating problems such as refusals to cooperate and incorrect addresses.

Workers contacted each household every six months over a three-year period for a total of seven interviews during this time. To avoid replacing the entire sample at the end of three years, the NCS staggered the beginning and ending points for each wave. Every six months, one-sixth of the households departed the study group and their replacements underwent the initial interview. Roughly 12,000 households were interviewed each month, making the survey process a year-round endeavor.

The NCS incorporated many features uncovered in the earlier exploratory studies. The panel design, for example, established a six-month bounding period for the study. The first interview was not used to estimate crime rates. Instead, it became the starting point or boundary. To guard against telescoping and memory decay, each subsequent interview was checked against previous reports.

One burden that confronted the NCS was the *mover-stayer problem*. Sampling of respondents was built on the residence, not the individual. If the original survey participants vacated the premises and somebody else moved in, the new tenants automatically joined the sample for the balance of the study period. Responses from the new residents were used even though bounding was not possible. The NCS made no effort to track the original respondents. Instead, it was assumed that the impact of relocation upon victimization estimates and the comparability of stable versus changed residences were minimal.

Unlike earlier generations, interviewers talked with each household member rather than just a single household representative. Exceptions to this rule occurred when the contact person was a child, when the parent objected to an interview with a minor, or when repeated attempts to contact an individual family member proved futile. In these cases, one person acted as a proxy for the entire household.

While the preceding is true regarding individual victimizations, crimes against the household were solicited from only one household representative. This procedure aimed to reduce interviewing time and to eliminate the overlap from talking with more than one person about the same things. Unfortunately, the selected household respondent may not always be aware of all crimes against the household or may not know all the details needed for accurate reporting.

The Business Victimization Survey

Along with the national survey, the NCS also launched a commercial victimization survey. This undertaking gathered information from businesses to assess their level of risk. The commercial survey, though, was discontinued in 1977 for two primary reasons. First, the sample of 15,000 businesses was too small to project reliable estimates. Second, the costs of the survey were not commensurate with the potential payoff.

City Surveys

Twenty-six large cities were selected for special surveys of both residents and businesses. A total of 12,000 households and 2,000 businesses were targeted for interviews in each city. While the single-city findings were interesting, there was a great deal of overlap with the national survey. The costs associated with these multiple projects were astronomical. Eventually, the city surveys were discontinued in 1975 after only three years of operation.

Fourth-Generation Victim Surveys

Today, we are in the fourth generation of victimization surveys. To emphasize this transition, the format and title of the national victim surveys have changed. The name is now the *National Crime Victimization Survey* (NCVS).

The redesign efforts began in 1979, partly as a response to issues raised in a National Academy of Science report (Penick & Owens, 1976). As before, a number of exploratory analyses were undertaken to test potential adjustments. Some of these considerations covered such items as improving accuracy of responses, identifying information by subgroups, adding new questions to tap different dimensions of crime and victim responses, and making the data more useful for researchers (Skogan, 1990; Whitaker, 1989).

Concern over recall accuracy returns to issues of question wording, bounding, memory decay, and telescoping. There was some worry that the *screen questions*—those inquiries that probe possible victimization experiences— could be misleading and in need of revision (Dodge, 1985). Redesign analysts suggested that improved screen questions could result in increased reports of crime by prodding the memory of respondents and providing clearer definitions of criminal victimization. To show how the NCVS does this, Table 2.5 displays screen questions used in both the individual and household surveys. Each respondent is asked the questions in Table 2.5 as a means of probing victimization experiences in the past six months. These responses are then used as the basis for in-depth questions about the specific victimization occurrences.

Table 2.5 NCVS Screen Questions*

36a.   I'm going to read some examples that will give you an idea of the kinds of crimes this study covers. As I go through them, tell me if any of these happened to you in the last 6 months; that is since_____. 20__

Was something belonging to YOU stolen, such as:

a)   Things that you carry, like luggage, a wallet, purse, briefcase, book—
b)   Clothing, jewelry, or cell phone—
c)   Bicycle or sports equipment—
d)   Things in your home—like a TV, stereo, or tools—
e)   Things outside your home such as a garden hose or lawn furniture—
f)   Things belonging to children in the household—
g)   Things from a vehicle, such as a package, groceries, camera, or CD—OR
h)   Did anyone ATTEMPT to steal anything belonging to you?

36b.   Did any incidents of this type happen to you?
36c.   How many times?
37a.   (Other than any incidents already mentioned,) has anyone:

a)   Broken in or ATTEMPTED to break into your home by forcing a door or window, pushing past someone, jimmying a lock, cutting a screen, or entering through an open door or window—
b)   Has anyone illegally gotten in or tried to get into a garage, shed, or storage room—OR
c)   Illegally gotten in or tried to get into a hotel or motel room or vacation home where you were staying?

37b.   Did any incidents of this type happen to you?
37c.   How many times?
40a.   (Other than any incidents already mentioned,) since_____, 20__, were you attacked or threatened OR did you have something stolen from you:

a)   At home, including the porch or yard—
b)   At or near a friend's, relative's, or neighbor's home—
c)   At work or school—
d)   In places such as a storage shed or laundry room, a shopping mall, restaurant, bank, or airport—
e)   While riding in any vehicle—
f)   On the street or in a parking lot—
g)   At such places as a party, theater, gym, picnic area, bowling lanes, or while fishing or hunting—OR
h)   Did anyone ATTEMPT to attack or ATTEMPT to steal anything belonging to you from any of these places?

40b.   Did any incidents of this type happen to you?
40c.   How many times?

*For each of these questions the respondent is asked to "Briefly describe incident(s)."
Source: Compiled by authors from Bureau of Justice Statistics (2008). National Crime Victimization Survey: NCVS- 1 Basic Screen Questionnaire. Washington, DC: Bureau of Justice Statistics.

To assess the impact of the changes in screen questions, half the interviews in 1992 were conducted using the old questions, while half the subjects were asked the new questions. A comparison of the two formats showed that the revamped queries produced 44% more personal victimization reports and 49% more property incidents (Kindermann, Lynch, & Cantor, 1997). As expected, reports for robbery, personal theft, and motor vehicle theft did not show substantial gains. However, rapes jumped by 157%, assaults rose 57%, burglaries increased by 20%, and theft moved upward by 27%. Inspection of the data led the analysts to believe that the new instrument made inroads into gray-area events. A *gray-area event* pertains to a victimization that does not conform to the usual common stereotype. For example, episodes involving nonstrangers as the aggressors showed marked increases with the new questions. It would appear, then, that the revisions worked as intended.

A shorter reference period was also examined as a means to improve recall. This option, however, was rejected. The increased costs were simply too prohibitive.

The problem of bounding came up in reference to the mover-stayer issue. If you recall, newly relocated respondents at a household marked for inclusion in the NCVS provided unbounded information during their initial interview. One solution called for basing the sample on respondents, as opposed to household addresses. However, such a move would require interviewers to follow sample members to their new residences for subsequent questioning. This option was not feasible because it increased survey costs substantially.

Another exasperating problem has been the inability to examine subgroups within the survey data. Because of legal restrictions protecting respondent identities, it is difficult to analyze victimization data in anything but the national aggregate. The redesign efforts have demonstrated that it is possible to produce limited information based on cities or states without violating subject confidentiality. Such an ability allows for more direct and meaningful comparisons with the UCR and other data sources.

A major goal of the redesign was to enhance the analytical worth of the survey. Despite the wealth of information contained in the NCVS, many researchers would like to capture data on other related topics. The redesign team considered the feasibility of adding special supplements that would supply data on selected topics. A variety of supplements have been conducted over the life of the NCVS, particularly since the redesign was fully implemented in 1993 (see Table 2.6). These supplements have examined respondent perceptions of offense severity, school crime, workplace violence, and identity theft, among other topics.

Another suggestion in the redesign was to conduct longitudinal analyses. To date, victimization studies have been restricted to cross-sectional approaches. It has not been possible to match a person's file with responses from an earlier interview. The redesign team strongly recommended that procedures for more longitudinal analyses be adopted.

The redesign also suggested the move to *computer-assisted telephone interviews* (CATI). This technique uses a computer to prompt the interviewer with the proper questions. It automatically skips questions whenever appropriate. Computerization should also eliminate miscoded data by accepting only legitimate responses during the interview.

Table 2.6 NCVS Supplements

National Survey of Crime Severity (1977)
- Asked respondents to rank severity of different offenses

Victim Risk Supplement (1984)
- Assessed perceptions of safety and crime prevention behavior

School Crime Supplement (1989, 1995, 1999, and biannually thereafter)
- Asked respondents ages 12–18 about school safety and security

Public-Police Contact Survey (1996 and every three years thereafter)
- Examined police use of force

Workplace Risk Supplement (2004)
- Assessed workplace violence and prevention efforts

Special Victimization Study (2006)
- Focused on stalking

Identity Theft Survey (2008)
- Assessed the extent and characteristics of identity theft

Source: Compiled by authors from Rand, M. R. (2010). National crime victimization survey, supplements. In B. S. Fisher & S. P. Lab (Eds.), Encyclopedia of victimology and crime prevention. *Los Angeles: Sage.*

The NCVS began carrying out the redesigned survey in 1988 and had the full survey overhauled and in place by the end of 1992. The current survey targets roughly 86,000 respondents in some 43,000 households nationally (Rennison, 2010). Typically, greater than 90% of the households and individuals respond to the survey requests, and the size of the sample results in little sampling error (Rennison, 2010). Undoubtedly, the NCVS will undergo further modification as victimization surveys continue to evolve and as the need for different sorts of information becomes more apparent. Victimization surveys have become a valuable tool within a very short time, both in the United States and other countries.

CRIME SURVEYS OUTSIDE THE UNITED STATES

While victimization surveys were pioneered in the United States, the importance of surveying the populace about crime victimization has been recognized around the world. Early non-U.S. surveys were conducted in The Netherlands; Zurich, Switzerland; and Stuttgart, Germany, in 1973 (Killias, 2010). The British initiated the ongoing British Crime Survey (BCS) in 1982 (Mayhew, 2010); the Dutch established one in 1983; and the Swiss began in 1984 (Killias, 2010). Beyond the individual country-based surveys, the International Crime Victims Survey (ICVS) was initiated in 1989, with new surveys in 1996, 2000, and 2005 (Killias, 2010).

 **WEB ACTIVITY**

A great deal of information on the National Crime Victimization Survey can be found on the Bureau of Justice Statistics website, along with links to different reports and surveys that have been conducted. These can be found at **http://www.bjs.gov/index.cfm?ty= dcdetail&iid=245**

The BCS is both similar to and different from the NCVS. First, until 2001, it was conducted every other year. Second, the BCS surveys only those aged 16 and over, and only one person per household. Third, the recall period in the BCS is one year, compared with the six-month window used in the NCVS (Mayhew, 2010). Another very important difference is the coupling of British census data to the BCS responses. This provides a richness not found in the NCVS and an ability to undertake more in-depth analyses of victimization in the community. Similar to the NCVS, the BCS has added special topics and questions over the years and uses computer-aided technologies (Mayhew, 2010).

WEB ACTIVITY

You can explore the British Crime Survey and compare it with the NCVS at **http:// www.crimesurvey.co.uk/**

The advent of the ICVS in 1989 opened the door to a wider view of victimization. Whereas both the NCVS and the BCS focus mainly on street crimes, the ICVS also includes questions on political corruption, hate crimes, slave trade, and other similar topics (Killias, 2010). The ability to make cross-country comparisons is also a major advancement. Unfortunately, while the ICVS has been conducted in 78 different countries, the United States has not participated. A number of concerns/problems have plagued the ICVS. Among these are small sample sizes in each country (typically less than 2,000), a five-year reference period, criticisms of CATI use in poorer and developing countries, and the lack of information gathered on ethnicity and other potential explanatory factors (Killias, 2010). Despite these problems, the ICVS offers insights otherwise unavailable.

COMPARING THE NCVS AND THE UCR

Recent years have witnessed a growing reliance on victimization survey data for assessing the crime problem. Perhaps the greatest reason for this change is the realization that the UCR suffers from systematic limitations. For some time now, criminologists have recognized that official reports underestimate how much crime there really is. Even the primitive early victim surveys uncovered much more crime than the UCR did. In addition, victim surveys capture data on the victim and the circumstances surrounding the criminal event. As a result, victimization surveys have earned an important niche in the measurement of crime.

According to the NCVS (Truman & Planty, 2012), there was almost 23 million crimes committed in 2011. In comparison, the UCR tabulated less than half as many Index Offenses in 2011 (Federal Bureau of Investigation, 2013). Even when one takes definitional differences into account, the gap between these two data sources is quite large. Clearly, victims reveal to interviewers incidents that have not come to the attention of the police. Table 2.7 shows that for most offenses, respondents report roughly half or less than half of

Table 2.7 Percent of Victimizations Reported to the Police, NCVS, 2008	
Offense	**% Reported**
Violent Crime:	**47.1**
Rape/sexual assault	41.4
Robbery	60.5
Aggravated assault	62.0
Simple assault	41.3
Property Crime:	**40.3**
Burglary	56.2
Motor vehicle theft	79.6
Theft	33.6
Source: Compiled by authors from NCVS data.	

their victimizations to the police. Aggravated assault (67%), robbery (66%) and motor vehicle theft (83%) are those offenses most often reported to the police. Cases of theft (36%) are the least reported offenses. Figure 2.1 graphically compares crime rates derived from both the UCR and NCVS for 2008. In virtually every category in which even rough comparisons can be made, the NCVS reveals higher offense levels, with the largest differences appearing in burglary and motor vehicle theft.

Victimization surveys also provide additional information not addressed by the UCR. For example, males are more likely to be violent crime victims than females, blacks have higher robbery and aggravated assault rates than whites, never-married individuals are more likely to be victimized, and persons with lower incomes have a higher risk of becoming crime victims in every category than people who are wealthier.

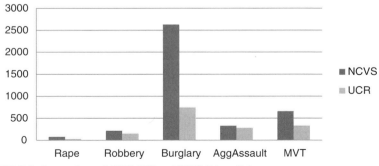

FIGURE 2.1 Comparison of 2008 UCR and NCVS Crime Rates.

AggAssault, aggravated assault; MVT, motor vehicle theft. *Source: Constructed by authors from UCR and NCVS data.*

Table 2.8 Victim–Offender Relationships in Violent Crime, NCVS, 2008	
Spouse	2.8%
Ex-spouse	2.0
Parent	0.6
Child	1.2
Other relative	3.9
Acquaintance	25.2
Casual acquaintance	13.9
Stranger	36.2
Don't know	5.3

Source: Maquire, K. (2013). Sourcebook of Criminal Justice Statistics [Online]. Retrieved December 3, 2013 from http://www.albany.edu/sourcebook/pdf/t3152008.pdf

Victimization data also provide a great deal of information about victim–offender relationships (see Table 2.8). This information, however, is primarily for crimes in which the victim and offender have personal contact. In 2008, 10.5% of all violent crimes were committed by family members. Strangers were involved in a high of 34% of all violent crimes and 54% of all robberies (Bureau of Justice Statistics, 2010b). Strangers committed 34% of all assaults, with a low of 26% of all sexual offenses (Bureau of Justice Statistics, 2010b). Acquaintances, either casual or well-known, make up 39% of the offenders, according to the NCVS.

REPEAT VICTIMIZATION

The growth of victimization surveys and the development of new data analysis techniques, particularly through the use of computer mapping, have generated increased interest in repeat victimization, or revictimization. *Repeat victimization* can be defined as the repeated occurrence of crime involving either the same victim or the same location. Even casual observation demonstrates that repeat victimization is common with some crimes. For example, it is not unusual for domestic violence victims to drop charges or refuse to cooperate with the prosecution, despite records of ongoing violent episodes. Sherman (1995) points out that police often receive repeated calls for service stemming from domestic violence at the same addresses.

In one of the earliest examinations of repeat victimization, Polvi et al. (1990) noted that the risk of being a repeat burglary victim is 12 times higher than expected, and this risk is more pronounced immediately after an initial burglary. This heightened risk persists for roughly three months and then levels off to normal expected levels.

Major victimization surveys, such as the National Crime Victimization Survey (NCVS), the British Crime Survey (BCS), and the International Crime Victim Survey (ICVS), demonstrate the existence of repeat victimization. The NCVS provides some insight through its questions dealing with *series victimizations.* "A series victimization is defined as six or more similar but separate crimes which the victim is unable to recall individually or describe in detail to an interviewer" (Bureau of Justice Statistics, 2003). The 2005 NCVS reveals that 4.1% of all crimes of violence are series victimizations. Similarly, 3.9% of all personal crimes and 0.5% of all property crimes fall into the series victimization category (Bureau of Justice Statistics, 2006a). Analysis of the BCS also shows that multiple victimization episodes are concentrated among relatively few victims. Ellingworth, Farrell, and Pease (1995), using BCS data from 1982 through 1992, point out that roughly one-quarter to one-third of all property crime is committed against people victimized five or more times within a one-year period of time. This means that almost two-thirds of victims are repeat victims. Similarly, roughly 50% of personal crimes appear as repeat victimizations (Ellingworth et al., 1995). Data from the 2000 ICVS appear in Table 2.9 and show that 46% of sexual crimes and 41% of assaults are repeats (Weisel, 2005). Burglary exhibits the lowest level of repeats, but even there it is 17% of offenses.

Another way of demonstrating revictimization using victimization data is to compare prevalence and incidence data. *Prevalence data* refer to the number of individuals who experience victimization over a period of time, whereas *incidence data* represent the total number of offenses that are reported during the same period. Any point at which the number of incidents exceeds the number of victims would indicate revictimization. Various analyses of survey data demonstrate the often concentrated nature of victimization. Pease (1998) notes that 2% of all respondents account for 41% of all property crimes, while

Table 2.9 Estimates of Repeat Victimization from the ICVS

Offense	Repeat Offenses
Sexual assault	46%
Assault	41
Robbery	27
Vandalism to vehicles	25
Theft from vehicles	21
Vehicle theft	20
Burglary	17

Source: Weisel, D. L. (2005). Analyzing Repeat Victimization. Problem-Oriented Guides for Police. Washington, DC: U.S. Department of Justice, Office of Community Oriented Policing Services.

1% account for 59% of the personal crimes. Farrell and Pease (2003) report that 25% of all burglaries in Charlotte, North Carolina, are repeat victimizations. Using data on 19 countries from the ICVS, Farrell and Bouloukos (2001) find that more than 40% of the sexual assaults and more than 30% of all assaults and robberies are repeats.

So far, the discussion has implicitly assumed that revictimization involves only the same victims. Revictimization, however, is not restricted in this way. Farrell (2005, 2010) notes that repeats can take a variety of forms. A *near repeat* is one in which a neighbor may be victimized in the same or a similar way as the initial victim (Johnson & Bowers, 2005). A *virtual repeat* involves a follow-up victimization of a similar person, place, or item, not necessarily nearby (Farrell, 2010; Pease, 1998). In virtual repeats the emphasis is on the method of offending or the similarity of the targets. Recognition of offenses as a repeat victimization, either as a near or virtual repeat, provides important information for assisting victims.

One problem with identifying repeat victimization involves the impact of short time frames within which repeats can occur. Ellingworth et al. (1995) note that most levels of repeat victimization in the BCS are probably under-reported because they rely on repeats only within a one-year time frame, which minimizes the potential for repeats before or after the survey boundaries. The problem of short time frames for repeat victimization is very evident when considering the NCVS. The NCVS reveals significantly lower repeat victimization compared with the ICVS for every category of victimization, including sexual offenses (51% repeats in the ICVS; 23% in the NCVS), assaults and threats (46% ICVS; 26% NCVS), and burglary (40% ICVS; 18% NCVS) (Farrell, Tseloni, & Pease, 2005). The reason for this is the six-month time frame used by the NCVS and the 12-month time frame used by the ICVS. Kleemans (2001) notes that 9% of repeat burglaries occur within one month, 30% occur within six months, and almost half occur within one year. Thus, the time frame under consideration makes a difference for the finding of repeat victimization.

Beyond documenting the extent of repeat victimization, research also provides information on the time frame of repeats. Pease (1998) notes that a great deal of revictimization tends to occur within a short period of time after the first victimization. Similar results appear in Bowers, Hirschfield, and Johnson's (1998) examination of repeat victimization of nonresidential locations and Johnson, Bowers, and Hirschfield's (1997) burglary study. In both analyses, the risk of repeats remains higher within relatively short periods of time after the initial victimization. Weisel (2005) demonstrates that the time frame for many repeats remains short for a range of offenses (see Table 2.10). For example, 15% of domestic violence repeats take place within one day, and 35% occur within five weeks (Lloyd, Farrell, & Pease, 1994). Similarly, 25%

Table 2.10 Time Frame for Repeat Victimization

Offense	Proportion of Repeats by Time Period	Where
Domestic violence	15% within 24 hours 25% within five weeks	Merseyside, England
Bank robbery	33% within three months	England
Residential burglary	25% within one week 51% within one month	Tallahassee, Florida
	11% within one week 33% within one month	Merseyside, England
Nonresidential burglary	17% within one week 43% within one month	Merseyside, England
Property crime at schools	70% within one month	Merseyside, England

Source: Weisel, D. L. (2005). Analyzing Repeat Victimization. *Washington, DC: U.S. Department of Justice, Office of Community Oriented Policing Services.*

 WEB ACTIVITY

You can read more about repeat victimization and responding to the problem in a guide from the Center for Problem-Oriented Policing at **http://www.popcenter.org/tools/repeat_victimization/**

of repeat burglaries occur within one week, and 51% occur within one month (Robinson, 1998). The information on the time frame of repeats can be useful for the introduction of prevention initiatives.

Evidence of repeat victimization, victim recidivism, or chronic victimization is not restricted to survey data or to individuals. Efforts to improve police effectiveness and efficiency have prompted the development of various techniques to identify what are known as crime *hot spots*. "Hot spots" are "small places in which the occurrence of crime is so frequent that it is highly predictable" (Sherman, 1995: 36). The use of computer mapping has enhanced the ability of most police departments to identify such places. Sherman, Garten, and Buerger (1989) noted that all domestic disturbance calls in Minneapolis came from only 9% of the places in town, all assaults occurred at 7% of the locations, and all burglaries took place at 11% of the places. Farrell and Pease (2003) noted that 1% of all Charlotte addresses account for 39% of all reported burglaries. Similar concentrations of offenses and calls for police service have been found in many other locations (see, for example, Block & Block, 1995; Spelman, 1995). What is not always demonstrated is whether the calls involve the same victims. While domestic violence calls to the same address probably have the same victim and offender (Farrell, Phillips, & Pease, 1995), repeated assault calls to a bar may involve different patrons every time. In either case, the value of the information is in its ability to inform responses to victimization.

Explanations for repeat victimization can generally be divided into two categories—risk heterogeneity and state dependence (Farrell et al., 1995).

Risk heterogeneity, or a flag explanation (Gill & Pease, 1998), suggests that the prior victimization or some other factor identifies the victim or location as an appropriate target for further victimization. As such, subsequent victimizations may be committed by different offenders who are attracted to the target by its apparent vulnerability or some other characteristic. Farrell et al. (1995) use the example of repeated fights at a bar as an indication of risk heterogeneity, where people looking for fights or interested in risky situations are attracted to establishments with a reputation for conflict. Those locations and/or the employees of those bars are then at a higher risk for repeat victimization.

Event dependency, or *boost explanations* (Gill & Pease, 1998), refers to situations in which (usually) the same offender commits another offense based on the past experiences with that victim or location. Successful past offending leads to another attempt against the same target. It is possible under this situation that a new offender commits a follow-up offense as a result of information shared between offenders. In this case, specific information about the target based on a past offense is the key to subsequent actions.

Revictimization information can be useful for developing responses by both potential victims and community agencies. Pease (1998) offers three conclusive findings based on studies of repeat victimization. First, "victimization is the best single predictor of victimization." Second, "when victimization recurs it tends to do so quickly." Finally, offenders take advantage of the opportunities that appear in the first offense. These findings do not mean that every victim will be victimized again in the future. Rather, they indicate that victims may be more vulnerable because of circumstances or lifestyle. Past victimization should be used to assess what factors contributed to the crime and what actions can be taken to mitigate future vulnerability. Just as people use knowledge of the victimization of others as a warning sign, so should a victim take heed. Unfortunately, for many victims, "Lightning *does* strike twice!"

Despite the increased interest in repeat victimization, there are several issues that require more attention. Perhaps the most pressing issue is to identify the extent of such activity. While the evidence shows that there is a good deal of repeat victimization, not all criminal acts are followed by another one against the same location or individual. Identifying which acts will result in a repeat victimization *prior* to the subsequent act is an elusive task. All of the existing research offers an after-the-fact analysis of the extent of the problem. It is possible, therefore, that interventions targeting past victims may result in a lot of unnecessary effort. On the other hand, such targeting should be more effective than interventions aimed at the general public, many of whom would never become a victim in the first place.

SUMMARY

How much criminal victimization is there in society? One thing that should be evident after working your way through this chapter is that criminologists and victimologists cannot provide an exact answer. However, by using different data sources, they can give some estimates as to the nature and extent of the victimization problem.

No matter which approach a researcher takes when he or she tackles this question, certain systematic problems have the potential to hamper those measurement efforts. The materials in this chapter shed light on what some of these obstacles are, how they impinge upon the data, and what can be done to minimize these intrusions. As you can see, victim surveys are very much like any other consumer product. People are constantly tinkering, updating, and refining these instruments to take advantage of the most current technology available.

KEY TERMS

boost explanations
bounding
British Crime Survey (BCS)
computer-assisted telephone
    interviews (CATI)
dark figure of crime
event dependency
flag explanations
forward record check
gray-area events
hot spots
household respondent
incidence data
Index Offenses
International Crime Victimization
    Survey (ICVS)
memory decay
mover-stayer problem
National Crime Survey (NCS)
National Crime Victimization
    Survey (NCVS)

National Incident-Based
    Reporting System (NIBRS)
near repeat
NORC survey
panel design
Part I Offenses
Part II Offenses
personal offenses
prevalence data
property offenses
repeat victimization
risk heterogeneity
reverse record check
screen questions
self-respondent
series victimizations
Supplemental Homicide Reports (SHR)
telescoping
Uniform Crime Reports (UCR)
victimization survey
virtual repeat

Explaining Victimization

INTRODUCTION

Explaining victimization is not that different from explanations for crime and delinquency. Most criminological theories attempt to understand why some people resort to criminal behavior while others do not. Victimologists

49

take a slightly different approach by focusing upon the not-so-victorious portion of the criminal–victim dyad. As we saw in Chapter 1, the concentration upon the victim led to an early reliance on the notion of victim precipitation. What did the victim do to deserve this type of treatment? While this idea does have some very real limits, victim involvement has yielded some fruitful insights when it comes to homicide victimization. As a result, some explanations focus upon theories that are based upon social interactionism and a cultural perspective. Other theories, particularly when considering property crimes, consider traditional criminological concepts, such as social strain and opportunity.

This chapter attempts to provide an overview of explanations for victimization and crime. It borrows heavily from the criminological discussion of what causes or leads to crime and delinquency, although the focus is often on the victimological side of the criminal–victim equation. The chapter also discusses some explanations that are more unique to victimology.

INTRAINDIVIDUAL THEORIES

Intraindividual theories locate the cause of deviant behavior inside a person. These explanations are frequently referred to as theories of *psychopathology*, or mental imbalances within the offender. They focus on what is wrong within the individual and address a variety of specific issues thought to cause abnormal behavior. Some of these items include substance use, mental illness, stress, depression, low self-esteem, intergenerational transmission of abuse, and other problematic areas. The perpetrator is seen as a disturbed or maladjusted individual who fails to exert sufficient control over his actions.

The earliest theories of crime often relied on general opinions that the offender was sick or disturbed. In essence, the offender was an aberration and did not reflect the norm in society. This belief fit well with the idea that interpersonal violence (IPV) was a private matter not to be dealt with by outsiders or, in the case of family violence, outside the home. In those instances where family violence came into the public spotlight, one could dismiss it easily as an isolated incident and of concern only to the immediate family.

Most early explanations of sexual assault portrayed rape and sexual violence as stemming from psychopathology. These explanations gained quick acceptance because they painted rape as a social aberration. One could attribute such undesirable behavior to the few deranged individuals who committed these acts. What made this perspective so lucrative was that it deflected attention away from society and the victim. In essence, they were blameless for the offense.

While some writers have attributed IPV to the mental illness of the offender, a more precise definition can be given to the topic by looking at individual factors that cause or contribute to the behavior. Alcohol and other drug consumption by either or both parties is a common research finding (Brookoff, 1997; Browne, 1987; Collins, 1989; Gelles & Straus, 1979; Hotaling & Sugarman, 1986; Kantor & Straus, 1987; Stuart et al., 2006). However, the fact that substance use is common in IPV cases does not isolate the causal mechanism at work. Two basic possibilities exist. First, the use of alcohol or other drugs may cause the offender to act or become abusive. The second alternative argues that alcohol and other drugs act as disinhibitors. They break down the barriers that normally would keep the offender from committing the act. Researchers have not yet learned which of these two possibilities is correct.

Stress, depression, low self-esteem, and similar factors are often proposed as causes of IPV (Hotaling & Straus, 1989; Pagelow, 1984). The basic argument is that the offender, when striking out against others, is venting frustration or anger at other people or things that he or she cannot deal with directly. For example, one cannot relieve stress at work by attacking the boss. Instead, one might search for a substitute and turn on an available family member who has little recourse. The abuser simply does not possess the tools with which to channel feelings in a more acceptable fashion. Often, socioeconomic conditions of the family are pointed to as a cause of low self-esteem or stress.

The intraindividual approach views child maltreatment as the product of some internal defect or flaw inside the abuser. Supposedly, personality deficiency leads "to a lack of inhibition in expressing frustration and other impulsive behavior" (Spinetta & Rigler, 1972: 299). If researchers can identify the disturbances present in child abusers, then the next step is to develop appropriate treatment plans. As one commentator (Melton, 2005: 11) explains:

> the assumption [is] . . . that the problem of child maltreatment was reducible to 'syndromes'—in effect, that abusive and neglectful parents were either very sick or very evil and that they thus could be appropriately characterized as 'those people' who were fundamentally different from ourselves.

Thus, the psychiatric model is attractive because it tries to locate and treat personality disorders that lead to child abuse.

Steele and Pollock (1974) conducted one of the first attempts to apply the psychiatric model to child abusers. They described their initial patient as a "gold mine of psychopathology." Those insights guided their analyses of 60 families over the next six years. The results revealed that child abusers did not monopolize any one particular diagnostic category. Instead, maltreaters exhib-ited disorders that spanned the entire spectrum of *psychopathology* or mental disorders. One phenomenon the researchers did focus upon, though, was role reversal.

Later research in this vein led Wright (1976) to coin the phrase *"sick but slick" parents*. Child maltreaters do not exhibit serious deficiencies on a battery of traditional psychological inventories. However, closer inspection shows that these subjects were not answering truthfully. Instead, the evaders gave what they thought were socially desirable responses. Thus, child abusers go to great lengths to project an image of themselves as normal parents—probably in order to deflect detection.

Critics point to four concerns that weaken support for the intraindividual approaches, particularly in relation to abuse. First, most inquiries rely upon clinical information as opposed to a random sample from some larger population. As a result, there is no way of knowing whether abusers who seek help form a typical cross-section of all offenders. Second, studies usu-ally lack an appropriate control group. The absence of a benchmark makes it difficult to determine whether attributes isolated as peculiar to abusers are unique or are shared with members of the larger population. Third, there is very little agreement among researchers about which exact charac-teristics distinguish abusers from nonabusers. Finally, much of the research is *ex post facto*. That is, it occurs after the act has taken place and registers very little predictive power.

SYMBOLIC INTERACTIONISM

A *symbolic interactionist* approach views behavior as a result of the interaction between two or more people. Most encounters are not planned and the process and outcome of the interactions are always uncertain. Symbolic interactionism proposes that every individual develops his or her self-image through a pro-cess of interaction with the surrounding world (Mead, 1934). How an indi-vidual sees himself or herself is determined by how that person thinks others see him or her. That is, a person's self-concept comes out of interaction with other people and the environment. If an individual perceives a positive image of himself or herself from others, the person will hold a positive self-image. Individuals view themselves in the way other people look at them.

The interaction between people also sets expectations and behaviors. For example, two people hired to do the same job in the same job setting will, over time, develop a leader–follower relationship. This will solidify as they interact with one another and will set expectations for how they will continue to inter-act. The position and roles people hold become set over time and repetition.

Some relationships are set by historical and social precedent. Husbands and wives hold certain roles and expectations in relation to one another. Parents and children also learn appropriate relations between one another.

The symbolic interactionism approach to explaining elder abuse acknowledges that individual roles change over time. Participants alter their expectations and reactions according to the new way in which they see and interpret the changing "reality." In essence, reality is the result of how people interpret what is going on around them and react to their surroundings.

For example, when parents switch roles with children, they expect the child to shower them with nurturance and love, rather than vice versa. When such a situation occurs, the parties can become frustrated and act out. When the child fails to provide emotional support (as evidenced, for example, by crying for a prolonged period, soiling diapers, or being unresponsive), the frustrated parent feels unwanted, rejected, and not loved by the child. Such feelings trigger an aggressive parental response that culminates in maltreatment. Steele and Pollock (1974) trace this infantilism back to the abuser's relationship with his or her own parents. According to them, parents maltreat children because of the inadequate relationship they had with their own parents.

Elder maltreatment signifies a dramatic *role reversal* for both the parent and the child. At an earlier point in time, the elderly person provided the basic income, made the major decisions, and acted as the head of the household. At that time the child was completely dependent on the parent. As years pass, parents relinquish their dominance. Parents whose well-being withers may come to rely heavily on the child—making extensive new demands and requiring more assistance than ever before. In essence, the parent and the child swap positions and take on new roles. Many individuals are either unprepared or unwilling to accept these new responsibilities. This frequently leads to abuse and neglect (Galbraith, 1989; Phillips, 1986).

As the aging person faces changing needs and begins to rely upon others for basic assistance, he or she redefines the situation in a variety of ways. In one sense, the parent may see himself or herself as a burden to the caregiver (Quinn & Tomita, 1986) and, in turn, may tacitly accept any maltreatment. Alternatively, the elderly individual may feel that the caregiver is too demanding, makes unreasonable requests, fails to do things when and how the parent wishes, or simply ignores the parent (Phillips, 1986; Shell, 1982). The older person may fight, yell, throw tantrums, invade the caregiver's privacy, or react in other inappropriate ways (Quinn & Tomita, 1986). The caregiver can similarly define the actions and demands of the elderly as inappropriate. These behaviors by both the older person and the caregiver can easily lead to abuse and neglect, or result in the interpretation of actions as abusive (Phillips, 1986).

Not all problems involve role reversal. The concept of *victim precipitation* fits the symbolic interactionist mold. As we mentioned in Chapter 1, early victimologists gave serious consideration to the idea of *victim precipitation*. They sought to learn what the victim did that triggered such a violent reaction. While Hans von Hentig and others debated how the dynamics of the criminal–victim dyad led to the victim's ultimate demise, it was Wolfgang's (1958) analysis of Philadelphia homicides that provided the necessary empirical support.

Wolfgang (1958) undertook an extensive review of police homicide records for all murders committed during the five-year period of 1948–1952 in Philadelphia. The one thing that struck Wolfgang was the realization that there was a significant amount of victim participation in some of these homicide events. Wolfgang (1958: p. 254) categorized 150 cases (26% of all the homicides) as victim-precipitated. In other words, the victims in these incidents initiated the violent encounter. They were the first party to display a weapon, throw a punch, or take other physically aggressive actions. When the other party retaliated, the violence escalated to a lethal response.

Luckenbill (1977) rekindled interest in victim actions when he addressed homicide as a "situated transaction." What he meant by a *situated transaction* was that the homicide culminated from a chain or series of discrete actions and reactions by the participants. The combination of the two actors, and possibly an audience, contributed to the development of a violent interaction. Luckenbill became intrigued by how the parties reacted to each other and whether the dynamics progressed in any regular patterns.

Tracing the hostilities, as well as the moves and countermoves displayed by the participants, led Luckenbill to conclude that these deadly struggles evolved in a series of predictable stages. What usually initiated these encounters was some type of an insult. The eventual victim may have said something rude, made an unwelcomed remark, or issued an obnoxious gesture toward the other party. The second stage consists of the recipient's assessment of these actions as offensive. The next stage, the response, appears to be absolutely critical to the final resolution of this conflict. The recipient's response could be to ignore the apparent insult, to dismiss the issuer as inconsequential, or to deal with the matter immediately. For instance, direct confrontation could involve a dare for the victim to restate the insult, an issuance of a retaliatory remark or gesture by the aggrieved party, or a physical challenge. The goal at this point is to do something to save face, degrade the initiator, or demonstrate superiority.

If the attempt to salvage one's social appearance fails, then the situation escalates to the fourth stage. At this point, both parties have elected neither to turn away nor to defuse the mounting disagreement. There could be more verbal challenges, accompanied by minor scuffling or further insults. Should neither party break off or end the grievance, a battle is imminent. A common strategy at this point is to assume an intimidating stance as a demonstration of pugilistic superiority or to display a weapon as proof of a tactical advantage. A failure to heed such a warning results in the ultimate demise of one of the parties. Thus, Luckenbill (1977) sees murder as the final outcome in a series of moves and counterstrategies negotiated continuously by the combatants.

Victim precipitation is a major contributing factor in serious violence. The key feature of these violent encounters is that they are provoked by an attack on one's "honor" and systematically evolve into a deadly "character contest." In essence, the nature of the instigating act is trivial compared with the final outcome. Combatants who were armed, intoxicated, and aggressive were more likely to be killed than those who were sober. These violent episodes then move to more threats and evasive actions. If a serious outcome is to be avoided, this is the time to de-escalate matters. However, for those incidents that do continue, the physical attack ensues next. Other applications of Luckenbill's "situated transaction" approach have found it to be helpful in reaching a better understanding of intimate partner homicide (Swatt & He, 2006) and how the "code of the street" leads to recurrent violence (Rich & Grey, 2005).

THE ROUTINE ACTIVITIES/LIFESTYLE MODEL

An alternative approach for explaining victimization that involves consideration of interaction between parties is the routine activities approach. Routine activities refer to the fact that individuals may place themselves at risk of victimization by their everyday behavior. Cohen and Felson (1979) demonstrate this possibility by examining social changes that have led to increasing property crime. They point out that the move to two-earner households has left homes unprotected during the day and allows for the purchase of more valuable and portable items. At the same time, increased mobility has led to a greater number of targets for offenders. Taken together, this convergence of suitable targets, lack of guardianship, and motivated offenders has allowed for greater levels of theft. Hindelang, Gottfredson, and Garofalo (1978) refer to this as a function of the lifestyle of the parties involved. That is, an individual's choice of behavior (i.e., lifestyle) influences the chances of becoming a victim. This approach is referred to as the *routine activities/lifestyle model*.

While traditionally used for property offenses, it is equally adept at explaining personal offenses. For a homicide, assault, or robbery to occur, it is necessary that the offender and victim be in the same place without a guardian. One example of this would be the following scenario:

> Two acquaintances frequent a bar where fights are a common occurrence. On one visit both individuals are cheering for opposing sports teams and make a wager on the outcome. Toward the end

of a close contest, a questionable call by an official determines the outcome of the game. Coupled with a good amount of alcohol consumption, the two parties come to blows; one person pulls a knife and stabs the other.

A similar scenario can be outlined for a robbery event:

A potential offender is in need of funds. Knowing that a local bar is frequented by college students who often leave inebriated and alone, the individual finds a location one block from the establishment on a road that is a major walkway back to the campus. Waiting at the location after 11:00 p.m. on Friday evening, the offender picks a lone patron and robs him as he heads back to his dormitory.

From a routine activities perspective, these offenses are partly attributable to the routine of the parties involved.

The value of the routine activities/lifestyle explanations is in understanding the social situations in which violent acts occur. These perspectives argue that our choices of where to go, what to do, and how to proceed (even when made innocently) influence the chances of becoming a victim. Recognition of this process may provide insight into personal offenses, like homicide and assault.

Routine activities have been used to explain in-school crime. Schools provide all the necessary factors for crime, according to routine activities theory. By bringing a large number of youths together, the school is making suitable targets (students and their belongings) available to potential offenders (other students) within a location where there is often nobody watching (a lack of guardians). Both the offender and the victim are required by law to attend school. Offenders can pick the time and place within the school for committing an offense. Moreover, despite all the best intentions in the world, teachers and staff cannot be watching every student at all times.

The routine activities explanation receives even more support when one considers the temporal nature of crime. An inspection of when youthful offending occurs shows that most juvenile crime is committed in the afternoon between roughly 3:00 and 4:00 p.m. (Office of Juvenile Justice and Delinquency Prevention, 1999). Specifically, almost 20% of juvenile violent crime and 14% of youthful sexual assaults take place between 3:00 and 7:00 p.m. on school days. This interval is precisely the time when youths are out of school and generally not under any direct supervision by a parent, teacher, or other adult guardian. In addition, a great deal of this victimization takes place near a school or along major routes used by youths going to or from school. Thus, the connection between schools and victimization is easy to delineate.

SOCIOCULTURAL EXPLANATIONS

Sociocultural explanations look for events that are external to the individual as the cause of behavior. These explanations have gained prominence as viable explanations for sexual battery and child maltreatment. They frequently focus on the traditional roles of males, females and children in society, thus they have a heavy historical orientation.

The sociocultural perspective views the abuse of women as an outcome of their historical treatment and the current patriarchal makeup of society (Brownmiller, 1975; Burgess & Draper, 1989; Dobash & Dobash, 1979). In other words, *patriarchy* creates a male privilege or structured inequality that portrays women as inferior and lacking in social power (Hunnicut, 2009). This approach has also been referred to as a feminist perspective. Brownmiller (1975) brought these arguments to the forefront when she pointed out that the historical place of women in society was one of subservience. Women belonged either to their fathers or to their husbands. Females were property; as such, they were subject to the wishes of the owner. In this context, any attack on a female was actually an affront against her master. Any compensation or retribution due to the possession's devaluation went to the owner, not to the female who was victimized. It is for similar reasons that warring armies use rape as a weapon to terrorize, intimidate, and taunt opposing forces (Brownmiller, 1975).

In updating the sociocultural explanation, rape is simply a means of showing and promoting male domination in a society in which formal ownership of females is no longer permitted. Rape is a means of guaranteeing the inequality between the sexes, with males occupying the upper niches of power. The sociocultural approach emphasizes the argument that rape is *not* a sexual offense. Instead, rape is an offense of *power*—a tool that enables men to exert power and control over women.

As one would expect, the sociocultural explanation gained a great deal of support from the women's movement. It became a clear challenge to the dominant male structure within society. Rape was also identifiable as perhaps the most heinous example of what was wrong with traditional sex roles. The sociocultural problems surrounding rape were highlighted further by the callous methods used by the criminal justice system when handling victims (Brownmiller, 1975; Holmstrom & Burgess, 1978) and by rape myths believed by many individuals (Koss & Leonard, 1984; Lottes, 1988).

The sociocultural approach also receives a great deal of support from discussions of date or acquaintance rape among college populations. Numerous authors point to the influence of peer support in sexual assault (see, for example, DeKeseredy & Kelly, 1995; Koss & Cleveland, 1997; Koss & Gaines, 1993; Martin & Hummer, 1989). Two peer networks often linked to sexual aggression are fraternities/sororities and athletics (Armstrong, Hamilton, & Sweeney, 2006; Boeringer, 1999; Gage, 2008; Humphrey & Kahn, 2000; Koss & Gaines, 1993; Martin and Hummer, 1989; Minow & Einolf, 2009; Stombler, 1994). In both cases, it is argued that offenders are challenged to prove their masculinity, maintain confidentiality, and support one's peers. The social setting of college life, coupled with broader social expectations of male and female behavior, enhances the probability of sexually aggressive activity.

Like sexual assault, child maltreatment is not of recent vintage. For most of history, children were looked at as family property. The ancient Romans believed that the father was endowed with the power of *patriae potestas* (Thomas, 1972). In other words, fathers had the right to sell, kill, or allow their progeny to continue to live. The ancient Greeks, especially the Spartans, practiced infanticide and abandonment of physically deformed newborns (deMause, 1974). The story of *Oedipus Rex* is testimony to the fact that these practices were accepted among both the lower and higher classes in society. Biblical stories also depict instances of child abuse, such as Abraham's aborted sacrifice of his son Isaac and King Herod's slaughter of the innocents. Other accounts of inhumane treatment have persisted down through the ages. Children were treated no differently from other property owned by the father (Whitehead & Lab, 2009).

Why were children treated in such ways? Both emotional and economic factors help explain this high degree of indifference toward children. First, the life expectancy was very short. The majority of infants died during the first year of life. Therefore, emotional attachments to newborns were avoided as a defense mechanism against the highly probable death of the infant. Second, families simply could not bear the burden of feeding and caring for another member. Children, because they could not work in the field and contribute to the household, represented a drain on the already limited family resources. This status was especially true for female offspring who would need a dowry in order to find a suitable husband.

Children who survived the first few years of life quickly found themselves thrust into the position of being "little adults" (Aries, 1962). There was no status of "childhood" as we know it today. As "little adults," children took part in all adult activities. They were expected to go to work and help support themselves. They received no formal education. Rather, schooling often entailed being sold into apprenticeship in order to bring money into the family and to provide a skill for the child.

This situation persisted into the Industrial Revolution. At that time, the severe economic competition for labor was fulfilled by exposing children to long and arduous work hours under unsafe conditions. The identification of "childhood" as a distinct station in life began to emerge slowly. Infant mortality showed signs of diminishing. Clergy, educators, and other child advocates stepped forward. As the statuses of "child" and "adolescence" emerged, there was a concurrent rise in concern over the treatment of children (Davis, Chandler, & LaRossa, 2004). Society started to realize that youths needed to be handled differently from adults.

While the acceptance of maltreatment waned, it did not disappear. The privacy of the home and the assumed sanctity of parental authority allowed much to take place out of sight. What happened within the protected confines of the home was considered to fall beyond the purview of society.

Besides the historical nature of sociocultural explanations, there also is a recognition of the place of people in the social structure as a contributor to crime and abuse. One typical characteristic of abusive families is their location in the lower social strata. Although one possibility is that social service agencies maintain more surveillance over these families, the etiological connection still fascinates researchers. Apparently, other variables act together to aggravate this situation. For example, Gil (1971) reports that one-half of the fathers were unemployed when they abused their children. Families that are cut off from neighbors and friends are prime candidates for internal hostilities (Garbarino & Gilliam, 1980). Family size and the amount of spacing between children often create havoc for parents. Unwanted pregnancies, large families, substance abuse, and unsupportive spouses may strain family resources and exacerbate an already tense living arrangement (Gelles, 1980; Smithey, 1997).

How society and culture have developed, what practices and beliefs have been carried over from past generations, and the social structure of the modern world are all related to crime and abuse. These explanations and factors are especially important for understanding family abuse. Implicit within these explanations is a belief that individuals learn what is appropriate and acceptable behavior.

LEARNING THEORY

Social learning theories have a long history in the study of deviant behavior. In this approach, behavior is learned through both formal and informal mechanisms, such as imitation, modeling, reinforcement, and explicit training. Essentially, these arguments posit that an individual learns behaviors and the attitudes that support those actions from the individuals and the world around them. Among the various learning theories that can be applied to crimes are: (1) modeling (Bandura & Walters, 1963); (2) differential association (Sutherland, 1939); and (3) differential identification (Glaser, 1956).

Modeling is perhaps the simplest form of learning theory. It suggests that people learn by copying or imitating the behavior of others. While it is assumed that most people will duplicate the actions of significant others, it is possible that some nondiscriminating viewers will mimic the activity of characters in the media.

Sutherland's (1939) *differential association* theory argues that most learning comes from interpersonal contacts that vary in frequency, duration, priority, and intensity. Individuals will act in accordance with the dominant input from the people with whom they have direct contact. Sutherland paid very little attention to the media—primarily because television did not yet exist in those days.

Glaser (1956), however, recognized the growing potential of the mass media to influence or mold behavior. *Differential identification* proposes that personal contact is not necessary for the transmission of behavioral guidelines. Both real and fictional presentations in the media, particularly television, can serve to define behaviors as either acceptable or unacceptable. In essence, differential identification is an explicit recognition that viewers can "model" or "imitate" what they see on the screen. This transference becomes problematic when the media grows preoccupied with depicting violence.

Media and Violence

Today, a great deal of the debate in learning theory involves the impact of the mass media on violent behavior. There is no dispute that the mass media is enamored with crime and violence. Violent crime is a major theme in both news and fictional media presentations, with 20% or more of television broadcast time often devoted to crime-related topics (see, for example, Dominick, 1978; Graber, 1977; Hofstetter, 1976). Even a casual observer cannot escape the centrality of crime to television. Recent years have seen a steady diet, as evidenced by shows such as "America's Most Wanted," "Unsolved Mysteries," "Law and Order," "CSI: Crime Scene Investigation," and the influx of telecasts such as Court TV.

Perhaps the most disturbing aspect of this proliferation of crime-related programming is that the presentations rarely resemble reality. Only the most sensational and horrific offenses make their way into the media. Violent crime, particularly murder, is overrepresented in comparison to its actual occurrence in the real world, and details are often distorted (Colomb & Damphousse, 2004; Dominick, 1978; Gerbner et al., 1980; Graber, 1980; Hofstetter, 1976; Paulsen, 2003; Skogan & Maxfield, 1981; Surette, 2011). In addition, it is rare for a story to focus on the consequences of the crime (e.g., being caught, prosecuted, and punished). Crime is glorified to some extent through its simple dominance in the stories. Such exposure may desensitize the public toward violence.

Various researchers have examined the potential of media presentations to influence behavior. At the simplest level, Gerbner et al. (1978; 1980) and Barrile (1980) have demonstrated that the general public give answers about crime that are more consistent with what is presented in the media than with what actually occurs. A more important concern, though, is whether media presentations can promote similar behavior among viewers. Belson (1978) reports that individuals with higher levels of exposure to realistic depictions of violence tend to commit more serious acts of violence. Similarly, studies of prize fights and fictionalized suicides find significant increases in homicide and suicide after these media presentations have been aired (Phillips, 1982, 1983).

The link between video game exposure and violent behavior has not escaped scholarly attention either. While some studies report a significant association, others claim that such an effect does not exist. Despite this lack of closure, some observers immediately pointed to being involved in excessively violent video gaming as a culprit in the 1999 Columbine High School shootings in which 13 people were killed and another 24 were injured, and in the 2007 massacre on the Virginia Tech campus that left 32 people dead and 25 wounded (Ferguson, 2007a). According to Ferguson (2007b), the literature on video game exposure is so replete with flaws that it is not possible to reach a definitive conclusion at this time. For one thing, researchers have not linked the measures commonly used to tap aggressive behavior with criminal violence. Another concern is that the typical subject pool of college or high school students overlooks the target group—persons who are predisposed toward violence. Finally, publication bias seems to have exerted an unwarranted impact on what papers are selected for print. In other words, journal editors are more prone to publish articles with significant findings and are more likely to turn down manuscripts that fail to unearth any significant relationships. This editorial slant, of course, predetermines what "knowledge" is readily available for consumption. All these concerns, in conjunction with a fresh look at the literature, led Ferguson (2007a: p. 481) to the worrisome conclusion that "researchers in the area of video game studies have become more concerned with 'proving' the presence of effects, rather than testing theory in a methodologically precise manner" (see Figure 3.1).

There are some claims that exposure to aggressive/violent pornography is coupled with violent criminal behavior (Donnerstein, 1980; Donnerstein & Hallam, 1978; Meyer, 1972; Shope, 2004; U.S. Attorney General's Commission on Pornography, 1986; Zillman, Bryant, & Carveth, 1981). For example, just before his execution, serial killer Ted Bundy blamed pornography for his violent escapades. Moreover, Andison's (1977) review of television violence research concluded there was a positive correlation between media presentations and violence. This relationship has grown stronger in more recent years, possibly due to accumulated exposure to media violence over time (Andison, 1977).

FIGURE 3.1 A person playing Call of Duty: Modern Warfare 2 on the Xbox 360.
The link between video game exposure and violent behavior is unclear. While some studies report a significant association, others claim that such an effect does not exist. *Credit: Tim Ireland/PA Wire URN:14108581 (Press Association via AP Images).*

Apart from these macro-level attempts to unravel a media–behavior link, there are numerous individual accounts of instances in which an individual imitates an act of violence seen on television or is prompted to violence by media presentations. While evidence on the media–violence link is not conclusive, there is at least qualified support for a causal connection. Huesmann and Malamuth (1986) suggest that, at the very least, excessive exposure to media violence can force some viewers to become more aggressive. It is uncertain, however, just how this causal mechanism actually works. While it is logical to assume that mass media depictions of violence prod some individuals to be violent, it is equally plausible that people who commit aggressive acts simply enjoy watching violence in the media. Despite the fact that researchers have not firmly established the direction of this relationship, there is little doubt that the mass media plays a role in the high levels of violence in society.

Learning Abuse in the Family

Social learning theory has spawned an interest in examining whether maltreatment leads to subsequent victim impairment, both for offspring and partners. A review of 29 empirical studies analyzing children who witnessed parental violence does find some connection with certain types of developmental problems (Kolbos, Blakely, & Engleman, 1996). More recent summaries of the existing literature concur and note that children who witness parental violence are also more likely to be maltreatment victims (Herrenkohl et al., 2008; Holt, Buckley, and Whelan, 2008). This exposure to multiple forms of violence and the simultaneous experience of different types of maltreatment prompted Finkelhor and his colleagues (2005, 2007) to coin the term *poly-victimization*. "Poly-victimization" means that maltreated children often fall prey to multiple forms, rather than a single type, of abuse and/or neglect. This realization is important because researchers who are unaware of this co-occurrence tendency might mistakenly attribute outcomes or effects to the wrong form of maltreatment.

There are other indications that being the victim of child maltreatment leads to subsequent delinquent behavior (Doerner, 1987; Doerner & Tsai, 1990; Fagan, 2005; Heck & Walsh, 2000; Kelley, Thornberry, & Smith, 1997; Lansford et al., 2007; Maas, Herrenkohl, & Sousa, 2008; Smith & Thornberry, 1995; Thompson et al., 2001; Widom, 1989; Widom & Maxfield, 2001; Zingraff et al., 1993). While researchers are starting to look at this linkage more thoroughly, it does appear that this relationship might vary according to the kind of maltreatment, the severity of the experience, and the frequency and duration of the victimization episodes. As this body of research becomes more sophisticated over the next several years, investigators should be able to achieve greater closure on this issue.

The principles behind social learning theory also lend credence to the notion of a *cycle of violence*. There is a fear that children who watch their parents engage in violent outbursts toward each other will come to accept these behaviors as permissible. Similarly, children who are maltreated run the risk of thinking that these behaviors are acceptable because their parents performed them. When these children grow up and form their own intimate relationships, these very same acts of violence are likely to surface.

Adherents to the "cycle of violence" thesis more commonly apply it to two forms of family violence. First, there is the popular notion that abused children will grow up to become child abusers. Second, there is the belief that children who witness spousal violence will become spouse abusers in their relationships. The U.S. Attorney General's Task Force on Family Violence (1984: pp. 2–3) summed up this view when it wrote:

> Children in violent homes "learn" violence in much the same way they learn any other behavior. They observe that violence is a normal way for people to treat one another and a normal way to solve problems. The family violence that occurs today is a time bomb that will explode years later as abused children become abusers of their own children or other children, and as children who watch one parent hitting the other repeat the example in their relationships or the community.

While some family violence researchers feel that this assessment is accurate, not all victimologists share this opinion. There is a great deal of debate over whether past victimization causes future offending. Some scholars maintain that there is still no sound empirical proof for the notion of intergenerational transmission of violence. As far as child maltreatment goes, Gelles and Cornell (1990: pp. 13–17) refer to the "cycle of violence" as a myth that hinders a full understanding of family violence. They reject this idea because it implies that maltreated children are imprinted or programmed to become abusers later in life. In other words, even if the linkage does exist, the definitive research needed to support this claim has yet to appear.

The idea of intergenerational transmission of violence has a fair share of adherents. The notion that parents instill an acceptance of violence in their offspring has appeared in the literature on child abuse and spouse abuse. Applying that same argument to elder abuse and neglect is a logical extension. Indeed, elder abuse researchers rely on child abuse and spouse abuse research to support their arguments (see Quinn & Tomita, 1986). The main difference appears in the outlet for the aggression. Rather than an abused child growing up and mistreating his or her child, the abused child grows up and retaliates against the parent who committed the initial abuse (Pillemer, 1986). However, this literature suffers from serious design flaws and weak empirical support.

The existence of contradictory evidence surrounding this ongoing debate suggests that a great deal of additional research is needed prior to making any final decisions about an intergenerational argument. The fact that past victimization may make the individual either an offender or a further victim indicates that different types of intervention may be useful once the initial victimization episode takes place. There is a clear need to identify the causal forces at work prior to making any fundamental policy decisions for addressing future behavior.

Learned Helplessness

According to Lenore Walker (1979), many battered women suffer from the syndrome she identifies as *learned helplessness*. The idea of learned helplessness centers upon three components. The first is the information a person has about what is going to happen. The second aspect is the knowledge or perception about what will happen. This component usually comes from past experiences (or lack thereof). The third portion is the person's behavior toward the event that takes place. Some people believe they cannot influence or control what is about to happen to them. As these perceptions mount and grow more overwhelming, the victim comes to believe she is helpless to alter her environment. In other words, she develops a belief that she is not in charge of the world around her and that she cannot change the flow of events. As a result, the victim becomes helpless in her struggle and may appear apathetic to some viewers.

The idea of learned helplessness follows from sociocultural explanations of the relative place of males and females in society. Some professionals contend that battered partners remain in destructive relationships for economic reasons. IPV victims may lack the monetary resources that would enable them to depart. They may have no place to go. They may not be able to support themselves financially. They may have young children that make support even more difficult. They lack marketable job skills. In short, the circumstances are such that some victims are unable to exert control over themselves or their environments. The perceived, or actual, inability to support oneself or gain employment may be an outcome of the historic role of women in society.

Interestingly, some authors view victims who tolerate such abuse as a psychopathological issue. In other words, if a person remains in a troubled relationship and still professes to love the batterer after he or she has beaten the partner, the victim must be sick or crazy. The problem with this perspective is the identification of which psychological traits are conducive to remaining in a violent relationship. Some observers point to *masochism*, or a desire to suffer, as the key ingredient. For whatever reason, victims who stay in a battering relationship harbor guilt feelings or other unresolved psychological problems that seem to welcome punishment. As a result, masochistic persons gravitate toward mates who will oblige their needs by hurting them. Another way to rephrase this notion is that these victims induce their partners to beat them to satisfy deep-seated inner urges to be beaten and hurt. This position fits the approach that Menachim Amir (1971) took when applying the concept of *victim precipitation* to forcible rape.

As you might imagine, not everyone accepts this orientation unequivocally (Hamberger, 1993; Pagelow, 1992, 1993). One scholar, in assessing this body of literature, notes:

> [T]here is little that would suggest either that women wish to bring the abuse onto themselves or simply that they are trapped in their homes without options. … The women were not passively accepting of abuse as most had attempted to get some sort of help but this did not change things. … If they are masochistic, they are staying for the abuse. An alternative is that they are staying in spite of the abuse or because of the positive aspects of the relationship. A strong possibility is that although women do have options, they do not feel that they do (Rounsaville, 1978: 17–18).

SUBCULTURAL THEORY

Subcultural theories take the position that there are groups and individuals in society that act in accordance with a set of subcultural norms that may violate the rules and regulations of the larger culture. Defining subculture is not an easy task. In the simplest sense, a *subculture* is a smaller part of a larger culture. While it must vary to some degree from the larger culture, it is not totally different. The subculture exists within and is part of the larger culture. In general, a subculture is a group of individuals who hold a set of values, beliefs, ideas, views, and/or meanings that differ to some degree from the larger culture.

From a subcultural perspective, delinquency and criminality are the result of individuals attempting to act in accordance with subcultural norms. This can occur in two ways. First, an individual acts according to subcultural mandates that, unfortunately, may be considered deviant by the larger society. This problem could be common for new immigrants who have traditionally acted according to one set of cultural proscriptions and are now faced with a different set of expectations in a new cultural setting. Second, deviance may result from the inability to join or be assimilated into a new or larger culture. Consequently, individuals may strike out against society because of the frustration faced in attempting to live according to the new cultural expectations.

Early Subcultural Explanations

Early subcultural explanations tended to focus on explaining delinquency and criminality among young adults. The emphasis was not from the victims' point of view, but rather what led the offenders to offend. Albert Cohen (1955), recognizing the concentration of delinquency among lower-class boys, proposed that these youths feel ill-equipped to compete in and cannot succeed in a middle-class society. This is compounded by the fact that they are expected to follow the goals and aspirations of the middle class. All youths are measured against a middle-class measuring rod that many cannot meet. The failure to succeed in terms of middle-class values leads to feelings of failure and diminished self-worth among the lower-class youths. As a result, these boys join together in groups and act in concert with the group (subcultural) norms instead of with the mandates of the larger culture. While this provides the youths with some degree of self-worth, status, and success, it also leads to *culture conflict*. That is, by following one set of cultural (or subcultural) practices, the individual is violating the proscriptions of another culture. In Cohen's study, adherence to the subcultural group's mandates means violating the laws of middle-class society.

Cohen (1955) identifies three aspects of the emergent "lower-class gang delinquency." He claims that the subculture is malicious, negativistic and nonutilitarian. In support of this contention, Cohen points out that the youths often steal items with the intent of causing trouble and harm for another person, not because they want the item. He sees much of the deviant activity as a means of tormenting others. The behavior brings about an immediate "hedonistic" pleasure instead of supplying any long-term need or solution to a problem. In general, there appears to be little point in the behavior besides causing trouble for the larger middle-class culture.

Walter Miller's (1958) subcultural explanation goes beyond the behavior of juveniles to include all lower-class males. Miller views the lower class as operating under a distinct set of cultural values, or focal concerns. These are: trouble, toughness, smartness, excitement, fate, and autonomy. Adherence to these lower-class focal concerns or values provides status, acceptance, and feelings of belonging for the lower-class individual (Miller, 1958).

At the same time that these values provide positive reinforcement in the lower-class world, they bring about a natural conflict with middle-class values. The goal of the lower-class individual is not to violate the law or the middle-class norms. Instead, the goal is to follow the focal concerns of their class and peers. Deviant behavior, therefore, is a by-product of following the subcultural focal concerns (Miller, 1958). Cohen (1955) saw deviance as a conscious reaction of lower-class youths striking out against the middle-class society and value system, because of the frustration faced in attempting to live according to the new cultural expectations.

Subcultures of Violence

Where the early subcultural approaches focused on youthful behavior, more recent discussions take a broader approach. Wolfgang and Ferracuti (1967), for example, posited a *subculture of violence* in which problems are solved through the use of violence. The members of this subculture hold values and beliefs that support the use of violence to solve conflicts.

The idea of subcultures has taken particular hold in discussions of homicide and assaultive behavior with the idea of a *regional culture of violence*. For years, the southern portion of the United States held the dubious distinction of leading the country in terms of homicide and assault victimization rates. As one might imagine, this *differential distribution of violent crime rates* has attracted considerable scholarly interest. What the phrase "differential distribution of violent crime rates" refers to is the fact that murder rates are not uniformly dispersed throughout time and space. In other words, if all things were equal, then all regional victimization rates should be equivalent to each other. The observed imbalance leads one to the question of how to account for these differences in rates.

Gastil (1971), examining homicide rates over a number of years, found a stable and intriguing pattern. Murder rates were quite pronounced in the South and these rates declined with distance away from this area. States bordering the South had elevated homicide rates, but these figures were not quite as high as those found in the Southern states. The states located furthest away from the South consistently showed the lowest homicide victimization rates. These observations led Gastil (1971: p. 414) to suspect that "persistent differences in homicide rates seem best explained by differences in regional culture."

According to Gastil (1971), there exists a distinctive Southern culture predating the Civil War that tolerates violence. Gastil points to a number of cultural vestiges as supporting evidence of this area's propensity toward violence, including slavery, gun ownership, dueling, a strong military tradition, frontier living, and an exaggerated sense of honor among males. This violent heritage renders Southerners distinctive from other Americans. The net impact of these cultural remnants is a desensitization toward the use of violence as an acceptable behavioral response.

People who are born and bred in the South become carriers of this "Southernness" culture. Not only do Southerners inculcate their offspring into this normative value system, they also transport these violent tendencies wherever they go. Gastil (1971) traced migration patterns out of the South to see how state murder rates mirrored settlement origins. To help track population shifts, Gastil constructed an *Index of Southernness*. States colonized by Southern-born persons receive top scores on this measure. Areas with sparse settlements of

Southerners rank at the bottom of the scale. Thus, Gastil's "Index of Southern-ness" is an attempt to track cultural diffusion through migratory patterns.

An empirical analysis of 1960 homicide victimization rates and census materials revealed a dramatic empirical relationship between the "Index of Southernness" and murder. As a result, Gastil (1971: p. 425) concluded that Southernness was responsible for the differential distribution of homicide vic-timization rates throughout the United States. This pronouncement, referred to as the *regional culture of violence thesis*, eventually spawned a large body of empirical studies.

The "regional culture of violence" thesis drew an immediate challenge. Loftin and Hill (1974) noted that instead of measuring culture directly, Gastil (1971) opted to substitute geographical location as a surrogate. These researchers reanalyzed state homicide rates, adding their own *Structural Poverty Index*, which reflected variables such as high infant mortality, low education, and low income. They also added a measure of income inequality to the analysis. Loftin and Hill (1974) found that the statistical power of Gastil's Index of Southernness diminished to virtually nothing. Instead, the Structural Poverty Index and the income inequal-ity measure were the strongest predictors of homicide levels. Essentially, then, these researchers raised serious doubts as to whether Southernness was the key to understanding the differential distribution of homicide victimization rates.

Another tack that researchers took moved away from the macro level and concentrated on the micro level. The thinking here was that Gastil's notion of a "culture of violence" hinges on the existence of a divergent normative value system. In other words, members of a subculture adhere to a distinctive attitudinal system that allows violence as a legitimate behavioral response. This belief system differs from the dominant culture and is directly responsible for higher rates of interpersonal violence among Southerners.

Despite repeated attempts, researchers have not been able to identify a sep-arate Southern tradition conducive to violence (Doerner, 1978a, 1979; Erlanger, 1974, 1975). In fact, there appears to be no attitudinal differences toward violence between Southerners and non-Southerners, or between non-Southerners and migrants who have left the region. Under these condi-tions, there does not appear to be any support for the existence of a divergent regional attitudinal structure. Thus, Gastil's contagion idea (that Southerners are carriers of a violent tradition who infect receiving areas) lacks foundation.

A second line of inquiry at the macro level raises questions about the homogen-eity of the "South." Gastil's Index of Southernness gives all the Southern states the same score. This means that Southernness must be distributed uniformly throughout the entire Southern region. Consequently, the South should dis-play similar homicide victimization rates across the states.

A look at homicide rates from 1940 through 1970 in 10-year intervals uncovers significant intraregional variation (Doerner, 1980). In other words, grave dissimilarities abound. A longitudinal analysis using the same data source that Gastil studied, the same point in time that Gastil examined, and the same spatial unit of analysis did not substantiate the assumption of regional homogeneity.

Alternative Cultural Differences

The failure of the empirical evidence to support Gastil's regional culture theory leaves the question of why homicide and assault are differentially distributed by region. Another approach is to ask the question in light of the fact that illegal violent acts range from mere threats or verbal taunts (assault) to minor injuries (simple battery) to very serious bodily harm (aggravated battery) to death (homicide). When viewed in this context, one can locate violent behavior on a continuum. In one sense, homicide is nothing more than a successful aggravated battery, while an aggravated battery could very well be a failed murder attempt.

Riveting attention entirely upon the outcome of an event ignores the fact that violence is a process and that death is only one possible consequence. Just because two combatants engage in a physical confrontation, with or without weapons, does not mean that this clash will culminate automatically in a death. Wounded fighters often sustain nonfatal injuries (Weaver et al., 2004). Furthermore, when they do incur critical, life-threatening damage, death is not necessarily imminent. Timely and appropriate medical intervention can play a key role in keeping an aggravated battery from slipping into a homicide statistic. Firearms were present in two out of every three homicide events in 2009, but only in one of every five aggravated assaults cases (Federal Bureau of Investigation, 2010a). This regularity may be due to the fact that firearm incidents require more medical attention than other injuries. Thus, it would seem that the potential impact of medical resources upon the production of lethality rates stemming from criminal violence deserves further examination.

One specialty area in the medical literature is trauma management. *Trauma*, in the medical sense, refers to any physical injury, without concern for the origin of the damage. Some examples of trauma include traffic accident injuries, industrial mishaps, suicide, poisoning, drowning, heart attacks, burns, stabbings, and gunshots. One prominent goal of trauma management is to reduce trauma-induced mortality.

In a review of the trauma management literature, Doerner (1983) looked at emergency transportation, field treatment, hospital emergency treatment, and post-operative recovery. One generalization that emerged was that rapid ambulance response time, coupled with the deployment of specially trained paramedics, increased the odds of patient survival. Medical experts refer to a period called the *golden hour*, the time period in which seriously injured people need medical attention if they are to survive (see Figure 3.2). A second finding is that most hospitals are not sufficiently equipped to handle serious trauma cases. They lack the appropriate technological facilities and do not have uniquely trained persons on staff. Instead, an ambulance with a critical injury case would be better advised to reroute to a specially designated trauma center. There the patient would receive more intensive care from specialized medical teams acquainted with the most current technology. However, all these measures still do not guarantee an automatic "save" from death. There is the ever-present danger of inaccurate patient assessment, post-operative infection, and other long-term complications.

It is important to realize that medical resources, just like homicide rates, are differentially distributed throughout time and space. The concentration and distribution of physicians is influenced by such considerations as degree of urbanization, community size, quality of life, and the availability of hospital facilities (Anderson, 1977; Begun, 1977; Eyles & Woods, 1983; Frenzen, 1991; Marden, 1966; Reskin & Campbell, 1976; Rushing, 1975; Rushing & Wade, 1973). One known outcome of greater medical specialization is a reduction in infant mortality rates and alterations in morbidity or sickness patterns (Anderson, 1977; Begun, 1977; Friedman, 1973). Given this evidence, it would not be unreasonable to expect that areas characterized by relatively fewer medical resources would exhibit higher lethality rates stemming from criminal violence, not because of the impact of Southernness, but due to the limited availability of adequate emergency medical care.

FIGURE 3.2 Firefighters and ambulance personnel work on a shooting victim in Buffalo, New York.
The "golden hour" refers to the critical time period in which seriously injured people need medical attention if they are to survive. *Credit: AP Photo/ The Buffalo News, Harry Scull Jr.*

Given this orientation, various authors have examined the impact of medical resources on homicide rates across areas. Doerner (1983; 1988) and Doerner & Speir (1986) report modest support for the impact of medical resources on homicide rates across areas. Others (Giacopassi & Sparger 1992; Hanke & Gundlach, 1995; Harris et al., 2002) note that medical resources have had a dramatic influence on the production of homicide and aggravated assault statistics.

The initial wave of research activity, therefore, suggests that the medical resources argument is plausible and deserves further consideration. Indeed, the victimological and emergency medical literatures acknowledge that

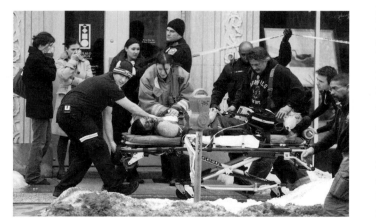

alcohol is a common ingredient in trauma incidents (Brookman & Maguire, 2005; Jurkovich et al., 1993; Lowenstein, Weissberg, & Terry, 1990; Riedel, Zahn, & Mock, 1985; Rivara et al., 1997; Soderstrom & Smith, 1993; Sutocky, Shultz, & Kizer, 1993; Wilbanks, 1984; Wolfgang, 1958; Woolf et al., 1991), both in terms of enhancing the initial traumatic event and in impeding the provision of medical services.

SITUATIONAL EXPLANATIONS

Situational explanations of crime and victimization reflect an array of factors that deal with the social, environmental, and economic situation of the victim and perpetrator. Some common factors include social strain, stress, dependence, and social isolation. The potential influence of each is discussed in turn.

Strain Theory

Strain theory considers deviance as a direct result of a social situation that places value on achievement but fails to provide the access to legitimate means for being successful. In order to understand strain theory, it is necessary to consider the fact that man is essentially *egoistic* (Durkheim, 1933) and requires satisfaction in his endeavors in order to be happy. In today's world, the trappings of success are manifested in what you own and how you measure up against others. The fact that some people have more than others and/or accumulate goods swiftly and with less effort than others may cause those less fortunate to feel betrayed, envious, or upset.

One response to the strain is finding alternative means for achieving success and/or obtaining wealth. Robbery, theft, and other property crimes are alternatives used by some to achieve. Agnew (1992) proposed a *general strain theory* that suggests that strain can come from several sources. These are: (1) the inability to achieve social goals, as outlined above; (2) the removal of desired or valued stimuli (such as losing one's home or job); and (3) being faced with negative stimuli. In each case, the individual may respond with criminal behavior. Rosenfeld and Fornango (2007) recently demonstrated that how the public perceives the economy and how it impacts them is related to robbery and property crime.

Strain has been used as an explanation for victimization at school. In the school arena students may feel strain from competition for grades. Instances in which a student is less successful than another may lead to striking out against those students who are achieving at higher levels or seeking out success in other anti-social or unacceptable ways, such as joining gangs or using illegal substances. This same type of strain may appear in the workplace.

Stress

Closely aligned to strain is the problem of stress. Stress can appear in a variety of settings (e.g., the home, school, or work) and from a variety of sources. Most discussion and interest in workplace victimization involves violence perpetrated by current or former coworkers on other employees. This format is the more typical portrayal seen in the news media. One major cause of violence by workers is stress (Braverman, 1999).

Some observers see stress as a leading cause of abuse and neglect (Phillips, 1986). According to this perspective, the perpetrator strikes out at the individual or situation that he or she perceives as causing tension. Some of the more significant stressors include the intensity or burden of caring for another person (O'Malley et al., 1983; Quinn, 1990; Quinn & Tomita, 1986; Schlesinger, 1988; Steinmetz, 1983, 1988), the economic strain that accompanies extended care (Champlin, 1986; O'Malley et al., 1983; Shell, 1982; Wolf & Pillemer, 1989), insufficient caregiver training (Steinmetz, 1988), and a lack of privacy between cohabiting adults (Anetzberger, 1989; Steinmetz, 1988). Steinmetz (1988) points out that elders sometimes feel they must resort to invading privacy, crying, yelling, or using guilt and other maneuvers to get what they want from their caregivers. A continued reliance upon these tactics can lead to tension, which the abuser may try to resolve by retaliating against the older person.

Dependency on other people for daily needs and special assistance often emerges as a major cause of maltreatment. Elderly persons may become victims because they rely so heavily upon the caregiver for subsistence. In reality, however, abusers tend to be economically dependent upon their victims (Anetzberger, 1989; O'Malley et al., 1983; Wolf & Pillemer, 1989). It appears that maltreatment is most likely to occur when the caregiver harbors a great deal of resentment toward the older person in his or her guardianship.

The social stress model emphasizes parents' lack of coping strategies (Belsky, 1978). In other words, when parents become stressed, their reactions include a sense of frustration and helplessness. This relative lack of power carries a feeling of not being in control, which makes it very easy for parents to lash out and vent their rage on their unprotected offspring.

Stress may come from a variety of different sources. Among the most obvious are personal conflicts between employees or family problems brought to work by an employee. Another important source of worry is the workplace itself. One major cause of violence by workers is stress (Braverman, 1999). Workplace bullying can be the initiating event for serious conflict. The downsizing or restructuring of an organization can place a great deal of stress and uncertainty on the workforce (Braverman, 1999). Competition for a position or the feeling that another, less worthy employee attained a position can precipitate conflict between employees. The dismissal of an individual from a job, whether legitimate or not, can make the person feel cheated (Schneid, 1999). Many of these situations can make a worker feel that the workplace is an unfair and unjust place (Greenberg & Alge, 1998). Individuals may feel a great deal of stress when they do not get what they feel is deserved. Greenberg and Alge (1998) note that when people perceive that decisions or procedures are unfair, aggression becomes one avenue of response. Stress also may be enhanced by physical characteristics of the workplace that cause discomfort for the employees (Chappell & DiMartino, 1998), such as extreme temperatures or overcrowding.

Support for the identification of stress as a leading contributor to workplace violence comes from the finding that most instances of violent behavior are not by new employees or employees who have caused trouble in the past (Schneid, 1999). Instead, a good deal of workplace violence is committed by individuals who have been model employees and can be considered dedicated workers. It is easy to see in these cases how changes in the workplace, such as reclassification of jobs, competition for promotion, or the dismissal of an employee, can bring about stress and possible violence. In essence, these types of changes contradict the individual's self-image vis-à-vis the job and his or her place on the job. Thus, the individual may feel betrayed and unfairly treated by the job and others at the place of employment.

Social Isolation

Another situational factor that contributes to victimization is social isolation. This is especially true in family violence and elder abuse. Lack of family support can exacerbate both dependency and stress (Anetzberger, 1989; Steinmetz, 1983, 1988). For example, an offspring who cares for a parent may resent the fact that other siblings are not providing similar assistance. Indeed, studies have found that abusive situations often involve frustrated caregivers with limited support systems at their disposal (Kosberg, 1988; Pillemer, 1986; Quinn & Tomita, 1986; Wolf & Pillemer, 1989). In similar fashion, it is not uncommon to find spouse abuse and child maltreatment in families that do not participate in social events and who tend to keep to themselves. This may be a response by the family to keep outsiders from recognizing signs of abuse. Taken together, dependence, stress, social isolation, and other situational factors can precipitate abuse and neglect as well as contribute to other causes of maltreatment.

Social Exchange

Closely related to both the situational and symbolic interactionist approaches is *social exchange theory*. Parties interact appropriately as long as both sides receive something in the exchange and each side feels that the other is treating him or her fairly (Galbraith, 1989). Typically, there is an assumption of equitable power or resources applied to the situation by both sides of the exchange. This explanation is particularly germane to elder abuse.

As the elderly grow increasingly dependent on others, they have increasingly less to offer in an exchange relationship (Phillips, 1986). If this inequity continues over a period of time, a strong imbalance may develop between the parties (George, 1986). The parties may allow this imbalance to accumulate because of a past mutual history (Cicirelli, 1986).

The aging person in an imbalanced exchange relationship may respond with feelings of guilt or distress (George, 1986) and recognize that he or she no longer has the power to control the relationship (Phillips, 1986). The caregiver may realize that the relationship is unfair. He or she may resent the fact that a valuable service is being provided with little or no return. That individual may opt to inflict punitive costs on the elderly person through abuse or neglect as a way to rectify the imbalance (Phillips, 1986). The mistreated member of the dyad may quietly accept the abuse or neglect in recognition of his or her dependent position in the exchange.

Social Attitudes

Another explanation for victimization, particularly elder abuse, involves social attitudes held by the parties involved. Attitudes can be considered situational as they develop out of the interaction between people and reflect larger social attitudes that may change over time. Quinn and Tomita (1986) point out that while attitudes themselves do not cause abuse or neglect, public opinion does make it easier for maltreatment to take place and thrive. *Ageism*, the stereotyping of older individuals and treating them differently because of their age, basically places the elderly in a devalued position (Hudson, 1988).

Various factors contribute to a general malaise about the elderly and their plight. The historical record of interaction between the generations provides some insight, just as the past plays a role in the plight of women and children. Older members of society have often kept rigid control over the family, yielding power only through death or major confrontations (Stearns, 1986; Steinmetz, 1988). The animosity that developed between parents and offspring in the past may be reappearing today when the elderly turn to the independent child for care and support.

A second attitudinal factor related to elder abuse may be that old age, particularly very old age, is an unknown in modern society (Quinn and Tomita, 1986). Families in the past century have moved away from extended households, even to the extent of being scattered across the country. This means that most citizens are isolated from aging family members and cannot readily assist them.

Coupled with longer life spans and medical advances that allow humans to live longer, people are faced with unknowns about being old. The elderly lack physical and economic power, and because they tend to be out of the workforce, they face a perception that they are useless.

Child maltreatment may reflect attitudes operating in an opposite fashion. As noted earlier, the historical patriarchal set up of the home and society provides justification for actions that are now considered misbehavior and abusive. The same can be applied to spousal assault. Social attitudes, both new and historical, provide an explanation for abuse and neglect in society.

SUMMARY

It should be evident that there is no single explanation for victimization. The explanation will vary by type of victimization, the context of the event, and the point of view of the individual investigating the event. This does not mean that theory cannot address victimization. Rather, the diversity in explanations demonstrates the variation in the field and the continued growth of victimology as a discipline. Generally, explanations can be grouped in the categories of intraindividual, symbolic interactionism, routine activities/lifestyle, sociocultural, learning, subcultural, and situational. It is important to note that these categories are not mutually exclusive and are not exhaustive. Rather, they simply serve to organize the discussion. Many discussions of victimization borrow from more than one category.

KEY TERMS

ageism
culture conflict
cycle of violence
differential association theory
differential distribution of violent crime rates
differential identification
egoistic
general strain theory
golden hour
Index of Southernness
learned helplessness
masochism
modeling
patriae potestas

patriarchy
poly-victimization
psychopathology
regional culture of violence
role reversal
routine activities/lifestyle model
"sick but slick" parents
situated transaction
social exchange theory
Structural Poverty Index
subculture of violence
symbolic interactionism
trauma
victim precipitation

Addressing the Impact of Victimization

The Costs of Victimization

LEARNING OBJECTIVES

After reading Chapter 4, you should be able to:

- Talk about why some people do not want to call the police after being victimized.
- Demonstrate the economic losses attributable to both property and personal victimization.
- Discuss the economic impact of fraud, identity theft, and cyber crime on victims.
- Relay what is meant by "the second insult."
- List different forms of noneconomic costs from victimization.
- Explain what intangible costs are.
- Discuss the economic costs of crime to society.
- List different costs borne by society in responding to victimization.

INTRODUCTION

This chapter takes a look at some of the costs associated with becoming a crime victim. As we all know, victims suffer at the hands of their criminals. Some people may be injured physically. Others may lose property during the attack. All will be gripped to some extent with fear and mental anguish. This aspect of their victimization experience will affect their quality of life and probably will not subside for quite a while.

Victims who turn to the criminal justice system for comfort and solace quickly learn that they run the risk of being exploited. The system, through its impersonal and detached mechanisms for sorting through cases, aggravates the victim's condition. For example, inconsiderate habits may force some victims to wait in hallways for a hearing to start, only to learn later that it has been canceled. No one bothered to telephone them. Other victims are bewildered by what is transpiring around them. No one has taken the time to explain what is happening in the case or why. Instead, these victims find system officials quickly shepherding them through the courthouse doors without so much as a simple "thank you." This chapter visits some of the problems that victims and witnesses encounter during their treks through the system.

Being victimized results in a number of both direct and indirect costs for the victim, his or her family, the community, and the criminal justice system. Victimization surveys provide insight into the costs associated with the crime. Beyond direct costs from the criminal event, victims and witnesses face additional losses when dealing with the authorities.

THE FIRST INSULT: CRIMINAL VICTIMIZATION

Early victim studies concentrated on documenting the calamity and woes that accompany the victimization experience. The Milwaukee Victim/Witness Project, for example, was undertaken to assess the difficulties stemming from the criminal episode (Knudten et al., 1976, 1977; Knudten & Knudten, 1981). In addition to sustaining physical injury and property loss or damage, a sizable proportion of victims reported losing time from work and their normal routines. They also endured emotional anguish and interpersonal complications with family members and friends. Despite their perception that these problems were serious, most victims forged ahead alone. Even though many social service agencies were in operation, victims remained largely unaware of service availability. As a result, relatively few victims received help coping with their crime-induced problems (Doerner et al., 1976). Table 4.1 illustrates the range of costs associated with crime for the victim and a host of other people.

Economic Losses

The direct economic loss due to crime can be large. It is possible to gain some insight into the loss from individual crimes through both official and self-report data. According to the 2011 UCR, burglary resulted in $4.8 billion in losses (Federal Bureau of Investigation, 2013). This works out to an average loss of $2,185. While these figures include burglaries of any structure, including businesses, the NCVS offers data on only household offenses. In the victimization data for 2008, 83% of the reporting households claimed to have monetary losses for total losses of more than $4.9 billion, with an average loss of $1,539 per residence (Bureau of Justice Statistics, 2010b). Over 24% of the households reported burglary losses between $100 and $500 (see Table 4.2). Another 40.2% of the households reported losses of more than $500 (Bureau of Justice Statistics, 2010b). These figures reveal a staggering economic impact from burglary that is attributable to the crime alone.

The impact of theft is equally great. Based on UCR figures, the average loss in larceny/thefts was $987 (Federal Bureau of Investigation, 2013). When

Table 4.1 List of Costs Associated with Crime

Costs of Crime	Party Who Directly Bears Cost
Direct Property Losses	
Losses not reimbursed by insurance	Victim
Losses reimbursed by insurance	Society
Administrative cost of insurance reimbursement	Society
Recovery by police	Society
Medical and Mental Health Care	
Costs not reimbursed by insurance	Victim/Family/Society
Costs reimbursed by insurance	Society
Administrative overhead of insurance coverage	Society
Victim Services	
Expenses charged to victim	Victim
Expenses paid by agency	Society
Temporary labor and training of replacements	Society
Lost Workdays	
Lost wages for unpaid workday	Victim
Lost productivity	Society/Employer
Lost School Days	
Foregone wages due to lack of education	Victim
Foregone nonpecuniary benefit of education	Victim
Foregone social benefits due to lack of education	Society
Lost Housework	Victim
Pain and Suffering/Quality of Life	Victim
Loss of Affection/Enjoyment	Family
Death	
Lost quality of life	Victim
Loss of affection/enjoyment	Family
Funeral and burial expenses	Family
Psychological injury/treatment	Family
Legal Costs Associated with Tort Claims	Victim or Family
"Second-Generation Costs"	
Future victims of crime committed by earlier victims	Future Victims
Future social costs associated with above	Society/Victims

Source: Miller, T. R., Cohen, M. A., & Wiersema, B. (1996). Victim Costs and Consequences: A New Look. *Washington, DC: National Institute of Justice, p. 11.*

Table 4.2 Selected Monetary Losses Due to Property Victimization, NCVS

Offense	% with Economic Loss	Gross Loss in Millions	Mean $ Loss	Median $ Loss	% Loss < $100	% Loss $100–$499	% Loss > $500
Household burglary	83.0	$4,906	$1,539	$380	20.9	24.6	40.2
Motor vehicle theft	91.0	$4,833	$6,077	$3,000	5.3	6.2	74.9
Household theft	96.8	$6,468	$524	$100	34.6	34.2	17.1

Source: Constructed by authors from Bureau of Justice Statistics (2010b) National Crime Victimization Survey, 2008, Statistical Tables. Washington, DC: Bureau of Justice Statistics.

extrapolated to the U.S. population, more than $6 billion was lost due to larceny in 2011. The NCVS also offers sobering statistics on theft loss. Based on 2008 data, those experiencing a purse-snatching lost an average of $110, and pick-pocket victims lost an average of $397. These two crimes had a combined loss of $46 million (Bureau of Justice Statistics, 2010b). Household theft losses averaged $524, with a total loss of more than $6.4 billion dollars in 2008 (Bureau of Justice Statistics, 2010b). There can be little doubt that theft has a major economic impact on both the individual and society.

While the actual number of motor vehicle thefts is not as high as other property crimes, the financial impact of the crime is large. The average loss due to motor vehicle theft was more than $6,089 in 2011. Nationally, the total loss was more than $4.3 billion (Federal Bureau of Investigation, 2013). Roughly three-quarters of the theft and loss was of automobiles. Victimization data present an equally troubling set of figures, with the average loss at $6,077 and a gross national loss of $4.8 billion (Bureau of Justice Statistics, 2010b). Overall, the NCVS reports a gross loss of more than $16 billion associated with property crime victimization in 2008.

It is also possible to look at monetary impacts from some personal crimes. When considering robbery, the UCR reports a total loss of $409 million in 2011 (Federal Bureau of Investigation, 2013). This is an average of $1,153 per offense. Robberies of banks incurred an average of $4,704 per event. Unfortunately, the UCR and NCVS do not offer any information on economic loss due to homicide, and the UCR offers nothing for assault. The NCVS, on the other hand, can provide some input to both assault and robbery. Table 4.3 offers insight into economic loss due to being an assault or robbery victim. Robbery victims incur a tremendous economic loss. More than three-quarters of the victims report economic loss, and the gross loss for the year is $885 million (Bureau of Justice Statistics, 2010b). Over 23% of the victims report losses in excess of $500. Fewer victims of assault report economic loss (only 6.8%), but the gross loss is over $1 billion. This seeming disparity in the figures for robbery and assault (more robbery victims with economic

Table 4.3 Selected Monetary Losses Due to Personal Victimization, NCVS

Offense	% with Economic Loss	Gross Loss in Millions	Mean $ Loss	Median $ Loss	% Loss < $100	% Loss $100–$499	% Loss > $500
Robbery	77.0	$885	$1,482	$140	29.6	34.3	23.5
Assault	6.8	$1,022	$236	$100	27.9	18.5	17.5

Source: Constructed by authors from Bureau of Justice Statistics (2010b) National Crime Victimization Survey, 2008, Statistical Tables. *Washington, DC: Bureau of Justice Statistics.*

loss but more dollars lost by assault victims) is due to the sheer number of assault victims compared with robbery victims and the costs of medical care.

Perhaps of equal concern is the dollar loss related to arson cases. In 2008, the average fire resulted in damages of just over $13,196 (Bureau of Justice Statistics, 2010b). This ranges from a low of $1,813 for "other" forms of property to a high of $68,394 for "industrial/manufacturing" fire. These dollar figures total almost $573 million in property loss due to arson.

There are other property offenses besides those that appear in the UCR Part I offense categories. Among these are offenses like identity theft, fraud, and cybercrime. Identity theft impacts victims in multiple ways. Most directly is the cost of the crimes, both to the individuals and to society. The NCVS reports that the average loss to the individual is $1,830 (Langton & Baum, 2010). The U.S. Government Accountability Office (GAO) (2002) put MasterCard and Visa fraud losses in 2000 at more than $1 billion and direct loss due to check fraud at $679 million.

Estimating the financial impact of mass-marketing fraud is extremely difficult. A survey in the UK puts the loss at more than $5.4 billion a year (UK Office of Fair Trading, 2006). Unfortunately, the U.S. Federal Trade Commission does not offer estimates for dollar losses in their data. The Federal Bureau of Investigation (2010a) places the estimated loss to U.S. adults between $23 billion and $25 billion per year. All of these figures reflect only direct losses from the crime itself.

The economic impact of cybercrime on society is not inconsequential. What information is available on cybercrime losses typically reflects its impact on businesses. A total of $867 million were lost by the 5,081 victimized businesses in 2005 (Rantala, 2008). This equates to an average loss of $170,636 per business. Of course, not all victims experience the same level of loss. More than 25% had a monetary loss between $10,000 and $99,000, with another 13% having losses in excess of $100,000.

These monetary estimates would escalate considerably if complete information were available on every single crime incident. At the same time, one should realize that these figures refer only to a handful of crimes. Other statutory violations (e.g., tax evasion, white-collar crime, corporate crime, and the like) need to be factored in to arrive at a more comprehensive assessment.

Noneconomic Costs

Crime victims suffer from a variety of ills beyond the direct monetary losses from victimization. First, many victims may not have insurance to cover any losses, or their insurance will not reimburse them for the type of loss they incurred. Certainly, falling victim to a mass-marketing inheritance scam is not something covered by insurance policies. In many cases the loss is borne solely by the victim. For victims without property insurance, even a burglary, arson, or motor vehicle theft leaves the individual with out-of-pocket losses for which there is no recompense.

Second, there are many different emotional consequences that may follow victimization. The Office for Victims of Crime (1998a) has pointed out that victims often experience shame, guilt, and self-blame for the event. Many victims opt not to tell anyone about the event out of a sense of guilt or shame. They may isolate themselves from others who they perceive might ridicule them for their lack of foresight or judgment that "allowed" them to be victimized. Indeed, some observers may condemn the victim as "getting what he deserved" (Office for Victims of Crime, 1998a). These emotional costs can be more debilitating than the financial losses resulting from the crime.

A third consequence of many types of crime is a lost sense of security in both the home and society. In the case of home burglary, victims lose the belief that they can be safe in their homes from the crime and turmoil that occur "out there." Whether the crime occurred when the resident was home or not, there is an increased sense of insecurity and anxiety that can permeate every facet of daily living. Where do you go to feel safe if you cannot do so in your home? Anxiety and a loss of trust also emerge as a result of any type of fraud. Victims may lose all sense of trust in banks/financial institutions, charities, the use of credit cards, or anything they equate with their victimization.

Adding to these measures of crime impact is the time lost by the victims. Victims often lose time from work or school (not to mention just relaxation time) as a result of the victimization. They spend time at the doctor, recuperating from an injury, talking to the police or prosecutor, coming to court, replacing lost or damaged goods, or doing other things related to the crime (see Table 4.4). Over 75% of robbery and over two-thirds of assault, household burglary and motor vehicle theft victims report losing at least one day of time due to the victimization (Bureau of Justice Statistics, 2010b). More than 60% of household theft victims report losing at least one day of work due to the victimization. It should also be noted that it is very difficult, if not impossible, to gauge the impact on lost productivity from the labor force even after the victim returns to the work site.

Beyond lost time from work, victims experience considerable lost time trying to resolve the problems. Eighteen percent of households report that problems

Table 4.4 Selected Non-monetary Losses Due to Victimization, NCVS

Offense	% Injured	% Requiring Medical Care	% with Medical Expenses	% Requiring Hospital Care	% Loss Work Time	% Loss < 1 Day	% Loss 1–10 Days	% Loss > 10 Days
Robbery	35.7	17.3	10.4	8.3	12.4	13.8	66.5	11.7
Assault	22.6	10.2	6.2	4.4	7.0	24.3	43.7	25.8
Household burglary	–	–	–	–	9.7	29.3	60.1	4.8
Motor vehicle theft	–	–	–	–	15.7	27.8	65.7	1.7
Household theft	–	–	–	–	5.7	36.1	58.3	2.9

Source: Constructed by authors from Bureau of Justice Statistics (2010b) National Crime Victimization Survey, 2008, Statistical Tables. *Washington, DC: Bureau of Justice Statistics.*

are ongoing, with another 17.2% reporting that it took more than one month to resolve the problems and 9.6% needing between one week and one month to address a theft (Baum, 2007). A survey by the Federal Trade Commission on fraud victimization reports that victims are harassed by collectors, are rejected for credit cards and loans, have accounts frozen, experience insurance problems, and may be subjected to criminal investigation or civil lawsuits (Synovate, 2007). These all add to the time loss and the impact of the initial victimization. See Figure 4.1.

Businesses also experience lost time as a result of unexpected business downtime. Businesses reported almost 324,000 hours of downtime due to some form of cybercrime, with two-thirds of that time due to a cyber attack (Rantala, 2008). Figures from the UK survey on mass-marketing fraud do not consider lost time in dealing with the event, a lost sense of security, or any other intangible loss, despite the fact that those losses are substantial.

A growing number of medical experts are becoming increasingly concerned with the implications stemming from interpersonal violence. One research team assembled a variety of data to construct an estimate of the medical costs associated with interpersonal violence during the calendar year 2000. Corso and colleagues (2007) compiled information on the expenses associated with medical care, lost wages due to a lack of labor force productivity, and other considerations. Their best indications are that fatalities due to homicide extracted a staggering $22.1 billion from the American economy.

There can be little doubt that victimization comes with high costs for both the victim and society. Not included in any of these figures are the intangible

 **WEB ACTIVITY**

The entire report by Miller, Cohen, and Wiersema can be found on this textbook's companion website at **http://booksite.elsevier.com/9780323287654**

harms of increased fear and anxiety brought on by the events. These other problems are much harder to quantify in any way, but may be the most problematic for many victims.

To help appreciate the magnitude of victimization costs, consider the following information (Miller, Cohen, & Wiersema, 1996: 1):

- Violent crime causes 3% of U.S. medical spending and 14% of injury-related medical spending.
- Violent crime results in wage losses equivalent to 1% of American earnings.
- Violent crime is a significant factor in mental health care usage. As much as 10–20% of mental health care expenditures in the United States may be attributable to crime, primarily for victims treated as a result of their victimization.

FIGURE 4.1 Victims of an alleged swindler wait in line to enter the courtroom for the arraignment of the suspect. Among the many things causing time lost by victims is time attending court, sometimes only to find that another court date has been scheduled. *Credit: AP Photo/The Canadian Press Graham Hughes.*

Beyond such obvious costs as injury, medical expenses, lost days from work, and economic loss, victimization generates a broader public impact. Many citizens, whether or not they have been victimized, report being afraid of crime, and the fear may manifest itself in various ways depending on the person involved and the basis for his or her anxiety. Some individuals fear walking on the streets in their neighborhood, while others fear physical attack within their own home. As a result, there may be a shift in physical functioning, such as high blood pressure and rapid heartbeat. Alternatively, the individual may similarly alter his or her behavior in certain places or avoid various activities. To a great extent, the source of the fear for the individual will determine the response to the fear.

Surveys report that more than 40% of the public are fearful of crime (Gallup, 1992; Skogan & Maxfield, 1981; Toseland, 1982). Survey results find that one-third of the public report that there are areas near their homes where they would be afraid to walk alone at night (Gallup, 2009; Maguire, 2010). Maguire (2013) reports that 20% of respondents worry frequently or occasionally about being murdered, 47% worry about having their home burglarized when they are not home, and 30% worry about burglary when they are home (see Table 4.5). More than two-thirds of high school seniors report worrying about crime and

Table 4.5 Concern about Crime Victimization (Percentage Reporting Frequent or Occasional Worry)

Concern	% Reporting Worry
Being victim of identity theft	67
Having your car stolen or broken into	44
Your home being burglarized when you are not there	47
Your home being burglarized when you are there	30
Getting mugged	34
Being attacked while driving your car	19
Being sexually assaulted	22
Getting murdered	20

Source: Maguire, K., ed. (2013) Sourcebook of Criminal Justice Statistics. University at Albany, Hindelang Criminal Justice Research Center (Table 2.39.2011). Retrieved on May 17, 2013, from http://www.albany.edu/sourcebook/tost_2.html#2_k.

violence (Maguire, 2010). A 2007 Gallup poll revealed that 48% of the participants avoid certain areas, 31% own a dog for protection, 23% bought a gun for self-defense, 31% installed a burglary alarm system, 14% carry mace or pepper spray, and 12% carry a gun or a knife for protection (Maguire, 2010). Obviously, fear of crime has become an added burden affecting both those victimized and the general public.

WEB ACTIVITY

Investigate people's fear and worry about crime and victimization by exploring data compiled on the Sourcebook of Criminal Justice Statistics' website at **http://www.albany.edu/sourcebook/tost_2.html#2_k**

Societal/System Costs

While the above information paints a serious picture of the impact of crime, the actual impact extends beyond the direct financial loss due to the crime or the time lost by victims as reflected in the UCR or the NCVS. Indeed, crime exacts a wide range of additional costs on the individual and society. Among these are the criminal justice system costs of investigating, arresting, prosecuting, adjudicating, and incarcerating/punishing the offender. Besides the direct crime losses suffered by the victims, there are the medical costs related to injuries and lost income, as well as *intangible costs*, which include pain and suffering, psychological impacts, and reduced quality of life. Yet another consideration is the costs associated with the offender's choice to pursue crime rather than socially acceptable forms of production (McCollister French and Fang, 2010).

Miller and colleagues (1996) combed through a variety of data sources, including the NCVS, to get a fuller picture of the costs and consequences of criminal victimization. They began by compiling a lengthy list of costs extracted by the victimization experience. As Table 4.6 shows, the annual loss due to just these

Table 4.6 Annual Losses Due to Crime During 1987–1990, in Millions, Expressed in 1993 Dollars[a]

Type of Crime	Medical	Other Tangible	Quality of Life	Total
Fatal Crime	$700	$32,700	$60,000	$93,000
Child Abuse	$3,600	$3,700	$48,000	$56,000
Rape and Sexual Assault	$4,000	$3,500	$119,000	$127,000
Other Assault or Attempt	$5,000	$10,000	$77,000	$93,000
Robbery or Attempt	$600	$2,500	$8,000	$11,000
Drunk Driving	$3,400	$10,000	$27,000	$41,000
Arson	$160	$2,500	$2,400	$5,000
Larceny or Attempt	$150	$9,000	$0	$9,000
Burglary or Attempt	$30	$7,000	$1,800	$9,000
Motor Vehicle Theft or Attempt	$9	$6,300	$500	$7,000
Total	$18,000	$87,000	$345,000	$450,000

[a]Totals may appear not to add up due to rounding.
[b]"Other Tangible" includes Property Damage and Loss, Mental Health Care, Police and Fire Services, Victim Services, and Productivity.
Source: Miller, T. R., Cohen, M. A., & Wiersema, B. (1996). Victim Costs and Consequences: A New Look. Washington, DC: National Institute of Justice, p. 17.

10 crime classifications reached $450 billion during the 1987–1990 period. These costs include not only medical costs and property loss, but also losses due to time loss, mental health care, and criminal justice system costs. These monetary estimates would escalate considerably if complete information were available on every single crime incident. At the same time, one should realize that these figures refer only to a handful of street crimes. Other statutory violations, such as fraud, mass-marketing fraud, identity theft, white-collar crime, and corporate crime, need to be factored in to arrive at a more comprehensive assessment. Similarly, Anderson (1999) estimates the annual cost of crime to U.S. society at $1.7 trillion!

Aos and colleagues (2001) computed the economic costs related to criminal justice system processing of individual crimes for the state of Washington. Their computations are based solely on the costs related to the various criminal justice system agencies involved in handling the offender and the offense as it moves through the system. Included are the costs to the police, courts, and correctional systems. Based on cost figures from the mid-1990s, the estimated cost of a homicide is $355,086; the cost of an aggravated assault is $56,790; and the cost of a robbery is $92,705 (Aos et al., 2001). While these figures are only for one state, it is reasonable to assume that other states would expend similar high dollar costs in processing these offenses.

WEB ACTIVITY

Details and discussion on calculating the economic costs of crime to society can be investigated at **http://www.wsipp. wa.gov/pub.asp?docid=03-01-1202**

Table 4.7 Tangible and Intangible Costs of Crime

Offenses	Victim Costs	Criminal Justice System Cost	Crime Career Cost	Total Tangible Costs	Pain and Suffering Costs
Murder	$737,517	$392,352	$148,555	$1,278,424	$8,442,000
Rape/Sex Assault	5,556	26,479	9,212	41,247	198,212
Aggravated Assault	8,700	8,641	2,126	19,537	13,435
Robbery	3,299	13,827	4,272	21,398	4,976
Motor Vehicle Theft	6,114	3,867	533	10,534	262
Arson	11,452	4,392	584	16,428	5,133
Household Burglary	1,362	4,127	681	6,170	321
Larceny/Theft	480	2,879	163	3,523	10
Stolen Property	n/a	6,842	1,132	7,974	0
Vandalism	n/a	4,160	701	4,860	0
Forgery/Counterfeiting	n/a	4,605	660	5,265	0
Embezzlement	n/a	4,820	660	5,480	0
Fraud	n/a	4,372	660	5,032	0

Source: Constructed by author from McCollister, K. E., French, M. T. & Fang, H. (2010). The cost of crime to society: New crime-specific estimates for policy and program evaluation. Drug and Alcohol Dependence 108:98–109.

In a recent analysis, McCollister and colleagues (2010) provide a detailed discussion of the data and computations on the costs of crime to society. The authors draw data from the UCR, National Incident-Based Reporting System (NIBRS), the NCVS, the Federal Emergency Management Agency, the U.S. Fire Administration (for arsons), the Bureau of Justice Assistance (for jail and prison data, criminal justice system employment data, and expenditures), and the Bureau of Labor Statistics (income and earnings). They also rely on data and input from other analyses, including the work of Miller et al. (1996) and Aos (2003). Table 4.7 presents the tangible and intangible costs for 13 crime types in 2008 dollars. The total costs range from a high of almost $9 million for each murder to a low of $3,533 for each larceny/theft. While these per crime figures are themselves staggering, multiplying the costs of homicides by the number of homicides in 2010 reveals a total cost of more than $132 billion just for this one offense category. Carrying out this same computation for all 13 crime categories reveals a total costs of more than $295 trillion in 2010!

The economic impact of crime on the individual and society is huge. Simply looking at the immediate loss due to the victimization itself is short-sighted. To these losses you need to add the costs of the criminal justice system, other costs to the victim and his or her family, pain and suffering, and lost productivity by the offender. While the actual level of crime has fallen in recent years, the staggering economic costs to the individual victims and to society cannot be ignored.

Summary

The data and figures on the impact of crime suggest that many victims, as well as the general public, become the "walking wounded." They endure their problems and tribulations in silence, often without help from external sources. On top of the crime-related losses come more difficulties when a victim's case finds its way into the criminal justice system. As the following section explains, these costs can be substantial.

THE SECOND INSULT: SYSTEM PARTICIPATION

A victim's problems have only just begun if the case is processed through the criminal justice system. The costs listed in Table 4.1 include a number of costs associated with the victim's decision to report the victimization to the authorities. A number of these costs accrue to the victims themselves. Others are borne by the criminal justice system and society at large.

The system extracts further costs as soon as people enter the halls of justice. In fact, the plight of victims and witnesses has led at least one prosecutor to chastise the system for victimizing its own patrons. Ash (1972: 390) describes typical system encounters in the following terms:

> [T]he witness will several times be ordered to appear at some designated place, usually a courtroom. ... Several times he will be made to wait tedious, unconscionable long intervals of time in dingy courthouse corridors or in other grim surroundings. Several times he will suffer the discomfort of being ignored by busy officials and the bewilderment and painful anxiety of not knowing what is going on around him or what is going to happen to him. On most of these occasions he will never be asked to testify or to give anyone any information, often because of a last-minute adjournment granted in a huddled conference at the judge's bench. He will miss many hours from work (or school) and consequently will lose many hours of wages. In most jurisdictions he will receive at best only token payment in the form of ridiculously low witness fees for his time and trouble.

A second feature of the Milwaukee Victim/Witness Project (discussed earlier) was to identify problems that the criminal justice system provoked for victims and witnesses (Doerner et al., 1976; Knudten et al., 1976; Knudten & Knudten, 1981). Interviewers learned that common problems for system participants included time loss, a corresponding reduction in income, time wasted waiting needlessly inside the courthouse, and problems getting to and from the courthouse. In addition, court appearances for subpoenaed witnesses translated into lost wages—a significant concern for many people. Waiting conditions were another critical problem. At the time of the study, all victims and witnesses reported to a large waiting room at the courthouse. Bailiffs would retrieve witnesses when it was time for their testimony. In one particular case, a sexual assault victim took a seat before the trial began. A number of other people shuffled in and out waiting for their cases to start. A few minutes later, much to her chagrin, the victim realized her suspected assailant was sitting next to her. Intimidation tactics can be very discomforting (Healey, 1995). In many cases, numerous delays and postponements can result in cases taking in excess of one year to resolve (Cassell, 1997). Needless to say, situations such as the one described here do nothing to alleviate the stress and anxiety associated with system participation.

Probably the best way to characterize the reactions of victims and witnesses would be to say that their courthouse experiences leave them bewildered and frustrated. Although victims have gone there to discharge a civic duty, they learn the hard way that the system takes undue advantage of their goodwill. They spend time away from work, lose money, and are not treated courteously (Norton, 1983: 146–147). As one research team explained:

> [T]here is a serious gap between . . . problems faced by crime victims and the help available to them. Unless this gap is bridged, victims may come to realize they stand a good chance of incurring even greater financial losses if they cooperate with the criminal justice system. The anticipated financial loss due to entrance into the system may be sufficient to deter such citizen involvement. It is ironic that the system which is designed to protect the constitutional rights of the offender fails even to recognize the victim's position and then turns around and wonders why its citizenry is apathetic (Doerner et al., 1976: 489).

Rather than claim apathy on the part of victims, it is more realistic to view the lack of participation in the criminal justice system as a rational choice. That is, victims make a *cost–benefit analysis* and see exacerbated costs accruing from system participation. Accordingly, the American criminal justice system is facing a critical loss of citizen trust and support.

Results from the 2007 National Crime Victimization Survey indicate that more than half the violent victimization episodes and 6 out of every 10 property victimizations go unreported to the police (Bureau of Justice Statistics, 2010a: Table 91). When interviewers ask these victims why they did not call the police, several consistent refrains emerge. Most often, victims report that the suspect was not successful and that nothing was lost. Others claim the police would not do anything or feel that the police would not want to get involved in the matter. Consequently,

WEB ACTIVITY

The issue of non reporting is a persistent problem. The NCVS routinely investigates this problem and you can find out more at **http://www.bjs.gov/index.cfm?ty=pbdetail&iid=4393**

victims turn to other officials or individuals besides the police (Bureau of Justice Statistics, 2010a). Other reasons typically revolve around apparent frustrations that nothing can be done to solve the situation. In short, many victims see no benefits to be gained from initiating contact with system representatives (Table 4.8).

These sentiments are not confined to the police. Many people harbor genuine doubts that the courts will punish an offender sufficiently once he or she is apprehended and prosecuted (Maguire & Pastore, 1996; Schneider, Burcart, & Wilson, 1976). They realize that there is no "truth in sentencing" for convicted felons. Homicide offenders, for example, usually net a 16-year state prison term from the courts. However, they typically spend only half this time behind bars. Judges solemnly pronounce 10-year terms for rapists, but often they are out in less than seven years. Robbers can expect to fulfill four-and-a-half years out of an eight-year sentence. Aggravated assault convicts often serve roughly three years, although their sentences officially extend for eight years (Maguire & Pastore, 2006). What this boils down to is that the system is not making good on its promises.

Given this climate, it is not surprising that Gallup reports that only 27% of its survey respondents expressed quite a lot or a great deal of confidence in the criminal justice system (Maguire, 2010). Citizen reluctance to become involved in the criminal justice system is reaching epidemic heights. A substantial number of victims and witnesses who have gone through the criminal justice process confide that they would not return if they could avoid doing so in the future (Cannavale & Falcon, 1976; Finn & Lee, 1987; Knudten et al., 1976;

Table 4.8 Reasons for Not Reporting Victimizations to the Police

Reason	Personal Crimes	Property Crimes
Reported to another official	15.1%	7.5%
Private or personal matter	20.4	6.3
Object recovered/offender unsuccessful	17.1	25.8
Not important enough	5.5	4.1
Insurance would not cover	0.2	2.2
Not aware of the crime until later	0.1	4.8
Unable to recover the property	0.0	5.6
Lack of proof	2.6	8.6
Police would not want to be bothered	9.0	14.8
Police inefficient, ineffective, or biased	3.8	5.4
Fear of reprisal	4.8	0.6
Too inconvenient or time-consuming	5.8	4.4
Other reasons	15.6	9.8

Source: Constructed by authors from Bureau of Justice Statistics (2010) Criminal Victimization in the United States, 2007: Statistical Tables. *Washington, DC: Bureau of Justice Statistics.*

Norton, 1983). System personnel complain that citizens are growing increasingly apathetic. However, such a self-serving portrayal is difficult to accept. An alternative description is that victims have grown disenchanted and are rebelling against further abuse. Because of past mistreatment, they are making a very deliberate and rational decision to bypass the criminal justice system.

Victims sustain costs both from the hands of their criminals and then by participating in the criminal justice system. In this sense, they face *double-victimization*. While victims may not be able to avoid the initial criminal victimization, they can choose to avoid the system, thus minimizing their losses. As one victim's mother put it:

> You have already been victimized, and you end up going through the victimization again from the system you are in. So what happens is, with all these choices, you end up trying to maintain integrity and security and sanity in hopes that the truth will come out and you feel good about the result. It is very hard. I don't know if we would go through it again (Cassell, 1997).

Unless these financial needs and system costs and consequences are addressed, victims and witnesses will continue to boycott the criminal justice system.

SUMMARY

It is easy to see why victims are reluctant to invoke or to re-enter the criminal justice system. Victims initially come into the halls of justice with hopes of minimizing their losses. However, after they complete the circuit and exit the system, they often realize they have maximized their losses instead. As a result, it should come as no surprise that system veterans claim they will avoid the system in the future whenever possible. This decision to boycott the legal system is not the product of an apathetic citizenry. It is a calculated and rational assessment—a silent protest. Avoiding system participation reduces victim exposure to further hardships and liabilities.

As we shall learn in the following chapters, the system has crafted responses designed to lure victims back. These responses are both financial and changes in how victims are handled in the system. It remains to be seen whether these efforts will be sufficient to maintain victim interest in current system operations.

KEY TERMS

cost–benefit analysis
double-victimization
intangible costs

Milwaukee Victim/Witness Project
second insult

CHAPTER 5

Remedying the Financial Impact of Victimization

INTRODUCTION

Victims lose not only as a result of the criminal act, but also from participating in the criminal justice process. The criminal justice system alienates the victim, making him or her feel like an outsider to both the offense and the system processes. The victim is little more than a witness for the state. The emphasis is not on making the victim whole. Rather, it is on processing the offender. Judging from citizen disillusionment with the criminal justice system, there is a clear need to take some bold steps to ameliorate the victim's suffering.

If a victim's decision to avoid formal contact with the criminal justice system stems from a rational cost–benefit assessment, then the system needs to entice victims back into the system with economic incentives.

There are a variety of ways whereby victims may recoup some of their monetary losses stemming from the victimization episode. Some alternatives include restitution, civil litigation, insurance payments, and victim compensation. While each method has the potential to restore the victim to his or her pre-crime state, the victim faces new obstacles when using these methods. Likewise, each option holds a different potential for drawing victims back into the criminal justice system. This chapter looks at restitution, civil litigation, insurance payments, and victim compensation as means of both restoring the victim's losses and bringing the victim back into the criminal justice system.

OFFENDER RESTITUTION

Offender restitution involves the transfer of services or money from the offender to the victim for damages inflicted by the offender. The idea of restitution predates the formal criminal justice system. Prior to the advent of a formal system of social control, victims were responsible for apprehending the offender and exacting payment for any loss or harm. Restitution was clearly outlined in various early laws, such as the Code of Hammurabi and the Justinian Code. The idea of offenders making restitution to their victims largely disappeared once the state assumed responsibility for apprehending and prosecuting offenders. While this new system of justice did not prohibit restitution, the practice gradually fell into disuse and was largely ignored.

The 1960s saw a renewed interest in offender restitution. A variety of factors contributed to this movement. They included the recognition of the victim in the 1967 President's Commission reports, the growing concern for identifying alternative methods for dealing with offenders, and the societal movement toward concern for crime victims. The awakening acceptance of restitution at that time was not accompanied by a myriad of new legislation. Rather, it was pointed out that restitution was an already existing sentencing option that the courts very rarely invoked.

The 1982 President's Task Force on Victims of Crime recommended that restitution become the norm in criminal cases. Later that same year, the Victim/Witness Protection Act went so far as to require federal judges to give a written explanation for why they did not require full restitution in a case. By 1990, 48 states had specific legislation dealing with restitution as a separate sentence or as an additional requirement to another sentence (Shapiro, 1990). Today, more than one-third of the states have a constitutional amendment that gives victims a right to restitution (Office for Victims of Crime, 2002a).

Some states have followed the federal lead and now require judges to make offender restitution a mandatory part of sentencing unless there are extraordinary circumstances to suggest otherwise (Office for Victims of Crime, 2002a). At least one state now imposes a civil restitution lien order upon convicted criminal offenders. A *civil restitution lien* means that the sentencing court, at the request of the victim, levies a claim against any real or personal property the convicted offender currently possesses or may come to own (see, for example, *Florida Statutes*, 2012, §960.29–960.297). What this means is that victims can recover any damages or losses from any assets the offender accrues.

WEB ACTIVITY

Many jurisdictions have established methods for both offenders and victims to see what is required in restitution and how to comply with restitution. An example can be found at **http://www. alleghenycounty.us/crim/restitution.aspx**

The Rationale for Restitution

The rationale for restitution involves the needs of victims. Victim losses are a key driving force behind the growth of restitution legislation and the use of court-ordered restitution. A survey of Pennsylvania judges revealed that compensating victims was the most important reason for restitution (Ruback & Shaffer, 2005). Other factors, however, are also apparent in the adoption of restitution as a sentencing alternative (see Table 5.1).

Many restitution programs are couched in terms of benefits for the offender. Rehabilitation is hailed as the most potent outcome (Barnett, 1981; Galaway, 1981; Hofrichter, 1980; Hudson & Galaway, 1980). Forcing the offender to pay or perform service to the victim allows the offender to see the pain and suffering that his or her actions caused. Rather than simply punishing the individual, restitution is supposed to provide a therapeutic or rehabilitative response to deviant actions. The rehabilitative argument is particularly appealing whenever restitution is tied to maintaining gainful employment or entering a job training program (Hillenbrand, 1990). In these instances, offenders help their victims while positioning themselves for legitimate opportunities in the future.

Table 5.1 Competing Rationales for Restitution

- Restoring the victim to the pre-victimization condition
- Rehabilitating the offender
- Providing a less restrictive alternative to incarceration
- Deterring the offender from future criminal activity

Proponents tend to regard restitution as a less restrictive alternative than normal processing, which most often would take the form of incarceration. Labeling arguments, which fault system intervention as the cause of further deviance, support restitution as a means of mitigating future offending. Rather than leading to deviance, restitution assists the offender in refraining from subsequent criminal activity.

Restitution also carries a deterrence effect (Tittle, 1978). Deterrence assumes that people will continue to commit deviant acts only as long as there is a positive payoff. By mandating repayment to the victim, restitution returns the offender—at least financially—to the exact same position held prior to the unlawful act. Coupling restitution with a fine or imprisonment can produce a negative balance between the outcome of the offense (assumed pleasure) and the system's response (pain). Following the basic hedonistic arguments underlying deterrence, the offender would be better off not committing the offense in the first place. Restitution, therefore, can produce a specific deterrent effect on the punished offender and may even provide general deterrence (i.e., influencing others through example).

Types of Restitution

Galaway (1981) outlines four variations on the general theme of restitution (see Table 5.2). The first, *monetary-victim restitution*, most closely fits the general public's impression of restitution. Under this arrangement, the offender makes direct monetary repayment to the victim for the actual amount of harm or losses incurred. While this is considered direct payment, in practice payments actually are routed through the court or probation office, which then turns the funds over to the victim. This process is particularly useful in cases in which the victim does not wish to have any further contact with the offender.

The second form is referred to as *monetary-community restitution*. This type of restitution entails payment by the offender to the community rather than to the actual victim. This option may be used for several reasons. For example, it may not be possible to identify a tangible victim in cases involving vandalism of public property. A victim may be unwilling to participate in a restitution program, or the court may be reluctant to use restitution to the victim in the sentencing of an offender. In some instances, this monetary-community restitution may actually be a method whereby the community simply recoups

---

Table 5.2 Types of Restitution

- Monetary payments to the victim
- Monetary payments to the community
- Service performed for the victim
- Service performed for the community

funds it previously made available to the victim. In essence, the community provided "up-front" restitution to the victim that would now be replaced by the offender.

The remaining restitution categories are closely aligned with the first two, except that they substitute service in place of financial payments. Both *service-victim restitution* and *service-community restitution* require the perpetrator to perform a specified number of hours or types of service (or both) in lieu of making cash payments. These forms of restitution are most common in situations in which the offender does not have the ability to make monetary compensation (such as in the case of unemployed individuals and juveniles). Service to the community may act as repayment for restitution that the community made on behalf of the offender or may be a way to pay for court costs and/or harm to the general populace. In any event, the important feature is that the offender must satisfy the debt established through his or her victimizing behavior.

Evaluating the Impact of Restitution

As with many programs, evaluations of restitution have evolved from simple examinations of attitudes and processes to studies of such outcomes as recidivism, cost savings, and diversion. In general, restitution has enjoyed a warm reception from victims, offenders, the general public, and system personnel (Gandy, 1978; Gandy & Galaway, 1980; Hudson & Galaway, 1980; Keldgord, 1978; Kigin & Novack, 1980; Novack, Galaway, & Hudson, 1980).

However, despite the general acceptance of restitution, relatively few offenders are required by the courts to pay restitution. Table 5.3 presents data showing that in only 18% of state felony cases and 12% of Federal District Court cases is the felon ordered to pay restitution as a part of the sentence. In the case of property offenses, where it is generally easier to document the amount of the loss, fewer than three out of 10 felons in state courts are ordered to pay restitution. Restitution orders clearly vary by the type of offense. The median level of restitution imposed in Federal District Courts is relatively low, ranging from a high of $8,157 in larceny cases to a low of $1,500 in firearms/weapons offenses.

The initial wave of restitution evaluations was mostly *process evaluations*; that is, the emphasis was on the number of offenders handled, the amount of time participants took to make restitution, the completion rate for restitution orders, and other similar program achievements. Those eligible to receive restitution include not only the crime victim, but also his or her family, insurance companies, victim support agencies, and government agencies that assist victims (Office for Victims of Crime, 2002a). The losses covered are likewise broad. Beyond costs for property loss or damage, restitution can cover medical

Table 5.3 Percent of Felons with a Penalty of Restitution and the Median Restitution Ordered

Conviction Offense	State Courts (%)	Federal District Courts (%)	Median ($)
All offenses	18%	12%	
Violent offenses			
Murder	13	31	6,423
Sexual assault	18	7	2,412
Robbery	18	51	6,020
Aggravated assault	18	20	2,000
Property offenses			
Burglary	27	64	2,100
Larceny	26	63	8,157
Drug offenses	14	1	1,500
Weapons offenses	8	9	1,500
Other offenses	13		

Source: Rosenmerkel, S., Durose, M., & Farole, D. (2009). Felony Sentences in State Courts, 2006, Statistical Tables. *Retrieved from http://bjs.ojp.usdoj.gov/content/pub/pdf/fssc06st.pdf; and Maguire, K. (2010).* Sourcebook of Criminal Justice Statistics *[Online]. Retrieved December 3, 2013 from http://www.albany.edu/sourcebook/*

expenses, lost wages, funeral expenses, mental health counseling, and other costs associated with the crime and its aftermath (Office for Victims of Crime, 2002a).

Most programs report a high offender compliance rate with restitution orders (Kigin & Novack, 1980; Lawrence, 1990; Schneider & Schneider, 1984). However, success varies according to the type and level of supervision provided to probationers (Ruback & Shaffer, 2005; Schneider & Schneider, 1984). For example, the use of specialized collection units, particularly those located outside of the courthouse, has been found to be less effective at collecting funds compared with those programs located within the courthouse (Ruback, Shaffer, & Logue, 2004; Ruback & Shaffer, 2005). The simultaneous imposition of other sanctions, such as fines and imprisonment, also may hinder or delay offender payments. The Office for Victims of Crime (2002b) suggests that all court-ordered payments be collected under a single system to address this problem. Finally, restitution programs have been found to be quite economical. They can handle a large number of individuals at a relatively low cost (Hudson & Galaway, 1980).

Studies that look at the impact of restitution on victims and offenders are known as *outcome evaluations*. The amount of money collected and funneled to victims is one key result that is assessed. Unfortunately, systematic information on the amount of restitution ordered is not available. What information does exist comes from sporadic reporting from different jurisdictions. In one analysis of felony probation, the Bureau of Justice Statistics reports an average restitution order of $3,368 (Cohen, 1995).

Another major outcome to assess is offender recidivism. Challeen and Heinlen (1978) report 2.7% recidivism for restitution clients, compared with 27% for similar offenders sentenced to jail. Recidivism declined in three of four programs by 10 fewer offenses per 100 youths (Schneider, 1986). A six-year follow-up of offenders who were diverted into a restitution program also showed significantly lower recidivism (Rowley, 1990). More recently, Ruback and associates (2004), examining the impact of restitution before and after it was made mandatory in Pennsylvania, found that offenders who paid a greater proportion of the ordered restitution had lower recidivism than those who did not make as many payments.

While these results appear encouraging, Schneider and Schneider (1984) caution that the value of restitution depends upon how well the program is administered. When restitution becomes an agency priority, the results are promising. However, outcome measures lag when restitution is handled as an added-on condition and is not a top agency concern. Programs that aggressively target restitution generate more successful performances and lower recidivism rates (Ervin & Schneider, 1990; Ruback, Ruth, & Shaffer, 2005; Ruback & Shaffer, 2005).

Problems and Concerns with Restitution

Despite both the theoretical attractiveness and positive outcomes of restitution, there are a variety of problems and concerns facing the practice. At the very outset is the need to apprehend and adjudicate the offender (Galaway, 1981; Hillenbrand, 1990). The Uniform Crime Reports shows that less than 20% of all property crimes (which are most amenable to restitution) are cleared by an arrest. Restitution, therefore, is possible a maximum of one-fifth of the time. Beyond arrest statistics, many offenders are not convicted, thereby mitigating any possibility of restitution.

The Office for Victims of Crime (2002a) notes that a major impediment to restitution is the victim's failure to request such compensation. While many states require prosecutors or the court to notify victims of their right to request restitution, there is no guarantee that such notification actually takes place. Notification also does not mean that the victims will make the request. One solution to these problems is to make restitution a mandatory part of sentencing in all criminal cases (Office for Victims of Crime, 2002a; Ruback et al., 2005).

A third stumbling block is the inability of offenders to pay restitution (Office for Victims of Crime, 2002a). Most offenders come from lower-class segments of society. It is naive to assume that these individuals will have the necessary means to make restitution. In some cases, statutes outline provisions in which restitution is ordered but commences at some future date when the offender will have the ability to pay (Office for Victims of Crime, 2002a). Another potential solution is assisting offenders in finding employment. The provision of jobs to offenders requires either public funds or substantial cooperation from the private sector, both of which may face problems. First, jobs may not be available. Second, opponents argue that more worthy law-abiding citizens are denied jobs in favor of offenders.

A fourth major issue is demonstrating and calculating the loss and the appropriate level of restitution (Office for Victims of Crime, 2002b). While a dollar figure for stolen or damaged property should be easy to identify, questions arise concerning depreciation for older, used property and the value of sentimental items for which monetary compensation is hard to determine. Some offenses may leave victims with psychological damage, for which setting a dollar figure may be more demanding. Difficulty also arises when attempting to set a level of service for restitution (Harland & Rosen, 1990). How much work or time offsets monetary loss, physical pain, or psychological suffering? In almost every attempt to order restitution, the court is asked to go beyond its legal expertise and become involved in the decisions that would be better made by a doctor, psychiatrist, economist, or accountant.

🌐 WEB ACTIVITY

Issues with restitution have been identified by many organizations. One such organization is the National Committee for the Prevention of Elder Abuse. They have offered their insight and comments at **http://www.preventelderabuse.org/elderabuse/issues/restitution.html**

Another major area of concern deals with the question of the proper philosophy of the criminal court. Thorvaldson (1990) argues that restitution moves the emphasis of the criminal justice system from society to the victim. Under restitution, the victim is seeking personal redress rather than acting on behalf of society. Consequently, restitution diminishes the importance of criminal processing and sentencing (Thorvaldson, 1990). Many individuals also see restitution as inappropriate for cases in which offenders receive a prison or jail term (Office for Victims of Crime, 2002a). Basically, critics claim that restitution shifts the court from a criminal orientation to a civil orientation. Instead of focusing on the offender, the victim becomes the focus of the process.

Several other issues carry potential problems for restitution. The current criminal justice system is not set up to administer such programs (Shapiro, 1990). Indeed, there is little coordination between agencies on monitoring restitution orders or sharing information on compliance with such orders (Office for Victims of Crime, 1998b). Further, there is little evidence that restitution will have a deterrent effect (Barnett, 1981). Clearly, there are still many reasons to question the efficacy of restitution.

While there are several stumbling blocks to restitution, there are many who believe that improving restitution requires taking steps to institutionalize

Table 5.4 Selected Recommendations from the Field for Restitution Programs

- Restitution orders should be mandatory and consistent nationwide.
- A coordinated, interagency response throughout the justice system is essential for the effective collection of restitution.
- Victims should be informed as early as possible in the justice process of their right to receive restitution from the offender.
- At the time of sentencing, courts should have sufficient information about both the victim and the offender to determine the amount of full restitution and a payment schedule.
- The use of technology can greatly enhance the tracking and payment of restitution orders.
- State legislation should make restitution payments a priority over other payments due from the offender, including fines, fees and restitution to entities other than the victim.
- Failure to comply with a restitution order should result in an extended sentence of the offender's community supervision.
- Civil remedies should be applied on a routine and consistent basis to assist crime victims in collecting restitution.
- Victims should have the right to petition to amend the payment schedule for restitution, the amount of restitution ordered, and any failure to order restitution.

Source: Compiled by authors from Office for Victims of Crime data.

the practice throughout the criminal justice process. Table 5.4 lists several recommendations made by the *New Directions* project (Office for Victims of Crime, 1998b). Among these recommendations are making restitution mandatory across the nation and making victims aware of their right to restitution. Of equal importance is the building of methods, techniques, and procedures for monitoring and enforcing restitution orders. Finally, the recommendations also include calls for ways in which victims can try to enforce restitution payments, notably through petitioning the court and resorting to civil actions.

CIVIL LITIGATION

Another method of redress for crime victims is the civil litigation arena. Civil lawsuits are the modern version of retribution/restitution practices from the past. The victim or the victim's family has the right to take civil action against offenders to recoup losses and to exact punitive damages. People sometimes call a civil lawsuit a tort action. A *tort* refers to a wrongful act that the *defendant* (the criminal) has committed against the *plaintiff* (the victim). This act has produced some type of loss, usually an injury or damage. The purpose of a tort action or civil litigation is for the plaintiff to recover monetary compensation from the defendant for any physical or psychological harm inflicted by the offender (Berliner, 1989). Thus, any civil lawsuit must be concerned with issues surrounding liability of the defendant and collectability or recovery of damages (Office for Victims of Crime, 1997).

There are some important benefits from filing civil suits (Dawson, 1989). Perhaps the most important aspect is the sense of control the victim regains through the court action. As long as the state is prosecuting the case in a criminal court, the prosecutor makes all the key decisions. The prosecutor, not the victim, decides whether to take the case to trial. The prosecutor, not the victim, can negotiate a plea settlement. The prosecutor, not the victim, decides what evidence to bring into court. Once the venue switches from the criminal court to a civil proceeding, the victim is no longer an outsider in the case. Instead, the victim and his or her ensuing problems are the central concern of the court case. The victim has the right to remain in the courtroom throughout the proceedings and has the final say in any settlement decision (National Center for Victims of Crime, 2001).

There are other advantages to pursuing a tort action. In civil suits the level of proof required is "a preponderance of evidence," whereas in criminal cases it is "proof beyond a reasonable doubt" (National Center for Victims of Crime, 2001). Even if the defendant is not found guilty in a criminal trial or if the prosecutor elects not to file charges, civil action may remain a viable alternative. In addition, a unanimous jury decision is not necessary in a civil proceeding. A majority or two-thirds decision is enough to gain a favorable verdict (see Figure 5.1). Berliner (1989) notes that juries tend to be sympathetic to victims in civil cases. Furthermore, the defendant (offender) can no longer refuse to testify by invoking the self-incrimination protection (Brien, 1992; Dawson, 1989; Office for Victims of Crime, 1997). The constitutional privilege against self-incrimination pertains to criminal proceedings, not civil action.

FIGURE 5.1 After one of the most notorious civil suits in recent history, family members of murder victim Denise Brown Simpson leave the Los Angeles County Superior Court House in 1997 after the jury found O.J. Simpson liable in the wrongful death civil suits against him.
The families of victims Denise Brown Simpson and Ronald Goldman brought civil suits after their disappointment over the acquittal of Simpson in the criminal trial for the murder. Credit: *AP Photo/Susan Sterner.*

Despite these advantages, there are a number of drawbacks to civil remedies. First, many victims are unaware of the option of pursuing a civil suit or how to find an appropriate attorney. These problems are exacerbated by the fact that many attorneys are unaware of this avenue of redress for crime victims. These problems are slowly being addressed by the establishment of referral agencies or groups around the country and through state legislation that emphasizes victims' rights to civil recourse (Office for Victims of Crime, 1998b). Second, as with restitution, the offender must be identified and located. There may be no possibility for civil action if the offender is unknown. Third, civil cases require the victim to hire an attorney and pay some filing fees before the proceedings begin (Barbieri, 1989). In effect, lower-income victims are barred from the civil system. Unless the victim is awarded a sizable sum of money, he or she may actually lose money after paying a guaranteed minimum fee to the attorney. Even with large awards, attorneys typically secure at least one-third of the award as a fee.

Fourth, some victims suffer further damage as a result of the lawsuit. Information about the victim's past behavior, character, and personal situation are all open to detailed scrutiny. This type of examination may cause further psychological and emotional harm to the victim (Barbieri, 1989). Fifth, civil suits are time-consuming and may take a period of years to resolve. During this interval the victim must have continued contact with the offender, which could bring further discomfort.

Finally, because most offenders have little or no income, there is little reason to expect any recovery even if the victim wins his or her suit. One innovation many states have attempted, to advance a victim's ability to attach an offender's assets, is the passage of so-called *"Son of Sam" provisions*. After New York serial murderer David Berkowitz (nicknamed "Son of Sam") was apprehended, he stood to gain millions of dollars by selling book and media rights to his story while his victims and their families received nothing. The idea that a criminal could gain a small fortune from his heinous acts prompted passage of a new law that allowed the state to confiscate any royalties and place the monies into the compensation fund.

WEB ACTIVITY

The Office for Victims of Crime published a good discussion of civil remedies and the issues using such approaches. This document can be found on this textbook's companion website at **http://booksite. elsevier.com/9780323287654**

Despite a flurry of similar legislation, these regulations were declared unconstitutional by the U.S. Supreme Court *(Simon & Schuster v. Members of the New York State Crime Victims Board et al., 1991)*. The Court ruled that this statute violated the First Amendment protections against censorship because it "singles out income derived from expressive activity for a burden the State places on no other income, and it is directed only at works with a specified content" (p. 487). As a result, these monies are no longer earmarked for confiscation and payment to crime victims. However, more recent incarnations of "Son of Sam" laws make it easier for victims to bring civil suits to collect any profits made by offenders as a result of their criminal activity (see Table 5.5).

Another possible avenue for victims is to file a *third-party civil suit* (Carrington, 1981; Castillo et al., 1979). In these instances, a victim sues a government entity, business, or corporation, such as a landlord, the managing corporation of a shopping center, or any other responsible body.

The argument developed during litigation of a *third-party suit* concerns the issue of whether the defendant's negligence failed to establish or to maintain a safe and protected environment. Here the victim must demonstrate two things.

Table 5.5 Possible Defendant Resources to Consider When Recovering a Civil Judgment

Source of Income
Wages
Benefits (pension payments and annuities)
Unearned income
Trust fund income
Tax refunds
Government entitlements

Property and Holdings
Personal property (cars, jewelry, etc.)
Real property (home, land, etc.)
Bank accounts
All debts owed to the defendant
Financial holdings (stocks, bonds, etc.)
Partnership interests
Future interests in real and personal property through wills, trusts, etc.

Source: Office for Victims of Crime (1997). Civil Legal Remedies for Crime Victims (2nd ed.). Washington, DC: U.S. Department of Justice, http://www.ncjrs.gov.txtfiles/clr.txt.

First, the criminal episode must be a foreseeable event. One can satisfy this requirement by documenting other offenses that have occurred on the premises or by showing that the area has a reputation for being a high-risk location. Second, either the third party must have failed to take appropriate steps to curtail further criminal events or its efforts must have fallen woefully short.

Suppose, for example, an unknown offender assaults and robs a tenant who is returning to his apartment in a housing complex. Neighbors have complained to the landlord on several occasions that the lighting in the halls is broken, nonresidents have been seen roaming the area, and there have been other similar criminal incidents in the past. Despite this information, the property manager has taken no remedial actions. Under these circumstances, a victim may be able to hold the landlord responsible for ignoring a known hazard.

Whether through civil litigation against an individual offender or against a third party, victims need to be made more aware of this avenue for recourse. The Office for Victims of Crime (1998b) has offered several recommendations to enforce the use of civil litigation (see Table 5.6). These recommendations range from simply informing victims of this response to developing consulting networks that can assist in litigation to changing the laws in order to allow victims more time in which to bring claims in civil court.

> **Table 5.6** Selected Recommendations from the Field for Civil Litigation
>
> - Crime victims should be fully informed of their legal rights to pursue civil remedies.
> - State and local networks of civil attorneys who have experience representing crime victims should be expanded.
> - Increased efforts should be made to identify consultants with the expertise to testify on issues relevant to victimization in civil and criminal cases.
> - Civil attorneys should provide training to victim service providers on civil remedies for crime victims.
> - Statutes of limitations for civil actions involving child abuse cases should be extended.
> - States should examine statutes of limitations for civil actions relating to other criminal acts to determine whether they should be extended to provide a meaningful opportunity for crime victims to obtain needed relief.
>
> *Source: Compiled by authors from Office for Victims of Crime data.*

PRIVATE INSURANCE

Another method for alleviating the losses due to crime entails private insurance. Most homeowner insurance policies have provisions for recovery of lost and damaged property. Likewise, health insurance policies typically allow payments for injuries sustained as a result of criminal incidents.

The use of insurance to offset the effects of crime does have several shortcomings. Foremost among these is that citizens must purchase the insurance. The fact that many people cannot afford insurance premiums effectively places such protection beyond their reach. Of course, this observation assumes that insurance is available to purchase in the first place. Many inner-city locations are in such crime-infested areas that private insurance companies refuse to do business there. This problem carries enormous ramifications. Lack of insurance leads to further gentrification and more urban decline in these blighted areas. This situation became so grave that the federal government now underwrites crime insurance for commercial enterprises and residents in high-crime areas.

Some people also argue that viewing insurance as a means of offsetting crime losses actually penalizes the victim further by assuming that it is the victim's responsibility to take action and avoid crime. Another problem is that most insurance policies have a deductible amount that reduces the cash outlay to victims. Deductibles of, say, $200 or $500 effectively eliminate any insurance payments for many crimes. In general, while insurance is a possible method for recouping losses, it is not an appealing means in many instances.

VICTIM COMPENSATION

Victim compensation takes place when the state, rather than the perpetrator, reimburses the victim for losses sustained at the hands of the criminal. While it is true that some victim compensation operations derive money from offender restitution, the state is the entity that has direct contact with the victim.

Table 5.7 Landmarks in Crime Victim Compensation

1963	First victim compensation legislation passed in New Zealand
1964	Victim compensation legislation passed in Great Britain
1966	California begins first victim compensation program in the United States
1977	National Association of Crime Victim Compensation Boards created
1984	Federal Victims of Crime Act passed
1986	States receive funding from Victims of Crime Act (VOCA) for first time
1988	VOCA amended to require states to pay benefits to domestic violence and drunk driving victims
2002	All 50 states, the District of Columbia, U.S. Virgin Islands, Puerto Rico, and Guam have established compensation programs

Victim compensation is not a new concept. These remedies once existed in such historical places as ancient Greece and Rome, biblical Israel, Teutonic Germany, and Saxony England (Jacob, 1976; Schafer, 1970). For a variety of reasons, this practice fell into disuse during the Middle Ages. Modern interest in victim compensation came about as a result of the advocacy efforts of Margery Fry. Fry, an English magistrate, played a prominent role in the passage of victim compensation laws in New Zealand in 1963 and in Great Britain in 1964 (Edelhertz & Geis, 1974) (see Table 5.7). In the United States, California launched its victim compensation program in 1966, followed next by New York and Hawaii. As one might imagine, there are a number of parallels between the Great Britain legislation and the American programs (Greer, 1994).

Federal efforts in the United States for victim compensation began in 1964 but did not win approval until passage of the Victims of Crime Act (VOCA) in 1984. The VOCA initiated a process whereby the federal government would provide victim compensation for federal offenses and federal funds for state compensation programs. The source of these funds came from fines, bond forfeitures, and special assessments levied on convicted individuals and businesses.

As Figure 5.2 shows, VOCA has been responsible for the flow of significant amounts of money into state compensation programs. The Crime Victims Fund has received more than $13 billion in deposits since it began in 1984. In 2010, the Crime Victims Fund generated more than $2.3 billion for distribution (Office for Victims of Crime, 2011).

The fluctuations in deposits since the late 1990s are attributable to several large fines paid by corporations (Derene, 2005). Fund disbursements fall into several prioritized categories (Office for Victims of Crime, 2011). In 2010, $20 million was set aside for investigating and prosecuting child abuse cases. Almost $39 million was set aside to improve services to victims in federal cases. More than $5 million went to the Federal Victim Notification System. OVC discretionary

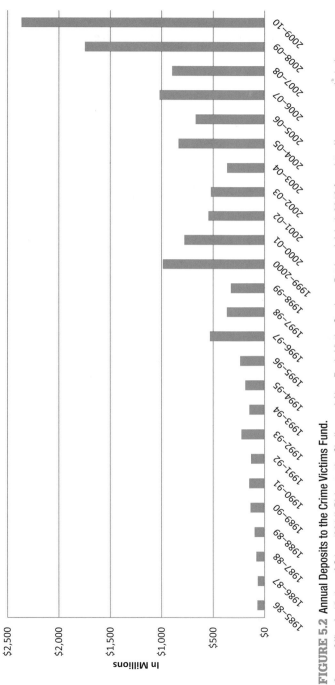

FIGURE 5.2 Annual Deposits to the Crime Victims Fund.

Source: Office for Victims of Crime (2011). Rising to the Challenge: A New Era in Victim Services. Retrieved July 4, 2013 from http://www.ovc.gov/pubs/ reporttonation2011/index.html.

grants received $32.1 million of the remaining funds. The remaining funds were divided between state victim compensation programs ($198 million) and state victim assistance programs ($421 million) (Office for Victims of Crime, 2011). All 50 states, the District of Columbia, and the U.S. Virgin Islands benefit from these funds. In FY 2010, more than $468 million was paid in state compensation to 168,070 claimants, an average of approximately $2,800 per claim (Office for Victims of Crime, 2011).

In addition to providing money, the VOCA helped standardize state crime compensation laws. The initial flurry to pass compensation provisions produced a variety of rules and regulations that differed from one state to the next. To be eligible to receive the federal VOCA funds, states had to follow a series of program guidelines. For instance, some states were granting compensation only to victims who were state residents. VOCA regulations called for the removal of state residency requirements, among other things. In order to reach a better understanding of just what victim compensation entails, the following sections describe some of the more salient characteristics of these statutes.

 **WEB ACTIVITY**

More information on the operations of the federal victim compensation program and funds can be found at **http://www.ovc.gov/pubs/reporttonation2011/index.html**

Philosophical Bases

Proponents feel that government has the obligation to provide victim compensation for two distinct reasons. The first view is the *social contract* argument. This perspective maintains that government, through its system of taxation and provision of services, engages in an unwritten contract to care for the safety and well-being of its citizens. Citizens, according to this perspective, have relinquished the power of law enforcement to government in exchange for protection. The experience of being a crime victim, through no fault of one's own, represents an affront to this agreement because the government has failed to keep its promise. As a result, it is incumbent upon government to restore victimized citizens to their former status.

The second philosophical position is the notion of *social welfare*. Government attempts to provide a minimum standard of living for its disabled, deprived, and unfortunate citizens. This position holds that innocent crime victims fall into this category because they suffer deprivations that are not self-induced. As a result, government should extend its welfare practices and come to the rescue of crime victims because they are, in effect, deprived.

The argument one chooses to embrace carries important ramifications for other features of victim compensation. For example, if one adheres to the social welfare view, one might endorse a "financial means test." In this scheme, only poor people should be eligible for compensation benefits. However, if one adopts the social contract notion, then compensation should be available to everybody, regardless of their financial status.

A third reason offered for victim compensation deals with the use of compensation as an enticement to lure victims back to the criminal justice system. Earlier we noted that many victims refrain from contacting the authorities because of the additional costs inherent in doing so. They are responding to a simple cost–benefit analysis. Compensation, however, can alleviate much of the monetary loss associated with the offense. Therefore, it is possible that compensation can tip the balance of the cost–benefit equation and bring victims back into the system. Not only does compensation carry the potential to promote good will between the criminal justice system and citizens/victims, it may also result in more crime clearances and (eventually) lower crime through the apprehension of more offenders.

Compensable Acts

Most programs restrict victim compensation to three categories of victims. The first group includes victims of personal injury crimes and the family members of victims who were killed. All expenses related to physical injuries, including mental health services/counseling and lost wages, are covered (National Association of Crime Victim Compensation Boards, 2007). Payments typically cover medical expenses, losses related to missed work, and mental health treatment of the victim (and family, in the case of the victim's death). Conversely, victims are rarely compensated for losses due to property crimes. Only a handful of states have provisions allowing payment for property loss or damage (Parent, Auerbach, & Carlson, 1992).

The second group is "Good Samaritans." Under *"Good Samaritan" provisions*, a person who is hurt or killed during an attempt to prevent a crime from taking place or while attempting to capture a suspected criminal is entitled to compensation. The thinking here is that society owes a special duty to anybody who acts above and beyond the normal duties of citizenship—that altruism should be encouraged, not discouraged.

The final category specifically includes anyone who is injured while coming to the aid of a law enforcement officer. Some states stipulate that people who do not help a police officer when he or she asks for assistance are guilty of a misdemeanor. Thus, it makes sense to compensate citizens when they act on behalf of a police officer.

There also are some people who are specifically not eligible for compensation. For example, most states prohibit compensation for law enforcement officers and firefighters. The thinking here is that their actions are part of the job and that other programs, such as workers' compensation, are more appropriate vendors (Parent et al., 1992). Other excluded persons include prison or jail inmates and individuals involved in organized crime.

Eligibility Restrictions

One restriction on compensation is to ensure that an offender is not "unjustly enriched." This is primarily a concern in domestic violence cases in which the victim still resides with the offender. Rather than simply exclude domestic violence victims from receiving compensation, the VOCA and its 1988 amendments require states to establish guidelines for determining whether compensation would be "appropriated by [the offender] or used to support him in a *substantial way*" (National Association of Crime Victim Compensation Boards, 2007). States are required to have written guidelines that apply to *all* crimes, not just domestic violence offenses. One way to alleviate such concerns is the use of provisions, such as those in Minnesota, that allow compensation if a domestic violence victim will prosecute the offending party or is in the process of seeking a legal separation or a divorce.

A number of states have a financial means test on the books. In other words, the victim must suffer a serious financial hardship before an award will be forthcoming. As we mentioned earlier, one philosophical basis for establishing a victim compensation program is the social welfare argument. While a financial hardship test stems from this orientation, it is also a mechanism to cap program expenditures. Interestingly, if a state compensation program operates under a financial hardship restriction, it is not eligible for federal victim compensation funds.

Another condition that affects eligibility is victim involvement or *contributory misconduct*. The victim must not share any criminal responsibility for the event. In other words, victim precipitation reduces one's standing for a compensation award. For example, suppose that John challenges Peter to a fight. Peter accepts and during this pugilistic event he breaks John's nose. Depending upon on how the state's provisions read, the compensation board may deny John's claim completely or it may reduce the size of the award in proportion to the amount of victim contribution to the criminal incident.

One additional eligibility criteria concerns the availability of other forms of assistance. Victim compensation is universally viewed as a *source of last resort*. That is, all other avenues for compensation must be exhausted before compensation benefits are forthcoming (National Association of Crime Victim Compensation Boards, 2007). Payments go to victims only after all alternate sources of funds are exhausted. Other sources include workers' compensation, disability benefits, insurance policies, offender restitution, private donations, Medicaid, Social Security, and possibly civil lawsuit awards. Any payments from a compensation program are reduced by an appropriate amount corresponding to funds received from such alternate sources. In order to avoid undue hardship on victims, programs typically make awards and subsequently recover any funds available from other sources.

Awards

States vary in the cap or limit they will pay per claim. Typically, caps range from $10,000 to $25,000, although the state of Washington has a $150,000 maximum while New York has no cap on payments for medical losses. Some states require a minimum loss in order to prevent the program from being inundated by frivolous claims that are costly to investigate. Many states also make emergency awards when victims or survivors face immediate financial hardship (Office for Victims of Crime, 1998b).

Crime compensation covers such items as lost wages, medical bills, prosthetics, funeral expenses, and, in some instances, mental health counseling. Most programs do not set aside any monies for pain and suffering or for property damage. Indeed, only five allow for pain and suffering, and eight make awards for property damage (Parent et al., 1992).

A recent addition to the items that victim compensation can pay is costs that arise from forensic medical examinations. A standard police investigatory practice is to transport sexual assault victims to a medical facility for physical examination. As Chapter 9 will explain, this examination consists of two parts, gathering physical evidence from the victim and providing medical treatment to the victim. Some compensation boards reimburse applicants for the medical portion of the examination but reject payment for the evidentiary aspects. This practice led a U.S. Department of Justice report (1986: 17) to comment that "[f]orcing sexual assault victims to bear this cost is tantamount to charging burglary victims for collecting fingerprints." The Victims of Crime Act of 1984 makes funds available for qualifying victim compensation programs to pay for forensic examinations.

The award itself can take several forms. The payout can be in a lump sum, in periodic installments, or in partial amounts. Some states permit victims in dire need to receive a small emergency award, pending the outcome of a full investigation. Some compensation agencies pay vendors (such as doctors and hospitals) directly to prevent victims from skipping out on their bills.

Funding

An important political issue for many people concerns funding sources. While some states extract monies from the general tax structure to underwrite victim compensation, a more popular funding mechanism is the offender. According to the National Association of Crime Victim Compensation Boards (2007), most state compensation programs receive funds primarily from fines and fees levied on offenders, with roughly one-third coming to the states from the Crime Victims Fund. Funding also comes from monies recouped through offender restitution payments to the state. Most programs receive *no* general revenue funds from the state.

Reporting Crime and Applying for Compensation

One prominent feature of victim compensation is its close alliance with the criminal justice system. Virtually every state requires the crime be reported to the police within a relatively short period of time (typically 72 hours). Victims also must cooperate fully with the police investigation and cooperate completely with the prosecution of the case should the state attorney or district attorney pursue that option. There are also deadlines for when victims must apply for compensation. Failure to abide by any of these requirements results in an automatic claim denial and the repayment of any compensation benefits that the victim may have received already. The Office for Victims of Crime's *New Directions* project (1998) calls for a relaxation of the reporting and claims time frames, and for allowing the initial report to be made to non-law enforcement agencies, such as counselors or medical personnel. The current requirements represent a very calculated attempt to bring victims back into the criminal justice system.

⊕ WEB ACTIVITY

A great deal of other information on victim compensation is available from the National Association of Crime Victims Compensation Boards at **http://www. nacvcb.org/** and the National Association of VOCA Assistance Administrators at **http://navaa.org/**

DOES VICTIM COMPENSATION WORK?

As noted earlier, a substantial number of victims elect not to report their victimizations to the police. Those victims who do contact the police may choose not to prosecute. One reason for this lack of involvement in the criminal justice process appears to be that victims realize they can minimize their losses by avoiding the legal system. If the decision to not cooperate with the system stems from an economic appraisal, then the system needs to lure victims back with financial incentives.

Some observers contend that victim compensation fits this bill. Failure to report the crime to the police, assist in the police investigation, and cooperate completely with the prosecution of the offender can automatically produce a compensation claim denial. Victim compensation, therefore, amounts to an economic incentive that serves to entice the victim back into the legal process. Compensation administrators routinely tout their programs as promoting greater victim cooperation with the legal machinery.

Macro-Level Effects

Victim compensation administrators generally assume that their programs increase victim participation in the criminal justice system. If this is correct, certain macro-level effects should appear. A *macro-level effect* refers to a change in some group or organizational characteristic. Because victim compensation laws mandate crime reporting, cooperation with the authorities, and participation in court cases, certain systematic effects should surface. Victim compensation programs should produce an increased rate of violent crimes known to the police, a higher proportion of known crime that is violent, and an increased proportion of violent crimes cleared by the police.

An examination of four states operating a victim compensation program found no support for any of these expectations (Doerner et al., 1976). A replication using victim compensation programs from several Canadian provinces did not uncover any evidence for the proposed effects (Doerner, 1978a). Because both studies utilized official data, it is possible that shortcomings within the data influenced the findings. As a result, another analysis examined self-reported victimization data (Doerner, 1978b). Utilizing the National Crime Panel Surveys from 26 cities made it possible to test two hypotheses. First, it was anticipated that compensating jurisdictions would record higher rates of violent crime reporting than would noncompensating areas. Second, it was expected that reporting rates for property crime in compensating and noncompensating jurisdictions would be similar in both types of jurisdictions because these offenses were not compensable. The findings revealed that areas with compensation programs had similar rates of reported violent and property crimes. Thus, these studies suggest that victim compensation did not stimulate an increase in crime reporting.

Although these studies failed to uncover any discernible effects, the possibility still exists that victim compensation programs do influence conviction rates. However, an analysis of Canadian provinces revealed similar conviction rates for violent and for property offenses in both compensating and noncompensating jurisdictions (Silverman & Doerner, 1979). As a result, the researchers concluded that victim compensation did not alter conviction rates.

In sum, these studies do not provide any consistent empirical evidence in support of the contention that victim compensation positively affects other components of the criminal justice system. This conclusion takes on much greater importance in view of the fact that the evidence is derived from studies conducted in two different countries and with data from official, as well as nonofficial, sources. Despite the conclusion of no macro-level or organizational effects, it still remains to be seen whether victim compensation programs generate any micro-level or individual effects.

Micro-Level Effects

Several researchers have pointed out that certain micro-level effects should materialize. A *micro-level effect* refers to any changes in a person, such as being more satisfied with the criminal justice system if a person received compensation. To test this assumption, Doerner and Lab (1980) mailed a questionnaire to victims who had applied for crime compensation in Florida. Following the advice of program officials, they divided the study participants into a group who received compensation and a group who was denied compensation. The expectation was that compensated victims would express more favorable attitudes toward criminal justice personnel and would be more likely to cooperate with these personnel in the future than noncompensated applicants.

The results showed that compensated victims were more satisfied with the crime compensation officials than were noncompensated victims. However, a similar sense of satisfaction did not accrue to the police, to the state attorney, or to the judge. While compensated victims were more likely to say that they would register a claim with the crime compensation program in the event of a future victimization, they were not inclined to cooperate with other system personnel. Thus, it would seem from this study that victim compensation programs do not generate a "spillover" or a halo effect to the remainder of the criminal justice system.

The foregoing results suggest that victim compensation programs have had little impact on the attitudes and views of the public toward the criminal justice system. This suggests that the future of compensation must not rely on arguments that it benefits the criminal justice system or society. Rather, an appeal to the social welfare and social contract arguments holds much more promise.

Problems and Concerns with Compensation

Besides the potential impact of compensation on the criminal justice system, it is possible to evaluate these operations in terms of the number of victims served and the extent of services provided. Early program evaluations found a number of readily identifiable deficiencies (Brooks, 1975; Doerner, 1977; Meiners, 1978). Just about every program was deluged by the number of claims it had received. Given the small number of staff, some claims required more than a year for processing. Rejection rates exceeded the 50% mark, and the availability of victim compensation remained a well-kept secret. These observations led one researcher to forecast that unless these problems were corrected, "victim compensation programs will not significantly reduce the plight of the crime victim in our society and will remain a prime example of a misguided social program" (Doerner, 1977: 109). More recently, Newmark and associates (2003) reported that 87% of claims were approved for payment.

These concerns appear to have diminished as the programs have matured. A phone survey of victims in six states revealed that the average processing time for claims is only 10 weeks (Newmark et al., 2003). At the same time, almost one-quarter of the victims believe this processing time is too long. The Office for Victims of Crime (1998b) offers several recommendations that could further increase the number of awards, as well as speed up the making of awards. These suggestions include the use of new technologies for filing and processing claims, greater cooperation between agencies in processing claims, and integrating victim compensation closer with other victim assistance functions and programs.

While recent figures on awards appear impressive, they fail to tell us the extent to which all eligible victims are being reached and served by compensation programs.

Considering the total number of compensable offenses reported to police, whether the victim was culpable, and the availability of insurance to cover losses, there were roughly 168,000 victims eligible for compensation in 1987 (Parent et al., 1992). Less than half of these crimes, however, resulted in a compensation claim. Many victims are not applying for or receiving compensation. One reason for this gap may be the relative anonymity within which many compensation programs operate (Newmark et al., 2003). That is, most victims do not know about the programs (McCormack, 1991). Greater outreach is needed to make victims aware of compensation programs (Office for Victims of Crime, 1998b).

SUMMARY

Crime victims face a host of problems, not the least of which are the financial costs accruing from the crime. This chapter has examined several mechanisms that victims can use to recoup some of their losses. There has been a great deal of resurgent interest in restitution over the past few decades. The problems with restitution, however, have prompted moves to other forms of recompense. Both civil litigation and insurance represent methods by which the victim takes an active role. Unfortunately, each requires a monetary outlay on the part of the victim beyond the loss due to the crime. Many victims simply cannot afford to turn to these alternatives. The final possibility discussed is the use of state victim compensation. Under this scheme, the state makes payments to crime victims. Innocent victims who cooperate with the criminal justice system receive compensation for their crime-related losses. Many victims, however, do not know about these programs and therefore fail to take advantage of these funds. The recent increase in federal participation and funding of victim compensation suggests that this scheme could well become the primary source of monetary aid to crime victims in the foreseeable future.

KEY TERMS

civil restitution lien
contributory misconduct
defendant
"Good Samaritan" provisions
macro-level effects
micro-level effects
monetary-community restitution
monetary-victim restitution
net-widening
offender restitution
outcome evaluations
plaintiff

process evaluations
service-community restitution
service-victim restitution
social contract
social welfare
"Son of Sam" provisions
source of last resort
third-party civil suit
tort
unjust enrichment
victim compensation
Victims of Crime Act (VOCA)

Remedying the Non-Financial Impact of Victimization

After reading Chapter 6, you should be able to:

- Chronicle the development of victim-witness management projects.
- Identify some of the recommendations issued by the New Directions project for prosecutors, police, the judiciary, and corrections.
- List different types of services usually provided by victim-witness programs.
- Explain how a victim-witness program blunts the "prosecutory assembly line" mentality.
- Talk about the two assumptions that underlie victim-witness service projects.
- Explain how derivative victims have come under the umbrella of victim services.
- Relay why compassion fatigue is an emerging concern.
- Convey how upgrading personnel qualifications and recognizing ethical considerations are professionalizing victim advocates.
- Evaluate whether victim-witness projects work.
- Address the criticism that witness management is simply a tool with which to manipulate victims.
- Define dispute resolution.
- Discuss the rationale for dispute resolution programs.
- Outline and discuss the common elements of dispute resolution.
- Provide evidence on the impact of dispute resolution.
- Provide a definition for restorative justice.
- Compare and contrast the basic premises of retributive justice and restorative justice.
- Discuss the advantages of restorative justice for victims, offenders, and the community.
- Provide a brief discussion of the background (history) of restorative justice.
- Discuss the theory of reintegrative shaming.

119

INTRODUCTION

While attempting to compensate victims for their monetary losses is a commendable goal, victims suffer in other ways. Victims of crime may experience a loss of confidence in themselves and their ability to protect themselves and their loved ones, or they may become apprehensive and fear that they will be victimized again in the future. Fear can lead victims to alter their normal routines. Victims may stay home due to fear of future attack; they may lock themselves in their homes to protect themselves; they may shy away from meeting new people due to a belief that they will be victimized; or they may needlessly spend money on security devices or weapons for protection. As noted in Chapter 2, many victims decide to avoid contacting the criminal justice system due to the problem of double victimization. One consequence of this is that the offender may never be caught and may continue to victimize others in the community.

Responses to victimization, therefore, require more than just attention paid to the financial losses incurred by the immediate victim and his or her family. More is lost as a result of a victimization, both for the victim and his or her family and for the community. A broader response is needed that addresses the needs of the victim and the community. This chapter examines new and innovative criminal justice system methods for addressing the needs of victims. Victim-witness assistance programs are one response that has emerged. Their goal has been to soften the impact of system participation so that victims would make good witnesses at the trial stage. This chapter also examines the idea of restorative justice as a means of addressing the needs of everyone impacted by criminal victimization.

PROSECUTORIAL-BASED VICTIM-WITNESS PROJECTS

The criminal justice community has recognized the need to address the looming problem of citizen noncooperation in order to save the system from crumbling. Starting in the mid-1970s, the federal government provided funding for victim-witness assistance programs housed in prosecutor offices. There were more than 265 such programs in place by the end of the decade (Viano, 1979).

Observers refer to these efforts as *victim-witness* or *victim/witness projects*. The underlying ideological thrust is witness management. Prosecutors render services to crime victims not out of compassion, but to cultivate or preserve the worth of the victims as witnesses for the state (Chelimsky, 1981). Thus, the focus is on minimizing witness discontent with system treatment in order to retain testimonial value.

Unfortunately, the initial federal funding started to dry up—beginning in the 1980s—and attempts to prompt local officials to take up the efforts met with limited success. Local victim-witness projects languished. The local efforts were not very adept at becoming institutionalized as permanently funded fixtures within local criminal justice budgets. Luckily, the political landscape underwent significant changes with the release of the report from the President's Task Force on Victims of Crime (1982).

The President's Task Force traveled throughout the country, holding public hearings and securing testimony. Time after time, the Task Force received disturbing accounts of how the criminal justice system routinely mishandled victims and witnesses. Citizens relayed the tragic details of their victimization experiences and further explained how their misfortunes had intensified when they turned to the criminal justice system for relief. Victims told how system officials shunned them, how becoming involved in the system had exacerbated or heightened their suffering, and how the halls of justice became just another ordeal to undergo.

Task Force members came to the conclusion that the criminal justice system had become a monstrous operation in dire need of immediate reform. If the plight of victims and witnesses was to be corrected, then the system needed improvement. For this reason, the Task Force issued a number of recommendations aimed directly at victim and witness concerns. Specifically, it urged prosecutors to communicate more closely with victims, seek greater victim input, protect them against any harassment, honor scheduled case appearances, return property promptly, and improve the overall quality of client services.

In 1986, the Department of Justice issued its assessment, *Four Years Later: A Report on the President's Task Force on Victims of Crime*, which monitored compliance with the Task Force's recommendations. The overall tone of the report was quite positive—almost buoyant. Victims and witnesses were making significant strides. Many efforts were underway to address the concerns raised by the Task Force. Assistant Attorney General Lois Herrington (U.S. Department of Justice, 1986: ii–iii) wrote the following message in her transmittal letter to the President of the United States:

> When you created the President's Task Force on Victims of Crime, the Nation began to listen and respond… . To date, nearly 75% of the proposals have been acted upon, led by a new Office for Victims of Crime in the Justice Department created expressly to implement the Task Force reforms… . We hope this document will help assure that the victim of crime will never be overlooked as an integral part of the criminal justice system.

Attention to victim-witness services did not die with these pronouncements. Officials have continued to monitor these efforts and make adjustments wherever necessary. In 1998, the Office for Victims of Crime issued an update, *New Directions from the Field: Victims' Rights and Services for the 21st Century.* This document was the culmination of a three-year project involving more than 1,000 individuals with varied backgrounds and expertise from across the United States. This report noted that, despite the recommendations and efforts proceeding from the 1982 Task Force report, "only a fraction of the nation's estimated 38 million crime victims receive much-needed services, such as emergency financial assistance, crisis and mental health counseling, shelter, and information and advocacy within the criminal and juvenile justice systems" (Office for Victims of Crime, 1998b: vii). Based on this pronouncement, the report called for a renewed emphasis and a refocus on assisting victims of crime.

WEB ACTIVITY

The New Directions report can be found at **https://www.ncjrs.gov/ovc_archives/directions/welcome.html**. The report covers many different agencies and professions. Investigate the possible contributions to victims' rights that could come from different sources.

In order to ensure that the earlier gains won on behalf of victims and witnesses would not be lost and to provide needed impetus for further changes, *New Directions* offered 250 recommendations addressing all parts of the criminal justice system, as well as related fields (such as health care, mental health, education, faith organizations, the business community, and the media). Recommendations specific to prosecutors appear in Table 6.1. Many of these guidelines reflect the same concerns and needs addressed in the 1982 Task Force Report.

Projects and Performance

The decision regarding what services a project should provide must begin with an overview of the models that currently exist. Most victim-witness assistance programs offer a very similar core of services (Finn & Lee, 1987; Tomz & McGillis, 1997; U.S. Department of Justice, 1986; Webster, 1988). Table 6.2 outlines the essential elements that appear in most programs.

Table 6.1 Selected Recommendations for Prosecutors

1. Prosecutors' offices should notify victims in a timely manner of the date, time, and location of the following: charging of defendant, pretrial hearings, plea negotiations, the trial, all schedule changes, and the sentencing hearing.

2. Prosecutors should establish victim-witness assistance units to ensure that victims of crime receive at least a basic level of service, including information, notification, consultation and participation.

3. Prosecutors should use the full range of measures at their disposal to ensure that victims and witnesses are protected from intimidation and harassment. These measures include ensuring that victims are informed about safety precautions, advising the court of victims' fears and concerns about safety prior to any bail or bond proceedings, automatically requesting no-contact orders and enforcing them if violated, and utilizing witness relocation programs and technology to help protect victims.

4. Prosecutors should advocate for the rights of victims to have their views heard by judges on bail decisions, continuances, plea bargains, dismissals, sentencing, and restitution. Policies and procedures should be put into place in all prosecutors' offices to ensure that victims are informed in a timely manner of these crucial rights in forms of communication they understand.

5. Prosecutors should make every effort, if the victim has provided a current address or telephone number, to consult with the victim on the terms of any negotiated plea, including the acceptance of a plea of guilty or nolo contendere.

6. Prosecutors should establish policies to "fast track" the prosecution of sexual assault, domestic violence, elderly and child abuse, and other particularly sensitive cases to shorten the length of time from arrest to disposition.

7. Prosecutors should adopt vertical prosecution for domestic violence, sexual assault, and child abuse cases.

8. Prosecutors' offices should establish procedures to ensure the prompt return of victims' property, absent the need for it as actual evidence in court.

Source: Office for Victims of Crime (1998b). New Directions from the Field: Victim's Rights and Services for the 21st Century. Washington, DC: U.S. Department of Justice.

Victim-witness projects, like many other social service agencies, keep statistics to track their performance and to justify their continued existence. Reports typically contain such items as the number of persons who used different project features, measures of client satisfaction, individual testimonials praising staff efforts, and commendations from system officials. These process-oriented figures are helpful when describing the level of service delivery and the type of activities in which staff members engage.

When these accounts stretch over time or multiple sites, one can obtain a better idea of the direction in which these ventures are moving. A number of states require prosecutors' offices to make services available to victims and witnesses. These services include notification and alerts; orientation and education; escort services; and counseling and assistance (DeFrances, Smith, & Does, 1996). Another way of looking at the provision of services is to consider the number of victims served. Table 6.3 shows the number of victims served in different capacities in 2009 and 2010 through programs funded by the Victim of Crime Act. It is important to note that many more victims receive assistance from local, state, and private programs and are not reflected in these data.

Table 6.2 Elements Essential for Victim-Witness Assistance Programs	
Emergency Services	**Court-Related Services**
–Shelter/food	–Witness reception
–Security repair	–Court orientation
–Financial assistance	–Notification
–On-scene comfort	–Witness alert
–Medical care	–Transportation
Counseling	–Child care
–24-hour hotline	–Escort to court
–Crisis intervention	**Post-Sentencing Services**
–Follow-up counseling	–Orientation
–Mediation	–Notification
Advocacy and Support Services	–Victim–offender reconciliation program
–Personal advocacy	–Restitution
–Employer intervention	**System-Wide Services**
–Landlord intervention	–Public education
–Property return	–Legislative advocacy
–Intimidation intervention	–Training
–Victim impact reports	
–Legal/paralegal counsel	
–Referral	
Claims Assistance	
–Insurance claims aid	
–Restitution assistance	
–Compensation assistance	
–Witness fee assistance	

One of the more striking facts that emerge from these reports on victim-witness projects is that they are swamped with referrals. Both the police and prosecutors are sending more clients to these projects for help, and there has been a sharp rise in victim self-referrals. The number of inquiries has risen so dramatically that some managers have had to expand the number of service providers on staff. In short, these programs seem to have become institutionalized fixtures within the criminal justice system.

Project Evaluation

In the past, some prosecutor offices were so clinical in how they handled witnesses that commentators dubbed these operations "the prosecutory assembly line" (Cannavale & Falcon, 1976). In stark contrast, victim-witness projects now concentrate on making the criminal justice system more user-friendly. For example, prosecutors have redesigned waiting areas to make them more comfortable, and efforts have been expended in returning property quickly to

Table 6.3 Number and Estimated Percent of Victims Served by VOCA Assistance Programs in 2009/2010

Assistance	Number of Victims	Estimated % Victims
Telephone information and referral	5,114,347	72
Criminal justice support and advocacy	4,408,947	62
Onsite information and referral	3,636,740	51
Follow-up	4,703,608	66
Crisis counseling	3,186,873	45
Personal advocacy	3,226,436	45
Help filing compensation claims	1,856,867	26
Shelter or safe house stay	730,712	10
Group treatment and support	933,536	13
Emergency legal advocacy	2,296,137	22
Therapy	540,133	8
Emergency financial assistance	610,373	8
Other	1,368,836	19
Total	31,202,025	

Source: Compiled by authors from Office for Victims of Crime (2011). Rising to the Challenge: A New Era in Victmin Surveys. Retrieved July 3, 2013 from http://www.ojp.usdoj.gov/ovc/pubs/reporttonation2011/index.html.

owners, filing applications for victim compensation, registering system participants for witness fees, and explaining court procedures to those with questions.

Notifying victims and witnesses about cancellations eliminates many unnecessary trips to the courthouse as well as the frustration that accompanies such trips. One major effort to address the problem of keeping victims and witnesses notified is the development of the *Statewide Automated Victim Information and Notification (SAVIN)* program. This system allows victims and witnesses to identify how (and if) they want to be kept abreast of cases.

WEB ACTIVITY

Visit the Bureau of Justice Assistance SAVIN website at **https://www.bja.gov/ProgramDetails.aspx?Program_ID=87**. Find out about the background of the program and the effectiveness of the system.

Two assumptions have guided these witness service provision attempts (Davis, 1983; Weigend, 1983). First, prosecutors want to ameliorate witness conditions because they feel that witness cooperation is essential to winning convictions. Second, the popular view is that victims and witnesses refuse to cooperate with system officials because the anticipated costs are too high. Thus, evaluation efforts gather data aimed at empirically refuting or supporting these two lines of thinking.

Despite the intuitive appeal behind these assumptions, there is some question as to whether these efforts actually carry a commensurate payoff. One jurisdiction established a victim-witness unit that handled only child sexual abuse cases and assessed whether witness cooperation could improve prosecution performance (Dible & Teske, 1993). The victim counselor who was assigned to this unit would follow a case throughout the entire process. This person would meet several times with the victim to establish a rapport with the child and to evaluate the validity of the complaint. Anatomically correct dolls were available so that the child could explain what had happened to him or her. Whenever the case went to the grand jury, judges allowed the victim counselor to take the place of the child on the witness stand and explain the details of the case. Finally, the counselor would accompany the child to the trial and offer support in whatever way was necessary. The researchers evaluated the performance of this program using a before-and-after intervention strategy. The results showed that once the program was operational, guilty trial verdicts increased from 38% to 72%, the severity of the convicted charges increased, and the number of sentences resulting in imprisonment rose. In short, the program was a prosecutorial success.

A recent response to intimate partner violence, the Judicial Oversight Demonstration Project, incorporated a strong victim advocacy/services component (Harrell et al., 2007). The program aimed to protect victims, reduce recidivism, and hold offenders accountable by coordinating community services and justice system action under the oversight of the judiciary. Victim services included a victim advocate working with victims, developing a safety plan for each victim, and providing needed interventions for each victim. The project was evaluated in Dorchester, Massachusetts, and Washtenaw County, Michigan. Results showed that victims reported more contact with victim services, a victim advocate and the receipt of more services (Harrell et al., 2007). Victims also reported satisfaction with the quality of the services and the response of the criminal justice personnel. Unfortunately, reduced repeat victimization is found only in Dorchester, meaning that no clear impact on recidivism is available (Harrell et al., 2007). In this case, the program had mixed results.

WEB ACTIVITY

The Office for Victims of Crime reports on many activities in support of victims' rights and services. There is also material on enforcement and evaluation of those activities. This can be found at **http://www.ojp.usdoj.gov/ovc/rights/overview_rights.html**

What is the key to program success? Why do some programs appear to be more effective than others? One possible explanation is that victims and witnesses seek only humane treatment, and giving them that will increase program effectiveness. Satisfied clients who have had a comfortable experience inside the halls of justice tend to express no reservations about returning again if the need arises (Kelly, 1984; Norton, 1983; O'Grady et al., 1992).

BEYOND THE PROSECUTOR'S OFFICE

Evidence and research on the effectiveness of prosecutorial efforts may be influenced by other elements and actors in the criminal justice system, and societal response to victims. Victim assistance needs to consider a wider range of individuals and agencies beyond the prosecutor's office. Among these are law enforcement, the judiciary, and corrections. While these groups have not been totally ignored in earlier efforts, such as the 1982 Task Force, the bulk of the emphasis and subsequent activity has been at the prosecutorial level. Law enforcement and the judiciary receive a great deal of attention in the *New Directions* report.

Recommendations for police policies and procedures for dealing with victims appear in Table 6.4. Interestingly, the very first recommendation made by the *New Directions* project for policing is for officers to provide victims with verbal and written notification of their rights at the earliest point in their contact (Office for Victims of Crime, 1998b). In itself, this would be a major change in the operations of most police agencies and would mirror the concern for offenders' rights currently accorded in the arrest process.

A second major recommendation is that the police should work with and use community agencies and resources to address the needs of crime victims. Emergency services, shelter, financial aid, and information are among the things that victims routinely need. The remaining recommendations revolve around making the investigation, arrest, and case preparation as inclusive of the victim as possible. Victims should be notified of all actions the police take, and the police should explain the process to the victims, both initially and as the case unfolds. In essence, the police should treat the victim as a key stakeholder in the system, rather than as a potential witness to be called if needed.

Recommendations directed at the judiciary often mirror the advice given to prosecutorial offices. They are set forth as a separate set of recommendations to emphasize the importance of judges in recognizing the needs of victims. Many of these recommendations deal with the inclusion of victims at various points in the court process—at pre- and post-release decisions, trial, plea bargaining, and sentencing (see Table 6.5). As with police, the recommendations open with the need to inform victims of their rights, just as with defendants. Judges are also called on to undergo training and education on victim issues and to assume a leadership role in addressing the needs of victims.

The role of the correctional system in aiding crime victims was also addressed in the *New Directions* report. As with the police, prosecutors, and judiciary, the thrust of the recommendations is to recognize the needs and concerns of victims. Again, information provision is a cornerstone of the recommendations, ranging from notifying victims of changes in an offender's status to

Table 6.4 Policies, Protocols, and Procedures for a Comprehensive Law Enforcement Response to Victims of Crime

Upon first contact with law enforcement, the responding officer should give victims verbal and written notification of their rights according to state or federal law.

Law enforcement agencies should utilize community partnerships to ensure that victims have access to the following emergency services, financial assistance, information and community programs:

- On-site crisis intervention, assistance, and support;
- Immediate referrals to community agencies;
- Transportation and accompaniment to emergency medical services;
- A brochure or other written resources that explain the expected reactions victims have to specific crimes;
- Written information about crime victim compensation and how to apply for it;
- Victims should not be charged for certain medical procedures or for costs arising out of the need to collect and secure evidence.

Protection from intimidation and harm:

- Notification about the procedures and resources available for protection;
- An explanation of anti-stalking rights, availability of emergency protection orders;
- Victim notification of the release of the accused and inclusion of no-contact-with-the-victim orders as conditions of the release.

Investigation:

- A verbal and written orientation to the investigation process;
- Procedures allowing a victim to choose an individual to accompany them to interviews;
- The name and telephone number of the law enforcement officer investigating the offense;
- A free copy of the incident and arrest report.

If an arrest has been made, victims should be notified of:

- The arrest of the offender;
- The next regularly scheduled date, time, and place for initial appearance;
- Any pretrial release of the offender;
- Their rights within the criminal and juvenile justice processes;
- Upon release of a suspected offender, notification of the date, time, and place of the next court appearance.

If there is no arrest within 7 days:

- Information about the right to notification of an arrest, providing the victim maintains a current address.

If the case has been submitted to a prosecuting attorney's office:

- Notification of the name, address, and telephone number of the prosecuting attorney assigned to the case.
- Prompt property return.

Source: Office for Victims of Crime (1998b). New Directions from the Field: Victim's Rights and Services for the 21st Century. *Washington, DC: U.S. Department of Justice.*

notification of the release of an offender from an institution (see Table 6.6). Correctional agencies are also prompted to take an active role in the collection and distribution of restitution, and to use victim impact panels in their work with offenders. Finally, there is a general concern with guaranteeing the safety of victims, as evidenced in calls to protect victims from intimidation, and notifying victims and the community of the release of sex offenders.

Table 6.5 Selected Recommendations for the Judiciary

- Judges should advise victims of their rights as routinely as they advise defendants of their rights.

- Judges and all court personnel at all levels of the court system must receive initial and continuing education on the law concerning victims' rights, the impact of crime on victims and their families, and how the judiciary can implement the spirit as well as the letter of these rights.

- Judges should facilitate the rights of crime victims and their families to be present at court proceedings unless the defendant proves that their presence would interfere with the defendant's right to a fair trial.

- Judges should consider victim and community safety in any pre-release or post-release decision.

- Before imposing a sentence, judges should permit the victim, the victim's representative, or, when appropriate, representatives of the community to present a victim impact statement.

- Judges should facilitate the input of crime victims into plea agreements and resulting sentences, and they should request that prosecuting attorneys demonstrate that reasonable efforts were made to confer with the victim.

- Judges have the responsibility to manage their cases and calendars to make victim involvement as feasible as possible.

- Judges should order restitution from offenders to help compensate victims for the harm they have suffered.

- Judges must take a leadership role in conceptualizing and advocating that the justice system encompass not only traditional adjudication and punishment but also holistic problem solving and treatment for victims as well as offenders.

Source: Office for Victims of Crime (1998b). New Directions from the Field: Victim's Rights and Services for the 21st Century. *Washington, DC: U.S. Department of Justice.*

Several clear themes permeate the recommendations targeted at the various parts of the criminal justice system. First, there is a call to recognize the rights of victims and to make certain that victims know about those rights. Second, the recommendations seek actions that will protect victims from further harm, particularly from their immediate offender. Third, victims should be included in virtually all phases of the criminal justice process, if they desire to do so. The system needs to notify victims of their rights to do so and seek ways to make that participation easier and meaningful. Finally, system employees need to undergo constant education on the needs and rights of victims. Simply outlining the rights is not enough if those persons charged with operating the criminal justice system are not aware of those mandates.

Criminal Justice Personnel Issues

It is the last of these themes that needs the greatest deal of work. Criminal justice personnel are asked to undertake such a wide array of different tasks, often with limited resources. It is not unreasonable to assume that new mandates will receive less than an enthusiastic response when the resources are not forthcoming to successfully implement them. Indeed, the staff of victim-witness projects often struggle to keep pace with staggering caseloads and mounting piles of paperwork. As the victim movement continues to grow and additional tasks are placed on the criminal justice system, agency staff find themselves fielding more requests to apply their expertise to nontraditional clients.

Table 6.6 Selected Recommendations for Corrections

- Correctional agencies should designate staff to provide information, assistance, and referrals to victims of crime.

- Correctional agencies should notify victims, upon their request, of any change in the status of offenders, including clemency or pardon, that would allow them to have access to the community or the victims themselves.

- Correctional agencies should place a high priority on ensuring the protection of victims from inmate intimidation, threats, or physical or other harm from offenders under their supervision.

- Correctional agencies should collect and distribute restitution payments consistent with the court's order to ensure that victims receive fair compensation from offenders who are incarcerated or released on probation or parole.

- Victims should have input into all decisions affecting the release of adult and juvenile offenders.

- To increase offender awareness of the consequences of their actions on victims' lives, correctional agencies for both adult and juvenile offenders should use victim impact panels and conduct courses about the effects of crime on people's lives.

- Crime victims should be notified of any violation of the conditions of an offender's probation or parole and should be allowed to provide input prior to or during the probation or parole violation hearing.

- When a sex offender is released, uniform community notification practices should be developed and implemented to promote public awareness and provide consistent protection for citizens from state to state.

Source: Office for Victims of Crime (1998b). New Directions from the Field: Victim's Rights and Services for the 21st Century. *Washington, DC: U.S. Department of Justice.*

Additionally, many service providers recognize that the victimization experience and its aftermath have ramifications that extend beyond just the person who is victimized. The victim's support system of family members and friends is affected as well. Because these people form an integral support foundation for the victim, extension of services is sensible in these instances. This increased outreach beyond concern for the offender and the immediate victim requires additional expansion of the criminal justice system.

Many criminal justice agencies and victim advocates are called on to offer their expertise to nontraditional victims. *Derivative victims*, while not direct crime victims, usually include persons whose lives have been touched by some tumultuous event (Tomz & McGillis, 1997). The trauma undergone by survivors of an attempted suicide, the processes induced from witnessing a traumatic event, or the emotional upheaval triggered by the unexpected death of a young person is sufficient to propel people into a morass of emotions. It is not unusual for mental health workers and first responders to experience *vicarious trauma* (Pearlman & Saakvitne, 1995; Way et al., 2004) or *compassion fatigue* (Boscarino, Figley, & Adams, 2004; Figley, 1995; Roberts et al., 2003). Compassion fatigue:

> refers to a physical, emotional and spiritual fatigue or exhaustion
> that takes over a person and causes a decline in his or her ability to
> experience joy or to feel and care for others. Compassion fatigue is
> a one-way street, in which individuals are giving out a great deal of

energy and compassion to others over a period of time, yet aren't able to get enough back to reassure themselves that the world is a hopeful place. It's this constant outputting of compassion and caring over time that can lead to these feelings (No Author, 2009).

Individuals exposed to a critical incident may find debriefing exercises to be beneficial as they try to sort through and juggle their own emotions. However, such reviews can trigger an adverse reaction if not done properly (Regehr et al., 2003). In short, victim advocates are learning that their skills are needed by a wide range of individuals.

Victim advocates, the people who service victim clients, need the appropriate background and training before they engage in helping behavior. When victim services first emerged as a fledgling area, many service providers were simply well-intended persons with a concern for others. Formal credentials, particularly when victimology was in its infancy, were nonexistent. Today, though, greater attention is being paid to formal pre-service and in-service training for criminal justice personnel and the staff of other agencies who come into contact with victims. Since 1995, roughly 1,800 practitioners have attended the 40-hour course at the National Victim Assistance Academies located on select university campuses (Caliber Associates, 2004). In addition, a number of states have instituted their own programs in an effort to upgrade the training that victim advocates receive. A national assessment of the Academy shows that students acquire the skills they desire and are satisfied with the training they receive. Students further report that the material is applicable to their current work (Caliber Associates, 2004). There is a growing recognition that employee preparation is one mechanism to ensure that quality services are being delivered to victims who need assistance. These efforts echo the recommendations regarding a greater emphasis on personnel development, education, and training found throughout the *New Directions* report.

DISSENTING VOICES

Not everyone is enamored with the direction that these system-based victim-witness projects have taken. Critics charge that bureaucrats, more interested in organizational survival than in client needs, have replaced zealous advocates. They contend that victim-witness projects have changed so that they no longer remain victim-oriented. In other words, virtually no effort is expended to address what this chapter labels as "the first insult." Instead, these projects concentrate on blunting only "the second insult," problems that stem from becoming involved with the criminal justice system.

Shapland (1983) cautions that many victim-witness programs are erected on what officials think their clients need—not necessarily what victims themselves want or need. Improvement of waiting conditions, provision of witness notification services, distribution of brochures outlining the criminal justice process, and similar strategies can be viewed as peripheral to clients—props designed to appease and manipulate people for ulterior purposes.

Under "ideal" conditions, victim programs would reach out to all victims (Weigend, 1983). However, current operations confine attention to preselected types of criminal victims. This client group is further restricted to just those victims who report the incident to the authorities. As we saw in Chapter 2, the attrition here is considerable. However, the pool becomes even smaller. Eligibility is reserved for those cases in which the police have identified and apprehended a suspect. Ultimately, the only victims who do get served are those whose cases culminate in the halls of justice.

Skeptics point out that the only value these victims hold to criminal justice officials depends upon how well they can serve those officials. As McShane and Williams (1992: 264) explain, "That which is passed off as victim assistance is, in reality, predicated on the needs of the prosecution rather than on the needs of the victim." Cries of foul from defendant quarters reinforce these concerns. A common complaint from defense attorneys is that granting concessions to victims affords the prosecutor an unfair advantage (Kelly, 1987, 1991). While the evidence to date does not support such an assertion, these statements serve as ongoing evidence to the tensions that victim-witness services elicit.

RESTORATIVE JUSTICE

The movement toward restorative justice seeks to address the needs of everyone impacted by the criminal act—the victim, the victim's family, the community, and the offender. Before defining and discussing restorative justice, we look at the attempt to shift some problems out of the formal criminal justice system and into dispute mediation or dispute resolution programs. Restorative justice techniques have been based on these types of programs, as well as other historical practices used by different cultural groups. These various efforts include victim-offender mediation, family group conferencing, and circle sentencing. This chapter examines the emergence of these alternatives for addressing the needs of victims, the community, and the offender.

Dispute Resolution

An immediate precursor to restorative justice, particularly in the United States, is dispute resolution, or dispute mediation. One can trace modern dispute resolution back to the early 1970s. During this time, a number of jurisdictions started programs to divert minor disputes out of the formal court system. While many programs were adjuncts to prosecutor's offices and the judiciary, others were sponsored by outside groups or organizations. These initial programs provided an arena in which victims and offenders could meet and work out mutually agreeable solutions.

Dispute resolution is a mechanism for achieving a number of goals simultaneously. First, the parties involved in the situation work together to resolve the problem rather than having some outside authority impose a solution. Second, any dispute that reaches a settlement is one less court case and alleviates some congestion in the court system. Third, this informal approach empowers victims by giving them a direct voice in their own matters. Victims retain complete veto power over the final outcome. Finally, dispute resolution provides the victim with a face-to-face encounter with the offender. This meeting enables the victim to vent anger and seek understanding—something that many victims deeply desire.

The approach of these programs appeals to a diverse audience and has spread rapidly. Prosecutors and judges welcome the chance to reduce overcrowded dockets, and victim advocates see a tremendous potential to help their clients. Its popularity is evident in the proliferation of programs operating in the UK, Canada, Australia, Denmark, Finland, Germany, and many other countries (Umbreit, 1997).

The cases found in dispute resolution take a variety of forms. Interpersonal disputes between family members and friends comprise a large portion of the cases brought to mediation. Domestic disputes, harassment, neighborhood nuisances, and landlord/tenant problems make up the bulk of the disputes. Merchant/customer disputes are more evident in programs that rely heavily on prosecutor's offices for referral. Mediation with juveniles is an attempt to keep the youth offender out of the formal system and eliminate the negative consequences of formal processing (Veevers, 1989).

Common Elements in Dispute Resolution Programs

The basic idea behind dispute resolution is to bring opposing parties together in an attempt to work out a mutually agreeable solution. While dispute resolution programs can vary in terms of the cases they handle or the procedures they use, they typically share five traits in common (Garofalo & Connelly, 1980a) (Table 6.7).

First, these programs involve a third-party mediator who monitors participant interaction. This arbitrator keeps the discussion focused and makes suggestions whenever the need arises. Most mediators are volunteers who are not affiliated with the formal justice system. Because of this independence, some people call these programs *neighborhood dispute resolution*.

A second characteristic is that many disputants have known each other over a period of time. Often, they are neighbors, friends, or family members (although store owners and customers can utilize such a program). This familiarity can be

---

Table 6.7 Common Traits of Dispute Resolution Programs

- A third-party mediator is involved.
- Disputants usually know each other.
- Participation must be voluntary.
- Processes are informal.
- Disputants are usually referred to the process by someone in the criminal justice system.

Source: Garofalo, J., & Connelly, K. J. (1980a). Dispute resolution centers, part I: Major features and processes. Criminal Justice Abstracts, *12, 416–436.*

---

helpful when trying to forge a compromise. It can also be a challenge because the dispute may be the result of a long-term issue or problem that may not be amenable to a short-term intervention.

Third, most programs insist that participation be completely voluntary. Both disputants must agree to handle the problem through the program. If either party declines to take part, the dispute moves back to the realm of more formal legal action.

Fourth, the actual resolution of a dispute follows a very informal process. Rules of evidence are not enforced, and attorneys are not allowed to attend these sessions. Instead, the process calls for discussion rather than rigid fact-finding. As one might expect, the mediator has a free hand to conduct each meeting as he or she sees fit.

The final characteristic is that most disputants enroll in the program after being referred to it by a member of the criminal justice system. Most often, the prosecutor has reviewed the case and decided that the interests of justice can be better served in a non-traditional manner.

 **WEB ACTIVITY**

Dispute resolution has grown across the United States. Perform a web search on "dispute resolution centers" and see how many hits come up. Pick one or two and investigate the similarities and differences across programs and centers.

Evaluation of Dispute Resolution

Dispute resolution programs are typically portrayed as an effective mechanism for addressing interpersonal disputes. This optimism about the programs would appear to indicate positive results. Unfortunately, evaluations of the programs have provided mixed reviews.

Perhaps the most important possible result of the programs from a victimological standpoint is the ability of the programs to serve the needs of crime victims. Clearly, the ability to arrive at a suitable settlement is a key element for victims. Evaluation efforts typically reveal that more than two-thirds of all participants report a satisfactory resolution, that most of the time the parties live up to the agreement, and most participants are happy with the outcomes (Anderson, 1982; Coates & Gehm, 1989; Cook, Roehl, & Sheppard, 1980; Felstiner &

Williams, 1982; McGillis & Mullen, 1977; Roehl & Cook, 1982). Similar results have been found for programs geared to juvenile offenders (Bridenback, Imhoff, & Blanchard, 1980; Reichel & Seyfrit, 1984; Umbreit & Coates, 1993).

Outcome studies that use official data, however, do not paint as consistently optimistic a portrait. These investigations compare recidivism levels for offenders who participate in dispute resolution against those who undergo normal system processing. While some studies report lower recidivism rates for those handled through dispute resolution programs (McGillis & Mullin, 1977; Sarri & Bradley, 1980; Smith & Smith, 1979; Vorenberg, 1981), other research finds no difference in subsequent court involvement between those who underwent mediation and those who did not (Davis, 1982; Davis, Tishane, & Grayson, 1980; Felstiner & Williams, 1979).

Two factors temper these findings. First, the fact that participation is voluntary suggests that those who agree to use this process are more likely to abide by the decision and to refrain from similar behavior in the future. Second, evaluations typically include only successful cases in which parties reach a mutually agreeable solution. There is no input from the failed cases. The inclusion of only successful mediation efforts virtually guarantees a positive outcome.

Additional considerations challenge the use of dispute resolution from a victim's point of view. First, many victims never have the opportunity to avail themselves of this service since both parties must agree to participate. Many case referrals never result in a meeting between the parties (Anderson, 1982; Coates & Gehm, 1989; Cook et al., 1980; McGillis & Mullen, 1977). Only those projects that mandate offender participation, such as some Victim-Offender Reconciliation Programs, can guarantee the willing victim a chance to meet with his or her offender.

Another concern is that dispute resolution efforts appear to arrive at lasting solutions only for property matters (Garofalo & Connelly, 1980b). When a property dispute is settled and the victim is made whole again, there is no ongoing problem with which to deal. Personal offenses between victims and offenders who are related to one another, or know each other, are often deeply traumatic events. Dispute resolution settlement provisions tend not to address the long-term root causes of problems. Thus, dispute resolution may not be an appropriate remedy for all kinds of crime victims. Despite these caveats about the success of dispute resolution, interventions such as these continue to find support.

The Growth of Restorative Justice

The success of and support for dispute resolution programs have been major factors in the growth of restorative justice programs that seek an alternative to formal criminal justice system intervention. Over the past 30 years there has been an increasing call for programs that pay more attention to the needs of victims. At the same time that victims are receiving more attention, there is a recognition that criminal justice processing of offenders is not effective at deterring crime and reducing victimization (McLaughlin et al., 2003). Consequently, there has been a growing demand for new methods of working with offenders. These apparent competing concerns (i.e., finding an alternative to the system for some offenses, assisting the victim, and intervening with offenders) suggest that any new intervention needs to serve a broader audience. The concept of *restorative (reparative) justice* seeks to use interventions that return the victim and offender to their pre-offense states. For victims, this means repairing the harm done, and for offenders, it means assuring that the action will not be repeated.

Discussions of restorative justice often begin with a comparison between this new idea and that of retributive justice. *Retributive justice* generally focuses on the law breaker and the imposition of sanctions for the purposes of deterrence, vengeance, and/or punishment. The formal criminal justice system operates primarily from a retributive justice approach. *Restorative justice* seeks to repair the harm that was done to both the victim and the community, while simultaneously changing the behavior of the offender. Table 6.8 contrasts some of the basic assumptions underlying both retributive and restorative justice.

Perhaps the primary difference between retributive and restorative justice is the role of the victim. Under retributive justice, a criminal act is viewed as an offense against society or the state, and the victim is nothing more than a witness for the state. Zehr and Mika (2003: 41) note that "crime is fundamentally a violation of people and interpersonal relationships." Restorative justice sees crime as an act against the victim and community, and the focus shifts from what is best for the state to repairing the harm that has been committed against the victim and community.

Restorative approaches seek to repair the harm done to the victim and community (Zehr & Mika, 2003), rather than focusing on punishment and deterrence. This requires a focus on the type of harm done and the desire of the victim and community for actions such as restitution and conciliation. The victim and community must be involved in the process in order to identify the harm and the appropriate responses desired by those victimized. The community, rather than the criminal justice system alone, should shoulder the burden of dealing with crime (Nicholl, 1999). Braithwaite (2003) points out that restorative justice seeks to restore the victims, restore harmony in society, restore social support for all parties, and restore the offenders.

This is accomplished by bringing together a range of interested parties in a non-confrontational setting, including the victim and the offender, as well as family members or friends, criminal justice system personnel, and members

Table 6.8 Assumptions of Retributive and Restorative Justice

Retributive Justice	Restorative Justice
Crime is an act against the State, a violation of a law, an abstract idea.	Crime is an act against another person or the community.
The criminal justice system controls crime.	Crime control lies primarily in the community.
Offender accountability defined as taking punishment.	Accountability defined as assuming responsibility and taking action to repair harm.
Crime is an individual act with individual responsibility.	Crime has both individual and social dimensions of responsibility.

Punishment is effective.
  a. Threat of punishment deters crime.
  b. Punishment changes behavior.
	Punishment alone is not effective in changing behavior and is disruptive to community harmony and good relationships.

Victims are peripheral to the process.	Victims are central to the process of resolving crime.
The offender is defined by deficits.	The offender is defined by capacity to make reparations.
Focus on establishing blame, on guilt, on past (did he/she do it?).	Focus on problem solving, on liabilities/obligations, on future (what should be done?).
Emphasis on adversarial relationship.	Emphasis on dialogue and negotiation.
Imposition of pain to punish and deter/prevent.	Restitution as a means of restoring both parties; goal of reconciliation/restoration.
Community on sideline, represented abstractly by State.	Community as facilitator in restorative process.
Response focused on offender's past behavior.	Response focused on harmful consequences of offender's behavior; emphasis on the future.
Dependence upon proxy professionals.	Direct involvement by participants.

Source: Adapted from Bazemore, G. S., & Umbreit, M. (1994). Balanced and Restorative Justice: Program Summary. *Washington, DC: U.S. Department of Justice; and Zehr, H. (1990).* Changing lenses. *Scottdale, PA: Herald Press.*

of the general community. The participants, as a group, seek to understand the actions that led to the criminal or antisocial behavior, reveal the feelings and concerns of all parties, negotiate or mediate a solution agreeable to everyone, and assist in implementing that solution (Bazemore & Maloney, 1994). Kurki (2000: 266) notes that "restorative justice is about relationships—how relationships are harmed by crime and how they can be rebuilt to promote recovery and healing for people affected by crime."

The Development of Restorative Justice

While many writers trace the growth of restorative justice in the United States to the dispute resolution/mediation programs from the 1970s, Braithwaite (1999: 2) argues that "[r]estorative justice has been the dominant model of criminal justice throughout most of human history for all the world's peoples."

As noted earlier in the book, there was no formal "criminal justice system" as we know it today throughout most of history. Victims and their families were expected to take action themselves to address the problems and repair the harm from the offense. The earliest codified laws, such as the Law of Moses, the Code of Hammurabi, and Roman laws, all outlined the responsibility of individuals to deal with criminal acts committed against them. The development of formal criminal justice systems, particularly the police and criminal courts, shifted the emphasis for taking redress from the victim to the state.

Many restorative justice practices being used today can be traced directly to historical traditions that have survived in indigenous cultures (Weitekamp, 2010). Of particular note are the practices of the Maori in New Zealand, the Aboriginal tribes in Australia, the Inuits in Alaska, and the First Nations tribes in Canada (Crawford & Newburn, 2003). While there is some debate over the degree to which restorative justice comes directly from the traditions of these groups (see Daly, 2002), there is little doubt that the ideas underlying restorative justice are not new in the last quarter century.

WEB ACTIVITY

Investigate the world-wide growth of restorative justice at the following websites: Restorative Justice Online (**http://restorativejustice.org/**); Center for Restorative Justice (**http://www.sfu.ca/crj.html**); Restorative Justice at Post-sentencing (**http://www.rjustice.eu/**). What other sources can you find? What do they tell you?

Theoretical Basis of Restorative Practices

The basic argument underlying restorative justice is that reactions to crime and harmful behavior should seek to repair the harm done to the individual, and society, while simultaneously reintegrating and addressing the needs of the offender. Braithwaite's (1989) *reintegrative shaming* rests on the assumption that the typical processing of offenders through the criminal justice system serves to isolate the offender and stigmatize him or her. This action marginalizes the offender (even more so than he or she may already be in society). In addition, it does nothing to correct the behavior or repair the harm done to the victim.

The underlying premise of Braithwaite's (1989) theory is that shame can be used in a positive fashion to bring the offender back into society. Under reintegrative shaming, the system needs to express its disapproval of the criminal activity, while simultaneously forgiving the offender for the action if the offender is willing to learn from the event and make reparations to the victim and society. The key is on "reintegration" rather than "stigmatization" (Braithwaite, 1989). The ability to employ reintegrative shaming effectively rests on shifting the focus of societal response from solely on the offender to a shared focus on the offending behavior, social disapproval (often by family, friends, and significant others), the needs of the victim and community, and a shared response to make things better (Harris, 2003) (see Figure 6.1).

Types of Restorative Justice

Restorative justice takes a variety of different forms, although they all attend to the same basic tenets. Indeed, "restorative justice" is often referred to as *transformative justice, social justice, "balanced and restorative justice", "peacemaking"*, or other terms. Braithwaite (2002) notes that many of these terms and programs have been incorporated into the more general idea of restorative justice.

The diversity in restorative programs can be seen in the extent to which they address the different goals of empowerment, restoration, reintegration, and emotional and social healing for the varied participants in the restorative process (Harris, 2003). *Empowerment* reflects the need for all interested parties to be involved in the process. This provides a sense of legitimacy for both the victim and the offender. *Restoration* simply refers to repairing the harm done to all participants. At the same time, retribution is disavowed as a legitimate response to the behavior. Restorative justice also seeks to *reintegrate* both the offender and the victim into the community, without the stigma of being an offender or being different from the other community members. Finally, there is a clear need to address the *emotional harm* that accompanies the behavior. Figure 6.2 presents a graphic depiction of the types of restorative justice programs and the degree to which they can be considered fully restorative.

The restorative practices typology represents an intersection of three different dimensions—a victim reparation orientation, an offender responsibility focus, and a communities of care domain—all indicated by a separate circle. Each of these dimensions contributes something to address crime and victimization, although each dimension alone offers only limited restoration. Victim reparation, for example, focuses exclusively on the needs of the immediate crime victim through things like victim compensation and victim services, and excludes concerns for the community or the offender. Similarly, the offender responsibility dimension relates to activities that help the offender understand his or her actions and take responsibility.

The intersection of different dimensions brings about greater restoration, with the greatest level of restoration occurring where all three dimensions overlap. It is within this intersection that full restoration can take place. Typical restorative justice practices that appear in this area are victim–offender

FIGURE 6.1 Volunteers talk to inmates during a class in the restorative justice program at the Columbia Correctional Institution in Portage, Wisconsin. Inmates participate in a graduation ceremony after completing a 25-session restorative justice program that teaches participants about coming to terms with their individual crimes and convictions. *Credit: AP Photo/Wisconsin State Journal, Kyle McDaniel.*

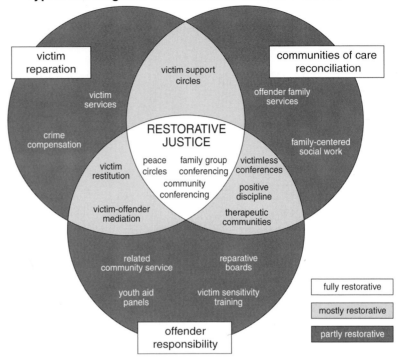

Types and Degrees of Restorative Justice Practice

FIGURE 6.2 Restorative Practices Typology.
*Source: McCold, P., & Wachtel, T. (2002). Restorative Justice Theory Validation. In E. G. M. Weitekamp &
H. Kernere (Eds),* Restorative Justice: Theoretical Foundations. *Portland, OR: Willan.*

mediation, family group conferencing, and circle sentencing. Each of these is discussed below.

Victim–Offender Mediation

Victim–offender mediation (VOM), also referred to as *victim–offender reconciliation programs* (VORPs), is a direct outgrowth of the early dispute resolution/dispute mediation programs of the early 1970s and is considered the oldest form of restorative justice (Umbreit, 1999). The first documented VOM program was one run by the Mennonites in Kitchener, Ontario, Canada, in 1973. Victim–offender mediation is typically a post-conviction process (although pre-conviction programs exist) in which the victim and the offender are brought together to discuss a wide range of issues. A trained mediator attends these meetings.

The basic premise of VOM is that the criminal incident and its consequences are complex and beyond the ability of the criminal code to address on its own (Nicholl, 1999). Where the formal criminal justice response to crime is to simply impose the sanction outlined in the statutes, VOM seeks to deal with the needs of both the victim and the offender. Perhaps the most important concern addressed in the VOM meetings is to identify for the offender the types and level of harm suffered by the victim as a result of the crime. The victim is given the opportunity to express his or her concerns about the crime and the loss incurred. At the same time, the offender is given the chance to explain why he or she committed the act and the circumstances that may underlie his or her behavior.

The aim of this discussion is for the two parties to gain an understanding of the other person as a starting point for identifying a response to the event. The focus of the meetings is on repairing the harm done to the victim, helping the victim heal (both physically and emotionally), restoring the community to the pre-crime state, and reintegrating the offender into society (Umbreit et al., 2003). Among the potential tangible outcomes for the victim may be the offender making monetary restitution or providing service to repair the harm done. Perhaps of equal importance are changes in behavior and attitude on the part of the offender.

Participation in VOM is voluntary for the victim, but the offender may be required by the court to participate as a part of the court process (Umbreit, 1999). Some programs allow for mediation to occur without the need for a face-to-face meeting between the victim and offender. This typically takes place only when the victim desires to participate in mediation but is reluctant to have any further direct contact with the offender.

Victim–offender mediation programs may be a part of the formal criminal justice system or may be run by other agencies that are not directly connected to the system. In some jurisdictions, mediation may be ordered by the judge in lieu of formal sentencing. A successful mediation may mean that the original conviction is vacated or expunged. On the other hand, the failure of an offender to participate in mediation or the failure of the mediation to reach an agreeable resolution may result in the offender being returned to the court for formal sentencing.

> **WEB ACTIVITY**
>
> Go to the Victim Offender Mediation Association website (**http://voma.org/**) and read about VOM, its history, goals, and the benefits from VOM.

Family Group Conferencing

Family group conferencing (FGC) finds its roots in indigenous practices of the Maori in New Zealand. Family group conferencing came to prominence in 1989 when New Zealand, responding to the increasing number of Maori youths being handled in the formal justice system, passed the Children, Young Persons and Their Families Act (Crawford & Newburn, 2003). This Act removed all youths aged 14–17 (with only a few exceptions for very serious offenders) from formal court processing and mandated that they be diverted to family group conferencing (Kurki, 2000). Since its inception in 1989, FGC has spread to Australia, the United States, Europe and other countries.

The greatest difference between FGC and VOM is the inclusion of family members, close friends, and other support groups of the victim and offender in the conferences. There is also the possibility of including criminal justice system personnel, including social workers, police officers, and an offender's attorney (Van Ness & Strong, 2010). The basic ideas of FGC were adapted by the police in Wagga-Wagga, Australia, in 1991 into a process known as *community group conferencing* (CGC) (McCold, 2003). One main difference between FGC and CGC is the possible inclusion of a broader set of support groups and community members to the conference (McCold, 2003). Figure 6.3 graphically depicts the potential involvement of different individuals and support groups in FGC and CGC. The expansion of participants from the victim, offender, and mediator in VOM to support persons and community representatives is very important in a variety of ways.

The conferences are led by a trained facilitator who serves in various roles. Most often the facilitator will make contact with all participants prior to the conference. At that time he or she will explain the process and the role of each individual. He or she will also emphasize the fact that the conference should conclude with a resolution to which all parties are in agreement. The facilitator leads the participants through a discussion of the facts of the case, the impact of the victimization on the parties, the feelings of all participants toward the action and the offender, and the development of a mutually agreed upon resolution (Nicholl, 1999). Families and support persons are expected to voice their feelings about the harm that was committed, their concern for the victim of the crime, their disappointment about the offender's behavior, and their suggestions as to how to resolve the problem. Of greater importance is that the support groups are expected to take some responsibility in monitoring the offender and making certain that any agreements are carried out after the conference (Kurki, 2000). While most conferences deal with more minor juvenile misbehavior, they can include serious offenses and repeat offenders (Kurki, 2000). Conferences can be held either pre- or post-trial and have become a part of police and pretrial diversion programs in many countries (McGarrell et al., 2000; Moore & O'Connell, 1994).

WEB ACTIVITY

New Zealand has been at the forefront of family-group conferencing. Visit the NZ government website and investigate the material they offer on this approach: **http://www.cyf.govt.nz/youth-justice/ family-group-conferences.html**

Neighborhood Reparative Boards

Neighborhood reparative boards (NRBs), or neighborhood accountability boards, have existed since the mid-1990s and typically deal with nonviolent youthful offenders. Not unlike other restorative practices, NRBs seek to restore the victims and community to pre-offense states, require the offender to make amends, and aid the offender in understanding the impact of his or her actions on the victim and community. Cases are referred to the boards by the court, most often prior to formal adjudication.

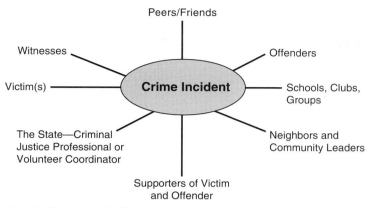

FIGURE 6.3 Parties Involved in Conferencing.
Source: Nicholl, C. G. (1999). Community Policing, Community Justice, and Restorative Justice: Exploring the Links for the Delivery of a Balanced Approach to Public Safety. *Washington, DC: Office of Community Oriented Policing Services.*

Despite the philosophical similarities between NRBs and other types of restorative conferencing, there are several key differences in how this approach operates. First, victims are not required to participate. Indeed, many early boards frowned on victim participation (Strickland, 2004), although victim participation is becoming more common. Second, while the conferences are often open to the public, actual participation is limited by the board and whom they wish to interview. The board questions the offender and examines statements made by members of the offender's family and others knowledgeable about the event (Bazemore & Umbreit, 2001). Third, the boards are composed of a small group of citizens who have been specially trained in conducting hearings and constructing appropriate sanctions.

At the conclusion of the hearing, the board undertakes private deliberations and outlines a suggested set of actions to be followed by the offender. If the offender agrees with the plan, the board oversees the offender's compliance with the terms and reports to the court about the success or failure of the offender (Bazemore & Umbreit, 2001). Typical conditions of agreements include restitution, apologies, and community service (Karp, 2001).

> ### 🌐 WEB ACTIVITY
>
> You can get more information on NRBs, along with an example session, by looking at the Community Reparative Boards document on this textbook's companion website at **http://booksite.elsevier. com/9780323287654**

Circle Sentencing

The fourth type of restorative justice program to be discussed is *circle sentencing.* Circle sentencing, sometimes referred to as *healing circles* or *peacemaking circles* (Bazemore & Umbreit, 2001), is based on Canadian First Nation practices and began formal operation in the early 1990s. Circle sentencing invites members from across the community to participate in determining the appropriate sanctions for offenders (Van Ness & Strong, 2006). As a sentencing procedure, this process typically occurs after a case is concluded and the offender is found guilty in court. Participants in sentencing circles typically include all of the parties found in FGCs, as well as general community members who wish to be included.

Sentencing circles may function as either a part of the court or separate from the court. In many jurisdictions, this sentencing alternative is used at the discretion of the trial judge and is not provided for under any statutory authority (Crawford & Newburn, 2003). Most cases handled by sentencing circles involve minor offenses, although some programs will consider more serious crimes (Stuart, 1996). A major difference between circle sentencing and the other forms of restorative justice is that this approach is regularly used with both adults and juveniles (Kurki, 2000).

Because of the fact that this process takes place post-conviction and can include a wide array of participants, circle sentencing normally requires a great deal of preparation before the actual circle convenes (Kurki, 2000). One common requirement is that the offender actively agrees to participate, even to the extent of requesting a circle (Nicholl, 1999). The facilitator is responsible for meeting with all participating parties. Those meetings are used to explain the process, outline the facts of the case for those who have more limited knowledge, answer any questions the parties may have, and make plans for the actual meeting. In many cases the offender will work on an initial plan to address the harms he or she committed, which will be presented when the circle meets (Nicholl, 1999). This extensive preparation may mean that the circle takes place months after the crime occurred and the court case concluded.

Every participant in the sentencing circle is given the opportunity to speak, express his or her feelings about the crime, and offer opinions and rationales about the outcome of the discussion. The intended outcome of the circle is consensus on a plan of action that may include a wide array of actions. Plans of action may include further meetings between the victim and offender, apologies by the offender, restitution, community service, treatment/rehabilitation programs (such as counseling or alcohol or other drug treatment), and/or explicit sentencing recommendations, including jail or prison time, to the trial judge (Nicholl, 1999; Van Ness & Strong, 2002). The decision of the circles is often binding on the offender and may be specifically incorporated into the official court record; failure to adhere to the decision may result in further criminal justice system processing or being returned to the circle (Van Ness & Strong, 2010).

🌐 WEB ACTIVITY

A list of the stages that occur in a sentencing circle can be found on this textbook's companion website at **http://booksite.elsevier.com/9780323287654**

Beyond the reparative plan for the offender, sentencing circles are meant to bring about action by all parties to the crime. The victim is supposed to receive support and be an active participant in healing him- or herself. The community's role is to identify the factors that led to the offending behavior and seek ways to eliminate those problems. These causal factors may be specific to the individual offender (such as lack of parental supervision or underage alcohol use) or may be due to larger social-structural issues (such as unemployment or the presence of gangs in the community).

Summary of Restorative Justice Types

While each of the forms of restorative justice discussed above takes a slightly different approach to repairing the harm done by the criminal act, all are considered fully restorative because they seek to address the needs of the victim, the offender, and the community. The variation between the approaches brings about restoration by attempting to build understanding between the parties, identifying the factors at work in the behavior, and arriving at a plan of action that is agreed to by all parties. The extent to which these restorative justice programs are successful is addressed below.

> 🌐 **WEB ACTIVITY**
>
> Examine the different restorative conferencing models side-by-side in the table found on this textbook's companion website at **http://booksite.elsevier.com/9780323287654**. Can you relate the major similarities and differences?

THE IMPACT OF RESTORATIVE JUSTICE

Restorative justice programs are intended to have a number of different possible outcomes, including repairing the harm done to the victim and rehabilitating the offender. Assessing the impact of the interventions, however, is more difficult. Many evaluations focus on victim and offender satisfaction with the process, and the level of compliance or completion of the agreed-upon settlement. Less common are analyses of the impact of the programs on subsequent offending by the offender. In addition, because very little research has been conducted on circle sentencing, most of the comments in this section refer to VOM and FGC.

Satisfaction and Compliance

Assessing the impact of restorative justice within a victimological context suggests that outcomes such as victim satisfaction, feelings of fairness by victims, and the completion of reparations are primary concerns. With very few exceptions, victims (as well as offenders) express satisfaction with the restorative process in which they have participated (Braithwaite, 1999). Evaluations of VOM typically reveal that between 75% and 100% of the participants express satisfaction with the mediation (Kurki, 2000). Similarly high levels of satisfaction arise from FGCs (Bazemore & Umbreit, 2001; Moore & O'Connell,

1994; Umbreit et al., 2003). The level of satisfaction is also reflected in feelings by participants that the process is fair (McCold, 2003; McGarrell et al., 2000; Umbreit, 1999; Umbreit & Coates, 1993; Umbreit et al., 2003). McCold and Wachtel (2002), rating restorative justice programs according to the degree to which they were fully restorative, mostly restorative, or not restorative, find that participants in fully restorative programs report higher levels of satisfaction and perceived fairness. Individuals from programs rated as not restorative report the lowest levels of satisfaction and fairness (McCold & Wachtel, 2002). These results contrast greatly with those found in analyses of the formal criminal justice system processing, where victims and offenders report lower satisfaction and feelings of fairness.

A companion to satisfaction is the ability of the meetings to achieve consensus on a solution and whether the parties carry through with the agreement. Again, there is evidence that most meetings culminate in an agreement and most parties comply with the settlement (Braithwaite, 1999; Kurki, 2000; Schiff, 1999; Umbreit & Coates, 1993). Restitution is a common component of many agreements, and evaluations reveal that 90% or more of the offenders in FGC comply with the ordered restitution (Wachtel, 1995). McGarrell et al. (2000) noted that participants in a conferencing program completed the program at a significantly higher rate than normal diversion clients.

This information on satisfaction and compliance must be tempered by the fact that participation in the programs is voluntary, particularly for victims. The fact that the program is voluntary may mean that only those individuals who are more amenable to the process to begin with are included in the programs. There may be a built-in bias in favor of positive results. Umbreit et al. (2003), for example, point out that only 40–60% of the victims and offenders who are asked to participate in VOM agree to do so. McCold and Wachtel (1998) report that almost six out of 10 FGC cases never materialize due to a refusal to participate. Similarly, an analysis of youth conferencing panels in England and Wales finds that only one-fifth of the victims participate (Crawford & Newburn, 2003). There is no way of knowing whether positive results are actually a function of the willingness to participate and effect change, or just the program itself.

Recidivism

Reducing reoffending is also an important restorative goal. While not always seen as a direct benefit to a victim, the ability to reduce recidivism is advantageous for individual victims and society as a whole. Unfortunately, there is relatively little research on offender recidivism found in the restorative justice literature. Part of the reason for this is the voluntary nature of many programs. One should expect to find lower recidivism from programs where only those who want to participate and want to try to change their behavior are included.

Despite this shortcoming, there is some evidence that restorative justice programs are able to reduce the level of subsequent offending.

Most evaluations of recidivism have appeared in relation to VOM programs. Umbreit and Coates (1993), comparing youths who participated in VOM with those undergoing typical juvenile justice processing in three states, report significantly less recidivism on behalf of the VOM sample. In their analysis of restorative justice conferences for youths in Indianapolis, McGarrell et al. (2000) report a 40% reduction in recidivism for the program youths compared with those undergoing normal system processing. Umbreit, Coates, and Vos (2001) provide evidence that youths completing VOM projects in two Oregon counties reduced their offending by at least 68% in the year after program participation compared with the year before the intervention. Finally, Nugent et al. (1999) note that both the level of reoffending and the seriousness of subsequent offenses are lower for youths who enter and complete VOM programs.

Examinations of recidivism from conferencing are less common, although those that do exist provide some positive assessments. Daly (2003), examining juvenile conferencing in South Australia, found significantly less recidivism by participants in the conferences. This is particularly true for conferences that are rated as highly restorative. Similarly, Hayes and Daly (2004) and Rodriguez (2005) uncovered reduced recidivism levels after conferencing and the results are strongest for first-time offenders who are participating in the programs. McCold (2003) claims that recidivism levels after conferencing are no higher than those found in traditional system processing. Latimer, Dowden and Muise (2005), in a meta-analysis of restorative justice programs, report that restorative justice is more effective at reducing recidivism than traditional criminal justice programs. This suggests that the restorative program has little impact on recidivism, although it may be more desirable than official court processing for other reasons.

While positive results on recidivism appear in several analyses, a great deal of additional research is needed on the impact of restorative justice programs. This is especially true for FGC and circle sentencing programs, which have not undergone as extensive evaluations as VOM. It is also important to note that almost all recidivism research has been completed on studies of youthful participants. With the growing interest in using restorative justice approaches with adult offenders, there is an even greater need to assess the potential of the approach. There remains a need to identify and understand the conditions under which different restorative justice programs work and do not work (Braithwaite, 2002).

Problems and Issues with Restorative Justice
Despite the growing popularity with restorative justice approaches, there are a number of problems and concerns that remain unanswered. Table 6.9 presents

Table 6.9 Key Concerns with Restorative Justice

- Lack of victim participation
- Emphasis on shaming and not enough on reintegration/reconciliation
- Inadequate preparation
- Inability to engender participation
- Problems with identifying appropriate participants
- Problems recruiting representative panels
- Coercive participation (particularly coercion of offenders)
- Net-widening
- Inadequate screening of cases
- Inability of participants (e.g., families, communities) to meaningfully contribute
- Lack of neutrality by participants and/or facilitator
- Inability to address serious violent crimes
- Inability to address long-standing interpersonal disputes
- Too victim-oriented
- Inability to protect constitutional rights of offenders
- Inadequate outcome evaluation

a number of concerns with restorative justice. Because a full discussion of critical issues is available elsewhere (see Ashworth, 2003; Feld, 1999; Kurki, 2000), only a few of the major concerns are presented here.

One problem is that restorative justice programs may be too ambitious in their attempt to solve very complex societal problems (Kurki, 2000). Simply gathering common citizens together to talk about a problem, and brainstorm possible solutions, is only the beginning of a much more complex process to address major social forces that may cause crime. Many problems involve long-standing interpersonal disputes that may not be amenable to simple mediation or conferencing.

A second concern, related to the first, is that restorative justice has been used primarily with less serious and property crimes. There is a great deal of debate over whether this approach can be used successfully with serious violent offenses (see Bannenberg & Rössner, 2003). This is especially true when offenses such as spouse abuse, sexual assault, aggravated assault, murder, and like crimes are considered. While few programs have directly assessed this question, there is some evidence that restorative justice can be used in these cases. For example, Umbreit et al. (2003) reported success using VOM with murderers and the families of their victims. Corrado, Cohen, and Odgers (2003) also found positive results (mostly in terms of satisfaction) for a VOM program dealing with serious and violent offenses in British Columbia. The strongest finding in these studies is the need for very lengthy and extensive preparation prior to the intervention.

Third, there exists a concern that, while voluntary, there is an underlying level of coercion in most programs. What makes this truly problematic is that many programs do not allow (or at least frown upon) the presence of defense attorneys, thus raising the issue of an accused's constitutional rights and procedural safeguards (Feld, 1999; Levrant et al., 1999). In some instances, the participation of the offender is actually coerced, as he or she is required to participate under threat of being processed in court. Compounding this problem is the need for the offender to admit to the act during the process. This is especially problematic if the intervention is taking place pre-adjudication.

A fourth concern with restorative justice is over how the "community" is defined and who is allowed to represent the community (Kurki, 2000). This can be a very important concern because the participants help mold the outcome and the expectations for the solution. The participants can bring a wide array of differing expectations. This may not be a problem in smaller, more homogeneous communities, such as Maori or Native American communities, but it can certainly be problematic in large, diverse cities.

Fifth, Feld (1999) notes that there is a distinct imbalance of power in most restorative justice programs. This is especially problematic when juvenile offenders must face not only the victim but also the victim's support groups, members of the criminal justice system, and sometimes strangers from the general community. The power differential must be a prime consideration in meetings.

A sixth area of concern deals with the issue of net-widening. *Net-widening* refers to the situation by which the introduction of a new program or intervention serves to bring more people under the umbrella of social control. This is especially problematic when the new programs are intended to take people currently being served in the formal justice system and divert them to the new program. The expectation is that the new programs will relieve some of the burden from the formal system while simultaneously offering a better response to the problems (Weitekamp, 2010). The extent to which restorative justice has resulted in net-widening is not clear, but there is a legitimate concern that this has occurred.

Another concern with restorative justice is the argument that admitting victims into the criminal justice process is threatening a system that traditionally has been oriented toward offender rights and that identifies society as the victim. Those favoring harsh punishment and those promoting rehabilitation or treatment tend to view the victim as getting in the way of dealing with offenders. The victim may want restitution and community service in lieu of punishment or may be looking for harsh punishment instead of treatment. Clearly, restorative justice proposes a new philosophy for the criminal justice system—particularly the corrections component. The offender-centered correctional system would be replaced by a system that attempts to accommodate diverse needs. Despite concerns such as these, restorative programming has spread to countries around the world and is being used with a wide array of problems and events within a relatively short time frame. Most suggestions to improve restorative justice revolve around either conducting rigorous evaluations of restorative justice programs or establishing oversight for restorative justice initiatives.

> ### 🌐 WEB ACTIVITY
>
> Can you think of areas where restorative justice could be improved? Come up with some ideas and then compare those to the ideas of Weitekamp that can be found on this textbook's companion website at **http://booksite.elsevier. com/9780323287654**

SUMMARY

System officials have tried to counter the move of victims to limit the costs of working with the criminal justice system by avoiding the system altogether. One method to change this has been to introduce victim-witness management projects into the system. Unfortunately, these efforts are reserved for only the small number of victims who eventually testify against their suspects. Restorative justice programs offer another method for addressing victim concerns and issues after an offense has occurred. The intent of these programs is multifaceted. There is a desire to restore the victim to the state he or she was in prior to the offense and to repair the more general harm that has been done to the larger community. Equally important is taking steps to rehabilitate the offender so that he or she does not commit future offenses. It remains to be seen whether these efforts will be sufficient to maintain victim interest in current system operations. It is difficult for anyone to argue against the notion that the offender, victim, criminal justice system, and the community all need and deserve attention. Both victim-witness projects and restorative justice attempt to address crime in such a way that the victim is a cornerstone participant.

KEY TERMS

circle sentencing	RISE
community group conferencing (CGC)	Statewide Automated Victim Information and Notification (SAVIN) program
compassion fatigue	
derivative victims	vicarious trauma
family group conferencing (FGC)	vicarious victimization
healing circle	victim advocate
net-widening	victim–offender mediation (VOM)
reintegrative shaming	victim–offender reconciliation
reparative justice	program (VORP)
restorative justice	victim-witness (victim/witness) projects
retributive justice	

Victim Rights

Victimology.
Copyright © 2015 Elsevier Inc. All rights reserved.

LEARNING OBJECTIVES

After reading Chapter 7, you should be able to:

- Explain the constitutional changes proposed by the President's Task Force.
- Understand the pros and cons behind this proposal.
- Outline the strategy behind the proposed Twenty-Sixth Amendment to the United States Constitution.
- Provide details as to what the proposed Twenty-Sixth Amendment encompassed.
- Convey why some people did not support the proposed amendments to the Constitution.
- Understand why the strategy switched to targeting state constitutional reform.
- Discuss the revived contemporary interest in a federal victim rights constitutional amendment.
- Trace legislative reforms at the federal level.
- Outline some of the guidelines regarding the treatment of federal victims and witnesses.
- Relay the provisions of the federal victims' "Bill of Rights."
- Talk about the two court rulings that focused on the federal crime victims' "Bill of Rights."
- Explore some of the guarantees that the states have extended to crime victims.
- List some of the concerns and remedies that critics have voiced over victim rights.
- Describe what a victim impact statement contains.
- Communicate the effect victim impact statements have had.
- Understand some of the constitutional issues surrounding death penalty cases.
- Appreciate how these constitutional issues affected the Supreme Court's reasoning with respect to victim impact statements.

LEARNING OBJECTIVES—CONT'D

- Outline case developments regarding federal Supreme Court rulings about victim impact statements.
- Talk about efforts to professionalize victim services.
- Appreciate the ethical concerns that can arise during the course of victim service delivery.

INTRODUCTION

The historic trend in formal systems of justice has been to look at crimes as transgressions against society and victims as witnesses for society. Recent years, though, have seen a gradual movement toward more victim participation in the justice process. Victims are gaining rights that restore them to greater prominence in the criminal justice system. Some of these rights are as simple as recognizing the victim's human dignity. Others outline procedures that allow victims to address the court and parole boards. Even more subtle changes include moving cases out of the formal justice system and into informal settings where victims seek to settle problems with the offenders.

Reasons for these new victim rights are easily identified. First, special interest groups have championed victim causes. They have pushed to balance the rights of the offender with the needs of the victim. Second, the justice system has experienced a great deal of dissatisfaction with how it handles victims. As we demonstrated in Chapter 4, victims derive little, if any, value from contact with the system. Except for fulfilling some vague notion of a "civic duty," victims have very little to gain—and much to lose—from system participation. Many victims never even have the satisfaction of knowing the outcome of their cases. The move toward procedures that give victims a louder voice is a way to make the system more responsive and to lure victims back into the halls of justice. Third, the justice system is overwhelmed by the volume of cases. Plea bargaining strategies, failure to file charges, time delays, inadequate sentences, and early prisoner releases due to overcrowding indicate that the system is not working well. Alternatives need to be developed.

This chapter looks at the attempt to reverse the historic trend of alienating victims from the resolution of criminal matters. Specifically, the chapter looks at two general trends that seek to make the victim an active participant at various stages of the justice system. We turn first to the passage of constitutional amendments. Then we will look at statutory provisions for victim rights. While this legal landscape is changing, there is still room for much improvement.

VICTIM RIGHTS AMENDMENT

Victim rights reform has taken several different paths in the United States. One strategy has involved efforts to gain passage of a federal constitutional amendment, commonly referred to as a *Victim Rights Amendment* (VRA), to guarantee victims certain rights when they participate in the criminal justice system. A parallel movement involved bids to change state constitutions by incorporating VRAs there as well. In this section we will look at how this movement has fared.

Federal Constitutional Reform

At the conclusion of its work, the President's Task Force on Victims of Crime (1982) issued a strong, stirring call for action. The President's Task Force (1982: 114) explained that "government must be restrained from trampling the rights of the individual citizen. The victims of crime have been transformed into a group oppressively burdened by a system designed to protect them." As a result, the Task Force proposed that the Sixth Amendment to the U.S. Constitution be modified to incorporate a new clause guaranteeing explicit rights to crime victims. As Table 7.1 shows, advocates envisioned that the addition of a single sentence would balance the constitutional standing of crime victims.

WEB ACTIVITY

The Final Report of the President's Task Force on Victims of Crime is available at **http://www.ojp.usdoj.gov/ovc/publications/presdntstskforcrprt/**

Supporters feel that a strong parallel exists between the historical conditions that spawned the original Bill of Rights and the current predicament of crime victims. Constitutional safeguards originally emerged from the colonists' determination to combat what they considered to be an unjust

---

Table 7.1 Proposed Change to the Sixth Amendment of the United States Constitution

In all criminal prosecutions the accused shall enjoy the right to a speedy and public trial, by an impartial jury of the State and district wherein the crime shall have been committed, which district shall have been previously ascertained by law, and to be informed of the nature and cause of the accusation; to be confronted with the witnesses against him; to have compulsory process for obtaining witnesses in his favor and to have the Assistance of Counsel for his defense. **Likewise, the victim, in every criminal prosecution shall have the right to be present and to be heard at all critical stages of judicial proceedings.**[*]

Proposed changes are highlighted for the reader.
Source: President's Task Force on Victims of Crime (1982). Final Report. Washington, DC: U.S. Government Printing Office, p. 114.

and oppressive system. The drafters of this document wove the notion of fair treatment for persons accused of crimes into a series of protections. This new formulation promised Americans such things as the right to a speedy trial, the right to confront one's accusers, the right to counsel, and freedom from cruel and unusual punishment. As one writer (Eikenberry, 1987: 33) put it, "The founding fathers wanted to ensure that the evils experienced by many innocent citizens at the hands of the English did not find their way into the newly found government."

Crime victims today find themselves in a posture reminiscent of the situation that this country's early settlers faced. The elevation of rights for the accused, coupled with the declining status of the victim, has left victims in a predicament. Even though victims have endured suffering through no fault of their own, the state is generally more concerned with protecting the rights of their transgressors.

The proposed change to the federal Constitution aims to restore the victim's legal standing and guarantee a certain degree of justice. The inclusion of a VRA in the federal Constitution, just like the extension of suffrage and the abolition of slavery, would provide a corrective mechanism for undoing past harms (Eikenberry, 1987). However, modifying the Constitution involves a slow, deliberate, and tedious process. Article 5 of the U.S. Constitution addresses the proper procedure for amending the document. Altering the Constitution is a two-part process. The first stage calls for the U.S. Congress to pass a resolution by a two-thirds vote of the House and a two-thirds vote of the Senate. There can be no further changes to the language of the amendment after this federal action has taken place. The second stage is triggered when Congress sends the resolution on to the states for ratification. Three-quarters of the state legislatures, or 38 of the 50 states, must vote to accept the resolution. Usually, the state ratification effort must take place within seven years of federal enactment, but Congress has extended that time limit on occasion in the past.

As the initial efforts floundered, advocates embraced a new tactic. A change of direction was heralded during a conference sponsored by the National Organization of Victim Assistance (NOVA) during January of 1986. After reviewing the recommendations proposed by the President's Task Force on Victims of Crime, participants offered an alternate strategy. Rather than trying to add language to embellish the Sixth Amendment, the suggestion was to create an entirely new Twenty-Sixth Amendment. This new amendment read:

> Victims of crime are entitled to certain basic rights including, but not limited to, the right to be informed, to be present, and to be heard at all critical stages of the federal and state criminal justice process to the

extent that these rights do not interfere with existing Constitutional rights (Young, 1987: 66–67).

Sponsors were in favor of a new amendment for at least three reasons (Young, 1987). First, forming a separate entry that dealt only with victims made the entire issue less confusing and objectionable. Victim gains would not hinge upon offender rights. Second, the new language was broader and much more inclusive. For example, it earmarked participation throughout the entire criminal justice process as its goal rather than restricting such participation to judicial proceedings. Third, it did not tamper with any rights of the accused. As a result, critics could not argue that victim rights were detrimental to existing protections afforded the accused.

These attempts to tamper with the federal Constitution drew resistance. Some observers countered that the entire effort to establish a national VRA was misdirected. Dolliver (1987) argued that the purpose behind the federal Bill of Rights is to protect against governmental infringement upon personal liberties. Because victim issues do not involve questions of freedom, they simply do not fit here. While one might commiserate with the unfortunate plight of crime victims, the "lack of uniformity in state statutes should hardly be an automatic recipe for a constitutional amendment" (Dolliver, 1987: 91).

Others found the proposed language to be too vague and overly encompassing. Lamborn (1987), for example, raised a number of perplexing questions as to the meaning of each phrase in the proposed federal amendment. His analysis ended with the following pronouncement (1987: 220):

> The failure of the proponents of the various proposals for a constitutional amendment on behalf of the victim to address the many complex issues raised by their proposals does not diminish the need for an enhanced role for the victim in the criminal justice process. That failure does, however, suggest that the campaign for a constitutional amendment is premature.

Supporters came to the grim realization that federal constitutional reform would be extremely difficult, if not impossible, in spite of their best efforts.

State Constitutional Reform

Given the lukewarm reception, support for any kind of national constitutional reform quickly dwindled. In fact, an assessment of the inroads gained after the 1982 President's Task Force (U.S. Department of Justice, 1986) ignored the entire issue of a federal VRA. Clearly, a new direction was needed.

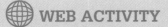 **WEB ACTIVITY**

The National Victims' Constitutional Amendment Network is making a concerted effort to safeguard victim rights. You can learn more about these activities by going to: **http://www.nvcap.org/index.html** for further details.

The method of reform was revisited and revised. Representatives from several victim advocacy groups had established an informal network for sharing ideas and information. Early in 1987, members of these groups decided to create a coalition called the National Victims' Constitutional Amendment Network (NVCAN). This group dedicated itself to promoting VRAs at the state, rather than the federal, level.

Targeting states became the preferred option for many reasons (Lamborn, 1987; Spencer, 1987). First, state VRAs would generate greater interest and more local support. Second, even though many states already had victim rights statutes on the books, there was no way to enforce these provisions. A state VRA would reinforce these arrangements. Finally, because state constitutions already protected criminals, it was reasonable to extend the same courtesy to crime victims.

At the present time, there are no provisions in the federal Constitution that deal with victim rights. However, 33 states, starting with California in 1982, have approved such constitutional measures. The map contained in Figure 7.1 shows the states in which voters have endorsed VRAs in their state constitutions.

State constitutional provisions typically address a set of common rights. Unfortunately, most people remain unaware of these rights, especially when it would be critically important to exercise these safeguards. As a result, NVCAN reviewed state statutes, perused agency policies, and then

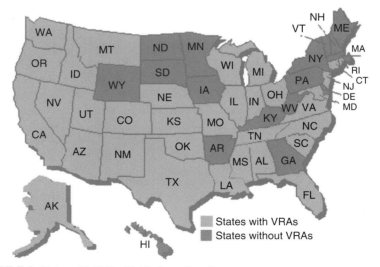

FIGURE 7.1 States with Victim Rights Amendments.
Source: National Victims' Constitutional Amendment Passage (2012a), State Victim Rights Amendments. Denver: National Victims' Constitutional Amendment Passage. Retrieved on May 9, 2013, from http://www.nvcap.org/stvras.html.

Table 7.2 Victims' Rights "*Miranda* Card" Model

We are sorry that you have become a victim of a crime. As a crime victim, you are entitled to specific rights. You have the right to:

- Be treated with dignity and respect.
- Be notified of all critical proceedings and developments in your case.
- Be notified of the status of the alleged or convicted offender.
- Be present at all hearings at which the defendant is entitled to attend.
- Be heard at critical proceedings.
- Restitution to be paid by the offender in cases that result in a conviction.
- Reasonable protection from the alleged or convicted offender before, during, and after the trial.
- Apply for victim compensation in cases involving violent crime (for more information, call [list number for compensation information]).
- Information about and referrals to services and assistance.
- Pursue legal remedies if your rights are violated.

Source: National Victims' Constitutional Amendment Network (2012b). Victims' Rights Education Project "Miranda Card." Denver, CO: National Victims' Constitutional Amendment Passage. Retrieved on May 9, 2013, from http://www.nvcap.org/vrep/NVCANVREPMirandaCard.pdf

interviewed key players and victims. This distillation helped NVCAN isolate critical or core rights that are common threads. Building upon this base, NVCAN then constructed a victim version of the popular *Miranda* rights cards that police officers routinely use to inform suspects of their rights. The thinking is that police officers could distribute this information during the initial investigation in order to make victims fully aware of their rights. That model card appears in Table 7.2 in a generic format. Obviously, it would be up to a local jurisdiction to tailor the exact language to its own state VRA.

In order to gain a better understanding of what a state VRA looks like, Table 7.3 reprints the Florida version, which was passed by 90% of the voters in November of 1988. Notice how the first section mirrors the Sixth Amendment of the federal

Table 7.3 Florida Victim Rights Amendment

Section 16. Rights of Accused and of Victims

(a) In all criminal prosecutions the accused shall, upon demand, be informed of the nature and cause of the accusation, and shall be furnished a copy of the charges, and shall have the right to have compulsory process for witnesses, to confront at trial adverse witnesses, to be heard in person, by counsel or both, and to have a speedy and public trial by impartial jury in the county where the crime was committed. If the county is not known, the indictment or information may charge venue in two or more counties conjunctively and proof that the crime was committed in that area shall be sufficient; but before pleading the accused may elect in which of those counties the trial will take place. Venue for prosecution of crimes committed beyond the boundaries of the state shall be fixed by law.

(b) Victims of crime or their lawful representatives, including the next of kin of homicide victims, are entitled to the right to be informed, to be present, and to be heard when relevant, at all crucial stages of criminal proceedings, to the extent that these rights do not interfere with the constitutional rights of the accused.

Source: Constitution of the State of Florida, Article 1, Section 16, Florida Statutes (2012).

Constitution and how the second section tracks the language of the proposed Twenty-Sixth Amendment. The construction of the victim addition was done in such a way as to facilitate ratification of the federal VRA once it passed Congress and went before the states.

The opposition to state constitutional amendments reflects concern over making changes to a document that serves as the basic foundation of our laws. Lamborn (1987) points out that many amendments are proposed without thorough investigation and discussion. Critics fear that victim rights bills tend to be more gut-level reactions than well-thought-out proposals. Consequently, there appears to be a conservative ideology underlying amendments that favor a "lock 'em up" philosophy.

Opponents of constitutional provisions also warn against eroding the rights of the accused in the haste to assist crime victims. Viano (1987) suggests that passage of constitutional amendments favoring crime victims will result in increased litigation over the treatment of victims, similar to what accompanied civil rights legislation. In essence, such constitutional amendments foster conflict between groups in society.

Rekindling Federal Constitutional Reform

The momentum achieved through state-level efforts was bolstered by a series of rulings issued by the trial court judge in the Oklahoma City bombing case. There, the defendant, Timothy McVeigh, was accused of detonating an explosion that toppled the federal building, killing 168 persons and injuring hundreds more. During pretrial motions, Judge Richard Matsch announced that he would set aside 45 courtroom seats for media representatives, 37 for public observers, and 16 chairs for the defense. There were no plans to accommodate any victims or survivors (Howlett, 1997). After the government provided a dozen places for victims, Judge Matsch issued an order on June 26, 1996, barring factual witnesses from the trial proceedings. What this ruling meant was that any victim who did not testify but exerted his or her right to attend the deliberations was not eligible to make a victim impact statement before the court during the sentencing phase.

This controversial decision ignited a number of reactions. The Department of Justice intervened, asking the judge to reconsider his decision. Victims and survivors filed their own motion, arguing that the judge's ruling abrogated or set aside the protections guaranteed under the federal Victims' Bill of Rights. One victim explained: "as it stands, I have to make the excruciating choice between testifying only in the sentencing phase and attending even one minute's worth of the trial" (Cassell, 1997).

The judge upheld his original position in a subsequent hearing, and an appeal to the federal District Court on October 4, 1996, produced no change. Bringing the case before the U.S. Court of Appeals for the 10th Circuit provided no immediate relief either. Judge Matsch steadfastly warned all parties that a potential avenue of appeal would be opened for the defendant if any victim attended the trial proceedings and gave victim impact testimony later during the sentencing phase. His position was that Rule 615 of the Federal Rules of Evidence at that time superseded the provisions of the Victims' Bill of Rights. The fear was that exposure to other victims' testimony during the trial might slant or taint the independent recollection of victims at the later sentencing phase (Cassell, 1997; Myers, 1997). Essentially, then, the legal protections contained in the federal Victims' Bill of Rights held a deep, hollow clang for the Oklahoma City bombing victims and their survivors.

In response to this controversy, Congress passed the Victim Rights Clarification Act (VRCA) the very next year. The VRCA, which appears in Table 7.4, removed the obstacle that hemmed in Judge Matsch. Today, victims are permitted to observe both portions of the criminal trial. The thinking behind this legislation is that while sequestering witnesses is intended to protect the defendant's basic right to a fair trial, impact statements deal with sentencing and bear no relationship to adjudication. As a result, the VRCA clarifies the victim's right to attend the full criminal trial and preserves the victim's right to address the court during sentencing proceedings.

These actions propelled a number of victim groups and other interested parties to merge into a unified force. Buoyed by successful campaigns to introduce state VRAs, lobbying efforts resurrected the earlier strategy of seeking support to amend the United States Constitution. This work culminated in Senate Joint Resolution 6, a proposal for a new amendment to the federal Constitution.

Table 7.4 The Victim Rights Clarification Act of 1997

Rights of victims to attend and observe trial

1. Non-Capital Cases—Notwithstanding any statute, rule, or other provision of law, a United States district court shall not order any victim of an offense excluded from the trial of a defendant accused of that offense because such victim may, during the sentencing hearing, make a statement or present any information in relation to the sentence.

2. Capital Cases—Notwithstanding any statute, rule, or other provision of law, a United States district court shall not order any victim of an offense excluded from the trial of a defendant accused of that offense because such victim may, during the sentencing hearing, testify as to the effect of the offense on the victim and the victim's family. …

Source: The Victim Rights Clarification Act of 1997, 18 U.S.C. § 3510.

A mounting wave of criticism quickly surfaced, and opponents echoed many of the concerns mentioned earlier. An editorial in *The New York Times* wondered whether support for constitutional reform amounted to anything more than mere political posturing by elected officials (Lewis, 1996). However, Kansas Attorney General Carla J. Stovall (1997) countered that the framers of the Constitution never intended for this document to be so sacrosanct as to not undergo modification. In fact, Congress has altered the Constitution 27 times already, extending protections to persons accused of crimes in 15 of these changes. In Stovall's (1997) view, "I do not believe it just that within our system no rights are guaranteed by the very same document to the victims of the very acts for which the accused have been arrested and guaranteed rights." Ultimately, the proposed amendment failed to gain passage.

Proponents took issue with such a pessimistic forecast and mounted another charge to bolster a consideration of victim rights at the federal level. Advocates went back to the drawing boards and emerged with a new bill for Congress to consider in the following session. Senator Jon Kyl (Arizona) and Senator Dianne Feinstein (California) attempted to rekindle interest in the victim rights issue by introducing a new constitutional amendment on April 1, 1998. This proposal wove its way through the Senate Judiciary Committee and was reintroduced in January of 1999 during the 106th Congress. A companion bill also made its way into the House of Representatives and gathered much support. However, the bill encountered obstacles in April of 2000, forcing the disappointed Senators Kyl and Feinstein to withdraw from further consideration what had become known as Senate Joint Resolution 3.

Undaunted by this experience, determined advocates continued to rally for a federal constitutional amendment. Senators Kyl and Feinstein introduced another resolution on January 1, 2003. That bill was referred to the Senate Judiciary Subcommittee, which held hearings and moved favorably on the proposal. The proposed amendment, which appears in Table 7.5, did not come up for a final vote.

Proponents and supporters came to the painful realization that they lacked a sufficient number of votes to gain Congressional passage. Rather than simply accept defeat and walk away, the decision was made to rechannel interests into the legislative, rather than the constitutional, reform effort. As Senator Feinstein (2004: S4262) explained:

> It is clear to me that passage of a Constitutional amendment is impossible at this time. If we tried, and failed, it could be years before we could try again. Victims of crime have waited years for progress, and a compromise approach, resulting in the bill now under consideration, will result in meaningful progress.

The latest development came when several House members introduced a resolution during the April of 2013. The language of that bill, contained in Table 7.6,

Table 7.5 Proposed Victim Rights Amendment to the United States Constitution, 2003

SECTION 1. The rights of victims of violent crime, being capable of protection without denying the constitutional rights of those accused of victimizing them, are hereby established and shall not be denied by any State or the United States and may be restricted only as provided in this article.

SECTION 2. A victim of violent crime shall have the right to reasonable and timely notice of any public proceeding involving the crime and of any release or escape of the accused; the rights not to be excluded from such public proceeding and reasonably to be heard at public release, plea, sentencing, reprieve, and pardon proceedings; and the right to adjudicative decisions that duly consider the victim's safety, interest in avoiding unreasonable delay, and just and timely claims to restitution from the offender. These rights shall not be restricted except when and to the degree dictated by a substantial interest in public safety or the administration of criminal justice, or by compelling necessity.

SECTION 3. Nothing in this article shall be construed to provide grounds for a new trial or to authorize any claim for damages. Only the victim or the victim's lawful representative may assert the rights established by this article, and no person accused of the crime may obtain any form of relief hereunder.

SECTION 4. Congress shall have power to enforce by appropriate legislation the provisions of this article. Nothing in this article shall affect the President's authority to grant reprieves or pardons.

SECTION 5. This article shall be inoperative unless it has been ratified as an amendment to the Constitution by the legislatures of three-fourths of the several States within 7 years from the date of its submission to the States by the Congress. This article shall take effect on the 180th day after the date of its ratification.

Source: Congressional Record (September 4, 2003). Senate Joint Resolution 1, 108th Congress, 1st Session. Retrieved on October 19, 2013, from http://www.gpo.gov/fdsys/pkg/BILLS-108sjres1rs/pdf/BILLS-108sjres1rs.pdf

differs somewhat from previous versions. As of this writing, the bill has been referred to a subcommittee for consideration. Its final status has yet to be determined.

While quite a few members of Congress endorse the notion of victim rights, their position is that these rights should be statutorily, not constitutionally, guaranteed. In order to harness these energies, lawmakers mobilized to create a crime victims' bill of rights. As we will see in the next section, these efforts were successful in gaining passage of a bill that incorporated a range of victim rights into already existing federal law.

VICTIM RIGHTS LEGISLATION

Another avenue to secure victim rights called for the passage of new laws and regulations that spelled out exact protections. Just like VRA reform, legislation was enacted mandating certain rights and privileges for crime victims and witnesses at the federal level. As Table 7.7 demonstrates, victim issues have garnered much publicity. This activity also prompted a parallel response at the state level. Both the federal and state arenas are visited in this section.

WEB ACTIVITY

You can track the progress of the federal Victim Rights Amendment by searching "Victim Rights Amendment" at the Library of Congress at **http://thomas.loc.gov/cgi-bin/query/z?c113:H.J.RES.40:**

WEB ACTIVITY

Every year the U.S. Department of Justice assembles a variety of materials to help local victim service groups promote National Crime Victims' Rights Week (see Figure 7.2). You can see those materials by going to **http://ovc.ncjrs.gov/ncvrw/**

Table 7.6 Proposed Victim Rights Amendment to the United States Constitution, 2013

Resolved by the Senate and House of Representatives of the United States of America in Congress assembled (two-thirds of each House concurring therein), That the following article is proposed as an amendment to the Constitution of the United States, which shall be valid to all intents and purposes as part of the Constitution when ratified by the legislatures of three-fourths of the several States:

Section 1. *The rights of a crime victim to fairness, respect, and dignity, being capable of protection without denying the constitutional rights of the accused, shall not be denied or abridged by the United States or any State. The crime victim shall, moreover, have the rights to reasonable notice of, and shall not be excluded from, public proceedings relating to the offense, to be heard at any release, plea, sentencing, or other such proceeding involving any right established by this article, to proceedings free from unreasonable delay, to reasonable notice of the release or escape of the accused, to due consideration of the crime victim's safety and privacy, and to restitution. The crime victim or the crime victim's lawful representative has standing to fully assert and enforce these rights in any court. Nothing in this article provides grounds for a new trial or any claim for damages and no person accused of the conduct described in section 2 of this article may obtain any form of relief.*

Section 2. *For purposes of this article, a crime victim includes any person against whom the criminal offense is committed or who is directly and proximately harmed by the commission of an act, which, if committed by a competent adult, would constitute a crime.*

Section 3. *This article shall be inoperative unless it has been ratified as an amendment to the Constitution by the legislatures of three-fourths of the several States within 14 years after the date of its submission to the States by the Congress. This article shall take effect on the 180th day after the date of its ratification.*

Source: Congressional Record (April 23, 2013). House Joint Resolution 40, 113th Congress, 1st Session. *Retrieved on May 9, 2013, from http://thomas.loc.gov/cgi-bin/query/z?c113:H.J.RES.40:*

FIGURE 7.2 Candles are lit at the National Observance and Candle-light Ceremony during the 2005 National Crime Victims' Rights Week. The ceremony marked the 25th observance of National Crime Victims' Rights Week. *Credit: AP Photo/Lawrence Jackson.*

Federal Legislative Reform

One alternative to making constitutional changes is to promote legislation that addresses victim concerns. This approach is clearly more palatable to many people. As Table 7.8 shows, the federal government has undertaken a variety of initiatives dealing with crime victims over the past four decades. Many of these bills have prompted the states to take parallel steps. A common federal strategy is to make funds available to states only if they incorporate specific features into their statutes and programs. As a result of this strategy, one will find much congruity between federal and state efforts.

These legislative developments often encourage further action. For example, the U.S. Attorney General has promulgated a set of guidelines for dealing with and assisting federal victims and witnesses to ensure that federal officials are complying with all pertinent federal directives (Office of the U.S. Attorney General, 2012). Table 7.9 lists the services that federal officials are mandated to deliver when dealing with crime victims. These rules attempt to make federal criminal procedures more accommodating and inviting to victims and witnesses.

Table 7.7 President Obama's Proclamation Declaring April 21 through 27, 2013 National Crime Victims' Rights Week

Every year, millions of Americans fall victim to crime through no fault of their own. These are people we know: families trying to rebuild after financial fraud or identity theft, grandparents spending their golden years in the shadow of elder abuse, children whose right to safety has been stolen away by violence or neglect. Many struggle to get help in the aftermath of a crime, and some never report their crime at all. During National Crime Victims' Rights Week, we reaffirm our solemn obligation to ensure they get the services they need—from care and counseling to justice under the law.

Thanks to thousands of victim assistance programs all across our country, we are making progress toward that goal. As dedicated advocates continue their important work, my Administration will continue to support them by raising awareness about victims' rights, making sure those rights are protected and practiced, and investing in training programs for law enforcement and other professionals. I was proud to sign the Violence Against Women Reauthorization Act into law last month, preserving and strengthening critical services for victims of abuse. We have continued to crack down on financial crimes that leave too many families struggling to get back on their feet. And we are stepping up our efforts in the fight against human trafficking, whether it occurs halfway around the world or right here at home.

Even now, we have more work to do. As an epidemic of gun violence has swept through places like Newtown, Aurora, Oak Creek, and cities and towns all across America, our country has come up against the hard question of whether we are doing enough to protect our children and our communities. As Americans everywhere have stood up and spoken out for change, my Administration has responded with reforms that give law enforcement, schools, mental health professionals, and public health officials better tools to reduce violent crime. But we cannot solve this problem alone. That is why I will continue to fight for common-sense measures that would address the epidemic of gun violence and help keep our children safe.

By working to prevent crime and extend support to those in need, we keep faith with our fellow citizens and the basic values that unite us. Let us renew that common cause this week, and let us rededicate ourselves to advancing it in the year ahead.

NOW, THEREFORE, I, BARACK OBAMA, President of the United States of America, by virtue of the authority vested in me by the Constitution and the laws of the United States, do hereby proclaim April 21 through April 27, 2013, as National Crime Victims' Rights Week. I call upon all Americans to observe this week by participating in events that raise awareness of victims' rights, and by volunteering to serve victims in their time of need.

IN WITNESS WHEREOF, I have hereunto set my hand this nineteenth day of April, in the year of our Lord two thousand thirteen, and of the Independence of the United States of America the two hundred and thirty-seventh.

BARACK OBAMA

Source: Office of the Press Secretary (2013b). Presidential Proclamation – National Crime Victims' Week, 2013, *April 20. Washington, DC: The White House. Retrieved on May 9, 2013, from http://www.whitehouse.gov/the-press-office/2013/04/20/presidential-proclamation-national-crime-victims-rights-week-2013*

Probably the most noteworthy feature in the federal legislative arsenal was the creation of the Crime Victims' Bill of Rights in 2004, which is summarized in Table 7.10. It is important to note that although it is called a *bill of rights*, it is not a national constitutional provision. These provisions illustrate how the federal government has expanded its policies and procedures for informing crime victims of their rights and for protecting their interests.

Table 7.8 Key Federal Victims' Rights Legislation

Year	Legislation
1974	Child Abuse Prevention and Treatment Act
1980	Parental Kidnapping Prevention Act
1982	Victim and Witness Protection Act
1982	Missing Children's Act
1984	Victims of Crime Act
1984	Justice Assistance Act
1984	Missing Children's Assistance Act
1984	Family Violence Prevention and Services Act
1985	Children's Justice Act
1988	Drunk Driving Prevention Act
1990	Hate Crime Statistics Act
1990	Victims of Child Abuse Act
1990	Victims' Rights and Restitution Act
1990	National Child Search Assistance Act
1992	Battered Women's Testimony Act
1993	Child Sexual Abuse Registry Act
1994	Violent Crime Control and Law Enforcement Act
1994	Violence Against Women Act
1996	Community Notification Act ("Megan's Law")
1996	Antiterrorism and Effective Death Penalty Act
1996	Mandatory Victims' Restitution Act
1997	Victims' Rights Clarification Act
1998	Crime Victims with Disabilities Act
1998	Identity Theft and Deterrence Act
2000	Trafficking Victims Protection Act
2001	Air Transportation Safety and System Stabilization Act (established September 11th Victim Compensation Fund)
2003	PROTECT Act ("Amber Alert" Law)
2003	Prison Rape Elimination Act
2003	Fair and Accurate Credit Transactions Act
2004	Justice for All Act
2006	Trafficking Victims Protection Reauthorization Act
2006	Adam Walsh Child Protection and Safety Act
2010	Tribal Law and Order Act
2013	Violence Against Women Reauthorization Act

Source: Adapted from National Center for Victims of Crime (2013). Landmarks in Victims' Rights & Services. 2013 National Crime Victims' Rights Week Resource Guide, *p. 19. Washington, DC: U.S. Department of Justice. Retrieved on May 9, 2013, from http://ovc.ncjrs.gov/ncvrw2013/pdf/2013ResourceGuide-Full.pdf*

Table 7.9 Federal Regulations Regarding Services to Victims

1. A responsible official shall
   a. inform a victim of the place where the victim may receive emergency medical and social services;
   b. inform a victim of any restitution or other relief to which the victim may be entitled under this or any other law and manner in which such relief may be obtained;
   c. inform a victim of public and private programs that are available to provide counseling, treatment, and other support to the victim; and
   d. assist a victim in contacting the persons who are responsible for providing the services and relief described in subparagraphs (a), (b), and (c).

2. A responsible official shall arrange for a victim to receive reasonable protection from a suspected offender and persons acting in concert with or at the behest of the suspected offender.

3. During the investigation and prosecution of a crime, a responsible official shall provide a victim the earliest possible notice of
   a. the status of the investigation of the crime, to the extent it is appropriate to inform the victim and to the extent that it will not interfere with the investigation;
   b. the arrest of a suspected offender;
   c. the filing of charges against a suspected offender;
   d. the scheduling of each court proceeding that the witness is either required to attend or, under section 10606(b)(4) of this title, is entitled to attend;
   e. the release or detention status of an offender or suspected offender;
   f. the acceptance of a plea of guilty or nolo contendere or the rendering of a verdict after trial; and
   g. the sentence imposed on an offender, including the date on which the offender will be eligible for parole.

4. During court proceedings, a responsible official shall ensure that a victim is provided a waiting area removed from and out of the sight and hearing of the defendant and defense witnesses.

5. After trial, a responsible official shall provide a victim the earliest possible notice of
   a. the scheduling of a parole hearing for the offender;
   b. the escape, work release, furlough, or any other form of release from custody of the offender; and
   c. the death of the offender, if the offender dies while in custody.

6. At all times, a responsible official shall ensure that any property of a victim that is being held for evidentiary purposes be maintained in good condition and returned to the victim as soon as it is no longer needed for evidentiary purposes.

7. The Attorney General or the head of another department or agency that conducts an investigation of a sexual assault shall pay, either directly or by reimbursement of payment by the victim, the cost of a physical examination of the victim which an investigating officer determines was necessary or useful for evidentiary purposes. The Attorney General shall provide for the payment of the cost of up to 2 anonymous and confidential tests of the victim for sexually transmitted diseases, including HIV, gonorrhea, herpes, chlamydia, and syphilis, during the 12 months following sexual assaults that pose a risk of transmission, and the cost of a counseling session by a medically trained professional on the accuracy of such tests and the risk of transmission of sexually transmitted diseases to the victim as the result of the assault. A victim may waive anonymity and confidentiality of any tests paid for under this section.

8. A responsible official shall provide the victim with general information regarding the corrections process, including information about work release, furlough, probation, and eligibility for each.

9. No cause of action or defense.

This section does not create a cause of action or defense in favor of any person arising out of the failure of a responsible person to provide information as required by subsection (b) or (c) of this section.

Source: Victims' Rights and Restitution Act of 1990, *42 U.S.C. § 10607.*

Table 7.10 Federal Crime Victims' Bill of Rights

Federal crime victims have the following rights under the Crime Victims' Rights Act (18 U.S.C. § 3771):

- The right to be reasonably protected from the accused.
- The right to reasonable, accurate, and timely notice of any public court proceeding, or any parole proceeding, involving the crime or any release or escape of the accused.
- The right not to be excluded from any such public court proceeding, unless the court, after receiving clear and convincing evidence, determines that testimony by the victim would be materially altered if the victim heard other testimony at that proceeding.
- The right to be reasonably heard at any public proceeding in the district court involving release, pleas, or sentencing, or any parole proceeding.
- The reasonable right to confer with the attorney for the Government in the case.
- The right to full and timely restitution as provided in law.
- The right to proceedings free from unreasonable delay.
- The right to be treated with fairness and with respect for the victim's dignity and privacy.

Source: U.S. Attorneys Office, Northern District of Illinois (2013). Victim Witness Unit: Crime Victims' Bill of Rights. *Chicago: U.S. Department of Justice. Retrieved on May 9, 2013, from http://www.justice.gov/usao/iln/rights.html*

Passage of the federal Crime Victims' Bill of Rights has been the subject of at least two interesting court cases. In *Kenna v. U.S. District Court* (2006), a father and son investment team had bilked scores of victims to the tune of almost $100 million. Both defendants pleaded guilty to the charges. More than 60 victims submitted victim impact statements. At the father's sentencing hearing, several victims, including the plaintiff Kenna, addressed the court and explained how their retirement savings were drained, businesses bankrupted, and lives ruined by the father's nefarious scheme. The court sentenced the father to 20 years in prison.

The son's sentencing hearing took place three months later. However, in this hearing, the judge declined to give any of the victims the opportunity to deliver a fresh set of remarks before the court. The judge stated that he had already listened to the victims at the last sentencing hearing and did not anticipate learning anything new. The judge then went ahead and sentenced the son to a little more than 11 years imprisonment.

Kenna filed a writ of *mandamus* in reaction to the judge's behavior. A writ of *mandamus* asks a higher court to order a lower court to act upon or refrain from, as the case may be, upholding the petitioner's rights. Kenna contended that the judge's refusal to allow victim input at the second sentencing hearing violated the fourth provision in the federal Crime Victim's Rights Act listed in Table 7.10 dealing with the "right to be reasonably heard." That safeguard, according to Kenna, guaranteed him allocution, or the right to speak before the court. The presiding judge, on the other hand, relied upon the word "reasonably." His position was that the language vested him with the authority to exercise discretion and limit victim testimony because the victims' views were already known. As a remedy, Kenna sought to have the sentence overturned and demanded that the judge be forced to listen to the victims and then resentence the defendant. The court of appeals agreed with Kenna. It advised the district court to conduct a new sentencing hearing and to allow Kenna and other victims in the cases to make oral presentations.

The federal Crime Victims' Bill of Rights was tested again in a second related development *(United States v. Wood, 2006)*. There, the defendant Wood had been found guilty of fraud and was scheduled for a sentencing hearing. However, the victims had plans to be out of the country on that day. Hence, they requested a later date for sentencing that would enable them to attend and speak before the court. The defendant objected to the delay, and the case made its way before the district court. After hearing this case, the district court relied upon the *Kenna* decision and found that the minor delay was a reasonable accommodation.

State Legislative Reform

While these federal actions were taking place, many states were devising their own ways to protect and assist crime victims. One prime example of these inroads is that all the states now have active victim compensation programs. Virtually every state in the union has passed its own legislation dealing with victim rights. In many respects, these provisions mirror federal efforts. As Table 7.11 outlines, Florida victims and witnesses are entitled to a number of rights. The introduction of victim rights legislation has not gone without criticism. For one thing, these additional measures and responsibilities translate into increased loads for beleaguered criminal justice workers. These actions may bring about some delays and greater costs in the court process.

Some people fear that greater participation may exacerbate harm to the victim. Although a number of states do not allow victims to be completely barred from attending the criminal's trial, some restrictions may apply. More worrisome, though, is that the victim must relive the traumatic events surrounding the crime during both the fact-finding and sentencing phases of a court case. Pointed questions by the defense can be a further detriment. This experience might be a cleansing event for some victims, but it may only intensify and prolong the hurt for others.

Another question involves the situation in which a victim is not notified or accorded his or her statutorily guaranteed rights. What avenues can victims pursue should the system not honor these rights? Many statutes spell out the steps expected of system personnel. Arizona, for example, requires that the prosecutor notify the court that he or she has made an honest effort to confer with the victim prior to arranging a plea agreement (Office for Victims of Crime, 2002a). However, there is little recourse if the prosecution does not comply with these procedures. In fact, some states include an explicit disclaimer that victims cannot take any legal action against system personnel who fail to follow the statute (Office for Victims of Crime, 2002a). Other jurisdictions rely on a more general immunity clause that prohibits the public from suing governmental agents for actions undertaken in good faith or without malice. One possible solution lies in the area of ethics standards. Victims may

---

Table 7.11 Florida Guidelines for Fair Treatment of Victims and Witnesses

Florida victims and witnesses are entitled to the following considerations:

- Information concerning services available to victims of adult and juvenile crime.
- Information for purposes of notifying victim or appropriate next of kin of victim or other designated contact of victim.
- Information concerning protection available to victim or witness.
- Notification of scheduling changes.
- Advance notification to victim or relative of victim concerning judicial proceedings; right to be present.
- Information concerning release from incarceration from a county jail, municipal jail, juvenile detention facility, or residential commitment facility.
- Consultation with victim or guardian or family of victim.
- Return of property to victim.
- Notification to employer and explanation to creditors of victim or witness.
- Notification of right to request restitution.
- Notification of right to submit impact statement.
- Local witness coordination services.
- Victim assistance education and training.
- General victim assistance.
- Victim's rights information card or brochure.
- Information concerning escape from a state correctional institution, county jail, juvenile detention facility, or residential commitment facility.
- Presence of victim advocate during discovery deposition; testimony of victim of a sexual offense.
- Implementing crime prevention in order to protect the safety of persons and property, as prescribed in the State Comprehensive Plan.
- Attendance of victim at same school as defendant.
- Use of a polygraph examination or other truth-telling device with victim.
- Presence of victim advocates during forensic medical examination.

Source: Florida Statutes *(2012)*, § 960.01.

---

be able to file complaints with a state ethics board that can levy disciplinary action for failure to comply with the law. However, it is likely that this recourse would bring very little satisfaction to the victim.

A recent development has been the establishment of special investigative units that look into complaints that system officials have usurped victim rights. An *ombudsman* is a neutral party who provides a checks-and-balances function and cuts through bureaucratic red tape in an effort to rectify problems or resolve disputes expeditiously. The Department of Justice, for example, has established the position of "Crime Victims' Rights Ombudsman" to handle any federal violations that may arise. Several states have also formed similar units that investigate complaints that system officials are not honoring a victim's rights. Usually, an ombudsman has the final voice, and this person's ruling is binding and not subject to appeal or review.

🌐 **WEB ACTIVITY**

One priority of the U.S. Department of Justice is to protect the rights of crime victims. The Crime Victims' Rights Ombudsman has the authority to act on complaints from victims that their rights have been infringed upon in federal cases. More information is available at **http://www.justice.gov/usao/eousa/vr/**

A more perplexing issue involves a debate over the goals of the criminal justice system. Increased attention to victim harm shifts sentencing from a preoccupation with rehabilitation to an emphasis on retribution and restitution. What this change does is refocus attention upon the needs of the victim. Critics protest that this alteration creates an imbalance and invites a diminution of offender rights. Others note that the call for harsher sanctions stretches an already overextended correctional system beyond its capacity. As one writer adroitly puts it:

> [I]n some respects, a new battle has replaced the old. Now, it is not victims fighting for a place in the system; the current consensus is that they belong. But a new battle now rages between the state and its own limited resources. Vying for these resources are overcrowded jails, rising crime rates, and competing welfare and infrastructure programs. Clearly, the rights of crime victims will not be secure until these issues are resolved (Calcutt, 1988: 834).

VICTIM IMPACT STATEMENTS

Perhaps one of the more significant steps in the crusade for victim rights has been the idea of a victim impact statement. A *victim impact statement* (VIS) allows the victim the opportunity to let the court know how the incident has influenced his or her life. Victims can describe the emotional and financial costs associated with the victimization and can outline what they consider to be an appropriate punishment. According to one former federal district court judge, such statements have at least four benefits:

> They not only provide information to judges, but also give possible therapeutic benefits to victims, educate defendants about the harms of their crime, and ensure that the sentencing process is viewed as fair by the broader public (Cassell, 2009: 648).

A VIS takes one of two formats. The first is a written account that usually accompanies the pre-sentence investigation report. Figure 7.3 reprints the VIS form that the South Carolina Attorney General recommends for use in that state. What makes this form interesting is that it was compiled after South Carolina had been involved in a U.S. Supreme Court case that will be discussed later in this chapter. The second format, called *allocution*, is an oral presentation. Here the victim him- or herself addresses the court during the sentencing phase.

WEB ACTIVITY

The California Department of Corrections and Rehabilitation has developed "A Guide for Writing Victim Impact Statements" that is available at **http://www.cdcr.ca.gov/Victim_Services/docs/Victim_Impact_Statement_Writing_Guide.pdf**

Two major streams of interest have trailed the VIS. The first area concerns research dealing with the effect of a VIS upon case processing. The second focus is upon the legal challenges that have risen regarding the use of a VIS in death penalty cases. Both topics are addressed in the following sections.

**South Carolina Attorney General
Victim Impact Statement**

CASE INFORMATION

Case: State v. _____

Charge: _____

Warrant: _____   Indictment: _____

VICTIM INFORMATION

Victim Name: _____   M ☐   F ☐

Contact Person: _____   Relationship: _____

Mailing Address: _____

City: _____   State: _____   Zip: _____

Home phone: _____   Work phone: _____

Cell phone: _____   Other phone: _____

E-mail Address: _____

NOTIFICATION REQUEST

Please check one of the following three statements:

☐   I absolutely want to be present for a guilty plea or other proceeding concerning this case.

☐   I would like to be present if it is convenient, but this is not absolutely necessary.

☐   I will come if I am needed, but do not care to be present otherwise.

Please check one of the following statements:

☐   I would like to be notified by the appropriate agencies of all post-trial proceedings involving the offender including, but not limited to appeals, probation, parole, etc.

☐   I do not want to be notified about post-trial proceedings involving the offender.

Please turn to the back of this form and complete accordingly

FIGURE 7.3 The South Carolina Victim Impact Statement Form.
Source: South Carolina Attorney General (2013). Victim Impact Statement. *Columbia: South Carolina Attorney General's Office. Retrieved on May 9, 2013, from http://www.scag.gov/wp-content/uploads/2011/03/VictimsImpactStatement.pdf.*

CRIME IMPACT

Please answer the following questions as appropriate to your case: (use an additional sheet if needed)

If and how has the crime affected you? (financially, mentally, physically, etc.)

Have you noticed any change in yourself since this happened? This might include changes in your personal habits, the way you deal with others, or the amount of tension or nervousness you feel.

Describe any physical injuries you suffered and medical treatment received as a result of the crime.

Have you received any counseling or psychological services because of the crime?

Did you suffer monetary loss due to the crime? If so, please summarize the loss below.

   Medical Expenses: _____

   Counseling: _____

   Lost Wages: _____

   Property Loss: _____

   Funeral Expenses: _____

   Other: _____

Did you recover any monetary loss? If so summarize below:

   Recovery from insurance: _____

   Victim Compensation (SOVA): _____

SIGNATURE REQUIRED

Thank you for taking time to complete this impact statement. Please sign indicating the statement was given truthfully and voluntarily:

_____   _____

Name of Victim / Contact person   **Date**

FIGURE 7.3 Continued

The Effect of Victim Impact Statements

The most surprising finding in virtually all victim impact statement studies is that large numbers of victims do not avail themselves of this opportunity. While local prosecutors in Texas provided impact forms to more than 91,000 victims during 2012, less than 19% of the recipients completed and returned these statements (Texas Department of Criminal Justice, 2013: 22). Other studies concur that around 10% of all victims make statements at sentencing hearings or parole board deliberations (Caplan, 2010; McLeod, 1987; Ranish & Shichor, 1985; Villmoare & Neto, 1987; Yun, Johnson, & Kercher, 2005). Obviously, a sizeable number of victims still do not avail themselves of these opportunities.

One reason for this stunning lack of participation is that many victims are not aware of the right to be present. In addition, in some instances, they cannot be located when the case reaches that stage of the criminal justice process (McLeod, 1987; Villmoare & Neto, 1987). But even when victims do know about this opportunity, they refrain from using it. Many victims are dissatisfied with the system, do not think their input is critical, fear retaliation, or are concerned for their own emotional well-being (Erez & Tontodonato, 1992; Villmoare & Neto, 1987).

For victims who do use the system, contrary to what skeptics had forecasted, not all of them use the VIS vindictively to seek the harshest punishment possible (Acker, 1992). Critics were concerned that VISs would supersede legal factors and that judicial punishment would comply with these subjective "victim pleas." One study found that the victim's presence in court, a VIS, and a request for incarceration all influenced the use of imprisonment as a sanction (Erez & Tontodonato, 1990). However, the VIS carried far less weight than legal variables and prior offense history in sentence determination. Other studies report that VISs have no impact on sentences, restitution orders, the speed of court procedures, or victim satisfaction (Davis & Smith, 1994, 1995; Davis, Henley, & Smith, 1990; Erez, 1990; Erez & Roeger, 1995; Erez & Tontodonato, 1992). In fact, one victimologist caustically commented that "requiring a victim impact statement and recommendation as part of the presentence report is a mere genuflection to ritualistic legalism" (Walsh, 1986: 1139).

There is an emerging body of literature that appears to contradict some of these earlier findings. Parsonage, Bernat and Helfgott (1994) found that parole boards are less likely to recommend inmates for release prior to sentence expiration when victims oppose such action. Luginbuhl and Burkhead (1995), in an experimental design that utilized college students as subjects, uncovered a tendency for these simulated jurors to vote for the death penalty when they had access to victim impact statements like the one the prosecution proffered in the *Booth* case (see the following section). Restricting the study group to just potential jurors who would emerge from *voir dire* as "death qualified" did not alter these findings.

Exposure to a VIS made subjects more prone to developing a favorable impression of the victim, heightening animosity against the defendant, and making jurors more inclined to favor capital punishment (Paternoster & Deise, 2011). Morgan and Smith (2005) reported that victim participation had a decided effect on parole board release decisions in Alabama. However, Caplan's (2010) explanation is particularly illuminating:

> New Jersey Parole Board members made over 6,500 parole release decisions in 2004. Assuming that they had no other work-related obligations but to decide release for 8 hours each day, board members would have less than 20 minutes to review each parole-eligible inmate's case file. Even at this pace—without taking breaks or performing other obligatory tasks—carefully considering every piece of input in addition to all other parole release factors may not be feasible. Therefore, it is reasonable to believe that . . . parole board members and other decision-makers do not adequately read and consider the input in order to save time and streamline the case-file review process (Caplan, 2010: 237–238).

Despite a number of empirical studies that find sentencing practices remain largely unaffected by victim input, VISs have generated tremendous legal concern. As the following section explains, even the federal Supreme Court became embroiled in the use of VISs during capital cases.

Federal Supreme Court Rulings

The practice of allowing a VIS has resulted in several significant U.S. Supreme Court cases. Initially, the Court barred the use of a VIS in death penalty cases. However, the Court later reversed itself to permit such information to be heard during the sentencing phase. A brief look at these major decisions will illustrate how case law has evolved in this area. However, first, it might be helpful to revisit some of the major issues that framed the death penalty at that time so we have an appropriate foundation for viewing the victim impact cases.

WEB ACTIVITY

You can examine the website of the U.S. Supreme Court by going to **http://www. supremecourt.gov/**

Background

The U.S. Supreme Court struck down the death penalty as cruel and unusual punishment in *Furman v. Georgia* (1972). Race had emerged as an important determinant of when the death penalty was imposed in rape cases. Black defendants were more likely to receive the death penalty when the victim was white than in intraracial incidents or instances in which the suspect was white and the victim was a minority member. In other words, social considerations, rather than legal variables, predicted sentencing outcomes.

The Florida state legislature reacted to *Furman* by enacting a revised statute aimed at removing any arbitrary or capricious intrusions (Ehrhardt et al., 1973). Essentially, the new law established what are called *mitigating* and *aggravating* circumstances. Four years later, the Court upheld the imposition of capital punishment as constitutional in *Gregg v. Georgia* (1976).

Aggravating circumstances render the crime more heinous or despicable (*Florida Statutes*, 2012: § 921.141(5)). Some examples include torturing the victim prior to death, a gang-style execution, a murder committed for pecuniary gain, assassinating a law enforcement officer or an elected public official to prevent him or her from discharging their duties, killing somebody while under confinement for a murder, killing a child under the age of 12, already being designated as a sexual predator, or killing somebody during the course of a felony. *Mitigating circumstances* are factors that make the crime somewhat more understandable (*Florida Statutes*, 2012: § 921.141(6)). Those include such items as mental impairment or a low IQ, a history of being abused as a child, being under extreme mental duress at the time of the incident, and young age.

Judges and juries are obligated to consider both mitigating and aggravating circumstances when deliberating over an appropriate sentence. The purpose behind introducing aggravating circumstances is "to demonstrate the victim's uniqueness as an individual human being and the resultant loss to the community's members by the victim's death" (*Florida Statutes*, 2012: § 921.141(7)). If the mitigating circumstances outweigh the aggravating circumstances, then the appropriate punishment would be life imprisonment. If, however, the aggravating circumstances are more prominent than the mitigating circumstances, then the death penalty would be the appropriate choice.

In addition to understanding the role of mitigating and aggravating circumstances in capital punishment cases, we should also be aware that the trial court must remain vigilant in protecting suspect rights. Inflammatory statements are not allowed, and items that would unduly prejudice jurors are not admissible. Given this background, we are now in a better position to appreciate the issues that were raised in a series of VIS decisions.

Booth v. Maryland *(1987)*

The Supreme Court first addressed the issue of the VIS in *Booth v. Maryland* (1987). Booth was convicted of two counts of first-degree murder in a case involving an elderly couple, Irvin Bronstein, age 78, and his wife Rose Bronstein, age 75. Booth robbed the Bronsteins in their home so he could buy some illicit drugs. Because Booth and the Bronsteins were neighbors, Booth felt compelled to kill them to prevent them from identifying him to the police. The suspect tied up the couple, gagged them, and then stabbed each victim numerous times. Jurors found Booth guilty of both killings. During the sentencing portion of the trial, the judge allowed the jury to hear the contents of a written VIS.

Booth's lawyer objected to the VIS, alleging that it contained a number of inflammatory statements that unduly biased the jurors. For example, the VIS described the victims as having "been married for fifty-three years," a father who "had worked hard all his life," and a mother "who was young at heart" (p. 510). They were "extremely good people who wouldn't hurt a fly," and the "funeral was the largest in the history" of the funeral parlor (p. 514). A granddaughter had to cancel her honeymoon in order to attend the funeral. The son stated that his parents were "butchered like animals" and that nobody "should be able to do something like that and get away with it" (p. 512). The daughter said "animals wouldn't do this," and she "could never forgive anyone for killing them that way" (p. 513). The caseworker who prepared the VIS concluded by writing, "It is doubtful that they [the survivors] will ever be able to fully recover from this tragedy and not be haunted by the memory of the brutal manner in which their loved ones were murdered and taken from them" (p. 515). Given the tone of these statements, Booth's lawyer argued that such characterizations were unduly prejudicial to his client.

The Supreme Court delivered a 5–4 judgment and ruled that a capital sentencing jury should not be exposed to a VIS during its deliberations. Introducing testimony about the sterling character of the victim runs the risk that the jury could make an arbitrary decision. In other words, instead of focusing completely upon the defendant, the jury might be tempted to impose the death penalty solely because the victim was an outstanding member of the community. The Court went on to say:

> One can understand the grief and anger of the family caused by the brutal murders in this case. … But the formal presentation of this information by the State can serve no other purpose than to inflame the jury and divert it from deciding the case on the relevant evidence. … The admission of these emotionally charged opinions as to what conclusions the jury should draw from the evidence clearly is inconsistent with the reasoned decision-making we require in capital cases (pp. 508–509).

Justice Scalia issued a dissenting opinion. There he wrote:

> To require, as we have, that all mitigating factors which render capital punishment a harsh penalty in the particular case be placed before the sentencing authority, while simultaneously requiring, as we do today, that evidence of much of the human suffering the defendant has inflicted be suppressed, is in effect to prescribe a debate on the appropriateness of the capital penalty with one side muted. If that penalty is constitutional, as we have repeatedly said it is, it seems to me not remotely unconstitutional to permit both the pros and the cons in the particular case to be heard (pp. 520–521).

South Carolina v. Gathers *(1989)*

In *South Carolina v. Gathers*, the U.S. Supreme Court extended this embargo to cover prosecutor comments made to a jury during the sentencing portion of a death penalty case. The victim Haynes had been in and out of a psychiatric facility several times. Among other things, Haynes thought he was a preacher and even used the term *Reverend Mister* when referring to himself (p. 807). He spent his days proselytizing and reading scripture to passers-by.

Gathers, with the help of some friends, beat Haynes viciously and eventually stabbed the victim to death. Afterward, Gathers went through Haynes's belongings to see if there was anything of value. A jury found Gathers guilty of first-degree murder and other charges.

During the sentencing phase, the prosecutor emphasized repeatedly that the deceased was an extremely religious person and a self-styled minister. The prosecutor read aloud portions of the victim's favorite religious tract to the jury. In the end, the jurors voted to impose the death penalty. Upon review, the South Carolina Supreme Court declared that the prosecutor "conveyed the suggestion appellant [Gathers] deserved a death sentence because the victim was a religious man" (p. 810).

The South Carolina Supreme Court, relying upon the *Booth* decision, overturned the sentence of death. It reasoned that the prosecutor's remarks implied that the death sentence was appropriate because the victim was such a religious person (p. 811).

An appeal to the U.S. Supreme Court brought a similar rebuff. The federal justices, in another 5–4 split decision, ruled that the prosecutor's description of the victim violated the standards erected in *Booth*. Justice Brennan, on behalf of the majority, declared:

> While in this case it was the prosecutor rather than the victim's survivors who characterized the victim's personal qualities, the statement is indistinguishable in any relevant respect from that in *Booth*. ... the prosecutor's argument in this case went well beyond that fact... (p. 811).

The dissenting opinions made it quite clear that there was considerable disenchantment, not only with the immediate decision, but also with *Booth* itself. Justice O'Connor, for example, wrote, "I remain persuaded that *Booth* was wrong when decided and stand ready to overrule it if the Court would do so..." (pp. 813–814).

Justice Scalia also echoed a similar sentiment in his dissenting remarks. There he wrote:

> Two Terms ago, when we decided *Booth v. Maryland*, I was among four Members of the Court who believed that the decision imposed

a restriction upon state and federal criminal procedures that has no basis in the Constitution. I continue to believe that *Booth* was wrongly decided, and my conviction that it does perceptible harm has been strengthened by subsequent writings pointing out the indefensible consequences of a rule that the specific harm visited upon society by a murderer may not be taken into account when the jury decides whether to impose the sentence of death. . . . I therefore think now the present case squarely calls into question the validity of *Booth*, and I would overrule that case (pp. 823–824) [citations omitted].

The tension among the Justices was quite evident. Even to the uninitiated, it was quite clear that the clouds were gathering prior to the storm. That test would come in the form of another case the Court would visit just two years later: *Payne v. Tennessee.*

Payne v. Tennessee *(1991)*

The VIS controversy continued until the Court reversed itself in the 1991 *Payne v. Tennessee* decision. In this case, Payne's girlfriend, who lived in an apartment directly across from the victims' residence, was not home. Frustrated by her absence, Payne gained access to Charisse Christopher's dwelling and accosted her. When Christopher resisted Payne's sexual overtures, Payne stabbed her 84 times. He also slashed Christopher's two-year-old daughter, who subsequently died, and her three-year-old son, Nicholas, who was left for dead, but miraculously survived his extensive knife wounds. At the conclusion of the trial, Payne was sentenced to death on two counts of murder.

During the sentencing phase, the jury learned about the duress Nicholas was facing. His grandmother testified, "He cries for his mom. He doesn't understand why she doesn't come home" (p. 814). The prosecutor reminded the jurors:

Nicholas' mother will never kiss him good night or pat him as he goes off to bed, or hold him and sing him a lullaby. . . . These are the things that go into why it is especially cruel, heinous, and atrocious, the burden that that child will carry forever (p. 816).

The jury imposed the death penalty upon Payne. Payne's lawyer appealed the sentence, arguing that any reliance upon the VIS comments of the grandmother and the prosecutor were highly prejudicial to his client and clearly violated both *Booth* and *Gathers.*

The federal Supreme Court granted *certiorari,* heard the case, and overturned its earlier rulings. As the majority opinion explained:

We thus hold that if the State chooses to permit the admission of victim impact evidence and prosecutorial argument on that subject, the Eighth

Amendment erects no *per se* bar. A State may legitimately conclude that evidence about the victim and about the impact of the murder on the victim's family is relevant to the jury's decision as to whether or not the death penalty should be imposed. There is no reason to treat such evidence differently than other relevant evidence is treated.

As a result of *Payne*, the courts are no longer required to suppress a VIS in a capital penalty case. If state law permits the prosecution to explain what repercussions the survivors have shouldered because of the incident, that information is appropriate for the jury to hear. Nothing in the Eighth Amendment forbids such testimony from consideration.

Kelly v. California *(2008)*

In this case, Kelly was convicted and sentenced to death for the murder of a 19-year-old woman. During the sentencing phase of the trial, the prosecutor played a 20-minute video that recounted the life of the victim from early childhood up until her demise.

Scenes of the victim swimming, riding a horse, and participating in other activities were accompanied by narration and soft background music. The final scene in the video consisted of a view of the victim's grave.

Kelly's attorney appealed the case to the U.S. Supreme Court. He maintained that the video was so laden with emotion that the trial judge should have withheld it from the jurors. However, the Supreme Court denied *certiorari* and declined to hear the case.

Justice Stevens disagreed and saw this case as an opportunity to clarify several issues surrounding VIS usage. He wrote:

In the years since *Payne* was decided, this Court has left state and federal courts unguided in their efforts to police the hazy boundaries between permissible victim impact evidence and its impermissible, "unduly prejudicial" forms. Following *Payne's* model, lower courts throughout the country have largely failed to place clear limits on the scope, quantity, or kind of victim impact evidence capital juries are permitted to consider (p. 6).

The Post-*Payne* Era

While the U.S. Supreme Court has entrenched victim impact statements firmly within the justice system, there are still a number of unresolved issues. Beloof (2003) divides VIS concerns into three components. They include: (1) the victim and his or her unique individual characteristics; (2) the impact the crime has had on the survivors; and (3) opinion regarding the appropriate sentence to be imposed. What are missing from the Supreme Court's rulings are operational guidelines for how to proceed (Blume, 2003; Burr, 2003; Cassell, 2009; Hoffman, 2003; Karp & Warshaw, 2009; Minot, 2012). For example, should the parties allowed to express a VIS be limited to immediate family members, or should derivative victims be allowed to as well? What format should a VIS take? Should poems, photographs, and other representations be allowed or limited (Younglove, Nelligan, & Reisner, 2009)? What kinds of expert witness testimony should judges allow (Blumenthal, 2009), and what kinds of instructions should judges issue to jurors regarding the VIS (Platania & Berman, 2006)? Should the defense be allowed to rebut the contents of a VIS, especially if it contains inflammatory or hearsay statements?

One avenue some states have adopted is to have the judge instruct the jury about the relevance of a VIS and the appropriate weight to attach to such testimony. For example, the Georgia Supreme Court suggested:

> In future cases in which victim impact evidence is given in the sentencing phase of a death penalty or life without parole case, the trial court should instruct the jury regarding the purpose of victim impact evidence. For example, the trial court might charge:

> The prosecution has introduced what is known as victim impact evidence. Victim impact evidence is not the same as evidence of a statutory aggravating circumstance. Introduction of victim impact evidence does not relieve the state of its burden to prove beyond a reasonable doubt the existence of a statutory aggravating circumstance. This evidence is simply another method of informing you about the harm caused by the crime in question. To the extent that you find that this evidence reflects on the defendant's culpability you may consider it, but you may not use it as a substitute for proof beyond a reasonable doubt of the existence of a statutory aggravating circumstance (*Turner v. The State*, 1997).

Some states have taken a different approach by constructing statutes that govern the types of victim impact evidence considered admissible and what kind of information is appropriate for juries to hear during the penalty phase. For example, *Florida Statutes* (2012: § 921.141(7)) reads:

> Once the prosecution has provided evidence of the existence of one or more aggravating circumstances as described in subsection (5), the prosecution may introduce, and subsequently argue, victim impact evidence to the jury. Such evidence shall be designed to demonstrate the victim's uniqueness as an individual human being and the resultant loss to the community's members by the victim's death. Characterizations and opinions about the crime, the defendant, and the appropriate sentence shall not be permitted as a part of victim impact evidence.

PROFESSIONALIZING VICTIM ADVOCACY

The last portion of Chapter 1 explained that the emergence of victimology and victim services was largely a grassroots effort undertaken by concerned citizens. Forty years ago, victim services was a fledgling area. Many service providers were either former victims or well-intended persons with a passionate concern for the welfare of others. Formal credentials were virtually nonexistent. Today, that landscape has changed dramatically. A warm smile and a sympathetic ear are no longer the only essential ingredients for becoming a victim service provider. As this book has shown, research findings have accumulated at a rapid pace, tasks have expanded, the need for coordinated responses has intensified, and the level of sophistication needed to discharge the advocacy role has grown immensely.

🌐 WEB ACTIVITY

Details regarding the National Victim Assistance Academy are available at **https://www.ovcttac.gov/views/TrainingMaterials/dspNVAA.cfm**

Victim advocates, the people who service victim clients, need an appropriate background and training before they engage in helping behavior. A growing emphasis is being placed upon pre-service and in-service training for criminal justice personnel and the staff of other agencies who come into contact with victims. For example, practitioners can attend a 40-hour course at the National Victim Assistance Academy. The national academy offers three tracks for direct service providers. The first segment focuses on entry-level aspects and provides a foundation for persons interested in launching a career in victim services. The second program takes people who are already working in the victim services field and goes into greater topical detail. The last path concentrates on leadership and management skills necessary to administer effective victim service programs.

A similar initiative to upgrade the training that victim advocates receive has taken hold at the state level. Starting in 1999, the federal Office for Victims of Crime began encouraging states to create their own localized versions of the national academy tailored to the backgrounds and needs of victim service providers (Neff, Patterson, & Johnson, 2012). As Figure 7.4 shows, 41 states have established their own victim assistance academies.

Some states have implemented formal credentials, short of licensing, as a way of recognizing the attainment of greater proficiency. As Table 7.12 shows, the Office of the Florida Attorney General urges service providers to upgrade their skills by offering a training curriculum that culminates in certification as a *victim practitioner*.

In another related development, representatives from various organizations banded together to form the National Victim Assistance Standards Consortium.

This multidisciplinary group sought input from service providers and policymakers throughout the country. The intent was to professionalize the field by establishing a set of minimum standards for programs and service providers. One product that emerged from these deliberations was a code of ethics. Table 7.13 presents these professional expectations. The intent is to help victim practitioners navigate perplexing issues that can arise as they strive to deliver the highest level of service possible.

WEB ACTIVITY

Interested in learning more about standards and practices regarding victim service providers? Then check out **http://ccfs. sc.edu/component/content/article/31-victim-assistance/103-national-victim-assistance-standards-consortium.html**

As the reader can see, there is a growing recognition that employee preparation is one mechanism to ensure that quality services are being delivered to victims who need assistance. These efforts echo the recommendations regarding a greater emphasis on personnel development, education, and training found throughout the *New Directions* report discussed in earlier chapters.

States with an OVC-funded SVAA

FIGURE 7.4 Location of State Victim Assistance Academies.
Source: Office for Victims of Crime (2013). State Victim Assistance Academies Locator, Washington, DC: U.S. Department of Justice. Retrieved on May 9, 2013, from http://www.ovc.gov/training/svaa.html

Table 7.12 The Florida "Victim Services Practitioner" Designation Requirements

Background

The Office of the Attorney General established the "Victim Services Practitioner Designation" in 1995 to document an individual's successful participation in the "Victim Services Practitioner Designation" course. A participant who completes the designation has been provided information on the basic issues and concerns related to victims of violent crime and the role of a victim advocate.

Initial Designation

An individual will automatically receive the designation of "Victim Services Practitioner" upon completion of all segments of the "Victim Services Practitioner Designation" course offered by the Office of the Attorney General, Florida Crime Prevention Training Institute (FCPTI).

Renewing the Designation

The "Victim Services Practitioner Designation" is valid for a period of four years from the date that appears on the "Victim Services Practitioner" designation certificate. It is the responsibility of the individual to renew his/her designation if he/she wishes to remain current. To renew the designation, a Victim Services Practitioner must meet the following requirements and file the appropriate forms and paperwork prior to the expiration of the designation:

- Applicant must have completed a minimum of 40 hours of additional victim services related training in a seminar, course or workshop setting;

- Of the 40 hours of training required above, at least sixteen (16) hours must be from victim advocate training courses offered through FCPTI; and

- Apply for renewal of the designation with the Office of the Attorney General and provide copies of all certificates on which you base the renewal, including a copy of your original designation certificate and any subsequent renewal certificates.

Expired Certificates

If an individual allows his or her designation to expire, he or she must complete all of the above requirements during a period not to exceed 12 months from the date of expiration.

In the event the individual has allowed the designation to expire for a period of more than 12 months from the date of the expiration, additional steps must be taken. The individual must complete 24 hours of Victim Advocate Training offered through FCPTI and an additional 16 hours of other victim services related training for a total of 40 hours within a 12-month period.

Source: Office of the Florida Attorney General (2013). Victim Services Practitioner Designation Requirements. *Tallahassee: Victim Services Professional Development Program. Retrieved on May 10, 2013, from http://www.fcpti.com/fcpti.nsf/pics/CFA429865A4BF-438852579D70058A8D4/$file/ATT7J2TQ.pdf*

Table 7.13 Ethical Standards for Victim Service Providers

A. Scope of Services

1. The victim assistance provider understands his/her legal responsibilities, limitations, and the implications of his/her actions within the service delivery setting and performs duties in accord with laws, regulations, policies, and legislated rights of persons served.
2. The victim assistance provider accurately represents his/her professional title, qualifications, and/or credentials in relationships with the people served and in public advertising.
3. The victim assistance provider maintains a high standard of professional conduct.
4. The victim assistance provider achieves and maintains a high level of professional competence.
5. The victim assistance provider who provides a service for a fee informs a person served about the fee at the initial session or meeting.

B. Coordinating within the Community

1. The victim assistance provider conducts relationships with colleagues and other professionals in such a way as to promote mutual respect, public confidence, and improvement of service.
2. The victim assistance provider shares knowledge and encourages proficiency in victim assistance among colleagues and other professionals.
3. The victim assistance provider serves the public interest by contributing to the improvement of systems that impact victims of crime.

C. Direct Services

1. The victim assistance provider respects and attempts to protect the victim's civil rights.
2. The victim assistance provider recognizes the interests of the person served as a primary responsibility.
3. The victim assistance provider refrains from behaviors that communicate victim blame, suspicion regarding victim accounts of the crime, condemnation for past behavior, or other judgmental, anti-victim sentiment.
4. The victim assistance provider respects the victim's right to self-determination.
5. The victim assistance provider preserves the confidentiality of information provided by the person served or acquired from other sources before, during, and after the course of the professional relationship.
6. The victim assistance provider avoids conflicts of interest and discloses any possible conflict to the program or person served, and also to prospective programs or persons to be served.
7. The victim assistance provider terminates a professional relationship with a victim when the victim is not likely to benefit from continued services.
8. The victim assistance provider does not engage in personal relationships with persons served that exploit professional trust or that could impair the victim assistance provider's objectivity and professional judgment.
9. The victim assistance provider does not discriminate against a victim or another staff member on the basis of race/ethnicity, language, sex, gender, age, sexual orientation, (dis)ability, social class, economic status, education, marital status, religious affiliation, residency, or HIV status.
10. The victim assistance provider furnishes opportunities for colleague victim assistance providers to seek appropriate services when traumatized by a criminal event or client interaction.

D. Administration and Evaluation

1. The victim assistance provider reports to appropriate authorities the conduct of any colleague or other professional (including oneself) that constitutes mistreatment of a person served or that brings the profession into dishonor.

Source: DeHart, D. D. (2003). National Victim Assistance Standards Consortium: Standards for Victim Assistance Programs and Providers. Columbia: Center for Child and Family Studies, University of South Carolina, pp. 59–65. Retrieved on May 12, 2013, from http://ccfs.sc.edu/images/pdfs/victimstandards.pdf

A LOOK AHEAD

Chapter 1 framed this book in the context of Mendelsohn's rendition of the field as "general victimology." At that point, readers were advised that this book was going to concentrate on a single component of that typology: criminal victimology. After considering so many different topics and broad issues, we think our readers would agree that this restriction certainly did not hinder the amount of materials we have visited and digested.

Several themes form the organizational backbone of upcoming chapters. Perhaps the most important guiding point is the notion of "double-victimization" introduced in Chapter 4. The whole idea that the system intensifies—rather than rectifies—victim suffering is a pivotal concern. Each chapter from this point forward will continue to amplify this dialogue by addressing various reform efforts intended to help transform the *criminal's* justice system into a more meaningful *victim's* justice system. While many of these efforts have blossomed and are making the "halls of justice" more user-friendly, we have tried to retain a critical (but not overly skeptical) eye. Simply put, some legal reforms have worked and others have not. As a consequence, many troublesome areas are still in need of solutions.

Another recurring concept that we have been careful to include wherever possible is the idea of victim precipitation. As the opening chapter explained, the original thrust within victimology was to unveil how victims contribute to their own demise. Despite an intense ideological backlash, remnants of victim-blaming continue to haunt victimological developments. We will see this theme when we turn to sexual battery, intimate partner violence, child maltreatment, elder abuse and neglect, and hate crimes. Rather than shy away from these accounts, we will include them for the reader's own evaluation. In many instances, this intense scrutiny of victim actions has acted as a springboard. It has stimulated a number of theoretical viewpoints. Sexual battery is now interpreted in terms of power and domination instead of sexual gratification. The question of "Why doesn't she leave him?" paves the way for understanding how learned helplessness and the cycle of violence immobilize victims of intimate partner violence. A reinterpretation of how alcohol influences social interaction patterns and impedes the delivery of medical services sheds a different light on homicide victimization. As you can see, the criticisms and flaws associated with the victim precipitation argument have launched many new perspectives.

Another common unifying thread that weaves its way throughout the upcoming chapters is the inclusion of a distinct practitioner orientation. For example, the sexual battery chapter places the victim's experience within the context of a crisis reaction. It also explores the activities that take place at different junctures throughout the criminal investigation process and introduces the Sexual Assault Nurse Examiner program. Similarly, the intimate partner violence chapter addresses how research has prompted policy changes in the ways that the police and the courts now provide services to battered women. Coping strategies for lessening the incidence of child maltreatment and elder abuse also make an appearance. Information on the steps involved in a death notification, as well as the bereavement stages that loved ones will encounter, helps to provide a more intense view of what service providers and their clients face during the aftermath of a horrible victimization episode. Victimization in the schools and at the workplace, traditionally thought to be safe places, also receives considerable attention. Recent events have made us realize that these locations have their own distinct patterns of victimization.

Those readers contemplating a possible career in the field of criminal justice should keep in mind that while the victim movement has been responsible for many changes, the ultimate success of these efforts hinges upon the people who work within the justice community. Remaining sensitive and compassionate to each victim's tragedies is the most essential ingredient to any meaningful social service delivery.

SUMMARY

The victim movement is maturing. Over the past three decades, there have been a number of serious initiatives to provide victims with rights. These efforts have continued to gather momentum. Laws now cover a wide range of areas, such as restitution, victim compensation, victim impact statements, notification of system procedures, protection of victims and witnesses, and consultation with victims. This coverage suggests that victim rights will continue to gain even more prominence.

Two issues must be kept in mind as this trend continues. First, there is still much to be learned about the plight of victims. Good intentions, no matter how noble, do not automatically guarantee that recipients are better off now than they were in the past. Only through constant monitoring and evaluation is it possible to gauge the effects of change.

Second, in our zeal to help victims, it is important to seek an equitable balance. In the past, many commentators have argued that the system has erred by becoming overly concerned with offender rights. The same argument can be used against victim rights if appropriate precautionary steps are not taken. A middle ground that balances everyone's interests must be sought. Consider Marquart's (2005: 330) remarks:

The American criminal justice system has come a long way in recognizing and clarifying the rights of both offenders and victims. The exclusion of victims from the process is now a thing of the past. How and where victims are heard and their exercise of power is still an unfolding process in our society.

Only when victims attain equitable footing with offenders will we be able to talk about a true justice system, rather than a *"criminal's* justice system." That is the challenge facing victimology.

KEY TERMS

aggravating circumstances
allocution
mitigating circumstances
ombudsman
victim advocate

victim impact statement (VIS)
victim practitioner
Victim Rights Amendment (VRA)
writ of *mandamus*

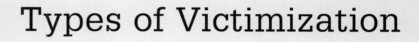

3

Types of Victimization

Traditional Crimes

LEARNING OBJECTIVES

After reading Chapter 8, you should be able to:

- List the persfonal and property crimes that appear in the Part I Offenses.
- Define criminal homicide.
- Assemble a picture of homicide victimization based upon UCR statistics.
- Explain why African Americans are overrepresented in homicide statistics.
- Offer a profile of youthful violence in America.
- Explore the development of the National Violent Death Reporting System.
- Distinguish a primary homicide from a non-primary homicide.
- Define aggravated assault.
- Discuss the difference between aggravated assault and simple assault.
- Explain the problems with measuring assault.
- Define robbery.
- Discuss how robbery is both a property and a personal crime.
- Discuss the extent of assault and robbery victimization.
- Relay the details of the death notification process.
- Discuss the grief process and its different stages.
- Explain some of the adjustments faced by survivors of homicide victims.
- List the five homicide survivor patterns and explain how they differ in response to the homicide event.
- Define burglary and discuss the elements of the definition.
- Discuss the extent and facts of burglary victimization.
- Provide a definition of larceny/theft.

INTRODUCTION

Whenever crime or victimization is discussed, the first image that comes to the mind of most people is the individual who has been the victim of a murder, rape, robbery, theft, or other crime typically handled by the police. It is these events that make up the annual crime figures reported each year by the government. These events also provide fodder for the television shows and movies that entertain us.

This chapter examines the forms of criminal victimization that typically comprise the activity of the criminal justice system. Specifically, we will consider the seven offenses that comprise Part I, Uniform Crime Reports Offenses: murder, robbery, assault, burglary, larceny/theft, motor vehicle theft, and arson (rape will be taken up in a subsequent chapter). A great deal of information is available on these offenses, including specifics on the number of offenses, the victims, and the impact of these crimes on both victims and society. Beyond these offenses, this chapter also looks at the growing problems of fraud, identity theft, mass-marketing fraud, and cybercrime.

PERSONAL CRIMES

The personal crimes of murder, robbery, and assault receive a disproportionate amount of attention from the public. In light of the physical harm from these crimes, this attention is not unexpected. The media also focuses on these offenses and enhances the public's concern over them. Interestingly, these crimes are not the most prevalent. That distinction rests with property offenses.

Homicide Victimization

According to the FBI's Uniform Crime Reports (UCR) (2013), there were 14,612 known homicides in the United States during 2011. Unlike most of the Index crimes, the FBI attempts to collect detailed data on reported homicides and makes this information available through *Supplementary Homicide Reports.* These reports seek data on both the victim and the offender, as well as the circumstances surrounding the event. Despite this fact, detailed information is not available for every one of these deaths. As a result, the UCR data offer a sketch based upon information derived from 89% of the known victim deaths.

The Federal Bureau of Investigation (2013) defines *criminal homicide* as the "willful (nonnegligent) killing of one human being by another… . The UCR Program does not include the following situations in this offense classification: deaths caused by negligence, suicide, or accident; justifiable homicides; and attempts to murder or assaults to murder… ." The FBI also omits from its tabulations traffic fatalities and deaths resulting from gross negligence.

Homicide victims are more likely to be males than females. In 2011, 78% of the deceased were males. In terms of race, 50% of the homicide victims were black and 46% white (FBI, 2013). This racial composition means that blacks experience an overrepresentation in homicide victimization. Considering that blacks make up approximately 13.5% of the American population, all things being equal, one would expect that they would account for 13.5% of all murder victims. Because the participation figure of 50% clearly exceeds the 13.5% population mark, victimologists regard blacks as being excessively represented in homicide statistics.

> ### 🌐 WEB ACTIVITY
>
> Detailed information on homicide can be found from the FBI UCR at **http://www.fbi.gov/about-us/cjis/ucr/crime-in-the-u.s/2011/crime-in-the-u.s.-2011/offenses-known-to-law-enforcement/expanded-offense-data** and the Supplemental Homicide Reports at **http://www.fbi.gov/about-us/cjis/ucr/crime-in-the-u.s/2010/crime-in-the-u.s.-2010/offenses-known-to-law-enforcement/expanded/expandhomicidemain**

Table 8.1 displays the age distribution of murder victims for 2011. These figures show that 497 deaths can be attributed to *infanticide* (child homicide). Victims under the age of 5 made up 3.9% of the homicide victimization pool. If we

Table 8.1 Age Distribution of U.S. Murder Victims, 2011

Age in Years	Number	Simple Percent	Cumulative Percent
Under 1	196	1.5	1.5
1–4	301	2.4	3.9
5–8	84	0.7	4.6
9–12	65	0.5	5.1
13–16	300	2.4	7.5
17–19	1,069	8.4	15.9
20–24	2,329	18.4	34.3
25–29	1,892	14.9	49.2
30–34	1,414	11.2	60.4
35–39	1,046	8.3	68.7
40–44	900	7.1	75.8
45–49	854	6.7	82.5
50–54	673	5.3	87.8
55–59	500	3.9	91.7
60–64	307	2.4	94.1
65–69	184	1.5	95.6
70–74	145	1.1	96.7
75+	278	2.2	98.9
Unknown	127	1.0	99.9
Total	12,664	100.0	99.9

Source: Constructed by authors from Federal Bureau of Investigation (2013). Crime in the United States 2011: Expanded Homicide Data Table 2. Washington, DC: U.S. Government Printing Office. Retrieved May 25, 2013, from http://www.fbi.gov/about-us/cjis/ucr/crime-in-the-u.s/2011/crime-in-the-u.s.-2011/tables/expanded-homicide-data-table-2.

expand the upper limit of childhood to 12 years of age, children account for 5.1% of all the homicide victimizations in the U.S. The most likely perpetrator in the majority of these cases is a parent or parent substitute. *Eldercide*, murders involving elderly victims, are less frequent in comparison.

A closer look at Table 8.1 shows that homicide victimization is concentrated among the younger segments of society. More than half of all homicide victims (53%) were between 17 and 34 years of age. In fact, since 1969, the leading cause of death among young black males is homicide (Bilchik, 1999). One commentator (Kellerman, 1994: 541) notes, "the number of 15- to 19-year-old African-American males who died from gunshot wounds in 1990 was 4.7 times larger than the number who died from acquired immunodeficiency syndrome, sickle cell disease, and all other natural causes of death *combined*" [emphasis in original]. Table 8.2 reinforces this depiction of homicide as a leading cause of

Table 8.2 Five Leading Causes of Death, United States 2000–2007, for Black Males

Rank	<1	1–4	5–9	10–14	15–24	25–34	35–44	45–54	55–64	65+	All Ages
						Age Groups					
1	Short Gestation 8,439	Unintentional Injury 1,651	Unintentional Injury 1,343	Unintentional Injury 1,486	Homicide 21,584	Homicide 17,335	Heart Disease 16,041	Heart Disease 42,493	Malignant Neoplasms 59,147	Heart Disease 168,539	Heart Disease 292,780
2	Congenital Anomalies 4,533	Homicide 708	Malignant Neoplasms 339	Homicide 510	Unintentional Injury 10,297	Unintentional Injury 10,664	HIV 13,718	Malignant Neoplasms 34,845	Heart Disease 58,049	Malignant Neoplasms 154,141	Malignant Neoplasms 261,359
3	SIDS 3,284	Congenital Anomalies 485	Homicide 195	Malignant Neoplasms 394	Suicide 3,034	Heart Disease 4,857	Unintentional Injury 12,714	Unintentional Injury 13,963	Cerebrovascular 11,030	Cerebrovascular 38,622	Unintentional Injury 70,870
4	Maternal Pregnancy Comp. 2,605	Malignant Neoplasms 271	Congenital Anomalies 161	Suicide 240	Heart Disease 1,680	HIV 4,539	Malignant Neoplasms 8,720	HIV 13,577	Diabetes Mellitus 9,371	Chronic Low. Respiratory Disease 23,971	Cerebrovascular 61,763
5	Placenta Cord Membranes 1,423	Heart Disease 221	Chronic Low. Respiratory Disease 120	Chronic Low. Respiratory Disease 202	Malignant Neoplasms 1,244	Suicide 3,367	Homicide 8,517	Cerebrovascular 8,137	Unintentional Injury 7,437	Diabetes Mellitus 23,969	Homicide 56,753

Source: National Center for Injury Prevention and Control (2010b). WISQARS Leading Causes of Death Reports, 1999–2007. Atlanta, GA: Centers for Disease Control and Prevention. Retrieved on July 21, 2013, from http://www.cdc.gov/injury/wisqars/LeadingCauses.html.

death among young black males in the United States. The information there shows that homicide is responsible for the untimely demise of young black males. At the same time, these figures fail to convey the toll sustained from the combined years of potential life lost whenever a person loses his or her life prematurely.

Relying upon annual homicide measures is not a completely accurate way of studying victimization. For example, overall homicide rates in the United States have declined over the past several years. These annual decreases, as pronounced as they are, can generate the impression that this problem is becoming less serious. As a result, researchers have turned to a new way of looking at homicide data. They refer to lifetime murder victimization rates—the chances of dying from a homicide—to study this social problem more closely.

Table 8.3 presents lifetime murder victimization rates for the year 1997, the most recently available data. Reading the table is counterintuitive—the larger the number, the smaller the chance of being a homicide victim. For example, in the total population, an individual has a 1 in 4,009 chance of being a murder victim over his or her lifetime. White males have a 1 in 3,774 chance, while

Table 8.3 1997 Lifetime Murder Victimization Rates by Race and Sex for the United States

Age	Total	White Male	White Female	Black Male	Black Female
0–4	207	241	684	35	171
5–9	214	248	731	35	184
10–14	215	249	741	35	186
15–19	217	251	753	35	189
20–24	250	284	825	41	206
25–29	328	356	953	57	243
30–34	419	442	1,088	76	290
35–39	534	544	1,309	101	368
40–44	678	663	1,588	133	481
45–49	860	820	1,876	174	638
50–54	1,109	1,032	2,280	231	826
55–59	1,388	1,304	2,714	269	998
60–64	1,752	1,660	3,259	354	1,204
65–69	2,203	2,076	3,597	464	1,552
70–74	2,686	2,607	3,896	544	2,012
75–79	3,376	3,338	4,585	690	2,099
80+	4,009	3,774	5,228	856	2,375

Source: Federal Bureau of Investigation (2000). Crime in the United States 1999: Uniform Crime Reports. Washington, DC: U.S. Government Printing Office, Table 5.2. Retrieved on July 21, 2013, from http://www.fbi.gov/about-us/cjis/ucr/crime-in-the-u.s/1999/99sec5.pdf.

black males have a 1 in 856 chance. Therefore, those with the highest odds of being murdered are black males, followed in order by black females, white males, and, finally, white females. The figures also show that the odds of victimization are highest in the younger ages, with the odds falling greatly after the late teens/early twenties.

Weapon involvement, especially with firearms, is a potent predictor of lethal and non-lethal injuries (Saltzman et al., 1992). In fact, despite the recent downturn in homicide rates at the turn of the century, firearms remain the second leading cause of injury-related deaths in the United States (Gotsch et al., 2001; National Center for Health Statistics, 2006). According to the UCR, firearms are used in two-thirds of all homicides. Almost three-quarters of firearms-related homicides involve handguns. Knives and other sharp objects account for an additional 13% of the homicides. Compared with weapon use in aggravated assaults (where, as in homicides, the intent of the offense is to cause bodily harm to the victim), homicides are three times as likely to involve a firearm.

One fundamental concern is that the United States does not have a comprehensive national clearinghouse that stockpiles data regarding violent deaths. In 2003, the Centers for Disease Control and Prevention (CDC) launched the *National Violent Death Reporting System* (NVDRS). Today, that effort involves 18 states. The ultimate goal is to collect information for all suicides, homicides, and unintentional firearms deaths in all 50 states. The NVDRS utilizes records from a variety of sources (death certificates, medical examiner reports, police files, crime labs, fatality review teams, etc.) to compile a more comprehensive picture of victims, offenders, and circumstances (Centers for Disease Control and Prevention, 2013).

Findings from the NVDRS provide interesting results. For example, more than 70% of the suspects who killed an intimate partner subsequently committed suicide (Karch et al., 2012). Problems in a romantic relationship stood out as a precursor of suicide in one-third of the cases in 2009 (National Violent Injury Statistics System, 2005). Alcohol or other drugs are found in one-third or more of the homicide victims. It is anticipated that the NVDRS and its expansion to more states will add some more interesting findings and will fuel policy developments in the prevention of violence.

> ### 🌐 WEB ACTIVITY
> You can read more about the NVDRS on the Centers for Disease Control and Prevention website at **http://www.cdc. gov/violenceprevention/nvdrs/**

The Federal Bureau of Investigation (2013) also reports that homicide is, for the most part, an intra-racial event. In other words, victims and offenders tend to share the same racial backgrounds. Black offenders killed 91% of the black homicide victims, and white perpetrators murdered 83% of the white homicide victims. Similarly, males were more likely to die at the hands of male killers (but so were female victims).

One important distinction that has emerged in the literature is the notion of non-primary versus primary homicide (Parker, 1989; Parker & Smith, 1979; Smith & Parker, 1980). A *non-primary homicide* is a situation in which the victim did not know the offender very well, if at all. A *primary homicide* means that both the victim and the offender shared a primary, or face-to-face, relationship. Primary homicides span a variety of relationships. Some examples of primary relationships are spouses, parents and their children, siblings, and people who are very close to one another. Cases involving men who murder their wives or lovers are referred to as *intimate femicide*. Recognition of the "battered woman syndrome," discussed in detail in Chapter 10, has unearthed situations in which women retaliate by killing their husbands or lovers. The act of *parricide*, children who kill their parents, has not escaped attention. One can subdivide parricide into cases involving *patricide* (where the father is the victim) or *matricide* (where the mother is the victim). As we saw in Chapter 2, most victims know their assailants. A person is more likely to be killed by someone with whom he or she is acquainted than by a complete stranger.

Assault Victimization

The second form of personal crime to be addressed is assault. The UCR breaks assaults into two categories—aggravated assault (an Index offense) and simple assault (a Part II crime). The UCR defines *aggravated assault* as "an unlawful attack by one person upon another for the purpose of inflicting severe or aggravated bodily injury" (FBI, 2013). The definition further indicates that this offense typically involves a weapon and that the act is likely to result in death or serious physical harm to the victim. It is reasonable to view aggravated assault as a close companion to homicide in that the difference between the two is often nothing more than simply the death or survival of the victim. All other assaults fall into the simple assault category.

Measuring assault poses some interesting challenges. The UCR gathers data on the number of reported aggravated assaults but only arrests for simple assaults. The data, therefore, reflect two different, albeit related, things. The 2011 UCR reports that there was a total of 751,131 aggravated assaults (FBI, 2013). This translates into an offense rate of 241.1 per 100,000 persons. Of those reported aggravated assaults, the UCR records only 397,707 arrests, for a rate of 128 per 100,000 persons. Simple assaults, which are only measured in terms of arrest, come in at 955,620 arrests. This translates to 399.9 arrests for every 100,000 persons (FBI, 2013).

Unlike with homicide, the UCR collects very limited data on the other Part I Offenses. There is no equivalent to the *Supplementary Homicide Reports* (SHR) for aggravated assaults. While the *National Incident-Based Reporting System* (NIBRS) has great potential, its limited adoption by agencies does not allow for meaningful assessment of assaultive behavior. Alternatively, the NCVS does offer additional information.

WEB ACTIVITY

Investigate data on assaults using the UCR and NCVS data: **http://www.fbi. gov/about-us/cjis/ucr/crime-in-the-u.s/2010/crime-in-the-u.s.-2010/ violent-crime/aggravatedassaultmain** and **http://www.bjs.gov/index.cfm?ty =pbdetail&iid=2173**

The NCVS respondents report a total of 5 million assaults in 2011 (Truman & Planty, 2012). More than three-quarters of these victimizations (3.9 million) were simple assaults, with the remaining being aggravated assaults. These figures equate to an overall rate of 1,940 assaults per 100,000 population. The rates for aggravated and simple assault are 410 and 1,530, respectively (Truman & Planty, 2012). In the only instance in which the UCR and NCVS can be compared, the number and rate for aggravated assault are both greater in the victimization data.

Examination of the NCVS data provide further insight into assaultive behavior. Table 8.4 presents information on assault rates by various victim characteristics (Rand, 2009). Several facts are immediately apparent. First, males are more victimized than females. Second, blacks are the most victimized racial group.

Table 8.4 Assault Rates (per 100,000) by Victim Characteristics, NCVS, 2008

	Total	Aggravated Assault	Simple Assault
Male	1,830	390	1,450
Female	1,430	280	1,150
White	1,590	300	1,280
Black	1,850	520	1,330
Other	1,130	280	850
Hispanic	1,240	350	890
Non-Hispanic	1,690	330	1,360
12–15	3,520	610	2,900
16–19	3,000	560	2,450
20–24	3,030	870	2,150
25–34	2,050	400	1,650
35–49	1,410	270	1,140
50–64	970	200	770
65+	270	40	230

Source: Rand, M. R. (2009). Criminal Victimization, 2008. Washington, DC: Bureau of Justice Statistics.

Third, respondents of Hispanic origin are less likely overall to be assaulted or be the victims of a simple assault, but are more likely to be aggravated assault victims. Finally, assault victimization generally decreases with age (Rand, 2009).

It is also possible to look at the relationship between victim and offender in victimization survey data. As we noted earlier, most homicide victims know their assailants. For female assault victims, the offender is most often someone they know (see Table 8.5). Indeed, in 69% of aggravated assaults and 73% of simple assaults the female is victimized by a nonstranger. Male victims know their offenders roughly 50% of the time in both categories of assault, with 42–43% of the male assaults being committed by a stranger.

Robbery Victimization

The last personal crime we consider in this chapter is robbery. The Federal Bureau of Investigation (2013) defines *robbery* as "the taking or attempting to take anything of value from the care, custody, or control of a person or persons by force or threat of force or violence and/or by putting the victim in fear." Many individuals think of robbery as a property crime due to the fact that the offense requires a theft or attempted theft. It is classified by the FBI as a personal crime because the theft requires a face-to-face confrontation between the victim and offender that involves the potential use of force in completing the theft offense.

Table 8.5 Relationship between Victim and Offender in Assaults, NCVS, 2008

	Aggravated Assault	Simple Assault
Male Victims:		
Nonstranger	51%	50%
Intimate partner	8	2
Relative	5	3
Friend/acquaintance	38	44
Stranger	43	42
Unknown	6	7
Female Victims:		
Nonstranger	69%	73%
Intimate partner	17	26
Relative	8	9
Friend/acquaintance	44	39
Stranger	29	23
Unknown	2	4

Source: Compiled from Rand, M. R. (2009). Criminal Victimization, 2008. Washington, DC: Bureau of Justice Statistics.

Both the UCR and NCVS provide data on robbery events. The UCR shows that there were 354,396 robberies reported to the police in 2011 (FBI, 2013). This equates to an offense rate of 114 robberies for every 100,000 people in the population. According to the most recent victimization data, there were 556,760 robberies in 2011, or a victimization rate of 220 (Truman & Planty, 2012). These data show that, as in other comparisons of official and self-reports of crime, there is a significant number of offenses that are not included in the official police records. This is evident in the fact that the NCVS reports roughly 200,000 more robberies than the UCR, as well as a rate that is almost twice the official rate.

If one were to guess about the type of robberies that are most prominent in our communities, it would be reasonable to assume that most offenses take place in banks and convenience stores. This is certainly the image that emerges from watching the local news and reading the newspaper each day. However, the actual location of most robberies is very different from this depiction (see Table 8.6). According to the Federal Bureau of Investigation (2013), more than four out of every 10 robberies occur on the street. Only 2.1% of robberies involve a bank, and convenience stores are the target of only 5.1% of the crimes. Of particular note is the fact that 17% of all robberies take place within a residence. Assuming that most of these are at the residence of the victim, the degree of fear and anxiety that results from the event is even more pronounced for these victims. Not only have they been threatened with force or violence and lost their property, the feeling of safety in their home has been taken from them.

WEB ACTIVITY

What other information can you gather on robbery from the FBI and NCVS? See **http://www.fbi.gov/about-us/cjis/ucr/crime-in-the.u.s/2010/crime-in-the-u.s.-2010/violent-crime/robberymain** and **http://www.bjs.gov/index.cfm?ty=pbdetail&iid=2173** for assistance.

Table 8.6 Robbery Locations, UCR, 2011

Location	Percent
Street	44
Residence	17
Commercial establishment	13
Convenience store	5
Gas station	2
Bank	2
Miscellaneous	17

Source: Compiled by authors from Federal Bureau of Investigation (2013). Crime in the United States 2011. Washington, DC: U.S. Government Printing Office. Retrieved May 29, 2013, from http://www.fbi.gov/about-us/cjis/ucr/crime-in-the-u.s/2011/crime-in-the-u.s.-2011/tables/robbery-table-1.

The NCVS also provides information on the specifics of robbery victimizations. As with most of the street crimes, males are victimized at a much higher rate than females (Rand, 2009). Interestingly, women are robbed more often by someone they know than by a stranger. Fifty-three percent of female robbery victims claim that the offender was a nonstranger, with 16% being an intimate partner and 15% being another family member. Conversely, only one-third of males are victimized by someone they know. Indeed, 61% of male robbery victims are targeted by strangers (Rand, 2009). Blacks are by far the most victimized racial group. The rate for black robbery victimization is 550 per 100,000 population, which is almost three-and-a-half times as high as for whites and almost twice the rate for other races. Similarly, those of Hispanic origin are much more victimized than are non-Hispanics. The age distribution follows a similar pattern to other offenses, with younger individuals being the most victimized and the rate falling almost linearly as age increases.

A final piece of information that can be gleaned from the UCR and NCVS about robberies is the use or presence of a weapon during the event. There are distinctly different results between the two data sources (see Table 8.7). The UCR data show that 41.3% of the events involved a firearm of some sort, followed closely by the absence of a weapon. The NCVS reveals that almost half of the reported robberies did not involve any weapon, and only 24% involved a firearm. These figures raise the question of how to explain the discrepancy. The most logical explanation is that victims who are confronted with a weapon are more likely to report their victimization to the police than are other victims. Because the NCVS data are not dependent on the decision to report an offense to the authorities, they would not be skewed toward events in which a weapon was present.

Summary

Personal victimization impacts a large number of people every year. Besides the number of events, these offenses impact people in a variety of ways. As we saw in Chapter 4, being a victim of personal crime comes with costs ranging

Table 8.7 Weapon Use in Robberies

Weapon	UCR	NCVS
Firearms	41%	24%
Knives/Cutting Instruments	8	11
Strong-arm/No Weapon	42	49
Other	9	4
Don't Know	–	11

Source: Compiled by authors from Federal Bureau of Investigation (2013), Crime in the United States 2011. Washington, DC: U.S. Government Printing Office. Retrieved May 29, 2013, from http://www.fbi.gov/about-us/cjis/ucr/crime-in-the-u.s/2011/crime-in-the-u.s.-2011/tables/robbery-table-3; and Rand, M. R. (2009). Criminal Victimization, 2008. Washington, DC: Bureau of Justice Statistics.

from monetary losses due to medical care and insurance, to property losses in robbery, to lost time from work. Such victimization also raises people's fear and anxiety in their daily lives and routine. Personal victimization comes with high costs to both the victim and society.

ASSISTING THE PERSONAL CRIME VICTIM

The impact of a personal victimization can take a variety of forms. Besides the economic impact associated with the loss of property due to a robbery or the medical costs associated with a homicide or assault, there are psychological and emotional impacts from the crime. The National Center for Victims of Crime (2008) lists a number of typical victim responses that fall into the realm of psychological/emotional issues. These include shock, anxiety, anger, disbelief, despair, fear, depression, helplessness, shame, and guilt. It is not unusual for those experiencing such things to withdraw into themselves and suffer on their own. Unfortunately, assistance for violent crime victims generally extends mainly to informing them of how to report the crime, work with the criminal justice system and, possibly, apply for compensation. There is little help in dealing with the other issues listed here. Homicide has received perhaps the most attention in terms of how to respond to personal victimization.

Death is a topic that many people prefer to avoid discussing. In fact, mortality is a taboo subject. Thinking about it can generate a sense of anxiety, so many people shun the subject. Whenever a person dies, someone must inform the next of kin or other survivors of the deceased. The notifier who delivers this message must be prepared to deal with a wide range of responses. The recipients of this communication start the coping process immediately upon hearing the news. The manner in which the initial notification is made can impact the grieving process. This portion of the chapter discusses death notification procedures and then moves to a treatment of the bereavement process.

Death Notification

Death notification is not a pleasant responsibility. Often, this task falls to law enforcement officers, victim advocates, or representatives from the medical examiner's or coroner's office. Many agencies have adopted formal policies similar to what appears in Table 8.8 to help their personnel with the delivery of death-related news. Even if an explicit policy does not exist, death notification procedures usually follow a four-step process (Byers, 1991; Hendricks, 1984): (1) information gathering; (2) control and direction; (3) assessment; and (4) referral.

The first step in any death notification is the information-gathering phase. The person who is to deliver the news should anticipate the types of questions

Table 8.8 Law Enforcement Agency Policy Regarding Death Notification Procedures

A. Notification Within the City

1. When the next-of-kin of a deceased, seriously injured or seriously ill person lives in the City, the officer should make all notifications in person whenever practical. However, if this is not practical, the officer should contact the Communications Center and request another officer be dispatched to the residence for notification.

2. The officer delivering the notification should have as much information as possible to enable him or her to carry out the notification in a professional and considerate manner. When possible, contact between officers or with the Communications Center should be via telephone.

3. The officer should make every reasonable effort to notify the next-of-kin during his or her tour of duty.
   a. The officer shall not leave notification up to the hospital or other authorities.
   b. The officer shall note in the offense report the name of the person notified, relationship and time accomplished.

4. The officer, when possible, should stand by after the notification has been made and render additional assistance to the next-of-kin and, when necessary:
   a. contact clergy;
   b. contact medical assistance;
   c. contact other family members.

Source: Tallahassee Police Department (2007). Policy Manual: Death Notification. Tallahassee, FL: City of Tallahassee.

that the recipients may ask and determine the appropriate responses to those inquiries. The most important element here is to obtain and verify the identification of the deceased. The name of the person, gender, age, address, and any other personal identifiers are of paramount importance. Similar information about the survivor(s) is also essential. Also valuable is information on the circumstances surrounding the death, including time and place. Prior to making the actual notification, the deliverer should confirm that he or she is at the correct location and has reached the appropriate party.

Step two in the death notification process is control and direction. It is the responsibility of the notifier to define the situation for the survivor by informing him or her of the unfortunate news. The deliverer should be factual, honest, and deliberate in the choice of words. Experts advise that it is best to avoid such euphemisms as "He's gone to a better place" or "She is looking down upon us now" (Byers, 1991; Hendricks, 1984). As the impact begins to take effect upon the survivor, the third phase—the assessment stage—begins to unfold.

The primary task of the notifier during the assessment stage is to gauge how the bereaved reacts to the disturbing message. Should the recipient show signs of self-blame, or self-destructive behavior such as suicide, the deliverer will need to rechannel, guide, or prod the person out of this frame of mind. If the situation worsens, other resources (such as a clergy member, a physician, a victim advocate, another survivor, or a neighbor) might be in a better position to assist. The objective of this phase is to ensure the well-being of the survivor(s).

The last stage is called *referral*. Survivors will become flooded with a number of concerns. They will need immediate information about how to make funeral arrangements, how to get the body released from the medical examiner's office, what police procedures must transpire, and the like. Once the situation is under control, the notifier has completed his or her assignment and may leave the scene.

> **WEB ACTIVITY**
>
> Read the article on death notification on the Officer.com website. What are the issues and the recommendations made for handling this task? **http://www.officer.com/article/10249064/death-notification-breaking-the-bad-news**

It is important to realize that leaving the scene does not mean that the situation has ended for the notifier. Emergency responders sometimes become deeply immersed in these events and have their own feelings to sort through once the formal assignment is completed (Hendricks, 1984; McCarroll et al., 1993; Walker, 1990). Many agencies will hold a debriefing session for members after a huge disaster or a major catastrophe has subsided. The intent is to relieve any stress reactions that workers may have developed during the crisis. These sessions allow workers to vent their feelings, receive information that they may have lacked during the incident, and begin readjusting to the daily routine.

The Bereavement Process

As we will learn in Chapter 9, people who experience a calamity inevitably find themselves in the midst of a crisis. The death of a significant other, particularly through a homicide, qualifies as a sudden, emotionally shattering event that can quickly propel survivors deep into a crisis state. Based upon what experts know about the crisis reaction repair cycle, recovery usually proceeds in a very predictable fashion.

The complete lack of any warning associated with most homicides denies survivors a chance to prepare beforehand for such excruciating news. Survivors do not have the luxury of *anticipatory grief*—the preparations that people can make to cushion the impact of death when a loss is imminent or expected to take place. For example, the diagnosis of a terminal illness in an elderly relative permits family members to brace themselves for the inevitable. This advance warning alerts people to what is coming, gives them time to search for appropriate coping mechanisms, and

> **WEB ACTIVITY**
>
> Explore a wide array of information and responses on grief due to personal crime at **http://www.fbi.gov/about-us/cjis/ucr/crime-in-the-u.s/2010/crime-in-the-u.s.-2010/violent-crime/robberymain**

enables survivors to adapt expeditiously to the loss. Homicide survivors lack this preparation. They are thrust into a crisis state unexpectedly without any prior warning or any chance to adjust their readiness.

Most homicide victims are men under the age of 40. This demographic profile means that the survivors of homicide victims will face a host of challenges. Generally speaking, it is easier to cope with timely, as opposed to "off-time," deaths (Detmer & Lamberti, 1991; Parry & Thornwall, 1992). At this point in the life cycle, most men have established a family unit. Their children will grow up without their father. The widow must assume all family responsibilities, including financial burdens. While Social Security and insurance may help defray some expenses, the role structure of the nuclear family unit often changes. Older children may take on more caretaking functions for younger siblings. Some women may find that they must re-enter the job market on a more sustained basis. In short, the survivors must make many adaptations to compensate for the loss of a loved one.

Relatively little research has been devoted to the response of homicide survivors to the loss of a loved one. Kübler-Ross (1969) outlined four stages to the *grief process*: (1) shock and denial; (2) anger; (3) isolation; and (4) acceptance/recovery. The first stage is shock and denial. Immediately after being informed of the death, the survivor reacts by denying that the information is true and tends to shut out all input concerning the event. This reaction is a short-term, self-protective mechanism that serves to cushion the blow. The second stage is anger. Here the survivor vents his or her rage, frustration, and anger toward anyone or anything available. This anger may be toward the bearer of the news, the doctors who could not save the victim, the offender, society, or even him- or herself. Third, the survivor tends to isolate him- or herself from others. Isolation reflects different emotions ranging from the uncertainty of how to deal with others to the feeling that there is no one to whom the survivor can turn. Finally, the survivor begins to resume some form of normal activities in the acceptance/recovery stage. While the death remains with the individual, the event is incorporated into the daily routine of the individual as he or she realizes that life must continue.

There is no predetermined timetable for grief resolution. It may take years before survivors can put the incident behind them. The bereavement process may be continuous and fluid, with members sometimes regressing to early stages. Recovery may be prolonged because of case processing by the criminal justice system. What little research that does exist on homicide survivors, though, suggests that these intense feelings diminish over time and the healing eventually tracks a typical recovery pattern (Horne, 2003; Kitson et al., 1991; Range & Niss, 1990).

There is also evidence that different survivors adapt and cope with homicide in various ways. Key (1992) identified five *homicide survivor patterns* based on his clinical experience with such individuals. These patterns are highly related to the lifestyle and social setting of the victim and the survivor. The five survival patterns correspond to: (1) the alcohol- or other drug-related murder; (2) the domestic violence homicide; (3) the gang-related murder; (4) the isolated sudden murder; and (5) the serial murder. The survivor in each of these situations reacts differently.

For example, in the alcohol- or other drug-related murder survivor pattern, the survivor typically knew of the victim's use and/or trafficking behavior. The survivor had some warning ahead of time that the victim was involved in potentially dangerous behavior and, consequently, was able to prepare somewhat for the loss of the victim. The survivor may even actually feel a sense of relief once the event occurs.

In the domestic violence homicide survival pattern, the survivor may feel some personal guilt for failing to intervene when early signs of abuse and problems emerged. The survivor may believe that if he or she had become involved, the victim may still be alive.

The gang-related homicide is typically expected by the survivor, who feels he or she had no control over the event. In many cases, the survivor may believe that the victim was also a homicide offender and it was only a matter of time until the offender became a victim.

The final two categories, isolated sudden murder survival pattern and the serial murder survival pattern, both reflect situations in which the death was totally unexpected. These are the scenarios that correspond to the classic image of an unsuspected homicide victimization. Here, the survivor experiences the typical grief pattern outlined earlier. There are feelings of denial, anger, self-blame, guilt, isolation, and eventual re-emergence to everyday reality. Key (1992) notes that these survival patterns are not exhaustive; not all possible patterns are included. Rather, he offers these patterns as illustrations of how various people respond to a homicide event in different ways based on the circumstances and background of both the victim and the survivor.

Critical to the bereavement process is the provision of support for the survivor. This support most likely begins with the police officer or physician who notifies the survivor and then lasts for a long period of time. An ideal support network can help with a myriad of different things facing the survivor. It certainly would include some offer of counseling, whether in an individual or a group setting. While one might assume that these services are common in our society, such assistance is often unknown to the survivor. One method that has emerged in many communities in recent years has been homicide support groups. These groups serve many immediate and long-term needs. In addition, they may involve themselves in community outreach programs, such as those teaching youths about the impact of homicide (Johnson & Young, 1992). Inevitably, the homicide survivor goes on with his or her life. The degree to which survivors receive assistance in that process, however, differs greatly from place to place.

PROPERTY VICTIMIZATION

People can suffer property victimization in a number of different ways. Some forms of property victimization tend to raise little fear or concern, such as the theft of a book or an item sitting idle in the yard. Others generate a great deal of anxiety and fear on the part of the victim. The best example of this is when an individual's home is burglarized (particularly if the person was present at the time). Other forms of property victimization can cause a lot of financial pain and hardship, but result in little actual fear, such as in the case of motor vehicle theft. The common denominator of all of the crimes is the financial loss that faces the victim.

Burglary

Of all the property crimes, burglary probably engenders the greatest level of angst. Indeed, in 2009, almost half of those responding to a Gallup poll reported worrying about their home being burglarized when they were not at home, and one-third worried about a burglary when they were at home (Maguire, 2010). These levels of worry cut across both males and females, as well as different races. This is understandable given the fact that it is in the home where people expect to be free from the dangers of the outside world. The very act of burglary destroys that perception and removes the "safe" sanctuary people count on having.

The FBI's UCR program defines *burglary* as "the unlawful entry of a structure to commit a felony or theft" (FBI, 2013). While most people think of burglary as involving their home, it is not confined to where an individual lives. A variety of structures can be the target of burglary, including a house, an apartment, a barn, an office or business, or a boat. Additionally, there is no need to have used force in entering the structure. Burglary can occur when an individual simply enters a structure without the legal right to do so. The key to the definition is that the person entering the structure is doing so with the intent to commit either a felony offense (such as an assault or rape) or a theft offense.

Burglary is not a rare event. According to the FBI's UCR, there were almost 2.2 million burglaries committed in 2011. Of these, 1.4 million were committed against a residence, with the balance involving a business (FBI, 2013). The NCVS also gathers information on burglaries, although it is limited to households. The 2011 NCVS uncovered more than 3.6 million household burglaries (Truman & Planty, 2012). It is important to note that the victimization data reveal more than a million more total offenses and approximately 2.5 times the number of burglaries against households.

Perhaps a better way to look at the offense data is to consider the offense rates. *Offense rates* reflect the number of offenses per some number of individuals (or other unit of analysis). The FBI typically calculates rates based on offenses per 100,000 individuals. Comparably, the NCVS offers rates per 1,000 individuals or households. The 2011 UCR burglary rate was 703.2 per 100,000 population (FBI, 2013), while the NCVS rate was 2,940 per 100,000 households (Truman & Planty, 2012). Unfortunately, there is no way to directly compare these numbers, because one relies on the number of people and the other uses the number of households. In either case, the figures show that burglary impacts a substantial number of people in the United States.

🌐 **WEB ACTIVITY**

Compare burglary data from the UCR and the NCVS. What unique things do you find? What value does each hold? **http:// www.fbi.gov/about-us/cjis/ucr/crime- in-the-u.s/2011/crime-in-the-u.s.-2011/ property-crime/burglary** and **http:// www.bjs.gov/index.cfm?ty= pbdetail&iid=2173**

The timing of burglaries often prompts surprise among the populace. Roughly half of all residential burglaries take place during the day. Meanwhile, for businesses, roughly one-third are during the day, with two-thirds at night (FBI, 2013). The reasons for this are actually pretty simple. It is during the day that most residences are empty and more attractive to potential offenders. Businesses, however, are occupied during the day (and often into the evenings) with both customers and staff, thus making them less attractive and pushing the offenders to more late night hours if they want to avoid contact with people.

Larceny/Theft

Larceny/theft is defined as "the unlawful taking, carrying, leading or riding away of property from the possession or constructive possession of another" (FBI, 2013). This definition covers a wide range of theft behaviors, including the simple taking of unattended property from any location (such as a yard or desk), theft of motor vehicle parts, theft from a store (i.e., shoplifting), or even picking someone's pocket or purse. Throughout these actions is the absence of a confrontation with the victim or the use of force to take the property. Among the theft offenses not covered under this heading are fraud, forgery, embezzlement, and similar offenses. Many times the victim may not even be immediately aware of the loss. Indeed, it is possible that the victim assumes that the property is simply lost, rather than stolen.

Larceny/theft is a very common offense. According to the Federal Bureau of Investigation (2013), there were almost 6.2 million offenses in 2011, accounting for two-thirds of all property crimes (see Table 8.9). The most common forms are from motor vehicles (24.8%) and shoplifting (17.5%). In terms of overall rate of offending, there are 1,649 larceny/thefts for every 100,000 persons. The 2011 NCVS reports almost 13 million personal thefts (Truman & Planty, 2012). Again, the victimization figures reveal twice as many offenses as the official police data. The victimization rates are similarly higher in the

Table 8.9 Types of Larceny/Theft, 2011

Type	Frequency	%
Pocket-picking	23,150	0.4
Purse-snatching	23,642	0.4
Shoplifting	940,903	17.5
From motor vehicles (except accessories)	1,330,396	24.8
Motor vehicle accessories	434,732	8.1
Bicycles	189,428	3.5
From buildings	635,582	11.8
From coin-operated machines	17,055	0.3
All others	1,774,967	33.1
Total	5,369,855	

Source: Adapted from FBI (2013). Crime in the United States 2011. Washington, DC: U.S. Government Printing Office. Retrieved June 1, 2013, from http://www.fbi.gov/about-us/cjis/ucr/crime-in-the-u.s/2011/crime-in-the-u.s.-2011/tables/table-23.

NCVS, with 10,420 thefts per 100,000 population (ages 12 and older). More than one in 10 households experiences a theft victimization each year.

Motor Vehicle Theft

The loss of a car is a major source of stress due to the fact that most everyone relies on a motor vehicle to get to and from work, school, shopping, entertainment, and appointments. Few cities have a transportation infrastructure that allows people to complete all their daily tasks without access to personal transportation. A broken-down car on the way to work causes great angst to many individuals. The loss of a motor vehicle due to theft similarly raises both anxiety and anger.

According to the Federal Bureau of Investigation (2013), *motor vehicle theft* involves "the theft or attempted theft of a motor vehicle." While most people think of cars (and some assume the FBI definition is "auto theft"), motor vehicle theft covers the theft of a wide range of land-based vehicles, including automobiles and trucks, motorcycles, buses, sport utility vehicles, and snowmobiles. Not covered in this classification are farm machinery, boats, airplanes, trains, and construction equipment.

Unlike many other offense categories, motor vehicle theft data are very similar across both official and victimization sources. In 2011, there were 715,373 motor vehicle thefts according to the Federal Bureau of Investigation (2013) and 628,070 reported by the NCVS (Truman & Planty, 2012). The rates for motor vehicle theft are 229.6 per 100,000 people (UCR) and 510 per household (NCVS). Explaining the high levels of reported motor vehicle theft in both official and victimization sources is easy and straightforward. Motor vehicles are a major expense for most any household, thus most are insured against loss.

In some cases, insurance is mandated, particularly if the vehicle is financed or the state requires some form of insurance. Most insurance policies require that the theft be reported to the authorities before any payments will be made. This fact results in a high level of official reports that mirror the unofficial reports.

Arson

The last of the UCR Part I property crimes is arson. According to the Federal Bureau of Investigation (2013), *arson* is "any willful or malicious burning or attempting to burn, with or without intent to defraud, a dwelling house, public building, motor vehicle or aircraft, personal property of another, etc." Unlike the other crime categories, the UCR does not offer any estimates on the extent of arson due to the variation in reporting practices by police agencies. Additionally, arson is not typically addressed in victimization surveys.

More than 52,000 arson cases were reported in 2011 by 15,640 law enforcement agencies (FBI, 2013). Nationally there were more than 18 arsons per 100,000 population. Fewer than 50% were of structures, and almost one-quarter were of some type of motor vehicle. In terms of structures, roughly 81% were occupied at the time of the offense.

OTHER ECONOMIC CRIMES

The property crimes discussed so far are often considered under the general heading of "street crimes." They are more common events that have faced many victims throughout the years. That does not make them unimportant or less problematic for the victims. What is missing from this group of offenses is the growing body of economic crimes that attack the victim through more subtle and often hidden ways.

These economic crimes have vestiges of some traditional property offenses, but also rely upon emerging electronic technology to prey on victims. A common cornerstone to these offenses is a type of fraud. What sets fraud apart from other property crimes is the secrecy and deception involved in the activity. Often, victims do not immediately know they have been victimized. Fraud is far from a new crime category. Indeed, fraud is a UCR Part II offense. The difference today is in how the fraud is completed. In this section we will look at four broad categories of offenses: fraud (in its more traditional forms), identity theft, mass-marketing fraud, and cybercrime against businesses.

Traditional Fraud

Fraud can be defined as "an act in which attempts are made to deceive with promises of goods, services, or financial benefits that do not exist, were never intended to be provided, or were misrepresented" (Office for Victims of Crime,

1998a). The key component of the definition is the use of deception in completion of the crime. Often this means that the victim is offered something or invited to participate in something that promises an attractive payoff, but requires the victim to provide information or finances in advance of the payoff. Unfortunately, the victim never realizes the promised payoff and loses what he or she initially provided.

The methods by which traditional fraud was carried out are wide and varied. Some of the common types of fraud include the following:

- Home repair schemes: The victim is asked for "up-front" money as an initial down payment or for "supplies;" the offender typically fails to return to complete the work; often targets the elderly.
- Appliance or auto repair schemes: Similar to home repair schemes, although the repair may not have been needed in the first place or was not completed at all.
- Insurance fraud: The victim is sold medical or life insurance that is worthless or not what was promised.
- Award scams: The victim wins a contest or prize but must pay a fee to process the transactions; the prize or contest may not exist or the fee paid is greater than the value of the prize.
- Membership fraud: The individual is sold a membership (sometimes a lifetime membership) in a club or business that either is nonexistent or goes out of business shortly after the sale.
- Financial or investment fraud: A financial advisor provides misleading or false information leading to losses by the victim; a loan requires a processing fee and once paid the loan is never awarded.
- Charity fraud: The offender solicits funds ostensibly on behalf of a charity; the charity either does not exist or the offender does not turn the funds over to the charity.
- 900 number phone scams: Victims are enticed to call a number and are billed for phone time at rates far in excess of what is normal; a caller may contact a regular phone number and then agrees to be transferred to another person, unaware that the transfer is to a premium charge line.

There is a wide range of other forms of fraud, as well as many variations on those listed above. Throughout these offenses the victim generally does not realize that he or she has been victimized until days, weeks, or months later.

Gauging the extent of fraud is very difficult. This is due largely to the secrecy of the initial act. A contributing factor to the lack of information is the reluctance of many victims to report the crimes. There is a level of shame felt by victims for being duped. On a more practical level, the UCR does not gather systematic data on fraud. What is collected by the UCR are figures on the number of arrests for fraud. In 2011, a total of 168,217 arrests were made. This translates into an arrest rate of 53.7 (FBI, 2013). The Office for Victims of Crime (1998a) suggests that roughly 85% of fraud offenses are not reported to the police. No other official sources of data exist on fraud, and victimization surveys generally do not include questions on this type of crime.

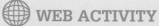

WEB ACTIVITY

Investigate fraud and responses to fraud at **http://www.stopfraud.gov/**

One of the few attempts to gauge the extent of fraud using survey methods was conducted in 1991 and published in 1995. Titus, Heinzelmann, and Boyle (1995) conducted a national phone survey of 1,246 households. Respondents were asked to report on their experience as a victim of 22 forms of fraud. The results show that 58% of the respondents had been the victim (or attempted victim) of at least one form of fraud over their lifetimes. Roughly one-third of those fraud events took place within the past year, and 48% of those events resulted in a successful fraud being committed. Among the most common and successful forms of fraud were appliance/auto repair, 900 number fraud, subscription, and warranty fraud (Titus et al., 1995).

Identity Theft

Identity theft is a common term heard in today's society, although the term *identity theft* was first introduced only a short time ago. McNally and Newman (2008) trace the root of the term to published newspaper reports in the late 1980s. There is no single accepted definition for identity theft, and it was not legally defined until passage of the Federal Identity Theft and Assumption Deterrence Act in 1998 (see Table 8.10). This is a relatively broad definition that covers a range of activities from use of false documents to the production of such documents. A more general, concise definition is that *identity theft* "refers to an instance in which an individual's personal information is used by another to facilitate an act of fraud" (McNally & Newman, 2008).

The information necessary for an individual to steal someone's identity can come from a wide array of sources. Newman (2008) outlines four primary sources: public records, commercial databases, employment/school records, and family records. A wide range of different documentation can be obtained from these sources. Included in these documents are birth certificates, death certificates, Social Security numbers, passports, credit card and revolving charge accounts, marriage licenses, school records, utility bills, addresses and phone numbers, and tax records. All of these items can be used by offenders in setting up fraudulent identities and accounts.

WEB ACTIVITY

The Federal Trade Commission has taken a lead in addressing identity theft and offers a great deal of information at **http://www.consumer.ftc.gov/features/feature-0014-identity-theft**

A primary concern is how potential offenders access these records and documentation in order to steal someone's identity. The methods vary, although the

> **Table 8.10** Federal Identity Theft and Assumption Deterrence Act
>
> Title 18 Section 1028 of the United States Code defines Identity Theft as when an individual:
>
> 1. knowingly and without lawful authority produces an identification document or a false identification document;
>
> 2. knowingly transfers an identification document or a false identification document knowing that such document was stolen or produced without lawful authority;
>
> 3. knowingly possesses with intent to use unlawfully or transfer unlawfully five or more identification documents (other than those issued lawfully for the use of the possessor) or false identification documents;
>
> 4. knowingly possesses an identification document (other than one issued lawfully for the use of the possessor) or a false identification document, with the intent such document be used to defraud the United States;
>
> 5. knowingly produces, transfers, or possesses a document—making implement with the intent such document—making implement will be used in the production of a false identification document or another document—making implement which will be so used;
>
> 6. knowingly possesses an identification document that is or appears to be an identification document of the United States which is stolen or produced without lawful authority knowing that such document was stolen or produced without such authority . . .; or
>
> 7. knowingly transfers or uses, without lawful authority, a means of identification of another person with the intent to commit, or to aid or abet, any unlawful activity that constitutes a violation of Federal law or that constitutes a felony under any applicable State or local law.
>
> *Source: Title 18,* United States Code, § 1028.

use of the Internet has largely moved the access into the electronic realm. One traditional method involves the simple theft of mail, which provides addresses, account numbers, personal information, and other items useful in appropriating an individual's identity. Another traditional method entails the theft of an individual's wallet, purse, or passport. A variation is an offender copying an individual's information provided in a legitimate transaction and using that information again later. In many cases the theft is committed by someone the victim knows.

Today, identity theft is closely aligned with the Internet and electronic records. As society has moved toward paperless records and the storage of information on computers, offenders no longer have to have physical access to the records. Instead, they can access the information over the Internet by either having lawful access to the files, or illegally gaining entry to the records by hacking into a computer system. *Phishing* is another method that involves acquiring information electronically by the offender posing as a legitimate business that requires the individual to provide personal information, including account information. These electronic methods can be used from next door or from around the world. Based on findings from a national survey of almost 5,000 adults conducted in 2006, most victims did not even know they were victimized or how it was done (56%) (Synovate,

Table 8.11 Methods by Which Information Is Taken

Method	Percent
Know the thief	16
Purchase or other transaction	7
From wallet	5
From a company	5
Mail	2
Computer hacking	1
Phishing	1
Some other way	7
Don't know	56

Source: Constructed by authors from Synovate (2007). Federal Trade Commission— 2006 Identity Theft Survey Report. *McLean, VA: Synovate.*

2007). Sixteen percent claimed to know the offender, and 7% noted that the theft was due to a past purchase or financial transaction (Table 8.11).

Identity theft can take a variety of forms. The NCVS has included questions on identity theft since 2004 (Baum, 2007). The Federal Trade Commission (FTC) has surveyed the public on identity theft since 2003 (Synovate, 2007). According to the NCVS, roughly 8.6 million households were the victims of identity theft in 2010 (see Table 8.12). Theft involving existing credit cards or other existing accounts is the most common form of identity theft. The establishment of new accounts and the theft of personal information are also prevalent forms of theft.

Information on identity theft offers a wealth of additional information. FTC data reveal that 61% of the existing accounts involved in identity theft are credit card accounts, followed by checking and savings accounts (33%), telephone accounts (11%), and Internet payment accounts (5%) (Synovate, 2007). The NCVS data show that most victims of identity theft are from households with

Table 8.12 Types and Extent of Identity Theft

Type	NCVS
Existing credit cards	4,625,100
Other existing accounts	2,195,900
Personal information	775,400
Multiple forms	975,500
Total	8,571,900

Source: Constructed by authors from Langton (2011). Identity Theft Reported by Households, 2005–2010. *Washington, DC: Bureau of Justice Statistics. Numbers have been rounded.*

incomes of $75,000 and more (Langton, 2011). Information from the NCVS suggests that this form of crime has been on the increase since the first survey was completed in 2003. Many victims fail to realize that a theft has occurred until long after the event. The most common means by which victims discovered the theft was the misuse or attempted misuse of a credit card (64.1%) (Langton, 2011).

Mass-Marketing Fraud

In recent years, fraud has greatly expanded to encompass the use of mass-marketing techniques. The Federal Bureau of Investigation (2010a) defines *mass-marketing fraud* as:

> fraud schemes that use mass-communications media—including telephones, the Internet, mass mailings, television, radio, and even personal contact—to contact, solicit, and obtain money, funds, or other items of value from multiple victims in one or more jurisdictions.

The U.S. Department of Justice (2010a) outlines two broad types of mass-marketing fraud. The first involves schemes that seek to obtain relatively small amounts of money from a large number of victims. In this case, the profit comes from the sheer number of individuals who are victimized. The second form seeks to maximize the return on a smaller number of potential victims; this type targets wealthier victims.

A unique feature of this type of fraud is the fact that the offenders can target victims virtually anywhere in the world. The use of mail, telephones, the Internet, and the mass media makes borders, whether physical or symbolic, almost meaningless. While there are a number of different mass-marketing fraud schemes, there are several commonalities in the approaches. First is the use of some form of mass communication to reach a wide range of potential victims spread over a large geographic area (often internationally). A second common feature is the attempt to convince victims to provide funds or access to funds in return for a promised service or benefit. Some of these schemes can appear very similar to those seen earlier under identity theft (see Figure 8.1).

The U.S. Department of Justice (2010a) outlines 11 types of mass-marketing fraud under three general headings (see Table 8.13). The forms under *advance fee fraud schemes* all share the common theme of enticing victims to send funds or pay fees in exchange for a promised item or service that would greatly benefit the victim. In all cases either the victim receives nothing or the item/service received is of greatly inferior value. *Bank and financial account schemes* involve getting victims to disclose personal and financial information that the offender can use to access the victim's funds or valuables. This activity typically involves contact over an electronic medium, such as the Internet or telephone. Finally, *investment opportunities schemes* entail the manipulation of stocks or securities to raise or lower their value. The offender, knowing that the information being used to alter the price is false, is able to make a profit by taking action on the true value at the expense of the victim who acts on the false information.

Gauging the extent of mass-market fraud schemes is not an easy task. Three main reasons can be offered for the lack of definitive data on these offenses. First, many of these offenses are relatively new crime forms, and both the public and the criminal justice system are playing catch-up in identifying and addressing them. Second, there is no systematic method for collecting and disseminating information on mass-market crimes. While the FBI and other agencies are working to gather such data, the work is still in its infancy. Third, many individuals either do not know they have been victimized or do not report the event to the authorities due to embarrassment and shame. Despite these facts, we can glean some information on the extent and impact of mass-marketing fraud.

Most of the information that is available is from victim surveys or complaints filed by victims. The UK Office of Fair Trading (2006) reports that almost half of their survey respondents had been approached by a scammer in some way over their lifetimes. Of those individuals, 8% had been the victim of some form of scam, with most of the events taking place in the past year. The survey report estimates that more than 3.2 million people (6.5% of the UK adult population) are victimized every year. In the United States, a Federal Trade Commission survey on consumer fraud claims that 10.8% of the U.S. adult population was victimized in 2011, with a total of almost 38 million fraud incidents (Anderson, 2013). Table 8.14 presents data on the types of fraud reported in the FTC survey. The most common form involves weight-loss products, followed by prize promotion and work-at-home programs. An alternative source of data comes from the Internet Crime Complaint Center. In 2012, the Center received 289,874 complaints (Internet Crime Complaint Center, 2013). Total losses exceeded $525 million with an average loss of $1,813. It is important to note that these data reflect only those incidents reported to that office and not victimizations reported to any other agency.

WEB ACTIVITY

Read more about mass-marketing fraud and responses for victims and society at **http://www.justice.gov/criminal/fraud/internet/**

FIGURE 8.1 Some of the 4,500 false documents found as a result of a month-long operation investigating mass-marketing fraud. Millions of people have handed over cash after being approached by scammers by e-mail, letter, or telephone. *Credit: SOCA/PA Wire URN:5207017 (Press Association via AP Images).*

Table 8.13 Types of Mass-Marketing Fraud

Advance Fee Fraud Schemes

- *Auction and Retail Schemes:* Offer high value items but require the victim to send money in advance. The scheme often fails to deliver the goods or sends poor quality goods.
- *Business Opportunity/"Work-at-Home" Schemes Online:* Victims are offered the chance to make lots of money but need to purchase materials or information in order to participate.
- *Credit Card Interest Reduction Schemes:* Offer to lower credit card debt in exchange for an up-front fee.
- *Inheritance Schemes:* The victim is told he or she has been named as a beneficiary and needs to make advance payments to pay for fees and taxes before the inheritance can be paid.
- *Lottery/Prize/Sweepstakes Schemes:* The victim is told he or she has won a prize but must pay fees or taxes before receiving the prize.
- *Online Sales Schemes:* "Buyers" of an item send a (counterfeit) check for more than the selling price of an item and then ask the seller (the victim) to wire the excess funds back.
- *"Romance" Schemes:* Online romances that lead to the victim sending money or valuables to the offender.

Bank and Financial Account Schemes

- *"Phishing:"* Emails and websites that get the victim to disclose personal and financial data.
- *"Vishing:"* Similar to phishing only using a telephone.

Investment Opportunities Schemes

- *"Pump-and-Dump" Schemes:* Falsely building up the value of a stock in order for the offender to dump his or her holdings for a profit.
- *Short-Selling ("Scalping") Schemes:* Similar to pump-and-dump in that false information is used to cause a decrease in a stock price.

Source: Compiled by authors from U.S. Department of Justice (2010a). Mass-Marketing Fraud. Retrieved December 6, 2013, from http://www.justice.gov/criminal/fraud/internet/.

Cybercrime Against Businesses

Cybercrime can be defined as "crime that occurs when computers or computer networks are involved as tools, locations, or targets of crime" (Newman, 2010). The growth of the Internet over the past two decades has greatly expanded the ability of offenders to target new and diverse victims. No longer is it necessary to be geographically proximate to the victim to commit an offense. Some of the frauds already discussed in this chapter rely on or use computer technology and the Internet to complete the event. Newman (2010) lists seven types of cybercrime: hacking into computer systems; privacy violations (i.e., spying on the victim's computer use); identity theft; phishing; information theft (typically for resale); denial of service (causing systems or the Internet to collapse);

Table 8.14 Estimated Number of Fraud Incidents, 2011

Type	Number of Incidents (millions)	Incidents per Victim
Weight-loss products	7.6	1.5
Prize promotions	2.9	1.2
Work-at-home programs	2.8	1.6
Unauthorized billing – Buyers' Clubs	2.3	1.2
Unauthorized billing – Internet services credit card	2.2	1.2
Insurance	2.2	1.7
Credit repair	2.0	1.2
Debt relief	1.7	1.1
Business opportunity	1.2	1.1
Advance fee loans	0.9	1.2
Mortgage relief	0.8	1.0
Pyramid schemes	0.7	1.1
Counterfeit check scams	0.6	1.3
Government job offers	0.6	1.2
Grant scams	0.2	1.0

Source: Constructed by authors from Anderson, K. B. (2013). Consumer Fraud in the United States, 2011: The Third FTC Survey. *Washington, DC: Federal Trade Commission. Retrieved June 4, 2013, from http://www.ftc.gov/reports/consumer-fraud-united-states-2011-third-ftc-survey.*

and virus attacks (releasing viruses into computers). What is not included in this list is the use of the Internet to promote deviant activities, such as child pornography or other sexual behaviors. In some cases these actions are committed for financial gain; in others it is simply to disrupt the activity of the victim.

As we have dealt with several forms of fraud and theft that use computers and the Internet earlier in this chapter, we will turn our focus here to cybercrime against businesses. Individuals and households are not the only victims of fraud and theft. Businesses are prime targets of a wide range of property offenses, and the growth of computers and the Internet has opened new avenues for exploiting businesses. Recognizing the threat potential of computer crime, the U.S. Department of Justice and the Department of Homeland Security inaugurated the National Computer Security Survey in 2005 (Rantala, 2008). Three forms of cybercrime were considered in the survey: *cyber attacks*—computer viruses, denials of service, and electronic vandalism or sabotage; *cyber theft*—theft of money, computer-based embezzlement, theft of intellectual property, fraud, and theft of data; and other incidents—adware, spyware, hacking, phishing, and so on.

In the 2005 survey, a total of 7,818 businesses responded, with two-thirds reporting some form of cyber attack (Rantala, 2008). Almost 60% reported a cyber attack, while 11% reported cyber theft, and one-fourth indicated some other form of cyber victimization. The most common form of cyber attack involved being infected with a virus. Most businesses were victimized more than once. In total, more than 22 million incidents of cybercrime were uncovered in the survey, with three-quarters of those incidents involving use of the Internet (Rantala, 2008).

The survey also provides some insight into the offenders in cybercrimes. A majority of suspected offenders (71%) are outsiders to the business, regardless of the type of incident (Rantala, 2008). Similarly, three-quarters of cyber attacks and 72% of other cyber incidents appear to be committed by outsiders. Conversely, 74% of the suspected offenders in cyber thefts are insiders, with the bulk of these suspects involved in embezzlement cases (Rantala, 2008). Despite the great number of events, especially when an insider is suspected to be the culprit, only 15% reported the crime to law enforcement. Businesses are more apt to report the events to other business organizations (Rantala, 2008).

It is easy to ignore cybercrime against businesses in discussions of victimization. Indeed, many discussions of crime victims focus on individuals and families as victims and fail to examine businesses as victims. This is unfortunate because the harm to businesses has implications for both society and individuals. For society, the loss incurred by businesses can have negative impacts on the viability of companies to stay in business and thus have an impact on communities and employees. For individuals, cybercrime against businesses can result in higher prices and costs of products as the businesses pass on the losses to the consumers. Individuals also suffer from lost work time and unemployment as businesses have to adjust to the victimizations. It is important to note that individuals and society suffer indirectly from the victimization of businesses.

Summary of Property Crime

Property crime is much greater than depicted in UCR and victimization reports of burglary, larceny/theft, motor vehicle theft, and arson. Recent years have seen a great growth in fraud offenses using computers, the Internet, and other electronic media. These are not new types of crimes; rather, they are a modern version of fraud crimes that have been around for a long time. The reach of these new fraud offenses places many more individuals in a vulnerable position, and the losses resulting from the offenses reach astronomical levels. Methods of addressing these offenses are still in the development stage. What also needs to be developed are means of assisting those who are victimized by property crimes.

ASSISTING THE PROPERTY CRIME VICTIM

Unlike with some personal crimes, there has been relatively little research on the impact of property crimes on victims or aid for victims of those crimes. Information on the impact of property crimes that is available generally reflects the same data that were presented in Chapter 4. The dollar loss is great. Unfortunately, there has been little attention paid to the non-monetary impact of property crime on victims. The clear exception to this is in the area of identity theft, where attention has been paid to the long-term impact of the crime on victims.

Aid to victims of burglary, larceny/theft, and arson is primarily monetary. Most aid comes from insurance coverage carried by the victims. Other sources of monetary aid could be by any civil court action or by restitution in criminal cases. As noted in Chapter 5, these require the offender to be identified, convicted/found liable, and have the resources to make the payments. Victim compensation is generally not available for property losses. Most other assistance for these victims is in the form of recommendations on what to do to avoid future victimization.

Aid to victims of fraud, particularly identity theft and mass-marketing fraud, is more prevalent, although still not extensive. The same issues with monetary recovery apply to these property crimes as to the others discussed above. One additional monetary source of assistance is the ability to have credit card fraud losses covered by the financial institution. This is limited, however, to the extent that the victim is aware of the fraud and informs the credit company in a timely fashion of the loss. Additionally, it is the responsibility of the victim to prove that the loss is not due to anything he or she did or did not do.

Beyond the immediate dollar losses, a victim of identity theft may need to spend considerable time and effort re-establishing his or her identity and creating new personal and financial records. In these cases, the Federal Trade Commission, prosecutor's offices, consumer groups and agencies, and many financial institutions have established assistance for the victims. In 2003, the Fair Credit Reporting Act was amended to require the three credit scoring agencies (Experian, TransUnion, and Equifax) to provide a yearly credit report to individuals free of charge, at the request of

WEB ACTIVITY

There are many national, local, and state agencies that provide recommendations to victims of crime, mostly in terms of protecting themselves. Typical sites are the National Center for Victims of Crime at **http://www.victimsofcrime.org/ help-for-crime-victims** and **http://www. victimassistanceprogram.org/**. Can you find others? What value do you see in the information?

WEB ACTIVITY

The FTC offers a great deal of information to consumers about identity theft at **http://www.consumer.ftc.gov/features/ feature-0014-identity-theft**. Another source of information is the National Criminal Justice Reference Service at **https://www.ncjrs.gov/spotlight/ identity_theft/facts.html** the individual. This provides individuals the ability to see what is happening in their name and to their financial accounts so that they can respond to any unauthorized activity.

SUMMARY

Traditional personal and property victimization are pervasive problems in society. Personal crime receives greater attention than property crime despite the fact that property crime is more prevalent. This is largely due to the fact that individual personal offenses are more heinous and often result in serious bodily injury or death. As such, personal offenses raise greater alarm and fear for the populace. They also provide more interesting fodder for both news programming and fictional media presentations. Despite these facts, property crime is much more common and has a major impact on both individuals and society.

The extent and impact of property crime is not small. The economic losses related to property crime are not inconsequential given the number of offenses. Losses from property crime alone easily reach into the billions of dollars each year. There is a clear need for additional attention to be paid to property crime victims, particularly in terms of understanding their plight and addressing their post-victimization needs. The needs of these victims are not totally different from those of personal crime victims, although the needs do diverge at some points. Before addressing those needs, we will turn to a discussion of personal crime victimization.

KEY TERMS

advance fee fraud scheme
aggravated assault
anticipatory grief
arson
bank and financial account scheme
burglary
clearance rate
criminal homicide
cyber attacks
cybercrime
cyber theft
death notification
Federal Identity Theft and
    Assumption Deterrence Act
fraud
grief process
homicide survivor patterns
identity theft

infanticide
investment opportunities schemes
intimate femicide
larceny/theft
mass-marketing fraud
matricide
motor vehicle theft
National Incident-Based Reporting
    System (NIBRS)
non-primary homicide
offense rates
parricide
patricide
phishing
robbery
Supplemental Homicide Reports (SHR)
Uniform Crime Reports (UCR)

Sexual Battery

After reading Chapter 9, you should be able to:

- Give the common-law definition of rape.
- Contrast rape with sexual battery.
- Tie the notion of spousal immunity to the idea of male power and domination.
- Differentiate between acquaintance rape and stranger rape.
- Discuss Supreme Court cases regarding child rape and the death penalty.
- Assemble a picture of forcible rape based on FBI UCR statistics.
- Sketch out some characteristics of sexual assault based upon victimization survey results.
- Compare and contrast UCR and NCVS statistics regarding rape.
- Discuss the shortcomings of the UCR and NCVS databases.
- Explain what the NCVS redesign has meant for sexual assault statistics.
- Critique independent efforts to gauge the extent of sexual assault among women.
- Draw a distinction between the incidence and the prevalence of sexual battery.
- Summarize the National College Women Sexual Victimization Study.
- Provide an overview of the National Violence Against Women Survey.
- Expound upon the problem of sexual violence at the national military academies.
- Be aware of several reasons why one should be cautious about sexual violence statistics.
- Relate the theme of male domination or power to sexual battery.
- Explain what "rape myths" are and what they do.
- Talk about what a crisis means.
- Understand the stages in the crisis reaction repair cycle.
- Analyze the rape trauma syndrome.

221

INTRODUCTION

Sexual battery is a devastating, dehumanizing experience. What makes this crime so crushing is that it is a direct attack on the person's self. Many victims suffer tremendous feelings of humiliation and degradation because of their assailants. Later, many of these same emotions are rekindled when the victim turns to the criminal justice system, expecting to find comfort and assistance.

This chapter opens with a presentation of what constitutes rape and sexual battery, along with some legal issues. To get a better sense of the prevalence of sexual battery in this country, we will look at official and unofficial data sources. A comparison of information contained in the Uniform Crime Reports with materials from the National Crime Victimization Survey reinforces the discussion in Chapter 2. Underreporting is a major drawback with this crime category.

The system is aware of the widespread reluctance to report sexual battery and to become involved with the authorities. Many states have rewritten their laws in an effort to dismantle the traditional barriers to victim cooperation. For example, rape has become redefined as sexual assault or sexual battery, and attention has been given to concerns with consent, the types of proof necessary to substantiate an allegation of sexual violence, and the character assassination tactics used to discredit victim testimony in court. Whether these reforms are working is an empirical question that we will probe. As Table 9.1 illustrates, sexual violence has gained recognition as a national problem in the United States.

Our discussion of sexual battery will delve into the personal tragedy that victims experience, the healing process these people face, and common coping strategies. This material will provide a backdrop for discussing how the police, hospital personnel, and the prosecutor respond to the victim.

Table 9.1 President Obama's Proclamation Declaring April 2013 as National Sexual Assault Awareness Month

In the last 20 years, our Nation has made meaningful progress toward addressing sexual assault. Where victims were once left without recourse, laws have opened a path to safety and justice; where a culture of fear once kept violence hidden, survivors are more empowered to speak out and get help. But even today, too many women, men, and children suffer alone or in silence, burdened by shame or unsure anyone will listen. This month, we recommit to changing that tragic reality by stopping sexual assault before it starts and ensuring victims get the support they need.

Sexual violence is an affront to human dignity and a crime no matter where it occurs. While rape and sexual assault affect all communities, those at the greatest risk are children, teens, and young women. Nearly one in five women will be a victim of sexual assault during college. For some groups, the rates of violence are even higher — Native American women are more than twice as likely to experience sexual assault as the general population. Moreover, we know rape and sexual assault are consistently underreported, and that the physical and emotional trauma they leave behind can last for years.

With Vice President Joe Biden's leadership, we have made preventing sexual violence and supporting survivors a top priority. Earlier this month, I was proud to sign the Violence Against Women Reauthorization Act, which renews and strengthens the law that first made it possible for our country to address sexual assault in a comprehensive way. The Act preserves critical services like rape crisis centers, upholds protections for immigrant victims, gives State and tribal law enforcement better tools to investigate cases of rape, and breaks down barriers that keep lesbian, gay, bisexual, and transgender victims from getting help. It also expands funding for sexual assault nurse examiner programs and sexual assault response teams, helping States deliver justice for survivors and hold offenders accountable.

Just as we keep fighting sexual assault in our neighborhoods, we must also recommit to ending it in our military — because no one serving our country should be at risk of assault by a fellow service member. Where this crime does take place, it cannot be tolerated; victims must have access to support, and offenders must face the consequences of their actions. Members of our Armed Forces and their families can learn more about the resources available to them at 1-877-995-5247 and www.SafeHelpline.org.

All Americans can play a role in changing the culture that enables sexual violence. Each of us can take action by lifting up survivors we know and breaking the silence surrounding rape and sexual assault. To get involved, visit www.WhiteHouse.gov/1is2many.

Together, our Nation is moving forward in the fight against sexual assault. This month, let us keep working to prevent violence in every corner of America, and let us rededicate ourselves to giving survivors the bright future they deserve.

NOW, THEREFORE, I, BARACK OBAMA, President of the United States of America, by virtue of the authority vested in me by the Constitution and the laws of the United States, do hereby proclaim April 2013 as National Sexual Assault Awareness and Prevention Month. I urge all Americans to support survivors of sexual assault and work together to prevent these crimes in their communities.

IN WITNESS WHEREOF, I have hereunto set my hand this twenty-ninth day of March, in the year of our Lord two thousand thirteen, and of the Independence of the United States of America the two hundred and thirty-seventh.

BARACK OBAMA

Source: Office of the Press Secretary (2013a). Presidential Proclamation – National Sexual Assault Awareness and Prevention Month Proclamation, 2013, March 29. Washington, D.C.: The White House. Retrieved on April 5, 2013, from http://www.whitehouse.gov/the-press-office/presidential-proclamation-national-sexual-assault-awareness-month.

DEFINING SEXUAL BATTERY

The definition of rape traditionally has been a matter of utmost concern. The common law view of rape dominated most state statutes well into the 1970s. According to *Black's Law Dictionary* (Garner, 2009: 1374), *rape* is the "unlawful sexual intercourse committed by a man with a woman who is not his wife through force and against her will." This definition is notable for several reasons. First, the victim status is restricted to females, and only males can be offenders. Second, the only act controlled under this approach is penile penetration. Third, husbands enjoy an automatic exemption from offender status. Fourth, an important element or ingredient is that the victim did not submit voluntarily to the act.

Over the years, lawmakers have altered the legal terminology involved with rape in a variety of ways. Many states have replaced the term *rape* with such phrases as "sexual battery," "deviant sexual conduct," and "sexual assault." These changes are more than just semantic. For one thing, they eliminate the gender bias inherent in the common law formulation. Today, it is possible for males to be victims and for females to be offenders. In addition, other forms of sexual abuse now fall under the purview of unwanted criminal intrusions. Some such acts would include oral, anal, and digital penetration, as well as fondling and the introduction of any other foreign objects into the victim's body. Finally, varying degrees of sexual battery replace the former all-inclusive single category of rape.

After years of relying upon the narrow common law definition of rape, U.S. Attorney Eric Holder recently announced that the Federal Bureau of Investigation is adopting a less restrictive definition of this offense. The purpose behind this change is to incorporate the more inclusive features of sexual battery. As Table 9.2 explains, the FBI will continue to track both the older definition of rape and the newer features associated with sexual battery over the next several years.

Spousal Rape

Under common law, a wife cannot accuse her husband of raping her while they are legally married. The underlying assumption is that the marriage vows provide an irretractable contractual arrangement to deliver exclusive sexual services upon demand. The marriage ceremony marks the formal transfer of the woman from her father's possession to the ownership of the husband. The practice of placing a premium on virginity, the institution of the dowry, and the tradition of relinquishing one's maiden name to assume the husband's surname all further reinforce the image of women as a commodity that males can buy and trade. This orientation maintains that a husband is free to do with his "property" as he sees fit (Ryan, 1995).

Despite this legal barrier, society recognizes that some unconscionable husbands do force their spouses to engage in unwanted sexual activity. It is not uncommon for coerced sexual behavior to occur in at least one of every 10 marriages (Finkelhor & Yllo, 1983; Russell, 1982). According to NCVS figures covering the years 2005 through 2010 (Planty et al., 2013: 4), a third of all rapes and sexual assaults in which females were the targets were committed by intimates (current or former spouses, boyfriends, or girlfriends). Friends and

Table 9.2 The Federal Bureau of Investigation Revises the Definition of Rape Used in the Uniform Crime Reports

Attorney General Eric Holder today announced revisions to the Uniform Crime Report's (UCR) definition of rape, which will lead to a more comprehensive statistical reporting of rape nationwide. The new definition is more inclusive, better reflects state criminal codes and focuses on the various forms of sexual penetration understood to be rape. The new definition of rape is: "The penetration, no matter how slight, of the vagina or anus with any body part or object, or oral penetration by a sex organ of another person, without the consent of the victim." The definition is used by the FBI to collect information from local law enforcement agencies about reported rapes.

The revised definition includes any gender of victim or perpetrator, and includes instances in which the victim is incapable of giving consent because of temporary or permanent mental or physical incapacity, including due to the influence of drugs or alcohol or because of age. The ability of the victim to give consent must be determined in accordance with state statute. Physical resistance from the victim is not required to demonstrate lack of consent. The new definition does not change federal or state criminal codes or impact charging and prosecution on the local level.

The longstanding, narrow definition of forcible rape, first established in 1927, is "the carnal knowledge of a female, forcibly and against her will." It thus included only forcible male penile penetration of a female vagina and excluded oral and anal penetration; rape of males; penetration of the vagina and anus with an object or body part other than the penis; rape of females by females; and, non-forcible rape.

Police departments submit data on reported crimes and arrests to the UCR. The UCR data are reported nationally and used to measure and understand crime trends. In addition, the UCR program will also collect data based on the historical definition of rape, enabling law enforcement to track consistent trend data until the statistical differences between the old and new definitions are more fully understood.

Source: Holder, E. (2012). Attorney General Eric Holder Announces Revisions to the Uniform Crime Report's Definition of Rape. Washington, DC: U.S. Department of Justice. Retrieved on April 16, 2013, from http://www.justice.gov/opa/pr/2012/January/12-ag-018.html.

acquaintances were responsible for an additional 38% of these violations. As Ferro, Cermele, and Saltzman (2008: 765) explain, "rapists are not strangers lurking in dark alleys or hiding behind bushes looking for their victims; rather the majority of rapes involve a victim and an offender who had a prior relationship before the rape occurred."

A common perception is that a sexual assault by a husband is not as serious as an attack by a complete stranger (Ferro et al., 2008; Frese, Moya, & Megias, 2004). However, Yllo (1999: 1060) writes, "When you are raped by a stranger, you live with a frightening memory; but when you are raped by your husband, you live with your rapist."

As mentioned earlier, the common-law interpretation, known as *spousal immunity*, is that a husband is incapable of raping his wife. If a jurisdiction follows this line of thinking, husbands enjoy an *absolute exemption* and are not prosecuted for spousal rape under any condition. Many states have relaxed their statutes to reflect the growing awareness that marital rape does exist and can have deep traumatic effects for the victim. These states may allow prosecution if the parties are separated, are in the process of obtaining a divorce, or have taken other steps to void or nullify the marriage. These laws grant what is known as a *partial exemption*. While this modification may appear to be an enlightened and progressive move, it does have its limits. A national survey of rape reform legislation cautions that states that "have removed the traditional immunity for spouses . . . have offset this change by providing relatively low penalties for conviction" (Berger, Searles, & Neuman, 1988: 342). Thus, what may appear at first to be a significant gain is sometimes really a very small concession.

Date or Acquaintance Rape

Another form of sexual assault that has emerged as a major topic of study is the category of *date rape* or *acquaintance rape.* This crime has garnered attention because it does not fit the stereotypical view of rape. To a large degree, many people assume that sexual assault occurs between individuals who do not know one another. They think the offender either stalks his or her prey or happens upon a victim and violently attacks that person. Date rape, however, does not fit that convenient mold. Rather, the victim and offender know one another and are engaged in friendly, noncombative interaction up until the attack. In many analyses, being "talked into" having sexual relations when the victim did not want to, submitting when inebriated, being made to feel guilty if refusing to have sex, or submitting after being given false promises (such as marriage) fall into the realm of sexual assault, although physical force or threats may not have been involved. The absence of the traditional stranger-to-stranger relationship and physical force sometimes leads some people to believe there must be some degree of consent in date or acquaintance instances, thereby negating a valid claim of rape.

WEB ACTIVITY

"Date rape drugs" are gaining more attention. You can find a balanced assessment of this problem at **http://www.isp. state.il.us/crime/daterapedrugs.cfm**

PUNISHING SEXUAL BATTERY

In the past, some juries have been reluctant to convict defendants on charges of rape or sexual battery for two general reasons. First, while physical evidence of sexual intercourse might be present, jurors had to wrestle with the issue of consent. Cases sometimes came down to a "he said/she said" type of presentation. Second, the death penalty loomed over the defendant in some instances. Given the finality of this punishment, juries were hesitant to convict in cases where the evidence was less than compelling.

When the Supreme Court struck down the death penalty in *Furman v. Georgia* (1972), it did so because capital punishment was being administered in a cruel, arbitrary, and capricious manner. State legislatures immediately went to work revising their death penalty laws. In 1976, the Supreme Court ruled that these efforts passed constitutional muster (*Gregg v. Georgia*, 1976). However, a number of issues pertaining to sexual assault remained unresolved. As a result, we need to visit two relevant Supreme Court rulings.

Coker v. Georgia (1977)

The State of Georgia, as did a handful of other states, allowed the imposition of the death penalty for the charge of rape if aggravating circumstances were present. In this case, Coker was serving time in prison for murder, rape, kidnapping, and aggravated assault when he escaped from that facility. During his quest for freedom, Coker burglarized a dwelling, robbed a couple at knifepoint, sexually assaulted the female victim, kidnapped her, and stole a vehicle. In light of his past criminal history and the commission of multiple felonies in this case, the jury returned a verdict of death.

Coker appealed his sentence on the grounds that the punishment was not commensurate with the crime. In other words, Coker's attorneys questioned whether the death penalty was appropriate for a non-capital offense. The Justices, in a 5–4 decision, agreed with Coker and wrote:

> That question, with respect to rape of an *adult* woman, is now before us. We have concluded that a sentence of death is a grossly disproportionate and excessive punishment for the crime of rape, and is therefore forbidden by the Eighth Amendment as cruel and unusual punishment [p. 592, emphasis added].

Kennedy v. Louisiana (2008)

The Court revisited the appropriateness of the death penalty in sexual battery cases where the victim was a child. Because the *Coker* decision specifically referred to an adult victim, many observers thought that the Court might be reserving the death penalty instead for child rape cases that did not involve a homicide. Louisiana law defined *child rape* as an adult having forcible sexual intercourse with a child under the age of 12. Furthermore, Louisiana punished child rape as a capital offense, meaning child rape was death penalty-eligible.

Kennedy v. Louisiana involved a situation where the defendant sexually battered his 8-year-old stepdaughter. The victim sustained multiple internal injuries and needed immediate emergency surgery as a result of the attack. The attending physician stated that this was the most brutal sexual assault case he had encountered during four years of practice. As the Court noted, the "crime was one that cannot be recounted in these pages in a way sufficient to capture in full the hurt and horror inflicted on his victim or to convey the revulsion society, and the jury that represents it, sought to express by sentencing petitioner to death" (p. 2).

Despite the abhorrence surrounding this criminal episode, the Court dismissed the suggestion that *Coker* only applied to adult victims and that the death penalty could be imposed for child rape. Instead, the Court reasoned that evolving standards of decency prevented the death penalty from being invoked in cases that did not involve a homicide. As the opinion explained, "resort to the [death] penalty must be reserved for the worst of crimes and limited in its instances of application" (p. 36). As a result, the sentence of death was vacated, and Kennedy was resentenced to life imprisonment.

As one might imagine, this 5–4 decision provoked a wide range of reactions. Death penalty opponents saw it as a logical boundary. Meanwhile, critics greeted the ruling with great disdain. As one writer put it:

> No matter how much life-long physical damage a man inflicts while raping a three-year old little girl, no matter how ritualistically he tortures her over hours or days, no matter how delicious he finds her sobbing agony and how coolly indifferent he is to her desperate need for subsequent care, no matter whether he has stolen her away from all she knows and kept her naked, starved, and terrorized in a pitch dark hole in the ground, no matter how many victims he has similarly brutalized or how often he repeats his cruelty with the same terrorized victim, so long as she survives the torment, he has a constitutional right to live out his natural life free of the threat that death will be visited upon him in punishment (Hurd, 2008: 351).

MEASURING THE EXTENT OF RAPE

As we learned in Chapter 2, estimates concerning the nature, extent, and distribution of crime vary considerably depending upon the source of that information. The category of forcible rape or sexual battery is no exception. The typical forums for gathering data on these criminal incidents are the Uniform Crime Reports (UCR) and the National Crime Victimization Survey (NCVS). Information from both these databases, as well as other undertakings, follows in this chapter.

UCR Information

The UCR describes forcible rape as "the carnal knowledge of a female forcibly and against her will" (FBI, 2012d). This category excludes statutory rape and other sex offenses. Using this definition, the UCR reveals that there were over 83,000 rapes known to the police in 2011. When one transforms the number of rapes known to the authorities during the calendar year 2011 into a crime rate, the resulting figure is approximately 53 offenses per 100,000 women.

NCVS Information

The emerging women's movement in the 1960s and 1970s assailed official rape statistics as too low and patently inaccurate. This position garnered a great deal of support from the early victimization surveys. The NORC (National Opinion Research Center) victimization survey, undertaken on behalf of the 1967 President's Commission, uncovered almost four times more rapes than what police reports had tallied. Despite a host of methodological problems with first-generation victim surveys, the issue of underreporting fueled skepticism about the reliability and validity of official crime counts.

After a great deal of refinement, the NCVS has emerged as a recognized source of information on crime victims. As you will recall from Chapter 2, the NCVS redesign modified the screen questions so as to more fully measure the extent of certain types of offenses, including sexual assault. Rather than simply probe sexual assault under a general question dealing with being attacked "in some other way," the redesigned survey specifically asks about rape, attempted rape, or any other type of sexual assault (Bachman & Saltzman, 1995). The expectation was that the new survey would uncover substantially more rape and sexual assault incidents than have materialized in the past (Kindermann, Lynch, & Cantor, 1997).

As expected, the level of reported sexual assault did increase under the redesigned format. According to the 1990 NCVS, there were 67,430 attempted rapes and 62,830 completed rapes in the United States. These figures jumped to 148,610 attempted rapes and 167,550 completed rapes in 1994, roughly a 243% increase for the combined categories (Bureau of Justice Statistics, 1997: 6). The 1994 figures translate into a combined rape/sexual assault victimization rate of 200 per 100,000 population aged 12 and above, compared with a rate of roughly 60 in 1990. However, more recent figures point to a dramatic decrease in rape and sexual assault victimization. For the year 2011, the NCVS recorded more than 243,000 rapes and sexual assaults, which translates into a rate of 90 per 100,000 persons (Truman & Planty, 2012).

Figure 9.1 presents some selected characteristics of rape incidents outlined in the NCVS. According to the charts, younger females are more likely to become rape victims. In addition, *nonstranger rapes* (which include "date rape" and "acquaintance rape," among other things) account for 73% of these sexual victimizations.

Comparing the UCR with the NCVS over Time

One way to address any similarities and disparities between police- and survey-derived victimization rates is to look at these data over time. If both sets of crime statistics are subject to similar influences, then they ought to move in unison. Should different forces affect one data set but not the other, then one

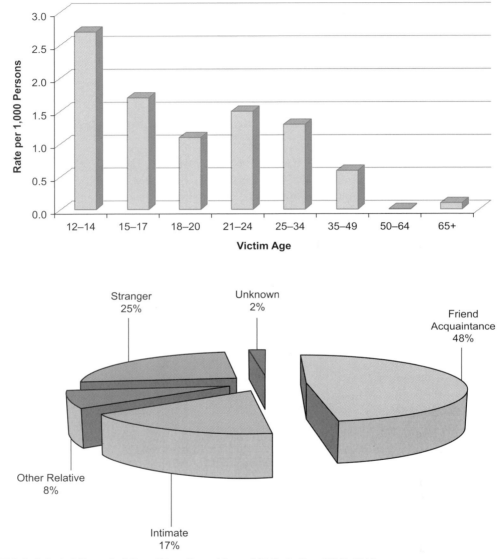

FIGURE 9.1 Selected Characteristics of Rape/Sexual Assault Victimization, NCVS, 2010.

Source: Adapted from Truman, J. L. (2011). Criminal Victimization, 2010. Washington, DC: Bureau of Justice Statistics.

should observe uncorrelated trends. One intrusion, the implementation of the redesigned NCVS in 1992, created an artificial increase in the number of rapes reported by respondents. As a result, researchers have adjusted the 1973–1991 data to make the entire series more compatible (Kinderman et al., 1997; Rand, Lynch, & Cantor, 1997). A second intrusion came with the introduction of

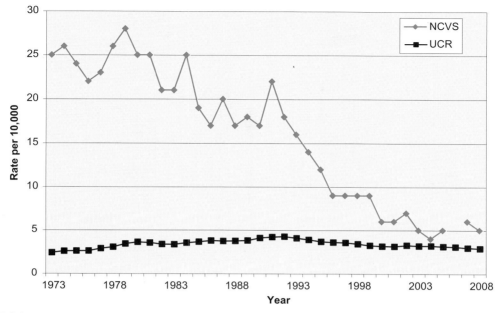

FIGURE 9.2 NCVS and UCR Rape Rates, 1973–2008.
Source: No Author (2010). National Crime Victimization Survey Crime Trends, 1973–2008. *Washington, DC: Bureau of Justice Statistics. Retrieved on July 12, 2010 from http://bjs.ojp.usdoj.gov/content/glance/rape.cfm. Compilation from UCR annual reports.*

some technical changes to the 2006 NCVS. The NCVS figure is suppressed for that year. Given these caveats, Figure 9.2 presents the rape victimization rates for both the UCR and the NCVS from 1973 through 2008.

The UCR forcible rape rates display a relatively steady climb from 1976 until 1992, at which point the rates started to decline. On the other hand, the victimization rape rates evidence a general downward trend throughout the data, even when considering the sudden jump due to the survey redesign. Both the data from 1976 to 1991 and those from 1992 to 2008 display a downward pattern, with the latter being very pronounced. While the UCR pattern is smooth, the NCVS exhibits steep bounces in both directions. As the two data sources do not track each other until about 1997, the next step is to find what systematic influences affect each data set.

A helpful way to visualize these trends might be to think of the area or gap between the NCVS and UCR rape rates in Figure 9.2 as possibly representing the "dark figure of crime." The immediate concern then is how to account for the observed changes over time. One possibility is that changes in traditional sex-role attitudes have relaxed the taboos once associated with rape. This liberalization, in turn, paves the way for greater reporting of such incidents. The underlying argument is that before this attitudinal shift, women were reluctant to report episodes that departed from "classic rape" stereotypes. For example, victims may have found it easier to report attacks in which the perpetrator brandished a weapon, was a complete stranger, or beat the victim. At the same time, however, victims would hide incidents involving acquaintances or relatives and alcohol use from public view (Fisher et al., 2003a).

To see if this notion was plausible, Orcutt and Faison (1988) analyzed attitudinal trends and victimization reporting habits from 1973 until 1985. They found that broader or more liberated perceptions of acceptable female behavior greatly affected whether the police were notified in nonstranger rape situations. Thus, Orcutt and Faison (1988) maintained that increases in rapes known to the police during this period could very well be a function of changing social mores. Other researchers also lend empirical support to this line of thinking (Bachman, 1993; Bachman & Saltzman, 1995; Baumer, Felson, & Messner, 2003; Baumer & Lauritsen, 2010).

Although the notion of an attitudinal shift carries considerable appeal, another alternative is just as lucrative. Criminologists know that organizational changes within the police bureaucracy influence the quantity and composition of official crime. Drawing upon this outlook, Jensen and Karpos (1993) counter that an increased presence of female law enforcement employees changes the quality of police interaction with victims. This gain, in turn, influences agency recording practices. More precisely, dispatchers and officers who are female have a heightened sensitivity toward sexual assault victims. These employees are in a better position to anticipate victim needs. A more sensitive posture, coupled with specialized investigatory units and connections with rape crisis centers, fosters greater citizen reporting and better police documentation of sexual assault cases.

A third reason for the UCR–NCVS discrepancy prior to 1992 is the realization that the victimization survey instrument did not contain any inquiries that deal directly with rape (Bachman & Taylor, 1994; Eigenberg, 1990). The individual screen questions eliciting reports of rape victimization were vague and evasive. This may have been because survey administrators regarded this area as delicate and highly sensitive. The NCVS redesign addresses this deficiency by including an item that uses a screen question asking about rape, attempted rape, and other types of sexual assault. Follow-up questions on any incidents are then conducted. This new procedure resulted in a 157% increase in identified incidents compared with the older approach (Kindermann et al., 1997). Consequently, data since the redesign have a better chance of mirroring the patterns in UCR data. However, researchers must still sort through an array of questions regarding validity and reliability before achieving accurate measures of violence against women (Fisher et al., 2003b; Gelles, 2000; Gordon, 2000; Schwartz, 2000).

More Recent Efforts

Sensitivity to these and other issues prompted two separate surveys to enlist national samples in an effort to arrive at a more comprehensive understanding of sexual violence. The first project was undertaken to secure sounder information from college women, and the second study focused on American women in general. The release of these details helps round out our current understanding of a number of issues. In fact, the college women survey is touted as "perhaps the most systematic analysis of the extent and nature of the sexual victimization of college women in the past decade" (Fisher et al., 2000a: 3). Finally, this section visits the problem of sexual violence at U.S. national military academies.

The National College Women Sexual Victimization Study

Acknowledging the limitations highlighted in the previous section, Fisher and colleagues drew a representative sample of almost 4,500 women enrolled in college during the fall of 1996. This effort, referred to as the *National College Women Sexual Victimization (NCWSV) Study*, borrowed the NCVS two-stage approach of utilizing screen questions and incident-relevant inquiries. However, one enhancement the researchers made was to add a larger number of, and more specific, screen questions. These initial queries avoided using legal terminology and relied more upon behavioral descriptions of the illicit acts. In other words, instead of asking respondents whether they had been raped, interviewers utilized a series of questions that described the exact behavior sought. The purpose behind this approach was to avoid any potential misunderstandings so that respondents could give the most accurate answers possible. It also enabled the investigators to collect data regarding attempted misconduct, threats with and without violence, sexual battery, stalking, and other aspects of sexual coercion.

> **WEB ACTIVITY**
>
> You can find more details about the National College Women Sexual Victimization Study by accessing the original report at **https://www.ncjrs.gov/pdffiles1/nij/182369.pdf**

The extrapolated results indicate that 5% of college women contend with rape or an attempted rape annually. If one realizes that many college students take five years to finish an undergraduate degree, then the actual risk rises into the vicinity of 20–25%. It might be more instructive to place the NCWSV number of incidents in a slightly different context. If a college had an enrollment of 10,000 female students, administrators could anticipate that one sexual battery would take place every day. One must also bear in mind that this estimate does not include other unwanted forms of sexual coercion such as harassing comments, obscene phone calls, coercion, voyeurism, and other sexually oriented behaviors. In short, these statistics paint a very unflattering portrait of an environment that many people naively assume is geared more toward intellectual and rational challenges.

The National Violence Against Women Survey

The National Institute of Justice and the Centers for Disease Control and Prevention combined forces to sponsor the National Violence Against Women (NVAW) Survey, which was carried out under the guidance of Tjaden and Thoennes (2000). The NVAW Survey, conducted from November of 1995 through May of 1996, involved 8,000 female and 8,000 male respondents. Its goal was to provide survey data on the prevalence, incidence, and consequences of violence against women.

WEB ACTIVITY

Further details about the National Violence Against Women Survey are available at **https://www.ncjrs.gov/pdffiles1/nij/181867.pdf**

Like the NCWSV, the NVAW Survey relied upon multiple behaviorally based queries to generate more detailed victimization information. The results showed that 17.6% of the women and 3% of the men indicated that they had been raped at least once during their lifetimes. In other words, "1 of 6 U.S. women and 1 of 33 U.S. men have been victims of a completed or attempted rape" (Tjaden & Thoennes, 2000: 13).

The researchers were careful to draw a distinction between the *incidence* of rape (the number of victimizations) and the *prevalence* of rape (the number of victims). National estimates based upon the NVAW data generate a total of 876,064 rape incidents with female victims and 111,298 incidents with male victims. By comparison, the 1994 NCVS figures include 432,100 incidents involving female victims and 32,900 cases with male victims. In terms of prevalence, these incidents registered more than 302,000 female victims and almost 93,000 male victims. Obviously, there were a substantial number of victims who reported multiple episodes. In addition, further analyses revealed that intimate partners were responsible for a number of these lifetime rape victimizations (7.7% of the female respondents and 0.3% of the male interviewees). These findings, along with further information regarding physical assault and stalking, confirm that violence against women is a major social problem in the United States.

Sexual Victimization at the National Military Academies

Traditionally, the United States military has been a male bastion. While women have entered the armed services for many years, they were typically relegated to work in stereotypical roles, such as the secretarial pool or hospital nurses. Even when wider access was granted, women were still restricted from entering combat duty, denied posts in other highly hazardous duty areas, and held to different physical fitness standards.

The military academies operate in a dual capacity. In addition to the mission of developing future military leaders, these institutions provide a college education to attendees. In other words, the military academies are institutions of higher education. It was not until the mid-1970s that the military academies began admitting female cadets into their programs. The integration of the two genders met with resistance. For example, the last all-male graduating class of the Air Force Academy sported tee-shirts and other attire imprinted with the logo "LCWB" or "Last Class Without Broads," one of the more staid euphemisms (Fowler, 2003: 59). Other practices contributed to an atmosphere that was hostile to women. A 2002 survey of the social climate at the Air Force Academy revealed that more than a quarter of the male cadets did not believe that women had a place on the campus. Virtually every female cadet expressed concern for her safety when she found herself alone at night (Fowler, 2003: 59). The practice of not allowing the doors to sleeping quarters to be locked at night fanned these fears.

It was against this backdrop that administrators became aware that sexual assault and sexual harassment were problematic issues. There were 142 allegations of sexual assault at the Air Force Academy during the 1993–2002 interim. Other estimates place the sexual victimization rate at 60% of cadets and midshipmen (Snyder, Fisher, Scherer, & Daigle, 2012). Of course, one must balance these figures against rampant nonreporting. A survey conducted in 2003 discovered that 80% of the female cadets who said they had been sexually assaulted did not report the incident (Fowler, 2003: 1). Almost one in five women said they became sexual assault victims during their stay at the Academy. Another four of five women in a 1995 campus survey were the targets of sexual harassment (Fowler, 2003: 16). A recent U.S. Department of Defense report confirms a similar nonreporting figure among all active-duty members throughout the entire military service in 2011 (Cronk, 2013).

While the Fowler report went on to advance a series of recommendations, Congress considered the problem serious enough to warrant an expanded look at all the national military academies. As a result, a task force was empanelled. Its charge boiled down to a very basic question. Starting with the premise that the military academies recruit only the "cream of the crop," the Task Force posed a simple question: "Why then, with such high-quality youth and high standards of discipline, do acts of sexual harassment and sexual assaults still occur?" (Howeing & Rumburg, 2005: 8) (see Figure 9.3).

The Task Force recognized, among other things, the existence of a sexually abusive environment on military campuses. It turned the spotlight squarely on the service academy culture. In an effort to defeat this milieu, the institutions must address social and institutional practices that devalue women (Houser, 2007; Suris & Lind, 2008). While a variety of reforms and victim services programs are currently being implemented (Wright, 2012), there is one very important point here. That is, these observations regarding the incidence

WEB ACTIVITY

More developments sponsored by the U.S. Department of Defense appear on its Sexual Assault Prevention and Response website located at **http://www.sapr.mil/**

of sexual violence at the military service academies stem from the very same vulnerable age groups that both the NCWSV and NVAW isolated.

A Word of Caution

In evaluating this information, however, there are several issues that one should keep in mind. First, the magnitude of many figures is inflated by focusing on "lifetime" occurrences or college surveys asking about "since you were 14" or any other similar ages. The data, therefore, appear high when compared with official and NCVS measures that tap only the past year.

Second, while often discussed as "date rape," the actions under consideration typically reflect a much broader category of *sexual coercion*. For example, verbal persuasion to engage in sex, promises of marriage, and making someone feel guilty are often lumped together with the use or threat of physical force in defining an experience as sexual assault. While these actions may entail coercion, there is a clear difference in magnitude and potential harm involved in the actions.

Third, most studies of date rape restrict their inquiries to college students. Furthermore, researchers often rely upon very select groups of students, such as undergraduates enrolled in psychology or criminal justice classes. A college sampling frame, while convenient, is not representative of society or of the 18- to 22-year-old general population.

Fourth, there is some compelling evidence that the format, style, and wording of questions help mold survey responses (Cook et al., 2011). There are ongoing efforts to distinguish *false positives* (nonvictims who report a victimization episode) from *false negatives* (victims who decline to report a victimization episode). For example, a comparison of the procedures employed by the NCWSV and NVACW led Fisher (2009) to conclude that relying upon questions containing specific behaviors offers more cues to participants and enables them to understand exactly what the question means. Shedding legal definitions and providing precise examples or descriptions optimize meaning, and appear to avoid unnecessary complications for many respondents (Thoresen & Overlein, 2009), and allow participants to recognize what constitutes sexual violence and to correctly identify incidents as rape situations (Fisher et al., 2003b). Other researchers, though, wonder whether such direct approaches are really a superior "gold standard" and would welcome more intensive research into what are appropriate self-report techniques (Cook et al., 2011; Krebs et al., 2011).

FIGURE 9.3

Vice Admiral G. L. Hoewing, Chief of Naval Personnel, speaks about a defense task force report on sexual harassment and violence at the U.S. military academies. Delilah Rumburg, executive director of the Pennsylvania Coalition Against Rape, is on the left. *Credit: AP Photo/ Dennis Cook.*

Fifth, there is a growing awareness that interview methodology can affect the quality and type of data obtained. How interviewers are trained prior to being deployed (learning about sexual violence in addition to learning how to conduct interviews), who the interviewers are (professional interviewers, lay persons, college students, former victims, advocates), and how they conduct the interview session (establishing rapport, enhanced listening skills, open-ended versus close-ended questions) can affect both response and disclosure rates (Campbell et al., 2009). In fact, some researchers purposively employ a style called *feminist interviewing*. Feminist interviewing strategies make an intentional effort to reduce the social status gap between the interviewer and the respondent by being empathetic, answering personal questions the interviewee may have of the interviewer, validating the person's feelings, offering reassurance, and being active listeners (Campbell et al., 2010).

Finally, caution must be used in blindly accepting interpretations advanced by "advocates." Gilbert (1993), while reviewing research on the magnitude of date rape, notes that almost three-quarters of the respondents in one study whom the researchers regarded as victims actually reported that they themselves did not think they had been a victim. He also points out that some "rape" questions fail to address whether the behavior was consensual or not—an important criterion to consider. Reliance upon such questionable assumptions results in incidence and prevalence rates that not only dwarf official data but also belie even the experiences of crisis assistance groups (Gilbert, 1993). Clearly, rape and sexual assault are greater problems than what official data would lead us to believe. At the same time, though, advocacy data probably err on the other extreme end of the spectrum by making unreasonable assumptions when measuring the problem. A safe conclusion is that rape is a much larger and more pervasive problem than the UCR and the NCVS figures indicate.

Rape Myths

Sociocultural explanations, frequently labeled as feminist in orientation, focus on the traditional roles of males and females in society. Brownmiller (1975) brought these arguments to the forefront when she pointed out that the historical place of women in society was one of subservience. Women belonged either to their fathers or to their husbands. Females were property; as such, they were subject to the wishes of the owner. In this context, any attack on a female was actually an affront against her master. Any compensation or retribution due to the possession's devaluation went to the owner, not to the female who was victimized. It is for similar reasons that warring armies use rape as a weapon to terrorize, intimidate, and taunt opposing forces (Brownmiller, 1975).

In updating the sociocultural explanation, rape is simply a means of showing and promoting male domination in a society in which formal ownership of females is no longer permitted. Rape is a means of guaranteeing the inequality between the sexes, with males occupying the upper niches of power.

The sociocultural approach emphasizes the argument that rape is *not* a sexual offense. Instead, rape is an offense of *power*—a tool that enables men to exert power and control over women.

As one would expect, the sociocultural explanation gained a great deal of support from the women's movement. It became a clear challenge to the dominant male structure within society. Rape was also identifiable as perhaps the most heinous example of what was wrong with traditional sex roles. The sociocultural problems surrounding rape were highlighted further by the callous methods used by the criminal justice system when handling victims (Brownmiller, 1975; Holmstrom & Burgess, 1978) and by rape myths believed by many individuals (Koss & Leonard, 1984; Lottes, 1988) (see Table 9.3).

The sociocultural approach also receives a great deal of support from discussions of date or acquaintance rape among college populations. Numerous authors point to the influence of peer support in sexual assault (see, for example, DeKeseredy & Kelly, 1995; Koss & Cleveland, 1997; Koss & Gaines, 1993; Martin & Hummer, 1989). Two peer networks often linked to sexual aggression

---

Table 9.3 Examples of Rape Myths

Rape myths are widely held, inaccurate beliefs about rape. Myths of rape give people a false sense of security by legitimizing sexual assault or denying that it even occurs. They often do this by blaming the victim for their experience or making excuses and minimizing their assault. In effect, these myths perpetuate sexual assault by not addressing the realities of rape.

- Sexual assault does not occur often.
- Women lie about being sexually assaulted to get revenge, for their own benefit, or because they feel guilty afterwards about having sex.
- Sexual assault is committed by strangers.
- The best way for a woman to protect herself from sexual assault is to avoid being alone at night in dark, deserted places such as alleys or parking lots.
- Women who are sexually assaulted ask for it by the way they dress or act.
- Rape only happens to young sexy women.
- Men who sexually assault women are either mentally ill or sexually starved.
- If a woman consents to have sex at the start of making out with her boyfriend, then she is not assaulted if she changes her mind, but her partner keeps on going.
- If a woman has had many sexual partners then she cannot be sexually assaulted.
- If a man pays for dinner or a movie, the woman owes him sex.
- When men become sexually aroused they have to have sex and cannot stop.
- If a woman is drunk or passed out from drinking too much it is okay to have sex with her.
- A woman cannot be raped if she does not want to be assaulted.

Source: Adapted from Women Against Violence Against Women (2013). Rape Myths. Vancouver, British Columbia, Canada: WAVAW Rape Crisis Centre. Retrieved on April 30, 2013, from http://www.wavaw.ca/mythbusting/rape-myths.

are fraternities/sororities and athletics (Armstrong, Hamilton, & Sweeney, 2006; Boeringer, 1999; Gage, 2008; Humphrey & Kahn, 2000; Koss & Gaines, 1993; Martin & Hummer, 1989; Minow & Einolf, 2009; Stombler, 1994). In both cases, it is argued that offenders are challenged to prove their masculinity, maintain confidentiality, and support one's peers. Intertwined with these peer associations is the use of alcohol. Alcohol contributes to sexual assault in numerous ways. It can reduce inhibitions, thwart the ability of a person to resist advances, increase the possibility of misreading another person's desires or intent, diminish feelings of responsibility, heighten miscommunication, increase offender aggressiveness, and promote "rape myths" (Abbey et al., 1996; Armstrong et al., 2006; Benson, Gohm, & Gross, 2007; Brecklin & Ullman, 2001; Corbin et al., 2001; Davis et al., 2006; Ehrhart & Sadler, 1985; Harrington & Leitenberg, 1994; Lundberg-Love & Geffner, 1989; Martin & Hummer, 1989; Pumphrey-Gordon & Gross, 2007; Ullman, Karabatsos, & Koss, 1999). It is important to note that alcohol influences both the offender and the victim. Harrington and Leitenberg (1994) found that the victim was "somewhat drunk" in 55% of the sexually aggressive situations they uncovered and that alcohol increased the degree of "acceptable sexual contact" (according to the victim) before the assault. While it is common to assume that most offenders consciously attempt to get the victim drunk, it is probably more likely that alcohol is used willingly by both parties, which, in turn, produces more opportunities for assault. The social setting of college life, coupled with broader social expectations of male and female behavior, enhances the probability of sexually aggressive activity.

THE AFTERMATH OF RAPE

Although they are enlightening, statistics about the number of offenses, debate over whether one data source is superior to another, and theoretical musing about the causes of sexual battery all present a rather sterile view of the problem. Such a focus loses sight of the victim's personal feelings and experiences. One key area of concern is the emotional repercussion that sexual violence unleashes upon the victim.

As soon as the sexual attack is over, the victim begins the task of facing a bewildering mixture of emotions and concerns. Perhaps the most immediate reaction is one of upheaval and confusion. The victim generally does not know what to do nor does he or she know whom to turn to for assistance. Many victims do not call the police right away, particularly if the offender was an acquaintance. If they do talk with anyone, it is often a family member, a close friend, or possibly someone at a rape crisis center.

A great deal of fear and anxiety can accompany this initial disorientation. The victim may second-guess his or her actions prior to and during the attack. He or she may fear potential retaliation from the assailant. He or she may envision disapproval, and even condemnation, from those who learn of the incident. Many victims worry about what will happen if the police and the criminal justice system become involved, and how people will respond to them afterward.

Crisis Reaction

Over the years, psychologists have learned that all these reactions are normal and follow a very typical pattern. A variety of events can contribute to or trigger a state of crisis. They may range from the bereavement or grief associated with death, the loss of a job, an unwanted pregnancy, or any other traumatic event that may surface throughout the course of life. What makes sexual victimization so disturbing is that it is the penultimate violation. As one team of psychological experts explains, "Short of being killed, there is no greater insult to the self" (Bard & Sangrey, 1986: 21).

A *crisis* develops whenever a situation poses a serious danger or threat to the person's self. This hazard is so monumental that the person who is at the center of this crisis has a great deal of difficulty coping with the circumstances. This imbalance, or lack of equilibrium, between what it takes to resolve the problem and the resources to combat the crisis renders the victim unable to climb out of the situation. As Bard and Sangrey (1986: 33) put it:

> The sudden, arbitrary, unpredictable violation of self leaves victims feeling so shattered that they cannot continue to function the way they did before the crime. Things fall apart, and victims are unable to pull themselves back together right away.

The severity and duration of a crisis depend upon three conditions. The first consideration is the degree to which the person's self is threatened. Insignificant events require very little, if any, attention or redirection. Devastating intrusions, on the other hand, command many more resources. They need constant attention and can be exhausting. The second factor is the person's ability at that precise moment to deal with a problem of such magnitude. Some people might be worn out from facing a series of calamities prior to this unexpected intrusion. Others might be refreshed and able to muster considerable inner strength to meet the challenge. Finally, the kind of intervention or help that a person receives immediately after the tragedy strikes can determine how long it takes to propel out of this helplessness and into recovery.

The Crisis Reaction Repair Cycle

While the time it takes to recuperate may vary from one person to the next, victims go through a very predictable sequence during their recovery. The *crisis reaction repair cycle* consists of three distinct stages. The first phase is called *impact*. The second phase is the *recoil* period. The final stage, *reorganization*, marks the end of the crisis reaction repair cycle. Although some people contend that this model neglects to explain which victims have these experiences and who will recover more quickly than another (Resick, 1990), it does provide a convenient backdrop for understanding the plight of the victim.

Impact

A single word that summarizes the *impact* stage is "shock;" "distress" is another appropriate descriptor. Victims run the entire gamut of emotions during this period. Some people go through denial. Expressions like "I can't believe this happened to me" are common. Other victims blame themselves and ask what they did to deserve this humiliation. Sometimes there are expressions of outrage, anger, and revenge. Confusion, fear, helplessness, guilt, self-pity, and feelings of worthlessness, if left unchecked, can ravage victims during this stage.

Many victims seek security and strong emotional support while dealing with and sorting out these feelings. Victims sense that they are vulnerable. They know they have lost control over themselves and their surroundings. As a result, victims sometimes interpret insensitive or judgmental comments as strong condemnations. Remarks such as "I can't believe you went there" or "What do you mean you don't know what happened?" can elicit harsh negative responses and devastate a person in need of some compassionate understanding.

The fear, anxiety, and shame that victims endure during the impact stage are not ill-founded. Sexual assault victims must combat various notions associated with rape and sexual battery. As explained in Chapter 1, the perception of victim precipitation is very much alive—especially in sexual battery situations. One common reaction is to "blame the victim" for the attack by claiming that he or she was in the wrong place at the wrong time. There might be other hints that the victim acted suggestively, dressed provocatively, or that she originally consented and later changed her mind.

Many victims have to grapple with a number of *rape myths.* These beliefs basically shift responsibility away from the offender and onto the victim. Far from relieving the victim's feelings and problems, they exacerbate them. Among these myths are such ideas as "many women wish to be raped" (Burt & Estep, 1981), "victims who fail to report to the police right away were not really raped" (Costin & Schwarz, 1987; Ehrhart & Sandler, 1985), and the "just world hypothesis" that "only those who deserve to be raped get raped" (Carmody & Washington, 2001; Lerner, 1980).

Recoil

The second phase of the victim's recovery is known as the *recoil* period. At this point, victims begin to adapt to the fact that the violation took place. The mending process helps reduce the sting of the emotions that appeared earlier. While these feelings still resurface from time to time, they are not as intense or devastating as they once were. In some cases, victims may move back and forth between the impact and the recoil stages. Over time, these swings become less frequent and less intense.

Many rape victims experience a condition known as *post-traumatic stress disorder* (PTSD). Clinicians who deal with sexual battery victims sometimes refer to these symptoms more narrowly as the *rape trauma syndrome* (Bassuk, 1980; Burgess & Holmstrom, 1974; Frazier & Borgida, 1992; Giannelli, 1997). In any event, this condition refers to a response to major, sudden tragedies.

Table 9.4 Diagnostic Criteria for Post-Traumatic Stress Disorder

A. The person has been exposed to a traumatic event in which both of the following were present:
  1. the person experienced, witnessed, or was confronted with an event or events that involved actual or threatened death or serious injury, or a threat to the physical integrity of self or others
  2. the person's response involved intense fear, helplessness, or horror

B. The traumatic event is persistently re-experienced in one (or more) of the following ways
  1. recurrent and intrusive distressing recollections of the event, including images, thoughts, or perceptions
  2. recurrent distressing dreams of the event
  3. acting or feeling as if the traumatic event were recurring (includes a sense of reliving the experience, illusions, hallucinations, and dissociative flashback episodes, including those that occur on awakening or when intoxicated)
  4. intense psychological distress at exposure to internal or external cues that symbolize or resemble an aspect of the traumatic event
  5. physiological reactivity on exposure to internal or external cues that symbolize or resemble an aspect of the traumatic event

C. Persistent avoidance of stimuli associated with the trauma and numbing of general responsiveness (not present before the trauma), as indicated by three (or more) of the following:
  1. efforts to avoid thoughts, feelings, or conversations associated with the trauma
  2. efforts to avoid activities, places, or people that arouse recollections of the trauma
  3. inability to recall an important aspect of the trauma
  4. markedly diminished interest or participation in significant activities
  5. feeling of detachment or estrangement from others
  6. restricted range of affect (e.g., unable to have loving feelings)
  7. sense of a foreshortened future (e.g., does not expect to have a career, marriage, children, or a normal life span)

D. Persistent symptoms of increased arousal (not present before the trauma), as indicated by two (or more) of the following:
  1. difficulty falling or staying asleep
  2. irritability or outbursts of anger
  3. difficulty concentrating
  4. hypervigilance
  5 exaggerated startle response

E. Duration of the disturbance (symptoms in Criteria B, C, and D) is more than 1 month.

F. The disturbance causes clinically significant distress or impairment in social, occupational, or other important areas of functioning.

Source: American Psychiatric Association (2000). Diagnostic and Statistical Manual of Mental Disorders—Fourth Edition, Text Revision *(DSM-IV-TR). Arlington, VA: American Psychiatric Association. Retrieved December 19, 2013, from http://www.ncbi. nlm.nih.gov/books/NBK83241/. Courtesy of the American Psychiatric Association.*

Table 9.4 outlines the four key criteria involved in PTSD. First, the stressor or event is such that it brings about a similar result in most people who experience it. Second, the individuals relive the initial experiences through flashbacks, nightmares, and other recollections. Third, those suffering PTSD display a lack of responsiveness and reduced involvement in everyday activities. Finally, the individuals experience a variety of potential problems, such as sleeplessness, headaches, self-blame, fear, and anxiety (Burgess, 1995). Victims often make major lifestyle changes so as to avoid situations similar to that involved in the earlier experience.

Sexual battery significantly affects the victim's self-esteem. Its impact has a lasting effect that diminishes very slowly over time. Depression is another common problem for sexual assault victims. Sometimes, even suicide might be a response to the depression brought on by rape experiences.

Reorganization

The last stage in the crisis reaction repair cycle is *reorganization*. Victims reach this point once they have sorted through their feelings and are able to put this traumatic event in perspective. As the intensity of their reaction begins to diminish, they are able to move on to other activities. Although from time to time victims will drift back to their unfortunate episode and think about what happened to them, they are no longer as preoccupied with these memories as they once were. These survivors have coped with the situation, reached a point of adjustment, and are now emerging out of the crisis.

Victims never attain a total or complete cure. They carry their emotional scars with them for the remainder of their days. Victims who do complete the repair cycle, however, are able to proceed with the rest of their lives. For those victims who are not able to complete this transition, the future may consist of a continuing struggle to find the answer to the question of "Why me?"

LEGAL REFORMS

As sexual violence and related concerns have grown over the years, societal and criminal justice responses have also changed. One area of reform that we already saw entailed the alteration of statutes governing rape or sexual battery. This section focuses on some of the other more prominent revisions. We discussed changes in the definition of rape and the issue of spousal immunity earlier in this chapter. Compulsory AIDS testing for offenders, removal of the corroboration requirement, and the enactment of shield provisions are additional areas of concern that will be taken up in the following pages. After we explore just what these changes are, we will take a look at whether they brought about the desired effect.

Compulsory AIDS Testing

A health concern that worries some sexual assault victims is the threat of sexually transmitted diseases (STDs). Sparking many policy considerations is the growing awareness of acquired immunodeficiency syndrome (AIDS), caused by the HIV virus, and its devastating effects. One issue is whether the criminal justice system should mandate testing for the HIV virus in sex offenders. Just about every state has some type of law governing mandatory HIV testing of sexual offenders (National Center for Victims of Crime, 1999). Some states have enacted pretrial compulsory testing for assailants, while others restrict this procedure to convicted offenders only. Table 9.5 contains an example of one such statute.

AIDS is spread through interpersonal contact. The usual sources of contamination include contact with tainted blood, sexual intercourse with an infected person, and the sharing of needles for injecting drugs. Medical advances have made it possible to determine whether HIV, a marker for AIDS, is present within the bloodstream. When a person tests *seropositive*, he or she is a carrier and has the potential to infect others.

Table 9.5 An Example of a Compulsory AIDS Testing Statute

(1) In any case in which a person has been convicted of or has pled nolo contendere or guilty to, regardless of whether adjudication is withheld, any of the following offenses, or the attempt thereof, which offense or attempted offense involves the transmission of body fluids from one person to another [sexual battery; incest; lewd, lascivious, or indecent assault or act upon any person less than 16 years of age; assault; aggravated assault; child abuse; aggravated child abuse; abuse of an elderly person or disabled adult; aggravated abuse of an elderly person or disabled adult; sexual performance by persons less than 18 years of age; prostitution; or donation of blood, plasma, organs, skin, or other human tissue] the court shall order the offender to undergo HIV testing . . . unless the offender has undergone HIV testing voluntarily or pursuant to . . . any other applicable law or rule providing for HIV testing of criminal offenders or inmates, subsequent to her or his arrest for an offense enumerated [see previous list] for which she or he was convicted or to which she or he pled nolo contendere or guilty. The results of an HIV test performed on an offender pursuant to this subsection are not admissible in any criminal proceeding arising out of the alleged offense.

(2) The results of the HIV test must be disclosed under the direction of the Department of Health, to the offender who has been convicted of or pled nolo contendere or guilty to an offense specified in subsection (1), the public health agency of the county in which the conviction occurred and, if different, the county of the residence of the offender, and, upon request pursuant to s. 960.003, to the victim or the victim's legal guardian, or the parent or legal guardian of the victim if the victim is a minor.

(3) An offender who has undergone HIV testing pursuant to subsection (1), and to whom positive test results have been disclosed pursuant to subsection (2), who commits a second or subsequent offense enumerated in paragraphs (1)(a)-(n), commits criminal transmission of HIV, a felony of the third degree. . .

(4) An offender may challenge the positive results of an HIV test performed pursuant to this section and may introduce results of a backup test performed at her or his own expense.

(5) Nothing in this section requires that an HIV infection has occurred in order for an offender to have committed criminal transmission of HIV.

Source: Florida Statutes (2012), § 775.0877.

Despite medical progress, there is still some ambiguity surrounding HIV laboratory testing. For one thing, the presence of HIV antibodies does not mean that a seropositive person has developed AIDS already. At the same time, a seronegative reading, while reassuring, is not necessarily conclusive. Once infection occurs, the virus requires an incubation period. This *window period* means that it may take several months for medical screening to detect any antibodies present in the carrier's bloodstream (Wieczorek, 2010). Thus, a negative report from one or even two points in time may not offer a guarantee of being disease-free.

What are the odds that sexual assault victims will become contaminated after the attack? One way to answer that question is to focus upon two related aspects. The first is to calculate the percentage of HIV cases within the offender population. The second is to determine the risk of viral infection from a single act of intercourse.

The Centers for Disease Control and Prevention (2006) places the risk of contracting HIV in consensual intercourse at around 0.1% per episode. While these odds are very low, many sexual assaults produce injuries and lacerations, an environment conducive to subsequent infection. While the Centers for Disease Control and Prevention has identified isolated cases in which a sexual assault victim has contracted HIV, the incidence is extremely rare (Wieczorek, 2010). Usually, initiating a series of antibodies and other drug regimens within 72 hours of the assault suffices to counteract any future problems. Follow-up testing and medical review over the next 1–2 weeks is a standard protocol.

An assessment of this situation has led to some protests against mandatory HIV-testing policy as an invasion of constitutional rights. For example, objections have surfaced concerning the suspect's right to privacy, the presumption of innocence, and whether pre-conviction testing violates search-and-seizure standards (McGuire, 1991; Smotas, 1991). At the same time, more than one-half of the states have enacted legislation making the intentional spread of HIV through sexual contact a crime. While there is some indication that media coverage sensationalizes and misrepresents the risk of disease transmission from HIV-related assaults (Flavin, 2000), the case law developing in this area is worth watching over the next few years.

Consent and Corroboration

The common law looked for corroborative or supporting evidence to validate a woman's claim that she had been the victim of a rape. If you will recall, the common-law definition appearing at the start of this chapter included an "utmost resistance" clause. Many juries hesitated to convict solely on the basis of the victim's testimony, especially if the death penalty was involved. They were afraid that the accuser might be harboring a vendetta and, for whatever reason, may try to "railroad" the man into prison (Ellis, 1992).

Typical supporting evidence would involve such things as timely notification to the police, the presence of semen, the use of a weapon by the offender, and (most notably) physical harm (Bourke, 1989; Spears & Spohn, 1996). The assumption was that any victim who was unwilling to submit to a sexual attack should resist to her utmost capacity. It was expected that a woman would submit only if her struggles would bring her to the brink of death. Under this reasoning, the "perfect" case would be the woman who was brutally beaten and exhibited massive physical injuries. Indeed, some people assumed that the absence of physical harm was tantamount to *prima facie* evidence that a rape did not take place.

Legal reforms eliminated the requirement that rape victims must fight ferociously for their lives. The reasoning employed was that no other victims are held to this defensive standard. As Table 9.6 attests, robbery victims are not expected to resist the robber before giving up their valuables. In the interest of justice, then, it is not fair to impose this extra burden upon sexual assault victims. As a result, when new sexual battery legislation was drafted, the resistance requirement was dropped. Of course, this move has raised new questions that have yet to be resolved (Stitt & Lentz, 1996).

The modification in the need for corroborative evidence also shows the change in the response to victims. Many jurisdictions no longer require proof of penetration or maximum resistance to the point of physical force. The protocol in effect at Antioch College, displayed in Table 9.7, makes consent an integral part at each step in order to avoid any possible misinterpretation by either party. As Winslett and Gross (2008: 558) explain, "preintimacy agreement between dating partners concerning sexual activity may reduce misperceptions of sexual intent."

These provisions underscore the debate over criminal liability and the absolute last point at which a person can withdraw consent. Essentially, the question is whether the victim can withdraw consent after the sexual act is underway. Common law generally holds that a rape cannot occur if a woman has agreed to participate and sexual intercourse has begun. However, some jurisdictions recognize post-penetration rape in those instances in which force is invoked to complete the act (Lyon, 2004). While legal developments are still taking place in this arena, Illinois has responded to this controversy by enacting a statute that affirms the right to withdraw consent at any time during the sexual encounter. Specifically, that law states "a person who initially consents to sexual penetration or sexual conduct is not deemed to have consented to any sexual penetration or sexual conduct that occurs after he or she withdraws consent during the course of that sexual penetration or sexual conduct" (720 *Illinois Compiled Statutes*, 2012: 5/11-1.70(c)).

As Table 9.8 demonstrates, there is still a reluctance to convict sexual batterers solely on the testimony of the victim for fear of a false claim. As a result, some

Table 9.6 "The Rape" of Mr. Smith

The law discriminates against rape victims in a manner which would not be tolerated by victims of any other crime. In the following example, a holdup victim is asked questions similar in form to those usually asked of a rape victim.

"Mr. Smith, you were held up at gunpoint on the corner of 16th and Locust?"

"Yes."

"Did you struggle with the robber?"

"No."

"Why not?"

"He was armed."

"Then you made a conscious decision to comply with his demands rather than to resist?"

"Yes."

"Did you scream? Cry out?"

"No. I was afraid."

"I see. Have you ever been held up before?"

"No."

"Have you ever given money away?"

"Yes, of course—"

"And did you do so willingly?"

"What are you getting at?"

"Well, let's put it like this, Mr. Smith. You've given away money in the past—in fact, you have quite a reputation for philanthropy. How can we be sure that you weren't contriving to have your money taken from you by force?"

"Listen, if I wanted—"

"Never mind. What time did this holdup take place, Mr. Smith?"

"About 11 P.M."

"You were out on the streets at 11 P.M.? Doing what?"

"Just walking."

"Just walking? You know it's dangerous being out on the street that late at night. Weren't you aware that you could have been held up?"

"I hadn't thought about it."

"What were you wearing at the time, Mr. Smith?"

"Let's see. A suit. Yes, a suit."

"An expensive suit?"

"Well—yes."

"In other words, Mr. Smith, you were walking around the streets late at night in a suit that practically advertised the fact that you might be a good target for some easy money, isn't that so? I mean, if we didn't know better, Mr. Smith, we might even think you were asking for this to happen, mightn't we?"

"Look, can't we talk about the past history of the guy who did this to me?"

"I'm afraid not, Mr. Smith. I don't think you would want to violate his rights, now would you?"

Source: Anonymous. "The Rape" of Mr. Smith. *Retrieved April 5, 2013, from http://www.holysmoke.org/fem/fem0235.htm.*

Table 9.7 The Antioch College Sexual Offense Prevention Policy

Consent is defined as the act of willingly and verbally agreeing to engage in specific sexual conduct. The following are clarifying points:

- Consent is required each and every time there is sexual activity.
- All parties must have a clear and accurate understanding of the sexual activity.
- The person(s) who initiate(s) the sexual activity is responsible for asking for consent.
- The person(s) who are asked are responsible for verbally responding.
- Each new level of sexual activity requires consent.
- Use of agreed upon forms of communication such as gestures or safe words is acceptable, but must be discussed and verbally agreed to by all parties before sexual activity occurs.
- Consent is required regardless of the parties' relationship, prior sexual history, or current activity (e.g., grinding on the dance floor is not consent for further sexual activity).
- At any and all times when consent is withdrawn or not verbally agreed to, the sexual activity must stop immediately.
- Silence is not consent.
- Body movements and non-verbal responses such as moans are not consent.
- A person cannot give consent while sleeping.
- All parties must have unimpaired judgement (examples that may cause impairment include, but are not limited to, alcohol, drugs, mental health conditions, physical health conditions).
- All parties must use safe sex practices.
- All parties must disclose personal risk factors and any known sexually transmitted infections. Individuals are responsible for maintaining awareness of their sexual health.

Source: Baya, M. J. (October 4, 1993). The Antioch College Sexual Offense Policy. Yellow Springs, OH: Antioch College. Retrieved on April 5, 2013, from http://www.mit.edu/activities/safe/data/other/antioch-code.

Table 9.8 Polygraph Tests Used to Corroborate Victim Allegations

CLEVELAND, Ohio – A Juvenile Court judge has ordered three teenage girls who were victims of sexual assault to submit to polygraph tests, baffling prosecutors and upsetting the victims.

Cuyahoga Juvenile Court Judge Alison Floyd ordered victims connected with four separate cases to be examined after she had found their attackers delinquent, the Juvenile Court equivalent of guilty.

"I believe even more damage was done by the judge letting the perpetrator know she was ordering the victim to take the polygraph. He apparently took this to mean the judge did not believe her and he used this to tell their peers that the judge did not believe her and was ordering her take a lie detector test," the mother wrote.

"It felt like the blame was back on her and she was being victimized, by not only him [again], but by the system as well."

Source: Dissell, R., & Atassi, L. (2010). Cuyahoga Juvenile Court Judge Alison Floyd orders sex assault victims to take polygraph tests. The Plain Dealer, March 19. Retrieved on April 5, 2013, from http://blog.cleveland.com/metro/2010/03/ juvenile_court_judge_alison_fl.html.

investigations have included a "lie-detector" test to establish the truthfulness of the victim. In light of this disparity, a number of states, including Florida (*Florida Statutes*, 2012: § 960.001(1)(t)), have banned the use of polygraph testing to establish the veracity of the victim's complaint. In addition, the federal funding initiatives contained in the Violence Against Women Reauthorization Act of 2013 (Public Law 113–4–March 7, 2013) require a prohibition against polygraph testing of sexual assault victims be in place before releasing grant monies.

Shield Provisions

Under common law, the burden of proof in a rape case fell squarely upon the victim. It was up to the victim to show that the accused forced her to engage in behavior to which she objected. A common tactic invoked by many aggressive defense attorneys was to attack the victim's credibility by making an issue of her sexual past. A typical strategy was to imply promiscuity from prior consensual sexual activity with men other than the defendant. Presumably, this information suggested a lack of chastity and, therefore, amply proved the victim's willingness to engage in sexual activity without any reliance on force. In essence, the criminal justice system placed the victim on trial and dealt with her in a callous fashion.

Many victims were reluctant to pursue formal charges under these skewed conditions. No other type of crime victim had to endure this kind of intense scrutiny. For example, lawyers did not probe the history of burglary or robbery victims to show they had a reputation or a proclivity for becoming victimized. As a result, reformers sought to introduce new standards that would protect or shield sexual assault victims from further trauma. To do so required a very delicate balance. As one group of experts explains (Call, Nice, & Talarico, 1991: 784–785):

> The controversy over rape shield laws has presented policy makers with a difficult dilemma: should they permit a defense strategy based on destroying the victim's reputation, a strategy that compounds victim trauma, may discourage reporting rapes, and may enable rapists to avoid punishment. Conversely, a strong shield law may generate complaints that it limits defendants' ability to have an adequate defense, thus violating due process.

The states have varied in their approaches to revising this portion of their sexual battery statutes. Three primary dimensions sprang from these efforts. First, there was the general issue of whether the victim's prior sexual history with others was relevant. Second, there was the more specific concern of whether the victim's prior sexual history with the accused should be admissible. Finally, the court would judge the relevancy of any evidence about the victim's sexual history *in camera*, that is, well out of public earshot. As you can see, the aim of these reforms was to protect the victim's privacy from any unnecessary public invasion.

One can rate a state's shield provisions as either strong (very restrictive and protective of victims) or weak (virtually no change from past practices), depending on how each of these three concerns are handled. While one might guess that more progressive states would respond more favorably to feminist pressures by embracing these changes, such is not the case. There is some indication that having a feminist agenda or a strong lobbying effort has not influenced these evidentiary reforms. Instead, it seems that these modifications reflect the much broader crime control strategy that was presented in Chapter 1 (Berger et al., 1988; Berger, Neuman, & Searles, 1991; Call et al., 1991).

Sex Offender Registration

The final legislative reform we will discuss is the proliferation of sex offender registration laws. These laws, often referred to as *Megan's Law* (which will be discussed further in Chapter 11), exist in every state and seek to provide both past victims and the general public with information regarding the presence of a convicted sex offender in the community. The premise underlying these laws is twofold. First, treatment protocols for sex offenders are far from perfect. The common belief is that recidivism rates for these criminals are quite high. Second, warning the public that a sex offender is living in their community alerts residents to take appropriate precautions and to be watchful of these people's activities.

One example of a *sex offender registration* law appears in Table 9.9. The Florida version shares many of the same features found in other state statutes. The precipitating offense need not be a violent rape. Instead, a host of "sexually oriented offenses" can trigger registration. Such crimes as rape, sexual battery, lewd and lascivious behavior, indecent exposure, other offenses that fulfill sexual needs of the offender (e.g., murder, kidnapping), and various sex crimes against children (e.g., kidnapping, pandering obscenity, compelling prostitution) can trigger these legal provisions. In addition, judges can impose registration requirements on convicted sex offenders because of the likelihood of future violations. Factors that judges can use when making this determination include multiple past convictions, evidence of deviant (not necessarily criminal) sexual behavior, past offenses involving torture or ritualistic acts, or prior nonsexual violent acts.

These laws instruct two main parties to take action. First, the offender must register with the local law enforcement agency where he or she intends to settle. This stipulation includes both the agency that has jurisdiction over the offender's permanent residence and any agency with jurisdiction over a temporary residence. Registration generally must occur within a few days of release from custody, movement into a new jurisdiction, or following a change of address. Second, the law enforcement agency with whom the registration occurs must notify a wide range of constituencies about the presence of the offender. Parties to be notified include neighbors of the offender, local educational institutions, nearby agencies that deal with children, and other local law enforcement agencies. The

Table 9.9 The Florida Sexual Predators Act Registration Requirements

(6) Registration.

(a) A sexual predator must register with the department through the sheriff's office by providing the following information to the department:

1. Name; social security number; age; race; sex; date of birth; height; weight; hair and eye color; photograph; address of legal residence and address of any current temporary residence, within the state or out of state, including a rural route address and a post office box, any electronic mail address and any instant message name required to be provided pursuant to subparagraph (g)4; home telephone number and any cellular telephone; date and place of any employment; date and place of each conviction; fingerprints; and a brief description of the crime or crimes committed by the offender. A post office box shall not be provided in lieu of a physical residential address.

(f) Within 48 hours after the registration required under paragraph (a) or paragraph (e), a sexual predator who is not incarcerated and who resides in the community, including a sexual predator under the supervision of the Department of Corrections, shall register in person at a driver's license office of the Department of Highway Safety and Motor Vehicles and shall present proof of registration. At the driver's license office the sexual predator shall:

1. If otherwise qualified, secure a Florida driver's license, renew a Florida driver's license, or secure an identification card. The sexual predator shall identify himself or herself as a sexual predator who is required to comply with this section, provide his or her place of permanent, temporary, or transient residence, including a rural route address and a post office box, and submit to the taking of a photograph for use in issuing a driver's license, renewed license, or identification card, and for use by the department in maintaining current records of sexual predators. A post office box shall not be provided in lieu of a physical residential address. ...

2. A sexual predator who vacates a permanent, temporary, or transient residence and fails to establish or maintain another permanent, temporary, or transient residence shall, within 48 hours after vacating the permanent, temporary, or transient residence, report in person to the sheriff's office of the county in which he or she is located. The sexual predator shall specify the date upon which he or she intends to or did vacate such residence. The sexual predator must provide or update all of the registration information required under paragraph (a). The sexual predator must provide an address for the residence or other location that he or she is or will be occupying during the time in which he or she fails to establish or maintain a permanent or temporary residence.

4. A sexual predator must register any electronic mail address or instant message name with the department prior to using such electronic mail address or instant message name on or after October 1, 2007.

(7) Community and Public Notification.

(a) Law enforcement agencies must inform members of the community and the public of a sexual predator's presence. Upon notification of the presence of a sexual predator, the sheriff of the county or the chief of police of the municipality where the sexual predator establishes or maintains a permanent or temporary residence shall notify members of the community and the public of the presence of the sexual predator in a manner deemed appropriate by the sheriff or the chief of police. Within 48 hours after receiving notification of the presence of a sexual predator, the sheriff of the county or the chief of police of the municipality where the sexual predator temporarily or permanently resides shall notify each licensed day care center, elementary school, middle school, and high school within a 1-mile radius of the temporary or permanent residence of the sexual predator of the presence of the sexual predator. Information provided to members of the community and the public regarding a sexual predator must include:

1. The name of the sexual predator;
2. A description of the sexual predator, including a photograph;
3. The sexual predator's current, temporary, and transient addresses, and descriptions of registered locations that have no specific street address, including the name of the county or municipality if known;
4. The circumstances of the sexual predator's offense or offenses; and
5. Whether the victim of the sexual predator's offense or offenses was, at the time of the offense, a minor or an adult.

Source: Florida Statutes *(2012) § 775.21.*

notification typically includes the name and address of the offender, a physical description, as well as the nature of the conviction offense.

🌐 **WEB ACTIVITY**

The National Sex Offender Public Web-site, sponsored by the U.S. Department of Justice, provides links to state sex offender registries. More information is available at **http://www.nsopw.gov/**

The move to offender registration has not been limited to state action. The federal government passed the Jacob Wetterling Crimes Against Children and Sexually Violent Offender Registration Act in 1995. What this legislation required, among other things, was that states must establish registries of convicted sex offenders or face a reduction in federal criminal justice funding. President Bush signed the Adam Walsh Child Protection and Safety Act into law on July 27, 2006. This initiative created a national sex offender registry, standardized the information each state entered, and integrated all the state files into a single source (White House News Release, 2006). The number of entries in the national sex offender registry exceeds 736,000 perpetrators.

As with any new legislation, several questions and challenges have arisen. One legal concern deals with the potential of these laws to further punish offenders once they have completed their sentences. This worry over double jeopardy, however, has fallen on deaf ears so far, with the U.S. Supreme Court upholding the right of the state to protect citizens in this way *(Kansas v. Hendricks,* 1997). A related concern involves attempts to impose the new laws on those already convicted and serving their sentences. Another issue relates to the impact of such laws on the offender's ability to find a home, locate a job, and be free from intimidation and harassment. There are some instances wherein an offender loses his or her job and must move due to actions taken by community members against him or her (Levenson & Cotter, 2005; Tewksbury, 2005). At what point does the community's right to know impinge on the rights of the offender to be secure in his or her home and to hold a job free from harassment? Each of these various concerns will be addressed in greater detail in Chapter 11.

All these efforts are predicated on the assumption that sex offenders are extremely dangerous to public safety and that they experience unusually high recidivism rates, thereby victimizing even more persons. For example, the legislative intent behind the Florida Sexual Predators Act (*Florida Statutes,* 2012: § 775.21(3)(a)) reads:

> Repeat sexual offenders, sexual offenders who use physical violence, and sexual offenders who prey on children are sexual predators who present an extreme threat to the public safety. Sexual offenders are extremely likely to use physical violence and to repeat their offenses, and most sexual offenders commit many offenses, have many more victims than are ever reported, and are prosecuted for only a fraction of their crimes. This makes the cost of sexual offender victimization to society at large, while incalculable, clearly exorbitant.

Using this kind of a sentiment as a springboard, Sample and Bray (2003) questioned whether these assumptions are grounded in empirical observations. The researchers relied upon offender criminal history information compiled by the Illinois State Police from 1990 until 1997. Their analysis revealed that sex offenders had one of the lowest rearrest rates for any crime and for the same original crime than did most other criminals. While these data provide little empirical support for the policy efforts that have arisen over the past few years, other commentators are not quite ready to dismiss legislative reactions as groundless or based on hysteria (Pallone, 2003; Wright, 2003). Instead, they suggest that it might be more fruitful to look at other avenues for greater effectiveness.

When dealing with legislative change, the genesis of the reform may not be as important as the impact of the new law. The real question is whether enacted legislative remedies are achieving the desired effects. The following section visits the question of whether legal reforms have worked as intended.

THE IMPACT OF LEGAL REFORM

Chapter 5 introduced two concepts that can be of use in addressing the question of whether these legal reforms have had the desired impact. Earlier, we talked about whether victim compensation legislation produced any macro-level or micro-level effects. If you will recall, a *macro-level effect* is a change in such global indicators as crime reporting rates, clearance rates, prosecution rates, conviction rates, and the like. The emphasis is on a broad societal impact. In contrast, a *micro-level effect* entails looking at a much smaller unit to see if there have been changes in such things as worker attitudes, client satisfaction, and so forth.

Both types of effects are helpful to look at when trying to evaluate whether legal reforms have worked. The following material examines whether changes in sexual assault laws have had the anticipated macro-level and micro-level effects.

Macro-Level Effects

The changes that legislators made in the sexual assault regulations were designed to make the criminal justice system more "victim-friendly." Modifying the elements of what constitutes sexual battery, removing some of the overly restrictive evidentiary barriers, and establishing shield provisions should lessen some of the trauma victims experience when seeking justice. These attempts to counteract biases that had come to typify sexual battery cases should encourage greater system participation. As a result, reformers were expecting to find increased crime reporting, higher arrest rates, more effective prosecution, and enhanced conviction rates.

Early studies gave hope that these legal reforms held promise. For example, it appeared that Michigan had experienced some significant gains in arrests and convictions (Caringella-MacDonald, 1984; Marsh, Geist, & Caplan, 1982).

However, subsequent evaluations have been less than enthusiastic about these changes (Bachman & Paternoster, 1993).

One research team studied the effect of definitional and evidentiary reforms in Illinois (Spohn & Horney, 1990). Using court cases from the Cook County Circuit Court allowed the researchers to monitor charges filed by the prosecutor, conviction records, and sentencing outcomes. What Spohn and Horney found was that legislative reforms had very limited, if any, direct impact. They explained that "passage of the rape shield law in 1978 had no significant effects on reports of rape or the processing of rape cases in Chicago. The results of the analysis of the 1984 definitional changes are inconclusive" (Spohn & Horney, 1990: 14).

Conclusions based upon data from a single jurisdiction suffer from an inability to generalize to other locations. One does not know whether the results are idiosyncratic or whether they accurately reflect broad trends. Such a shortcoming points out the need to look at several jurisdictions and various degrees of reform efforts.

After closely examining a number of state statutes, Horney and Spohn (1991) selected six evaluation sites: Atlanta, Detroit, Chicago, Houston, Philadelphia, and Washington, DC. Using records from 1970 until 1984, the researchers gathered information regarding filed reports, indictments, convictions, and sentencing practices. Even after isolating the different types of changes in the various locations, there was no evidence of any systematic or dramatic impact. Another study that looked at the impact of legal reform in Canada upon arrests and subsequent prosecution also found no effect (Schissel, 1996). A reanalysis of the National Violence Against Women Survey (see earlier in this chapter) reveals only subtle changes in reporting practices (Clay-Warner & Burt, 2005). In other words, it appears that rape reforms have not introduced any sweeping changes into system operations.

Micro-Level Effects

The lack of any noticeable macro-level effects perplexed some observers. However, others did not regard these dismal outcomes as being out of the ordinary. They pointed out that the system has a long history of failures in attempting to mend flaws. Whenever outsiders try to correct current practices, system officials have ample opportunities to circumvent the desired goals.

Mindful of the gap between how the law appears on the books and how it is implemented, Horney and Spohn (1991) interviewed judges, prosecutors, and defense attorneys in six cities for clues. What they found was instructive.

While shield provisions outline what types of evidence are considered relevant and provide for *in camera* hearings, private sidebars rarely occur. Instead, informal courtroom norms govern the players. Prosecutors, well aware of how the judge eventually would rule, simply concede and do not try to block the admission of certain kinds of evidence. As Horney and Spohn (1991: 155–156) explain:

> If a defendant is acquitted because the judge ignored the law and either admitted potentially relevant evidence without a hearing or allowed the defense attorney to use legally inadmissible evidence, the victim cannot appeal the acquittal or the judge's decisions. If, on the other hand, the judge followed the law and refused to admit seemingly irrelevant sexual history evidence, the defendant can appeal his conviction. All of the consequences, in other words, would lead judges and prosecutors to err in favor of the defendant.

What this finding seems to indicate is that the major players in the courtroom drama have the capability to thwart reform efforts. The results show a huge gap between the law as it appears on the books and the law in action.

Summary of Legal Reform

Legislative reform does not guarantee improvement in the plight of the victim or the activity of the criminal justice system. Simply changing the law guarantees neither compliance nor impact. In some cases, the system can accommodate the change by altering procedure rather than outcome. In more recent actions, such as sex offender registration laws, enough time has not gone by yet for an impact to materialize. In some other instances, there has been little, if any, systematic study devoted to the effect of the legislation.

RESPONDING TO SEXUAL ASSAULT VICTIMS

A number of jurisdictions have adopted a *Sexual Assault Response Team* (SART) approach when responding to sexual assault victims. The purpose of a SART is to combine representatives from law enforcement, victim advocacy, forensic nursing, and the prosecutor's officer in a joint effort to provide seamless case handling. The intent is to lessen the aggravation that many victims experience after they report the incident and enter the criminal justice system. SART is designed to make the victim's needs, not the system's needs, the top priority. The discussion that follows explains the role of each SART member.

The Police

The police response is mobilized as soon as there is notification that a sexual assault has taken place. Police call-takers and dispatchers perform a gatekeeper role to the police system (Doerner, 2012). After the call-taker sorts through the information being relayed, he or she is in a position to categorize the incident, determine the most appropriate agency response, and start mobilizing resources. Table 9.10 outlines some of the considerations for which dispatchers are responsible when initiating a SART response.

Table 9.10 Dispatcher Protocol Checklist in a SART Format

- Check safety (weapons, injuries, direction of travel of suspect, etc.).
- Check special language/access needs.
- Confirm victim/s safety and medical needs; activate Emergency Medical Services as needed.
- Seek suspect information; description, direction of travel, vehicle, etc.
- Provide SANE related evidentiary advisories—not to bathe, change clothes, comb hair, brush teeth, touch any articles or furniture the assailant may have touched, etc.
- When a SART-trained officer is on duty, the SART-trained officer will be dispatched to the scene. When a SART-trained officer is not on duty, a uniform officer will be dispatched to the scene.
- Dispatcher is to remain on the line with the victim, if practical, until officers arrive, especially if the victim is alone and/or the scene is not safe.
- If it is obvious through the discussion that the incident is a sensitive crime and venue is confirmed, dispatch may activate the SART (SART-trained officer, advocate, SANE) immediately upon the approval of the shift commander.

Source: Wisconsin Coalition Against Sexual Assault (2011). Wisconsin Adult Sexual Assault Response Team Protocol. Madison: Wisconsin Office of Justice Assistance, p. 20. Retrieved on April 5, 2013, from http://www.wcasa.org/file_open.php?id=203.

Upon arrival at the scene, the responding officer must assess the victim's physical and emotional condition and then initiate appropriate actions. The primary officer has three major responsibilities in a sexual assault case. They are as follows:

- protect, interview, and support the victim;
- collect and preserve evidence that can assist in the apprehension and prosecution of the offender;
- investigate the crime and apprehend the offender (National Sheriffs' Association, 2010: 43).

Once this stage is concluded, the officer usually tries to get some details on what has taken place and may enlist the aid of a victim advocate. Victims normally go to a medical facility for treatment. Evidence collection (especially DNA sampling, if possible) takes place at the crime scene, as well as at the hospital. At this point, the initial investigation usually concludes with an interview in an effort to gather more information about the incident and the assailant.

The view of police indifference and insensitivity toward rape victims is widespread and not without some empirical support. A national survey of police officers uncovered a prevailing attitude of suspicion and lack of concern for rape victims (LeDoux & Hazelwood, 1985). A significant number of police officers, like the general population, subscribe to rape myths. Often, police officers classify rape cases as unfounded, based on their perceptions of the offender and the victim (Sanders, 1980). While this decision-making is not unlike what takes place in other kinds of cases, it does indicate a consistent style of indifference.

One factor that may reflect the criminal justice system's stance toward rape victims is the level of reporting by victims. According to a detailed analysis by the NCVS, two out of every three women who were rape or sexual assault victims during the 2005–2010 interval chose not to disclose their victimization episodes to the police (Planty et al., 2013: 7). Typically, sexual battery is the least reported offense in the NCVS (Chen & Ullman, 2010). One possible reason for this nonreporting is the nonsupportive reaction of the police to such allegations. Cumbersome, insensitive, and inappropriate questions that drill victims to expose any holes or inconsistencies in their allegations can change the emphasis of the case from what the accused did to what the victim did or did not do (Patterson, 2011a, 2011b).

Concern over this callous handling has led many agencies to institute changes in how they process sexual assault cases. Many departments have established specialized investigatory units whose exclusive responsibility is to handle sexual battery calls. Other strategies call for greater supervisory review over cases that are inappropriately closed, deemed to be unfounded, or not worthy of further investigation (Police Executive Research Forum, 2012). Steps have been taken toward training officers to employ crisis counseling techniques, establishing closer ties with rape crisis centers, deploying victim advocates to the crime scene, dispatching female patrol officers to assist sexual assault victims, and developing relationships with doctors and medical services for better treatment of victims. The result of such initiatives is officers who are more sympathetic toward, and hold more positive attitudes about, victims of sexual assault (Campbell, 1995; Campbell & Johnson, 1997; Kinney et al., 2007; Temkin, 1996).

The Hospital

A standard procedure when dealing with sexual assault victims is to arrange for the provision of medical care. The goals enumerated in Table 9.11 underscore the fact that the hospital becomes a very crucial link for many victims. The purpose of seeking emergency medical treatment for sexual assault victims is actually twofold. The first goal is to receive medical assistance; the second is to preserve materials for evidentiary purposes.

Medical Examination

One of the more pressing needs in a sexual assault case is to attend to the victim's physical well-being. For some victims, this need is rather apparent. There may be bleeding, contusions, bumps, broken bones, or other obvious injuries that require immediate medical treatment. Other victims may be hurt even though they do not display any outward signs of injury.

Many hospitals have established specific procedures aimed at minimizing the emotional trauma that victims experience. A support person—either a victim advocate or a specially trained nurse—will remain with the victim throughout the physical examination. Most hospital procedures allow sexual assault victims to bypass the usual registration procedures in the public intake area. Instead, medical personnel escort the victim to a private room in order to spare the victim further embarrassment and to help the survivor re-establish a sense of control.

Table 9.11 What Does a Sexual Assault Nurse Examiner (SANE) Do?
Mission Statement
The primary mission of a SANE program is to meet the needs of the sexual assault victim by providing immediate, compassionate, culturally sensitive, and comprehensive forensic evaluation and treatment by trained, professional nurse experts...
Program Goals
■ To protect the sexual assault victim from further harm. ■ To provide crisis intervention. ■ To provide timely, thorough, and professional forensic evidence collection, documentation, and preservation of evidence. ■ To evaluate and treat prophylactically for sexually transmitted diseases (STDs). ■ To evaluate pregnancy risk and offer prevention. ■ To assess, document, and seek care for injuries. ■ To appropriately refer victims for immediate and follow-up medical care and follow-up counseling. ■ To enhance the ability of law enforcement agencies to obtain evidence and successfully prosecute sexual assault cases.
Source: Ledray, L. E. (1999). SANE: Sexual Assault Nurse Examiner: Development and Operation Guide. *Washington, DC: Office for Victims of Crime, pp. 8–9. Accessed on April 27, 2013, from http://www.ojp.usdoj.gov/ovc/publications/infores/sane/saneguide.pdf.*

A promising development has been the introduction of the *Sexual Assault Nurse Examiner* (SANE). A SANE is a registered nurse who has acquired advanced training and is able to provide specialized service to sexual assault victims. This person works as a forensics nurse. A *forensics nurse* bridges the fields of medical care and criminal justice. In addition to providing physical and emotional treatment, he or she collects evidence that will aid the law enforcement investigation and prosecutory efforts. As Table 9.11 explains, this approach takes a holistic view of victim needs while, at the same time, remaining cognizant of legal and forensic concerns.

Essentially, the SANE coordinates service delivery and guides the victim through the entire process. The first SANE program began operating in the mid-1970s. Today, there are numerous programs in place, and that number continues to expand. Unfortunately, it is too early to reach a definitive conclusion as to how well these programs are working in achieving their goals (Campbell, Patterson, & Lichty, 2005; Greeson & Campbell, 2013). It is safe to say, though, that there are some preliminary indications that SANE programs do promote post-assault recovery and play an important role in generating more thorough law enforcement investigations, capturing more critical evidence, and subsequent prosecutions (Campbell et al., 2005; Campbell et al., 2012a; Campbell, Patterson, & Bybee, 2012b; Fehler-Cabral, Campbell, & Patterson, 2011; McLaren, Henson, & Stone, 2010).

The medical examination addresses the immediate physical injuries, the prevention or treatment of sexually transmitted diseases (STDs), and the possibility of pregnancy. The likelihood of becoming pregnant after a sexual assault ranges from 5–30% (Shulman, Muran, & Speck, 1992). In addition to external forms of trauma, it is not unusual for sexual assault victims to sustain internal gynecological injuries. These conditions, if left untreated, could lead to long-term complications.

One problem that can have extremely important ramifications is *sexually transmitted disease* (*STD*). Because most assailants have not been apprehended or tested at this point, the risk of an STD infection is unknown. Precautionary measures designed to combat gonorrhea, syphilis, chlamydia, or other STDs may be warranted. For example, Baker and associates (1990) note that almost one-half of the rape victims in their study identified AIDS as a primary worry. However, there is some concern that detection of exposure to the HIV virus is neither timely nor reliable and could impede emotional recovery (Bowleg & Stoll, 1991). Undoubtedly, anxiety over this issue will escalate as the incidence of AIDS and other STDs continues to grow (Centers for Disease Control and Prevention, 2012; Ledray, 1999).

Forensic Examination

Evidence preservation begins long before the victim reaches the hospital doors. Sometimes sexual assault victims may feel defiled or dirty. They may have a strong desire to take a shower, change clothes, brush their teeth, or wash their hands before going to the hospital. Doing so could destroy potentially valuable evidence. As a result, police dispatchers and investigators normally advise sexual assault victims to delay these activities. They also ask these victims to carry a fresh set of clothing to the hospital so that items worn during the attack can be impounded and preserved as evidence.

A frequent stumbling block to the forensic portion of the emergency room examination has been that it placed physicians in an awkward position (Best, Dansky, & Kilpatrick, 1992). Once the attending physician finished treating the victim, the *forensic examination* was underway (though the victim might not be cognizant of it). Many doctors lacked appropriate training in evidence collection (Campbell et al., 2005; Carrow, 1980; Hilberman, 1976; Martin & Powell, 1994; Sproles, 1985) or conveyed a less than sympathetic attitude toward the victim (Campbell, 2005; Martin & Powell, 1994; Temkin, 1996). Consequently, they relied upon police investigators for instructions as to what to do in these situations. The outcome, as one might well guess, was often haphazard and far from systematic. These gaps could hinder successful prosecution of the attacker. The SANE program discussed earlier is designed to sidestep these problems.

Many states responded to a federal initiative and formulated *rape kits* to alleviate this evidentiary problem. The Office of the Florida Attorney General (2010), in conjunction with the Florida Department of Law Enforcement, has instituted one such standardized protocol. These kits include a preprinted set of instructions for the physician to follow, report forms to complete, containers for collecting hair samples and fingernail scrapings, swabs and slides for extracting fluid specimens, blood sample containers, and other tools for gathering trace evidence. Once the attending physician or SANE completes the forensic examination, the police investigator impounds the kit and submits it to the crime laboratory for evidence analysis.

A related issue that has commanded attention is who should pay for the evidentiary or forensic examination. A follow-up to the 1982 President's Task Force on Victims discovered that it was a common practice for hospitals to bill sexual assault victims for the evidence collection. The federal Violence Against Women Act prohibits participating hospitals or medical carriers from billing victims for sexual assault examinations (U.S. Department of Justice, 2013, p. 55). Today, state victim compensation programs usually underwrite the cost of this evidence gathering. Florida, for example, does not allow providers to bill victims for the medical exam. Instead, the Office of the Attorney General will reimburse vendors up to $500 for these expenses (*Florida Statutes*, 2012: § 960.28). If this recourse is not available, then either the investigating agency or the prosecutor's office is usually responsible for payment.

The Prosecutor

In the past, many prosecutors have been reluctant to take sexual battery cases to trial. Prior to the implementation of the legal reforms presented earlier, prosecutors were leery of pursuing cases in which the victim did not sustain any visible physical injuries. The issue of consent was a huge stumbling block, particularly if there was a jury trial. Often, the determining factor in the case was the victim's demeanor and credibility on the stand. In fact, Konradi (1996) reports that the clothes a victim wears to court, the appropriate display of emotion while testifying, rehearsing testimony, and other pretrial preparations help survivors negotiate the criminal justice process and sway the odds in their favor. In addition, it may very well be that some jurors, unbeknown to the prosecution, harbor rape myths or inaccurate beliefs, like the ones described earlier in this chapter, that may sway their perceptions (Long, 2008; Scalzo, 2007; Wisconsin Office of Justice Assistance, 2009).

Critics have not hesitated to question prosecutorial decisions and case attrition. A common complaint is that prosecutors refuse to file charges and fail to prosecute an inordinate number of suspects. In very broad terms, it is typical for only about one-half of the victimizations reported to the police to result in an arrest. In turn, only about one-half of the arrests culminate in a prosecution, and far fewer end in a conviction.

Some studies indicate that the attrition in prosecution and conviction is due to actions of the victim (Horney & Spohn, 1991; Spears & Spohn, 1996;

Spohn & Spears, 1996). For example, victims who take "risks," such as hitch-hiking, using alcohol or other drugs, or going to the offender's home, have a greater likelihood of their case being dismissed than other victims. In one sense, these people do not fit the normal profile of a "genuine victim." As Chapter 6 explains, "the prosecutory assembly line" concentrates on winning in court. One way to achieve this goal is to take on "convictable" cases and to discard those cases that might present more of a challenge (Alderden & Ullman, 2012). In terms of the case handling by the system, a detailed comparative analysis has shown that rape cases move through the system just like any other major felony (Galvin & Polk, 1983). Despite this "business as usual" approach, there is still room for improvement in the way prosecutors handle sexual assault cases.

SUMMARY

Sexual violence has been an instrumental rallying point in the growth of the victim movement in the United States. Many of these issues led to the revision of the criminal justice system to make it more protective of victims. Sexual battery victims suffer much emotional trauma and endure a burdensome recovery process. In order to expedite the healing, new legislation and interventions have emerged. These reforms aim to relocate victims from a position in which they are blamed to one in which they receive help. Due to the relatively short time since rape and sexual assault have emerged as major policy concerns, there is a need for more research, improved training of system workers, and further development of informed systems of intervention.

KEY TERMS

absolute exemption	post-traumatic stress disorder (PTSD)
acquaintance rape	prevalence
child rape	psychopathology
crisis	rape kit
crisis reaction repair cycle	rape myths
date rape	rape trauma syndrome
false negatives	recoil
false positives	reorganization
forensic examination	seropositive
forensics nurse	sex offender registration
in camera	Sexual Assault Nurse Examiner (SANE)
impact	Sexual Assault Response Team (SART)
incidence	sexually transmitted disease (STD)
macro-level effect	sociocultural explanations
micro-level effect	spousal immunity
nonstranger rape	window period
partial exemption	

Intimate Partner Violence

LEARNING OBJECTIVES

After reading Chapter 10, you should be able to:

- Talk about how men have dominated women historically.
- Address historical trends in intimate partner violence (IPV).
- Estimate the extent of IPV.
- Recognize the different types of IPV.
- Explain how researchers measure IPV.
- List some shortcomings with how researchers measure IPV.
- Define IPV.
- Tie in lethality with IPV.
- Address the trends in IPV over the past dozen or so years.
- Understand what the battered woman syndrome means.
- Explore how patriarchy influences violence against women.
- Explain how the cycle of violence builds.
- Explore the role of alcohol in IPV.
- Connect the power and control wheel with IPV.
- Summarize how the laws of arrest hampered police intervention in IPV in the past.
- Assess the non-arrest options available to the police.
- Summarize the Minneapolis Experiment and its findings.
- List three criticisms of the Minneapolis Experiment.
- Relate pro-arrest and mandatory arrest policies to the Minneapolis Experiment.
- Explain how legislatures have relaxed the misdemeanor rule.
- Talk about why there are refuge houses and how they are funded.
- Compare and contrast internal validity with external validity.
- Summarize the replications of the Minneapolis Experiment.
- Explore the prosecutorial response to IPV.

INTRODUCTION

When one thinks of crime and criminals, the image that most often comes to mind is that of stranger-to-stranger violations. In actuality, however, you are more likely to be killed or beaten by a person you know than by a total stranger. Furthermore, the violent offender is probably not just a passing acquaintance or somebody you nod to at the grocery store. It is more than likely that person will be an immediate family member or someone with whom you share a very close personal relationship.

Every day hundreds of husbands brutalize their wives. Much of this violence is hidden from the public eye. It frequently takes place in private, behind closed doors, where no one can see the physical infliction or hear the anguished pleas for help. In addition, if people should hear the muffled sounds of a beating, many would not intervene, based on the belief that "a man's home is his castle."

It is only recently that we have come to realize the amount of human suffering that takes place within families. Gradually, this internal domestic strife is becoming more exposed to public view. Society finally is starting to recognize the problem of intimate partner violence (IPV) as a major public health hazard. Twenty-two percent of the nonfatal violent incidents experienced by women from 2001 through 2005 involved altercations with an intimate partner, compared with 4% of similar male victimizations (Catalano, 2007).

This chapter deals with violence between husbands and wives or other conjugal cohabitants. We look at the pervasiveness of this problem and at the types of statutory provisions that govern these behaviors. We also examine how academicians account for IPV. As you will see, the IPV problem has dropped into the laps of law enforcement personnel and they have assumed responsibility as first responders. The primary reason why the police deal with IPV is that no other public agency operates seven days a week, 24 hours a day, 365 days a year. Because they did not anticipate these tasks, law enforcement agencies often lack the resources and skills required to deal with this form of violence. Despite this shortcoming, police departments and the rest of the criminal justice community continue to look for ways to combat this social problem.

A BRIEF HISTORY OF INTIMATE PARTNER VIOLENCE

The domination of men over women has strong historical roots. Early Roman law treated women as the property of their husbands, a custom reinforced by biblical passages, Christianity, English common law, and the mores of American colonists (Dobash & Dobash, 1977–78, 1979; Edwards, 1989; Pleck, 1989). As property, women were subject to the control of their fathers or husbands, who held the power of life and death over them.

Women have held no legal standing throughout most of history. Any harm committed against a woman was viewed as an offense against the father or husband, not her. Consequently, it was the male "owner" who sought vengeance or compensation for his loss. At the same time, a female could not be a culpable party. The father or the husband was the one held responsible for any injurious action by his woman. Buzawa and Buzawa (1990) point out that husbands or fathers were expected to punish women. In fact, many Western cultures proscribed official punishment of women in their legal codes.

The legal movement in this country to restrict wife beating can be divided into roughly three stages. The first period occurred in the mid-1600s, when the Puritans in Massachusetts enacted laws against wife beating and family violence (Pleck, 1989). Pleck points out, however, that these laws were rarely enforced. This laxity was due, in large part, to the strong belief in family privacy and the acceptance of physical force by the husband as a valid form of discipline.

A second upswing in concern over IPV appeared in the late 1800s, when states began passing laws restricting family violence. Worries over immigration, rising crime, the use of alcohol, and other factors prompted the passage of laws restricting family conflict and allowing for outside intervention (Pleck, 1989). Some states even mandated public flogging as a punishment for beating women. As with the earlier movement, however, these laws and punishments were seldom enforced (Pleck, 1989).

While these protective actions were evolving, some nineteenth-century state supreme court decisions continued to condone wife beating. However, husbands were advised that physical chastisement should not exceed the boundaries of good taste (Dobash & Dobash, 1977–78; Pleck, 1979). It is important to note that it was not until the early part of the twentieth century that women in the United States gained *suffrage*, the right to vote (see Table 10.1).

The fate of the Equal Rights Amendment (ERA) is another example of the diminished status held by women. The first Equal Rights Amendment was proposed on December 23, 1923. However, it languished in Congress for years and never got out of committee. Another version of the ERA was approved by the House in 1971 and by the Senate in 1972. However, this effort eventually failed because only 35 out of the necessary 38 states had ratified the ERA when the time for consideration expired. More recently, a resolution reviving the ERA was introduced in the Senate (S. J. Res. 10) (see Table 10.2) and is currently under consideration. The point remains, though, that women have a lesser status than men and have encountered strong resistance to achieving parity.

🌐 WEB ACTIVITY

You can track the progress of the federal Equal Rights Amendment by accessing the Library of Congress at **http://thomas. loc.gov/cgi-bin/query/z?c113:H.RES.61. IH:**

The third stage of interest in IPV is the one currently in effect. The 1960s saw the beginning of general social unrest and demands for equality. Concerns over rape, intimate partner abuse, and family violence became rallying cries for the emerging women's movement. Calls for greater police intervention into domestic violence replaced family privacy issues. It was during this time that physicians and social workers became vocal about family violence and brought these problems to the attention of society (Pleck, 1989). Remarkably, not a single research article in the *Journal of Marriage and the Family*, a premiere scholarly outlet in this area, addressed the issue of family violence prior to 1969 (Wardell, Gillespie, & Leffler, 1983). Reflecting on the historical paucity of interest in IPV, Dobash and Dobash (1977–78: 427) pointed out that:

Table 10.1 The 19th Amendment to the United States Constitution, Granting Women the Right to Vote

AMENDMENT XIX

Passed by Congress June 4, 1919. Ratified August 18, 1920.

The right of citizens of the United States to vote shall not be denied or abridged by the United States or by any State on account of sex.

Congress shall have power to enforce this article by appropriate legislation.

Source: National Archives Experience (n.d.). Constitution of the United States. Washington, DC: National Archives. Retrieved May 13, 2013, from http://www.archives.gov/exhibits/charters/constitution_amendments_11-27.html.

> **Table 10.2** Senate Joint Resolution 10, Proposing an Amendment to the Constitution of the United States Relative to Equal Rights for Men and Women, March 5, 2013
>
> Resolved by the Senate and the House of Representatives of the United States of America in Congress assembled (two-thirds of each House concurring therein), That the following article is proposed as an amendment to the Constitution of the United States which shall be valid, to all intents and purposes, as part of the Constitution when ratified by the legislatures of three-fourths of the several States:
>
> SECTION 1. Equality of rights under the law shall not be denied or abridged by the United States or by any State on account of sex.
>
> SECTION 2. The Congress shall have the power to enforce, by appropriate legislation, the provisions of this article.
>
> SECTION 3. This article shall take effect 2 years after the date of ratification.
>
> *Source: Congressional Record (March 5, 2013).* Senate Joint Resolution 10, 113th Congress, 1st Session. *Retrieved on May 13, 2013, from http://thomas.loc.gov/cgi-bin/query/z?c113:S.J.+Res.+10:*

[W]ife-beating is not, in the strictest sense of the words, a "deviant," "aberrant," or "pathological" act. Rather, it is a form of behavior which has existed for centuries as an acceptable, and, indeed, a desirable part of a patriarchal family system within a patriarchal society, and much of the ideology and many of the institutional arrangements which support the patriarchy through the subordination, domination and control of women are still reflected in our culture and our social institutions.

Perhaps the greatest breakthrough for interest in IPV was the publication in 1984 of the Minneapolis Experiment, which evaluated the effectiveness of arresting abusive husbands. This research, which will be discussed in more detail later in this chapter, generated a great deal of policy change, spawned widespread debate in the academic community, and prompted a series of replications.

The renewed interest in IPV has gone relatively unabated. While some feminist scholars lament that research involving violence against women continues to be housed in specialized and separate disciplinary silos (Basile, 2009; Ford, 2009; Jordan, 2009), IPV continues to be a leading issue within the larger framework and growth of victimology. The criminal justice system has adapted by altering different policies and procedures for dealing with abusive offenders and their victims. Academic interest has also kept pace. A casual inspection of most library holdings will uncover a large selection of materials dealing with IPV.

THE EXTENT OF INTIMATE PARTNER VIOLENCE

Estimates about how often IPV occurs show some variation from one study to the next. Sometimes the definitions that researchers employ are responsible for these differences. Despite these apparent differences, victimologists would agree that there are several types of IPV. As Table 10.3 shows, there are at least

---

Table 10.3 Types of Domestic Violence

We define domestic violence as a pattern of abusive behavior in any relationship that is used by one partner to gain or maintain power and control over another intimate partner. Domestic violence can be physical, sexual, emotional, economic, or psychological actions or threats of actions that influence another person. This includes any behaviors that intimidate, manipulate, humiliate, isolate, frighten, terrorize, coerce, threaten, blame, hurt, injure, or wound someone.

- **Physical Abuse:** Hitting, slapping, shoving, grabbing, pinching, biting, hair-pulling, etc. are types of physical abuse. This type of abuse also includes denying a partner medical care or forcing alcohol and/or drug use upon him or her.

- **Sexual Abuse:** Coercing or attempting to coerce any sexual contact or behavior without consent. Sexual abuse includes, but is certainly not limited to, marital rape, attacks on sexual parts of the body, forcing sex after physical violence has occurred, or treating one in a sexually demeaning manner.

- **Emotional Abuse:** Undermining an individual's sense of self-worth and/or self-esteem is abusive. This may include, but is not limited to constant criticism, diminishing one's abilities, name-calling, or damaging one's relationship with his or her children.

- **Economic Abuse:** Is defined as making or attempting to make an individual financially dependent by maintaining total control over financial resources, withholding one's access to money, or forbidding one's attendance at school or employment.

- **Psychological Abuse:** Elements of psychological abuse include—but are not limited to—causing fear by intimidation; threatening physical harm to self, partner, children, or partner's family or friends; destruction of pets and property; and forcing isolation from family, friends, or school and/or work.

Source: Office on Violence Against Women (2013). What is Domestic Violence. *Washington, DC: U.S. Department of Justice. Retrieved on May 13, 2013, from http://www.ovw.usdoj.gov/domviolence.htm.*

---

five major forms of IPV. They include physical abuse, sexual abuse, emotional abuse, economic abuse, and psychological abuse.

One well-known survey instrument, the Conflict Tactics Scale (CTS), is used frequently to assess the extent of marital violence. The CTS represents a range of responses to conflict, extending from nonviolent to violent actions. Respondents are asked to indicate how often each response was resorted to in the past year. Using the original version of the CTS, Straus, Gelles, and Steinmetz (1980) found that 16% of the subjects reported at least one violent episode within the previous year. More than one-fourth of these people acknowledged participating in at least one violent confrontation with their partner during the marriage.

While the CTS enjoyed wide usage when it was introduced, it had some limitations (Dobash et al., 1992). First, only one member of a household was typically surveyed. This shortcoming meant that there were no comparative data against which to gauge the responses. Lack of validation is especially problematic because husbands tend to see less violence than do wives (Browning & Dutton, 1986). Second, these data were limited in terms of assessing the degree of conflict. There was no indication as to the kind of object used in various categories, the number of times an act occurred during each instance, the degree of force used, or differences in the strength of the combatants

(Frieze & Browne, 1989). Third, there was no information on the severity of the actual harm, if any, inflicted. Finally, there was rarely any information gathered on the length of the marriage, age of the parties, family socioeconomic conditions, or other demographic characteristics.

Despite these shortcomings, the CTS carried at least three benefits (Schafer, 1996). First, reliance upon a standardized protocol makes it much easier to compare results from one project to the next and to develop a continuous body of knowledge. Second, using a standardized questionnaire may serve as a tool to minimize subject memory decay. As discussed in Chapter 2, recall problems are a source of constant worry for survey researchers. Finally, using a standardized set of questions over many different settings makes refinements and improvements possible.

These considerations prompted Strauss and his associates to produce more refined versions of the instrument (Straus et al., 1996; Straus & Douglas, 2004). The revised scale includes more items pertaining to abuse, documents psychological abuse, delves into different forms of sexual violence, and includes outcome measures such as injury. Efforts at establishing the reliability, validity, and applicability of this revised protocol continue. In fact, at least one observer (Langhinrichsen-Rohling, 2005) considers the creation of the CTS and its ensuing development as the most fertile advance in IPV research.

 **WEB ACTIVITY**

Many researchers have used the Revised Conflict Tactics Scale (CTS2). You can view a copy of this instrument at **http://fluidsurveys.com/s/conflict-tactics/?ef**

Gelles and Straus (1988) claim that approximately 25% of all couples will experience abuse during their lifetimes. As one research team succinctly explained, "the percentage of women who will experience partner violence victimization is far greater than the percentage of women who experience breast cancer" (Logan et al., 2006: 177).

IPV figures, whether official or self-reported, undercount the actual level of abuse and are subject to a great deal of speculation. One reason for inaccuracy may be that many studies fail to register the number of times violence occurs in a relationship, opting instead to simply count whether any abuse has occurred. Looking at the number of times abuse occurred, Straus (1978) reported an average of three beatings a year.

Another problem is that many studies refer only to married couples. Studies of courtship patterns reveal violence between dating partners is a common occurrence (Katz, Tirone, & Schukrafft, 2012; Sikes, Walley, & Hays, 2012). Apparently, some people view this period as a "training ground" for marital interaction. In addition, researchers tend to overlook the amount of violence that occurs within same-sex couples (Lockhart et al., 1994).

Finally, reconciling disparate research results is often difficult due to differences in study design. Besides using different definitions of abuse, the data sources also vary (such as police records, social service agencies, single-city surveys, or estimates by "experts"). As a result, researchers suspect that the actual number of IPV cases is close to 50% of all couples (Feld & Straus, 1989). The inescapable conclusion generated from these and other projects is that IPV is an all-too-frequent act. See Table 10.4 for a way to assess whether abuse is taking place in a relationship.

With the redesign of the National Crime Victimization Survey (NCVS) discussed earlier in Chapter 2, comes more detailed information regarding IPV. The term *intimate partner violence* includes physical episodes involving current or former spouses, boyfriends, and girlfriends (Catalano, 2012a). Figure 10.1 displays these figures from 1993 through 2009. While female victimization rates show a decline over the years, the gap between the female and male victimization rates remains pronounced. Females are more likely than males to experience harm at the hands of their intimates. Four out of every five victims of intimate partner violence during this period were female (Catalano, 2012a: 3). Females were IPV victims in more than 775,000 cases in 2009.

Table 10.4 Am I Being Abused?

Does your partner:

- Embarrass you with put-downs?
- Look at you or act in ways that scare you?
- Control what you do, who you see or talk to, or where you go?
- Stop you from seeing your friends or family members?
- Take your money or Social Security check, make you ask for money or refuse to give you money?
- Make all of the decisions?
- Tell you that you're a bad parent or threaten to take away or hurt the children?
- Prevent you from working or attending school?
- Act like the abuse is no big deal, it's your fault, or even deny doing it?
- Destroy your property or threaten to kill your pets?
- Intimidate you with guns, knives or other weapons?
- Shove you, slap you, choke you, or hit you?
- Force you to try and drop charges?
- Threaten to commit suicide?
- Threaten to kill you?

Source: National Domestic Violence Hotline (2013a). Am I Being Abused? Austin, TX: National Domestic Violence Hotline. Retrieved on October 22, 2013, from http://www.thehotline.org/is-this-abuse/.

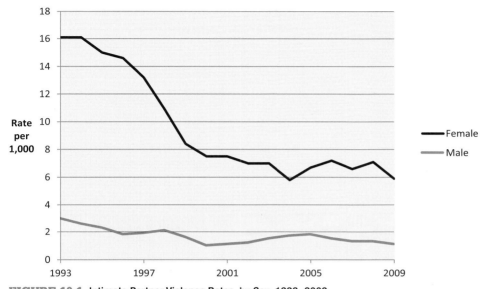

FIGURE 10.1 Intimate Partner Violence Rates, by Sex, 1993–2009.

Source: *Adapted from Catalano, S. (2012a).* Intimate Partner Violence, 1993–2010. *Washington, DC: Bureau of Justice Statistics, p. 10. Retrieved on May 13, 2013, from http://www.bjs.gov/content/pub/pdf/ ipv9310.pdf.*

The recognition of IPV as a public health issue prompted the Centers for Disease Control and Prevention to sponsor The National Intimate Partner and Sexual Violence Survey (NISVS) in 2010. Lifetime estimates of IPV indicate that one of every three women and one of every four men in this country will become victims of some form of IPV during their lifetimes (Black et al., 2011). Approximately 7 million women and 5.7 million men reported experiencing sexual battery, physical violence, and/or stalking by an intimate partner within the past year alone. We will touch upon the consequences and ramifications that accompany a problem of this magnitude throughout the remainder of this chapter.

Any discussion of IPV must recognize that these incidents have the potential to escalate into lethal confrontations. The Federal Bureau of Investigation (2012a) reports that 14,612 homicides occurred throughout the nation in 2011. The Supplementary Homicide Reports (FBI, 2012b), which contain a rich array of data, have information available on 12,664 of these cases. Tabulations based on these files reveal that 79% of the victims knew their assailants, while 21% were murdered by strangers. As the reader can see, homicide victims are more likely to expire from injuries they sustain at the hands of people whom they

WEB ACTIVITY

If you are interested in learning more about The National Intimate Partner and Sexual Violence Survey, go to **http:// www.cdc.gov/violenceprevention/ nisvs/**

know rather than complete strangers. This tidbit is exactly what we learned in Chapter 1 from Wolfgang's (1958) classic study of homicide in Philadelphia.

IPV is not restricted to husbands hurting their wives. Sometimes, women batter their mates. When the idea of women striking their mates was first introduced (Steinmetz, 1977–78, 1978a), some commentators dismissed this notion as a "red herring" or a misleading distortion of the real problem (Fields & Kirchner, 1978). The idea of *sexual symmetry*, that women are equally as violent as their partners, overlooks the degree to which serious injuries are inflicted, whether the act was initiated in self-defense, and the intensity of the response (Dobash et al., 1992). People who adhere to the family violence perspective would welcome greater attention to this and other related topics. However, those who endorse a strict feminist viewpoint would reject this call because it ignores the relationship between gender and power (Stalans & Lurigio, 1995). Perhaps the best summary of this situation came when Henning, Renauer, and Holdford (2006: 6) wrote:

> Those arguing that IPV is a gendered crime with female victims and male offenders will highlight the fact that most of the women in our sample were primary victims. People arguing that women are just as violent as men and that the criminal justice system is biased against males will point to the "female batterers" we identified. Our opinion is that both pieces of information are important and must be acknowledged for the field to advance beyond the highly polarized debate that continues to fuel a growing backlash against domestic violence initiatives.

Part of the reason behind using the more expansive term *intimate partner violence*, as opposed to *spouse abuse*, is the growing recognition that violence also occurs within same-sex relationships (Kuehnle & Sullivan, 2003; Lockhart et al., 1994; Younglove, Kerr, & Vitello, 2002). Some writers have concluded that violence within same-sex couples takes place at about the same rate as it does in heterosexual pairings or even higher (Aulivola, 2004; Finneran & Stephenson, 2012; McClennen, 2005; Messinger, 2011; Stanley et al., 2006). Instead of painting the issue of spouse abuse along gender lines where women are victims and men are the aggressors, the suggestion these observers make is to recast the issue in terms of intimate partner violence and focus upon violence within primary relationships.

Women sometimes strike back at their assailants. Research over the past three decades shows that approximately three-quarters of the homicides involving a male partner death were preceded by instances of IPV perpetrated upon the female partner (Campbell et al., 2007: 247). The fact that these women were IPV victims has led lawyers to raise the *battered woman syndrome* as a self-defense explanation, a concept we will delve into later in this chapter. The argument is that these women were so traumatized by previous beatings that they simply seized the opportunity to kill their assailants to prevent any further victimization episodes. In any event, situations such as those typified here caused one author to remark, "A man's home may be his castle, but a woman's home too often is her dungeon" (Costa, 1984: 8).

THE CYCLE OF VIOLENCE AS BACKDROP

As Chapter 3 explained, contributing to a sense of helplessness is the reality that battered women are not beaten every minute of the day. Instead, there is a *cycle of violence*, which gradually builds their feelings of being powerless and unable to alter their plight. Walker sees this cycle as consisting of three distinct stages: (1) the tension-building phase; (2) the battering episode; and (3) the reconciliation period.

The *tension-building phase* may be accompanied by minor assaults. During this period, the woman believes she can deflect her husband's bullying. She may calm the situation by conceding to his wishes or by staying out of his way. Her goal is not to prevent the battering behavior but to avoid it. She becomes grateful that small displays of abusive behavior are not as serious as what they could be. Sometimes, she may even make excuses for the man's behavior. Her general perception is that these incidents are isolated events that will end once the irritant is removed. Thus, she is able to rationalize these outbursts.

The second part of the cycle, the *battering episode*, is the culmination of the frustrations experienced in the first stage. At this point, the man is out of control and acts in a rage. As Walker (1979: 55) explains:

> He starts out wanting to teach the woman a lesson, not intending to inflict any particular injury on her, and stops when he feels she has learned her lesson. By this time, however, she has generally been very severely beaten.

A common rationalization regarding these volatile outbursts is the man's claim that he did not fully realize what he was doing because he had been drinking. This *disinhibition* account acts to transfer responsibility away from the abuser and to characterize alcohol as the real culprit. In other words, the alcohol weakened the man's normal behavioral restraints, thus triggering atypical and uncontrollable violence, sometimes with even more severe consequences (Graham et al., 2011). As noted earlier, however, the evidence for alcohol as a cause of IPV is unclear. This fact has prompted some researchers to conclude that although "there is more than a 'kernel of truth' in the drunken bum theory of wife beating, the findings also provide the basis for demythologizing this stereotype" (Kantor & Straus, 1987: 224). One counselor probably had the best handle on this situation when he stated, "While I can't say drinking is the cause of domestic abuse, it definitely pours gasoline on the fire" (Healey, Smith, & O'Sullivan, 1998: 6).

The final phase is the *reconciliation period*. Here the batterer transforms himself into a very apologetic, tender, and loving character. Pleas for forgiveness and promises of a better future often cloud the anger and fear the victim has experienced at the hands of her partner. As Walker (1979: 58) puts it:

> The batterer truly believes he will never again hurt the woman he loves; he believes he can control himself from now on. He also believes he has taught her such a lesson that she will never again behave in such a manner, and so he will not be tempted to beat her.

It is not uncommon for the batterer to shower the victim with tokens of affection during this period. A bouquet of flowers may appear unannounced. Declarations of love abound. There may be many little thoughtful things, reminiscent of romantic days gone by, to prove the insistence of a loving relationship. However, the cycle-of-violence perspective implies that this period too shall pass.

As the couple's relationship proceeds through this cycle again and again, the wife's physical and psychological well-being become compromised. As the Power and Control Wheel contained in Figure 10.2 shows, numerous practices trap the victim in this environment. She might assess her marriage as a failure, but not be able to take any remedial steps. There may be strong religious beliefs, family pressures, and other social considerations that prevent action. Postponement of any resolution to the beatings permits the cycle to continue without any end in sight (Eisikovits, 1996). The woman is trapped; she simply learns to live with the violent spasms that characterize the relationship. The learned helplessness perspective centers on the emotional dependency that develops during an intimate relationship. As society expects, the woman becomes more enthralled with her husband. Simultaneously, an economic dependency also surfaces within the household. One writer (Pagelow, 1984: 313) sizes up the situation quite deftly:

> When a woman leaves her abuser, her economic standard of living very likely takes a drastic drop. If she has dependent children, she must take into consideration the lives and welfare of her children, who have roughly one chance out of two of dropping below the poverty level (two out of three for minority children). Is it any wonder that many battered women remain with their abusers for many years, sometimes until the children have grown up and left home?

 WEB ACTIVITY

The Duluth Model is a leading tool for helping us understand and erase domestic violence. For a fuller understanding of this problem, visit the website at **http://www.theduluthmodel.org/**

POLICE INTERVENTION

The first point at which society typically becomes involved in domestic disputes is when a police officer is summoned to an abusive episode. More than likely, this incident is not the first time that the couple has engaged in a violent confrontation

FIGURE 10.2 The Power and Control Wheel.
Battering is one form of domestic or intimate partner violence. It is characterized by the pattern of actions that an individual uses to intentionally control or dominate his intimate partner. That is why the words "power and control" are in the center of the wheel. A batterer systematically uses threats, intimidation, and coercion to instill fear in his partner. These behaviors are the spokes of the wheel. Physical and sexual violence holds it all together—this violence is the rim of the wheel. *Source: Domestic Abuse Intervention Programs (n.d.). The power and control wheel. Duluth, MN: Domestic Abuse Intervention Programs. Retrieved May 14, 2013, from* http://www.theduluthmodel.org/pdf/PowerandControl.pdf.

with each other. Historically, officers who respond to a call involving IPV have had a variety of alternatives at their disposal: making an arrest, counseling the parties, referring the couple to professional counseling, threatening to make an arrest, separating the parties, or advising the victim to sign a formal complaint. This portion of the chapter explores some of these options and their limits.

The Arrest Option
While one of the more awesome powers entrusted to police officers is that of arrest, there are several restrictions that limit its utility. The first consideration is the distinction between reasonable suspicion and probable cause.

Reasonable suspicion permits an officer to intrude into a situation to investigate whether a crime has been committed, is being committed, or is about to occur. Probable cause, on the other hand, is more stringent. *Probable cause* means that the facts and circumstances are sufficiently strong enough to make the officer conclude that the accused is the one who committed the crime under investigation. If probable cause is present, the officer can make a legitimate or lawful arrest. If probable cause is absent, the arrest lacks proper foundation. There is not a lawful custodial situation. Any officer who willfully violates this provision may be the subject of a series of administrative, criminal, and civil penalties.

A second major consideration lies in the distinction between a misdemeanor and a felony offense. The general rule of thumb is that an officer may effect a lawful arrest for a felony offense, either with or without an arrest warrant, as long as probable cause exists. In a misdemeanor case, though, an officer can make a *warrantless arrest* only if the transgression has taken place in his or her presence. This restriction, called the *misdemeanor rule*, can hamper effective police intervention, particularly in situations in which many offenses are misdemeanors, such as IPV.

One recommendation issued by the U.S. Attorney General's Task Force (1984) called for states to revise their provisions concerning arrests in family violence. The Violence Against Women Act of 1994 reiterated this position by linking receipt of certain federal funds with revisions to state laws that created an exception to the misdemeanor rule in domestic violence situations. As a result, the states have responded by relaxing the misdemeanor rule in IPV situations (Zeoli, Norris, & Brenner, 2011). In other words, an officer can make a legitimate warrantless arrest even though he or she did not observe the crime being committed. The probable cause element, though, has not changed. It still remains the essential ingredient in the decision to take an individual into custody.

WEB ACTIVITY

The International Association of Chiefs of Police, in conjunction with the U.S. Department of Justice Office on Violence Against Women, has produced a training package to help officers address intimate partner violence. You can see the materials by going to **http://www.theiacp.org/ PublicationsGuides/ResearchCenter/ Projects/ViolenceAgainstWomen/ PoliceResponsetoViolenceAgainst Women/tabid/372/Default.aspx**

Another important determinant in how the police handle a domestic disturbance is whether the suspect is at the scene when the police arrive. If the abuser has left the premises, the officer may not be able to make an immediate arrest. At this point, the officer must assess the extent of injury to the victim. If the injuries are serious and require medical attention, then more than likely the crime is an aggravated battery, which is a felony in most jurisdictions. This classification means the officer can initiate a warrantless arrest. However, if the injuries are minor or nonvisible, then it might be difficult to establish that a crime took place. If probable cause is lacking or if the misdemeanor rule is in effect, then the officer is powerless to make a legitimate warrantless arrest. The only thing that will enable the police to arrest the abuser is if the victim signs an affidavit, and that process usually takes some time.

An *affidavit* is an official complaint in which the victim outlines the details of the offense and swears under oath that the individual named in the accusation is the offender. The completion of this legal document and the issuance of a warrant by a judge give the police proper authority to arrest the suspect on a misdemeanor charge.

Should the suspect be present at the scene when the officers arrive, an evaluation of the arrest option is in order. Bear in mind that if the state legislature has not made IPV an exception to the usual misdemeanor rule, then the officer cannot arrest the abuser for a misdemeanor without observing a violation firsthand. However, if the elements for a felony offense fit, the officer may have probable cause for an immediate arrest.

Non-Arrest Options

If an arrest is not possible, or if the officer elects not to pursue the arrest option immediately, a variety of other options are at the officer's disposal. The officer may engage in a *mediation* effort. Ideally, this choice involves talking with each party privately to learn each participant's version of what took place. The officer may suggest one or more ways in which to handle disputes of this nature in the future. Alternatively, he or she may try to extract a promise from the disputants that they will not engage in another confrontation after the officer leaves. The officer then exits, in the belief (or hope) that accord has been re-established.

In other instances, the officer may suggest the couple contact a minister, a counselor, or some other social service agency. The problem with this *referral* option is:

> that it depends upon the efforts of the citizen for initial contact with the agency to which he is referred. Many of those involved in domestic disturbances are prevented from seeking assistance by their own fear, ignorance, or lack of initiative (Parnas, 1967: 934–935).

As one psychologist adroitly recognizes, "Regardless of the potential danger, the parties have the Constitutional right to refuse help" (Bard, 1980: 114). In other words, the police are powerless to compel individuals to seek family counseling—even if this recourse is in the best interests of the couple.

Another common tactic is to either threaten or cajole the parties into peaceful behavior. As one veteran commented, "What can a police officer tell a person who has been married 20–25 years! You just have to be a good con artist" (Parnas, 1967: 948). Usually this option comes with the reminder that a return visit by the police will trigger the arrest of either one or both parties.

Perhaps the most typical response is to separate the combatants. Officers do not have the legal authority to order an inhabitant out of his or her own house. However, one prevalent strategy is to request that the perpetrator leave for a "cooling off" period. Sometimes the request may go unheeded or the occupant might assert the right to remain on the premises. In this situation, the officer might try to regain the upper hand by reminding the uncooperative party of the dire consequences of an arrest. Confronted with a hostile subject and a lack of legitimate alternatives, the officer might enlist the help of the woman. The officer might even offer to drive the woman to a relative's house or to place her and the children, if any, in a domestic violence shelter for the evening.

THE MINNEAPOLIS EXPERIMENT

Victim advocates and women's groups have long argued that the police need to take a more proactive role in dealing with domestic violence situations. In particular, they have called for the authorities to make arrests of offenders rather than resorting to non-arrest alternatives. Underlying these arguments is the assumption that arrest will curb future IPV acts effectively.

The Minneapolis Police Department, working with the Police Foundation, agreed to serve as a testing site for an investigation into the impact of arrest in IPV cases. The purpose of the study was to determine how effective various police responses were in preventing further episodes of domestic violence (Sherman & Berk, 1984). These responses included: (1) an automatic arrest; (2) having one party leave for a "cooling off" period; and (3) counseling or referral to a social service agency.

Each officer participating in the field experiment received a report pad. This pad instructed him or her about which option to invoke on a particular call. While these actions were predetermined in advance via a randomized fashion, officers could deviate from the guidelines whenever the situation demanded a more appropriate response. Situations allowing for deviation included when the offense was a clear felony, when the officer felt threatened, and when the victim demanded action. To see how well each intervention strategy worked, staff members telephoned civilian complainants biweekly over the following six-month period. The purpose of these telephone contacts was to elicit information about any more domestic violence by the suspect.

Profiles of victims and suspects revealed that 60% were unemployed, a considerably higher figure than the area's general 5% unemployment rate. Three out of five suspects had a prior arrest record, and almost one-third of the suspected men had a violent arrest history. Eighty percent of the abusers had assaulted the woman at least once during the previous six months. The police had responded to more than one-half of these earlier violent confrontations.

One-half of the couples were not married to each other at the time of the study. In short, these men and women appeared to be tormented couples.

Two outcome measures were analyzed. The first indicator tapped whether the police had to return to the residence for another domestic squabble during the six-month follow-up period. The other measure came from the telephone interviews. It indexed any victim reports of repeated violence with the same suspect.

The police blotters showed that officers returned to 26% of the households in cases in which the initial strategy was to issue a warning and separate the parties for a brief "cooling off" period. Police recidivism figures reached the 18% mark for those settings in which the officer took the counseling approach and registered 13% when the officer exercised the arrest option. The telephone accounts showed a high of 37% repeaters stemming from the counseling tactic. The low was 19% in the cases in which the initial response was an arrest. In short, arrest appeared to be the most efficient way of preventing more IPV between the original combatants.

The researchers combed their data to learn whether an incapacitation effect clouded the results. *Incapacitation* refers to the fact that an offender is unable to recidivate while in confinement. If most of the arrested individuals spent the next six months in jail, the results would not be very impressive. However, further analysis revealed that incapacitation held very little influence on the findings. Almost one-half of the detained suspects were released from confinement within 24 hours of the arrest. Only 14% remained in jail one week after their arrest. Thus, it does not appear that an incapacitation effect contaminated or impinged upon the results.

These findings contradict the belief that an arrest merely aggravates an already tense interpersonal situation and that the best course of action is minimal police involvement. First, there was no indication of a revengeful violent escapade once the arrested male returned home. Second, the separation did not produce economic hardships for these women. (Some observers have commented that many wives shy away from the arrest alternative because they rely upon their husbands for a steady income to maintain the household.) Third, the results are even more impressive when one considers the abundant arrest histories—particularly violent confrontations with their wives—that these men had logged.

While proponents embraced these results and used them to lobby for more sustained police action in IPV cases, the researchers themselves were not quite as enthusiastic. Besides reciting the familiar refrain for replicative studies, Sherman and Berk (1984: 270) issued some conservative remarks:

> [A]rrest and initial incarceration alone may produce a deterrent effect, regardless of how the courts treat such cases ... . Therefore, in jurisdictions that process domestic assault offenders in a manner

similar to that employed in Minneapolis, we favor a presumption of arrest; an arrest should be made unless there are good, clear reasons why an arrest would be counterproductive. We do not, however, favor requiring arrests in all misdemeanor domestic assault cases. Even if our findings were replicated in a number of jurisdictions, there is a good chance that arrest works far better for some kinds of offenders than others and in some kinds of situations better than others.

REACTION TO THE MINNEAPOLIS EXPERIMENT

The recognition of IPV as a social problem, as well as the publicity surrounding the Minneapolis Experiment, heralded reaction on several fronts. As one might expect, academicians found flaws in the Minneapolis Experiment. However, mounting public pressure meant the legal system could not sit by idly until scholarly debate resolved these questions. As a result, police enforcement policies changed, and legislatures revamped their criminal codes. What we shall do in this section of the chapter is explore some of these ramifications.

Agency Directives

At one time, many police agencies adhered to a strategy of minimal intervention in IPV disturbances. What this directive amounted to was that officers would not resort to an arrest if they could avoid such action. Such a stance did not tend to bother officers, particularly in light of the mistaken perception that domestic disturbances were the most dangerous calls for police to handle (Garner & Clemmer, 1986; Hirschel, Dean, & Lumb, 1994; Stanford & Mowry, 1990). However, advocacy efforts and lawsuits forced agencies to rescind these informal "no arrest" policies.

The findings from the Minneapolis Experiment forced law enforcement agencies to reconsider their stance. While some administrators maintain a public image of full enforcement, actual field practices fall short of this mark. *Full enforcement* means the police arrest every violator for every illegal act whenever possible. Because such a goal is often impractical, officers engage in selective enforcement. *Selective enforcement* means the police arrest only some violators for some of their actions some of the time. In other words, individual officers are free to exercise their discretion when deciding whom to arrest and whom not to arrest.

Discretion vests officers with considerable latitude in the performance of their duties. It also raises two major concerns (Doerner, 2012: 278). First, the lowest-ranking members of the agency are the ones who determine how official policy translates into action. Second, quite often these decision makers are the least accountable members of the agency. That is, their decisions are rarely subject to review. Hence, there are no assurances that actions out in the field correspond to policy guidelines.

One way to circumvent the thorny problem of officer discretion is to remove it. That is exactly what many agencies did when they revamped their IPV guidelines. They outlawed selective enforcement. These new directives, sometimes called *pro-arrest policies* or *mandatory arrest policies,* informed police officers that they must make an arrest whenever feasible in IPV situations. Others, known as *presumptive arrest policies,* assume that an arrest will be made in every case. A decision to not arrest requires a written justification by the officer. Probable cause requirements persist in these new policies. Failure to conform to agency rules and regulations can result in disciplinary action and, if appropriate, termination from employment. In fact, failure to respond appropriately to domestic violence situations also might create a civil liability exposure (Blackwell & Vaughn, 2003). Thus, officers and their agencies have an incentive to adhere to statutory and policy guidelines.

These changes have not come easily. First, many rank-and-file officers resent what they perceive to be an unwarranted encroachment upon their discretion (Steinman, 1988). While there are some indications that mandatory arrest policies work and that officers comply with these directives (Balenovich, Grossi, & Hughes, 2008; Dichter et al., 2011; Hirschel et al., 2008; Phillips & Sobol, 2010; Simpson et al., 2006), there is other evidence that officers either disagree with or fail to follow mandatory arrest policies (Gover, Paul, & Dodge, 2011; Ho, 2000). For instance, Mignon and Holmes (1995) note that two-thirds of all domestic violence offenders in 24 Massachusetts communities were *not* arrested, despite the existence of a mandatory arrest statute. While arrests increased after the law took effect, compliance remains well below 100%. Second, some suspects taken into custody have sued, claiming that mandatory arrest policies unfairly discriminate against males. In other words, if they were not males, officers would not arrest them for IPV. Most of these efforts have faltered.

Some police administrators, in an effort to appease all parties, have shied away from a mandatory arrest policy and have chosen to express a *preference* for an arrest solution. Table 10.5 contains an example of a written policy directive governing police handling of IPV situations in the Miami area.

Legislative Reform

Many state legislatures have responded to the problem of IPV with reforms on several fronts. As noted earlier, one popular approach has been to relax the misdemeanor rule. To bypass this restriction, some state legislatures have declared IPV to be an exception to the usual misdemeanor rule. This legislative maneuver removes the "in the presence of an officer" requirement. As a result,

Table 10.5 An Example of Police Policy Guidelines Regarding Domestic Violence Arrests

1. When probable cause has established that an act of domestic violence has occurred, an arrest shall be made pursuant to Florida Statutes 741.29. Remember, as it relates to Domestic Violence, the officer need not have witnessed the incident.

2. Factors that should **NOT** be considered in making an arrest:
   a. Marital status, sexual orientation, race, religion, profession, age, disability, cultural, social or political position, or socioeconomic status of either party.
   b. Ownership or tenancy rights of either party, if suspect has not been living at home.
   c. Victim's request that an arrest not be made.
   d. Emotional state of the victim, including belligerence.
   e. Belief that the victim will not participate with criminal prosecution or that the arrest may not lead to a conviction.
   f. Verbal assurances that the abuse will stop.
   g. Denial by either party that the abuse occurred when there is evidence of domestic abuse.
   h. Lack of a court order and/or injunction against the subject.
   i. Chemical dependency or intoxication of the parties, if evidence of domestic violence is apparent.
   j. Disposition of previous police calls involving the same victim or suspect.
   k. Cultural bias.
   l. Presence of children or the immediate dependency of children on the suspect.
   m. Immigration status.

3. Officers will not threaten, suggest, or otherwise indicate:
   a. The possible arrest of all parties.
   b. The removal of the children from the home.
   c. Any report to immigration authorities with the intent of discouraging requests for intervention by law enforcement by any party or in any attempt to control either party.

4. Cross-Arrests: This policy strongly discourages making cross-arrests except where clearly necessary. The following factors should be considered, in addition to factors already listed, in determining the primary aggressor:
   a. Physical size between the parties.
   b. Evidence gathered from witness accounts.
   c. Severity of injury to each party.
   d. Defensive injuries.
   e. Existence of an injunction, and/or stay away order in effect against either party.
   f. Background questions/history and/or prior reports of:
       i.   History of sexual abuse
       ii. Violence
       iii. Economic abuse
       iv. Coercion or threats
   g. Disability rendering one party more vulnerable.

5. If cross-arrests are made, the facts supporting each arrest must be clearly documented.

6. When an arrest cannot be made due to lack of probable cause, the officer will do the following:
   a. Fill out a report.
   b. Explain to the victim why an arrest is not being made.
   c. Advise the victim that he/she can have their case reviewed by the State Attorney's Office.
   d. Encourage the victim to contact local domestic violence service providers.
   e. Advise the victim that the incident report will be sent to the local domestic violence shelter.
   f. Advise the victim to notify the agency of any additional incidents or new information.
   g. Contact advocate at the officer's police department if available.
   h. Write a domestic report.
   i. Contact the Department of Children & Family Services Abuse hotline at 1-800-96 ABUSE (22873), if there are children involved or living (temporarily or permanently) at the location.

Source: Police Chief's Association of Miami-Dade County (2009). Domestic Violence Protocol for Law Enforcement 2009. Miami: Police Chief's Association of Miami-Dade County. Retrieved on May 14, 2013, from http://www.dvsacmiami.org/Committees/ LERC/DV%20Protocol%20for%20Law%20Enforcement%202009.pdf.

a police officer may make a bona fide warrantless arrest for a misdemeanor even though he or she did not witness the violation itself.

Another legislative remedy that gives police officers an immediate response aims to provide safe temporary housing. One fear that victims harbor is that the arrested party will return home from jail and embark upon a revengeful rampage. The only alternative available to many women, and one that is often suggested by responding police officers, is to pack their belongings and move their children to a temporary location where they can hide. However, many people do not have the resources to pursue this option. Some are poor; others live too far away from family and friends.

Some social service groups have responded by establishing *refuge houses* or *domestic violence shelters*. The purpose of these places is to provide the battered woman a safe haven where she can live until she decides what to do about the abusive marital situation. The location of these refuge houses remains a well-guarded secret to ensure safety from angry partners who might appear on the premises for retaliation. More recently, some shelters have begun publicizing their presence in an effort to mobilize greater public support (Belluck, 1997). No matter which approach is taken, these havens require considerable finances for housing, furniture, food, clothing, upkeep, and staffing. As Table 10.6 shows, these escalating costs have prompted some state legislatures to mandate surcharges on marriage licenses and divorce settlements to underwrite IPV centers.

A number of other legislative changes have taken place. Florida police officers who are investigating an incident involving IPV are required by state law to file a written report even if there is no arrest in the matter (*Florida Statutes*, 2012, § 741.29). That report must contain an explanation of why no arrest was made. In addition, officers must give IPV victims a brochure regarding their rights and remedies and document that action in the written report.

Other changes are directed at the judiciary. In Florida, persons arrested on a charge of domestic violence are not entitled to bail; they must remain in jail for a mandatory first appearance hearing before a judge who then makes a bail decision (*Florida Statutes*, 2012, § 741.2901(3)). In addition, there is a minimum mandatory five-day jail sentence for anyone convicted of domestic violence (*Florida Statutes*, 2012, § 741.283). Furthermore, any person convicted of domestic violence in Florida is automatically placed on probation for one year and must attend a batterer's intervention program (*Florida Statutes*, 2012, § 741.281).

Academic Concerns

Partly due to the tremendous popular and legislative interest in the Minneapolis results, many researchers turned a critical eye toward the project and viewed it as more suggestive than definitive. Flaws in the experiment's

---

Table 10.6 How Florida uses Marriage Fees to Combat the Problem of Spousal Abuse

(1) Every marriage license shall be issued by a county court judge or clerk of the circuit court under his or her hand and seal. The county court judge or clerk of the circuit court shall issue such license, upon application for the license, if there appears to be no impediment to the marriage. ... The county court judge or clerk of the circuit court shall collect and receive a fee of $2 for receiving the application for the issuance of a marriage license.

(2) The fee charged for each marriage license issued in the state shall be increased by the sum of $25. This fee shall be collected upon receipt of the application for the issuance of a marriage license and remitted by the clerk to the Department of Revenue for deposit in the Domestic Violence Trust Fund. The Executive Office of the Governor shall establish a Domestic Violence Trust Fund for the purpose of collecting and disbursing funds generated from the increase in the marriage license fee. Such funds which are generated shall be directed to the Department of Children and Family Services for the specific purpose of funding domestic violence centers, and the funds shall be appropriated in a "grants-in-aid" category to the Department of Children and Family Services for the purpose of funding domestic violence centers. From the proceeds of the surcharge deposited into the Domestic Violence Trust Fund as required under s. 938.08, the Executive Office of the Governor may spend up to $500,000 each year for the purpose of administering a statewide public-awareness campaign regarding domestic violence.

(3) Further, the fee charged for each marriage license issued in the state shall be increased by an additional sum of $7.50 to be collected upon receipt of the application for the issuance of a marriage license. The clerk shall transfer such funds monthly to the Department of Revenue for deposit in the Displaced Homemaker Trust Fund created in s. 446.50.

(4) An additional fee of $25 shall be paid to the clerk upon receipt of the application for issuance of a marriage license. The moneys collected shall be forwarded by the clerk to the Department of Revenue, monthly, for deposit in the General Revenue Fund.

(5) The fee charged for each marriage license issued in the state shall be reduced by a sum of $32.50 for all couples who present valid certificates of completion of a premarital preparation course from a qualified course provider registered under s. 741.0305(5) for a course taken no more than 1 year prior to the date of application for a marriage license. For each license issued that is subject to the fee reduction of this subsection, the clerk is not required to transfer the sum of $7.50 to the Department of Revenue for deposit in the Displaced Homemaker Trust Fund pursuant to subsection (3) or to transfer the sum of $25 to the Department of Revenue for deposit in the General Revenue Fund.

Source: Florida Statutes *(2012),* § 741.01.

---

design, implementation, and analysis have proved troublesome. In fact, some people considered these limitations serious enough to "make it more appropriate to consider the Minneapolis study a pilot study rather than an experiment with decisive implications for changing national policy" (Binder & Meeker, 1988: 350).

One issue that generated a skeptical reaction involved external validity. *External validity* is another way of asking how generalizable are the results of a study (Campbell & Stanley, 1963: 5). Are the results obtained in Minneapolis applicable to just Minneapolis, or do they apply to other locations? As one critic explains:

> The problem is not that the Minneapolis experiment was a single study; the problem is that it was a *Minneapolis* experiment. Had Sherman and Berk designed a study that collected data from ten cities

simultaneously and had the results been consistent across locations, I would not have called for replication . . . (Lempert, 1989: 155).

A second volley of criticisms focused upon internal validity. *Internal validity* raises the question of whether the treatment caused the outcome or whether outside influences contaminated the experiment (Campbell & Stanley, 1963). For example, the officers who participated in the study volunteered for this duty. Some of these officers became much more extensively involved in producing the data than did others (Binder & Meeker, 1988; Gartin, 1995a). Indeed, three officers supplied the vast majority of all the cases included in the study. Furthermore, officers found it necessary to deviate from the randomly assigned treatment to make an arrest in a number of incidents. While this impact may appear to be negligible (Berk, Smyth, & Sherman, 1988), there is a hint that other complications may be at work (Elliott, 1989; Gartin, 1995b; Weiss & Boruch, 1996).

A third area of concern involves a cost–benefit assessment (Binder & Meeker, 1988; Lempert, 1989; Meeker & Binder, 1990). Do the benefits of making a misdemeanor arrest outweigh the costs? What impact do such misdemeanor arrests have on the victim and/or on local jail bed capacities? Is the arrest option an efficient use of scarce police resources? Would other intervention techniques provide more efficient strategies? The following section looks at some of these issues.

The Minneapolis Experiment Replications

The criticisms outlined here, along with a host of other questions, led to the funding of six replication projects. The chosen sites were Milwaukee, Omaha, Charlotte, Colorado Springs, Miami, and Atlanta. While the studies were replications, each site employed a slightly different research design. Rather than use the exact same battery of possible interventions, the replications tested a variety of police responses, including arrest, mediation, varying lengths of jail confinement, protective orders, and verbal warnings. The most important departure from the Minneapolis study was the increased control over random assignment of responses. In most sites, the dispatcher (or someone else removed from the scene of the disturbance) assigned the response type to officers. In essence, officer discretion was greatly curtailed in the replications.

The results of the replications failed to confirm the Minneapolis findings. In general, there was little evidence that any treatment was significantly better than another at reducing subsequent domestic violence (Sherman, 1992). In Charlotte, for example, arrest did not reduce domestic assaults (Hirschel et al., 1991; Hirschel, Hutchinson, & Dean, 1992), and there is some evidence that recidivism increased after arrests (Sherman, 1992). Similarly, Dunford, Huizinga, and Elliott (1989) reported no difference in recidivism within six months of the initial police contact in Omaha. Further, Sherman (1992) pointed to evidence of escalating abuse in Omaha at the one-year mark.

Sherman (1992), inspecting the reports and data from five of the six replication sites, suggested that arrest has a possible *criminogenic effect*. That is, arresting an offender may cause greater subsequent offending. The only clear deterrent effect of arrest appears in an analysis of apprehensions that resulted from the issuance of an arrest warrant (Dunford, 1990). In this instance, arrest warrants were randomly obtained for Omaha cases in which the offender was not present when police initially responded. Those individuals arrested on a warrant were clearly deterred from further abuse compared with those suspects not arrested. With this exception, arrest either had no effect or was found to increase subsequent abuse.

Sherman (1992) attempted to probe the reasons for the discrepancies between the initial Minneapolis study and the replication projects. First, differences may be due to demographic variation from study to study. Offenders who were employed, married (as opposed to cohabiting), and better educated seem to be deterred by arrest. Individuals with lower stakes in conformity may increase their offensive behavior after an arrest. Second, greater recidivism occurs in longer follow-up time frames, indicating that short-term deterrence may precede even greater long-term abuse. Finally, despite differences and flaws in study designs, there were few consistent differences. Therefore, one cannot attribute variations in results to the research methodology.

While the replication projects greatly tempered the enthusiasm generated by the initial Minneapolis Experiment, Garner, Fagan, and Maxwell (1995) suggested that the conclusions were far from clear. The authors pointed out a variety of questionable assumptions made in the different analyses. A reanalysis of data from all these research sites reported more favorable results. Maxwell, Garner, and Fagan (2001) asserted that much more detailed and methodical inspection of the data reveals that arresting batterers appears to reduce future IPV. At the same time, a substantial number of perpetrators who were not arrested did not engage in any subsequent aggressive actions against their partners. A closer look at the pooled data prompted Maxwell, Garner, and Fagan (2002: 66) to conclude that "compared with nonarrest interventions, arrest provides additional safety to female victims of intimate partner assault." However, when offenders did recidivate, they generated approximately seven new assaults within a six-month window. Obviously, the differential impact of arrest on IPV requires further study before researchers can come to a definitive conclusion.

Prosecutorial and Judicial Action

While most attention has been paid to the actions of the police in IPV cases, the victim also can turn directly to the court through the office of the prosecutor.

While it is true, then, that not all cases reach the court through an initial police arrest, victims bring few cases (IPV or otherwise) to the prosecutor. The police remain the largest "supplier" of cases for the court.

Evidence exists that there is a high level of attrition in domestic violence cases once they reach the prosecutorial stage. Buzawa and Buzawa (1990) identify a number of reasons for this attrition. First, victims see that there are both immediate and potential costs involved in going through with a case. Among these costs are the possibility of retaliation by the accused, lost time from work, lost income from the accused, and lack of companionship. Second, many victims change their mind about prosecuting after filing charges. They may no longer see the action as important enough to prosecute or may simply lose interest in the case. Third, victims may feel guilty and assume some of the blame for the abusive act. Fourth, some victims may be using the court for purposes other than to prosecute the offender. Some participants may be looking to benefit from *therapeutic jurisprudence*, the healing and sense of empowerment one may gain from moving forward with the case (Cattaneo, Dunn, & Chapman, 2013). They may be trying to teach the accused a lesson, gain revenge, or confirm their own status as a victim, or they may have other reasons that do not require completion of prosecution (Eisikovits, 1996; Fischer & Rose, 1995; Gondolf et al., 1994; Smith, 2000).

Each of these reasons for case attrition can contribute to yet another factor—pressure by the prosecutor or state attorney to drop the charges. Based on prior experiences of victims failing to carry through with charges, prosecutors are reluctant to prepare and begin proceedings when they feel it is likely that the victim may withdraw at a later date. Prosecutors, therefore, often influence victims to drop charges by suggesting that the victim was an active participant in the abuse situation. The lack of a clear victim makes a case more difficult to prosecute.

Despite claims that prosecutors often summarily dismiss domestic violence cases, evidence from different jurisdictions reveals that prosecutors make decisions on the basis of case merit more than on the type of case. For example, Schmidt and Steury (1989) note that in cases in which charges were not brought, 45% were a result of the fact that victims did not wish to pursue the case, and another 30% of the cases rested on questionable legal grounds. Only 14% of the cases were deemed not important enough to pursue. Similarly, Sigler, Crowley, and Johnson (1990), in a statewide survey of judges and prosecutors, found that the failure to prosecute was due primarily to victims recanting their testimony or a lack of evidence. The most important factor uncovered in the literature is the level of cooperation by the victim. A lack of cooperation often leads to dismissals or a failure to bring charges (Elliott, 1989).

This discussion on whether to prosecute presupposes that such an intervention will make a difference. There have been few studies regarding the impact of prosecution in domestic violence cases. Elliott (1989), in a review of such studies, notes that court actions tend to have little impact on subsequent violence. This conclusion is echoed in studies that show that no one court sanction is more effective in reducing recidivism or promoting victim satisfaction (Davis et al., 2008; Gross et al., 2000; Klein & Crowe, 2008; Klein & Tobin, 2008). In fact, evidence is mounting that court-ordered mandatory counseling generally has no impact on subsequent domestic violence (Labriola et al., 2007). However, it does appear that one subgroup—those men who attend most or all sessions—have much more to lose if they are rearrested and so they refrain from repeat IPV (Feder & Dugan, 2002; Gordon & Moriarty, 2003). The most notable instance in which prosecution reduces violence is in cases in which past violence was less common and not as serious. These conclusions, however, are drawn from few studies, and much more research is needed before suggesting any significant policy changes.

Besides filing criminal charges against an abusive partner, there is the possibility of taking civil action against the offender. Unfortunately, a woman who has made the decision to leave her partner is usually too destitute to pay the attorney fees and filing costs associated with divorce or other civil petitions. Some states now provide a simplified mechanism to secure an *injunction*, or what some people call a *restraining order* or a *protection order*, against the abuser. As of mid-2006, Florida alone had more than 153,000 protective orders in its computerized record-keeping system (Florida Domestic Violence Fatality Review Team, 2007). Kentucky recorded over 11,000 domestic violence orders in 2007 (Logan, Walker, & Hoyt, 2012). One estimate places the annual number of domestic violence injunctions issued in the United States at 1.2 million (Sheeran & Meyer, 2010: 3).

Under these provisions, the clerk of the court supplies a preprinted, fill-in-the-blanks form to request an injunction or court protection order against the violent party. The clerk also explains how to complete the form. He or she can waive the filing fees if the victim is unable to pay court costs. The clerk also assists in the preparation of these materials. The judge can issue a temporary restraining order on an *ex parte* basis. In other words, the offender does not have to be present in order for the judge to take official action. Any violation of a protective order can constitute either a contempt-of-court charge or a separate criminal violation, and any law enforcement officer may then arrest the offender, which is a significant repercussion for men who do not want others to know about their behavior (Eisikovits, 1996; Fischer & Rose, 1995; Sorenson & Shen, 2005; U.S. Department of Justice, 2002; Wallace & Kelty, 1995). In fact, the federal Violence Against Women Act requires judges to enforce injunctions that have been issued outside their states (Eigenberg et al., 2003).

Despite these protections, less than one-half of the women who secure a temporary restraining order go on to obtain a permanent, final order (Zoellner et al., 2000). Perhaps, the process for filing and getting a permanent (as compared to a temporary) court order remains too cumbersome and tedious for these victims (Durfee, 2009; Logan, Shannon, & Walker, 2006). Another possibility is that the experience of obtaining a restraining order might dissuade some women from seeking further formal action. Women may become wary and noncommittal if they encounter court personnel who are intimidating, condescending, nonsupportive, or overly bureaucratic (Bell et al., 2011; Wan, 2000). However, there is some evidence that a legislative commitment to combat domestic violence can pay dividends. There are some indications that injunction or protective order provisions substantially reduce IPV violence, although the possibility of ineffective enforcement and subsequent stalking does emerge as a valid victim concern (Diviney, Parekh, & Olson, 2009; Dugan, 2003; Kothari et al., 2012; Logan & Walker, 2009a, 2010a). One study projected that IPV injunctions produce an annual savings of $85 million (costs borne by the justice system, health care services, employers, etc.) for Kentucky taxpayers (Logan et al., 2012: 1148). Table 10.7 displays an example of a petition form for a court injunction. Notice how it contains a series of fill-in-the-blanks and check-offs to facilitate filing.

There are a number of other proposals aimed at improving the prosecutorial and judicial responses to domestic violence. One such idea has been the introduction of victim advocates into the prosecutor's office and the courtroom. The availability of such individuals can help demystify the court process, provide support to the victim, and assist in the successful prosecution of the case. Closely related to this change is the appointment of specific attorneys to handle domestic violence cases and the use of "vertical adjudication," whereby a single prosecutor handles the case from start to finish (Durfee, 2009; Visher, Harrell, & Newmark, 2007: 4). In one jurisdiction, having investigating officers take digital photographs of victim injuries and preserving this evidence resulted in more guilty pleas, a greater number of convictions, and longer sentences (Garcia, 2003). Pretrial domestic violation probation units educate arrested persons about their bond conditions, especially if there is a no-contact-with-victim order, and verify that suspects have acquired an alternative living arrangement (Visher et al., 2007). Finally, many jurisdictions have sought to de-emphasize punishment in domestic violence cases and to promote treatment for both the offender and the victim.

> **WEB ACTIVITY**
>
> The American Bar Association has established a Commission on Domestic and Sexual Violence that serves as a clearinghouse. You can access those resources at **http://www.americanbar.org/groups/domestic_violence/resources.html**

Another strategy has entailed efforts to curtail dropping domestic violence cases at the prosecutorial level. As one veteran prosecutor explains:

> Experienced domestic violence prosecutors understand . . . domestic violence victims often stay with their abusers, regularly minimize their abuse, recant, request the dismissal of charges against their batterers, refuse to testify for the prosecution, or testify on behalf of their batterers (Long, 2008: 21).

Table 10.7 Petition for an Injunction for Protection Against Domestic Violence

Before me, the undersigned authority, personally appeared Petitioner____(name)____; who has been sworn and says that the following statements are true:

(a) Petitioner resides at:____(address)____
   (Petitioner may furnish address to the court in a separate confidential filing if, for safety reasons, the petitioner requires the location of the current residence to be confidential.)

(b) Respondent resides at:____(last known address)____

(c) Respondent's last known place of employment____(name of business and address)____

(d) Physical description of respondent:
   Race:____
   Sex:____
   Date of birth:____
   Height:____
   Weight:____
   Eye color:____
   Hair color:____
   Distinguishing marks or scars:_____

(e) Aliases of respondent:_____

(f) Respondent is the spouse or former spouse of the petitioner or is any other person related by blood or marriage to the petitioner or is any other person who is or was residing within a single dwelling unit with the petitioner, as if a family, or is a person with whom the petitioner has had a child in common, regardless of whether the petitioner and respondent are or were married or living together, as if a family.

(g) The following describes any other cause of action currently pending between the petitioner and respondent:
   _____

   The petitioner should also describe any previous or pending attempts by the petitioner to obtain an injunction for protection against domestic violence in this or any other circuit, and the results of that attempt:
   _____
   Case numbers should be included if available.

(h) Petitioner is either a victim of domestic violence or has reasonable cause to believe he or she is in imminent danger of becoming a victim of domestic violence because respondent has (mark all sections that apply and describe in the spaces below the incidents of violence or threats of violence, specifying when and where they occurred, including, but not limited to, locations such as a home, school, place of employment, or visitation exchange):
   _____committed or threatened to commit domestic violence defined in s. 741.28, Florida Statutes, as any assault, aggravated assault, battery, aggravated battery, sexual assault, sexual battery, stalking, aggravated stalking, kidnapping, false imprisonment, or any criminal offense resulting in physical injury or death of one family or household member by another. With the exception of persons who are parents of a child in common, the family or household members must be currently residing or have in the past resided together in the same single dwelling unit.
   _____previously threatened, harassed, stalked, or physically abused the petitioner.
   _____attempted to harm the petitioner or family members or individuals closely associated with the petitioner.
   _____threatened to conceal, kidnap, or harm the petitioner's child or children.
   _____intentionally injured or killed a family pet.
   _____used, or has threatened to use, against the petitioner any weapons such as guns or knives.
   _____physically restrained the petitioner from leaving the home or calling law enforcement.
   _____a criminal history involving violence or the threat of violence (if known).
   _____another order of protection issued against him or her previously or from another jurisdiction (if known).
   _____destroyed personal property, including, but not limited to, telephones or other communication equipment, clothing, or other items belonging to the petitioner.
   _____engaged in any other behavior or conduct that leads the petitioner to have reasonable cause to believe he or she is in imminent danger of becoming a victim of domestic violence.

Continued

Table 10.7 Petition for an Injunction for Protection Against Domestic Violence—*Cont'd*

(i) Petitioner alleges the following additional specific facts: (mark appropriate sections)

_____Petitioner is the custodian of a minor child or children whose names and ages are as follows:

_____

_____Petitioner needs the exclusive use and possession of the dwelling that the parties share.
Petitioner is unable to obtain safe alternative housing because: _____

_____Petitioner genuinely fears that respondent imminently will abuse, remove, or hide the minor child or children from petitioner because:_____

(j) Petitioner genuinely fears imminent domestic violence by respondent.

(k) Petitioner seeks an injunction: (mark appropriate section or sections)

_____Immediately restraining the respondent from committing any acts of domestic violence.

_____Restraining the respondent from committing any acts of domestic violence.

_____Awarding to the petitioner the temporary exclusive use and possession of the dwelling that the parties share or excluding the respondent from the residence of the petitioner.

_____Awarding temporary custody of, or temporary visitation rights with regard to, the minor child or children of the parties, or prohibiting or limiting visitation to that which is supervised by a third party.

_____Establishing temporary support for the minor child or children or the petitioner.

_____Directing the respondent to participate in a batterers' intervention program or other treatment pursuant to s. 39.901, *Florida Statutes*.

_____Providing any terms the court deems necessary for the protection of a victim of domestic violence, or any minor children of the victim, including any injunctions or directives to law enforcement agencies.

Source: Florida Statutes *(2012),* § *741.30(3)(b).*

Such "no-drop" or mandatory prosecution policies, like the guidelines that appear in Table 10.8, seek to force victims to carry through with the case and have the state assume the burden of the prosecution (Buzawa & Buzawa, 1990; Davis & Smith, 1995). The thinking behind these no-drop policies is to let the offender know that it is the state, not the victim, pursuing the case and to make abusers accountable for their actions (Berliner, 2003). This practice also extends the time an IPV case is involved in the courts and keeps the batterer under formal scrutiny for a longer period of time (Peterson & Dixon, 2005). Critics, though, question the advisability of coercing victims into prosecution without a fuller understanding of the ramifications (Flemming, 2003; Ford, 2003; Humphries, 2002). Despite the appearance of being harsh, two-thirds of the shelter residents in one study favored mandatory prosecution policies (Smith, 2000).

WEB ACTIVITY

AEquitas: The Prosecutors' Resource on Violence Against Women is dedicated to improving justice for women. Its resources can be accessed at **http://www.aequitasresource.org/**

As recent U.S. Supreme Court cases illustrate, some evidentiary risks or hurdles can accompany a no-drop policy. Among other things, the Sixth Amendment to the U.S. Constitution guarantees defendants the right to confront and cross-examine their accusers. However, when the victim declines to testify or refuses to appear in court, the defendant does not have the opportunity to impeach the witness. Typically, the state is not able to proceed in such instances

Table 10.8 An Example of a Prosecutor's Domestic Violence Guidelines That Contain a "No-Drop" Clause

The District Attorney has established a no-drop policy as it pertains to victims wishing to drop charges against defendants. All victims who inquire about dropping charges are referred to the victim coordinator. This policy does not mean the District Attorney's office will not reduce or dismiss a case; it means the decision is the responsibility of the District Attorney, not the victim. It is the State of Alabama vs. the Defendant, not the Victim vs. the Defendant. Crime victims wishing to discuss the possible reduction or dismissal of charges in a pending case must schedule an appointment with a victim coordinator.

Multiple reasons exist for this policy. Some victims who are being coerced or feel compelled to drop charges have changed their minds and cooperated with the prosecution after talking with a victim coordinator, while other victims who inquire about our no-drop policy are relieved to discover they do not carry the burden and responsibility of pressing charges and prosecuting the case. The no-drop policy also gives victim coordinators the opportunity to further research a case and present a more complete profile to the prosecutor, who then has the opportunity to review the file and make better-informed decisions about the pending case.

Source: Domestic Violence Prosecution Committee (2004). Guidelines for Prosecution of Domestic Violence Cases. *Montgomery: Alabama Coalition Against Domestic Violence, p. 22. Retrieved on May 16, 2013, from http://www.acadv.org/Prosecutionguidelines.pdf.*

without relying on hearsay evidence. However, one exception to hearsay is *forfeiture by wrongdoing.* If the defendant impedes the prosecution by threatening, intimidating, or actually harming the victim, then he or she forfeits any Sixth Amendment protections against statements made outside the courtroom. As the U.S. Supreme Court explained, "one who obtains the absence of a witness by wrongdoing forfeits the constitutional right to confrontation" (*Davis v. Washington*, p. 18).

Crawford v. Washington (2004)

During a police investigation into a nonfatal stabbing episode, both Crawford and his wife, who witnessed the altercation, made statements that implicated Crawford as the assailant. However, when the case went to trial, Crawford claimed that he had acted in self-defense. His wife declined to testify, citing the husband–wife privileged relationship. As a result, the prosecutor was left with a weak case.

The prosecutor tried to salvage the case by introducing earlier statements the wife made during an interrogation session at the police station, in an effort to show the stabbing was not done in self-defense. Part of the prosecutor's reasoning was that the marital exemption only applied to in-court testimony. Crawford countered that his wife's unavailability as a witness denied him the right to confrontation as guaranteed under the Sixth Amendment. Eventually, the court allowed the jury to hear the taped interrogation session and the jury went on to convict the defendant of assault.

The case made its way to the U.S. Supreme Court. There, after considerable analysis, the Justices decided in favor of Crawford. Admitting testimonial statements without affording the defendant the opportunity to cross-examine the witness amounts to a fundamental violation of the Sixth Amendment.

Davis v. Washington (2006)

This ruling actually involved two separate cases. In the first situation, McCottry dialed 911 immediately after her boyfriend Davis left her residence, and reported that Davis had just beaten her. The victim gave the authorities the suspect's name and a physical description. Two officers responded, observed McCottry's injuries, and took a report. Eventually, the police were able to arrest Davis. When the case came to trial, the victim McCottry failed to appear. Instead of just dropping the case, the prosecutor introduced the 911 tapes as evidence of the assault and the jury found Davis guilty. Later, Davis appealed his conviction on the grounds that he was denied the opportunity to confront and cross-examine his accuser.

In the second instance, the police responded to another domestic disturbance. Upon arrival, the officers found the victim Hammon outside on the porch. After gaining her consent to enter the premises, the officer observed signs of a struggle in the living room and located the suspect inside the kitchen. Based upon their observations, what the victim told them, and the contents of the affidavit the victim had written under oath and signed at the scene, the officers arrested Hammon for domestic battery. When the case went to trial, the victim failed to appear. The prosecutor introduced the affidavit as evidence in the victim's absence. Although the defendant's lawyer objected to the affidavit because its author was not available for cross-examination, the trial judge admitted the statement under the "excited utterance" exception. Hammon was convicted and subsequently appealed on the basis of the Sixth Amendment because he was not able to cross-examine the accuser.

Upon review of these cases, the Supreme Court drew a distinction between *testimonial* and *nontestimonial statements.* As the Court explained:

> Statements are nontestimonial when made in the course of police interrogation under circumstances objectively indicating that the primary purpose of the interrogation is to enable police assistance to meet an ongoing emergency. They are testimonial when the circumstances objectively indicate that there is no such ongoing emergency, and that the primary purpose of the interrogation is to establish or prove past events potentially relevant to later criminal prosecution (p. 7).

Using this distinction, the Court reasoned that the information generated during McCottry's 911 telephone exchange fell under exigent circumstances and did not constitute testimony for the purpose of proving guilt. In contrast, the Hammon situation had already concluded, was relatively calm, and did not involve any immediate danger. As a result, the Court concluded that the McCottry 911 tape was nontestimonial and, therefore, admissible without triggering any Sixth Amendment protections. On the other hand, the affidavit in Hammon was testimonial and the defendant had the right to conduct a cross-examination of the victim.

Giles v. California (2008)

Giles shot and killed his ex-girlfriend Avie during the course of an argument. About three weeks earlier, Giles had battered Avie and threatened to kill her. Avie contacted the police after that incident and the officer wrote a report.

When the murder case went to trial, the prosecutor introduced the statements that Avie had made to the investigating officer in the earlier incident. Giles objected on the grounds that he could not possibly cross-examine the witness. But the trial court allowed the evidence because California law permitted out-of-court statements when the victim was not available as long as they involved threats or injuries to the victim and those statements were trustworthy. Giles was found guilty and appealed his conviction to the California Court of Appeal. That court applied the *forfeiture by wrongdoing doctrine* and ruled that Giles had lost his right to cross-examine Avie because he was responsible for her murder.

The Supreme Court remanded *Giles* back to the state court with instructions to consider whether the defendant murdered Avie in order to prevent her testimony in court. In other words, forfeiture by wrongdoing would be appropriate only if the defendant murdered the victim in a deliberate effort to keep her from testifying against him:

> Acts of domestic violence often are intended to dissuade a victim from resorting to outside help, and include conduct designed to prevent testimony to police officers or cooperation in criminal prosecutions. Where such an abusive relationship culminates in murder, the evidence may support a finding that the crime expressed the intent to isolate the victim and to stop her from reporting abuse to the authorities or cooperating with a criminal prosecution—rendering her prior statements admissible under the forfeiture doctrine. Earlier abuse, or threats of abuse, intended to dissuade the victim from resorting to outside help would be highly relevant to this inquiry, as would evidence of ongoing criminal proceedings at which the victim would have been expected to testify (p. 23).

Summary of Judicial Action

These three rulings have some chilling implications for no-drop policies and victimless prosecutions. Some observers think it would behoove the system to concentrate more on the reasons why IPV victims do not testify against their attackers. Making victims safer from their batterers, addressing economic security, recognizing that a battering relationship constitutes an ongoing emergency, introducing more expert witness testimony about the devastating effects of IPV, and crafting more workable forfeiture-by-wrongdoing strategies would do much to help empower victims in the post-*Giles* era (Bailey, 2009; Ewing, 2007; Hussain, 2009).

COORDINATING SYSTEM APPROACHES

Instead of thinking that any single agency can have a major impact on IPV, it is more reasonable to assume that coordinated efforts of several agencies will be more effective. Coupling arrest with aggressive prosecution, for example, may reduce subsequent offending more than arrest alone. Indeed, one criticism of the Minneapolis Experiment and its replications was the lack of information on what happened to the offender after the arrest. Unfortunately, relatively few analyses look at broader-based system approaches.

Tolman and Weisz (1995) reported on one coordinated arrest and prosecution program in Illinois. DuPage County instituted a program that included a pro-arrest policy, as well as prosecution based on complaints signed by the police when victims refused to do so. While officers can sign complaints in many jurisdictions, it is not very common, because the refusal of victims to sign generally signifies a future lack of cooperation with the prosecution. In the DuPage program, the prosecution actively worked to gain victim participation in the case. Analyzing 690 domestic abuse cases, Tolman and Weisz (1995) found the highest recidivism levels in cases of arrests with no convictions. Conversely, arrests ending in conviction displayed the lowest recidivism rates. The authors argue that this system approach is more effective than individual agency initiatives.

Another cooperative arrangement holding potential for stemming IPV entails coupling victim or social service agencies with the criminal justice system (Ahmad & Mullings, 1999; Spence-Diehl & Potocky-Tripodi, 2001). The use or inclusion of victim or social service agencies has become increasingly common in recent years. Many police departments will call on specially trained individuals to assist in responding to IPV or sexual assault cases. Similarly, prosecuting attorneys often rely on victim advocates and social service agencies to help guide victims through legal proceedings, encourage victims to carry through with a prosecution, and conduct danger assessments. Concern for the ongoing safety of IPV victims has prompted some jurisdictions to evaluate the volatility of the victim's situation. While there are several standardized protocols currently in use (Campbell et al., 2003; Campbell, Webster, & Glass, 2009), they typically rely upon themes similar to those that appear in Table 10.9. In fact, some evidence suggests that this attention enhances victim cooperation immensely (Dawson & Dinovitzer, 2001).

Table 10.9 Prominent Risk Factors in an IPV Danger or Lethality Assessment

- Is there a history of domestic violence?
- Does the perpetrator have obsessive or possessive thoughts?
- Has the perpetrator threatened to kill the victim?
- Does the perpetrator feel betrayed by the victim?
- Is the victim attempting to separate from the perpetrator?
- Have there been prior calls to the police?
- Is there increasing drug or alcohol use by the perpetrator?
- What is the prior criminal history of the perpetrator?
- Is the perpetrator depressed?
- Does the perpetrator have specific "fantasies" of homicide or suicide?
- Does the perpetrator have access to or a fascination with weapons?
- Has the perpetrator abused animals/pets?
- Has the perpetrator demonstrated rage or hostile behavior toward police or others?
- Has there been an increase in the frequency or severity of the violence (whether documented or not)?
- Has the perpetrator been violent toward children?
- Has there been strangulation involved and how often?
- Is there a history of stalking behavior?

Source: State of Nevada Advisory Council for Prosecuting Attorneys (2006). Nevada Domestic Violence Prosecution Best Practice Guidelines. Reno: State of Nevada Advisory Council for Prosecuting Attorneys. Retrieved on May 16, 2013, from http:// nvpac.nv.gov/uploadedFiles/nvpacnvgov/Content/Resources/DV_Best_Practice_Guidelines.pdf.

A recent effort in Milwaukee provides a good illustration that the "go-alone" approach often invites failure. Prosecutors in that city unilaterally decided to accept more IPV cases for court action by relaxing the emphasis on victim cooperation. However, there was no corresponding effort to enlist the help of other members of the criminal justice system. Police officers did not receive any training or instruction on how to improve evidence-gathering at crime scenes, victim advocates were not prepared for the increased number of clients, court resources were not increased to handle an expanding docket, and the prosecution staff did not grow. As Davis, Smith, and Taylor (2003: 279) termed it, this situation "was a recipe for disaster." The flood of case filings resulted in substantial delays from start to finish, a rise in pretrial repeat offenses, lower conviction rates, and enormous victim dissatisfaction. These misguided experiences led the authors to warn that "good intentions do not always result in good public policy" (Davis et al., 2003: 280).

Relatively little empirical research has been conducted looking at the use of victim advocates and social service agencies. In one report, Davis and Taylor (1997) analyzed the impact of a program that combined the police with social workers in New York City. This program, the Domestic Violence Intervention Education Project (DVIEP), involved crisis response teams in two main functions. One was to follow up on IPV calls handled by routine patrol. The second function involved educating the public about family violence and invoking system response. The authors were able to make random assignments of IPV cases to either the DVIEP program or normal police intervention. Similarly, the education program was randomly assigned to different households. Unfortunately, the evaluation showed no impact on subsequent self-reports of IPV or on the seriousness of subsequent abuse. On the other hand, the project significantly increased the willingness of respondents to call for police assistance (Davis & Taylor, 1997). It would appear that the project had its greatest impact on altering the amenability of victims to recognize their victimization as a problem and one that required some form of intervention. What is missing from the evaluation is any assessment of the quality of the intervention, especially across cases, and the extent to which the program prompted other positive responses on the part of the victims.

More attention needs to be paid to systemic responses to IPV. These efforts are not uncommon. Unfortunately, few have undergone rigorous evaluation, leaving the programs with little more than faith in their abilities. It would be advantageous to know what type of cooperative intervention works best and in what settings each is most appropriate. As Miller (2006: 1125) explains:

> [A] single solution, such as a single domestic violence intervention program or a mandatory arrest, prosecution, and counseling program for known abusers, is untenable. We know that not all IPV abusers should be arrested. And we know that some abusers, if not incapacitated, will continue a pattern of intimate terrorism that will result in severe, chronic, or permanent injury or death. Imagine a highly curable illness (e.g., bronchitis) that affects 19% of the women in the general population and a different type of illness (e.g., a mutated flu virus) that can threaten the lives of 2% of the women. Are those numbers big enough to warrant therapeutic or preventive strategies? Are they different enough to warrant different responses?

MORE RECENT RESPONSES

Besides making legislative changes that allow greater police action, such as relaxing the misdemeanor rule, most jurisdictions have responded to IPV by enacting laws aimed at threatening behavior and situations. Perhaps the most notable of these efforts is the growth of anti-stalking laws, outlawing gun possession by domestic violators, court-ordered mandatory counseling for convicted batterers, granting clemency to battered women convicted of killing their partners, installation of a national hotline, and impaneling fatality review teams.

Stalking Laws

While the word "stalking" may bring an immediate picture to mind, there is no single accepted definition of what the term means. According to Wright and colleagues (1997: 487), *stalking* "is the act of following, viewing, communicating with, or moving threateningly or menacingly toward another person." The inclusion of "viewing" and "communicating with" in the definition may surprise some readers. These kinds of actions, however, can create a great deal of anxiety and fear, especially if they are part of a repeated pattern or coupled with other activities.

The NCVS recently conducted a Supplemental Victimization Survey that explored stalking experiences (Catalano, 2012b). In addition to the components of inducing fear in the victim and taking place on multiple occasions, the survey focused on the following unwanted behaviors:

- Making unwanted phone calls;
- Sending unsolicited or unwanted letters or e-mails;
- Following or spying on the victim;
- Showing up at places without a legitimate reason;
- Waiting at places for the victim;
- Leaving unwanted items, presents, or flowers; and
- Posting information or spreading rumors about the victim on the Internet, in a public place, or by word of mouth (Catalano, 2012b).

The combination of action with both fear and repetition can be seen in Florida's stalking statute, displayed in Table 10.10.

The three key features of most anti-stalking codes are the existence of threatening behavior, criminal intent by the offender, and repetition in the activity. These three factors are important because there is no other law violation involved in most instances. For example, in the absence of an anti-stalking code, simply following someone around is not illegal, even though it might be construed as harassment (Sheridan, Davies, & Boon, 2001). In fact, some professions, such as private investigation or journalism, typically require one person to follow another. Determining threat or criminal intent is not easy. The usual standard, however, involves recognizing what a "reasonable person" would fear or find acceptable. The requirement for repeated action or a pattern of activity also helps to outline what constitutes stalking. It is important, therefore, for legislation to allow for the distinction between different types of "following" behavior. One example of this evolving notion would be the phenomenon of *cyberstalking*, which refers to harassment conducted via the Internet, e-mail, spyware, cell phones, global positioning systems, or other means of electronic communication (Southworth et al., 2007).

As far as IPV goes, stalking often takes place once the victim has decided to end the "cycle of violence." As mentioned earlier, the cycle of violence progresses

---

Table 10.10 The Florida Stalking Statute

(1) As used in this section, the term:

(a) "Harass" means to engage in a course of conduct directed at a specific person that causes substantial emotional distress in such person and serves no legitimate purpose.

(b) "Course of conduct" means a pattern of conduct composed of a series of acts over a period of time, however short, evidencing a continuity of purpose. The term does not include constitutionally protected activity such as picketing or other organized protests.

(c) "Credible threat" means a verbal or nonverbal threat, or a combination of the two, including threats delivered by electronic communication or implied by a pattern of conduct, which places the person who is the target of the threat in reasonable fear for his or her safety or the safety of his or her family members or individuals closely associated with the person, and which is made with the apparent ability to carry out the threat to cause such harm. It is not necessary to prove that the person making the threat had the intent to actually carry out the threat. The present incarceration of the person making the threat is not a bar to prosecution under this section.

(d) "Cyberstalk" means to engage in a course of conduct to communicate, or to cause to be communicated, words, images, or language by or through the use of electronic mail or electronic communication, directed at a specific person, causing substantial emotional distress to that person and serving no legitimate purpose.

Source: Florida Statutes *(2012),* § 784.048.

---

through three distinct stages: the tension-building phase, the battering episode, and the reconciliation period. However, once the woman is determined to abandon the abusive relationship, the male partner may be at a loss as to how best regain control over her. When the mollifying behaviors that worked so well before fizzle, the male may resort to stalking activity or threats in an effort to thwart her escape and re-establish control over the victim (DeKeseredy et al., 2006; Logan & Walker, 2009b, 2010b; Melton, 2007a, 2007b; Norris, Huss, & Palarea, 2011; Roberts, 2005). This behavior is so common that Logan and Walker (2009b) resort to the term *partner stalking.*

Many state codes have been challenged on a number of fronts. The most strenuous objections have focused on the perceived ambiguity and extensive breadth of the statutes (Bjerregaard, 1996; Sohn, 1994; Thomas, 1997). For example, critics have charged that terminology such as "repeatedly" and "intent to cause emotional distress" is too vague, thus rendering the statutes unconstitutional. Other challenges attack provisions that outlaw such things as "contacting another person . . . without the consent of the other person" or "following" another person. The contention is that this wording is so broad that it criminalizes constitutionally protected behaviors. In almost every case, the courts have rejected these arguments and upheld the constitutionality of stalking laws.

Penalties for stalking depend upon past violations, as well as the extent of any injury or threat. Misdemeanor violations typically allow for a jail term of up to one year. Felony violations, however, can carry substantial penalties, particularly if there are aggravating circumstances, such as the use of a weapon, the violation of a restraining order, or a prior conviction. These penalties may include imprisonment or fines of $10,000 or more. It is also possible that stalking may constitute a violent crime for purposes of "three strikes" laws in some states, resulting in life sentences without parole.

WEB ACTIVITY

The Stalking Resource Center, maintained by the National Center for Victims of Crime, offers a wide range of information about stalking that you can find at **http://www.victimsofcrime.org/ our-programs/stalking-resource-center**

Despite the growth of stalking legislation, research on the topic is just now making its appearance. Most discussions point to media accounts of well-known, spectacular stalking incidents, typically involving celebrities or politicians, or actions resulting in murder (Hickey, 2012; Marquez & Scalora, 2011). Much more common is stalking of women by ex-husbands or ex-boyfriends (see Figure 10.3). Information gleaned from the National Intimate Partner and Sexual Violence Survey reveals that "approximately 1 in 6 women in the United States has experienced stalking at some point in her lifetime in which she felt very fearful or believed that she or someone close to her would be harmed or killed as a result" (Black et al., 2011: 29). More pointedly, the Supplemental Victimization Survey to the NCVS estimates that 5.3 million adults in this country are the victims of stalking or harassment every year, with 70% of these perpetrators being intimate partners or friends and acquaintances (Catalano, 2012a).

FIGURE 10.3 Domestic violence survivor Kathy Haley was stalked and ultimately shot and paralyzed by her husband.
Credit: AP Photo/Don Edgar.

The extent to which stalking laws will impact the level of domestic abuse is unknown at this time. Most statutes are too new to have undergone extensive impact analysis. It is unclear, for example, to what extent these laws are being used by victims and enforced by the police and the courts. The fact that the statutes have withstood constitutional challenges suggests that they should receive attention as a legitimate tool in the fight against IPV.

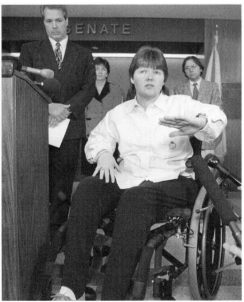

The Lautenberg Amendment

Congress passed a bill, introduced by Senator Frank R. Lautenberg, that banned gun ownership by any person ever convicted of a misdemeanor domestic violence charge (see Table 10.11). This amendment to the Gun Control Act of 1968 took effect on September 30, 1996. A number of states followed this federal strategy by either changing their own IPV statutes to prohibit abusers from possessing firearms or including similar language in the provisions of a restraining order (Nathan, 2000).

The goal behind this initiative is to combat violence against women. IPV homicides made up 16% of all homicides committed in this country between 1980 and

Table 10.11 An Excerpt from the Lautenberg Amendment

(g) It shall be unlawful for any person–

(8) who is subject to a court order that–

(A) was issued after a hearing of which such person received actual notice, and at which such person had an opportunity to participate;

(B) restrains such person from harassing, stalking, or threatening an intimate partner of such person or child of such intimate partner or person, or engaging in other conduct that would place an intimate partner in reasonable fear of bodily injury to the partner or child; and

(C) (i) includes a finding that such person represents a credible threat to the physical safety of such intimate partner or child; or

(ii) by its terms explicitly prohibits the use, attempted use, or threatened use of physical force against such intimate partner or child that would reasonably be expected to cause bodily injury; or

(9) who has been convicted in any court of a misdemeanor crime of domestic violence, to ship or transport in interstate or foreign commerce, or possess in or affecting commerce, any firearm or ammunition; or to receive any firearm or ammunition which has been shipped or transported in interstate or foreign commerce.

Source: 18 U.S.C. § 922.

2008. More than two-thirds of the murder victims killed by current or former spouses died from gunshot wounds (Cooper & Smith, 2011). As Table 10.12 shows, a greater awareness of the explosive nature of IPV situations has prompted authorities to become more meticulous about seizing firearms when appropriate.

Opposition to this initiative formed very quickly, and a flurry of outcries soon crystallized. Opponents argued that extending a weapons ban to persons *ever* convicted of domestic violence was nothing more than an *ex post facto* law and patently unconstitutional. In other words, additional penalties were being applied to cases that were already concluded and to situations in which individuals had already completed their sentences. Proponents maintained that the critics were wrong: the new laws made possession of a weapon by convicted IPV offenders after the passage date a completely new charge. Because the language outlawed a new behavior, it did not violate the prohibition against *ex post facto* laws.

Observers also noted that the weapons ban meant that law enforcement officers and members of the military with IPV histories fell under these provisions. These persons could not perform essential job functions if they were not allowed to carry a firearm. Efforts to gain a public-interest exemption for these groups have failed (Nathan, 2000).

A Supreme Court decision (*U.S. v. Hayes*, 2009) lends further support to the weapons ban. Hayes was convicted in 1994, prior to this federal law taking effect, of misdemeanor battery on his wife. However, West Virginia did not have a specific domestic violence statute on the books at that time. Hence, Hayes was convicted under the generic battery statute. In 2004, officers

---

Table 10.12 Recommended Strategies for Law Enforcement Seizure of Firearms and Ammunition When Enforcing Domestic Violence Civil Protection Orders

■ Attempt to verify the existence of firearms through dispatch and mobile data terminals, call history, prior experience with the parties, and firearm registries while en route to the scene.

■ Make inquiries as to the presence and location of firearms after arrest and separation of the parties.

■ Seize firearms and ammunition in a respondent's possession when serving protection orders, as permitted under state or federal law.

■ Inform the respondent fully about restrictions on firearms and ammunition.

■ Identify if firearms have been transferred before an officer's arrival and explain to the third party that transferring the firearms back to the respondent may be illegal.

■ Ensure that the third party is eligible to take possession of the firearms prior to releasing the firearms to the party.

■ Ensure weapons are not returned until appropriate.

Source: Adapted from Sheeran, M., & Meyer, E. (2010). Civil Protection Orders: A Guide for Improving Practice. Reno, NV: National Council of Juvenile and Family Court Judges. Retrieved on May 16, 2013, from http://www.ncjfcj.org/resource-library/publications/civil-protection-orders-guide-improving-practice.

---

determined that Hayes had a rifle and several other firearms in his house. The officers arrested Hayes, and he was convicted of violating the federal weapons ban. Hayes appealed his conviction, maintaining that his 1994 conviction was not a qualifying offense because West Virginia did not have a specific domestic violence statute at that time. After analyzing the circumstances and determining that Hayes had committed a simple battery on his spouse, the Supreme Court rejected his argument and upheld his conviction.

Finally, others contended that these provisions violated the equal protection clause because harsher penalties were being exacted from misdemeanants than from felons (Nelson, 1999). In other words, convicted felons could petition to have their civil rights restored. If successful, they could lawfully possess a firearm. No corresponding reinstatement procedure exists for misdemeanants. To date, the Lautenberg Amendment has survived these and other challenges.

Court-Ordered Mandatory Counseling

One lingering problem with relying upon mandatory arrest policies as the most appropriate or sole solution to the problem of IPV is that arrest by itself is generally an ineffective response. What an arrest platform amounts to, especially in the absence of any follow-up intervention, is a *Scared Straight* tactic. In other words, fear becomes the overriding motivational factor. While it is true that the deterrence doctrine is an important underpinning for how the criminal justice system operates, it is not always the most efficient practice. As a result, therapeutic interventions that seek to prevent a relapse have become an essential strategy. In fact, Florida, like other states, now requires judges to sentence convicted abusers to participation in a batterer's intervention program (*Florida Statutes*, 2012: § 741.281). Although this strategy is appealing, one must bear in mind that there is often a considerable delay between arrest and program enrollment. What this section explores, then, is whether self-initiated or court-mandated participation works better, whether the counseling should deal with only one or both parties in the relationship, and whether therapeutic intervention is a meaningful route to travel.

One scheme for envisioning how treatment produces change within a person is to cast any transformation, whether the topic be abusive action or addictive behavior like cigarette smoking, into a five-step model (Cancer Prevention Research Center, 2013). The initial phase, the *precontemplation stage*, is a point at which the person, although he or she may recognize the need to stop engaging in destructive behavior, has no set timetable or goals in place. The *contemplation stage* gets the person ready for what is to come. Here, the subject recognizes the need for modification and starts thinking about the best way to embark upon this process. The *preparation stage* occurs when the individual devises a plan and is ready to implement it. The *action stage* comes when the person achieves the goals and makes headway in terms of eradicating the objectionable behavior. Finally, the *maintenance stage* calls for eternal vigilance. At this point, the person must continue the newly learned behavior and not succumb or give in to pressures to revert back to the old destructive behavior.

Abusive partners who wish to alter their violent behavior need a supportive therapeutic environment in which to complete this transition. Until now, abuser participation in therapeutic activities has been largely voluntary or one-sided. Batterers who seek counseling may start with all the best intentions in the world. Given the myriad of defenses that one may conjure up to defend previous actions, the therapist faces a Herculean task with these clients. Usually, a self-referred patient, no matter how energetic and dedicated, is fragile but amenable to treatment (Dutton & Starzomski, 1994). Should the counselor critically confront the client and abruptly challenge his or her fundamental thinking, the chances are that the self-referred person will not return for a second session (Murphy & Baxter, 1997). In such a case, any hopes for change are dashed.

A second important consideration for the therapist is whether to deal with one or both parties in the abusive relationship. Therapists who engage in couples therapy have several focal points in mind. They are aiming to eliminate any psychological or physical violence, to convince the clients to accept responsibility for escalating to violent behavior when arguing, to have clients learn self-control, to establish better communication between the couple, to promote more enjoyable activity for the couple, and to instill the idea that each partner should treat the other with respect (O'Leary, 1996).

While this protocol may appear reasonable, critics express serious reservations about it. There is a fundamental disagreement with how the problem is conceptualized. As McMahon and Pence (1996: 453) explain, "such terms as *spousal abuse, physically aggressive couples*, or *abusive relationships* … hide the fact that the phenomenon under discussion is primarily men's violence toward their wives or female partners." When the therapist approaches violent behavior as a symptom of a much larger underlying problem, all the counselor does is deflect attention away from treating the violent behavior. What the therapist should be addressing is the abuser's reliance on violence, not probing for tensions within the relationship, and certainly the counselor should not imply that the wife bears responsibility for helping the male partner change his behavior.

There is some evidence that battered women and mental health workers have divergent perceptions of IPV and that this lack of a common definition undermines the utility of seeking help. There is often a very fine line that separates aggression from violence (Bailey, Buchbinder, & Eisikovits, 2011) and this distinction pits a feminist orientation against a patriarchal approach. The therapist's failure to assess the situation appropriately produces two types of victim disenchantment: disenchantment through avoidance and disenchantment through action.

According to Eisikovits and Buchbinder (1996), *disenchantment through avoidance* arises when the counselor sidesteps the issue of violence. Rather than initiate a discussion of the battering, many therapists stand back and wait for the victim to broach the topic. This avoidance or lack of guidance leaves many victims wondering about the therapist's interest. Therapists, on the other hand, try hard to maintain some professional distance when dealing with clients. Instead of seeing this stance as a professionalization strategy, however, victims view it as aloofness or coldness. In other words, what battered women expect from their counselors is quite different from the services they receive.

A second avenue, *disenchantment through action*, further cements the woman's frustration with the therapeutic relationship. Many therapists open a couples session by asking the male to give his version of what is taking place within the relationship. Quite often, the male will make some effort to debunk the woman's rendition. Immediately the woman is thrust into the position of having her truthfulness being evaluated. Furthermore, by transforming the battering into an indicator of tensions within the relationship, the therapist paints the woman as a co-source of the disharmony. As Eisikovits and Buchbinder (1996: 436) explain:

> For battered women, violence is their life, but for the social worker, it is a symptom. Due to self-disclosure, many battered women tend to develop the illusion of interpersonal closeness, whereas social workers respond with "correct," professional role relationships. Social workers attempt to place violence in context, corroborate the women's story, and bring the men into the process to make them part of the solution

rather than the problem. Such behaviors are interpreted by the women as evidence of distance and betrayal.

As you can see, there are many complex issues endemic to the role of therapeutic intervention. While the common assumption is that counseling can cure whatever ails the people in an IPV relationship, there are a number of questions that require a critical examination first. At the same time, this discussion has not even delved into the question of which kinds of treatment are more suitable than others, which protocols produce the best success rates, and at what cost (Gondolf, 2008, 2009; Huss & Ralston, 2008; Jones, 2000; Price & Rosenbaum, 2009; Taylor, Davis, & Maxwell, 2001). One helpful distinction Chapter 5 developed was the difference between a process and an outcome evaluation when addressing restitution practices. If you recall, a *process evaluation* focuses on counting the number of clients served, time spent in the program, number of sessions, and other markers that deal with volume measures. An *outcome evaluation*, in contrast, concentrates on documenting the impact a program has altering client behavior. Riger and Staggs (2011: 66) use this distinction to illustrate a major shortcoming in how domestic violence programs are held accountable:

> most states that fund domestic violence services collect some form of evaluation data from the agencies that they fund. Typically, the data collected describes the activities of agencies. Less often, evaluation data assess the impact of services on clients. Even less frequently, evaluations assess the extent to which agencies achieve previously specified performance goals.

While this area will experience further research and greater development, one thing is certain. Even though court-mandated therapeutic intervention may appear to be a reasonable and satisfactory solution, it is not a simple universal antidote to the problem of IPV. A "one-size-fits-all" approach simply will not work.

Executive Clemency

One post-conviction remedy, executive clemency, provides a course of redress to women imprisoned for killing their husbands or boyfriends. *Executive clemency* means the state governor, either alone or in consultation with a board or panel, commutes or reduces the original court-imposed sentence to a lesser punishment. This humanitarian effort usually comes about after doubts surface regarding the sufficiency of the evidence presented at trial, additional evidence becomes unveiled after the trial is concluded, overlooked aspects of the case gain prominence, the sentence is overly harsh when balanced against mitigating factors, or a host of other reasons (Acker & Lanier, 2000). In capital punishment cases, executive clemency sets aside the death penalty and usually substitutes life imprisonment in its place (Freilich & Rivera, 1999; Pridemore, 2000).

When such a request is filed by an IPV survivor, the claim usually involves the "battered woman's syndrome" (BWS) as an extenuating circumstance or a form of self-defense. Under normal conditions, a person involved in a physical confrontation has the legal obligation to retreat whenever possible. One can become the aggressor and initiate an attack in self-defense only if that person is cornered and has no immediately available avenue of escape. The BWS contends that the lethal or violent response by the woman who is in an ongoing abusive relationship represents the culmination of the cycle of violence and learned helplessness. While an opportunity to get out of harm's way might have been present at the time of the incident or the immediate conditions may not have amounted to a genuine threat to the woman's overall health or well-being, her past experiences have convinced her that no other feasible alternative exists. In short, she is cornered in her own home (Orr, 2000) where "castle doctrine" protections apply (see Table 10.13).

Table 10.13 The Castle Doctrine

Kathleen Weiand was charged with first-degree murder for the 1994 shooting death of her husband Todd Weiand. Weiand shot her husband during a violent argument in the apartment where the two were living together with their seven-week-old daughter. At trial Weiand claimed self-defense and presented battered spouse syndrome evidence . . . in support of her claim. Weiand testified that her husband had beaten and choked her throughout the course of their three-year relationship and had threatened further violence if she left him.

Under Florida statutory and common law, a person may use deadly force in self-defense if he or she reasonably believes that deadly force is necessary to prevent imminent death or great bodily harm. ... Even under those circumstances, however, a person may not resort to deadly force without first using every reasonable means within his or her power to avoid the danger, including retreat. ... There is an exception to this common law duty to retreat "to the wall," which applies when an individual claims self-defense in his or her own residence. ... An individual is not required to retreat from the residence before resorting to deadly force in self-defense, so long as the deadly force is necessary to prevent death or great bodily harm.

The privilege of nonretreat from the home, part of the "castle doctrine," has early common law origins. ... It is not now and never has been the law that a man assailed in his own dwelling is bound to retreat. If assailed there, he may stand his ground and resist the attack. He is under no duty to take to the fields and the highways, a fugitive from his own home. ... Flight is for sanctuary and shelter, and shelter, if not sanctuary, is in the home. ... The rule is the same whether the attack proceeds from some other occupant or from an intruder.

Imposition of the duty to retreat on a battered woman who finds herself the target of a unilateral, unprovoked attack in her own home is inherently unfair. During repeated instances of past abuse, she has "retreated," only to be caught, dragged back inside, and severely beaten again.

What [the duty to retreat] exception means for a battered woman is that as long as it is a stranger who attacks her in her home, she has a right to fight back and labors under no duty to retreat. If the attacker is her husband or live-in partner, however, she must retreat. The threat of death or serious bodily injury may be just as real (and, statistically, is more real) when her husband or partner attacks her in home, but still she must retreat.

In conclusion, we hold that there is no duty to retreat from the residence before resorting to deadly force against a co-occupant or invitee if necessary to prevent death or great bodily harm. ...

Source: Excerpted from Weiand v. State, *732 So. 2d 1044 (Fla. 1999).*

Thus, lashing out at the abuser is the only convincing way to end this torment.

The formulation of the BWS as a legal defense had to contend with the portrayal of this phenomenon as either an excuse or a justification. Mental health workers paint BWS as a post-traumatic stress disorder, a mental state. Feminists, on the other hand, object to this depiction. They argue that BWS is a normal response to an extremely abusive relationship (Gagné, 1996). This distinction frames the contours of an important legal battle. As Dressler (2006: 463) explains, "justifications focus on the act; excuses focus on the actor."

The stakes involved here are very high. The excuse route would call for the woman to admit that she committed the act but maintain that she lacked responsibility for the deed. Insanity issues would arise here. The justification path requires a similar admission. However, here the perpetrator would point to recognizable mitigating circumstances. The insanity excuse, if believed, could lead to a civil commitment in a mental health facility for treatment. On the other hand, the justification excuse, if compelling, could result potentially in exoneration (Sigler & Shook, 1997: 368).

Generally speaking, five criteria are necessary for clemency consideration under the BWS:

1. the applicant must be a woman;
2. she must be incarcerated for murder of an intimate partner;
3. she must document a history of abusive behavior from her intimate partner;
4. she must have completed a portion of the imposed sentence; and
5. she must have an acceptable outlook on her experience.

This post-conviction remedy is an important strategy when attempting to undo previous miscarriages of justice. Once the courts began recognizing BWS as a viable self-defense argument, convicted women started to avail themselves of this new concept. Introducing evidence that documented the existence of an abusive relationship and bringing this new information to an executive clemency board for review offer new hope to women who previously were unable to convince the trial court that this experience was a legitimate justification for the events that had unfolded.

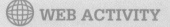 **WEB ACTIVITY**

The Michigan Women's Justice and Clemency Project advocates on behalf of women who were convicted of murdering their abusers. Their website houses a variety of educational materials and can be found at **http://www.umich.edu/~ clemency/**

National Telephone Hotline

We often tend to think of crime as an urban phenomenon and forget that problems, such as domestic violence, know no boundaries. These interpersonal difficulties also occur in rural areas and among culturally diffuse groups where remoteness may compound these difficulties. Unfortunately, many agriculturally based areas lack a sufficient population density and tax base to support a variety of community service and outreach programs. This recognition has prompted officials to establish a national hotline in an effort to reach out to underserviced constituencies.

This national hotline (1-800-799-SAFE) is available seven days a week, 24 hours a day. Specialists can handle inquiries, make local referrals, and offer advice to callers. Interpreters, who can communicate in more than 170 different languages, ensure that no ethnic group goes unserved. The hotline handles over 23,000 calls every month (National Domestic Violence Hotline, 2013b). This mammoth effort is an attempt to make sure that the problem of domestic violence does not go unanswered in any segment of society.

> ### 🌐 WEB ACTIVITY
>
> The National Domestic Violence Hotline attempts to provide callers with program referrals and other resources. Its activities can be found at **http://www.thehotline.org/**

Fatality Review Systems

Many states have established *fatality review teams* to dissect cases involving domestic violence, homicides, and suicides. While the exact team composition varies from one state to the next, it is common for participants to hail from the law enforcement sector, prosecutor's offices, medical examiner or coroner staff, victim advocates, probation services, the judiciary, and the academic community. The purpose of these reviews is to study domestic violence deaths and near-fatal incidents in an effort to learn about the underlying dynamics and to improve formal responses. These panels review the history of the participants, examine the events that eventually culminated in such violence, and try to identify possible intervention strategies that could prove useful in preventing future tragedies. While the exact authority of these panels varies, most bodies can gain access to confidential records, such as hospital charts and investigative case files. Usually, the information gleaned from these varying sources is exempt from discovery and legal proceedings. In other words, what is learned from these reviews becomes protected information.

These team reviews try to identify "red flags" or early warning signs so that local agencies can take appropriate action whenever they encounter a situation with similar characteristics (Hassler et al., 1999). For instance, procuring an injunction, fleeing to another state, and prior violence are all telltale signs that should alert authorities to the potential for escalation or an elevated risk of violence at the hands of the estranged batterer. As we mentioned previously in the discussion on stalking, the decision to leave an abusive and possessive partner is a critical juncture that often triggers a violent response. Educating health care professionals, judges, prosecutors, victim advocates, and law enforcement personnel about the dangers associated with these and similar circumstances could aid in reaching more accurate lethality assessments and providing appropriate services. For example, some jurisdictions have found that using a dangerousness assessment scale immediately after arrest helps judges decide what steps are appropriate to take in order to ensure the safety of the victim (Goodman, Dutton, & Bennett, 2000; Weisz, Tolman, & Saunders, 2000). Another possibility, electing not to purge expired injunctions from computer files, could provide an extensive data bank that would help social service providers better understand the couple's past and design a more appropriate response to the current crisis. In short, our current understanding of the dynamics that underlie IPV is insufficient when one considers the enormous consequences that all too often accompany this suffering.

WEB ACTIVITY

The Florida Coalition Against Domestic Violence hosts information about a number of projects, including the statewide domestic violence fatality review team. More details appear at **http://www.fcadv.org/**

SUMMARY

Intimate partner violence is gaining broad recognition as a pressing social problem. People who profess to love one another hurt each other regularly. Abusive behavior appears to be almost an integral part of these relationships. It may be very difficult for an outsider to comprehend why anyone would tolerate being victimized repeatedly in this way. However, as the learned helplessness perspective explains, many people are trapped into staying in an abusive relationship. Fleeing from the abuser is not always a viable option.

Some people look to the criminal justice system—particularly the police—to provide effective relief to IPV victims. While police folklore holds that nonintervention is a more suitable stance, the Minneapolis Experiment suggested otherwise. That study reported less intimate partner violence after the police took the abuser into custody. While there are some doubts over the wisdom of basing public policy upon the outcome of a single study, many law enforcement agencies reacted almost immediately. They instituted policies that instructed officers to make an arrest for IPV whenever possible. More recent studies, however, suggest that these policies may have been implemented too hastily. The more prudent path for the criminal justice system to pursue in IPV matters is to retain an open mind and be willing to try different approaches as research and practice dictate. As Davis and Smith (1995: 551) explain:

> We have come a long way in changing how the criminal justice system responds to domestic violence cases. Significant reforms have included mandatory arrest policies, no-drop prosecution practices, civil restraining orders, and batterer treatment programs. Unfortunately, research findings on these reforms have not been encouraging, and it is unclear whether these reforms are making victims safer from harm or changing batterers' violent behavior.

KEY TERMS

action stage

affidavit

battered woman syndrome

battering episode

contemplation stage

criminogenic effect

cyberstalking

cycle of violence

disenchantment through action

disenchantment through avoidance

disinhibition

domestic violence

domestic violence shelter

ex parte

ex post facto law

executive clemency

external validity

fatality review teams

forfeiture by wrongdoing

full enforcement

incapacitation

injunction

internal validity

intimate partner violence

learned helplessness

maintenance stage

mandatory arrest policy

masochism

mediation

Minneapolis Experiment

misdemeanor rule

outcome evaluation

partner stalking

patriarchy

precontemplation stage

preparation stage

presumptive arrest policy

pro-arrest policy

probable cause

process evaluation

psychopathology

reasonable suspicion

reconciliation period

referral

refuge house

selective enforcement

sexual symmetry

sociocultural explanations

stalking

suffrage

tension-building phase

testimonial and nontestimonial statements

therapeutic jurisprudence

warrantless arrest

Child Maltreatment

LEARNING OBJECTIVES

After reading Chapter 11, you should be able to:

- Show how historical practices devalued children.
- Understand what is included under the term *child maltreatment*.
- Talk about how child maltreatment was discovered and who discovered it.
- Explain why it took so long to recognize child maltreatment.
- Distinguish abuse from neglect.
- Expand upon the different types of child maltreatment.
- Understand what the "shaken baby syndrome" entails.
- Elaborate on some indicators of the different types of child maltreatment.
- Outline the provisions that appear in child maltreatment laws.
- Discuss the purpose of mandatory reporting and the idea of net-widening.
- Relate reporting provisions to the "good faith" standard.
- List the items that should be included in a child maltreatment report.
- Discuss the intention behind a central register.
- Identify some problems that still remain in child maltreatment laws.
- Explore how the child welfare system operates.
- Gain a feeling for the prevalence of child homicide and child maltreatment.
- Link what we know about child maltreatment to its data sources.
- Interpret the relationship between child maltreatment, social class, and surveillance bias.
- Present some coping strategies aimed at fighting child maltreatment.
- Provide an overview of home visitation programs.
- Explain what a "safe haven" is and what it aims to accomplish.
- Convey what "Megan's Law" did.
- Connect the Adam Walsh Act with sex offender registration and notification.
- Analyze civil commitment as a strategy to combat sex offender recidivism.
- Convey what a "Children's Advocacy Center" entails.

311

INTRODUCTION

One of the sadder experiences children endure is victimizations perpetrated by family members. Some parents routinely beat their offspring; others deny them food and affection. Still others sexually molest children. Until recently, these victims had no special legal safeguards. Many states placed the welfare of children under "cruelty to animals" provisions. Fortunately, the diligent efforts of child advocacy groups have changed that picture. As Table 11.1 illustrates, child maltreatment has become a prominent national concern.

 **WEB ACTIVITY**

The American Humane Association has expanded its mission to include the protection of children. For more details, visit the website at
http://www.americanhumane.org/

Research in the area of child maltreatment has revolved around three questions. First, how widespread or prevalent are child abuse and neglect? Second, what are the correlates of child maltreatment? Third, what causes people to engage in this type of behavior? In addition to these concerns, this chapter probes what is meant by child abuse and neglect, what child abuse laws cover, and some strategies that people have suggested to combat this problem.

THE DISCOVERY OF CHILD MALTREATMENT

Child maltreatment is not of recent vintage. For most of history, children were looked at as family property. The ancient Romans believed that the father was endowed with the power of *patriae potestas* (Thomas, 1972). In other words, fathers had the right to sell, kill, or allow their progeny to continue to live. The ancient Greeks, especially the Spartans, practiced infanticide and abandonment of physically deformed newborns (deMause, 1974). The story of Oedipus Rex is testimony to the fact that these practices were accepted among both the lower and higher classes in society. Biblical stories also depict instances of child abuse, such as Abraham's aborted sacrifice of his son Isaac

Table 11.1 President Obama's Proclamation Declaring April 2013 National Child Abuse Prevention Month

America is a country where all of us should be able to pursue our own measure of happiness and live free from fear. But for the millions of children who have experienced abuse or neglect, it is a promise that goes tragically unfulfilled. National Child Abuse Prevention Month is a time to make their struggle our own and reaffirm a simple truth: that no matter the challenges we face, caring for our children must always be our first task.

Realizing that truth in our society means ensuring children know they are never alone — that they always have a place to go and there are always people on their side. Parents and caregivers play an essential part in giving their children that stability. But we also know that keeping our children safe is something we can only do together, with the help of friends and neighbors and the broader community. All of us bear a responsibility to look after them, whether by lifting children toward their full potential or lending a hand to a family in need.

Our Government shares in that obligation, which is why my Administration has made addressing child abuse a priority. Since I took office, we have advocated for responsible parenting and invested in programs that can give our sons and daughters a strong start in life. I was also proud to sign measures into law that equip State and local governments with the tools to take on abuse, like the CAPTA Reauthorization Act and the Violence Against Women Reauthorization Act.

Together, we are making important progress in stopping child abuse and neglect. But we cannot let up — not when children are still growing up looking for a lifeline, and not when more than half a million young people are robbed of their basic right to safety every year. So this month, let us stand up for them and make their voices heard. To learn more about ending child abuse and how to get involved, visit www.ChildWelfare.gov/Preventing.

NOW, THEREFORE, I, BARACK OBAMA, President of the United States of America, by virtue of the authority vested in me by the Constitution and the laws of the United States, do hereby proclaim April 2013 as National Child Abuse Prevention Month. I call upon all Americans to observe this month with programs and activities that help prevent child abuse and provide for children's physical, emotional, and developmental needs.

IN WITNESS WHEREOF, I have hereunto set my hand this twenty-ninth day of March, in the year of our Lord two thousand thirteen, and of the Independence of the United States of America the two hundred and thirty-seventh.

Source: Office of the Press Secretary (2013a). Presidential Proclamation—National Child Abuse Prevention Month, 2013, March 29. Washington, DC: The White House. Retrieved on May 20, 2013, from http://www.whitehouse.gov/the-press-office/2013/03/29/presidential-proclamation-national-child-abuse-prevention-month-2013.

and King Herod's slaughter of the innocents. Other accounts of inhumane treatment have persisted through the ages. Children were treated no differently from other property owned by the father (Whitehead & Lab, 2013).

Why were children treated in such ways? Both emotional and economic factors help explain this high degree of indifference toward children. First, life expectancy was very short. The majority of infants died during the first year of life. Therefore, emotional attachments to newborns were avoided as a defense mechanism against the highly probable death of the infant. Second, families simply could not bear the burden of feeding and caring for another member. Children, because they could not work in the field and contribute to the household, represented a drain on the already limited family resources. This status was especially true for female offspring who would need a dowry in order to find a suitable husband.

Children who survived the first few years of life quickly found themselves thrust into the position of being "little adults" (Aries, 1962). There was no status of "childhood" as we know it today. As "little adults," children took part in all adult activities. They were expected to go to work and help support themselves. They received no formal education. Rather, schooling often entailed being sold into apprenticeship in order to bring money into the family and to provide a skill for the child.

This situation persisted into the Industrial Revolution. At that time, the severe economic competition for labor was fulfilled by exposing children to long and arduous work hours under unsafe conditions. The identification of "childhood" as a distinct station in life began to emerge slowly. Infant mortality showed signs of diminishing. Clergy, educators, and other child advocates stepped forward. As the statuses of "child" and "adolescence" emerged, there was a concurrent rise in concern over the treatment of children (Davis, Chandler, & LaRossa, 2004). Society started to realize that youths needed to be handled differently from adults. Local school boards have become enmeshed in long debates over the merits and utility of corporal punishment. As the map contained in Figure 11.1 shows, there is a concerted effort to ban the application

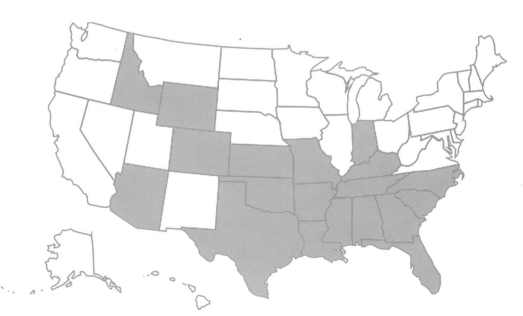

FIGURE 11.1 States Banning Corporal Punishment in Schools.

States in blue have laws permitting corporal punishment in schools. *Source: Center for Effective Discipline (2013).* Corporal Punishment and Paddling Statistics by State and Race. *Canal Winchester, OH: The Center for Effective Discipline. Retrieved on May 20, 2013, from* http://www.stophitting.com/index.php?page=statesbanning.

of corporal punishment in schools in the United States. Organizations such as the American Academy of Pediatricians, the American Psychological Association, and the United Nations Committee on the Rights of the Child (2013) have taken a formal stance against corporal punishment. At the last count, at least 24 countries, mostly European nations, have outlawed corporal punishment of children (Zolotor & Puzia, 2010). At the same time, Florida courts view corporal punishment as a parental privilege and place disciplinary measures outside the scope of child maltreatment statutes (*Kama v. State*, 1987; *Raford v. State*, 2002; *Wilson v. State*, 1999). In other words, it is not possible for a parent to commit a simple battery against his or her child when administering physical punishment. Of course, if disciplinary measures exceed the level of good taste, then felony charges might be appropriate.

While the acceptance of maltreatment waned, it did not disappear. The privacy of the home and the assumed sanctity of parental authority allowed much to take place out of sight. What happened within the protected confines of the home was considered to fall beyond the purview of society.

Until relatively recently, child abuse was not easy to detect. John Caffey, a pediatric radiologist, published a study in 1946 outlining bone damage of mysterious origin that he found in some of his young patients. While not accusing parents of being the direct source of these injuries, Caffey (1946) noted that some parental explanations of various accidents were preposterous. Caffey's discovery prompted other physicians to conduct similar investigations. These researchers also stopped short of blaming parents for the intentional infliction of the observed injuries. Eventually, Caffey (1957) came to suspect that parents were responsible for this "unspecified trauma." However, this accusation still did not clarify whether the injuries were intentional or accidental.

The first public denunciation of parents as intentional abusers of their offspring appeared in the early 1960s. In a groundbreaking publication, Kempe et al. (1962) abandoned the term *unspecified trauma* and introduced a new phrase, *the battered-child syndrome*. The Kempe's radiological research team (1962: 107) applied this new terminology to "young children who have received serious physical abuse, generally from a parent or foster parent."

WEB ACTIVITY

The legacy of Dr. C. Henry Kempe continues through the work of The Kempe Foundation for the Prevention and Treatment of Child Abuse and Neglect. Visit the website at **http://www.kempe.org**

This discovery launched a movement aimed at eradicating this newly found concern. Before detailing those efforts, though, two questions arise. First, why did it take so long to discover child abuse, especially because it is such a serious problem? Second, why did radiologists, and not some other medical group, such as pediatricians, discover this phenomenon?

UNDERSTANDING THE DISCOVERY OF CHILD MALTREATMENT

Four obstacles impeded the recognition of these injured children as victims of abuse (Pfohl, 1977). First, although emergency-room physicians dealt with the physical aftermath of brutal beatings, they did not understand what they saw. Second, physicians were unable to bring themselves to realize that parents would beat their children or inflict such severe wounds deliberately. A third hurdle was the confidential doctor–patient relationship. Physicians generally regarded the parent, not the child, as their client. Disclosing confidential information to the authorities would violate ethical standards. Such action could subject the physician to civil liability and professional censure. Finally, testifying in court would place physicians in the awkward position of having to defend their medical expertise and diagnosis to laypersons.

Concerning the question of why radiologists were the discoverers, Pfohl (1977) explains that radiologists differed from physicians in four important ways. First, radiologists examine X-rays, not people. They can be more objective because they have no direct contact with the patient. Second, the goal of radiology is to discover new diagnostic categories, whereas direct-care providers simply identify a condition and place it into a logical, already existing category. Third, the doctor–patient relationship was not a stumbling block because the patient is the person who is being X-rayed. The fourth and most important point deals with the issue of professional control.

Pediatric radiology was a peripheral medical specialty during the 1950s. It lacked professional prestige. Instead of dealing directly with patients, radiologists conducted research alone in isolated laboratories. This separation from patients also meant that radiologists did not make glamorous life-or-death decisions. As a result, child abuse offered a unique opportunity for this marginal branch to become more integrated into the mainstream medical profession. After all, it involved the clinical task of diagnosis. Making the correct assessment could spell the difference between life and death for a young patient.

The term *battered-child syndrome* was born. Adding the word "syndrome" after the term *battered child* created a new medical diagnostic category. These facts, coupled with the advances of other professions whose goal was to "cure" abusers through therapy, elevated the discovery of child abuse to prominence. Child abuse became an integral component of medical parlance.

A SURVEY OF CHILD MALTREATMENT LAWS

Immediately after the "discovery" of child abuse, state legislatures raced to enact new laws. A wave of legislative adjustments followed in the late 1960s and early 1970s. The task was to respond to aspects that were overlooked in the hasty lawmaking process. Except for some minor tinkering, maltreatment statutes have remained largely intact since that time. The passage of a federal law dealing with child abuse and neglect brought greater standardization to state statutes.

Although abuse and neglect fall under the broad and more encompassing term of *maltreatment*, they are two distinct phenomena. *Abuse* is the commission of an act upon the child, while *neglect* refers to the omission of a caretaker function.

To gain a more thorough understanding of child maltreatment laws, our analysis focuses upon a limited range of topics. First, we review the statutory definitions of abuse and neglect. Next, we direct our attention to provisions governing who should report such incidents, what the report should contain, and the central register. Finally, the discussion concludes by pointing out some problem areas that remain.

Statutory Definitions

Most state laws define abuse and neglect in very general terms. The purpose behind this approach is to encourage the reporting of as many suspected cases as possible. By casting out a broad net, the hope is to uncover instances of maltreatment that might otherwise go undetected. Critics, though, charge that such an expansive definition invites excessive governmental intervention.

Abuse generally refers to any nonaccidental infliction of injury that seriously impairs a child's physical or mental health. Most statutory definitions outlaw sexual abuse, sexual exploitation, pornography, and juvenile prostitution. Some jurisdictions make it a point to exclude reasonable disciplinary measures such as controlled spanking of a child by a parent, guardian, or custodian. Although corporal punishment is a common corrective method in this country, there is the fear that it could lead to maltreatment. Most states fail to define emotional abuse explicitly, although virtually every state includes the term in its provisions.

Neglect is the withholding of life's essentials. These necessary ingredients include food, clothing, shelter, and medical treatment. Some states recognize that parents may hold religious beliefs that prohibit them from seeking medical care. They place such persons outside the scope of the neglect definition. However, if the child's condition involves a life-threatening situation or serious disability, the courts will not hesitate to intervene and order the administration of appropriate medical treatment. Some statutes also mention such offenses as failure to make child support payments, alcoholic or substance-dependent parents who cannot supervise their offspring properly, permitting a child to be habitually truant from school, and family abandonment.

The federal Child Abuse Prevention and Treatment Act (42 U.S.C. 5101, *et seq.*) captures the essence of these statutory details. It defines child maltreatment in terms of three components. First, the act or failure to take appropriate action must produce an unacceptable risk of serious physical or emotional harm, death, sexual abuse, or exploitation. Second, the target of this maltreatment is a child, usually a person under the age of 18 years. Finally, the perpetrator is a parent or caretaker who bears responsibility for the child's welfare and well-being.

As one might imagine, there are a variety of behaviors that fall under the rubric of child maltreatment. Table 11.2 attempts to capture the breadth of these activities by displaying the major types of child maltreatment along with definitions and examples for each category. Table 11.3 lists a less common, but just as harmful, behavior.

Table 11.2 Major Types of Child Abuse and Neglect

Physical abuse is nonaccidental physical injury (ranging from minor bruises to severe fractures or death) as a result of punching, beating, kicking, biting, shaking, throwing, stabbing, choking, hitting (with a hand, stick, strap, or other object), burning, or otherwise harming a child, that is inflicted by a parent, caregiver, or other person who has responsibility for the child. Such injury is considered abuse regardless of whether the caregiver intended to hurt the child. Physical discipline, such as spanking or paddling, is not considered abuse as long as it is reasonable and causes no bodily injury to the child.

Neglect is the failure of a parent, guardian, or other caregiver to provide for a child's basic needs. Neglect may be:
- Physical (e.g., failure to provide necessary food or shelter, or lack of appropriate supervision)
- Medical (e.g., failure to provide necessary medical or mental health treatment)
- Educational (e.g., failure to educate a child or attend to special education needs)
- Emotional (e.g., inattention to a child's emotional needs, failure to provide psychological care, or permitting the child to use alcohol or other drugs)

Sexual abuse includes activities by a parent or caregiver such as fondling a child's genitals, penetration, incest, rape, sodomy, indecent exposure, and exploitation through prostitution or the production of pornographic materials.

Emotional abuse (or psychological abuse) is a pattern of behavior that impairs a child's emotional development or sense of self-worth. This may include constant criticism, threats, or rejection, as well as withholding love, support, or guidance. Emotional abuse is often difficult to prove and, therefore, child protective services may not be able to intervene without evidence of harm or mental injury to the child. Emotional abuse is almost always present when other forms are identified.

Abandonment is now defined in many States as a form of neglect. In general, a child is considered to be abandoned when the parent's identity or whereabouts are unknown, the child has been left alone in circumstances where the child suffers serious harm, or the parent has failed to maintain contact with the child or provide reasonable support for a specified period of time.

Substance abuse is an element of the definition of child abuse or neglect in many States. Circumstances that are considered abuse or neglect in some States include:
- Prenatal exposure of a child to harm due to the mother's use of an illegal drug or other substance
- Manufacture of methamphetamine in the presence of a child
- Selling, distributing, or giving illegal drugs or alcohol to a child
- Use of a controlled substance by a caregiver that impairs the caregiver's ability to adequately care for the child

Source: Child Welfare Information Gateway (2008). What Are the Major Types of Child Abuse and Neglect? Washington, DC: U.S. Department of Health and Human Services, Children's Bureau. Retrieved on May 20, 2013, from http://www. childwelfare.gov/pubs/factsheets/whatiscan.cfm.

Table 11.3 The "Shaken Baby Syndrome"

What is "Shaken Baby Syndrome?"

Shaken baby syndrome is a type of inflicted traumatic brain injury that happens when a baby is violently shaken. A baby has weak neck muscles and a large, heavy head. Shaking makes the fragile brain bounce back and forth inside the skull and causes bruising, swelling, and bleeding, which can lead to permanent, severe brain damage or death. The characteristic injuries of shaken baby syndrome are subdural hemorrhages (bleeding in the brain), retinal hemorrhages (bleeding in the retina), damage to the spinal cord and neck, and fractures of the ribs and bones. These injuries may not be immediately noticeable. Symptoms of shaken baby syndrome include extreme irritability, lethargy, poor feeding, breathing problems, convulsions, vomiting, and pale or bluish skin. Shaken baby injuries usually occur in children younger than 2-years-old, but may be seen in children up to the age of 5.

What is the prognosis?

In comparison with accidental traumatic brain injury in infants, shaken baby injuries have a much worse prognosis. Damage to the retina of the eye can cause blindness. The majority of infants who survive severe shaking will have some form of neurological or mental disability, such as cerebral palsy or mental retardation, which may not be fully apparent before 6 years of age. Children with shaken baby syndrome may require lifelong medical care.

Source: National Institute of Neurological Disorders and Stroke (2010). NINDS Shaken Baby Syndrome Information Page. Bethesda, MD: National Institutes of Health. Retrieved on May 21, 2013, from http://www.ninds.nih.gov/disorders/shakenbaby/shakenbaby.htm.

The Reporter

A significant element of child abuse laws is the mandatory reporting provisions. Any person who witnesses or learns of a child maltreatment incident has the obligation to report the occurrence to the authorities. Anyone who knowingly fails to make such a report may risk a criminal penalty. In addition, it is common for state laws to designate members of certain professions as mandatory reporters. According to one review of state child maltreatment laws (Child Welfare Information Gateway, 2012a: 2), those persons typically required to report suspected cases of maltreatment include the following:

- Social workers;
- Teachers, principals, and other school personnel;
- Physicians, nurses, and other health care providers;
- Counselors, therapists, and mental health professionals;
- Childcare providers;
- Medical examiners or coroners; and
- Law enforcement officers.

As already mentioned, medical personnel championed the early battle against child maltreatment. However, physicians initially were very reluctant to report suspected cases of abuse or neglect. In fact, when states were drafting their original child abuse laws, the American Medical Association opposed any provision that required doctors to report suspicious cases (No Author, 1964). One reason for this stance was a fear of legal and professional repercussions.

Most states normally regard doctor–patient interaction as a *privileged relationship*. A privileged relationship means there is an inviolable, nonintrudable bond between two parties. The physician cannot reveal any information gathered in that confidential capacity without first obtaining the patient's consent. Should a doctor break that trust, he or she could face a civil lawsuit and professional censure. Some other privileged discussions are conversations attorneys hold with their clients and the confessions that ministers hear from their penitents.

Because the traditional doctor–patient privileged relationship could hinder physician reporting of suspected abuse and neglect, many states created an exemption. Today, the doctor–patient privileged relationship does not exist in child maltreatment cases. In addition, states have extended this protection by granting *legislative immunity* to any person who makes a child maltreatment report in *good faith*. That is, if a person contacts the authorities out of genuine concern for the child's well-being, he or she cannot be sued if the allegation turns out to be false. However, the obstacles of identifying, understanding, diagnosing, and then dealing with child protective services are still challenging steps for attending physicians today (Flaherty, Jones, & Sege, 2004; Flaherty et al., 2006; Leventhal, 1999; Levi, Brown, & Erb, 2006).

The Report

State statutes require that reporters contact authorities about alleged maltreatment as quickly as possible. Some states stipulate that the initial disclosure can be an oral statement, followed a short time later by a written report. The purpose of an oral report is to avoid any cumbersome bureaucratic delays when a child is at risk. The written report must include the victim's name, parents' identity, address, and nature of the injuries. It should also contain color photographs and X-rays, if possible. It also must indicate whether there are other siblings in jeopardy. Table 11.4 details some of the observations that are useful in trying to establish whether an abusive or neglectful situation exists.

One area of intense legislative debate in some jurisdictions was the issue of to whom to submit the report. Most statutes designate a public social service agency as the primary recipient of child abuse and neglect reports. However, such an arrangement is not satisfactory for at least three reasons. First, most social service agencies conduct their business on a nine-to-five, Monday through Friday schedule. Lack of availability and the inability to research family records at night, on weekends, or on holidays become key concerns. One way to circumvent this difficulty is to establish a 24-hour telephone hotline. People who are worried about a child's situation can contact the hotline at any time and on any day of the week to file a confidential report. The counselor will ask a series of questions, gather all the pertinent information, and compile it on an intake form. Figure 11.2 displays the form used by the Florida Abuse Hotline. The counselor will determine whether an immediate intervention or

---

Table 11.4 Some Indicators of Child Maltreatment

Consider the possibility of **physical abuse** when the child:
- Has unexplained burns, bites, bruises, broken bones, or black eyes.
- Has fading bruises or other marks noticeable after an absence from school.
- Seems frightened of the parents and protests or cries when it is time to go home.
- Shrinks at the approach of adults.
- Reports injury by a parent or another adult caregiver.

Consider the possibility of **neglect** when the child:
- Is frequently absent from school.
- Begs or steals food or money.
- Lacks needed medical or dental care, immunizations, or glasses.
- Is consistently dirty and has severe body odor.
- Lacks sufficient clothing for the weather.
- Abuses alcohol or other drugs.
- States that there is no one at home to provide care.

Consider the possibility of **sexual abuse** when the child:
- Has difficulty walking or sitting.
- Suddenly refuses to change for gym or to participate in physical activities.
- Reports nightmares or bedwetting.
- Experiences a sudden change in appetite.
- Demonstrates bizarre, sophisticated, or unusual sexual knowledge or behavior.
- Becomes pregnant or contracts a venereal disease, particularly if under age 14.
- Runs away.
- Reports sexual abuse by a parent or another adult caregiver.

Consider the possibility of **emotional maltreatment** when the child:
- Shows extremes in behavior, such as overly compliant or demanding behavior, extreme passivity, or aggression.
- Is either inappropriately adult (parenting other children, for example) or inappropriately infantile (frequently rocking or head-banging, for example).
- Is delayed in physical or emotional development.
- Has attempted suicide.
- Reports a lack of attachment to the parent.

Source: Constructed by authors from Child Welfare Information Gateway (2013). What is Child Abuse and Neglect? Recognizing the Signs and Symptoms. Washington, DC: U.S. Department of Health and Human Services, Children's Bureau. Retrieved on May 21, 2013, from https://www.childwelfare.gov/pubs/factsheets/whatiscan.cfm.

---

a routine investigation is warranted and notify either law enforcement or child protective services.

Second, although search-and-seizure guidelines empower the police to make warrantless entries into houses or other structures if an emergency exists, such lawful powers do not extend automatically to non-sworn personnel acting as governmental agents.

Third, it is not uncommon for the perpetrator to be present when the child protective services worker arrives. Because of the potential explosiveness involved and possible violence directed against the social worker, many states also include the police as an appropriate agency to handle child maltreatment reports (Cross, Finkelhor, & Ormrod, 2005). The offender's presence

FLORIDA ABUSE HOTLINE Fax Transmittal Form
To Report Abuse/Abandonment/Neglect/Exploitation
Fax Number: 1-800-914-0004

Please do not fax multiple allegations of abuse or neglect for multiple families at a time.
By submitting them **one** at a time, they will likely get processed **faster**.

REPORTER INFORMATION

This information is required for mandatory reporters. Refer to Chapters 39 and 415, Florida Statutes.

Today's Date: _____

Your Last Name: _____ Your First Name: _____ MI: _____

Your Occupation: _____ Your Agency: _____

Address: Street # _____ Street Name: _____ City: _____ Fax #: _____ Zip Code: _____ County: _____ Phone #: _____ State: _____

VICTIM INFORMATION

If the victim is a child, list other children in the home. If the victim is an adult, describe disability and how he/she is impaired in the ability to care for or protect self in the DESCRIPTION OF INCIDENT section on page 2.

ADDRESS where the victim is currently located:

Street # _____ Street Name: _____ City: _____ Zip Code: _____ County: _____ State: _____

Home Telephone Number: _____ Work Telephone Number: _____

	LAST NAME	FIRST NAME	DOB	SEX	RACE	SSN	IS THIS PERSON A VICTIM?
(1)							☐ Yes ☐ No
(2)							☐ Yes ☐ No
(3)							☐ Yes ☐ No
(4)							☐ Yes ☐ No
(5)							☐ Yes ☐ No

PERSON(S) RESPONSIBLE FOR ALLEGED ABUSE, NEGLECT, ABANDONMENT OR EXPLOITATION

	NAME	DOB	SEX	RACE	SSN	RELATIONSHIP TO VICTIM
(1)						
(2)						
(3)						

CONFIDENTIAL

FLORIDA ABUSE HOTLINE Fax Transmittal Form

DESCRIPTION OF INCIDENT

Please describe what happened, when and where the incident occurred, the frequency of occurrence, and a description of injuries and/or threat of harm.

WHAT happened?

WHEN did the incident occur?

WHERE did the incident occur?

Description of injuries/threat of harm:

FOR ADULT VICTIMS ONLY: Describe the adult victim's disability and how the victim is impaired in the ability to care for or protect self.

OTHER INDIVIDUALS

Please list others who might be aware of the abuse/abandonment/neglect/exploitation of the victim.

NAME	RELATIONSHIP TO THE VICTIM	ADDRESS	HOME PHONE	WORK PHONE

DO NOT SEND COPIES OF MEDICAL NOTES, CASE FILES, ARREST REPORTS, OR SIMILAR DOCUMENTS.

Revised 12/2004   Page 2   **CONFIDENTIAL**

FIGURE 11.2 The Florida Abuse Hotline Reporting Form.

Source: Florida Abuse Hotline (2004). Florida Abuse Hotline Fax Transmittal Form to Report Abuse/Abandonment/Neglect/Exploitation. Tallahassee: Department of Children and Families. Retrieved on May 20, 2013, from http://www.dcf.state.fl.us/programs/abuse/docs/faxreport.pdf.

may fuel antagonisms. For example, if the child is in danger, the investigator may place the minor in *protective custody*. In this situation, the worker terminates parental custody for the time being, removes the child from the home, and places him or her in foster care for safekeeping pending judicial review at a later date. In addition to arousing parental anger, this step can stir up resentments within the child. As one victim told the U.S. Attorney General's Task Force (1984: 15):

> Why should I have been taken out of my home? I was the victim. I had [done] nothing. I did nothing wrong. My father should have been taken out, not me.

The Central Register

A critical component of child maltreatment laws is the establishment of a central register. A *central register* is a depository that stores records of all allegations of child abuse and neglect. Register users can index cases by the child's name, parent's name, and perpetrator's name. While many states have had such a tool for some time now, a federal hotline now exists.

WEB ACTIVITY

The National Resource Center for Permanency and Family Connections houses information regarding state child abuse registries. You can locate that website at **http://www.hunter.cuny.edu/socwork/ nrcfcpp/downloads/policy-issues/State_ Child_Abuse_Registries.pdf**

The purpose of this record-keeping system is to help in the diagnosis by tracking relevant case histories. In the past, some enterprising abusers skirted detection by taking the child to a different hospital or a new doctor every time the child needed medical attention. This strategy usually succeeded because the attending physician lacked access to any previous medical records. With the central register, chronic abusers have a more difficult time eluding detection.

Some Trouble Spots

Although child abuse and neglect laws have undergone much revision, some gaps remain. One troublesome area revolves around definitional aspects. Most states have an expansive construction of what constitutes abuse and neglect. They cast as wide a net as possible in the hope that valid cases of maltreatment do not go undetected. However, not everyone views maltreatment in the same way. Social workers and police officers, for example, may regard instances of maltreatment as being more serious than do doctors and lawyers (Giovannoni & Becerra, 1979; Saunders, 1988). Even teachers (Webster et al., 2005) and pediatricians (Levi et al., 2006) disagree among themselves as to how to categorize cases. Differences also exist between groups such as police, mental health therapists, and child protection services workers (Cross et al., 2005; Deisz, Doueck, & George, 1996; Everson et al., 1996).

These divergent definitions can strain already scarce resources by compelling a small staff to investigate a large number of allegations. For example, four out of every five reports alleging child maltreatment during 2011 turned out to be unfounded or unsubstantiated (Child Welfare Information Gateway, 2012b: 17). Such a high rate of unfounded allegations is a source of concern that scarce resources are being diverted away from children who really do need attention (Melton, 2005).

A second problem is that not all states place the same degree of emphasis on child maltreatment. Designated violations range from misdemeanors in some states to felonies in other states. Even though the United States does have a national data collection system in place for child abuse and neglect, it may be that variations in state reports stem from differing definitions (Whitaker, Lutzker, & Shelley, 2005).

A related issue is the level of proof required to initiate a social service intervention. Most child protective services regard the "proof beyond a reasonable doubt" standard, the criterion for a criminal court conviction, as being far too rigid. The fear is that too many children in need of help would go unserved if this legalistic criterion is invoked. Similarly, the "probable cause" standard that police officers must use when making an arrest is also considered overly restrictive. As a result, many states rely upon a much more lenient threshold of "some credible evidence" to identify circumstances that trigger official action (Cross & Casanueva, 2009).

A fourth difficulty involves the lack of reporting. Despite statutory protection, many professionals are still reluctant to report suspected instances of maltreatment. Some develop *countertransference*—a sense of guilt, shame, or anxiety that leads to nonreporting (Pollak & Levy, 1988). Others either waiver in their initial assessment that the situation is serious, or they fear that an interruption in an ongoing treatment program would halt any progress already made (Kalichman, Craig, & Follingstad, 1990; Willis & Wells, 1988; Zellman, 1990a,b).

Finally, the issue of training has not received sufficient attention. Teachers, for example, spend much time in direct contact with children. One might think that teacher preparation courses and state licensing requirements would devote detailed attention to the topic of child abuse and neglect. Perhaps one solution would be for legislation to require specific instruction to all workers whose occupational duties involve routine contact with children (Crenshaw, Crenshaw, & Lichtenberg, 1995; Lamond, 1989; U.S. Attorney General's Task Force, 1984).

WEB ACTIVITY

The State of Virginia now requires applicants seeking or renewing a teacher's license to first complete a training module on how to recognize and intervene when suspicions of child maltreatment arise. You can find those training materials at **http://www.doe.virginia.gov/teaching/licensure/child_abuse_training.shtml**

THE CHILD WELFARE SYSTEM

Once a report of child maltreatment is initiated, the child welfare system moves into action. Much like the criminal justice system, the child welfare system is a conglomeration of numerous public and private entities as opposed to a unified model. Some of the system's responsibilities include investigative duties, foster care, medical services, mental health treatment, substance abuse counseling, employment assistance, and welfare options. All of these activities are united by the same goal of protecting the best interests of the child.

Figure 11.3 is a diagram of the child welfare system. Upon receipt of a child maltreatment allegation, Child Protective Services (CPS) conducts an evaluation of the information. *Screening* takes place at this point. If it appears that the conditions in the report do not constitute abuse or neglect, the case is removed from the system. On the other hand, if the case merits a closer look, a *referral* is made and the file is routed for further processing. In 2011, CPS handled 3.4 million allegations, of which 39% were screened out and 61% were screened in (Child Welfare Information Gateway, 2013a).

The second stage, the investigation, may take place immediately if the circumstances warrant or—if there is no danger to the child—shortly thereafter. As mentioned earlier, the child may be removed from the household and placed in *protective custody* if his or her safety is imperiled. The CPS investigator will interview family members, will make a risk assessment, and may contact other parties, such as doctors, teachers, and neighbors. Once the CPS worker has gathered all the information possible, the case will be marked as "unsubstantiated" or "substantiated." An *unsubstantiated* disposition means the allegation is unfounded and the case is closed. In other words, there is not enough evidence to support the claim that the child was maltreated or is at risk of being maltreated. A *substantiated* disposition means that the CPS investigation concurred that maltreatment had occurred or is taking place, or that the child's well-being is at risk. Child maltreatment statistics for 2011 in the United States reveal that 3.7 million children were monitored and approximately one out of every five were substantiated as a maltreatment case (Child Welfare Information Gateway, 2013b: 17).

The third stage involves processing substantiated cases. If the situation involved a one-time incident and the child is not at any further risk, the case may be terminated. Sometimes, the determination may be that unfavorable conditions exist and that the family and/or child may benefit from receiving some type of social services. In other instances, CPS may route the case to the juvenile dependency court for formal handling. In 2011, 36% of the victims received some type of social service after the CPS investigation was concluded, and approximately 223,000 victims were placed in foster care (Child Welfare Information Gateway, 2013a: 89–91).

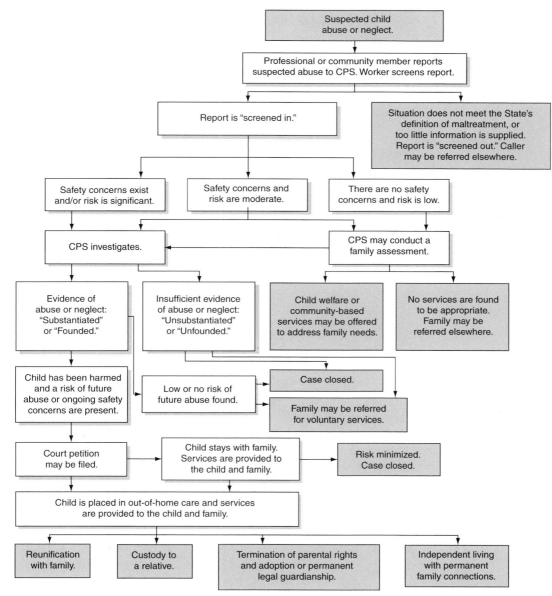

FIGURE 11.3 The Child Welfare System.

Source: Child Welfare Information Gateway (2013a). How the Child Welfare System Works, p. 9. Washington, DC: U.S. Department of Health and Human Services, Children's Bureau. Retrieved on May 21, 2013, from https://www.childwelfare.gov/pubs/factsheets/cpswork.pdf.

THE INCIDENCE OF CHILD MALTREATMENT

Measuring child maltreatment is very difficult. These acts usually take place out of the public eye. As a result, it is a very difficult offense to detect. The neighbors rarely see it, and the police have a hard time discovering it. When it is detected, the victim may be too young to explain what happened. As a result, nobody really knows how pervasive child abuse is.

 **WEB ACTIVITY**

The Child Welfare Information Gateway, an arm of the U.S. Department of Health and Human Services, houses a wealth of information about child abuse and neglect. You can access this collection at **https://www.childwelfare.gov/**

Although the incidence of child maltreatment remains elusive, the National Child Abuse and Neglect Data System (Child Welfare Information Gateway, 2013c: 19) estimates that 676,569 children were victims of abuse and neglect in 2011. Sadly, 1,545, or 2.1 of every 100,000 American children, died from maltreatment in 2011 (Child Welfare Information Gateway, 2013c: 56). In other words, four to five children die from maltreatment every day in this country, with 82% being under the age of four. According to the *Uniform Crime Reports*, 196 murder victims in 2011 were infants. Another 301 homicide victims came from the one- to four-year-old age bracket, while an additional 84 criminal homicide victims were between the ages of five and eight (Federal Bureau of Ivestigation, 2012b).

Most observers would agree that these numbers underestimate the true extent of child fatalities due to maltreatment. One review team examined medical examiner records for 1985–1994 in North Carolina. They contended that child abuse statistics actually underestimate the true number of child homicide cases by 60% (Herman-Giddens et al., 1999). A similar investigation in Colorado showed that half the maltreatment deaths during 1990–1998 were misclassified (Crume et al., 2002). A national review illustrates how inconsistent coding might mask the underlying cause of death. Klevens and Leeb (2010) determined that many cases labeled as malnutrition actually stemmed from the infliction of head trauma. To combat this problem, all the states in this country now employ *child fatality review teams* (Douglas & Cunningham, 2008). These groups combine the expertise of child protective services workers, law enforcement officers, coroners and medical examiners, health care workers, prosecutors, and others to investigate child deaths to determine whether maltreatment was involved. Some signs that may suggest abuse or neglect include severe head trauma, the shaken baby syndrome (see Table 3.11), injuries to the abdomen or thorax areas, scalding, drowning, suffocation, poisoning, and chronic neglect. Over the years, these review teams have issued recommendations regarding such aspects as educational campaigns to increase awareness, training, protocols for law enforcement officers

 **WEB ACTIVITY**

The National Center for Child Death Review is an important resource in the effort to combat child maltreatment. Its website is available at **http://www.childdeathreview.org/**

and coroners to follow during death investigations and autopsies, highlighting common risk factors, and increasing interagency coordination (Douglas & Cunningham, 2008; Palusci, Yager, & Covington, 2010).

The Children's Bureau, housed in the U.S. Department of Health and Human Services, compiles yearly figures on child maltreatment in the United States based on information provided by state child protective service agencies. According to the best available estimates, authorities received reports involving 3.4 million children alleged to be maltreatment victims in 2011. However, investigators were able to substantiate the allegations in only 18.5% of the cases (Child Welfare Information Gateway, 2013c). A *substantiated allegation* means that sufficient evidence existed to confirm the reporting person's suspicions. In other words, the case did involve child maltreatment.

It is important to realize that child maltreatment figures may not reflect actual changes in the level of maltreatment. It is possible that a heightened awareness of child abuse has led to greater reporting of maltreatment by the public, more intensive investigative efforts, and better methods for tabulating the data by interested agencies. Given the historical treatment and place of children in society, it is very likely that the growing numbers are the result of better counting rather than a rampant escalation of abusive incidents. Figure 11.4 contains a visual depiction of the different types of substantiated maltreatment involved in cases handled during 2011. As you can see, neglect tops the list.

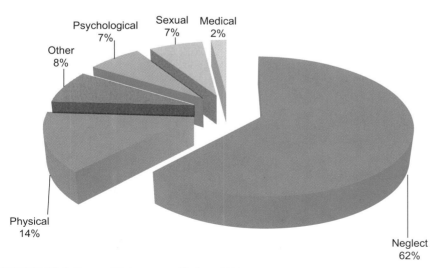

FIGURE 11.4 Types of Maltreatment Victims, 2011.

Source: Compiled from Child Welfare Information Gateway (2012b). Child Maltreatment 2011, *pp. 44–45. Washington, DC: U.S. Department of Health and Human Services, Children's Bureau. Retrieved on May 21, 2013, from http://www.acf.hhs.gov/sites/default/files/cb/cm11.pdf.*

Table 11.5 lists some child maltreatment statistics. As alarming as these statistics may be, the reader should bear one thing in mind: No one yet has compiled an accurate count of the number of crippling injuries or the physical and mental retardation cases that stem from this kind of violence. All that we can do at this point is to make ballpark estimates of what suffering our children endure.

One way to grasp the impact of child maltreatment is to look at the monetary costs associated with this type of victimization. Earlier in Chapter 4, we explained that victims sustain a host of direct and indirect costs as a result of being victimized. Direct costs pertain to the immediate consequences. These outlays include expenditures for physical health problems and mental health problems, as well as expenses incurred by the child welfare, law enforcement, and judicial sectors. Indirect costs refer to long-term or secondary effects. This category includes special education, extended health costs, subsequent juvenile delinquency, future adult criminality, and lost productivity from the labor force.

Another helpful distinction is to separate child maltreatment statistics into prevalence and incidence reports. When applying this approach to the costs associated with child maltreatment, *prevalence* estimates tally the expenses that occur over a period of time, while *incidence* estimates calculate the lifetime costs. All told, one model puts the lifetime costs of child abuse and neglect

---

Table 11.5 Selected Child Maltreatment Statistics, 2011

- An estimated 3.4 million referrals, involving the alleged maltreatment of approximately 6.2 million children, were made to Child Protective Services (CPS) agencies in 2011.

- Approximately three-fifths of the referrals were screened in for investigation or assessment by CPS agencies.

- Approximately one-fifth of the investigations or assessments found at least one child to be a victim of abuse or neglect; approximately four-fifths of the investigations or assessments determined that the child was not a victim of maltreatment.

- The most common report sources were education personnel, legal and law enforcement personnel, social services staff, and medical personnel.

- Children in the age group of birth to 1 year had the highest rate of victimization at 21.2 per 1,000 children of the same age group in the national population.

- More than 75% of victims suffered neglect.

- More than 70% of child fatalities were attributed to neglect only or a combination of neglect and another maltreatment type.

- More than 80% of the children who died due to child abuse and neglect were younger than 4-years-old.

- More than 80% of perpetrators of child maltreatment were parents.

- Two-fifths of victims who received services were removed from their homes and received foster care services.

Source: Compiled from Child Welfare Information Gateway (2013b). Child Maltreatment 2011: Summary of Key Findings. Washington, DC: U.S. Department of Health and Human Services, Children's Bureau. Retrieved on May 21, 2013, from https:// www.childwelfare.gov/pubs/factsheets/canstats.pdf.

cases that emerge each year at about $124 billion in 2010 dollars (Fang, Brown, Florence, & Mercy, 2012). Another estimate is that child maltreatment drains $220 million every day from the national economy (Gelles & Perlman, 2012).

A WORD OF CAUTION REGARDING OFFICIAL MALTREATMENT STATISTICS

Many people think of child abuse victims as being infants or small children. Quite often, however, the data source itself can influence what one finds. Clinical studies, which are based on counseling records, usually reveal that the very young are victims. Yet surveys show that child maltreatment spans all ages. Survey data generally record a high proportion of nonwhite victims, whereas clinical studies do not. This relationship probably reflects differential accessibility. Many African Americans, because of their impoverished status, are unable to afford private therapy.

A common finding in family violence research is the relationship between child maltreatment and social class. Reliance upon official records usually shows that maltreatment cases are concentrated at the lower end of the social class spectrum. It is possible that lower-class people resort to violence more often to resolve misunderstandings (Gelles, 1973; Wolfgang & Ferracuti, 1967). At the same time, official abuse and neglect statistics contain an inherent slant. Because members of the lower class come under the watchful eyes of service providers more often, higher rates of detected maltreatment and other problematic conditions should come as no surprise. In other words, it is entirely possible that child maltreatment is just as prevalent in the middle and upper classes as it is in the lower class. "Surveillance bias" may be responsible for this so-called "empirical regularity." As Chaffin and Bard (2006: 301) explain, *surveillance bias* "refers to any increased, systematic outcome-related scrutiny that may exist for some individuals or groups but not others." With respect to families that have been flagged for child abuse or neglect intervention, surveillance bias means that "service participants may be more likely to be reported for maltreatment than comparable nonservice participants because they are subject to greater scrutiny by virtue of interacting with service providers and service systems" (Chaffin & Bard, 2006: 301–302). The critical difference is that members of the middle and upper classes have the advantage of more resources. As a result, they can escape monitoring, while those of the lower class are not as fortunate. Given this orientation, Gelles (1975; 1980) recommends that attention be focused more upon the "gatekeepers"—the system personnel who have the power to confer the label of child maltreatment. One should keep these admonitions in mind when reading profiles such as the one that Table 11.6 contains.

At least one researcher has taken this suggestion to heart. Handelman (1979) investigated a variety of alleged maltreatment cases that were referred to a social service agency for official investigation. Taking an organizational approach,

---

Table 11.6 Who Commits These Acts?

There is no single profile of a perpetrator of fatal child abuse, although certain characteristics reappear in many studies. Frequently, the perpetrator is:

- a young adult in his or her mid-20s;
- without a high school diploma;
- living at or below the poverty level;
- depressed; and
- may have difficulty coping with stressful situations.

Source: Child Welfare Information Gateway (2013c). Child Abuse and Neglect Fatalities 2011: Statistics and Interventions. Washington, DC: U.S. Department of Health and Human Services, Children's Bureau. Retrieved on May 21, 2013, from https://www.childwelfare.gov/pubs/factsheets/fatality.pdf.

Handelman showed how agency emphasis upon certain carefully selected details influenced the degree of intervention required in each case. In other words, the imposition of the label "child abuse" depended upon the presence or absence of certain cues. They included the social worker's interpretation of what constitutes abuse and neglect, the client's amenability to accepting the label of child abuse, and the caseload the worker was currently handling.

The definitional ambiguity surrounding child abuse and neglect, coupled with bureaucratic mandates, may influence the official designation of problem families as abusive families. On the other hand, the system may overlook and discard actual cases of child abuse because the workload is sufficiently high to keep all agency workers fruitfully occupied.

SOME COPING STRATEGIES

What can be done to ensure that all children have a safe home and a loving atmosphere in which to grow and develop? One option that the state does exercise is to rescind parental custody and place children in foster homes or in other alternative housing. Such a procedure comes into play in only the most extreme circumstances and is a last-ditch effort. But what else can be done? Some people have suggested public health screening for detection. Others think parenting classes are the key to prevention. Another group advocates the development of profiles of offenders and victims to enhance detection. Further suggestions include more active law enforcement, self-help groups, and legal changes that would increase deterrence. These latter solutions would avoid governmental intrusion into one's domicile. The following sections explore some of these options.

Home Visitation

One social policy option that attracts interest is a home visitation and health screening program. Proponents suggest that public health workers should conduct routine home visits where there are young children and newborns

(Leventhal, 2001; Prevent Child Abuse America, 2003). In fact, the U.S. Advisory Board on Child Abuse and Neglect (which no longer exists) is on record as recommending universal implementation of home visits. These home visits would serve a dual purpose. The first goal would be prevention. Workers could help new at-risk parents adjust to their offspring by showing them how to care for infants and allaying parental apprehensions. The second objective would be to uncover hidden cases of maltreatment and other adverse developmental conditions. Such a strategy would avoid the haphazard detection techniques now in use.

Although this proposal is appealing, it has some drawbacks. One criticism is that it invites unwarranted governmental intrusion. Two types of errors would surface (Light, 1973; Warner & Hansen, 1994). A *false positive error* would occur when a worker misclassifies a nonabused child as a maltreatment case. A *false negative error* entails not diagnosing a child as abused when that child really is a maltreatment victim. Critics fear that these two errors could be high enough to render this approach questionable at best. Proponents counter that a greater emphasis on personnel training and a multistage checking system would avoid the embarrassment of making false accusations and impugning caregivers. However, false allegations can have far-reaching implications for both the accused and the accuser (Hershkowitz, 2001).

The Healthy Families Florida Program, displayed in Table 11.7, is part of a national initiative sponsored by Prevent Child Abuse America (PCA). PCA has developed a network of state chapters whose goal is to promote prevention programs. To date, this program is in place in more than 400 locations across the nation (PCA, 2013).

The Florida program, as well as similar efforts throughout the country, was modeled after the heralded Hawaii Healthy Start Program, which began in the early 1990s. While these programs have enjoyed a warm reception, some questions remain about their effectiveness in combating child abuse. Some common findings include small, if any, reductions in child maltreatment (Duggan et al., 2004b; Duggan et al., 2007; Gessner, 2008), poor client monitoring and inadequate training of workers (Caldera et al., 2007; Duggan et al., 2004a), and the need for a fuller understanding of which service delivery modes are most beneficial and cost-effective (DePanfilis, Dubowitz, & Kunz, 2008; DuMont et al., 2008). When taken together, these shortcomings make it nearly impossible to determine the program's overall success. Much of this difficulty stems from the gaps between what the program looks like on paper and what it evolves into when placed into action (Gomby, 2007). Thus, a fair assessment is that analysts still do not understand what portions of the program work, the conditions under which they work, which clients benefit the most, and which service providers are more efficient.

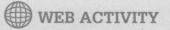 **WEB ACTIVITY**

The Healthy Families America network sponsors programs in a number of states. You can find out if your state is a participant by going to the website: **http://www.healthyfamiliesamerica.org/home/index.shtml**

Table 11.7 The Healthy Families Florida Program

What is Healthy Families Florida?

Healthy Families Florida is a nationally accredited, statewide program that is proven to prevent child abuse and neglect before it ever starts. Healthy Families Florida provides community-based home visitation services focused on promoting child health and development and positive parent–child interaction.

What are the goals of Healthy Families Florida?

- Prevent the incidence of child abuse and neglect
- Enhance parents' ability to create stable and nurturing home environments
- Increase parents' ability to develop positive parent–child relationships
- Promote child health and development
- Promote family self-sufficiency
- Ensure that the families' social and medical needs are met
- Ensure families are satisfied with services

Who is eligible for Healthy Families?

Services are offered to expectant families and families of newborns that live in targeted high-risk geographic areas and who are voluntarily assessed as having risk factors that place them at risk of child maltreatment and other adverse outcomes. These risk factors include but are not limited to:

- Single parenting
- Inadequate housing/income
- Less than high school diploma or GED
- Limited awareness of discipline options
- Late prenatal care (12 weeks or later)
- Unrealistic expectations about child development
- Abuse or neglect experienced in childhood/adolescence
- Raised by alcoholic/drug-addicted/mentally unstable caregiver
- Current maternal depression
- Witness to domestic violence in childhood/adolescence
- Multiple children in home
- Prior CPS involvement
- Limited contact with close friends and/or family
- Instability of care during childhood
- Past abusive relationships (not related to childhood)
- Parent verbalizes need to physically punish a child 1 year or younger
- A sense of hopelessness
- Child or other family member with special needs
- Parent is less than 18-years-old
- Negative verbalization about baby
- Upon knowledge of pregnancy continued smoking, drinking or using drugs
- Expressed fear of violence in the home

Source: Healthy Families Florida (2010–2011). Frequently Asked Questions. Tallahassee: Florida Chapter of Prevent Child Abuse America. Retrieved on May 22, 2013, from http://www.healthyfamiliesfla.org/faqs.html.

Obviously, a "one-size-fits-all" approach is flawed. Instead, there is a need to continually adapt to client needs and to absorb recommended changes that flow from further empirical evaluations. The challenge is to remain focused and continue working toward the goal of making needed improvements in the lives of children.

Education

The education effort aims to demystify child rearing by providing parents with instruction in child development. Some observers contend that the high school curriculum should contain a family course. Others advocate continuing adult education projects at hospitals, schools, churches, and social service agencies.

In their study of child maltreatment fatalities among children under the age of five, Klevens and Leeb (2010) attributed two out of every three deaths to *abusive head trauma* (AHT). AHT is associated with the shaken baby syndrome (see Table 11.3). Because the shaken baby syndrome is so detrimental to children, the National Center on Shaken Baby Syndrome and other groups have devised prevention programs. One such effort, the "Love Me . . . Never Shake Me" program, targets hospitalized mothers who have just given birth. The materials explain that babies often cry and, in some instances, may seem inconsolable and may cry for what seems to be an unbearable amount of time. Appropriate reaction strategies are then presented to the viewer. Indications are that the program reinforces what some mothers already know, increases awareness in those parents who are not versed in this area, and provides coping techniques that mothers can use (Center for Family Safety and Healing, 2013; Deyo, Skybo, & Carroll, 2008; Fujiwara et al., 2012). One shortcoming, though, is that the program is not geared toward fathers. Research shows that male caregivers are responsible for more than half the deaths associated with the shaken baby syndrome (Klevens & Leeb, 2010). Yet, unfortunately, this program overlooks fathers.

> **⊕ WEB ACTIVITY**
>
> The National Center on Shaken Baby Syndrome is dedicated to creating greater public awareness of the shaken baby syndrome. Its resources are available at **http://www.dontshake.org/**

Although an educational approach appears attractive, it is not the simple cure one might wish it to be. This option could not be implemented within a very short period of time. Issues regarding course content, development, and funding have to be resolved. Moreover, once in place, this alternative would require several years before yielding any returns.

Safe Haven Laws

Safe haven laws (SHLs) represent an effort to deal with baby abandonment and infanticide. For a variety of reasons, a parent may want to hide the birth of a baby, not be in a position to assume the responsibility of raising that child, or lack sufficient resources to keep a newborn. In the past, some parents have reacted by leaving their newborns unattended in the hope that somebody would discover the abandoned infant and rescue him or her. Infants have been located in restrooms, garbage dumpsters, doorways, and other less-than-optimal locations. In some tragic cases, these babies escaped notice, went undetected, and subsequently died (see Figure 11.5).

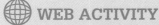 WEB ACTIVITY

The National Safe Haven Alliance concentrates on saving the lives of babies who are abandoned. Its activities can be seen at **http://www.nationalsafehavenalliance.org/**

Texas was the first state to enact an SHL in 1999. Since then, every state has addressed the issue of legally surrendering a child, although the exact provisions vary from one state to the next (Child Welfare Information Gateway, 2010). Table 11.8 displays the Florida version of an SHL. When you read that statute, you will see that it specifically defines what constitutes a newborn, mentions what locations are appropriate drop-off points, protects the identity of the parent, removes the threat of arrest or prosecution, and views the relinquishment as legally surrendering and not abandonment.

Because these statutes are of relatively recent vintage, a considerable body of evaluative research does not exist yet. Hence, the current literature is more thought-provoking than definitive. For instance, Pruitt (2008) encountered a situation where not a single Texas agency was tasked with tracking how many babies were illegally abandoned and how many were legally surrendered, let alone how many had survived or died. She attempted to sidestep this difficulty by scouring Texas newspapers for relevant stories of abandoned and surrendered newborns. Her efforts uncovered a total of 82 abandonment and 11 surrender cases from 1991 through 2006. Of course, these small sample sizes precluded Pruitt from carrying out a detailed examination of the Texas SHL. Other Texas media-based accounts have yielded highly disparate counts (Pertman & Deoudes, 2008). The lack of any records and the absence of any case details, coupled with the absence of a public awareness campaign, make it impossible to assess whether SHLs reduce the number of illegal infant abandonments (Atwood, 2008; Oberman, 2008; Pertman & Deoudes, 2008). As Pertman and Deoudes (2008: 100) explain:

> As long as safe havens remain society's principal means of addressing unsafe infant abandonment—even though we do not truly know whether they work— the very real risk is that the problem is, in fact, not being dealt with at all.

Hammond, Miller, and Griffin (2010) have urged future researchers to focus on a number of problematic aspects. First, there is a need to uncover just who these "at-risk" mothers and babies are. Second, the promise of anonymity when surrendering babies makes it very difficult for

FIGURE 11.5 Boston Fire Commissioner Paul Christian, left, and Boston Mayor Thomas Menino, right, place a "Baby Safe Haven" sticker on the door of a firehouse in Boston's West Roxbury district.
The Safe Haven Act of Massachusetts allows a parent to legally surrender newborn infants seven days old or younger at a hospital, police station, or manned fire station without facing criminal prosecution. *Credit: AP Photo/Steven Senne.*

researchers to gain insight into why these women chose this course of action. Third, any database is restricted to just those cases where the authorities knew that an infant death took place. Illegally abandoned babies who died because nobody found them may continue to remain hidden. Finally, the relatively small number of infanticides makes it difficult to draw firm conclusions about life-saving interventions and fosters exaggerated claims of program effectiveness.

Given the tenor of these observations, lingering doubts will continue to trail SHLs until much more accurate and detailed data become available.

Parents Anonymous

Parents Anonymous is a nonprofit national organization with local chapters. Local groups consist of parents who feel they are maltreating, or are in danger of maltreating, their children. The national organization operates a 24-hour hotline that parents can call when they need to vent their frustration or anger. Hopefully, talking to a sympathetic person who has encountered

WEB ACTIVITY

Parents Anonymous is credited with helping parents and caregivers cope with the stress of raising children. You can find a guide to this group's successful parenting practices at
http://parentsanonymous.org/

Table 11.8 The Florida Safe Haven Law

(1) As used in this section, the term "newborn infant" means a child who a licensed physician reasonably believes is approximately 7 days old or younger at the time the child is left at a hospital, emergency medical services station, or fire station.

(2) There is a presumption that the parent who leaves the newborn infant in accordance with this section intended to leave the newborn infant and consented to termination of parental rights.

(3) Each emergency medical services station or fire station staffed with full-time firefighters, emergency medical technicians, or paramedics shall accept any newborn infant left with a firefighter, emergency medical technician, or paramedic. The firefighter, emergency medical technician, or paramedic shall consider these actions as implied consent to and shall:
(a) Provide emergency medical services to the newborn infant to the extent he or she is trained to provide those services, and
(b) Arrange for the immediate transportation of the newborn infant to the nearest hospital having emergency services.

(5) Except when there is actual or suspected child abuse or neglect, any parent who leaves a newborn infant with a firefighter, emergency medical technician, or paramedic at a fire station or emergency medical services station, or brings a newborn infant to an emergency room of a hospital and expresses an intent to leave the newborn infant and not return, has the absolute right to remain anonymous and to leave at any time and may not be pursued or followed unless the parent seeks to reclaim the newborn infant. When an infant is born in a hospital and the mother expresses intent to leave the infant and not return, upon the mother's request, the hospital or registrar shall complete the infant's birth certificate without naming the mother thereon.

(9) A newborn infant left at a hospital, emergency medical services station, or fire station in accordance with this section shall not be deemed abandoned and subject to reporting and investigation requirements under s. 39.201 unless there is actual or suspected child abuse or until the department takes physical custody of the child.

(10) A criminal investigation shall not be initiated solely because a newborn infant is left at a hospital under this section unless there is actual or suspected child abuse or neglect.

Source: Florida Statutes *(2012), § 383.50.*

similar feelings will curb any violence directed at a child. In some ways, Parents Anonymous resembles the Alcoholics Anonymous network.

In order to meet the ideals outlined in Table 11.9, the members of each local chapter gather for weekly meetings to discuss their successes and failures, both as parents and as crisis interventionists for fellow members. Because membership is anonymous, no definitive evaluations were available until recently.

The National Council on Crime and Delinquency (2007, 2008), funded by the Office of Juvenile Justice and Delinquency Prevention, partnered with Parents Anonymous to determine what impact the program had on participants. The researchers interviewed a sample of 206 parents from around the country at three points in time: when they first joined the program, one month later, and then six months later. Parents who participated fully in the program showed dramatic improvements when compared with parents who started but then

---

Table 11.9 Parents Anonymous

Who Attends the Parents Anonymous® Group?

Parents Anonymous® Groups welcome any parent or individual in a parenting/caregiver role seeking support and positive parenting strategies regardless of the age or special challenges of their children. Parents may be married, divorced, single, grandparents, stepparents, foster parents, teen parents, or even aunts and uncles. Parents at risk or involved with Child Protective Services, domestic violence, homeless shelters, correctional and/or substance abuse programs also attend. In Parents Anonymous®, our important message is "Asking for Help is a Sign of Strength,®" meaning that we celebrate each person's individual journey of change the minute they commit to attend a Parents Anonymous® Group.

What Happens in a Parents Anonymous® Group?

- Parents are welcomed to the Parents Anonymous® Group and receive information about how the group operates.
- Parents are invited to share responsibility for planning and operating the Parents Anonymous® Group including engaging in outreach activities to recruit parents to the program.
- Parents provide vital emotional support, talk and problem-solve with other parents about parenting issues and personal challenges.
- Parents determine their own goals, how they are achieved and when they are met.
- Parents receive a variety of Parents Anonymous® program materials such as the *I Am a Parents Anonymous® Parent* along with newsletters such *Across the Nations*, which feature stories written by parents for parents.
- Parents give and receive support from other parents during and after meetings. Our motto is the more you give, the more you get!
- Parents have access to the National Parent Helpline® in between meetings to address their issues.
- Parents expand their network of support with others to help reduce stress and isolation.
- Parents learn about community resources and how to link to them.
- Parents have the opportunity to take on meaningful leadership roles in their family, the Parents Anonymous® Group and their community.

Source: Parents Anonymous® Inc. (2013). Adult Group. Claremont, CA: Parents Anonymous® Inc. Retrieved on May 22, 2013, from http://parentsanonymous.org/programs/parents-anonymous-groups/adult-group/.

dropped out of the self-help group. The more involved parents became with the program, the greater the benefits they derived from participation. All in all, the only existing independent assessment of the Parents Anonymous program indicates that it is a very promising avenue.

Counseling

Another avenue for dealing with child abuse cases emphasizes a treatment or rehabilitation approach. This response seeks to help both the victim and the offender, often involving the entire family. Most treatment interventions revolve around individual and group counseling. Various studies report that treatment programs are successful at engendering more assertiveness in victims and opening up communication about the event and related problems (Maddock, Larson, & Lally, 1991; Owen & Steele, 1991; Woodworth, 1991). At the same time, however, some distrust and suspicion of the offender remain after treatment, and therapy can have a negative impact on the family unit (Levitt, Owen, & Truchsess, 1991; Maddock et al., 1991; Woodworth, 1991). Wright (1991) evaluated the impact of removing the offender from the home (a common step in familial sexual abuse) and concluded that this action often leads to divorce, distant relations between the missing parent and children, financial hardship, and failed attempts at reconciliation.

Perhaps the most notable result of intervention studies is the almost universal finding that more services are needed than are typically available. Indeed, it may be the absence of available and appropriate services that is the cause of negative treatment outcomes. Among the needs most often cited are increased financial assistance, extended treatment and counseling, more clarity and structure in the expectations of all participants, and the provision of tangential services for related problems such as alcohol and other drug dependence (Levitt et al., 1991; Woodworth, 1991; Wright, 1991).

Children's Advocacy Centers

A *Children's Advocacy Center* (CAC) is an umbrella organization, independent of the criminal justice system, that brings together child protective services workers, law enforcement officers, the prosecutor's office, educators, mental health counselors, and medical personnel in an effort to provide a coordinated response and seamless service delivery to maltreated children. This multidisciplinary team approach is designed to keep children from being shuttled from one agency to the next and to provide a variety of services under one roof. The first CAC opened its doors in 1985 in Huntsville, Alabama. Since then, the concept has expanded, and there are now more than 700 CACs operating throughout the country (National Children's Alliance, 2013).

The goal of a CAC is to minimize the trauma child victims undergo and to provide a safe and comfortable atmosphere. One notable service CACs provide is videotaped forensic interviews. Among other things, videotaping reduces the number of interviews/interviewers, preserves testimony for later use, documents the tone of the session and the conditions under which the interview took place, and allows an assessment of the child's veracity (Chandler, 2000). In fact, an independent assessment of "best practices" specifically praised a multidisciplinary team approach, trained forensic interviewers, videotaping interviews, and the CAC model as being among the "best practices" to utilize when conducting child maltreatment investigations (Jones et al., 2005).

WEB ACTIVITY

More information about the National Children's Advocacy Center is available at **http://www.nationalcac.org/**

One promising interview technique is the NICHD Investigative Interview Protocol. Developed under the auspices of the National Institute of Child Health and Human Development, a team of researchers worked to develop a strategy that police officers and child protective services workers could use when dealing with child maltreatment victims. In the past, interviewers tended to employ leading questions, words that children did not understand, and other suggestive practices that interfered with the child's recall. The NICHD approach, which requires extensive training and practice, is very different from standard interrogation practices. It divides the interview into several distinct phases. During the introduction phase, the interviewer greets the child, explains what the meeting is about, assures the child that it is acceptable not to know all the answers, and then has the child respond to a series of questions that are markedly right or wrong to assess the child's cognitive abilities. The next stage helps establish rapport by simply conversing with the child. The interview continues by having the child relay things that took place during a recent birthday, day in school, or other event. Once the child has demonstrated a capacity for participating, the interview then moves to the purpose of the investigation. Care is taken to utilize open-ended questions or prompts that enable the child to provide a narrative. Interviewers purposively avoid issuing a narrow range of questions that focus on specific things. Toward the end of the session, the interviewer returns to nebulous responses and asks for clarification. One can find the most recent version of this protocol and further details in an article written by Lamb et al. (2007). Guidelines issued by the National Children's Advocacy Center (2011) also describe the fluid structure of this protocol. A very similar model has received an endorsement from the American Prosecutors Research Institute (Walters et al., 2003), as well as the American Bar Association (2009) and at least one prosecutor (Giles, 2009).

WEB ACTIVITY

You can track the latest developments with the NICHD interview protocol at **http://nichdprotocol.com/**

In sum, CACs appear to be a very sensible approach and have received some positive evaluations (Cross et al., 2008; Jones et al., 2005). While research efforts are starting to accumulate, a sufficient body of research does not currently exist upon which to base a definitive statement as to the role that CACs play and how well they play it.

Sex Offender Registration and Notification

Sex offender registration and notification (SORN) means that when convicted offenders are released from confinement, they must advise the authorities periodically of where they are living and working. There have been two major developments, and we will visit both. The first is the establishment of SORN laws; the second is the current effort by the federal government to standardize how the states approach SORN.

Megan's Law

Megan Kanka was a seven-year-old girl who resided in a small New Jersey town. Her neighbor, Jesse K. Timmendequas, lived across the street. Timmendequas had a dark secret that nobody in the neighborhood knew about. He had been convicted twice of sex offenses against children and had just been released from prison. He was also living with two other sex offenders whom he had met while in prison. On July 29, 1994, Timmendequas promised Megan that she could play with his puppy if she went inside his house. She did. It was there that he sexually assaulted Megan and strangled her to death with a belt before disposing of her body.

Public outrage over this death spurred state legislatures to pass new laws commonly referred to as *Megan's Laws*. While the exact details vary from state to state, the core requirement calls for public notification whenever a sex offender is released from prison into the community. This notification gives local authorities the ability to track the whereabouts of sex offenders in the community.

These laws typically classify sex offenders into three risk categories with commensurate notification responsibilities (Brooks, 1996). The lowest tier is reserved for convicted offenders who have made numerous adjustments and are least likely to recidivate. The usual requirement is that the state must notify the victim and local law enforcement agencies that the offender has been released from custody and is back in the community. The second level is the *sexual offender*. This person is deemed to be a "moderate risk," and an additional notification is made to local schools and youth organizations (e.g., Boy Scouts, Girl Scouts, sports and recreation centers). The highest risk category, *sexually violent predator*, is reserved for the most dangerous offenders with the most proclivity for recidivism. In these instances, the entire community is alerted about the offender's release. Community meetings, press releases, as well as flyers and posters complete with photographs, criminal history, the offender's new address, place of employment, and vehicle tag all serve to advertise this person's presence in the area. The hope, of course, is that enhanced community awareness will spur greater parental supervision over their children and reduce any opportunity for the criminal to reoffend.

States and local governments have enacted additional residency restrictions in a bid to keep sex offenders away from potential targets. Florida, for example, forbids sex offenders from living within 1,000 feet of a school, daycare facility, park, or playground (*Florida Statutes*, 2012: § 775.215). However, some 150 Florida cities and counties have gone a step further by passing local ordinances that impose a more stringent 1,500- or 2,500-foot buffer (Zandbergen & Hart, 2009; Zandbergen, Levenson, & Hart, 2010). Enterprising localities elsewhere have begun converting vacant lots into pocket parks in a concerted effort to displace sex offenders from those neighborhoods (Lovett, 2013). In many instances, these bans have the effect of zoning sex offenders out of the entire jurisdiction.

The Adam Walsh Act

President George W. Bush signed the Adam Walsh Child Protection and Safety Act of 2006 into law during the summer of 2006. This Act supersedes all previous federal legislation regarding SORN and introduces a new series of rules and regulations designed to standardize SORN practices and to create the National Sex Offender Registry. States that do not adhere to these new directives forfeit a portion of the federal monies they normally receive. As one might imagine, it took some time for Department of Justice administrators to digest this new law and to release implementation guidelines to the states. In light of this unforeseen delay and other complications, the U.S. Attorney General has extended the state compliance deadline and provided more funds to the states. Even so, only 16 states are in substantial compliance with these directives as of this writing (U.S. Department of Justice, 2013d). Hence, this new system is still evolving.

⊕ WEB ACTIVITY

The National Sex Offender Public Website, sponsored by the U.S. Department of Justice, provides links to all state registry sites. You can explore its features by going to **http://www.nsopw.gov/**

The federal guidelines establish three classes of sex offenders. Tier I contains the least risky sex offenders. This group is expected to register annually for a period of 15 years.

Tier II, reserved for more serious offenders, must contact authorities semi-annually for a 25-year period. The last category contains the serious sexually violent predators. They must reregister every three months for the rest of their lives. Registration means that offenders must provide a DNA sample, fingerprints, Social Security number, home and work addresses, vehicle description, and other information. Juveniles who match certain restrictions also fall under this purview.

The new provisions require the states to alter some of their existing procedures. Prior to the Adam Walsh Act, some states relied upon risk assessment instruments to classify individual offenders. The new SORN system substitutes the offense severity of the crime for which a person was convicted. In addition, states whose system does not match the federal three-tiered classification system need to revise their guidelines.

Some researchers are starting to investigate the implications of realigning sexual offenders into the new classification system. They probably will uncover a number of glitches and inconsistencies. For instance, there are some indications that less serious offenders are being sorted into higher dangerousness categories even though their risk of recidivating is minimal, that the inclusion of juveniles who are at least 14-years-old might amount to unwarranted net-widening, and that the operational and budgetary implications of absorbing this new mandate deserve greater scrutiny (Freeman & Sandler, 2010; Harris & Lobanov-Rostovsky, 2010; Harris, Lobanov-Rostovsky, & Levenson, 2010).

The operational implications of absorbing a bigger pool of registrants and the administrative burden of periodic contact, especially during the current economic downturn, and the gains to be derived from this new system are not fully understood at this time. In short, the implementation of these federal SORN directives will be of considerable interest to researchers, the criminal justice community, and the general public.

Other Considerations

The U.S. Supreme Court addressed an allied issue in *Smith v. Doe* (2003). Two convicted sex offenders in Alaska protested the fact that their pictures and other personal information were posted on an Internet website. The respondents argued that because they were convicted and sentenced prior to the passage of this statute, *ex post facto* protections exempted them from the retroactive application of the new law's provisions.

After hearing arguments, the Supreme Court held that the *ex post facto* clause did not apply in this instance for several reasons. First and foremost, the creation of this sex offender registry was done for civil, not criminal, purposes. Because the goal of the statute is to protect the public, as opposed to imposing punitive measures on offenders, this law is civil and not criminal in nature. *Ex post facto* provisions extend only to criminal penalties. Second, many punishments during colonial times were intended to shame or humiliate offenders. The intention of the current register is not to disgrace convicted sex offenders but to provide meaningful information for the greater public good. Third, placing identifying details on the Internet does not expose offenders to a heightened level of ridicule. Widespread publicity is necessary for this notification to be effective and work as intended. Fourth, the register does not restrict the movement of the persons listed on that site. Convicted sex offenders are free to live and work anywhere they choose, as long as they comply with the registration requirements.

Finally, even though the intent is to generate a deterrent effect, one of the hallmarks of criminal legislation, the statute is merely a regulation and not a new punishment. As a result of these considerations, the U.S. Supreme Court upheld the posting of sex offender information as serving a legitimate social function.

In the wake of these and other court rulings, researchers have begun studying the collateral experiences of sex offender registrants (Barnes et al., 2009; Casaday, 2009; Levenson & Cotter, 2005; Tewksbury, 2005; Tewksbury & Lees, 2007; Vandiver, Dial, & Worly, 2008; Zgoba, Levenson, & McKee, 2009). Being stigmatized as a sex offender does carry serious social repercussions. There are reports of registrants being fired from their jobs or enduring other employment restrictions once their status became known. Others have been denied housing, treated rudely, and subjected to other forms of harassment. Additional complaints center around the lack of a process for differentiating between a 10-year or lifetime registration and the inability to get removed from the list if one's risk to society diminishes or is nonexistent. As Table 11.10 shows, juveniles charged with a sex crime for having engaged in consensual sex relations with an under-aged partner may now have a formal avenue for avoiding sex offender registration requirements under so-called "Romeo and Juliet" laws. Obviously, a "one-size-fits-all" mentality that lumps together all types of behaviors under the single rubric of "sex offense" does not make for sound policy in every instance.

Table 11.10 The Florida "Romeo and Juliet" Law

(1) For purposes of this section, a person shall be considered for removal of the requirement to register as a sexual offender or sexual predator only if the person:

    (a) Was or will be convicted or adjudicated delinquent of a violation of [sexual battery, lewd or lascivious behavior, child pornography] . . . and the person does not have any other conviction, adjudication of delinquency, or withhold of adjudication of guilt for a violation of [sexual battery, lewd or lascivious behavior, child pornography];

    (b) Is required to register as a sexual offender or sexual predator solely on the basis of this violation; and

    (c) Is not more than 4 years older than the victim of this violation who was 14 years of age or older but not more than 17 years of age at the time the person committed this violation.

(2) If a person meets the criteria in subsection (1) and the violation . . . was committed on or after July 1, 2007, the person may move the court that will sentence or dispose of this violation to remove the requirement that the person register as a sexual offender or sexual predator. The person must allege in the motion that he or she meets the criteria in subsection (1) and that removal of the registration requirement will not conflict with federal law. The state attorney must be given notice of the motion at least 21 days before the date of sentencing or disposition of this violation and may present evidence in opposition to the requested relief or may otherwise demonstrate why the motion should be denied. At sentencing or disposition of this violation, the court shall rule on this motion and, if the court determines the person meets the criteria in subsection (1) and the removal of the registration requirement will not conflict with federal law, it may grant the motion and order the removal of the registration requirement. If the court denies the motion, the person is not authorized under this section to petition for removal of the registration requirement.

Source: Florida Statutes (2012), § 943.04354.

Civil Commitment

The problems and failures associated with sex offender management have brought the dawning recognition that current ways of dealing with sex offenders are sometimes ineffective. Many sex offenders have lengthy criminal histories, are not amenable to treatment, and will recidivate after release. As a result, some states have instituted civil commitment procedures for mentally ill sex offenders in an effort to prevent future victimization. In other words, once a dangerous sex offender completes his or her prison sentence, the state will initiate legal proceedings to confine this person indefinitely in a mental institution. As the statement of legislative intent in Florida's involuntary commitment statute explains:

> Sexually violent predators generally have antisocial personality features which are unamenable to existing mental illness treatment modalities, and those features render them likely to engage in criminal, sexually violent behavior. The Legislature further finds that the likelihood of sexually violent predators engaging in repeat acts of predatory sexual violence is high . . . that the prognosis for rehabilitating sexual violent predators in a prison setting is poor, the treatment needs of this population are very long term, and the treatment modalities for this population are very different . . . (*Florida Statutes*, 2012: § 394.910).

This strategy of confining offenders civilly after they have completed their criminal sentence has come under fire for a number of reasons. First, critics argued that this approach was nothing more than an *ex post facto* law. It imposed additional punishment long after the criminal court had adjudicated the matter. Second, there is the question of *double jeopardy*. Essentially, the offender is being punished twice for the same act. Third, the prospect of a lifetime commitment after completing the terms of incarceration amounts to cruel and unusual punishment. Finally, additional confinement violates plea bargain terms.

The U.S. Supreme Court ruled on this matter in *Kansas v. Hendricks* (1997). Hendricks was a convicted sex offender who had already served a 10-year prison term. As he neared release, the state sought to commit Hendricks to a mental institution as an uncured sexually violent predator. During that trial, Hendricks freely admitted that he quit the therapy program the prison offered, that he had a long history of sexually assaulting children, that he felt that he suffered from *pedophilia* (a sexual attraction toward children), and that he had no control over his urges to molest children. The jury found that Hendricks suffered from a mental abnormality and posed a danger to others; they agreed that he met the criteria for being classified as a sexually violent predator. The judge, then, issued a civil commitment order. Hendricks appealed it on the grounds that Kansas had violated his due process rights and double jeopardy and *ex post facto* protections.

The Supreme Court ruled against Hendricks in a 5–4 decision. It held that the Kansas statute had built in a sufficient number of procedural checks to provide for due process and protect against overzealous application. Furthermore, the Court found that Kansas had distanced the civil commitment procedures from any criminal proceeding and, therefore, the statute was not punitive in nature. The Justices ruled that Kansas was correct to incapacitate Hendricks as a way of protecting society even though no effective treatment was available for his mental abnormality.

A similar ruling on this topic came in the case of *U.S. v. Comstock* (2010). *Comstock* raised the question of whether the federal government had the power to civilly commit a federal prisoner, considered to be dangerous, after completing a term of incarceration for a federal sex crime. The defendants in this case maintained that Congress had overextended itself and did not have the constitutional power to enact a civil commitment statute for sexual predators. In other words, Article I of the Constitution restricts the creation of federal crimes to counterfeiting, treason, and piracy and crimes committed on the high seas. Enacting a civil commitment statute that detains uncured sexual predators exceeds the powers contained in the Constitution. The Court rejected this argument by a 7–2 margin. As Justice Alito (p. 3) explained, "it is necessary and proper for Congress to provide for the civil commitment of dangerous federal prisoners who would otherwise escape civil commitment as a result of federal imprisonment."

Amber Alert

In January of 1996, a nine-year-old girl, Amber Hagerman, was pedaling her bicycle down the street. The driver of a black pickup truck pulled over, grabbed Amber, and shoved her into the vehicle. He then sped off. Bystanders who witnessed the event notified the police. However, the investigation did not turn up any additional evidence or leads. Amber had vanished in broad daylight. Her body was found four days later. Amber had been murdered.

Local community members were stunned by this incident and the inability of the police to locate Amber in a timely manner. Gradually, this concern over child safety underscored the need for rapid dissemination of information to the public (see Table 11.11). As a result, a plan developed whereby local radio stations and television channels would broadcast vital information so that anybody spotting the victim and/or the abductor could notify the authorities. Cell phone companies, Internet service providers, the trucking industry, and billboard owners have also become partners. Today, all 50 states have some form of an Amber Alert system in place.

These Amber Alert plans operate under the premise that there is precious little time to waste once a stranger kidnaps a child. The fear is that the suspect intends to kill the victim and will do so within the next several hours. Hence, time is of the essence.

Table 11.11 The Letter that Launched the Amber Alert Program

Jennifer Grim
KDMX 102-9 FM
Addison, Texas

Dear Jennifer,

As we discussed on the telephone Friday, January 19, concerning the Amber Hagerman tragedy, it occurred to me that in the vast majority of abduction cases we hear about, children are being put into vehicles and transported from the point of abduction, point A, to somewhere, point B. Considering the population density of the metroplex area, that seems virtually impossible to complete without being seen by someone. In Amber's case, for example, I'm sure a number of people saw her in that black pickup truck but simply did not know what they were seeing. To remedy this, I would like to suggest an emergency system be set up so that when a verified 911 call is placed, all the radio stations in the area would be notified immediately and they would interrupt programming to broadcast an emergency alert, giving whatever information and descriptions that are pertinent. In this way, thousands of people would be alerted within minutes of an occurrence, greatly minimizing the chance of successful escape. Naturally, citizens would be advised not to interfere, but simply call in any sightings of the suspect vehicle or persons. Also, a great number of my colleagues and clients feel that this type of a response system may act as a strong deterrent, since possible perpetrators would be aware that virtually everyone on the roads etc. would be looking for them.

I want to thank you and Kim Ashly for your interest and support of this idea. I sincerely hope this plan or something similar be enacted so children of the Dallas/Ft. Worth area may experience their childhood as a time of joy, rather than one of fear and apprehension.

If you are able to gather support of this Emergency Broadcast Plan, my one request is that it be known as Amber's Plan.

Sincerely,

Diana Simone

Source: Simone, D. (2010). "The Letter that Launched Amber Alert." The Amber Advocate, 4(1), 5. Retrieved on May 27, 2013, from http://www.amberalert.gov/newsroom/pdfs/advocate_1004.pdf.

According to federal guidelines (U.S. Department of Justice, 2013a; Uzzell, 2012), the Amber Alert system should be activated only if four conditions are met. They include:

- Law enforcement officials must conduct an initial investigation and confirm that a child has been abducted;
- There must be some indication that the child is endangered;
- There must sufficient information available to make a recovery plausible; and
- The case must be entered into the National Crime Information Center, the FBI computerized index of criminal justice information.

The National Center for Missing and Exploited Children (2012) advises there were 158 Amber Alerts covering 197 children issued during 2011. Seventy percent of these cases involved a noncustodial parent, 24% pertained to a nonfamily member, and the remainder were either lost, injured, missing, or runaway children. In terms of age, 58% of the Amber Alerts involved children under the age of four. Two-thirds of the recovered

🌐 WEB ACTIVITY

The U.S. Department of Justice is the driving force behind the national Amber Alert program. More details appear at the website: **http://www.amberalert.gov/**

children were located within six hours of the activation. Five children were deceased when they were found.

While these numbers might appear to be impressive, some observers are not so sure. They question whether Amber Alerts are being used appropriately (Griffin et al., 2007; Griffin & Miller, 2008; Griffin, 2010; Hammond, Miller, & Griffin, 2010; Zgoba, 2004). As mentioned earlier, this system was designed to intervene in situations in which strangers abducted a youngster and that child was in danger of being harmed. The abundance of parental suspects and the absence of life-threatening situations make it difficult to determine whether the program is working as intended.

Legal Reform

Participation in criminal justice system proceedings can be a traumatic experience for children. In fact, the American Bar Association (1996) requires attorneys to consider the child's well-being carefully before deciding whether the victim should testify in court. However, victim testimony is a crucial component in an adversarial system of justice. Without a victim's account, most cases are simply not prosecutable. As a result, some jurisdictions employ victim counselors to help combat the emotional upheaval that victims incur and to sustain victim credibility by increasing cognitive recall. The content of these disclosures may fall under the protection of victim-counsel or privilege laws in some states (Office for Victims of Crime, 2002c). Table 11.12 contains provisions that allow Florida judges to close the courtroom and to allow a hearsay exception when dealing with child abuse cases.

Any reform effort must weigh victim trauma against the defendant's constitutional rights. The defendant has the right to confront and to cross-examine witnesses under the Fourteenth Amendment of the United States Constitution. Back in Chapter 10, when we were exploring intimate partner violence, we introduced the U.S. Supreme Court decisions *Crawford v. Washington* (2004) and *Giles v. California* (2008). *Crawford* dealt with the admissibility of testimonial statements when the declarant was unavailable, and *Giles* involved forfeiture by wrongdoing when the defendant caused the declarant to be unavailable to testify in court. How these cases will impact child abuse cases in which the victim is too afraid to testify and how they affect the admissibility of CAC-videotaped interviews is the subject of much legal speculation at this time (Fox, 2009; Phillips, 2005).

There is the right to a public trial under the Sixth Amendment, and the public has the right to access the proceedings under the First Amendment. The difficulty, then, becomes one of balancing victim trauma induced by system participation against the defendant's interests. As we stressed in Chapter 1, this is the criminal's, not the victim's, justice system.

Table 11.12 Florida Trial Guidelines Involving Child Victims and Child Witnesses

Closing the Courtroom

When the victim of a sex offense is testifying concerning that offense in any civil or criminal trial, the court shall clear the courtroom of all persons upon the request of the victim, regardless of the victim's age or mental capacity, except that parties to the cause and their immediate families or guardians, attorneys and their secretaries, officers of the court, jurors, newspaper reporters or broadcasters, court reporters, and, at the request of the victim, victim or witness advocates designated by the state attorney may remain in the courtroom.

Hearsay Exception

Unless the source of information or the method or circumstances by which the statement is reported indicates a lack of trustworthiness, an out-of-court statement made by a child victim with a physical, mental, emotional, or developmental age of 11 or less describing any act of child abuse or neglect, any act of sexual abuse against a child, the offense of child abuse, the offense of aggravated child abuse, or any offense involving an unlawful sexual act, contact, intrusion, or penetration performed in the presence of, with, by, or on the declarant child, not otherwise admissible, is admissible in evidence in any civil or criminal proceeding if:

1. The court finds in a hearing conducted outside the presence of the jury that the time, content, and circumstances of the statement provide sufficient safeguards of reliability. In making its determination, the court may consider the mental and physical age and maturity of the child, the nature and duration of the abuse or offense, the relationship of the child to the offender, the reliability of the assertion, the reliability of the child victim, and any other factor deemed appropriate; and

2. The child either:
   a. Testifies; or
   b. Is unavailable as a witness, provided that there is other corroborative evidence of the abuse or offense. Unavailability shall include a finding by the court that the child's participation in the trial or proceeding would result in a substantial likelihood of severe emotional or mental harm... .

Source: Florida Statutes *(2012)*, § *918.16(2)*; Florida Statutes *(2012)*, § *90.803(23)(a)*.

Some states in this country relax the hearsay rule when the following circumstances are present: a child victim is under the age of 11, he or she is involved in a child abuse case, and the trustworthiness of a statement made out of court and not under oath can be established. The *hearsay rule* disallows statements made by a third party because the court cannot evaluate that person's credibility and, thus, the defense is unable to impeach that testimony. Judges waive the hearsay rule only under very narrow circumstances.

WEB ACTIVITY

The National Association of Counsel for Children devotes its effort to educating judges and lawyers who work in the best interests of the child. See its website at **http://www.naccchildlaw.org/**, which contains a wealth of information.

Another mechanism to reduce victim trauma is the use of *in camera* proceedings (Brancatelli, 2009). One such effort has been to allow child victims to testify outside the courtroom in less formal, less threatening surroundings. This practice allows the judge to interview a child in private and to videotape the testimony for the trial. An example of a state statute allowing for this practice is reproduced in Table 11.13.

Although the use of *in camera* proceedings is innovative, it has encountered some legal objections. First, some defendants have argued that such

---

Table 11.13 An Example of a Statute Allowing Videotaping of Testimony in Child Sexual Abuse Cases

(1) On motion and hearing in camera and a finding that there is a substantial likelihood that a victim or witness who is under the age of 16 or who is a person with mental retardation as defined in s. 393.063 would suffer at least moderate emotional or mental harm due to the presence of the defendant if the child or person with mental retardation is required to testify in open court, or that such victim or witness is otherwise unavailable as defined in s. 90.804(1), the trial court may order the videotaping of the testimony of the victim or witness in a case, whether civil or criminal in nature, in which videotaped testimony is to be utilized at trial in lieu of trial testimony in open court.

(4) The defendant and the defendant's counsel shall be present at the videotaping, unless the defendant has waived this right. The court may require the defendant to view the testimony from outside the presence of the child or person with mental retardation by means of a two-way mirror or another similar method that will ensure that the defendant can observe and hear the testimony of the victim or witness in person, but that the victim or witness cannot hear or see the defendant. The defendant and the attorney for the defendant may communicate by any appropriate private method.

Source: Florida Statutes *(2012), § 92.53.*

---

proceedings violate their constitutional right to confront and cross-examine witnesses. These complaints have been quashed by allowing the defense counsel to attend the out-of-court questioning. In addition, the courts have ruled that the defendant does not have to be physically present in the same room with the witness. A suitable alternative arrangement is to have the defendant view witness testimony from another location via closed circuit television.

A second objection deals with the right of the public to have access to the trial. Sufficient precedent exists that the public has limited access to observe judicial proceedings without jeopardizing the legal process. A similar third objection deals with the defendant's right to a public trial. Precedence is mixed on this point. After reviewing a variety of cases, Melton (1980: 282) concluded that "embarrassment and emotional trauma to witnesses simply do not permit a trial judge to close his courtroom to the entire public." While *in camera* proceedings may avoid inducement of unnecessary trauma, not all courts have reached a definitive conclusion about the conditions under which it is permissible.

Perhaps Vandervort (2006: 1415) captured this dilemma in the following remarks:

> Videotaping has often been opposed by prosecutors and urged by defense advocates. This has largely been a quixotic debate that has taken place in a vacuum with advocates for either side advancing their perceived interests and without consideration of how other investigative methods and tools might complement the use of videotaping. Moreover, the broader community's interests have been largely absent from this debate. Our findings suggest that, at least

when used as part of a carefully thought-out investigative protocol, videotaping has a deleterious impact upon defendants' interests and a very positive impact on prosecutor's efforts to successfully prosecute child sexual abuse cases.

SUMMARY

It has taken our society much time to recognize that child maltreatment exists. Once discovered, states implemented laws forbidding the victimization of children. Maltreatment, however, tends to take place behind closed doors. It often involves victims who are unable to defend themselves, making detection difficult. While reporting laws aim to remedy this dilemma, they have had a boomerang effect. About three-quarters of all child maltreatment complaints are graded as unfounded or unsubstantiated.

Other coping strategies have surfaced. Together, they suggest that the eradication of child abuse and neglect is everybody's responsibility. One way to place this mandate in perspective is to realize that somewhere in this country another child probably died from maltreatment during the time it took you to read this chapter.

KEY TERMS

abuse
abusive head trauma
Adam Walsh Act
battered-child syndrome
central register
child fatality review teams
children's advocacy center
countertransference
double jeopardy
ex post facto law
ex post facto research
false negative error
false positive error
good faith
hearsay rule
in camera
legislative immunity

maltreatment
Megan's Laws
neglect
patriae potestas
pedophilia
poly-victimization
privileged relationship
protective custody
referral
screen out/screen in
sex offender registration and
    notification (SORN)
sexual offender
sexually violent predator
shaken baby syndrome
substantiated allegation
surveillance bias

Crime and the Elderly

After reading Chapter 12, you should be able to:

- Account for the rising interest in the elderly.
- Link changes in life expectancies with population shifts.
- Show how the American population is "graying."
- Comment on the political role of the elderly.
- Give some characteristics of older Americans.
- Explain who the elderly are.
- Convey what the underrepresentation of the elderly in victimization statistics means.
- Talk about age patterns in victimization statistics.
- Visit the idea of a "magnitude issue" and link it to the traditional lack of interest in crime among the elderly.
- Separate "fear of crime" into two components.
- Discuss the objective and the subjective odds of elder victimization.
- Understand what is meant by the fear–crime paradox.
- Tie "vicarious victimization" to fear of crime.
- Distinguish risk from vulnerability.
- List four risk factors for the elderly.
- Outline three vulnerability factors for the elderly.
- Compare and contrast elder abuse with elder neglect.
- Estimate how much elder maltreatment takes place.
- Relay various shortcomings associated with official estimates of elder maltreatment.
- Discuss the extent of institutional elder abuse.
- Talk about some possible causes of institutional elder abuse.
- Evaluate whether mandatory abuse reporting laws are effective.
- Understand the role of Adult Protective Services.
- Recognize the limitations of current social service provisions.

Victimology.

INTRODUCTION

Perhaps the most recent concern to emerge in victimology is the topic of the elderly and their unfortunate victimization experiences. The popular notion is that seniors enter an idyllic period, sometimes called the *twilight years* or the *golden years*, as they approach the end of the life cycle. The journey of life now becomes transformed into a joyous, calm, and carefree celebration. There is a sense of accomplishment and an accompanying serenity. The idea that the older generation is owed a debt of gratitude for their unselfish sacrifices and should be cherished pervades even the message contained in President Obama's recent Presidential Proclamation recognizing "Older Americans Month" (see Table 12.1).

The grim reality is that nothing could be further from the truth for some seniors. They live in impoverished conditions and watch as their quality of life dwindles. The conditions associated with advancing age render them more vulnerable to stranger-to-stranger crimes. In addition, some seniors also

---

Table 12.1 President Obama's Proclamation Declaring Older Americans Month

For half a century, communities in every corner of our country have come together to honor older Americans in a special way during the month of May. We carry that tradition forward again this year by recognizing their accomplishments, sharing their stories, and showing support and appreciation for our elders.

With groundbreaking advances in medicine and health care, Americans are living longer and achieving more. Many seniors are using a lifetime of experience to serve those around them. Even after decades of hard work, men and women are taking on new roles after retirement – organizing, educating, innovating, and making sure they leave the next generation with the same opportunities they had. It is a commitment that shines brightly in programs like Senior Corps, which connects more than half a million people to service opportunities from coast to coast.

As older Americans strive to lift up their neighborhoods, my Administration is working to make sure they get the tools they need to make a difference. We are helping more seniors get involved in volunteer service and give back to those around them. We are also finding new ways to make sure seniors live with dignity as full members of their communities—from improving access to health care to broadening employment opportunities. And to ensure older Americans have resources they can count on, my Administration will continue to protect and strengthen Medicare and Social Security not just for this generation, but also for those to come.

Our seniors deserve the best our country has to offer. This month, we pay tribute to the men and women who raised us, and we pledge anew to show them the fullest care, support, and respect of a grateful Nation.

NOW, THEREFORE, I, BARACK OBAMA, President of the United States of America, by virtue of the authority vested in me by the Constitution and the laws of the United States, do hereby proclaim May 2013 as Older Americans Month. I call upon all Americans of all ages to acknowledge the contributions of older Americans during this month and throughout the year.

IN WITNESS WHEREOF, I have hereunto set my hand this thirtieth day of April, in the year of our Lord two thousand thirteen, and of the Independence of the United States of America the two hundred and thirty-seventh.

BARACK OBAMA

Source: Office of the Press Secretary (April 30, 2013). Presidential Proclamation – Older Americans Month, 2013. *Washington, DC: The White House. Retrieved on June 13, 2013, from http://www.whitehouse.gov/the-press-office/2013/04/30/presidential-proclamation-older-americans-month-2013.*

experience mistreatment from within their own social circles. The cycle of life has entrapped these individuals.

Because interest in elder victimization has begun to sprout, a number of unanswered questions and issues have emerged for consideration. The entire field of elder victimization is still in the process of defining its parameters. For ease of presentation, we divide the subject matter into two major subheadings: criminal victimization and elder maltreatment. *Criminal victimization* refers to the commission of acts against the elderly that would be criminal violations regardless of the victim's age. Certainly, abuse and neglect fall into this category. However, they differ from other crimes in that they specifically target the elderly because of their diminished capacity. The status of being elderly provides the opportunity for this type of victimization.

Before diving into this topic, we need to visit two allied concerns. The first is to explain why there is an upswing in interest about the elderly; the second is to explore just who the elderly are. After that, we will be in a much better position to turn to issues involving crime among the elderly and elderly maltreatment.

THE RISE OF INTEREST IN THE ELDERLY

The elderly population has captured interest from many quarters for a number of reasons. This section of the chapter explores some of those reasons. They include demographic changes in the population, political action, and social consciousness.

Demographic Change

One major reason for the keen interest in elder affairs stems from the graying of the American population. Two forces are operating here. The first is the change in the average life expectancy, and the second is the overall growth of the elderly population itself. Let us take a brief look at each.

One underlying development that has boosted interest in the elderly is due, in large part, to medical advances. Changes in nutrition, healthier lifestyles, the availability of medical resources, and advances in medical knowledge have increased the life expectancy of both men and women. *Life expectancy* refers to the number of years that the average person should live. The life expectancy for a man born in 1900 was 46 years; it was 48 years for a woman. A male baby born in 1950 could expect to live until age 66, while a female infant averaged 71 years. By 2000, the life expectancy had climbed to 74 years for males and 79 years for females. The 2008 figures come in at 76 and 81 years, respectively (Arias, 2012). The most recent data indicate that a child born in 2011 would live almost until his or her 79th birthday, about 30 years more than if he or she had been born in 1900 (Administration on Aging, 2012). This steady increase in life expectancies suggests that the absolute number of senior citizens in the United States will continue to grow.

Figure 12.1 depicts the number of older Americans from 1900 through 2010, and then projects these population figures out to 2050. The population of persons 65 and over started out at 3 million in 1900, rose to 40 million in 2010, and is expected to top out at 88.5 million in 2050. Persons over the age of 85 numbered slightly more than 100,000 in 1900. That group grew to 5.5 million in 2010 and is projected to reach 19 million by 2050. Approximately 3 million Americans celebrated their 65th birthday during 2011 (Administration on Aging, 2012). Another way to look at these numbers is that 20% of the American population will be 65 or older by the year 2030 (Federal Interagency Forum on Aging-Related Statistics, 2012).

As already demonstrated, there has been a dramatic surge in the number of elderly people in this country since 1900, and projections show that this trend should continue well into the twenty-first century. As Table 12.2 demonstrates, the increased number of elderly raises a variety of issues and concerns for society, including health care, Social Security viability, and also crime victimization. The absolute increase in the number of elderly should equate with an increased number of crimes against the elderly.

> ### 🌐 WEB ACTIVITY
>
> The U.S. Census Bureau deals with much more than just counting the number of people in this country every 10 years. A look at its website will lead you to appreciate how population dynamics can have far-reaching effects: **http://www.census.gov/**

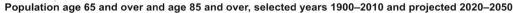

Population age 65 and over and age 85 and over, selected years 1900–2010 and projected 2020–2050

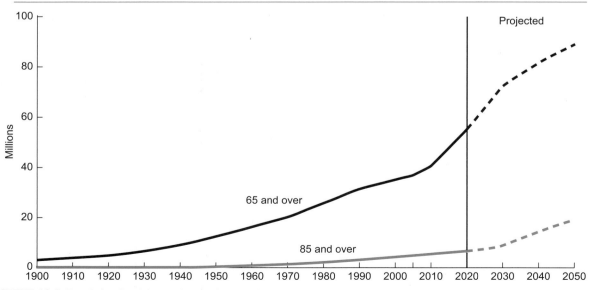

FIGURE 12.1 Population Aged 65+ and 85+, 1900–2050.

Source: *Federal Interagency Forum on Aging-Related Statistics (2012). Older Americans 2012: Key Indicators of Well-Being. Washington, DC: U.S. Government Printing Office, p. 2. Retrieved on June 13, 2013, from http://www.agingstats.gov/agingstatsdotnet/Main_Site/Data/2012_Documents/Docs/EntireChartbook.pdf.*

Table 12.2 Characteristics of Older Americans, 2012

- The older population (65+) numbered 41.4 million in 2011, an increase of 6.3 million or 18% since 2000.
- The number of Americans aged 45–64—who will reach 65 over the next decades—increased by 33% during this decade.
- Over one in every eight, or 13.3%, of the population is an older American.
- Persons reaching age 65 have an average life expectancy of an additional 19.2 years (20.4 years for females and 17.8 years for males).
- Older women outnumber older men at 23.4 million older women to 17.9 million older men.
- Older men were much more likely to be married than older women—72% of men vs. 45% of women.
- About 28% (11.8 million) of noninstitutionalized older persons live alone (8.4 million women, 3.5 million men).
- Almost half of older women (46%) age 75+ live alone.
- The population 65 and over has increased from 35 million in 2000 to 41.4 million in 2011 (an 18% increase) and is projected to increase to 79.7 million in 2040.
- The 85+ population is projected to increase from 5.7 million in 2011 to 14.1 million in 2040.
- The median income of older persons in 2011 was $27,707 for males and $15,362 for females.
- The major sources of income as reported by older persons in 2010 were Social Security (reported by 86% of older persons), income from assets (reported by 52%), private pensions (reported by 27%), government employee pensions (reported by 15%), and earnings (reported by 26%).
- Social Security constituted 90% or more of the income received by 36% of beneficiaries in 2010 (23% of married couples and 46% of non-married beneficiaries).
- Almost 3.6 million elderly persons (8.7%) were below the poverty level in 2011.

Source: Administration on Aging (2012). A Profile of Older Americans: 2012, p. 1. Washington, DC: U.S. Department of Health and Human Services. Retrieved on June 13, 2013, from http://www.aoa.gov/AoAroot/Aging_Statistics/Profile/2012/docs/2012profile.pdf.

Political Action

Another factor in the growth in visibility of elder issues is political astuteness. Given their numbers, the elderly form a considerable voting constituency. Voter registration and voter turnout tend to increase noticeably with age. People over 45 years of age constitute a formidable voting bloc because they go to the polls and cast votes in considerably greater numbers than younger persons (File, 2013; File & Crissey, 2013). Age-based advocacy groups have the resources and savvy to lobby elected officials. Perhaps the most notable of these groups is AARP (formerly the American Association of Retired Persons). AARP is active in promoting legislation on a variety of topics important to individuals aged 50 and over. Among the issues addressed by AARP in recent years are health care benefits and costs, employment opportunities for seniors, improved conditions in group residential living centers, and crime against the elderly.

🌐 WEB ACTIVITY

The American Association of Retired Persons has evolved into a potent political force and has extended its reach into many more areas. For more information, visit the group's website at **http://www.aarp.org/**

WEB ACTIVITY

Look at some legislative activities regarding the interests of elderly persons by exploring what the National Silver Haired Congress does at **http://natlshc.org/**

Not to be overlooked is the practice of state *Silver-Haired Legislatures* and a national "Silver-Haired Congress." The Silver-Haired Legislature is a mock legislative assembly consisting of older persons, usually at least 60-years-old. These so-called "representatives" convene periodic meetings to discuss legislative remedies to issues confronting the elderly. They also elect their own set of officials, usually mirroring the positions held by various elected governmental officials, who run the legislative session. This group will meet in the state capital chambers, hold a variety of committee hearings, debate new proposals, and eventually pass "bills" aimed at resolving these matters. The outcomes of these mock assemblies are conveyed to the state's governor, cabinet members, and state legislators. It is not uncommon for bills endorsed by a Silver-Haired Legislature to pick up sponsors from actual state politicians and, ultimately, make their way into state statutes (see Figure 12.2). In Florida, for example, there are sentencing enhancements when the victim is 65 years of age or older, even if the offender does not know the victim's actual age (*Florida Statutes*, 2012, § 784.08). Similar provisions exist for theft (*Florida Statutes*, 2012, § 812.0145), as well as abuse, neglect, and exploitation of elderly persons (*Florida Statutes*, 2012, § 825.101(5); § 825.104).

Social Consciousness

A final reason for increased attention to elder abuse and neglect may be the general trend to take up the causes of oppressed and/or underprivileged segments of society. In this sense, interest in elder abuse is a logical extension of the concern over women's and children's issues.

FIGURE 12.2
A member of the Silver Haired Legislature takes the microphone during a three-day session at the Statehouse in Columbia, South Carolina.
The group's 152 representatives champion legislative priorities of voters over age 60 in counties across the state. *Credit: AP Photo/Mary Ann Chastain*

DEFINING THE ELDERLY

At one time, it was relatively easy to define elderliness. Most people worked until they reached the age of 65, and then they retired, subsisting on a pension and Social Security benefits. Federal legislation eventually lowered the threshold for Medicaid and Medicare to 62 years of age. Suddenly, more and more pension plans opened their retirement windows to younger participants. Companies found themselves in jeopardy of "graying." In order to provide promotional opportunities for younger workers and to restructure their workforce, some businesses began offering special incentives for early retirement packages. They attempted to lure younger persons, who were in their mid- to late 50s, into retirement. As you can see, gauging elderliness in terms of retirement eligibility soon lost any intrinsic meaning.

Gerontologists, people who study the aging process, tend to be critical of efforts to link old age to chronological years of life. Much to their dismay, many researchers quickly adopted the calendar age as a convenient reference point (Schaie, 1988). This simple definition overlooked the complexity of the aging process. As Maddox and Wiley (1976: 9) explain, "aging connotes three distinct phenomena: the biological capacity for survival, the psychological capacity for adaptation, and the sociological capacity for the fulfillment of social roles."

Victimologists began to realize that lumping all people over the age of 65 into a single category did not produce a homogeneous group (Fattah & Sacco, 1989). There were significant variations that were being masked by this designation. As a result, efforts were made to expand the senior citizen category. Some researchers separated "early old age" (age 64–74) from "advanced old age" (age 75 and older). Other schemes recognized that there were important differences between the "old," the "very old," and those over 85—the "old old" (Fattah & Sacco, 1989). The reader should be sensitive to this concern and be aware that classifying the elderly into a single group can do more disservice than good.

CRIMINAL VICTIMIZATION OF THE ELDERLY

While crime pervades much of modern society, it does not reach all social groups equally. Perhaps the best source of information on who is victimized is the National Crime Victimization Survey (NCVS). Based on NCVS data, the most victimized people are blacks, males, people from the lower economic strata, and the young. The elderly, in contrast, experience relatively low levels of victimization.

An inspection of census information, along with NCVS data, bears out this point (see Table 12.3). Victimization levels are highest among the younger age categories and consistently decline with each successive age group. As we shall see in a moment, the lowered odds of victimization will be an important point. A second aspect to note deals with the issue of an uneven age distribution in victimization statistics. While persons aged 65 and over make up 15% of the population, they experience only 1.7% of the violent crime victimizations and 8.3% of the property victimizations reported to the interviewers. If all things were equal, one would expect that the 65+ age group would be involved in 15% of the victimizations. What this situation means, then, is that there is an *underrepresentation* of the elderly in victimization statistics.

Looking further at Table 12.3, those persons in the 50–64 range comprise 26% of the population, but account for only 6.2% of the personal victimizations

Table 12.3 Distribution of Age Groups in the Population and in Victimization

	Personal Victimization			Property Victimization	
Age Group	Population Percentage	Victimization Percentage	Age Group	Population Percentage	Victimization Percentage
12–15	6.5	23.1	12–19	13.3	37.8
16–19	6.8	27.0			
20–24	8.3	19.0	20–34	24.4	21.3
25–34	16.0	13.5			
35–49	26.1	9.6	35–49	26.1	19.3
50–64	21.2	6.2	50–64	21.2	13.4
65+	15.0	1.7	65+	15.0	8.3
Total	99.9	100.1		100.0	100.1

Source: Population information compiled from U.S. Census Bureau (2010). Table 7: Resident population by age and sex: 1980 to 2007. Statistical Abstract of the United States 2009. Washington, DC: U.S. Census Bureau. Retrieved on June 13, 2013, from http://www.census.gov/prod/2008pubs/09statab/pop.pdf. Victimization information compiled from U.S. Department of Justice (2010b). Table 3: Victimization rates for persons age 12 and over, by type of crime and age of victims and Table 19: Victimization rates by type of crime and age of head of household. Criminal Victimization in the United States, 2007—Statistical Tables. Washington, DC: Bureau of Justice Statistics. Retrieved on June 13, 2013, from http://bjs.ojp.usdoj. gov/content/pub/pdf/cvus0701.pdf.

and 13.4% of the property incidents. Once again, this older age group is underrepresented in victimization statistics relative to its presence in the population.

Looking at the other side of the age spectrum, respondents in the 12–15 age bracket make up 6.5% of the population, but experience 23% of the violent victimizations. Another way to put it is that this age group is *overrepresented* in violent crime. Generally speaking, violent victimization rates for all personal crime categories decrease across age groups from ages 20–24 through age 65 and over (see Figure 12.3). A similar pattern holds true for property victimization (see Figure 12.4). Essentially, then, both these figures show a clear negative linear relationship between victimization and age. Thus, one could conclude that the overall objective odds of falling prey to the criminal element are very small for senior citizens and much larger for the younger segments of the population.

The underrepresentation of the elderly in victimization incidents, coupled with relatively small crime rates for this age group, led Payne (2011) to suspect that a *magnitude issue* was another contributing reason for the lack of attention being paid to crime among the elderly. In other words, the low levels of elderly victimization became interpreted as evidence that crime against the elderly was not a serious social problem since it was a rare occurrence. As we shall see in the following section, separating the *objective* from the *subjective odds of victimization* is important because fear of crime can have a devastating impact on the quality of life for many senior citizens.

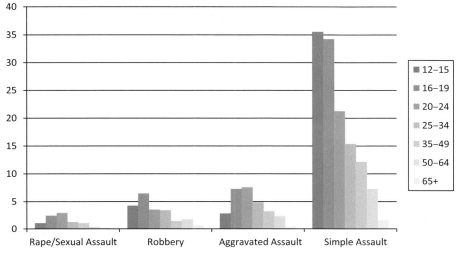

FIGURE 12.3 Personal Victimization Rates by Victim Age.
Source: Compiled from U.S. Department of Justice (2010b). Table 3: Victimization rates for persons age 12 and over, by type of crime and age of victims. Criminal Victimization in the United States, 2007—Statistical Tables. *Washington, DC: Bureau of Justice Statistics. Retrieved on June 13, 2013, from http://bjs.ojp.usdoj.gov/content/pub/pdf/cvus0701.pdf.*

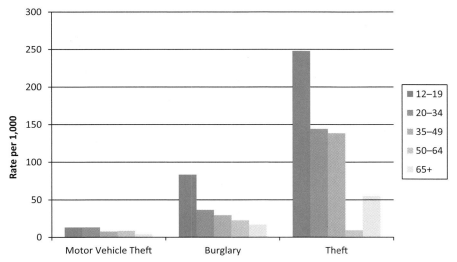

FIGURE 12.4 Property Victimization Rates by Age of Head of Household.
Source: Compiled from U.S. Department of Justice (2010b). Table 19: Victimization rates by type of crime and age of head of household. Criminal Victimization in the United States, 2007—Statistical Tables. *Washington, DC: Bureau of Justice Statistics. Retrieved on June 13, 2013, from http://bjs.ojp.usdoj.gov/content/pub/pdf/cvus0701.pdf.*

FEAR OF CRIME

While the actual victimization experience directly impacts a finite number of people, a much larger portion expresses a genuine fear of becoming crime victims. *Fear of crime* consists of two parts: (1) the actual odds of being victimized and (2) the subjective or perceived risk of victimization. We just used the victimization survey results to depict the objective odds of becoming a crime victim. Now it is time to turn to the second component, the subjective odds of becoming a crime victim.

Fear of crime has captured the attention of a substantial number of Americans. Many people are of the opinion that crime continues to march upward unabatedly. Figure 12.5 tracks a series of annual polls spanning the 2000–2011 period. Respondents were asked two similar questions regarding their perceptions of crime. The first item read, "Is there more crime in the U.S. than there was a year ago, or less?" The wording of the second query was, "Is there more crime in your area than there was a year ago, or less?" The graph in Figure 12.5 shows that 47% of the respondents in 2000 thought the level of crime in this country had increased compared with the previous year. By 2011, that proportion had risen to 68%. The impression was that local crime also showed a similar upward climb. In 2000, 34% of the participants indicated that crime in their area had increased compared with the previous year. By 2011, 48% of the people in the survey said local crime was on the rise.

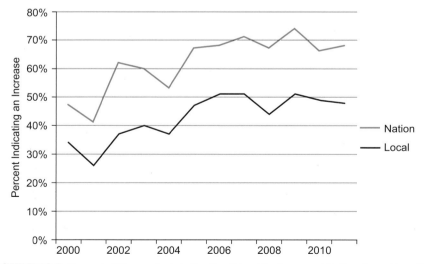

FIGURE 12.5 **Percent of Respondents Indicating Crime Has Increased Nationally and Locally by Year, 2000–2011.**

Source: Compiled by authors from K. Maguire (Ed.) (2013). Source of Criminal Justice Statistics. Albany, NY: Hindelang Criminal Justice Research Center. Retrieved on June 13, 2013, from http://www.albany. edu/sourcebook/pdf/t2332011.pdf and http://www.albany.edu/sourcebook/pdf/t2352011.pdf.

Another survey asked Americans whether they worried about a variety of possible victimization episodes. As Figure 12.6 shows, two out of every three people were apprehensive about identity theft. Slightly less than half the sample were concerned about their homes and cars being burglarized. A third expressed uneasiness about getting mugged, their children's safety at school, and acts of terrorism. One of every five respondents fretted about being sexually assaulted, murdered, or attacked while driving.

Interestingly, the level of fear (one's subjective odds) consistently outdistances both official and victimization measures of actual crime (one's objective odds). For example, Skogan and Maxfield (1981) note that while almost half of all Americans fear crime, official records show only about 6% of the population become actual crime victims. Furthermore, the annual Index Offense rates reported by the Federal Bureau of Investigation show a general decline since 2000, a trend that is also corroborated by the national victimization surveys (Truman & Planty, 2012). Thus, it appears that the American preoccupation with crime is not in sync with the actual risk of victimization.

Fear of crime is not constant across demographic groups. In general, fear is highest among urban dwellers, females, blacks, the poor, and the elderly. This elevated fear among the elderly contrasts dramatically with the fact that older persons are the least likely to become crime victims. This paradoxical discrepancy between the objective level of victimization and the subjective perception

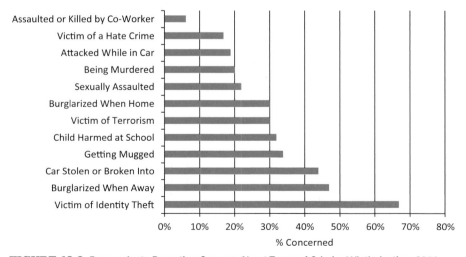

FIGURE 12.6 Respondents Reporting Concern About Types of Criminal Victimization, 2011.
Source: K. Maguire (Ed.) (2013). Sourcebook of Criminal Justice Statistics. Albany, NY: Hindelang Criminal Justice Research Center. Retrieved on June 13, 2013, from http://www.albany.edu/sourcebook/pdf/ t2392011.pdf.

about the odds of becoming a victim has attracted prolonged debate in the research community.

Explaining the Fear–Crime Paradox

One would expect that because crime against the elderly is relatively low, there should be a corresponding reduced fear of crime for that group. When the level of fear is incongruent with the supposed cause of fear (crime in this case), it becomes necessary to find alternative explanations for that fear. Attempts to explain the fear–crime differential typically fall into three related discussions. Those that deal with the way fear is measured and the issues of differences in risk and vulnerability (either real or perceived) among the elderly.

Measuring Fear

No universally accepted definition of fear has emerged in the literature. Consequently, measures of fear vary by the definition used by different researchers. Ferraro (1995) provides one of the most recognized definitions. He defines *fear of crime* as "an emotional response of dread or anxiety to crime or symbols that a person associates with crime." The key to this definition is the required emotional response from the victim. As a result, fear can be elicited by different events or situations, depending on what evokes emotions in varied individuals. The elderly, therefore, may respond as being fearful in situations that do not evoke the same response in younger respondents.

Ferraro (1995: 8) points out that fear measures often tap more than emotions. For example, many studies ask respondents to rate their assessment of safety in a specific neighborhood or area, or to provide an opinion on whether crime is increasing or decreasing over a period of time. In both of these cases, the research is tapping more of a value judgment or a person's general knowledge than any real emotional reaction to crime. The emotional component is more directly tested in surveys that ask about how much respondents worry about being victimized (Ferraro, 1995; Ferraro & LaGrange, 1988). Unfortunately, many studies claiming great fear of crime rely on questions that do not assess the emotional state of the victim. One example of those questions is the key query from the NCVS, which asks "How safe do you feel, or would you feel, being out alone in your neighborhood at night?" While bordering on an emotional response, the question is so broad and hypothetical that it would not fit Ferraro's definition.

Take a look at the graph appearing in Figure 12.7, where survey participants answered affirmatively to the question "Is there any area right around here— that is, within a mile—where you would be afraid to walk alone at night?" The black line reflects the view of people over the age of 50, while the blue line refers to respondents in the 18–20 age bracket. The material indicates that

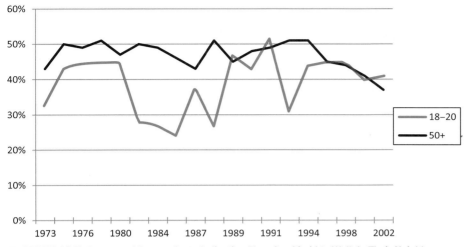

FIGURE 12.7 Percent of Respondents Indicating They Are Afraid to Walk in Their Neighborhood at Night by Age Group and Survey Year.

Source: Compiled by authors from K. Maguire (Ed.) (2013). Sourcebook of Criminal Justice Statistics. *Albany, NY: Hindelang Criminal Justice Research Center. Retrieved on June 14, 2013, from http://www. albany.edu/sourcebook/pdf/t2372011.pdf.*

the elderly have a heightened level of fear compared with the younger group. Sometimes this gap is pretty large; at other times, the lines converge. In general, though, the elderly are much more perturbed about crime.

Do Ferraro's criticisms mean that the fear data in Figure 12.7 are meaningless? Is there nothing to be gained from surveys purporting to measure fear? Does this mean that the elderly are really not fearful? In each case, the answer is no. While no definitive statement can be made about fear, what the varying measures do offer is some insight into the related issues of risk and vulnerability, at least as they are perceived by the elderly. *Risk* typically refers to the chances of becoming a victim of crime, while *vulnerability* deals more with the susceptibility to crime and the harm that accompanies victimization. In some instances, the same factors enhance both risk and vulnerability. For the elderly, there are particular risks and vulnerability factors that may help explain their inordinate fear of crime. It is to these discussions that we now turn.

Risk

Possible risk factors for the elderly include their economic resources, where they live, whether they live alone, and their diminished physical abilities. The economic status of an elderly person can have a great impact on other facets of life. Almost 3.6 million elderly individuals had household incomes below the poverty level in 2011, with another 2.4 million living below 125% of the poverty level (Administration on Aging, 2012). This equates to 14.5% of the elderly U.S. population. Indeed, the median income in 2011 for elderly persons was $27,707 for males and $15,362 for females (Administration on Aging, 2012).

Dour economic conditions often dictate that many elderly live in older, deteriorating neighborhoods; in areas that are more ethnically diverse due to turnover of older homes to younger tenants; and in neighborhoods with more transient populations. These types of neighborhoods are often very crime-prone. They frequently attract deviants as residents and draw outsiders who commit crime. The prevalence of crime in these areas, whether directed against the elderly or not, exacerbates feelings of fear and loss of safety among the aged (McCoy et al., 1996).

Additionally, many senior citizens lack financial reserves and live in homes needing repairs. To the extent that confidence games play a role in the level of crime, older people living in rundown housing may respond more favorably to offers of seemingly "bargain" repairs. Economic factors also may force the elderly to walk or to use public transportation, which may increase both real and perceived risks of victimization.

The fact that many elderly people live alone also increases risk by making them more suitable crime targets. Roughly 28% of all older Americans reside by themselves, with 36% of women and 19% of men over the age of 65 living alone (Administration on Aging, 2012). Dealing with a single individual lessens both resistance and chances of identification of intruders. There appears to be a relationship between living alone and victimization. The 2011 NCVS shows that people who were never married, divorced, or separated have much higher violent victimization rates than people who are married or widowed (Truman & Planty, 2012).

The generally diminished physical abilities of the elderly also contribute to actual and perceived risk. If the offender is a young male, an elderly victim is at a clear physical disadvantage. In terms of violent crime victims who were aged 65 or older, 73% of their offenders were strangers and 19% of their lone assailants were under 20 years old, compared with 68% when there were multiple offenders (U.S. Department of Justice, 2010b). Both the anonymity of offenders and the age differential serve to enhance the fears of the elderly.

Going beyond simply identifying potential risk factors, Stafford and Galle (1984) have considered exposure to risk in assessing fear of crime. They argue that the elderly are overly victimized given their exposure to risk. Stafford and Galle (1984) claim that by adjusting the level of fear in terms of the degree to which different demographic groups are exposed to victimization opportunities, the discrepancy between fear and victimization greatly diminishes. In the study, the elderly still express higher levels of fear than expected, but not to the great extent found in other studies. Ward, LaGory, and Sherman (1986) present similar evidence that fear is related to the differential risk introduced by varying environmental situations. Warr (1984), however, cautions that fear cannot be totally explained by differences in risk. Age continues to play a role in the level of fear even after accommodations are made for differential risk.

Vulnerability

Because risk alone does not completely explain the level of fear among the elderly, vulnerability helps round out the picture. *Vulnerability* refers to the ease of being victimized and the impact the crime has upon the victim. The assumption is that people who would suffer the greatest pain or loss from a victimization episode will be the most fearful. For the elderly, vulnerability is a key concern. Among the many factors that increase elder vulnerability are physical attributes, financial concerns, and social connections.

Declining physical strength and increasing health problems contribute much to a sense of vulnerability. Only 44% of the elderly rate their health as excellent or very good, and almost all elderly individuals have at least one chronic health condition (Administration on Aging, 2012). The most common chronic ailments are hypertension (72% of the elderly), arthritis (51%), heart disease (31%), and cancer (24%) (Administration on Aging, 2012). The National Center for Health Statistics (2012) reports that older people are more likely to contend with eyesight and hearing impairments, visit physicians, utilize hospital outpatient departments, and require emergency services more often, and account for a disproportionate share of health care expenditures in this country.

These medical facts suggest that the elderly are not as capable as younger persons of warding off physical attacks, are likely to be more prone to injury, and are in need of more medical assistance than other segments of the population. Data from victim surveys support this point. For example, the likelihood of injury and medical attention because of a crime increases with victim age (Bachman & Meloy, 2008; U.S. Department of Justice, 2010b). It is not unusual for crime-related injuries to aggravate pre-existing health problems (Burt & Katz, 1985).

Economic liability often accompanies criminal victimization. The elderly have reduced incomes. Much of that money is derived from fixed sources, such as Social Security, pension funds, and investments (Administration on Aging, 2012). Any loss, no matter how small, can be burdensome to the elderly. Many elderly cannot afford more medical expenses, insurance premiums, and property replacement costs.

Besides such tangible factors as physical harm and economic losses, social isolation can compound the impact of victimization. As we have discussed elsewhere in this text, social support is an important part of coping with the aftermath of crime. This is no less true for the elderly. Older victims who suffer physical injury may need assistance with normal daily activities during their recuperation. They may also need help repairing damaged property, shopping for replacement goods, or straightening up the mess left by intruders. Sometimes victims blame themselves for the crime. Social support is important for placing the event in its proper perspective and alleviating any feelings of guilt. The presence of a support network can also help the victim realize that the world is not all bad, and that the victimization should not be the central focus of what to expect in the future.

Many elderly do not have access to a suitable support system. A number of factors contribute to the social isolation of the elderly. First, the transience of today's society means that the families of the elderly are scattered around the country, often due to employment requirements. Second, old age often brings the death of one's spouse and friends, which results in living alone. Third, due to economics, many elderly live in transient and ethnically diverse neighborhoods. Any one, or a combination, of these factors can make a person feel lonely and isolated. A victimization experience can further fuel these feelings. Social isolation, therefore, intensifies the physical and economic impacts by reducing one's sense of well-being.

Vicarious Victimization

The sustained interest in crime against the elderly is also a result of the influence of the mass media. Victimologists refer to this phenomenon as *vicarious victimization*. People who have had no actual victimization experiences themselves become acutely aware of others who were preyed upon by criminals. The receiver absorbs this information and speculates that "it could have happened to me." This indirect attribution heightens one's fearfulness, even though the actual odds of victimization may be remote.

Patterns of television viewing and newspaper consumption, both of which portray a great deal of sensationalistic reports, contribute to fear of crime. Victimization of the elderly has emerged as an issue that commands media attention. Different media routinely present stories or issue warnings about con artists operating scams on area residents, particularly the elderly. Despite the relative rarity of crimes against the elderly, the prominence they receive in the media propels them into the consciousness of the general public.

ELDER ABUSE AND NEGLECT

Like victimology in general, it is only recently that abuse and neglect of the elderly have surfaced as topics worthy of study. Some observers credit Steinmetz (1978) with introducing the idea of *elder abuse* into contemporary focus. This is not to say that maltreatment of the elderly did not exist prior to this time. There have always been tensions between the young and the old that have resulted in various forms of mistreatment.

An examination of pre-modern Western society shows that disagreements over property rights resulted in physical conflict, including death, between parents and their offspring. Pre-industrial American parents often used economic power to control their adult children, leading to strained family relationships (Steinmetz, 1988). Due to this economic bondage, children often despised and isolated their parents, waiting until such a time that they could rid themselves of the parent. The idea that the young have always venerated their elders down through the ages is a myth.

Family patterns changed during the Industrial Revolution (Stearns, 1986). There were fewer households mixing different generations under the same roof. Retirement support systems made their debut, reducing the financial dependency of the older generation on younger family members. Better economic situations also made medical care more accessible. A new industry of caregivers, such as geriatric nurses and social workers, made it possible for people outside the immediate family to provide suitable alternative living arrangements. All these factors spelled a period of relative calm between parents and their grown children. More than likely, it is this ebb that accounted for the lack of attention paid to abuse and neglect of the aged.

Defining the Problem

While many commentators point to elder abuse and neglect as a problem, there is little agreement on exactly what constitutes abuse and neglect. A number of problems appear in attempts to provide a definition of abuse/neglect. First, many definitions fail to distinguish abuse from neglect. As we explained in the chapter on child maltreatment, many researchers view abuse as a more active form—and neglect as a more passive form—of mistreatment. Second, some definitions require the perpetrator to act with "intent." They ignore the possibility of abuse or neglect that is unintentional yet still problematic for the victim. Instead, harm may be the result of the failure of a caregiver to provide for needs of the victim. Third, some definitions assume that the victim must depend upon the perpetrator for physical or mental care. One might construe this feature as a legal requirement to provide care before an act is considered abuse. It also ignores the possibility that a perpetrator may be dependent on the victim and commits abusive acts as a means of exerting power. Finally, some definitions include the idea of self-neglect. Many writers, however, view self-neglect as a distinctly different problem from abuse and neglect inflicted by a third party.

The National Research Council (2003: 40) undertook an analysis of the state of the evidence on elder abuse and offered the following definition of elder mistreatment:

> "Elder mistreatment" . . . refer[s] to (a) intentional actions that cause harm or create a serious risk of harm (whether or not harm is intended) to a vulnerable elder by a caregiver or other person who stands in a trust relationship to the elder or (b) failure by a caregiver to satisfy the elder's basic needs or to protect the elder from harm.

This definition excludes self-neglect and victimization by strangers. While both of these situations are of interest, they are significantly different from the remaining actions that are encompassed by the definition. The definition includes a wide array of behaviors committed by family members and other caregivers (such as staff at nursing homes), both intentionally and unintentionally, against an elderly individual.

The definition offered above, like many definitions of abuse and neglect, includes a wide range of diverse types of maltreatment, with varying degrees of agreement among users. For example, the term *physical abuse* can mean different things to different people. Few would disagree that physical attacks against the elderly represent abuse, particularly when perpetrated by someone who is responsible for the victim's well-being. However, some consider the deliberate withholding of care as physical abuse, while others might call the same act "neglect" (Wolf & Pillemer, 1989). Even when researchers do separate abuse from neglect, they may disagree on the contents of each (Galbraith, 1989). This definitional ambiguity hampers discussion of the issues and the comparison of findings from one study to the next.

Table 12.4 contains a breakdown of various forms of elder abuse and neglect outlined by the National Center on Elder Abuse. These categories are fairly representative of those found in past research and various state laws. In this categorization, the distinction between abuse and neglect relies mainly on whether the offender is a caretaker of the victim. The failure of a caretaker to fulfill that role generally results in a determination that neglect, either active or passive, is present. Abuse, on the other hand, does not rest on an obligation to provide care. That is, anyone can commit an abusive act. One can divide abuse further into various categories of physical, psychological/emotional, and material exploitation.

WEB ACTIVITY

Combating the problem of elder abuse and neglect requires a multi-faceted approach. One umbrella organization that aims to coordinate policy and program delivery is the National Center of Elder Abuse located at **http://www.ncea.aoa.gov/**

> **Table 12.4** Forms of Elder Abuse and Neglect
>
> The following types of abuse are commonly accepted as the major categories of elder mistreatment:
>
> - **Physical Abuse**—Inflicting, or threatening to inflict, physical pain or injury on a vulnerable elder, or depriving them of a basic need.
> - **Emotional Abuse**—Inflicting mental pain, anguish, or distress on an elder person through verbal or nonverbal acts.
> - **Sexual Abuse**—Non-consensual sexual contact of any kind, coercing an elder to witness sexual behaviors.
> - **Exploitation**—Illegal taking, misuse, or concealment of funds, property, or assets of a vulnerable elder.
> - **Neglect**—Refusal or failure by those responsible to provide food, shelter, health care or protection for a vulnerable elder.
> - **Abandonment**—The desertion of a vulnerable elder by anyone who has assumed the responsibility for care or custody of that person.
>
> *Source: National Center on Elder Abuse (2013a). What Is Abuse? Orange, CA: Administration on Aging, Department of Health and Human Services. Retrieved on June 14, 2013, from http://www.ncea.aoa.gov/faq/index.aspx.*

Today, most researchers rely on categorizations of abuse and neglect rather than viewing them as a single concept. However, these categorizations do not resolve all definitional problems. Using the categories in Table 12.4 as an example, one can find several apparent problems. First, the components of a caretaking "obligation" are not always clear. Who decides an individual's obligation? What actions are required, as opposed to being simply "nice to do?" Second, some actions may cause more than one type of maltreatment. For example, physically striking an individual can engender fear and intimidation (i.e., psychological abuse) as well as physical abuse. Similarly, material exploitation deprives the victim of his or her property and may also result in an inability to provide needed care (i.e., neglect). Finally, because much research is based on official records of various government and social service agencies, the categories may not correspond to the legal classifications used to define the problem at that location. It is apparent that definitional problems are an unresolved issue in the study of elder abuse. As a result, we will remind the reader of these issues whenever they affect issues discussed in the chapter.

THE INCIDENCE OF ELDER MALTREATMENT

Identifying just how much mistreatment of the elderly takes place is not an easy undertaking. The National Research Council (2003) points out several weaknesses that permeate attempts to enumerate the extent of elder abuse and neglect. Among the problems found throughout both published and unpublished reports are unclear and inconsistent definitions, unclear and inadequate measures, incomplete professional counts, lack of population-based data, and a lack of prospective data.

The first two problems are relatively easy to understand and simply point out that the study of elder maltreatment has yet to embrace a single definition of abuse and neglect and, as a consequence, tends to use a wide array of different measures when trying to count the extent of abuse/neglect. The problem of "incomplete professional counts" refers to the fact that many attempts to count abuse/neglect rely on the reports of a select group of individuals or agencies. Thus, the results of those counts basically provide anecdotal evidence rather than reliable counts of the problem. The "lack of population-based data" is a similar problem in that, even when an attempt to undertake a broad-based study is made, the results are not necessarily representative of the entire population. Finally, the prospective data issue deals with the fact that most counts are based on a review of already collected records and primarily reflect the actions of the agencies. What is needed is to identify a population of elderly individuals and trace their experiences (prospectively) over time in order to uncover the maltreatment they experience.

Beyond the problems noted by the National Research Council, measures of maltreatment may be hampered by the unwillingness and inability of elders to report their victimization. Older adults may be reluctant to report instances of abuse or neglect for a number of reasons (Acierno, 2003; Payne, 2011). First, the perpetrators of elder abuse are often family members. The victim may want to protect the offender or regard the situation as a private matter not meant for outside viewing. The victim, therefore, may be unwilling to notify anyone. Second, the victim may think that he or she somehow contributed to the situation and, therefore, is at fault. Third, the victim may fear retribution by the offender if the victim reports the abuse. Additionally, the victims may feel embarrassed for allowing the victimization to occur, or may feel stigmatized as a result of reporting the incident. Reporting of abuse may also be impeded by a victim's physical inability to report the event. Eyesight problems, hearing loss, speech impediments, or memory loss can all make reporting problematic. Other reasons why elderly victims may be reluctant to contact authorities are the fact that victims may depend on the offender for daily care and support, or the victim simply does not recognize the abuse as such or, as often happens in financial theft, may not be aware of what has happened. Given these possible influences on reporting behavior, it is safe to conclude that reported estimates mark the lower boundaries of elder abuse and neglect.

The National Research Council (2003) claimed that between one and two million members of the senior population have been the victim of some form of abuse. Projections from other studies reveal that this figure is not farfetched (Pillemer & Finkelhor, 1988; Tatara & Cyphers, 1998), although the actual figure may extend as high as 2.5 million victims (Hudson, 1988). The National Center on Elder Abuse (NCEA) has conducted several studies on the extent of abuse/neglect.

In 2004 the NCEA surveyed Adult Protective Services (APS) agencies in all 50 states. *Adult Protective Services* are those "services provided to elders and

Table 12.5 Reports of Abuse of Persons Age 60+ to Adult Protective Services, 2004

Estimated Total Number	381,430	
Estimated Rate per 1,000	8.3	
Cases Received	253,426	(32 states)
Investigated Cases	192,243	(20 states)
Substantiated Cases	88,455	(24 states)

Source: Constructed by authors from Teaster, P. B., et al. (2007). The 2004 Survey of State Adult Protective Services: Abuse of Adults 18 Years of Age and Older. *Washington, DC: National Center on Elder Abuse, pp. 19–20. Retrieved on June 15, 2013, from http://www.ncea.aoa. gov/Resources/Publication/docs/APS_2004NCEASurvey.pdf.*

to vulnerable adults with disabilities who are, or who are in danger of, being abused, neglected, or financially exploited, who are unable to protect themselves, or who have no one to adequately assist them" (Teaster et al., 2007: 36). These agencies are the clearinghouse for information/data on elder abuse in all states. The NCEA estimates that there were 381,430 cases of abuse in 2004 giving a rate of 8.3 cases for every 1,000 persons age 60 and over (see Table 12.5). While these numbers are lower than other figures, it is important to note that these instances reflect only those cases reported to specific government agencies or officials. In relation to the earlier figures, official data appear to include a small minority of all cases.

The NCEA study also provides some insight into the various types of abuse and neglect. Relying on data for only substantiated cases reported to APS agencies, Figure 12.8 shows that the most common type of mistreatment is self-neglect (37% of cases). Caregiver neglect accounts for another 20% of the cases, while emotional/psychological/verbal abuse and financial/material exploitation each appear in 15% of all cases. Interestingly, physical abuse appears in only one out of 10 cases of elder maltreatment. These data suggest that perhaps the most easily recognized form of abuse (i.e., physical abuse) is less common than types of maltreatment that may be easier to hide from view.

Besides looking at simple raw numbers, many reports offer estimates of the prevalence of abuse in the elderly population. A recent national estimate places the number of victims at slightly more than 10% of the aged population (Acierno et al., 2010). Similarly, a self-report study of New York state residents puts the annual incidence at 7.6% of the elderly population (Lachs, Psaty, Psaty, & Berman, 2011). Another confirmation of this level emerges from a South Carolina survey (Amstadter et al., 2011; Begle et al., 2011). Obviously, the "golden years" are full of trials and tribulations for some elderly Americans.

While there may seem to be some consistency across studies in the reported levels of elder abuse, there are many factors that one should keep in mind

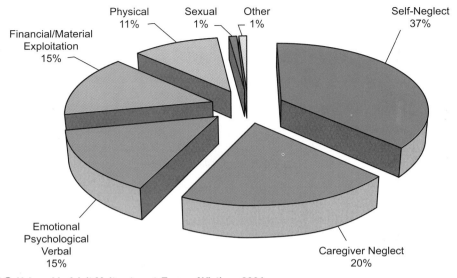

FIGURE 12.8 Vulnerable Adult Maltreatment: Types of Victims, 2004.

Source: Adapted from Teaster, P. B., et al. (2007). The 2004 Survey of State Adult Protective Services: Abuse of Vulnerable Adults 18 Years of Age and Older. *Washington, DC: National Center on Elder Abuse, p. 25. Retrieved on June 15, 2013, from http://www.ncea.aoa. gov/Resources/Publication/docs/APS_2004NCEASurvey.pdf.*

when considering the extent of maltreatment. Many social service providers and researchers claim that these estimates grossly underreport the actual level of maltreatment. The greatest difficulty with many estimates is that most are based on official statistics, and, as you may recall from Chapter 2, official statistics require notification by the victim or someone else. Hence, the dark figure of crime is a looming problem.

INSTITUTIONAL MALTREATMENT

The living situation of the victim plays an important role in determining possible correlates of elder abuse and neglect. While many people might think that strangers commit most of the elder abuse and that they do so in impersonal institutional surroundings, such is not the case. Indeed, most senior citizens do not even live in institutions. Only 3.6% of the elderly reside in nursing homes or other institutional settings, although the number increases greatly with age (Administration on Aging, 2012). An inspection of the raw numbers reveals that there are approximately 1.5 million persons living in licensed nursing homes (Administration on Aging, 2012). Consequently, while only a small percentage of elders are at risk of being mistreated in these facilities, there are many elderly at risk on any given day.

Extent of Institutional Maltreatment

Unfortunately, there has been very little study of elder maltreatment in residential facilities. What data do exist, however, suggest that abuse and neglect are not uncommon. Pillemer and Moore (1989), surveying staff in nursing homes, report that more than one-third of the respondents witnessed at least one episode of physical abuse, while 8 out of 10 saw incidents of verbal or psychological abuse in a 12-month period. Interestingly, 10% admitted committing physical abuse themselves, and 40% admitted verbal/psychological abuse. MacDonald (2002) notes that 58% of nursing home staff witnessed other staff yelling at residents; 11% witnessed staff threatening residents; 21% saw residents being pushed or shoved; and 12% observed staff slapping residents. The most common form of physical abuse is the use of excessive restraints (MacDonald, 2002).

One problem with staff surveys is that they often focus on reports of witnessing mistreatment. What may occur in these studies is that a large number of respondents may observe the same events, thus resulting in a larger percentage of respondents reporting the abuse. This deficiency is demonstrated to some degree by the fact that self-reports of inflicting abuse in the same studies is smaller than the figures for witnessing maltreatment. Surveys of residents and their families are an alternative means of gauging maltreatment in the institutions. Data from a survey of a Georgia nursing home residents and their families reveal that 44% of the respondents reported physical abuse, while 48% reported rough treatment on the part of the staff (Atlanta Long-Term Care Ombudsman Program, 2000). A Michigan survey suggests that older adults undergo *poly-victimization*. That is, elderly persons who experience one type of abuse are also likely to be victims of multiple forms of maltreatment (Post et al., 2010).

Theft is another form of abuse believed to be very common in institutional settings. While most of the evidence is anecdotal or based on the impressions of workers in nursing homes (see, for example, Harris, 1999; Harris & Benson, 1996), one survey of nursing home employees found that 4% admitted to theft, and 10% observed other employees stealing from residents (Harris & Benson, 1996). In one survey of patients, 50% claimed to have had property stolen from their room (Kruzich, Clinton, & Kelber, 1992). Other forms of institutional abuse involve fraudulent medical billings, unnecessary physical or chemical restraint, and social isolation.

While these limited survey data suggest that maltreatment is common in institutional settings, few nursing homes or residential care facilities are cited for such behavior. Doty and Sullivan (1983) noted that only 7% of the nursing homes in the United States were reprimanded for abuse in 1980. A report of the U.S. House of Representatives found that only 10% of nursing homes were cited for actual harm to residents over a two-year time period (Hawes, 2003). A U.S. General Accounting Office (GAO) review (2002) found that only one of 26 audited facilities in Illinois had incurred a civil monetary penalty. These figures are significantly smaller than those found in surveys of staff or residents. One reason for this discrepancy may be that the events are not being reported to the authorities or oversight agencies in the different jurisdictions.

WEB ACTIVITY

The Centers for Medicare and Medicaid Services (CMS) have a goal of ensuring that Americans receive appropriate health care. A visit to that website, **http://www.cms.gov/**, will enable you to see what concerns CMS address.

Another possible reason for the low numbers of cases in official abuse reports may be the fact that many events are simply not reported in a timely enough fashion, thus resulting in a determination that the event was unfounded (Payne & Fletcher, 2005). This is the position taken by the General Accounting Office (2002). Despite the fact that the Centers for Medicare and Medicaid Services (the oversight agency for nursing homes) mandates various reporting guidelines for abuse and neglect allegations, the GAO notes that most state agencies are not promptly notified in accordance with regulations. Indeed, almost two-thirds of the reports are made two or more days after the required deadline (GAO, 2002). This delay is problematic because it makes it difficult, if not impossible, for the investigating agencies to undertake a meaningful investigation. After a delay it is often difficult to talk to witnesses, the witnesses or victims cannot recall the event clearly, or the evidence is no longer available for the police or other investigators. Based on these findings, the GAO (2002) made several recommendations to improve the identification and investigation of abuse in residential settings (see Table 12.6).

In response to these suggestions, Medicare and Medicaid officials have embarked upon a series of routine on-site inspections aimed at improving the quality of care provided by nursing homes (GAO, 2011a). This activity includes interviews with staff, talking with residents, observation of staff members as they perform their duties, and a review of medical records and other documentation. Other oversight efforts involve more intensive monitoring of nursing homes that exhibit chronic deficiencies (GAO, 2010) and substandard facilities purchased by for-profit groups (GAO, 2011b). The hope, of course, is that these efforts will provide a more suitable environment for Americans during their "golden years."

Causes of Institutional Maltreatment

What factors contribute to abuse in settings that, at least nominally, exist to care for the well-being of the elderly? Pillemer (1988) offers a model containing four interrelated sets of factors. The first of these are *exogenous factors*, which reflect the influence of the larger community on institutional operations. For example, a relatively small number of nursing homes and available

---

Table 12.6 GAO Recommendations for Protecting Nursing Home Residents

- Ensure that state survey agencies immediately notify local law enforcement agencies or Medicaid Fraud Control Units when nursing homes report allegations of resident physical or sexual abuse or when the survey agency has confirmed complaints of alleged abuse.

- Accelerate the agency's [Centers for Medicare and Medicaid Services] education campaign on reporting nursing home abuse by (1) distributing its new poster with clearly displayed complaint telephone numbers and (2) requiring state survey agencies to ensure that these numbers are prominently listed in local telephone directories.

- Systematically assess state policies and practices for complying with the federal requirement to prohibit employment of individuals convicted of abusing nursing home residents and, if necessary, develop more specific guidance to ensure compliance.

- Clarify the definition of abuse and otherwise ensure that states apply that definition consistently and appropriately.

- Shorten the state survey agencies' time frames for determining whether to include findings of abuse in nurse aide registry files.

Source: U.S. Government Accountability Office (2002). Nursing Homes: More Can Be Done to Protect Residents from Abuse. *Washington, DC: U.S. General Accounting Office, p. 27. Retrieved on June 28, 2013, from http://www.gao.gov/products/ GAO-02-312.*

---

beds mean that clients have few choices and that poor quality facilities will still be in demand. Similarly, low unemployment in the community may result in fewer qualified workers available for employment in these settings (Bennett et al., 1997).

The *nursing home environment* is a second source from which maltreatment may arise. Institutions that have a custodial orientation and fail to emphasize resident needs will tend to have greater levels of abuse. Similarly, poor supervision, low staff-to-patient ratios, lower pay, and high staff turnover can all contribute to less concern for the elderly patient. As one health care worker explained:

> You see the staff outside smoking cigarettes and the little old ladies wandering the halls just looking for somebody (DeHart, Webb, & Cornman, 2009: 364).

A third area of potential concern involves *staff characteristics*. Pillemer (1988) notes that younger staff members and those with less education tend to show less concern for the elderly. These individuals take a more custodial view toward their duties. Workers who experience higher levels of stress and burn-out also contribute to the incidence of abuse (Harris, 1999).

The final category of factors reflects *patient characteristics*. Elderly patients who are in poor health and have poor or deteriorating social abilities pose additional challenges and place greater demands on institutional staff. A sizeable number of nursing home residents suffer from some form of dementia, making the patient more resistant to care. Consequently, some staff may respond in inappropriate ways. Look at one situation a health care worker relayed to researchers:

> I came in one day, and there was a little man out here with a bucket
> and a mop. . . . The staff member gave him the bucket for urinating in
> the corner. [The staff member] was making [the resident] clean it up.
> And I'm thinking this [staff member] might think that, "Well, if he does
> that, I'll make sure he cleans it up and then that will teach him not to
> do it again." Someone's not going to learn not to urinate in the corner.
> They wouldn't be here anyway if they were able to not urinate in the
> corner (DeHart et al., 2009: 371).

A patient who tends to wander the halls, for example, may be subjected to bed restraints as a means of controlling the behavior. Exacerbating the incidence of abuse may be the social isolation of an elder. The absence of visitors means that abuse and neglect can take place with little chance of discovery. For example:

> The feeding issue is always a problem, particularly if they can't feed
> themselves . . . it would take an hour to an hour-and-a-half to feed [the
> resident] and not force feed her. Or [the staff member] just say, "to
> hell with it" and go to Ensure or put in a stomach tube (DeHart et al.,
> 2009: 364).

Table 12.7 displays various signs or indicators of potential abuse in institutions. Different indicators correspond to different forms of maltreatment. Financial exploitation may be indicated by missing property, the inability of the residents to purchase essentials, and/or the misappropriation of a resident's allowance. Signs of physical abuse include unexplained injuries or bruises, poor hygiene, unexplained accidents, or the need for excessive or repeated medication. A lack of basic amenities or inadequate resources could reveal a state of neglect. Heightened anxiety, agitation, withdrawal or fear, isolation from other patients or visitors, and unkempt residents may indicate emotional abuse.

 WEB ACTIVITY

Florida is a retirement destination for many people after they leave the work force. The State of Florida recognizes the economic impact this group has and the special needs that develop with the aging process. The Florida Agency for Health Care Administration, which you can visit at **http://ahca.myflorida.com/**, represents one way in which the elderly are protected.

Responding to Institutional Maltreatment

Most jurisdictions have passed legislation specifically to address the incidence of institutional abuse and neglect. Ohio, for example, prohibits any "person who owns, operates, or administers, or who is an agent or employee of, a care facility" from committing abuse or neglect "against a resident or patient of the facility" (*Ohio Revised Code*, 2013, § 2903.34). The onus for investigating and enforcing criminal violations of this law falls on the state attorney general, not local law enforcement. Claims for civil liability can be handled at either the state or local level. At the federal level, the 1987 Nursing Home Reform Act outlines various forms of prohibited activity,

Table 12.7 Warning Signs of Elder Abuse

Financial Exploitation

- Lack of affordable amenities and comforts in an elder's home.
- Giving uncharacteristically excessive gifts or financial reimbursement for needed care and companionship.
- A caregiver has control of an elder's money but fails to provide for the elder's needs.
- An older adult has signed property transfers (power of attorney or will, for example) but is unable to comprehend what the transaction means.

Physical Abuse

- Inadequately explained fractures, bruises, welts, cuts, sores, or burns.
- Unexplained sexually transmitted diseases.

Neglect

- Lack of basic hygiene or appropriate clothing.
- Lack of food.
- Lack of medical aids (e.g., glasses, walker, dentures, hearing aid, or medications).
- Person with dementia left unsupervised.
- Person confined in bed is left without care.
- Home is cluttered, dirty, or in disrepair.
- Home lacks adequate facilities (stove, refrigerator, heating and cooling, plumbing, or electricity).
- Untreated bed sores or pressure ulcers.

Emotional Abuse

- Unexplained or uncharacteristic changes in behavior, such as withdrawal from normal activities, or unexplained changes in alertness.
- Caregiver isolates the elder (doesn't let anyone in the home or speak to the elder).
- Caregiver is verbally aggressive or demeaning, controlling, or uncaring.

Source: Adapted from National Center on Elder Abuse (2013b). Warning Signs of Elder Abuse. Orange, CA: Administration on Aging, Department of Health and Human Services. Retrieved on June 28, 2013, from http://www.aoa.gov/AoA_Programs/ Elder_Rights/YEAP/docs/Fact%20Sheets/AoA-119%20YEAP%20InfoFact%20Sheets_WarningSigns%28nm%291.4c.508.pdf.

including abuse, neglect, and the unwarranted use of restraints. More recently, as noted earlier, the GAO (2002) made suggestions for improving the reporting and investigation of abuse in residential facilities as a first step to addressing this problem. As Table 12.8 demonstrates, there is also a growing awareness that nursing home residents have the right to certain expectations.

RESPONDING TO ELDER MALTREATMENT

Societal response to elder abuse and neglect is still very much in the developmental stages. Only within the past two decades or so has formal legislation dealt specifically with the rights and needs of older Americans. The Family Violence Prevention and Treatment Act of 1984 was perhaps the earliest legislation to prohibit elder abuse. In the same year, amendments to the Older Americans Act mandated that states assess the need for abuse services, identify

---

Table 12.8 Rights of Florida Nursing Home Residents

Each resident shall have the right to:

- Civil and religious liberties.
- Private and uncensored communication.
- Visitation by any individual.
- Organize and participate in resident groups.
- Participate in social, religious, and community activities.
- Examine results of recent facility inspections.
- Manage his/her own financial affairs.
- Be fully informed, in writing and orally, of services available at the facility.
- Refuse medication and treatment and to know the consequences.
- Receive adequate and appropriate health care.
- Privacy in treatment and in caring for personal needs.
- Be informed of medical condition and proposed treatment.
- Be treated courteously, fairly, and with the fullest measure of dignity.
- Be free from mental and physical abuse, corporal punishment, and from physical and chemical restraints except those ordered by resident's physician.
- Choose physician and pharmacy.
- Retain and use personal clothing and possessions.
- Have copies of rules and regulations of the facility.

Source: Adapted from Florida's Long-Term Care Ombudsman Program (2010). Resident's Rights. Tallahassee: Florida Department of Elder Affairs. Retrieved on June 27, 2013, from http://ombudsman.myflorida.com/ResidentsRights.php.

---

existing programs, and address the problem of elder abuse (Rinkle, 1989). The reauthorization of the Older Americans Act in 1993 included new initiatives dealing with the protection of the elderly, including an ombudsman program, abuse and neglect prevention programs, and legal assistance. Of course, the impact of these initiatives will have to be assessed in the future. Amid the growing number of legislative initiatives, perhaps the most noteworthy and successful has been the promotion of mandatory elder abuse reporting laws.

Mandatory Reporting

At first glance, it appears reasonable to assume that mandatory reporting is a good first step in dealing with elder maltreatment. Interestingly, however, there has been a great deal of resistance to mandatory reporting and numerous criticisms of these efforts. Most states now have some form of mandatory reporting law for abuse that, either implicitly or explicitly, covers elder maltreatment. As noted earlier, the Centers for Medicare and Medicaid Services mandates several procedures that facilities receiving federal funds and reimbursement for services must follow, and these regulations require reporting of abuse and neglect to state-level agencies.

Table 12.9 offers excerpts from Florida law governing the mandatory reporting of elder abuse. A couple of important observations can be drawn from the contents. First, reporting requirements are restricted primarily to public employees or employees of agencies that would most likely have contact with potential

Table 12.9 Mandatory Reporting Provisions in Florida

Any person, including, but not limited to, any:
1. Physician, osteopathic physician, medical examiner, chiropractic physician, nurse, paramedic, emergency medical technician, or hospital personnel engaged in the admission, examination, care, or treatment of vulnerable adults.
2. Health professional or mental health professional … .
3. Practitioner who relies solely on spiritual means of healing.
4. Nursing home staff; assisted living facility staff; adult day care center staff; adult family-care home staff; social worker; or other professional adult care, residential, or institutional staff.
5. State, county, or municipal criminal justice employee or law enforcement officer.
6. Any employee of the Department of Business and Professional Regulation conducting inspections of public lodging establishments … .
7. Florida advocacy council member or long-term care ombudsman council member; or who knows, or has reasonable cause to suspect, that a vulnerable adult has been or is being abused, neglected, or exploited shall immediately report such knowledge or suspicion to the central abuse hotline.

Source: Florida Statutes *(2012), § 415.1034.*

victims. Persons not included in these categories have no legal obligation to make a report of suspected abuse. Second, the specificity of who must report suspected abuse varies somewhat from state to state. In Florida, bank employees and inspectors of public lodging establishments must report. Third, although Table 12.9 does not display this information, the "good faith standard" we encountered in the child maltreatment chapter is also extended to elder maltreatment. Finally, all privileged communications (i.e., doctor–patient, husband–wife, etc.), with the exceptions of lawyer–client and clergy–penitent, are rescinded in cases of elder maltreatment (*Florida Statutes*, 2012, § 415.1045(3)).

The greatest criticism of such efforts has been that they do little more than encourage reporting. Often, these reporting laws fail to define elder abuse and neglect, to identify to whom maltreatment is to be reported, to impose penalties for failure to report abuse, and to outline what to do with the reports once they are made (Blakely & Dolon, 1991; Payne, 2011; Quinn & Tomita, 1997; Roger & Ursel, 2009; Thobaben, 1989). A number of other problems also have been identified with mandatory reporting laws. First, the laws typically deal only with the reporting of abuse and fail to provide resources to follow up on the reports, or to do something about the problem (Anetzberger, 1989). Second, critics claim that these laws intrude into the privacy of the individual. The best example of this contention involves laws requiring physicians to report suspected cases of abuse, which critics contend violates client–physician confidentiality (Crystal, 1986; Macolini, 1995; Rodriguez et al., 2006). Third, mandatory reporting is seen as reinforcing ageism by focusing on the victim rather than the offender (Anetzberger, 1989; Payne, 2011; Quinn, 1990; Quinn & Tomita, 1997). *Ageism* refers to stereotyping all older individuals as being in need of protection and treating them differently because of their age. These laws identify the victim of maltreatment and often prompt reactions that may include removing the victim from the home or blaming the victim for the abuse, rather than focusing on the perpetrator (Crystal, 1986). Fourth, there is a need to create public awareness campaigns that inform social service workers and the general populace about elder maltreatment (Gironda et al., 2010; Roger & Ursel, 2009). A fifth criticism is that these efforts place the elderly into a category with children, the mentally ill, and others who are incapable of making decisions for themselves. These laws, therefore, fail to treat the elderly as adults and, consequently, degrade the elderly victim.

The move toward greater protection for the elderly is evident in the introduction passage of the Elder Justice Act, which President Obama signed into law on March 23, 2010. The Act contains a variety of provisions. Central to the bill are the detection, prevention, and prosecution of elder abuse. Also included is the establishment of an Advisory Board on Elder Abuse, Neglect, and Exploitation within the Office of the Secretary of Health and Human Services, which mandates the collection and dissemination of data on elder maltreatment, creates an infrastructure at the federal and state levels for addressing elder maltreatment, takes steps to improve long-term care, and requires screening of employees of nursing facilities. As you can see, the intent and the breadth of these provisions point to the increasing concern over elder abuse and neglect.

Social Service Provision

One expected outcome of mandatory reporting laws and other legislation is that social service professionals will be alerted to the problem and will take appropriate actions. Surveys of various social service professionals reveal that nurses, social workers, and the clergy are among those who most often deal with, and who are most knowledgeable about, elder maltreatment (Anderson, 1989; Dolon & Hendricks, 1989). Interestingly, while one might assume that the police would be a primary source of immediate contact and aid, law enforcement is minimally involved—even when mandated to receive reports of abuse (Dolon & Hendricks, 1989; Fiegener, Fiegener, & Meszaros, 1989). The relative lack of police involvement may be due to the fact that often the most common form of maltreatment identified by social service workers is self-neglect (Burnett et al., 2006; Fiegener et al., 1989; Payne & Gainey, 2005; Poythress et al., 2006). The questionable legal status of self-neglect serves to remove the police from the equation.

Beyond identifying which social service workers are most involved in dealing with elder abuse, research has surveyed these professionals about their views of service needs. The need for additional training in elder abuse issues is perhaps the most common response (Blakely & Dolon, 1991; DeHart et al., 2009; Dolon & Blakely, 1989; Fiegener et al., 1989; Gironda et al., 2010; Payne, 2010). A second commonly expressed opinion is that there is room for more and improved resources to deal with abuse. Blakely and Dolon (1991), based

on a national survey, identify a number of other needs, including greater cooperation between agencies (see Figure 12.9), more public awareness, increased
numbers of staff to deal with elder abuse, and stronger elder abuse legislation.
What these responses tell us is that social service efforts to deal with elder maltreatment are still in their infancy and that much more remains to be done.

In an attempt to address the issues of elder abuse and neglect, many jurisdictions have established agencies, or offices within agencies, with the specific mandate of responding to those needs (such as Adult Protective Services).
Often these efforts are backed by state legislation and are attached to agencies

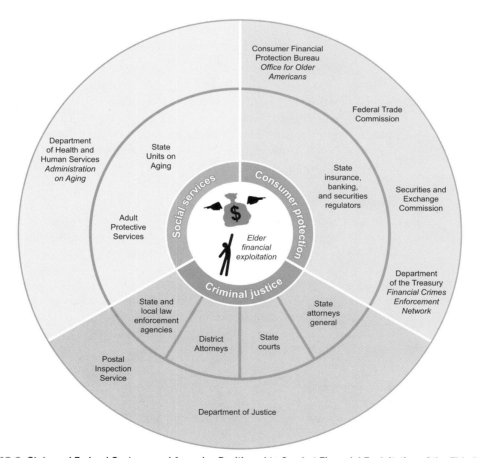

FIGURE 12.9 **State and Federal Systems and Agencies Positioned to Combat Financial Exploitation of the Elderly.**
Source: U.S. Government Accountability Office (2012). Elder Justice: National Strategy Needed to Effectively Combat Elder Financial
Exploitation, *p. 6. Washington, DC: U.S. Government Accountability Office. Retrieved on June 28, 2013, from http://www.gao.gov/
products/GAO-13-110.*

such as health and human services departments. Today, every state has some form of protective service devoted to the elderly.

Figure 12.10 illustrates how the Florida Adult Protective Services (APS) is designed to work. The first decision to be made upon receipt of a maltreatment report is whether the circumstances constitute an emergency. A *vulnerable adult* refers to a person who is incapable of performing normal daily living activities or is unable to protect him- or herself because of a physical or mental impairment (*Florida Statutes*, 2012, § 415.102(27)). If the case does not involve a vulnerable adult living in a precarious situation, the non-emergency route is initiated. The non-emergency process calls for a court hearing within 14 days of receiving a petition for protective services. The purpose of this hearing is to determine whether the person in question requires additional services or the court's protection. If the conditions do amount to an emergency, the process is expedited and a speedier determination is reached.

While their primary task revolves around investigations of abuse and neglect, these APS offices may also be responsible for such disparate activities as licensing nursing homes, funding research, and training social service workers. The fact that every jurisdiction has some form of APS is not indicative of a growing consensus on the problems of elder abuse and neglect. There remains a great deal of diversity in definitions, legislation, legal requirements, and interventions across the various jurisdictions.

Research

Perhaps the largest key to responding to elder maltreatment is increasing our knowledge about the problem and appropriate responses. The work of the National Research Council (2003) points out the weaknesses and limitations that permeate the current knowledge about the problems. Based on their extensive review of the extant literature, the NRC offers a comprehensive research agenda that, if undertaken and completed, would greatly enhance our knowledge and understanding of elder abuse and neglect (see Table 12.10). The results of this research endeavor would be improved responses and interventions to help the elderly victims of abuse.

SUMMARY

As the number of elderly persons steadily increases, society faces new problems and issues. For victimology, the elderly emerge as the subject of interest in two broad areas. First, they are victims of the same crimes as everyone else. Second, they occupy a special niche as victims of abuse and neglect.

More is known about general crimes committed against the elderly because of the great similarity to crime against the rest of society. Theft, burglary, assault,

Case Management Process

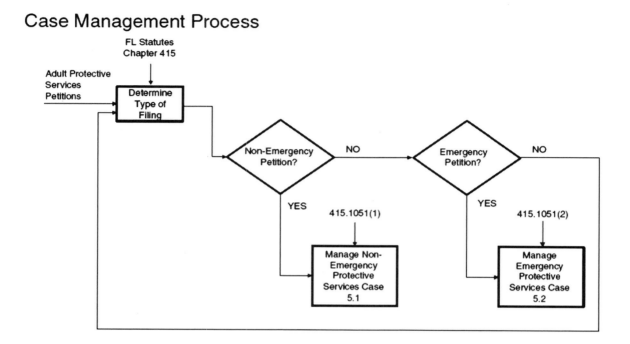

Non-Emergency Protective Services

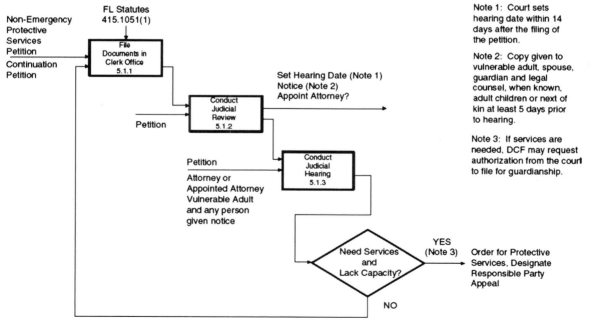

FIGURE 12.10 The Florida Adult Protective Services Process.

Source: Supreme Court of Florida (2003). Probate, Guardianship, & Mental/Medical Health Functional Requirements Document. *Tallahassee, FL: Office of the State Courts Administrator. Retrieved on June 27, 2013, from http://www.floridasupremecourt.org/clerk/adminorders/2003/forms/Probate%20FRD%20final%202-03.pdf.*

Emergency Protective Services

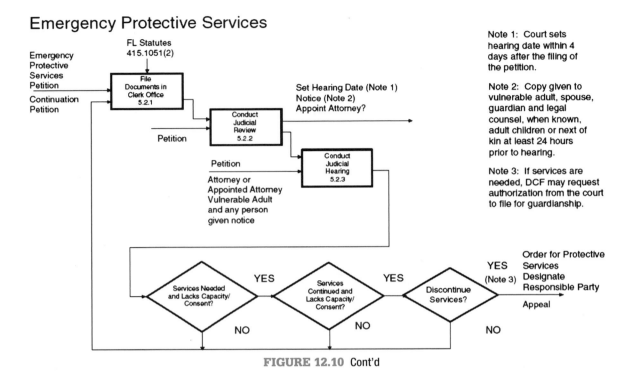

FIGURE 12.10 Cont'd

Table 12.10 Recommended Research Agenda of the National Research Council

- Basic research on the phenomenology of elder mistreatment is a critical early step in the further development of the field.
- Development of widely accepted operational definitions and validated and standardized measurement methods for the elements of elder mistreatment is urgently needed to move the field forward.
- Population-based surveys of elder mistreatment occurrence are feasible and should be given high priority by funding agencies.
- Funding agencies should give priority to the design and fielding of national prevalence and incidence studies of elder mistreatment.
- [N]ew methods of sampling and identifying elder mistreatment victims in the community should be developed in order to improve the validity and comprehensiveness of elder mistreatment occurrence estimates.
- Studies are greatly needed that examine risk indicators and risk and protective factors for different types of elder mistreatment.
- Substantial research is needed to improve and develop new methods of screening for possible elder mistreatment in a range of clinical settings.
- Research on the effects of elder mistreatment interventions is urgently needed.
- An adequate long-term funding commitment to research on elder mistreatment must be made by relevant federal, state, and private agencies.

Source: Compiled from National Research Council (2003). Elder Mistreatment: Abuse, Neglect, and Exploitation in an Aging America. *Washington, DC: National Academies Press.*

and other such offenses are traditional realms of interest for the criminal justice system. The greatest difference regarding crime against the elderly falls not in the crime itself, but rather in the impact of that crime upon the victim.

Elder maltreatment, however, poses a relatively new problem for the criminal justice system. While abuse may not be a new occurrence, it is a phenomenon that is gaining attention. Victimologists are beginning to identify the intricacies of the problem, probe its causes, and offer some solutions. However, a great deal of additional work remains to be done at both the theoretical and practical levels. A short decade or two of work has not been sufficient to do much more than identify elder abuse and neglect as a major problem and offer the sketchiest of responses. As one legal expert opines (Kohn, 2012: 328), a more fruitful approach might be to integrate aging issues within the context of civil rights:

> It is, therefore, time we begin to clearly frame the discourse over aging in civil rights terms. Doing so is imperative from a law reform perspective. It is also a way to create a climate in which an elder rights movement can emerge. Such framing has energized past civil rights movements. It can now energize our nation's next big civil rights movement: the elder rights movement.

KEY TERMS

Adult Protective Services (APS)
ageism
elder abuse
elder neglect
exogenous factors
fear of crime
gerontologists
institutional abuse
life expectancy
magnitude issue
mandatory reporting
nursing home environment

objective odds of victimization
patient characteristics
poly-victimization
risk
sentinel agency
Silver-Haired Legislature
staff characteristics
subjective odds of victimization
vicarious victimization
vulnerability
vulnerable adult

Hate Crime

LEARNING OBJECTIVES

After reading Chapter 13, you should be able to:

- Distinguish a hate crime from a regular crime.
- List the type of classes that are protected under the hate crime designation.
- Explore three factors that typically intersect before there is a resolution to the hate crime problem.
- Discuss the various areas that hate crime provisions have targeted.
- Sketch out the federal response to the problem of hate crime.
- Link the term *sentencing enhancement* to hate crime.
- Probe issues surrounding the First Amendment and hate crime laws.
- Provide an overview of hate crime statistics generated by the UCR Program.
- Show how the NCVS addresses issues that the UCR Program does not address.
- Compose a picture of hate crime victimization based upon NCVS information.
- Explain the roles that third-party watch groups have taken with regard to hate crime.
- Visit the complexities which victims must contend with as they negotiate their way through the hate crime reporting process.
- Elaborate on prosecutorial strategies pertaining to hate crime charges.
- Visit Supreme Court case decisions that address penalty enhancements.

INTRODUCTION

What follows is a snapshot of some incidents that took place recently (Florida Commission on Human Relations, 2009). They include the following descriptions:

> The victim was run down as she rode her bicycle on a Daytona Beach sidewalk. Thomas Cato was charged with aggravated battery and simple battery. The victim allegedly heard Mr. Cato say, "(N-word) must die". . . . Nekedia suffered badly broken bones and emotional scars. She was released from the hospital a week after the incident and is currently in therapy.

> Upon arriving at the church, members of the Macedonia Baptist Church on Lipscomb Street found messages such as "KKK," "666," and racially derogatory comments painted across the building.

> A teenager was arrested and charged with simple assault and trespassing after police said he hung a noose in his African-American neighbor's tree.

> Villazano confessed to detectives after the 2 a.m. killing . . . telling them he shot Oscar Mosqueda after the victim made an embarrassing sexual advance towards him inside the late-night club event . . . . Villazano told police he was embarrassed because he isn't gay. One witness to the shooting, Wesley Rosser, said he found it unlikely Villazano would have been surprised by being hit on at the event, which featured men in drag.

Despite apparent differences in terms of the victim's race, religious orientation, gender, and sexual orientation, these episodes share one thing in common. That is, they were fueled by a bias or prejudice that the perpetrator harbored.

What is a hate crime? A *hate crime* or *bias crime*, one can use the terms interchangeably, is "an act committed or attempted by one person or group against another—or that person's property—that in any way constitutes an expression of hatred toward the victim based on his or her personal characteristics" (Bondi, 2012: 6). Another explanation is that hate crimes "include all types of crime where the offender is motivated by specific characteristics of the victim, including the victim's race, ethnicity, religion, or sexual orientation" (Office of Justice Programs, 2011).

An important component to a hate crime is the offender's perception of the victim. Whether the victim is actually a member of a protected group is immaterial. The relevant point is that the perpetrator perceives the victim possesses this characteristic and then acts because he or she thinks the victim belongs to that group.

This chapter, then, explores how the notion of a hate crime came into being and what the various statutory responses look like. It also examines some court challenges and then tries to determine how many hate crimes occur annually in this country. A quick look at how the law enforcement and prosecutor sectors have reacted reveals some complexities that forced the U.S. Supreme Court to step in and address.

HATE CRIME LEGISLATION

Laws banning bias-based crime have taken a double-barreled approach. The states, and even some local governments, have drawn up their own rules and regulations outlawing this type of behavior. In addition, Congress has enacted legislation at the federal level. In order to frame this picture, we will look at the initiatives that have occurred at both levels. First, though, we need to establish an appropriate background for understanding the emergence and recognition of this social problem.

A Backdrop

Usually, three distinctive elements must intersect before a meaningful collective response is generated. First is the occurrence of a particularly horrendous or outrageous event, such as a cross-burning or a heinous bias-motivated death. Sometimes called a *trigger event*, this incident captures attention, promotes public disbelief, and prompts a sustained moral outcry. In some instances, this element may materialize only after there has been an accumulation of these distasteful episodes.

Second, media attention keeps the issue squarely in the forefront of the public's mind, and this coverage becomes an influential force. This fueling may come in the form of reporting other similar incidents or documenting reaction in other locales. Editorials, speeches at rallies, protests, and other public events lend the impression that the situation will continue to spiral out of control unless pre-emptive and authoritative action is taken. At some point, all this publicity and attention creates what is known as a *moral panic*. A moral panic means that a social problem is considered to be so pervasive and damaging that it threatens core values and beliefs. The impression in the public's mind is that this danger has grown so immense and is so destructive that an immediate regulatory solution must be crafted to combat this force.

A third ingredient materializes when potent interest groups enter the scene. These organizations have accumulated experience in shaping and waging campaigns. Proponents, such as the Anti-Defamation League, local church and civic leaders, and other watchdog groups, undertake activities to spread their messages. Opponents, such as the Ku Klux Klan and right-wing extremists, mobilize their members and make their own positions available for public consumption. The result is a raucous and extremely cantankerous atmosphere.

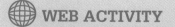 **WEB ACTIVITY**

The Anti-Defamation League has devoted considerable energy to eradicating hate crime and bias crime. For more details, visit the website at **http://www.adl.org/**

Studies tracing the diffusion of hate crime laws and interviews with key informants (Becker, 1999; Colomb & Damphouse, 2004; Grattet, Jenness, & Curry,

Table 13.1 The Florida Cross-Burning Statute

It shall be unlawful for any person or persons to place or cause to be placed in a public place in the state a burning or flaming cross or any manner of exhibit in which a burning or flaming cross, real or simulated, is a whole or a part.

Source: Florida Statutes *(2012), § 876.17.*

1998; Jenness & Grattet, 1996) confirm the crucial roles that each of these factors have played in the enactment of hate crime legislation. It would be safe to say that these statutory protections will assume even greater importance as the American population becomes increasingly diversified.

The State Response

In 1978, California became the first state to target hate crime. A handful of other states passed similar legislation in quick succession. However, the movement remained largely dormant until the late 1980s when more states began to adopt similar legislation addressing this concern. Today, at least 45 states have some type of hate crime legislation in place (Anti-Defamation League, 2013; Smith & Foley, 2010) (see Tables 13.1 and 13.2).

Many of the provisions in state laws were sparked by the model legislation drafted by the Anti-Defamation League in 1981. While the exact format of these legislative reactions has not always been the same from one location to the next, there are some identifiable common threads. Generally speaking, state lawmakers have pursued provisions that address:

- Bias-motivated violence based on race, color, ethnicity, religion, sexual orientation, homeless status, physical or mental disability, or age;
- Enhanced criminal penalties;
- Cross-burning and other symbolic displays;
- Wearing masks or hoods in public;
- Institutional vandalism of public monuments and places of worship;
- Civil rights protection;
- Training for law enforcement officers; and
- Data collection and information dissemination.

Table 13.2 The Florida Prohibition Against Wearing Masks or Hoods in Public

No person or persons over 16 years of age shall, while wearing any mask, hood, or device whereby any portion of the face is so hidden, concealed, or covered as to conceal the identity of the wearer, enter upon, or be or appear upon any lane, walk, alley, street, road, highway, or other public way in this state.

Source: Florida Statutes *(2012), § 876.12.*

The Federal Response

Congress tackled the issue of discrimination when it enacted the Civil Rights Act of 1964 (42 U.S.C. § 2000e). This legislation outlawed unfair employment practices. In other words, hiring, promoting, or firing workers because of that person's race, color, sex, national origin, or religion became illegal. After formulating these affirmative action measures, Congress went on to pass the Civil Rights Act of 1968 (25 U.S.C. § 1302). This law extended civil rights protections by guaranteeing equal access to housing. It prohibited any form of discrimination when it came to selling, renting, or financing homes, residences, apartments, and other living facilities.

The saga against bias gained further momentum with the passage of the Hate Crime Statistics Act of 1990 (28 U.S.C. § 534). This initiative instructed the U.S. Attorney General to compile information regarding bias-motivated crimes in a more systematic fashion. As the Federal Bureau of Investigation was already operating the Uniform Crime Reporting Program, it was put in charge of this new data collection effort. Since then, the Federal Bureau of Investigation has produced annual reports devoted exclusively to hate crime incidents and their characteristics. Congress renewed its efforts in this arena when it approved the Matthew Shepard and James Byrd Jr. Hate Crime Prevention Act in 2009 (18 U.S.C. § 249), named after two hate crime victims.

Matthew Shepard was a young college student attending the University of Wyoming. One night, Shepard accepted a ride home from two men he had just met. Instead of driving Shepard straight home, the assailants took him to an out-of-the-way place. There the men beat Shepard unconscious, tied him to a fence, and left him to die. A passerby found Shepard still alive and contacted the authorities. However, Shepard slipped into a coma and succumbed to his injuries a few days later.

After being arrested, the defendants admitted they had assaulted Shepard because he had made homosexual advances toward them. Although the two suspects were charged with murder, they could not be prosecuted for a hate crime because Wyoming had not passed such a state law. Afterwards, the victim's parents established the Matthew Shepard Foundation to advocate on behalf of people who have nontraditional sexual orientations.

James Byrd Jr., a black person, died a horrific death at the hands of three white supremacists. His assailants chained Byrd by his ankles to the back of a pickup truck and then dragged him down a bumpy road for three miles. Medical evidence suggested that Byrd remained conscious during this ordeal until his head and arm became severed from his body. The State of Texas has executed one suspect in this case. A second accomplice remains on death row, and another suspect is serving a life sentence. In an interview a few months prior to his execution, the death row inmate told a news reporter "I have no regrets. I'd do it all over again, to tell you the truth" (Phillip, 2011) (see Figure 13.1).

These two cases were instrumental in the passage of a new federal hate crime law, aptly named the "Matthew Shepard and James Byrd Jr. Hate Crime Prevention Act." Its provisions, among other things, now extend coverage to include violence targeting people who are gay, lesbian, bisexual, and transgendered.

PUNISHING HATE CRIME

When state legislators set out to craft a strategy that dealt with the issue of hate crime, they had to make a strategic decision. Were they going to write an entirely brand-new set of laws or were they going to utilize existing laws and merely increase penalties? No matter which avenue was chosen, the way in which lawmakers handled this situation would inevitably result in litigation.

Sentencing Enhancement

As Table 13.3 shows, Florida decided to increase the degree of a criminal act if the perpetrator attacked the victim because of any animosity or bias toward a class of persons. If the offender selected the victim solely because of his or her race, color, heritage, religion, sexual orientation, homeless status, disability, or old age, then the incident became more heinous than usual. The presence of such an aggravating circumstance is met by a *sentencing enhancement*. In other words, if any of these conditions are present, the judge can raise the applicable penalty allowed under sentencing guidelines.

The question of whether the judge has the legal authority to mete out a more severe sanction than usual in a hate crime incident became the focal point of one U.S. Supreme Court case (*Wisconsin v. Mitchell*, 1993). The defendant, Mitchell, instructed a group of black youths to attack an adolescent who was walking down the street solely because that teenager was a Caucasian. The victim was hospitalized and laid in a coma for four days. A trial jury later found Mitchell guilty. The judge sentenced him to four years imprisonment, two years for the aggravated battery charge, and an additional two years because the situation involved a racially tinged crime. Mitchell appealed the sentence on the grounds that the hate crime sentencing enhancement was unconstitutional because it violated his

FIGURE 13.1 Ricky Jason displays a photograph of James Byrd Jr. outside the Texas Department of Criminal Justice Huntsville Unit before the execution of Lawrence Russell Brewer on September 21, 2011. Brewer was convicted for his participation in chaining Byrd to the back of a pickup truck, dragging him along a rural East Texas road, and dumping what was left of his body outside a church cemetery in 1998. *Credit: AP Photo/David J. Phillip.*

Table 13.3 A Hate Crimes Statute That Provides for Sentencing Enhancements

(1) (a) The penalty for any felony or misdemeanor shall be reclassified as provided in this subsection if the commission of such felony or misdemeanor evidences prejudice based on the race, color, ancestry, ethnicity, religion, sexual orientation, national origin, homeless status, mental or physical disability, or advanced age of the victim:

    1. A misdemeanor of the second degree is reclassified to a misdemeanor of the first degree.
    2. A misdemeanor of the first degree is reclassified to a felony of the third degree.
    3. A felony of the third degree is reclassified to a felony of the second degree.
    4. A felony of the second degree is reclassified to a felony of the first degree.
    5. A felony of the first degree is reclassified to a life felony.

(1) (b) As used in paragraph (a), the term:

    1. "Mental or physical disability" means that the victim suffers from a condition of physical or mental incapacitation due to a developmental disability, organic brain damage, or mental illness, and has one or more physical or mental limitations that restrict the victim's ability to perform the normal activities of daily living.
    2. "Advanced age" means that the victim is older than 65 years of age.
    3. "Homeless status" means that the victim:
        a. Lacks a fixed, regular, and adequate nighttime residence; or
        b. Has a primary nighttime residence that is:
            (I) A supervised publicly or privately operated shelter designed to provide temporary living accommodations; or
            (II) A public or private place not designed for, or ordinarily used as, a regular sleeping accommodation for human beings.

(2) A person or organization that establishes by clear and convincing evidence that it has been coerced, intimidated, or threatened in violation of this section has a civil cause of action for treble damages, an injunction, or any other appropriate relief in law or in equity. Upon prevailing in such civil action, the plaintiff may recover reasonable attorney's fees and costs.

(3) It is an essential element of this section that the record reflect that the defendant perceived, knew, or had reasonable grounds to know or perceive that the victim was within the class delineated in this section.

Source: Florida Statutes *(2012), § 775.085.*

First Amendment rights. Essentially, Mitchell maintained that the hate crime statute punished him for holding bigoted thoughts and biased beliefs. The Supreme Court disagreed and upheld the judge's imposition of a penalty enhancement as appropriate.

First Amendment Protection

The issue of First Amendment protection, among other things, arose again in another federal Supreme Court proceeding (*Virginia v. Black*, 2003). Two separate cases were consolidated in a consideration of the constitutionality of Virginia's anti-cross-burning statute. The State of Virginia had enacted a law that prohibited all instances of cross-burning due to the terror that such an act induced in victims. In addition, the statute had another provision that equated the burning of a cross with *prima facie* evidence of intent to intimidate. It was this part of the statute that the Supreme Court struck down. Because the Court upheld the constitutionality of cross-burning statutes, we will concentrate on this aspect.

The defendant in the first case sponsored a Ku Klux Klan (KKK) rally on his private property. People who had gathered on the side of the road and neighbors living on an adjacent property could hear and see portions of the event. At the end of the meeting, the participants set a 30-foot cross on fire. The sheriff, who had been watching the rally from the side of the road, then entered the property and arrested the organizer on the charge of cross-burning.

The second case involved two quarreling next-door neighbors. One night, the defendants decided to burn a cross in the victim's front yard. The victim was of African-American descent. When he saw the charred remains of the cross, the victim became fearful for his well-being and that of his family.

The Supreme Court opinion noted that Scottish tribes in the fourteenth century burned crosses as a way to signal others of impending danger. This practice was also done for other lawful usages. However, the Ku Klux Klan adopted cross-burning as a ceremonial ritual and also as a way to frighten African Americans and their civil rights sympathizers. In short time, cross-burning became the violent trademark of the KKK and morphed into a symbol of hatred. As the opinion explained (*Virginia v. Black*, 2003: 357):

> when a cross burning is directed at a particular person not affiliated with the Klan, the burning cross often serves as a message of intimidation, designed to inspire in the victim a fear of bodily harm. Moreover, the history of violence associated with the Klan shows that the possibility of injury or death is not just hypothetical. The person who burns a cross directed at a particular person is often making a serious threat, meant to coerce the victim to comply with the Klan's wishes unless the victim is willing to risk the wrath of the Klan.

The defendants maintained that the First Amendment protects freedom of speech and that cross-burning fell within this blanket. The Court countered that while the First Amendment does protect freedom of speech, this safeguard does not automatically extend to every single expression. For example, "fighting words" and "true threats" lie outside the protection of the First Amendment. As the Court explained (*Virginia v. Black*, 2003: 359), *true threats* directed against a person:

> encompass those statements where the speaker means to communicate a serious expression of intent to commit an act of unlawful violence to a particular individual or group of individuals.

As a result, provisions of state statutes that ban cross-burning do not fall within the scope of the First Amendment and, therefore, are considered to be constitutional (Ruane & Doyle, 2007).

Other Developments

Buoyed by these developments, some proponents have explored the possibility of establishing similar statutes that deal with the hangman's noose (Barger, 2008). The *hangman's noose* refers to the manner in which a rope is coiled and tied prior to executing a person via hanging. It is also a very vivid symbol associated with lynchings, particularly of black people in the South (Klanwatch Project, 2011). Given its offensiveness and power to intimidate, Congress decried the use of this repulsive object and adopted the formal resolution that Table 13.4 displays.

Table 13.4 U.S. Senate Resolution Regarding the Hanging of Nooses

Whereas, in the fall of 2007, nooses have been found hanging in or near a high school in North Carolina, a Home Depot store in New Jersey, a school playground in Louisiana, the campus of the University of Maryland, a factory in Houston, Texas, and on the door of a professor's office at Columbia University;

Whereas the Southern Poverty Law Center has recorded between 40 and 50 suspected hate crimes involving nooses since September 2007;

Whereas, since 2001, the Equal Employment Opportunity Commission has filed more than 30 lawsuits that involve the displaying of nooses in places of employment;

Whereas nooses are reviled by many Americans as symbols of racism and of lynchings that were once all too common;

Whereas, according to Tuskegee Institute, more than 4,700 people were lynched between 1882 and 1959 in a campaign of terror led by the Ku Klux Klan;

Whereas the number of victims killed by lynching in the history of the United States exceeds the number of people killed in the horrible attack on Pearl Harbor (2,333 dead) and Hurricane Katrina (1,836 dead) combined; and

Whereas African-Americans, as well as Italian, Jewish, and Mexican-Americans, have comprised the vast majority of lynching victims, and, by erasing the terrible symbols of the past, we can continue to move forward on issues of race in the United States: Now, therefore, be it

    Resolved, That it is the sense of the Senate that—

    (1) the hanging of nooses is a reprehensible act when used for the purpose of intimidation and, under certain circumstances, can be criminal;

    (2) incidents involving the hanging of a noose should be investigated thoroughly by Federal, State, and local law enforcement, and all private entities and individuals should be encouraged to cooperate with any such investigation; and

    (3) any criminal violations involving the hanging of nooses should be vigorously prosecuted.

Source: Congressional Record (December 13, 2007). Senate Resolution 396, 110th Congress, 1st Session. *Washington, DC: Government Printing Office. Retrieved on July 5, 2013, from http://www.gpo.gov/fdsys/pkg/BILLS-110sres396ats/pdf/BILLS-110sres396ats.pdf.*

MEASURING THE EXTENT OF HATE CRIME

As previously discussed, estimates concerning the nature, extent, and distribution of various types of crimes depend upon the source of that information. Hate crime, especially because it has gained formal recognition only recently, is not an exception. The typical sources of data are the Federal Bureau of Investigation through its Uniform Crime Reporting Program, the National Crime Victimization Survey, and independent third-party watch groups.

UCR Information

The Federal Bureau of Investigation expanded its crime coverage to include hate crime in the mid-1990s. The 1990 Hate Crime Statistics Act (28 U.S.C. § 534) instructed the Federal Bureau of Investigation to integrate hate crime into its national data collection efforts. These offenses pertain to incidents "that are motivated, in whole or in part, by the offender's bias against a race, religion, sexual orientation, ethnicity/national origin, or disability" (Federal Bureau of Investigation, 2012a). Of course, this expansion meant a program needed to be developed and that law enforcement personnel had to be trained in the investigation, recognition, and reporting of hate crime. The first report, released in 1990, had a humble beginning. It compiled data from 11 states that had started gathering such information on their own. By 1996, the Federal Bureau of Investigation program had grown to cover about 84% of the American population (Federal Bureau of Investigation, 1997). By 2011, the coverage had expanded to 14,575 participating agencies and blanketed 92% of the nation's inhabitants (Federal Bureau of Investigation, 2012a). Figure 13.2 presents a condensed copy of the report form that local agencies complete and forward to the Federal Bureau of Investigation whenever they encounter a bias-crime.

The Federal Bureau of Investigation received reports of more than 6,200 hate crime incidents in the United States during the calendar year 2011. These incidents are reflected in Figure 13.3, which plots the various types of hate crime committed since 2000. Several points emerge from that diagram. First, the most frequent type of hate crime involves racial intimidation. While 71% of the victims are black, a sizeable number of these events involve white victims. Second, offenses that target people because of their physical or mental disabilities occur the least often. Third, the number of incidents based upon the victim's religion, sexual orientation, and ethnicity remains relatively constant

WEB ACTIVITY

The Federal Bureau of Investigation has produced an annual report on hate crime in the United States since 1990. For more information, access the website at **http://www.fbi.gov/about-us/cjis/ucr/hate-crime/2011/resources/about-hate-crime-statistics** (Federal Bureau of Investigation, 2012c).

WEB ACTIVITY

Some states compile their own annual report on hate crimes that have taken place within their boundaries. You can locate more information about hate crime in Florida by visiting the website at **http://myfloridalegal.com/webfiles.nsf/WF/RWHN-93HMH4/$file/2011Hate CrimesReport.pdf**

1-699 (Rev. 05-14-2012) Expires 06-30-15   **HATE CRIME INCIDENT REPORT**   OMB No. 1110-0015

Initial ☐   Adjustment ☐   ORI ☐☐☐☐☐☐☐☐☐   Date of Incident ___/___/___
                                                             Month   Day   Year

Incident No. ☐☐☐☐☐☐☐☐☐☐☐☐   **Page** ☐ **of** ☐ **of Same Incident**

Offense Information

Enter an offense code and the number of victims for each bias motivated offense.

	Offense Code	Number of victims
Offense #1	☐☐	☐☐☐
Offense #2	☐☐	☐☐☐
Offense #3	☐☐	☐☐☐
Offense #4	☐☐	☐☐☐
Offense #5	☐☐	☐☐☐

01 Murder
02 Rape
03 Robbery
04 Aggravated Assault
05 Burglary
06 Larceny-Theft

07 Motor Vehicle Theft
08 Arson
09 Simple Assault
10 Intimidation
11 Destruction/Damage/Vandalism

Location Information

Check one location for Offense #1.

01 ☐ Air/Bus/Train Terminal
02 ☐ Bank/Savings and Loan
03 ☐ Bar/Night Club
04 ☐ Church/Synagogue/Temple/Mosque
05 ☐ Commercial/Office Building
06 ☐ Construction Site
07 ☐ Convenience Store
08 ☐ Department/Discount Store
09 ☐ Drug Store/Dr.'s Office/Hospital
10 ☐ Field/Woods
11 ☐ Government/Public Building
12 ☐ Grocery/Supermarket
13 ☐ Highway/Road/Alley/Street
14 ☐ Hotel/Motel/etc.
15 ☐ Jail/Prison
16 ☐ Lake/Waterway
17 ☐ Liquor Store
18 ☐ Parking Lot/Garage
19 ☐ Rental Storage Facility
20 ☐ Residence/Home
21 ☐ Restaurant
23 ☐ Service/Gas Station

24 ☐ Specialty Store (TV, Fur, etc.)
25 ☐ Other/Unknown
37 ☐ Abandoned/Condemned Structure
38 ☐ Amusement Park
39 ☐ Arena/Stadium/Fairgrounds/Coliseum
40 ☐ ATM Separate from Bank
41 ☐ Auto Dealership New/Used
42 ☐ Camp/Campground
44 ☐ Daycare Facility
45 ☐ Dock/Wharf/Freight/Modal Terminal
46 ☐ Farm Facility
47 ☐ Gambling Facility/Casino/Race Track
48 ☐ Industrial Site
49 ☐ Military Installation
50 ☐ Park/Playground
51 ☐ Rest Area
52 ☐ School-College/University
53 ☐ School-Elementary/Secondary
54 ☐ Shelter-Mission/Homeless
55 ☐ Shopping Mall
56 ☐ Tribal Lands
57 ☐ Community Center

If more than one offense occurred, enter a location code for each additional offense having a different location than Offense #1.

	Location Code
Offense #2	☐☐
Offense #3	☐☐
Offense #4	☐☐
Offense #5	☐☐

FIGURE 13.2 FBI Hate Crime Incident Report Form.

Source: Federal Bureau of Investigation (2012b). UCR Reporting Forms: Hate Crime Incident Report. *Washington, DC: U.S. Government Printing Office. Retrieved on July 6, 2013, from http://www.fbi.gov/about-us/cjis/ucr/reporting-forms/hate-crime-incident-report-pdf.*

Bias Motivation Information

Check up to five bias motivations for Offense #1.

Race

11 ☐ Anti-White
12 ☐ Anti-Black or African American
13 ☐ Anti-American Indian or Alaska Native
14 ☐ Anti-Asian
15 ☐ Anti-Multiple Races, Group
16 ☐ Anti-Native Hawaiian or Other Pacific Islander

Religion

21 ☐ Anti-Jewish
22 ☐ Anti-Catholic
23 ☐ Anti-Protestant
24 ☐ Anti-Islamic (Muslim)
25 ☐ Anti-Other Religion
26 ☐ Anti-Multiple Religions, Group
27 ☐ Anti-Atheism/Agnosticism

Ethnicity

32 ☐ Anti-Hispanic or Latino
33 ☐ Anti-Not Hispanic or Latino

Sexual Orientation

41 ☐ Anti-Gay (Male)
42 ☐ Anti-Lesbian
43 ☐ Anti-Lesbian, Gay, Bisexual, or Transgender (Mixed Group)
44 ☐ Anti-Heterosexual
45 ☐ Anti-Bisexual

Disability

51 ☐ Anti-Physical Disability
52 ☐ Anti-Mental Disability

Gender

61 ☐ Anti-Male
62 ☐ Anti-Female

Gender Identity

71 ☐ Anti-Transgender
72 ☐ Anti-Gender Non-Conforming

If more than one offense occurred, enter up to five bias motivations for each additional offense having a different bias motivation than Offense #1.

	Bias #1	Bias #2	Bias #3	Bias #4	Bias #5
Offense #2					
Offense #3					
Offense #4					
Offense #5					

Victim Information

Check all applicable victim types for each offense listed above.

	Offense #1	Offense #2	Offense #3	Offense #4	Offense #5
1 Individual*	☐	☐	☐	☐	☐
2 Business	☐	☐	☐	☐	☐
3 Financial Institution	☐	☐	☐	☐	☐
4 Government	☐	☐	☐	☐	☐
5 Religious Organization	☐	☐	☐	☐	☐
7 Other	☐	☐	☐	☐	☐
8 Unknown	☐	☐	☐	☐	☐

*Indicate the number of Individuals (persons) who were victims in the incident.

Total number of victims.

Total number of victims 18 and over.

Total number of victims under 18.

FIGURE 13.2   cont'd

Offender Information

Indicate the number of Individuals (persons) who were offenders in the incident.

Total number of offenders. If unknown, enter 00.

Total number of offenders 18 and over. If unknown, enter 00.

Total number of offenders under 18. If unknown, enter 00.

Bias Motivation Information

Check one race and one ethnicity.

Race

1 ☐ White
2 ☐ Black or African American
3 ☐ American Indian or Alaska Native
4 ☐ Asian
5 ☐ Group of Multiple Races
6 ☐ Unknown
7 ☐ Native Hawaiian or Other Pacific Islander

Ethnicity

H ☐ Hispanic or Latino
N ☐ Not Hispanic or Latino
M ☐ Group of Multiple Ethnicities
U ☐ Unknown

This report is authorized by Title 28, Section 534, U.S. Code, and the Hate Crime Statistics Act of 1990. Even though you are not required to respond, your cooperation in using this form to report hate crimes known to law enforcement during the quarter will assist the FBI in compiling timely, comprehensive, and accurate data regarding the incidence and prevalence of hate crime throughout the Nation. Please submit this report quarterly, by the 15th day after the close of the quarter, and any questions to the FBI, Criminal Justice Information Services Division, Attention: Uniform Crime Reports/Module E-3, 1000 Custer Hollow Road, Clarksburg, West Virginia 26306; telephone 304-625-4830, facsimile 304-625-3566. Under the Paperwork Reduction Act, you are not required to complete this form unless it contains a valid OMB control number. The form takes approximately 7 minutes to complete. Instructions for preparing the form appear below.

GENERAL

This report is separate from and in addition to the traditional Summary Reporting System submission. In hate crime reporting, there is no Hierarchy Rule. Offense data (not just arrest data) for Intimidation and Destruction/Damage/Vandalism of Property should be reported. On this form, all reportable bias motivated offenses should be included regardless of whether arrests have taken place. Please refer to the publication *Hate Crime Data Collection Guidelines and Training Manual* for additional information.

QUARTERLY HATE CRIME REPORT

At the end of each calendar quarter, each reporting agency should submit a single Quarterly Hate Crime Report, together with an individual Hate Crime Incident Report for each bias motivated incident identified during the quarter (if any). If no hate crimes occurred during the quarter, the agency should submit only the Quarterly Hate Crime Report.

The Quarterly Hate Crime Report should be used to identify your agency, to state the number of bias motivated incidents being reported for the calendar quarter, and to delete any incidents previously reported that have been determined during the reporting period not to have been motivated by bias.

HATE CRIME INCIDENT REPORT

The Incident Report should be used to report a bias motivated incident or to adjust information in a previously reported incident. Include additional information on separate paper if you feel it will add clarity to the report.

FIGURE 13.2 cont'd

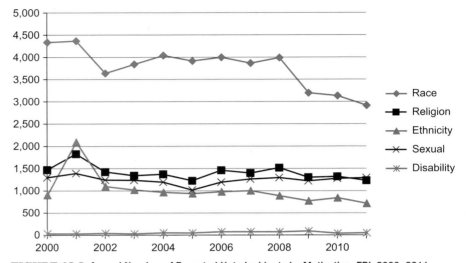

FIGURE 13.3 Annual Number of Reported Hate Incidents by Motivation, FBI, 2000–2011.
Source: Compilation from UCR annual reports. Retrieved on July 5, 2013, from http://www.fbi.gov/about-us/cjis/ucr/ucr-publications.

over time. Other statistics indicate that almost two-thirds of the religion-based crimes involve Jewish people, and 60% of the sex-based offenses are directed against male homosexuals.

One can also categorize hate crime incidents according to whether they were aimed at a person, property, or involved other violations. As Figure 13.4 shows, the majority of the incidents involve direct contact with a person. However, a large proportion of the incidents involve property transgressions (vandalism, property damage, burglary, theft, arson, etc.).

NCVS Information

As mentioned earlier in Chapter 2, one nagging problem that trails the Uniform Crime Reports and other police-generated data are that they reflect only those crimes that come to the attention of the authorities. Many victims, for whatever reason, opt not to contact the police or become further involved in the criminal justice system. As a result, official data sources are haunted by the *dark figure of crime* (incidents of which the police are not aware and/or do not record). It is for this reason that victimologists and criminal justice researchers turn to alternative data sources to arrive at a more complete picture of crime. Fortunately, the NCVS does provide some information about hate crime.

 **WEB ACTIVITY**

The full NCVS hate crime report for 2003–2011 is available at **http://www.bjs.gov/content/pub/pdf/hcv0311.pdf**

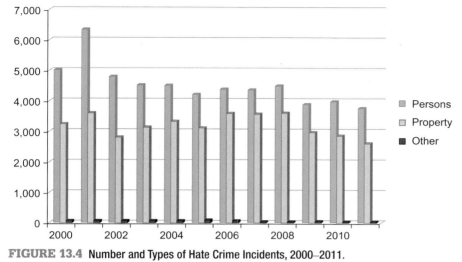

FIGURE 13.4 Number and Types of Hate Crime Incidents, 2000–2011.

Source: Compilation from UCR annual reports. Retrieved on July 5, 2013, from http://www.fbi.gov/about-us/cjis/ucr/ucr-publications.

The NCVS began capturing hate crime data in 2003. It uses the same definition that appears in the Hate Crime Statistics Act, which is also utilized by the Federal Bureau of Investigation. Simply put, hate crime refers to "crimes that manifest evidence of prejudice based on race, gender or gender identity, religion, disability, sexual orientation, or ethnicity" (28 U.S.C. § 534). The categorization relies upon the victim's perception that a bias-motivated transgression was aimed against him or her.

Figure 13.5 presents the number of hate crimes the NCVS uncovered during the 2004–2011 interval. While both the violent and property hate crime victimizations dipped at the beginning of the series, the violent confrontations climbed before dropping again. The property incidents were relatively stable. The figure also demonstrates that the overwhelming majority of hate crime episodes were violent. Nine out of every ten hate crimes involved a personal attack.

The major advantage of the NCVS is its ability to tap into the dark figure of crime and capture incidents that have gone undetected by the authorities. The police were contacted in a little over one-third of the violent hate crimes that took place between 2007 and 2011. When asked why they had not called the police, a quarter responded that the police could not or would not help and another quarter stated that it was a private or personal matter that they would handle in another way (Sandholtz et al., 2013). The leading motivation underlying these cases was racial bias. The remainder of the incidents was evenly divided among religious background, sexual orientation, and ethnicity (Sandholtz et al., 2013). Other research reveals that black victims of hate crime are much less likely to

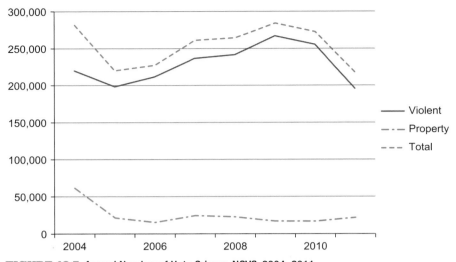

FIGURE 13.5 Annual Number of Hate Crimes, NCVS, 2004–2011.

Source: Sandholtz, N., Langton, L., & Planty, M. (2013). Hate Crime Victimization, 2003–2011. *Washington, DC: Bureau of Justice Statistics. Retrieved on July 6, 2013, from http://www.bjs.gov/content/pub/pdf/hcv0311.pdf.*

notify the police compared with white persons (Zaykowski, 2010). The outline of the key decision points that hate crime victims must sift through appears in Table 13.5 and illustrates the complexities of this entire process.

Third-Party Watch Groups

There are a number of independent organizations whose mission is to monitor the activities of various hate crime groups. The two most prominent watch groups are the Anti-Defamation League (2013) and the Southern Poverty Law Center (2001).

The Anti-Defamation League (ADL) was founded more than 100 years ago to deal with anti-Jewish sentiments. Its objectives have evolved beyond anti-Semitism to include efforts against racism and other forms of bigotry. It maintains a keen interest in such white supremacist groups as the Aryan Brotherhood and other derivatives of the neo-Nazi movement. The ADL was instrumental in drafting a model statute that formed the basis for many of today's hate crime laws.

 WEB ACTIVITY

The Southern Poverty Law Center maintains a website at **http://www.splcenter.org/**

The Southern Poverty Law Center (SPLC) is another nonprofit group dedicated to battling racial and social injustice. Established initially during the Civil Rights Movement, the SPLC drew attention from its efforts to help dismantle the Ku Klux Klan, white supremacists, and allied segregation advocates. The SPLC has adopted the strategy of suing hate groups in civil court in order to drain their financial reserves.

Table 13.5 Key Decision Points in Hate Crime Reporting

1. Victim understands that a crime has been committed.

2. Victim recognizes that hate (of the victim's real or perceived minority status or attribute) may be a motivating factor.

3. Victim or another party solicits law enforcement intervention.

4. Victim or another party communicates with law enforcement about motivation of the crime.

5. Law enforcement recognizes the element of hate.

6. Law enforcement documents the element of hate and, as appropriate, charges suspect with civil rights or hate/bias offense.

7. Law enforcement records the incident and submits the information to the Uniform Crime Report, Hate Crime Reporting Unit.

Source: McDevitt, J., et al. (2000). Accuracy of Bias Crime Statistics Nationally: An Assessment of the First Ten Years of Bias Crime Data Collection: Final Report, *p. 34. Boston: Northeastern University. Retrieved on July 6, 2013, from http://www.jrsa.org/pubs/reports/bjs_bias_crime_data.pdf.*

The SPLC also monitors hate crime activity throughout the country. One SPLC estimate (Southern Poverty Law Center, 2001) is that there are as many as six to seven times more hate crimes than what the Federal Bureau of Investigation acknowledges. One reason for this gap is what the SPLC terms *false zeroes*. Matching media reports of hate crime incidents against official reports revealed a number of discrepancies. For instance, one practice in several states was to substitute an unverified value of zero, indicating that no hate crimes had occurred in the jurisdiction, for agencies that were non-participants and had not submitted a report. Thus, it is difficult to determine whether a zero value indicates a lack of hate crimes occurring or reflects nonreporting.

Another reason for the existence of false zeroes is that while some states had developed a form for documenting each individual hate crime incident, there was no summary or aggregate form to report that no such crimes had taken place.

SYSTEM RESPONSES TO HATE CRIME

Members of the criminal justice system have begun to make more vigorous efforts to confront hate crime victimization. Some of these efforts have confronted obstacles that demand a different approach. As a result, the law enforcement response and the prosecution efforts are singled out in this section.

The Law Enforcement Response

As we have just seen, one of the major reasons for the disparity between official and unofficial statistics are reporting and recording practices. In addition to the key decisions that victims must make, many hate crime targets are reluctant to contact the authorities. Minority members might not fully trust the police.

People from other cultures might have a distorted view of who the police are and what they do in this country. The antipathy against Arabs and Muslims generated by such historical events as the September 11, 2001, bombing of the World Trade Center in New York City might amount to an expected backlash against a "new enemy" (Disha, Cavendish, & King, 2011; Zaykowski, 2010). Some other reports may get channeled to civilian third parties, especially on college campuses, who neglect to relay the information to law enforcement officials (Wessler & Moss, 2001). In short, there are ample reasons why the full array of hate crimes might not be coming to the attention of the proper authorities.

One effort to short-circuit these difficulties is to provide additional resources to police officers and sheriff deputies. These endeavors typically come in two forms. The first strategy is to instruct sworn personnel about the contents of hate crime laws. This effort can involve both academy and periodic in-service training. Basic recruit training in Florida, for example, incorporates a module on hate crime. There, academy participants learn about what the elements of a hate crime are, what they should emphasize in the narrative portion of the incident report, and how to alert the State Attorney's Office of a hate crime contained in an arrest affidavit (Florida Criminal Justice Standards & Training Commission, 2013: 321). Other pre-service segments about human diversity and special population groups aim to sensitize trainees to the wide varieties of people they will encounter during the course of their duties.

The second avenue is to sensitize investigators to some of the more prominent signs or indicators that may accompany a bias-motivated incident. Some victims might not be aware of the underlying tone of hatred that prompted their experiences. The absence of an offender in custody might make it more difficult to impute motivation. However, a more thorough and detailed investigation that is attuned to the nature of such episodes might pick up on some subtle signs. As Table 13.6 shows, paying greater attention to details and being aware of things to watch for could produce dividends and help clear a case.

The Prosecution Response

The burden of combatting hate crime does not fall solely upon the shoulders of the law enforcement community. State attorneys or prosecutors also represent an important cog in the wheel of justice. Unfortunately, data regarding the number of hate crime cases that make it to intake, are investigated, get filed, and how they weave their way through the court system are lacking. According to one source, only 5% of the 643 bias crime cases investigated in a New Jersey county from 2001 until 2004 underwent prosecution (Phillips, 2009). Similarly, prosecutors in Texas have filed only 18 hate crime law violations in the 12 years since 2001 (Gillis, 2013) and have averaged less than one hate crime conviction per year (Dexheimer, 2012). While it is not known whether the possible

---

Table 13.6 Key Indicators for Law Enforcement Officers That a Hate Crime May Have Occurred

The main difference between a hate crime and other crimes is that a perpetrator of a hate crime is motivated by bias. To evaluate a perpetrator's motives, you should consider several bias indicators:

- Perceptions of the victim(s) and witnesses about the crime.

- The perpetrator's comments, gestures or written statements that reflect bias, including graffiti or other symbols.

- Any differences between perpetrator and victim, whether actual or perceived by the perpetrator.

- Similar incidents in the same location or neighborhood to determine whether a pattern exists.

- Whether the victim was engaged in activities promoting his/her group or community—for example, by clothing or conduct.

- Whether the incident coincided with a holiday or data of particular significance.

- Involvement of organized hate groups or their members.

- Absence of any other motive, such as economic gain.

The presence of any of these factors does not confirm that the incident was a hate offense, but may indicate the need for further investigation into motive.

Source: International Association of Chiefs of Police (2001). Responding to Hate Crimes: A Police Officer's Guide to Investigation and Prevention. *Alexandria, VA: International Association of Chiefs of Police. Retrieved on July 9, 2013, from http://www.theiacp.org/tabid/299/Default.aspx?id=120&v=1.*

---

sentencing enhancements made defendants more amenable to accepting a plea bargain, some observers find these numbers to be disconcerting.

These concerns led McPhail and Jenness (2005) to probe the calculus that Texas prosecutors invoke when deciding how to proceed with a hate crime case. Two goals guide prosecutorial discretion in charging. The foremost objective of a prosecutor is to strike a solid plea-bargain arrangement if possible. If that avenue fails, then the case proceeds to trial, where winning becomes paramount. In any event, Table 13.7 showcases some of the substantive things that can help prosecutors frame a criminal violation as a hate crime incident.

Prosecutors have two general strategies in mind when they enter the courtroom for a trial. The first concern is to decrease the complexity of a case, and the second consideration is to minimize the risk of losing a case. As we shall see in a moment, relying upon a sentencing enhancement can insert the case into a legal labyrinth. For example, in addition to convincing the jury that a specific crime took place, the prosecutor has the added burden of showing that it was a hate-motivated incident. As a result, many prosecutors are happy to meet the

Table 13.7 Questions that Prosecutors Should Consider When Determining Whether to File Hate Crime Charges

1. Did the offender(s) use words, symbols, or acts that are or may be offensive to an identifiable group?

2. Are the victim and offender members of different racial or ethnic groups? If so, has there been past hostility or tension between these two groups? Has the victim's group been subject to prior similar criminal acts or harassment?

3. Is the victim the sole member of his or her group, or one of a small number of members living or present in the neighborhood where the crime occurred?

4. Has the victim recently moved to the area in which the incident took place?

5. Does the incident appear timed to coincide with any holiday or observance of significance to a certain group or community, such as religious holiday or ethnic celebration?

6. Has the victim or victim's group been involved in recent public or political activity that makes the individual a likely target for hate-motivated violence?

7. Does the offender appear to belong to or does the manner of the commission of the crime appear to involve an organized hate group such as the Ku Klux Klan or Neo-Nazi organization? When the offender is wearing clothing that indicates membership in such a group, the arresting agency should seize the clothing as evidence. If the offender has tattoos indicating such an affiliation, photos of the tattoos should be taken at the time of charging.

8. Does the defendant, in a post-arrest interview or in statements made before or during the commission of the crime, recognize the victim to be a member of a potential "target" group?

9. Has there been recent news coverage or media exposure of similar events?

10. Does the defendant have a prior history involving hate-motivated conduct?

11. Is the attack particularly vicious?

Source: Heffernan, C. J. (2001). Hate Crime: A Prosecutor's Guide. Chicago: Governor's Commission on Discrimination & Hate Crimes. Retrieved on July 9, 2013, from http://www.google.com/url?sa=t&rct=j&q=&esrc=s&source=web&cd=5&ved=0CFcQFjAE&url=http%3A%2F%2Fileeta.org%2FTrainers_resources%2FHate%2520Crime%2520Pros%2520Guide_ashley.ppt&ei=SovcUY2mH43y9gTTklGIDg&usg=AFQjCNGZm9AmGaq_ywtdxXw_dripbpgqxw&sig2=cdJY65TrNu2avmd4EmFnSQ&bvm=bv.48705608,d.eWU.

minimum threshold and avoid muddying a case with additional fanfare. As McPhail and Jenness (2005: 115) explain:

> Prosecutors desire the lowest charge for the highest payoff, and many times hate crime enhancements add to their burden without increasing their reward, especially in first-degree felony cases. The ability to address a bias motivation in the punishment phase rather than the guilt/innocence phase, which removes risk while potentially gaining increased punishment via jury outrage rather than penalty enhancement, also acts against the charging of hate crimes.

Part of the prosecutorial reluctance to wade through a hate crime charge stems from two federal Supreme Court decisions. In the first case, a black family moved into what had formerly been an all-white neighborhood. The defendant, Apprendi, registered his displeasure at this incursion by firing several bullets into the dwelling. After being arrested, Apprendi admitted to shooting because he did not want any minority members living in the area. Later, Apprendi would deny making that biased statement. Eventually, both sides reached a plea-bargain agreement that called for a sentence in the range of 10 to 20 years imprisonment. The judge, however, ignored this arrangement. Instead, he used the hate crime motivation as a penalty enhancement and doubled the sentence.

Apprendi subsequently appealed his sentence. His position was that the judge's reliance upon a sentencing factor to depart from the statutorily established sentencing band violated due process. For one thing, a sentencing factor requires a finding based upon only a preponderance of evidence rather than the more stringent proof beyond reasonable doubt standard. Second, Apprendi maintained the appropriate fact-finding entity would be a jury and not the presiding judge.

The U.S. Supreme Court found Apprendi's arguments persuasive. The Court ruled in his favor and established a very clear-cut rule. It held that:

> Other than the fact of a prior conviction, any fact that increases the penalty for a crime beyond the prescribed statutory maximum must be submitted to a jury, and proved beyond a reasonable doubt (*Apprendi v. New Jersey*, 2000, p. 490).

The Court recently affirmed its *Apprendi* rule when it decided *Alleyne v. United States* (2013). Alleyne had used a firearm during the course of a robbery. The sentencing statute called for a five-year term of imprisonment for using or carrying a firearm during the course of a crime. That penalty could increase to a minimum term of seven years if the firearm was brandished and to 10 years if the suspect fired the weapon. The jury found beyond a reasonable doubt that even though Alleyn possessed a firearm during the incident, he did not brandish or display the gun. That finding made the five-year sentence the applicable benchmark. However, the judge applied the weaker preponderance-of-evidence standard and imposed a seven-year term, the minimum sentence for brandishing a weapon. These actions led the defendant to argue that the sentencing judge had violated his right to a jury trial under the Sixth Amendment. The U.S. Supreme Court sided with Alleyne when it wrote:

> Apprendi's definition of "elements" necessarily includes not only facts that increase the ceiling, but also those that increase the floor. Both kinds of facts alter the prescribed range of sentences to which a defendant is exposed and do so in a manner that aggravates the punishment (*Alleyne v. U.S.*, 2013, pp. 6–7).

As you can see, prosecuting a case as a hate crime does add some twists and turns for prosecutors to negotiate during a trial. As a result, pursuing a hate crime penalty enhancement might not always be an optimal strategy for a prosecutor to pursue.

SUMMARY

Hate crimes are based upon a distorted view of individuals. They harbor prejudice, tension, discrimination, and bias based upon ascribed characteristics. Various groups have suggested a number of initiatives to promote tolerance of people who may not resemble us, but who are still seeking similar things. The Anti-Defamation League, for example, has developed a campaign titled "Imagine a World without Hate" in an effort to appreciate a diverse population. The Southern Poverty Legal Center has put together a call for community action that mobilizes people and channels their energy into a positive force. University and colleges have initiated awareness campaigns to encourage respect for others and to create an atmosphere of inclusiveness on their campuses. All these efforts are geared toward promoting a fundamental principle that the founders of this country debated vigorously and purposively included in the Declaration of Independence they penned in 1776:

> We hold these truths to be self-evident, that all men are created equal, that they are endowed by their Creator with certain unalienable Rights, that among these are Life, Liberty and the pursuit of Happiness.

KEY TERMS

bias crime	moral panic
dark figure of crime	sentencing enhancement
false zeroes	trigger event
hangman's noose	true threats
hate crime	

Victimization at Work and School

INTRODUCTION

Many of the foregoing discussions of victimization revolve around actions tied to the home of the victim and/or the offender. Indeed, as we have seen, one of the perplexing problems with much family violence is how to shed light on actions that take place behind closed doors, hidden from the rest of society.

411

Not all victimization, however, takes place inside the home. One reason we focus on victimization at home is the fact that the home is where many victims and offenders have the most contact. Two other prime locations for victimization are the workplace and school.

The workplace and school are two prime locations for violence and victimization for a variety of reasons. Perhaps the easiest explanation revolves around the idea of routine activities. As we discussed in Chapter 3, the *routine activities perspective* posits that crime is more likely where and when three things coincide: (1) a suitable target, (2) a motivated offender, and (3) an absence of guardians. Both the workplace and schools typically bring these three key ideas together. The fact that most adults hold a job and most youths, by law, must attend school satisfies the first condition. This same fact also addresses the second condition of having a motivated offender. Going to work or school brings a variety of individuals together. It is from these groups of individuals that the potential offenders and victims emerge. The third factor, a lack of guardians, may be an unfortunate part of many schools and places of employment. The schools and employers may not focus on or be prepared to offer protection to those parties who frequent their locations. The need to take protective measures may not have arisen in the past. Thus, the employer or school has failed the victim more through ignorance than because of an uncaring attitude.

Paying greater attention to the role of security and preventing victimization at work and at school is a relatively recent phenomenon. The media, researchers, and various agencies have given increased attention to workplace and school victimization, particularly in terms of violent episodes in recent years. The best illustration of this focus can be found in the attention paid to the problem in the media. Shootings at work and at school are headline news, and coverage often persists on television for weeks or months after the event. Violent events, therefore, are seen as part and parcel of going to work or school.

This chapter investigates victimization, particularly violence, at work and at school. The chapter is divided into separate discussions of work and school. For each type of victimization, the chapter attempts to define the problem, provide an overview of the extent of victimization at work and school, offer potential explanations for the behavior, and visit potential responses. Points of similarity between work and school, such as in the case of teacher victimization, are noted throughout the discussion. A separate but related topic, sexual harassment, is considered at the end of the chapter.

VICTIMIZATION AT WORK

While many different crimes occur at work against the agency or the employees, most discussions of workplace victimization revolve around the problem of violence. Interest in workplace violence has increased in recent years, largely due to media presentations of killings at work. Indeed, violence directed by an employee or ex-employee against others at the workplace has popularly come to be known as *going postal*, a reference to a few highly publicized incidents of violence by postal workers at the workplace. Workplace violence, however, is not confined to a single action or location.

Defining Workplace Victimization

No single, agreed-upon definition of *workplace violence* appears in the literature. A wide range of actions can be subsumed under the idea of workplace violence, including homicide, assault, robbery, rape, intimidation, harassment, threats, and even verbal and psychological aggression. The National Institute of Occupational Safety and Health (NIOSH) defines *workplace violence* as "violent acts, including physical assaults and threats of assault, directed toward persons at work or on duty." Unfortunately, this definition fails to address issues of intimidation, harassment, bullying, or verbal aggression. The fact that those omitted forms of violence are harder to measure is perhaps the most notable reason for adopting a more limited working definition.

Some definitions limit workplace violence to situations in which the offender is a current or former employee at the workplace. Other delineations consider any violent act committed against an employee on the job, whether the offender is a client, another employee, or a complete stranger. The offender also may be a relative or close acquaintance of the victim who is bringing a problem or confrontation from home or elsewhere into the workplace.

Another consideration in defining workplace violence is identifying what constitutes the workplace. Most people think in terms of a specific location, such as a store, factory, office, or school. At the same time, the workplace can be considered in a broader sense. Many jobs require employees to work outdoors and move around a wide geographic area. Water meter readers, police officers, firefighters, real estate salespersons, taxi drivers, and many others do not have just one "place" of business. Rather, their place of business varies across both time and space. Thus, most investigations of locational violence tend to consider the workplace as being wherever the employee is on duty, and not just an identifiable geographic location.

Based on these considerations in defining workplace violence, a typology of violence has developed over time (see Table 14.1). Initially developed by the California Occupational Safety and Health Administration, the typology has been modified by others. The current typology offers four categories of workplace violence. Type 1 reflects violence by offenders who intend to commit a crime. Included here are offenses such as robbery, theft, trespassing, and terrorism, which are related more to the opportunity to commit a crime than to the individuals involved. Type 2 workplace violence involves actions in which there is a customer/client relationship and violence emerges during the

Table 14.1 Typology of Workplace Violence

Type	Description
I. Criminal Intent	The perpetrator has no legitimate relationship to the business or its employee, and is usually committing a crime in conjunction with the violence. These crimes can include robbery, shoplifting, trespassing, and terrorism. The vast majority of workplace homicides (85%) fall into this category.
II. Customer/Client	The perpetrator has a legitimate relationship with the business and becomes violent while being served by the business. This category includes customers, clients, patients, students, inmates, and any other group for which the business provides services. It is believed that a large portion of customer/client incidents occur in the health care industry, in settings such as nursing homes or psychiatric facilities; the victims are often patient caregivers. Police officers, prison staff, flight attendants, and teachers are some other examples of workers who may be exposed to this kind of WPV [workplace violence], which accounts for approximately 3% of all workplace homicides.
III. Worker-on-Worker	The perpetrator is an employee or past employee of the business who attacks or threatens another employee(s) or past employee(s) in the workplace. Worker-on-worker fatalities account for approximately 7% of all workplace homicides.
IV. Personal Relationship	The perpetrator usually does not have a relationship with the business but has a personal relationship with the intended victim. This category includes victims of domestic violence assaulted or threatened while at work, and accounts for about 5% of all workplace homicides.

Source: NIOSH (2006). Workplace Violence Prevention Strategies and Research Needs, NIOSH Publication No. 2006–144. Atlanta: Centers for Disease Control and Prevention. Retrieved on July 21, 2013, from http://www.cdc.gov/niosh/docs/2006-144/pdfs/2006-144.pdf.

business transaction. A wide variety of individuals fall into this relationship category, including customers, clients, patients, inmates, students, and anyone else served by a business. Type 3 involves worker-on-worker confrontations, including past employees. The fourth and final type involves a personal relationship between the victim and offender from outside the workplace. Wives, husbands, boyfriends, girlfriends, children, siblings, friends, and other acquaintances all fall into this group. While explanations for victimization in the workplace are not mutually exclusive across the types (for example, stress at home may have an impact on altercations between coworkers), these categories provide an organizing theme for looking at causation.

The Extent of Workplace Victimization

Systematic analyses of workplace violence are rare, relative to more general studies of violence and victimization in society. While we hear about crime and violence regularly on television and in other media, very little of that information deals with the workplace. Indeed, workplace violence mainly appears in the media only when a mass shooting or homicide takes place at work. This statement, however, does not mean that data on workplace violence do not exist.

Liberty Mutual produces an annual report on workplace safety. In 2010, assaults and violent acts were the tenth leading cause of injuries at work, accounting for 1.3% of all workplace injuries at a cost of $64 million (Liberty Mutual, 2012). While the level is small, this indicates that such acts have increased more than 10% from 1998 to 2010. The Bureau of Labor Statistics [BLS] (2012) reports that homicide is the fourth most frequent cause of work-related fatalities, with 458 homicides occurring at workplaces in 2011, with 358 involving a firearm. While high, this is the fewest number ever reported by the Bureau of Labor Statistics. In fact, the number of workplace homicides has been cut in half since the peak of 1,080 in 1994. The bulk of all workplace homicides involve male victims (96% in 2011). Beyond homicides, workplace violence also appears as assaultive behavior.

WEB ACTIVITY

The Bureau of Labor Statistics provides a great deal of information on fatalities and injuries on the job. Visit **http://www.bls.gov/iif/oshcfoi1.htm** and find out what information is available for investigating victimization at work.

Another way to look at workplace violence is to consider the prevalence of the problem across work sites. According to a BLS survey, 5.3% of more than 7.3 million establishments experienced at least one violent incident in 2005 (Bureau of Labor Statistics, 2006). Table 14.2 provides data on the percent of establishments experiencing different types of workplace violence. In terms of fatal workplace shootings in 2010, over one-quarter were in the retail setting, followed by government (17%) and leisure/hospitality (15%) (Bureau of Labor Statistics, 2013). Figure 14.1 shows fatal workplace shootings by industry.

One of the broadest-based attempts to look at workplace violence may be the National Crime Victimization Survey (NCVS). The NCVS asks respondents to identify where their victimization took place. The survey shows that there were more than 1.7 million crimes of violence committed at the workplace or while at work from 1993 to 1999. This number represents 18% of all victimizations reported over the seven-year time period (Duhart, 2001). It is noteworthy that most of those violent victimizations are simple assaults, which account for three-quarters of all acts of violence at work.

Table 14.2 Percent of Establishments Experiencing Workplace Violence in Past 12 Months

	Any Incidents	Criminal	Customer/Client	Coworker	Domestic Violence
Total	5.3	2.2	2.2	2.3	0.9
Private industry	4.8	2.1	1.9	2.1	0.8
State government	32.2	8.7	15.4	17.7	5.5
Local government	14.7	3.7	10.3	4.3	2.1

Source: Bureau of Labor Statistics (2006). Survey of Workplace Violence Prevention. Washington, DC: U.S. Department of Labor. Retrieved on July 21, 2013, from http://www.bls.gov/iif/oshwc/osnr0026.pdf.

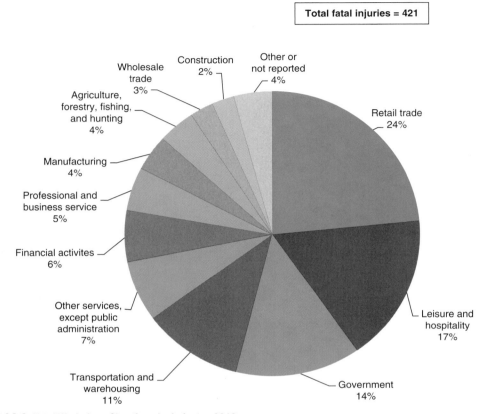

Total fatal injuries = 421

Wholesale trade 3%

Construction 2%

Other or not reported 4%

Agriculture, forestry, fishing, and hunting 4%

Manufacturing 4%

Professional and business service 5%

Financial activites 6%

Other services, except public administration 7%

Transportation and warehousing 11%

Retail trade 24%

Leisure and hospitality 17%

Government 14%

FIGURE 14.1 Fatal Workplace Shootings by Industry, 2010.

Source: Bureau of Labor Statistics (2013). Workplace Homicides from Shootings. *Washington, DC: U.S. Department of Labor. Retrieved on July 17, 2013, from http://www.bls.gov/iif/oshwc/cfoi/osar0016.htm.*

While victimization at work is not an insignificant problem, some workers are more likely to be a victim at work than others. Using data from the NCVS, Duhart (2001) computed the number and rate of victimizations for individuals working in different occupations from 1993 to 1999 (see Table 14.3).

Perhaps not unexpectedly, individuals working in law enforcement are victimized at a higher rate than almost all other occupations. Police officers are the most victimized, both in terms of raw numbers (almost 1.4 million victimizations) and victimization rate (261 per 1,000). Corrections officers are the second most victimized given the number of people in that position (i.e., the rate of violent victimizations), and those working in private security also face a high level of violence. There is also a relatively high rate of victimization for those employed in the mental health field. The results for law enforcement and mental health should not be surprising given the type of job and the kinds of people with whom these employees must deal. Besides

Table 14.3 Occupations of Victims of Violent Victimization in the Workplace, 1993–1999

Occupation	Number	Rate per 1,000 Workers
Medical		
Physicians	71,300	16.2
Nurses	429,100	21.9
Technicians	97,600	12.7
Mental Health		
Professional	290,900	68.2
Custodial	60,400	69.0
Teaching		
Elementary	262,700	16.8
Junior High	321,300	54.2
High School	314,500	38.1
College/University	41,600	1.6
Special Education	102,000	16.7
Law Enforcement		
Police	1,380,400	260.8
Private Security	369,300	86.6
Corrections Officers	277,100	155.7
Retail Sales		
Convenience/Liquor Store	336,800	58.9
Gas Station	86,900	68.3
Bartender	170,600	81.6
Transportation		
Taxicab Driver	84,400	128.3
Bus Driver	105,800	38.2
Total[a]	**4,720,100**	**38.3**

[a]*Total includes occupations not otherwise listed in the table.*
Source: Duhart, D. T. (2001). Violence in the Workplace, 1993–99. Washington, DC: Bureau of Justice Statistics.

law enforcement, the highest rates of victimization appear for taxi drivers (rate of 128.3 per 1,000), followed by those working in retail sales. There is also a relatively high rate for junior high school teachers (rate of 54.2 per 1,000). Why do certain occupations display higher levels of victimization? Perhaps the best explanation entails the factors outlined under the routine activities perspective. Many jobs put workers into situations in which there is a great deal of contact with the public, and often that contact occurs in isolation from coworkers or some form of supervision. Stores, gas stations, and bars, for example, often have a single employee at work at a time. The worker, therefore, is isolated. That is, there is an absence of guardians. In other settings, such as retail sales and service occupations like taxi driving, there is an assumption that a suitable target (i.e., cash) is available, thus making those individuals good targets for offending. Yet another factor is dealing with special populations.

The varied measures of workplace violence offer a number of important insights. First, the commonly held beliefs about workplace violence are generally wrong. Most of the violence is related to other criminal acts and is not the result of a disgruntled worker or ex-employee. Second, the most dangerous occupations are often those in which the employees have tacitly accepted a degree of risk by the very nature of the job, such as law enforcement or mental health workers. Third, the level of risk is closely related to occupations in which the victim works alone and/or the job requires employment at night and early mornings when the employee is isolated from others. Fourth, a significant portion of all victimizations, both violent and theft, occur at work or when the victim is on duty. These findings offer insights that are useful for understanding workplace victimization and responses to this problem.

Workplace Bullying

Not all workplace victimizations involve fatal acts or physical assaults. In fact, a precursor to and potential cause of these serious physical assaults may be bullying in the workplace. According to the Workplace Bullying Institute (2010), workplace bullying is

> repeated, health-harming mistreatment of one or more persons (the targets) by one or more perpetrators that take one or more of the following forms: verbal abuse; offensive conduct/behaviors (including nonverbal) which are threatening, humiliating, or intimidating; work interference—sabotage—which prevents work from getting done.

Bullying also can destroy relationships and lead to failure on the job. Other components of bullying are harassment, emotional abuse, disrespect, and incivility.

Gauging the extent of workplace violence is typically accomplished through surveys of workers or employees. A 2007 survey by the Employment Law Alliance [ELA] reports that 44% of the responding workers claim that their boss is abusive (ELA, 2007). Similarly, the 2010 U.S. Workplace Bullying Survey found that 35% of workers had been bullied at work. This number represents an estimated 53.5 million workers (Namie, 2013). Finally, the Society for Human Resource Management and the Ethics Resource Center (2008) reported that one-third of the responding human resource managers had observed bullying

Table 14.4 Forms of Workplace Bullying (% Responding)

Verbal Abuse	52.2%
Behaviors/Actions	52.5
Abusive Authority	46.9
Interfering with Work Performance	45.4
Destruction of Workplace Relationships	30.2
Other	5.4

Source: Namie, G. (2007). U.S. Workplace Bullying Survey. Retrieved October 25, 2013, from http://www.workplacebullying.org/multi/pdf/WBIsurvey2007.pdf.

behavior in the workplace. While certainly not definitive, the consistency across these surveys suggests that workplace bullying is a significant problem.

The workplace bullying behavior of individuals can take a variety of forms. Table 14.4 shows the types of tactics used by bullies in the workplace. Verbal abuse is reported by 52% of the U.S. Workplace Bullying Survey respondents. This type includes actions such as swearing, shouting, and name calling. A range of behaviors/actions, including threats, intimidation, humiliation, and offensive actions, also are reported by 53% of the respondents (Namie, 2007). Forty-seven percent claim to be victims of abuse of authority. This form includes denials of advancement, undeserved negative evaluations, unsafe working conditions, lack of clear direction, and failure to give proper credit for work. Interfering with performance at work is reported by 45% of the respondents (Namie, 2007).

The source of workplace bullying can be virtually anyone within the work setting. At one extreme are customers and clients who intimidate employees in one way or another. A second source of bullying is coworkers. At the other end of the continuum are supervisors/bosses/employers who commit bullying activity. According to the U.S. Workplace Bullying Survey, the most prevalent form of bullying is that directed at subordinates by bosses (73%), followed by peer offenders (18%) and subordinates against supervisors (9%) (Namie, 2007). (This survey did not consider actions by outside clients.) Beyond their position in the workplace, bullies are more often male (60%) and act alone (68%). Females, Hispanics, and older workers are more likely to be targeted (Namie, 2007).

WEB ACTIVITY

The Workplace Bullying Institute offers information on the extent of bullying and possible responses for individuals and employers. Go to its website (**http://www.workplacebullying.org/**) and investigate responses to workplace bullying.

Clearly, workplace bullying is both pervasive and problematic. At least one-third of survey respondents claim to be victims, and the forms of victimization are significant. At the very least, this behavior makes the workplace a threatening venue for workers. At the extreme, this behavior could be a trigger for, or a precursor to, serious violent aggression. It is to the causes of workplace victimization that we now turn.

Intervention and Prevention

As in any situation in which victimization is a potential concern, the best recourse is to take steps to prevent the problem in the first place. Indeed, the Occupational Safety and Health Act of 1970 addresses the issue of workplace safety in what is known as its *general duty clause*, which states:

> Each employer shall furnish to each of his employees employment and a place of employment which are free from recognized hazards that are causing or are likely to cause death or serious physical harm to his employees (29 U.S.C. 645(a)(1)).

This clause is most often used in connection with physical considerations of a workplace that pose a potential hazard to employees, such as hazardous waste, exposed wiring, slippery floors, and the lack of railing around open pits. While potential violence is not typically considered under this clause, violent acts clearly fall under this section of the Act. Employers, therefore, have a duty to provide a workplace free from violence, whether that violence is between employees or involves individuals from outside the workforce. The form of the response will vary from workplace to workplace.

The Occupational Safety and Health Administration (OSHA) (2002) provides a list of recommendations for protecting employees against workplace violence (see Table 14.5). These measures can be grouped into two general categories: those the employer should take and those the employee should enact. Some of the suggestions fall into the realm of physical design changes that can enhance security, such as improved lighting or alarms, protective enclosures, and inaccessible safes. Other recommendations relate to maintaining contact with workers in the field, working in pairs or groups, and making certain that vehicles and equipment are in good working condition. Employees should also learn how to recognize, avoid, and diffuse problematic situations. Beyond these recommendations, OSHA (2002) provides guidelines for what employees should do following a violent incident on the job, including reporting the act, receiving medical attention, and discussing the event with others.

Protective measures, such as those appearing in Table 14.5, are limited mainly to actions that fit Type 1 violence in which there is clear criminal intent. What they do not address are actions between coworkers or problems brought to the workplace by family members or acquaintances. Beyond the general methods, NIOSH provides a breakdown of prevention efforts according to the four major types of workplace violence (see Table 14.6). The overarching

Table 14.5 OSHA Recommendations for Protecting Employees Against Violence

Employer Actions

- Provide safety education for employees.
- Secure the workplace—locks, video surveillance, lighting, alarms, ID badges, guards.
- Provide drop safes to limit cash on hand.
- Provide cell phones and hand-held alarms for field staff.
- Keep informed of location of field employees.
- Properly maintain employer-provided vehicles.
- Develop policies and procedures for home visits and field work.

Employee Actions

- Learn to recognize, avoid, or diffuse potentially violent situations.
- Alert supervisors to any concerns about safety or security.
- Avoid traveling alone to unfamiliar locations or situations.
- Carry minimal cash.

Source: Occupational Safety and Health Administration (2002). Workplace Violence. OSHA Fact Sheet. Retrieved October 25, 2013, from https://www.osha.gov/OshDoc/data_General_Facts/factsheet-workplace-violence.pdf.

recommendation is to establish policies and procedures, and then educate the staff on those measures.

Braverman (1999) outlines five key elements that all employers should develop for preventing victimization in the workplace. The successful implementation of these factors can address all forms of workplace violence. First, the employer needs to establish *clear policies and procedures* to guide all elements of the work environment (Braverman, 1999). The absence of policies and procedures leaves both employees and outsiders uncertain about how things are to be done, when they are to occur, and so on. Second, all members of the workplace need *training* in all aspects of the policies and procedures. Third, the employer and the employees need *access to medical and mental health expertise* in order to assess and address potential problematic situations and individuals. This expertise can alert the workplace to problems before they get out of hand, as well as give individuals an alternative source of response apart from violent activity. Fourth, the employer needs to establish *clear, commonsense policies and procedures for terminations and layoffs*. This step is especially important for heading off feelings of injustice and a lack of fairness in the decision-making processes at work. Finally, the employer needs to be able to identify *signals for violence* in order to take appropriate actions before the violence actually occurs (Braverman, 1999). This knowledge can be fed back into the mental health and training activities of the overall violence prevention plan.

> **WEB ACTIVITY**
>
> Visit the Occupational Safety and Health Administration website (**https://www.osha.gov/SLTC/workplaceviolence/**) and investigate risk factors, prevention programs, and training materials available to address workplace violence.

Table 14.6 Prevention Strategies Specific to Types of Workplace Violence

Type I—Criminal Intent

- Environmental interventions
  - Cash control
  - Lighting control (indoor and outdoor)
  - Entry and exit control
  - Surveillance (e.g., mirrors and cameras, particularly closed-circuit cameras)
  - Signage
- Behavioral interventions
  - Training on appropriate robbery response
  - Training on use of safety equipment
  - Training on dealing with aggressive, drunk, or otherwise problem persons
- Administrative interventions
  - Hours of operation
  - Precautions during opening and closing
  - Good relationship with police
  - Implementing safety and security policies for all workers

Type II—Customer/Client Violence

- Adequate staffing, skill mix
  - Address need to serve the client adequately to avoid problems
- Training
  - Focus on hazards and early recognition of violence, de-escalation techniques, communication skills
- Accreditation criteria tied to workplace violence prevention
  - Specify and train on specific requirements addressing violence prevention

Type III—Worker-on-Worker

- Evaluating prospective workers
  - Establish a hiring process that screens potential employees
- Training in policies and procedures
  - Establish process for reporting behaviors; orientation training that addresses these issues
- Focus on observable behaviors
  - Observation and reporting of changes in behavior; timely and consistent responses

Type IV—Personal Relationship Violence

- Training in policies and reporting
  - Provide information on the nature of personal/intimate partner violence; training on cues and traits; establish clear policies for reporting
- A culture of support
  - Support for victims; assurance of no penalties for those who come forward; confidentiality; training of all staff; provide avenues of help for perpetrators

Source: Adapted by authors from NIOSH (2006). Workplace Violence Prevention Strategies and Research Needs. NIOSH Publication No. 2006-144. Cincinnati: NIOSH. Retrieved on July 21, 2013, from http://www.cdc.gov/niosh/docs/2006-144/pdfs/2006-144.pdf.

Responses to Workplace Victimization

While the prevention ideas outlined previously hold the potential of mitigating the level and amount of victimization in the workplace, they do little to address the failures of the workplace to protect victims. What recourse do victims have after being victimized at work? Who can be held accountable for the victimization? As in any other situation in which an individual is a crime victim, the victim can turn to a variety of sources for assistance. Victim compensation, restitution, and civil action against the offender are all possible sources of help. Another possible source of assistance to employees is workers' compensation. *Workers' compensation* is basically an insurance plan in which employers participate (typically mandated by law) that makes payments to employees who are hurt on the job. The employer pays premiums into the compensation system on behalf of all employees. Workers can draw on the funds if an injury is job-related.

Another source of victim assistance may come from *third-party lawsuits*. As discussed earlier in this book, a third-party lawsuit is one in which a victim can sue someone other than the offender due to the failure of the third party to take action that would have mitigated a foreseeable problem. In the case of workplace violence, the employer has a duty to take action to provide a safe work environment to its employees. The occurrence of victimization at work may signal the failure of the employer to respond to a known problem or a problem about which the employer should have known.

Schneid (1999) lists various bases on which a victim can claim employer negligence in a third-party lawsuit. The first involves *negligent hiring*, in which an employer knew or should have known that the individual posed a risk to others. A second related issue is the *negligent retention* of an employee who already works for the employer and is a known risk to others. Both of these issues raise concerns over the proper screening of potential and current employees. Third is *negligent supervision*. In this situation, the employer may be unable to dismiss a potential problem worker, but should recognize that the person poses an unacceptable risk and needs to be closely monitored on the job. The failure to carry out the needed supervision may allow the violence to occur. A fourth basis for a suit may involve *negligent training*. While the failure to train employees adequately to use equipment or do the job properly is probably the most common form of negligence under this heading, it is also possible that the training should include how to deal with problem clients or coworkers. The failure to provide that training may allow violence to take place. Perhaps the clearest form of negligence involves *negligent security*. The employer has a duty to safeguard employees, the workplace, and the public from known problems. These problems may have appeared in the past and the employer simply ignored the problem rather than taking proactive steps to avoid its reoccurrence (Schneid, 1999).

Under each of these forms of negligence, the victim can make a claim against the employer for loss and damages due to the victimization. As discussed in Chapter 5, this recourse does not require the actual offender to be caught, to be convicted, or to have resources to pursue. The onus falls on the employer. The task for the victim, however, is to hire an attorney and prove that the employer knew, or should have known, of the potential problem. The burden is on the victim to prove the negligence. This action can take time and resources that many victims do not have.

Responding to victimization at work is a relatively new issue for most agencies. While violence and crime at work are not new problems, they have become recognized and studied in recent years. Many organizations have not given the problem of workplace violence much attention in the past. A great deal of additional research and work should be directed at victimization on the job.

VICTIMIZATION AT SCHOOL

Victimization and violence at school have become major concerns in recent years. This emphasis is due largely to several isolated events that have received major media attention. Perhaps the most notable example is the mass murder at Columbine High School in Colorado, where two students planned and carried out lethal attacks on fellow students. Similarly, heinous crimes on college campuses, such as the rape and murder of Jeanne Clery in her college dorm room at Lehigh University in Pennsylvania, have raised concerns over safety on college campuses. The reality of victimization at schools, however, is far from what is portrayed in the media. Lethal violence is relatively rare, and most victimizations involve property offenses or minor confrontations. In this part of the chapter, we outline the problem of victimization in schools and discuss the responses that institutions should take to address these problems. We will first address victimization in junior and senior high schools before turning our attention to institutions of higher education.

Victimization in Junior and Senior High Schools

In contrast to the earlier discussion of the workplace, where the emphasis was generally on violent acts, the literature on schools takes a broader approach to victimization. School violence, including acts such as murder, assault, and rape, represent the most serious form of victimization at school. It is typically these acts that find their way onto the evening news and frame the problem for the general public. School victimization, however, includes another entire realm of actions that typically receives less attention. Included here are theft offenses, vandalism, bullying, and verbal altercations. As will be seen, this latter group is much more prevalent in schools, although it rarely finds its way into the media or many discussions. It is important, therefore, to consider both violent and nonviolent forms of victimization when discussing the academic setting.

Besides listing the types of actions to consider, it is equally important to recognize the targets and the locations of the victimization when discussing schools. One major assumption held by many people is that victimization in schools takes place between students. This assumption, however, neglects the fact that teachers and staff members are also potential victims. Indeed, the discussion earlier in this chapter shows that victimization against teachers is not an insignificant problem. A second consideration is where the victimization takes place. School victimization covers more than just the school building or the playground. Students in transit to and from school, whether walking, riding a school bus, or using public transportation, are generally considered under the auspices of the school. Any action against them in those venues is considered a form of victimization at school. This realization also means that one can extend "victimization at school" to include the time immediately before and immediately after the school bell rings.

Beyond the actual victimization of students, teachers, or staff, it is important to consider the level of fear felt by the members of the school environment. Fear can affect more individuals than just actual crime victims. Its influence can be particularly debilitating if the fear keeps youths from going to school or concentrating on studies. The purpose of the school can become secondary to the safety concerns of the students. It is important, therefore, to examine the level of fear and the consequences of fear in schools.

The Extent of School Victimization

Recent years have seen an increased interest in assessing the extent of victimization at school. Several large-scale analyses of victimization and crime, as well as numerous smaller projects, provide insight into this problem and how this phenomenon may be changing over time. Luckily, the data do not come exclusively from one source or point of view. Instead, information is available from students, teachers, and administrators. It looks at both individual experiences with victimization and crime experienced as a school (i.e., reports on the level of crime for an entire school).

Public interest in school crime typically revolves around homicide and mass killings in schools. Certainly, media portrayals of sensational killings at schools—such as at Columbine High School in Colorado in 1999, Westside Middle School in Jonesboro, Arkansas, in 1998, and Sandy Hook Elementary in 2012—lead to the impression that lethal violence is a relatively common event that is occurring with ever greater frequency. The reality of the situation, however, is that homicide at school is a rare event (see Table 14.7). For the 2010–2011 academic year, there were only 11 homicides at schools (Robers et al., 2013). These results are not atypical and show that homicide is a very rare event at school, despite the picture drawn in the media.

Beyond homicide, victimization at schools is not rare. One major source of data from students is the NCVS. Data from the 2011 NCVS appear in Table 14.8. The data indicate that 49 out of every 1,000 youths ages 12–18 report being

Table 14.7 Homicides of Youths

School Year	Total Student, Staff, and Non-Student School-Associated Violent Deaths	Homicides at School	Total Homicides
1992–93	57	34	2,713
1993–94	48	29	2,922
1994–95	48	28	2,705
1995–96	53	32	2,552
1996–97	48	28	2,229
1997–98	57	34	2,106
1998–99	47	33	1,781
1999–00	37	14	1,566
2000–01	34	14	1,503
2001–02	36	16	1,503
2002–03	36	18	1,548
2003–04	45	23	1,465
2004–05	52	22	1,551
2005–06	44	20	1,689
2006–07	63	30	1,811
2007–08	48	21	1,743
2008–09	44	17	1,591
2009–10	35	19	1,595
2010–11	31	11	–

Source: Adapted by authors from Robers, S., Kemp, J., & Truman, J. (2013). Indicators of School Crime and Safety: 2012 (NCES 2013-036/NCJ 241446). National Center for Education Statistics, U.S. Department of Education, and Bureau of Justice Statistics, Office of Justice Programs, U.S. Department of Justice. Washington, DC. Retrieved on July 21, 2013, from http://nces.ed.gov/pubs2013/2013036.pdf.

victimized at school. The highest rates of victimization across most demographic categories appear in theft offenses, followed by violent crimes. Breakdowns by gender, race/ethnicity, and age reveal some interesting results. First, the rate of violent victimization is much higher for males, but it is similar in other categories. Second, blacks have a much higher rate for total crime and theft.

Based on figures such as those seen here, some people have suggested that the problem of school crime is rather small. Indeed, relatively few students are ever the victim of any serious violent victimization, and the percent of property victimizations is also small. What can be lost in these figures, however, is the number of youths who are victimized. According to the NCVS, roughly 1.2 million students ages 12–18 were victims of nonfatal crimes at school in 2011 (Robers et al., 2013). This figure translates into about 648,600 thefts and 597,500 violent crimes. What these numbers show is that, despite the relatively low rate, the actual number of victims at school is significant. At the same time, the level of reported victimization at school has declined steadily from 1993 to 2011.

Table 14.8 Rate (per 1,000) of Student-Reported Victimization at School by Selected Characteristics, 2011[a]

Student Characteristics	Total	Theft	Violent[b]	Serious Violent[c]
Gender				
Male	57	29	28	4
Female	41	22	19	3
Race/Ethnicity				
White	46	24	23	3
Black	70	40	30	11
Hispanic	45	21	24	2
Other	43	24	18	—
Age				
12–14	55	21	34	6
15–18	44	30	14	2
Total	49	26	24	4

[a]Data for students aged 12 to 18.
[b]Violent crimes include rape, sexual assault, robbery, aggravated assault, and simple assault.
[c]Serious violent crimes include the violent crimes except for simple assault.
Source: Robers, S., Kemp, J., & Truman, J. (2013). Indicators of School Crime and Safety: 2012 (NCES 2013-036/NCJ 241446). National Center for Education Statistics, U.S. Department of Education, and Bureau of Justice Statistics, Office of Justice Programs, U.S. Department of Justice. Washington, DC. Retrieved on July 21, 2013, from http://nces.ed.gov/pubs2013/2013036.pdf.

Besides being victimized by thefts or violent acts, students are common targets of bullying behavior. According to the 2011 *NCVS: School Crime Supplement*, roughly 28% of all students reported being bullied at school and 9% report being a victim of cyberbullying (Robers et al., 2013). Bullying is more prevalent against females, whites, younger youths, and in public schools. Bullying behavior does decrease with grade level. An inspection of the types of bullying reported in Table 14.9 shows that several categories are actually forms of criminal victimization, although the students report it as bullying.

Students are not the only potential victims at school. Teachers, administrators, and other staff also can be targets. Data from surveys of teachers show that a significant number have been the victims of force or threats of force at school. According to the National Center for Educational Statistics, more than 444,000 teachers were physically attacked or threatened with injury by a student during the 2007–2008 school year (Dinkes et al., 2009). This represents approximately 10% of all teachers. The level of teacher victimization, therefore, is not insignificant and should not be ignored in discussions of school crime.

Table 14.9 Types of Bullying at School, 2011

Type of Bullying	Percent of Students Reporting
Made fun of, called names, or insulted	18.6
Subject of rumors	18.3
Threatened with harm	5.0
Pushed, shoved, tripped, or spit on	7.9
Tried to make do things did not want to do	3.3
Excluded from activities on purpose	5.6
Property destroyed on purpose	2.8
Cyberbullying	9.0

Source: Robers, S., Kemp, J., & Truman, J. (2013). Indicators of School Crime and Safety: 2012 (NCES 2013-036/NCJ 241446). National Center for Education Statistics, U.S. Department of Education, and Bureau of Justice Statistics, Office of Justice Programs, U.S. Department of Justice. Washington, DC. Retrieved on July 21, 2013, from http://nces.ed.gov/pubs2013/2013036.pdf.

 **WEB ACTIVITY**

The full report on school crime for 2012 can be found at **http://nces.ed.gov/pubs2013/2013036.pdf**. What other information is available in the report? Of what value is the information?

Responses to School Victimization

Beyond the immediate problem of victimization at school, we need to be concerned about how individuals respond to both the real and perceived levels of crime and victimization. Typical responses to real or perceived victimization at school generally fall into three categories: fear, avoidance, and self-protection. Each of these has implications for the students and the educational system.

Fear of crime is a common problem expressed by students. According to the 2011 NCVS, 3.7% of students feared attack or harm at school, and 2.4% feared attack or harm on the way to or from school (Robers et al., 2013). These figures suggest that the school is a more fearful place than the outside community for youths. As we showed in earlier chapters, fear can be a debilitating factor for some people. In relation to students and schools, it can cause youths to focus on noneducational endeavors, thus degrading the learning environment and potentially harming the long-term potential of students to succeed in school or at work. This fear can also lead to other immediate responses.

Two responses are avoidance behavior and the carrying of weapons to school (Table 14.10). Staying home from school due to fear of victimization is a common response for some youths. The 2011 *NCVS: School Crime Supplement* reports that 5.5% of students avoid school, school activities, and/or specific places at school due to fear of attack or harm (Robers et al., 2013). A variety of other studies have reported similar proportions of youths who skip school due to fear (Lab & Clark, 1996; Lab & Whitehead, 1994; Metropolitan Life, 1993;

Table 14.10 Responses of Students to Victimization and Fear in School, 2011

Avoidance Behavior:	5.5%
School activities	2.0
Stayed home from school	0.8
Avoided places	4.7
Entrances	0.9
Hallways or stairs	2.5
School cafeteria	1.8
Restrooms	1.7
Other places	1.1
Carrying Weapons to School	**5.4**

Source: Compiled by authors from Robers, S., Kemp, J., & Truman, J. (2013). Indicators of School Crime and Safety: 2012 *(NCES 2013-036/NCJ 241446). National Center for Education Statistics, U.S. Department of Education, and Bureau of Justice Statistics, Office of Justice Programs, U.S. Department of Justice. Washington, DC. Retrieved on July 21, 2013, from http://nces.ed.gov/pubs2013/2013036.pdf.*

Ringwalt et al., 1992). While the youths may be attending school, the quality of the education they receive is diminished. Some students may go hungry, suffer discomfort because they are afraid to use restrooms, arrive late for classes due to using only certain stairways or hallways, or refrain from taking part in enriching extracurricular activities. In essence, the school experience is far from an ideal nurturing atmosphere. The ultimate form of this avoidance is quitting school. Students who drop out are not included in surveys of students. Thus, the number of youths who report avoiding school due to fear in most studies is an undercount of who is taking this action.

Another form of response involves self-defense actions, particularly carrying weapons for protection. According to data from the *Youth Risk Behavior Survey* conducted by the Centers for Disease Control and Prevention, 5.4% of high school students reported carrying a weapon to school at least once in the past 30 days (Dinkes et al., 2009). Lab and Clark (1996) found that 24% of the respondents carried a weapon to school for protection at least once over a six-month time period. Even higher levels of weapon possession at school emerge in studies of inner-city schools (see, for example, Sheley, McGee, & Wright, 1995). Among the weapons carried for protection are guns, knives, brass knuckles, razor blades, spiked jewelry, and mace (Lab & Clark, 1996).

Unfortunately, while bringing a weapon to school may make a youth feel safer, such devices have the potential of causing more problems than they solve. One negative outcome is that being caught with a weapon can lead to expulsion, criminal prosecution, and other sanctions against the student who is trying to protect him- or herself. A second possibility is that if the student is attacked and does try to use the weapon, the level of violence and victimization may escalate. That is, a fistfight can become a shooting, or a theft can result in an aggravated assault. The victim may be more seriously harmed, or the victim may become the offender. Yet another consequence is that schools can become armed camps where the administration is forced to take progressively intrusive measures to keep weapons out of school.

Regardless of which response is taken to actual or potential victimization, the atmosphere and the activity in the schools shift away from education. Learning becomes a secondary concern to safety and protection. Students and teachers never quite devote their entire attention to the lesson plan. Everyone in the school is victimized.

Addressing School Victimization

Schools have taken a wide array of actions to deal with actual and potential crime and victimization. Perhaps the first step is to identify factors and indicators of potential violence. Table 14.11 presents one list of warning signs identified by more than 500 experts on school violence and victimization, coming from diverse backgrounds and experiences. Among these signs are past violent behavior, verbal aggression, lack of parental supervision, a preoccupation with violence, gang participation, depression or withdrawal, past trauma, and substance abuse. While these traits cannot definitively identify students who will be violent at school, students displaying these signs should be given added attention or referred to appropriate sources of intervention.

🌐 **WEB ACTIVITY**

The National School Safety Center (**http://www.schoolsafety.us/**) addresses a wide range of victimization and safety issues for schools. What kinds of suggestions and materials can you find on its website for addressing school safety?

Often, the most visible and immediate response is to introduce measures that impose greater physical control over students, teachers, administrators, visitors, and the school grounds. Typical responses include the call for installing metal detectors at entrances, locking all but one door to outsiders, requiring everyone to wear identification badges, installing closed-circuit television monitors, and hiring guards for the hallways and the building. Unfortunately, these prevention efforts typically assume that the offenders and the threats come from outside the school and that most of the problems are addressed once students are screened into the building. What these efforts overlook is that most of the crimes take place between offenders and victims who are students, each of whom has a right (and expectation) to be in the school.

Beyond the simple introduction of physical security devices and methods is the heavy reliance on harsh discipline and control measures. Suspension and expulsion from school are common responses to violence and repeated

Table 14.11 Warning Signs of Potential Violence

- Has engaged in violent behavior in the past.
- Has tantrums and uncontrollable angry outbursts abnormal for someone that age.
- Continues exhibiting anti-social behaviors that began at an early age.
- Forms and/or maintains friendships with others who have repeatedly engaged in problem behaviors.
- Often engages in name calling, cursing, or abusive language.
- Has brought a weapon or has threatened to bring a weapon to school.
- Consistently makes violent threats when angry.
- Has a substance abuse problem.
- Is frequently truant or has been suspended from school on multiple occasions.
- Seems preoccupied with weapons or violence, especially those associated more with killing humans than with target practice or hunting.
- Has few or no close friends despite having lived in the area for some time.
- Has a sudden decrease in academic performance and/or interest in school activities.
- Is abusive to animals.
- Has too little parental supervision given the student's age and level of maturity.
- Has been a victim of abuse or been neglected by parents/guardians.
- Has repeatedly witnessed domestic abuse or other forms of violence.
- Has experienced trauma or loss in the home or community.
- Pays no attention to the feelings or rights of others.
- Intimidates others.
- Has been a victim of intimidation by others.
- Dwells on perceived slights, rejection, or mistreatment by others; blames others for his/her problems and appears vengeful.
- Seems preoccupied with TV shows, movies, video games, reading materials, or music that expresses violence.
- Reflects excessive anger in writing projects.
- Is involved in a gang or anti-social group.
- Seems depressed/withdrawn or has exhibited severe mood or behavioral swings, which appear greater in magnitude, duration, or frequency than those typically experienced by students that age.
- Expresses sadistic, violent, prejudicial, or intolerant attitudes.
- Has threatened or actually attempted suicide or acts of unfashionable self-mutilation.

Source: International Association of Chiefs of Police (2000). Guide for Preventing and Responding to School Violence. *Washington, DC: International Association of Chiefs of Police.*

transgressions by students. Unfortunately, these actions do little to address the factors that may cause the problem, and often represent only a quick fix for larger underlying problems in the school. In addition, these responses sometimes force the offending party to drop out of school and cause further problems down the road (Adams, 2000). Closely related to suspension and expulsion are zero-tolerance policies that often lead to a greater reliance on suspension and expulsion. Such stances do not allow the schools to address the differing needs of transgressors (Adams, 2000). Anti-bullying legislation has been enacted in some states as well (see Figure 14.2).

Recognizing the limitations of such physical prevention methods, schools have also attempted to implement a variety of programs and policies to deal with crime and aggression in the schools. One general approach is to institute some form of conflict management or resolution program. These programs appear under a variety of different names, including dispute resolution, peer mediation, and conflict resolution. While the approach of the programs may vary, their purpose is to teach students to recognize conflict and learn appropriate ways of channeling aggression and resolving problems before they can escalate further. Several programs of this type have shown success, such as the Resolving Conflict Creatively Program (DeJong, 1993), the Responding in Peaceful and Positive Ways program (Farrell & Meyer, 1997), and the work of Olweus (1994, 1995) to address bullying problems in schools. One advantage of these interventions is that they attempt to address the needs of both the victims and the offenders. The victims are active participants in responding to any actions against them and can seek redress for losses or injuries, while the offender can learn appropriate methods for dealing with anti-social behavior and impulses.

Where these varied responses may address issues of school security, prevent future problems in school, and satisfy the need to assist offenders, they often leave the victim on the outside of the response (the notable exceptions are some forms of conflict resolution). There are differing ways that a school can respond to the needs of the victim, as well as students who are indirectly victimized by criminal actions taking place at school. Many of those responses mirror the responses offered in other chapters. Other responses, however, may be geared to the unique nature of the school, where a large number of individuals must be considered in the wake of different actions.

College Campus Victimization

Crime on college campuses has vaulted to the forefront of social concern as the result of highly publicized shootings on campus (such as the shootings at the Virginia Polytechnic Institute and State University in 2007). For years, many colleges and universities were reluctant to reveal crime data. Administrators were concerned about the kind of image such information might project about their institutions. Worries abounded that negative publicity might hurt student recruitment and adversely affect enrollments. Consequently, systematic collection of crime data from colleges was rarely possible, and the information was largely unavailable.

The situation changed with congressional approval of the Jeanne Clery Disclosure of Campus Security Policy and Campus Crime Statistics Act (20 U.S.C. 1092). Jeanne Clery, a 19-year-old college freshman at Lehigh University in Pennsylvania, was raped and murdered

FIGURE 14.2 Massachusetts Governor Deval Patrick pauses during a bill signing at the Statehouse in Boston, May 3, 2010.
The bill is meant to crack down on school bullies and requires teachers to report bullying to principals. *Credit: AP Photo/Steven Senne.*

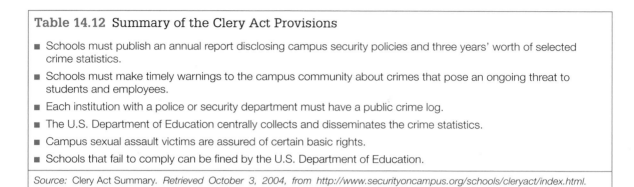

Table 14.12 Summary of the Clery Act Provisions

- Schools must publish an annual report disclosing campus security policies and three years' worth of selected crime statistics.
- Schools must make timely warnings to the campus community about crimes that pose an ongoing threat to students and employees.
- Each institution with a police or security department must have a public crime log.
- The U.S. Department of Education centrally collects and disseminates the crime statistics.
- Campus sexual assault victims are assured of certain basic rights.
- Schools that fail to comply can be fined by the U.S. Department of Education.

Source: Clery Act Summary. *Retrieved October 3, 2004, from http://www.securityoncampus.org/schools/cleryact/index.html.*

in her dormitory room by another student whom she did not know. The suspect, who was apprehended, entered the dormitory through a series of doors that had been left ajar. Later, it was revealed that the university had received numerous complaints about propped-open doors in that same dormitory in previous months. In addition, there were other security lapses and a lack of available information about campus safety.

Dissatisfaction with how the university handled the investigation and other aspects of the matter prompted the victim's parents to lobby for a campus crime disclosure law. Those efforts were successful at the state level and paved the way for a national campaign. In 1990, a new federal directive took effect, mandating that colleges and universities make certain crime statistics public. There have been several modifications and amendments to the original provisions over the years. Table 14.12 summarizes the currently existing provisions.

The Extent of College Student Victimization

The Clery Act requirements have resulted in more than 6,000 colleges and universities forwarding victimization statistics and other information to the U.S. Department of Education for tabulation. Table 14.13 contains the total number of known crimes that took place on college campuses throughout the entire country during 2009. These tallies are further divided according to the type of college or university. The counts reveal that burglary is the most common crime on campuses, followed by aggravated assaults, forcible sexual assaults, and robberies. Murder and nonforcible sexual assaults are relatively infrequent events. Interestingly, there does appear to be some variation according to the type of institution. Four-year colleges and universities are responsible for the largest number of violent victimization episodes, followed by two-year schools and other kinds of programs.

While these data are interesting, they are silent on several fronts. For example, the information in Table 14.13 pertains to victimizations that have taken place

Table 14.13 Number of Known On-Campus Violent Crimes, 2009

Type of Institution	Murder/ Nonnegligent Manslaughter	Forcible Sex Offenses	Nonforcible Sex Offenses	Robbery	Aggravated Assault	Burglary
Public, 4-year or above	8	1,208	41	675	1,203	10,816
Private nonprofit, 4-year or above	6	1,137	11	511	701	9,153
Private for-profit, 4-year or above	0	8	1	89	47	305
Public, 2-year	2	210	13	275	473	2,298
Private nonprofit, 2-year	0	10	1	23	46	220
Private for-profit, 2-year	0	5	1	90	69	282
Public, less-than-2-year	0	9	4	11	82	85
Private nonprofit, less-than-2-year	1	2	0	73	8	38
Private for-profit, less-than-2-year	0	1	0	118	46	172
Total	16	2,590	72	1,865	2,675	24,069

Source: U.S. Department of Education (2013). Campus Security: Data on Campus Crime. Washington, DC: U.S. Department of Education. Retrieved on July 21, 2013, from http://www2.ed.gov/admins/lead/safety/campus.html#data.

on college campuses. While the Department of Education now requires schools to document crimes that take place on property adjacent to their campuses, local authorities are typically responsible for recording those reports. The availability and accuracy of these statistics are subject to a host of influences. In addition, these numbers do not provide a full picture of the collegiate experience. Rising enrollments mean that many institutions lack sufficient housing for their students. This shortage forces college enrollees to look for off-campus housing and commute to campus. Victimization episodes that arise from the collegiate lifestyle, but take place away from the campus gates, tend not to make their way into institutionally generated statistics. Another influence, the dark figure of crime stemming from student-victims not contacting the authorities (Fisher et al., 2003a, b; Hart, 2003), can also affect the accuracy of these reports.

WEB ACTIVITY

You can investigate the level of crime and victimization at your institution and for schools across the country using data compiled by the U.S. Department of Education at **http://ope.ed.gov/security/**. Look at statistics for your institution and compare them to another one. What does it show?

Addressing Campus Crime

In the past, most responses to crime on college campuses simply reflected law enforcement and security efforts found in the general community. Prevention activities primarily involved educating and working with students to take

---

Table 14.14 Ohio Campus Security Checklist

Does your campus have a safety and security plan? Has it been reviewed and updated since April 2007? Please check all of the following that apply to your campus:

1. Protocols are in place to address the behavior of students, faculty, staff, and guests who are disruptive or pose a significant potential risk of harm and a clear response protocol exists if a student or other person on campus is engaged in or actively threatening violence.
2. Faculty, staff, and students know how to identify and what to do if someone poses a risk of harm to self or others.
3. Campus authorities have a clear understanding of relevant laws.
4. Responses to actual or potential threats are coordinated with on and off campus safety forces.
5. Protocols are established for both internal and external communications with all who need to know, including students, faculty, staff, administrators, safety officials, hospitals, and media.
6. Procedures are in place to mobilize support required during a crisis, including vital staff, mental health personnel, communications staff, and facility operational staff.
7. A plan is in place for business continuity and resumption/recovery.
8. Resources are available to address emotional, physical, and other human needs following an incident.
9. Plans are developed to return essential staff and personnel to campus.

Source: Task Force on Ohio College Campus Safety and Security (2007). Report to Governor Ted Strickland. *Columbus: Ohio Board of Regents. Retrieved on July 21, 2013, from http://www.uc.edu/content/dam/uc/publicsafety/docs/TaskForceon CampusSecurityFinalReport.pdf.*

---

precautions and call for assistance when faced with criminal behavior. This general state of affairs has changed greatly since the 2007 Virginia Tech shootings. Most institutions and states have taken steps to develop emergency response plans and made proactive efforts to head off serious violent actions on campus.

One example of efforts at campus safety is the actions of the Task Force on Ohio College Safety and Security. This task force was charged with ensuring that all college campuses in Ohio are safe and prepared to address security breaches. Outcomes of this task force include the creation of a clearinghouse on campus safety information, clarification of legal issues facing colleges when identifying and investigating potential offending students, developing safety training courses for security personnel, and workshops on safety issues. The task force also promulgated a Campus Safety Checklist (see Table 14.14) with which campuses can assess their preparation to address safety problems and concerns.

WEB ACTIVITY

The University System of Ohio has produced a campus safety guidebook that can be found on this textbook's companion website at **http://booksite.elsevier. com/9780323287654**. What kinds of information can you find in that material on making a campus safe?

SEXUAL HARASSMENT

Another problem facing both employees and students is that of sexual harassment. *Sexual harassment* differs from most other forms of victimization, including sexual assaults, in two primary ways. First, sexual harassment often does not involve an actual physical assault. Rather, harassment can manifest itself in subtle ways, such as sexually suggestive comments, unwanted touching, risqué jokes and pornography, or blatant demands for sexual contact. In most cases, these actions take place within work or educational settings where both the offender and the victim are required to be in close contact. This consideration means that the offender and victim are acquaintances. The second distinguishing feature of sexual harassment is that the criminal justice system rarely deals with these infractions. Instead, sexual harassment falls into the realm of civil or administrative law and remedies.

While no universally accepted definition of sexual harassment exists, most definitions outline unacceptable actions that fall into two broad categories. The first is *quid pro quo* harassment, wherein the offender requires sexual contact in exchange for employment, better working conditions, high grades, or other favorable treatment. In essence, the offender sets up an exchange arrangement in which sex is the cost to be paid by the victim. Most people would recognize this first category as a violation of the rights of others. The actual threat does not have to be carried out for the action to constitute sexual harassment. The threat is enough in and of itself.

The second category deals with the creation of a *hostile environment.* Under this form, the harassment may be as subtle as displaying calendars of naked people at work, telling crude sexual jokes, touching a person, or commenting about how "sexy" a person looks in certain clothing. In each case the victim, intentionally or unintentionally, is made to feel uncomfortable. While some individuals may not perceive these actions as harassment, others will be impacted negatively by the activity. This second form, therefore, is more difficult to identify and requires individuals to express their feelings about such actions to the offending party. The true problem begins when the offender continues a practice after being informed about the transgression. The hostile environment situation does not require the loss of a job, benefits, or other factors in order to prove harassment (Rubin, 1995).

Both of these forms of sexual harassment appear in Section 1604.11 of the Federal Regulations governing the *Equal Employment Opportunity Commission* (EEOC) (see Table 14.15). While the definition is specific to employment situations, many institutions have tailored it to fit the unique nature of their own environments. Universities, for example, typically add language that applies the same conditions to actions that interfere with the ability of a student to learn. It is not uncommon to see definitional policies developed to meet the specific needs of different agencies and settings.

The Extent of Sexual Harassment

Gauging the extent of sexual harassment depends on the definition used and the target of the investigation. There is no ongoing national data collection

> **Table 14.15** The EEOC Definition of Sexual Harassment
>
> Section 1604.11 Sexual Harassment.
>
> Unwelcome sexual advances, requests for sexual favors, and other verbal or physical conduct of a sexual nature constitute sexual harassment when:
>
> (1) submission to such conduct is made either explicitly or implicitly a term or condition of an individual's employment,
>
> (2) submission to or rejection of such conduct by an individual is used as the basis for employment decisions affecting such individual, or
>
> (3) such conduct has the purpose or effect of unreasonably interfering with an individual's work performance or creating an intimidating, hostile, or offensive working environment.

program for sexual harassment. Rather, what knowledge we have is based primarily on various surveys. Further complicating the measurement of the problem is the fact that most surveys target specific groups, such as students or faculty at a single university, or heavily female-dominated employee groups like nursing. Thus, the results are typically not generalizable to the overall population. Other measurement problems include the failure of respondents to report harassment due to embarrassment or fear of retaliation, and the failure of some people to define a sexual situation as harassment even though it may fit the legal definition.

Despite these measurement problems, numerous studies provide insight into the frequency with which sexual harassment occurs. In one early study, 17% of the female students reported sexual advances, and 14% claimed to receive unwanted sexual invitations. McKinney (1990), studying 156 faculty at one institution, reports that almost 14% of the female respondents and 9% of the male respondents felt they had been sexually harassed by a coworker. In a national survey of college faculty, 6.8% of the respondents reported harassment, with women reporting almost five times more incidents than men (Dey, Korn, & Sax, 1996). Using results from female employees, Gutek (1985) advises that 53% had been negatively impacted (i.e., being fired or denied promotions or raises) due to refusing sexual advances at work. Studies of the general public, while rarer, have uncovered even greater levels of harassment. For example, Wyatt and Riederle (1995) find 44% of women from the Los Angeles area claim to have been sexually harassed at work, and 45% report harassment in social settings. Finally, Swisher (1995) notes that the number of sexual harassment claims made to the EEOC more than doubled from 1991 to 1993 (3,300 complaints compared with 7,300 complaints). EEOC data on the number of sexual harassment charges brought to their agency or Fair Employment Practices agencies around the country show even greater numbers of harassment (see Table 14.16). In 2011, there were more than 11,000 cases filed (Equal Employment

WEB ACTIVITY

The EEOC offers a great deal of information on sexual harassment in the workplace and ways of addressing the problem. Visit the website at **http://www. eeoc.gov/eeoc/publications/fs-sex.cfm** and report on what you find.

Table 14.16 Sexual Harassment Charges, 2003–2011

	FY 2003	FY2006	FY 2009	FY 2011
Receipts	13,566	12,025	12,696	11,364
Percent of Charges Filed by Males	14.7%	15.4%	16.0%	16.3%
Resolutions	14,534	11,936	11,948	12,571
Resolutions by Type:				
Settlements	12.3%	12.2%	11.6%	10.9%
Withdrawals with Benefits	8.9%	9.8%	10.8%	9.1%
Administrative Closures	24.8%	23.8%	23.7%	21.0%
No Reasonable Cause	46.1%	47.5%	47.7%	53.0%
Reasonable Cause	7.9%	6.7%	6.3%	6.1%
Merit Resolutions	29.1%	28.7%	28.6%	26.1%
Monetary Benefits (millions)*	$50.0	$48.8	$51.5	$52.3

The data reflect charges filed with the EEOC and cooperating state and local Fair Employment Practices agencies. The total of individual percentages may not always sum to 100% due to rounding.
*Does not include monetary benefits obtained through litigation.
Source: Equal Employment Opportunity Commission (2013). Sexual Harassment Charges EEOC & FEPAs Combined: FY 1997– FY 2011. Retrieved on July 18, 2013, from http://www.eeoc.gov/eeoc/statistics/enforcement/sexual_harassment.cfm.

Opportunity Commission, 2013). The vast majority of these cases involve a female complainant, although there has been a slight increase in the percent of cases where the complainant is male.

Responses to Sexual Harassment

As noted earlier, responses to sexual harassment generally fall outside the realm of the criminal justice system. Instead, victims can take a variety of steps to address harassment, ranging from taking personal action to invoking the legal system. Most organizations have sexual harassment policies that outline the problem, the expectations for workers, and the procedures for resolving these issues. Where these actions fail, victims can invoke various equal employment statutes and protections or take direct action in civil court. No matter what avenue is chosen, however, the victim is put under additional unwarranted stress and inconvenience.

The resolution of sexual harassment cases can take a variety of forms. Table 14.16 provides some insight into the outcomes of cases brought to the EEOC. Interestingly, the number of resolved cases often exceeds the number of new cases due to the fact that some cases are carried over from one year to the next and other agencies transfer cases to the EEOC. Most of the complaints are resolved through administrative closures or "no reasonable cause" (almost three-quarters). These categories typically represent findings that harassment did not occur or that the complainant did not follow through with the case. "Merit Resolutions" represent the next major form of case resolution; they include situations in which a settlement has been made, or a case has been withdrawn, because the complainant has received some form of desired benefit. This outcome is a growing form of resolution, with 26% of the cases during 2011 being settled in this manner. Interestingly, while most cases do not end with a finding that harassment actually occurred, the cases in which claims of harassment are upheld result in significant monetary benefits. In 2011, $52.3 million was awarded to complainants.

Beyond the responses outlined in Table 14.16, companies can be compelled to take steps in response to harassment by their employees. This action is due to the fact that employers and educational institutions have a legal responsibility to provide an harassment-free environment in which to work and learn. These actions can be divided into two groups: measures to stop the harassment and make certain it does not recur, and measures to correct the effects of the harassment.

The EEOC offers a variety of examples of these actions. To stop harassment, the employer can give warnings or reprimands to offenders, transfer or reassign an individual, force offenders into counseling, demote or monetarily sanction the person, closely monitor the individual in the future, or even discharge the offender (Equal Employment Opportunity Commission, 1999). At the same time that steps are taken to deal with the harasser and the situation, things can be done to help the victim directly. For example, if leave or some other form of time off was taken by the victim due to the incident, the employer can restore that lost time. A victim who left employment due to harassment could also be offered full reinstatement to the job. The employer may also review the personnel file of the victim and expunge any negative comments or evaluations related to the behavior of the harasser (Equal Employment Opportunity Commission, 1999). Various responses should be considered when dealing with harassment cases.

Sexual harassment is a problem that has received increased attention in recent years, particularly with the increase of females in the workplace. As such, many employers and schools are having to deal with this emerging issue and develop new policies and procedures. It is not unusual for businesses and educational institutions to initiate mandatory training on sexual harassment for all staff members. The hope is that such an initiative will limit the number of sexual harassment incidents. At the very least, it helps to mitigate the liability of the employer or school if an incident does occur. Clearly, sexual harassment is a problem that must be addressed.

SUMMARY

Being victimized at work or at school can be particularly traumatic because most workers and students assume they are safe at these locations. Except for those individuals employed in the criminal justice system or in another security position, people have a right to expect that their employer or school has taken steps to secure them and their property. Workers and students are pursuing lawful activities, and any form of victimization represents a violation of their expectations. Schools and employers can be held liable for failing to take reasonable precautions that would attempt to guarantee the safety of those in their care or employment. It is important that employers and schools take preventive measures before a victimization takes place, outline remedial actions to take in the event of a victimization, and prepare plans to aid and assist anyone who is victimized (directly or indirectly) while on the job or at school. All of these actions must be dynamic and able to adjust to situations as they arise. As such, no set of responses can consider all possible events. Instead, the responses should outline processes, rather than specific outcomes.

KEY TERMS

Equal Employment Opportunity
   Commission (EEOC)
general duty clause
going postal
hostile environment harassment
National Crime Victimization Survey:
   School Crime Supplement Stress
National Institute of Occupational
   Safety and Health (NIOSH)
negligent hiring
negligent retention
negligent security

negligent supervision
negligent training
Occupational Safety and Health
   Administration (OSHA)
quid pro quo harassment
routine activities perspective
sexual harassment
strain
third-party lawsuits
workers' compensation
workplace bullying
workplace violence

References

Abbey, A., Ross, L. T., McDuffie, D., & McAuslan, P. (1996). Alcohol, misperception, and sexual assault: How and why are they linked? In D. M. Buss & N. M. Malamuth (Eds.), *Sex, power, conflict: Evolutionary and feminist perspectives*. New York: Oxford University Press.

Acierno, R. (2003). Elder mistreatment: Epidemiological assessment methodology. In National Research Council (Ed.), *Elder mistreatment: Abuse, neglect, and exploitation in an aging America*. Washington, DC: National Academies Press.

Acierno, R., Hernandez, M. A., Amstadter, A. B., Resnick, H. S., Steve, K., Muzzy, W., et al. (2010). Prevalence and correlates of emotional, physical, sexual, and financial abuse and potential neglect in the United States: The national elder mistreatment study. *American Journal of Public Health, 100*, 292–297.

Acker, J. R. (1992). Social sciences and the criminal law: Victims of crime—Plight vs. rights. *Criminal Law Bulletin, 28*, 64–77.

Acker, J. R., & Lanier, C. S. (2000). May god—or the governor—have mercy: Executive clemency and executions in modern death-penalty systems. *Criminal Law Bulletin, 36*, 200–237.

Adams, A. T. (2000). The status of school discipline and violence. *The Annals, 567*, 140–156.

Addington, L. A. (2010). National incident-based reporting system (NIBRS). In B. S. Fisher & S. P. Lab (Eds.), *Encyclopedia of victimology and crime prevention*. Los Angeles: Sage.

Administration on Aging. (2012). *A profile of older Americans: 2012*. Washington, DC: U.S. Department of Health and Human Services. Retrieved on June 13, 2013, from http://www.aoa.gov/AoAroot/Aging_Statistics/Profile/2012/docs/2012profile.pdf.

Agnew, R. (1992). Foundation for a general strain theory of crime and delinquency. *Criminology, 30*, 47–87.

Ahmad, J., & Mullings, J. L. (1999). *Family violence units. Texas Law Enforcement Management and Administrative Statistics Program Bulletin (Vol. 6, number 5)*. Huntsville, TX: Police Research Center, Sam Houston State University.

Alderden, M. A., & Ullman, S. E. (2012). Creating a more complete and current picture: Examining police and prosecutor decision-making when processing sexual assault cases. *Violence Against Women, 18*, 525–551.

American Bar Association. (1996). *Standards of practice for lawyers who represent children in abuse and neglect cases*. Chicago: American Bar Association. Retrieved on June 2, 2013, from http://www.americanbar.org/content/dam/aba/administrative/child_law/repstandwhole.authcheckdam.pdf.

American Bar Association. (2009). *Resolution 101D*. Chicago: American Bar Association. Retrieved on June 2, 2013, from http://www.americanbar.org/content/dam/aba/migrated/domviol/ABA_Policies/134_1_3.authcheckdam.pdf.

American Psychiatric Association. (2000). *Diagnostic and statistical manual of mental disorders—Fourth edition, text revision (DSM-IV-TR)*. Arlington, VA: American Psychiatric Association. Retrieved on April 5, 2013, from http://dsm.psychiatryonline.org.proxy.lib.fsu.edu/content.aspx?bookid=22&sectionid=1891137#3357.

Amir, M. (1971). *Patterns in forcible rape*. Chicago: University of Chicago Press.

Amstadter, A. B., Zajac, K., Strachan, M., Hernandex, M. A., Kilpatrick, D. G., & Acierno, R. (2011). Prevalence and correlates of elder mistreatment in South Carolina: The South Carolina elder mistreatment study. *Journal of Interpersonal Violence, 26*, 2947–2972.

Anderson, D. A. (1999). The aggregate burden of crime. *Journal of Law and Economics, 42*, 611–642.

Anderson, J. G. (1977). A social indicator model of a health services system. *Social Forces, 56*, 661–687.

Anderson, K. (1982). *Community justice centers: Alternatives to prosecution*. Paper presented at the National Symposium on Victimology.

Anderson, K. B. (2013). *Consumer fraud in the United States, 2011: the third FTC Survey*. Washington, DC: Federal Trade Commission. Retrieved on June 4, 2013, from http://www.ftc.gov/os/2013/04/130419fraudsurvey.pdf.

Anderson, T. B. (1989). Community professionals and their perspectives on elder abuse. In R. Filinson & S. R. Ingman (Eds.), *Elder abuse: Practice and policy*. New York: Human Sciences Press.

Andison, F. S. (1977). TV violence and viewer aggression: A culmination of study results, 1956–76. *Public Opinion Quarterly, 41*, 314–331.

Anetzberger, G. J. (1989). Implications of research on elder abuse perpetrators: Rethinking current social policy and programming. In R. Filinson & S. R. Ingman (Eds.), *Elder abuse: Practice and policy*. New York: Human Sciences Press.

Anonymous. (2013). *"The rape" of Mr. Smith*. Retrieved on April 5, 2013, from http://www.holysmoke.org/fem/fem0235.htm.

Anti-Defamation League. (2013). *Pioneering hate crime legislation and advocacy: ADL's legacy of addressing violent bigotry in America*. New York: Anti-Defamation League. Retrieved on July 7, 2013, from http://www.adl.org/assets/pdf/combating-hate/Hate-Crimes-2-pager.pdf.

Aos, S. (2003). *The criminal justice system in Washington State: Incarceration rates, taxpayer costs, crime rates, and prison economics*. Olympia, WA: Washington State Institute for Public Policy.

Aos, S., Phipps, P., Barnoski, R., & Lieb, R. (2001). *The comparative costs and benefits of programs to reduce crime*. Olympia, WA: Washington State Institute for Public Policy.

Arias, E. (2012). *United States life tables, 2008. National Vital Statistics Reports, 61* (3). Hyattsville, MD: National Center for Health Statistics. Retrieved on June 13, 2013, from http://www.cdc.gov/nchs/data/nvsr/nvsr61/nvsr61_03.pdf.

Aries, P. (1962). *Centuries of childhood*. New York: Knopf.

Armstrong, E. A., Hamilton, L., & Sweeney, B. (2006). Sexual assault on campus: A multilevel, integrative approach to party rape. *Social Problems, 53*, 483–499.

Ash, M. (1972). On witnesses: A radical critique of criminal court procedures. *Notre Dame Lawyer, 48*, 386–425.

Ashworth, A. (2003). Is restorative justice the way forward for criminal justice? In E. McLaughlin, R. Fergusson, G. Hughes & L. Westmarland (Eds.), *Restorative justice: Critical issues*. Thousand Oaks, CA: Sage.

Atlanta Long-Term Care Ombudsman Program. (2000). *The silenced voice speaks out: A study of abuse and neglect of nursing home residents*. Atlanta, GA: Atlanta Legal Aid Society. Retrieved on June 27, 2013, from http://www.atlantalegalaid.org/abuse.htm.

Atwood, T. C. (2008). Comment: National council for adoption's responses to the Texas safe haven study. *Child Maltreatment, 13*, 96–97.

Aulivola, M. (2004). Outing domestic violence: Affording appropriate protections to gay and lesbian victims. *Family Court Review, 42*, 162–172.

Bachman, R. (1993). Predicting the reporting of rape victimizations: Have rape reforms made a difference? *Criminal Justice and Behavior, 20*, 254–270.

Bachman, R., & Meloy, M. L. (2008). The epidemiology of violence against the elderly: Implications for primary and secondary prevention. *Journal of Contemporary Criminal Justice, 24*, 186–197.

Bachman, R., & Paternoster, R. (1993). A contemporary look at the effects of rape law reform: How far have we really come? *Journal of Criminal Law and Criminology, 84*, 554–574.

Bachman, R., & Saltzman, L. E. (1995). *Violence against women: Estimates from the redesigned survey*. Washington, DC: Bureau of Justice Statistics.

Bachman, R., & Taylor, B. M. (1994). The measurement of family violence and rape by the redesigned National Crime Victimization Survey. *Justice Quarterly, 11*, 499–512.

Bailey, B., Buchbinder, E., & Eisikovits, Z. (2011). Male social workers working with men who batter: Dilemmas in gender identity. *Journal of Interpersonal Violence, 26*, 1741–1762.

Bailey, K. D. (2009). The aftermath of *Crawford* and *Davis*: Deconstructing the sound of silence. *Brigham Young University Law Review, 2009*, 101–155.

Baker, T. C., Burgess, A. W., Brickman, E., & Davis, R. C. (1990). Rape victims' concerns about possible exposure to HIV infection. *Journal of Interpersonal Violence, 5*, 49–60.

Balenovich, J., Grossi, E., & Hughes, T. (2008). Toward a balanced approach: Defining police roles in responding to domestic violence. *American Journal of Criminal Justice, 33*, 19–31.

Bandura, A., & Walters, R. H. (1963). *Social learning and personality development*. New York: Holt, Rinehart and Winston.

Bannenberg, B., & Rössner, D. (2003). New developments in restorative justice to handle family violence. In E. G. M. Weitekamp & H. Kerner (Eds.), *Restorative justice in context: International practice and directions*. Portland, OR: Willan Pub.

Barbieri, M. K. (1989). Civil suits for sexual assault victims: The down side. *Journal of Interpersonal Violence, 4*, 110–113.

Bard, M. (1980). Functions of the police and the justice system in family violence. In M. R. Green (Ed.), *Violence and the family*. Boulder, CO: Westview Press, Inc.

Bard, M., & Sangrey, D. (1986). *The crime victim's book* (2nd ed.). New York: Brunner/Mazel Publishers.

Barger, A. (2008). Changing state laws to prohibit the display of hangman's nooses: Tightening the knot around the First Amendment. *William and Mary Bill of Rights Journal, 17*, 263–292.

Barnes, J. C., Dukes, T., Tewksbury, R., & De Troye, T. M. (2009). Analyzing the impact of a statewide residence restriction law on South Carolina sex offenders. *Criminal Justice Policy Review, 20*, 21–43.

Barnett, R. E. (1981). Restitution: A new paradigm of criminal justice. In B. Galaway & J. Hudson (Eds.), *Perspectives on crime victims*. St. Louis, MO: C.V. Mosby.

Barrile, L. G. (1980). *Television and attitudes about crime*. Ph.D. Dissertation, Boston College.

Basile, K. C. (2009). Advancing the study of violence against women: Response to Jordan. *Violence against Women, 15*, 428–433.

Bassuk, E. L. (1980). A crisis theory perspective on rape. In S. L. McCombie (Ed.), *The rape crisis intervention handbook: A guide for victim care*. New York: Plenum Press.

Baum, K. (2007). *Identity theft, 2005*. Washington, DC: Bureau of Justice Statistics.

Baumer, E. P., & Lauritsen, J. L. (2010). Reporting crime to the police, 1973–2005: A multivariate analysis of long-term trends in the National Crime Survey (NCS) and National Crime Victimization Survey (NCVS). *Criminology, 48*, 131–185.

Baumer, E. P., Felson, R. B., & Messner, S. F. (2003). Changes in police notification for rape, 1973–2000. *Criminology, 41*, 841–872.

Baya, M. J. (October 4, 1993). *The Antioch College sexual offense policy*. Yellow Springs, OH: Antioch College. Retrieved on April 5, 2013, from http://www.mit.edu/activities/safe/data/other/antioch-code.

Bazemore, G., & Maloney, D. (1994). Rehabilitating community service: Toward restorative service in a balanced justice system. *Federal Probation, 58*, 24–35.

Bazemore, G., & Umbreit, M. (2001). *A comparison of four restorative conferencing models*. Washington, DC: U.S. Department of Justice, Office of Juvenile Justice and Delinquency Prevention.

Beare, M. (2002). Organized corporate criminality—Tobacco smuggling between Canada and the U.S. *Crime, Law and Social Change, 37*, 225–243.

Becker, P. J. (1999). The creation of Ohio's ethnic intimidation law: Triggering events, media campaigns, and interest group activity. *American Journal of Criminal Justice, 23*, 247–265.

Begle, A. M., Strachan, M., Cisler, J. M., Amstadter, A. B., Hernandez, M., & Acierno, R. (2011). Elder mistreatment and emotional symptoms among older adults in a largely rural population: The South Carolina elder mistreatment study. *Journal of Interpersonal Violence, 26*, 2321–2332.

Begun, J. W. (1977). A causal model of the health care system: A replication. *Journal of Health and Social Behavior, 18*, 2–9.

Bell, M. E., Perez, S., Goodman, L. A., & Dutton, M. A. (2011). Battered women's perceptions of civil and criminal court helpfulness: The role of court outcome and process. *Violence Against Women, 17*, 71–88.

Belluck, P. (1997). Women's shelters disclosing their locations, despite risk. *New York Times, August, 10*, A1, A17.

Beloof, D. E. (2003). Constitutional implications of crime victims as participants. *Cornell Law Review, 88*, 282–305.

Belsky, J. (1978). Three theoretical models of child abuse: A critical review. *Child Abuse & Neglect, 2*, 37–49.

Belson, W. (1978). *Television violence and the adolescent boy*. Westmead, England: Saxon House.

Bennett, G., Kingston, P., & Penhale, B. (1997). *The dimensions of elder abuse: Perspectives for practitioners*. London: Macmillan.

Benson, B. J., Gohm, C. L., & Gross, A. M. (2007). College women and sexual assault: The role of sex-related alcohol expectancies. *Journal of Family Violence, 22*, 341–351.

Berger, R. J., Neuman, W. L., & Searles, P. (1991). The social and political context of rape law reform: An aggregate analysis. *Social Science Quarterly, 72*, 221–238.

Berger, R. J., Searles, P., & Neuman, W. L. (1988). The dimensions of rape reform legislation. *Law & Society Review, 22*, 329–349.

Berk, R. A., Smyth, G. K., & Sherman, L. W. (1988). When random assignment fails: Some lessons from the Minneapolis spouse abuse experiment. *Journal of Quantitative Criminology, 4*, 209–223.

Berliner, L. (1989). Another option for victims: Civil damage suits. *Journal of Interpersonal Violence, 4*, 107–109.

Berliner, L. (2003). Making domestic violence victims testify. *Journal of Interpersonal Violence, 18,* 666–668.

Berryman, J. (2000). Russia and the illicit arms trade. *Crime, Law and Social Change, 33,* 85–104.

Best, C. L., Dansky, B. S., & Kilpatrick, D. G. (1992). Medical students' attitudes about female rape victims. *Journal of Interpersonal Violence, 7,* 175–188.

Biderman, A., & Reiss, A. (1967). On exploring the "dark figure" of crime. *Annals of the American Academy of Political and Social Sciences, 374,* 1–15.

Bilchik, S. (1999). *Promising strategies to reduce gun violence.* Washington, DC: U.S. Department of Justice, Office of Juvenile Justice and Delinquency Prevention.

Binder, A., & Meeker, J. W. (1988). Experiments as reforms. *Journal of Criminal Justice, 16,* 347–358.

Bjerregaard, B. (1996). Stalking and the First Amendment: A constitutional analysis of state stalking laws. *Criminal Law Bulletin, 32,* 307–341.

Black, M. C., Basile, K. C., Breiding, M. J., Smith, S. G., Walters, M. L., Merrick, M. T., et al. (2011). *The National Intimate Partner and Sexual Violence Survey (NIPSVS): 2010 summary report.* Atlanta: National Center for Injury Prevention and Control, Centers for Disease Control and Prevention. Retrieved on May 17, 2013, from http://www.cdc.gov/ViolencePrevention/pdf/ NISVS_Report2010-a.pdf.

Blackwell, B. S., & Vaughn, M. S. (2003). Police civil liability for inappropriate response to domestic assault victims. *Journal of Criminal Justice, 31,* 129–146.

Blakely, B. E., & Dolon, R. (1991). Elder mistreatment. In J. E. Hendricks (Ed.), *Crisis intervention in criminal justice/social service.* Springfield, IL: Charles C. Thomas Publisher.

Block, R. L., & Block, C. R. (1995). Space, place and crime: Hot spot areas and hot places of liquor-related crime. In J. E. Eck & D. Weisburd (Eds.), *Crime and place.* Monsey, NY: Criminal Justice Press.

Blume, J. H. (2003). Ten years of *Payne*: Victim impact evidence in capital cases. *Cornell Law Review, 88,* 257–281.

Blumenthal, J. A. (2009). Affective forecasting and capital sentencing: Reducing the effect of victim impact statements. *American Criminal Law Review, 46,* 107–125.

Boeringer, S. B. (1999). Associations of rape-supportive attitudes with fraternal and athletic participation. *Violence Against Women, 5,* 81–90.

Bondi, P. (2012). *Hate crimes in Florida 2011.* Tallahassee: Florida Office of the Attorney General. Retrieved on July 8, 2013, from http://myfloridalegal.com/webfiles.nsf/WF/RWHN-93HMH4/ $file/2011HateCrimesReport.pdf.

Boscarino, J. A., Figley, C. R., & Adams, R. E. (2004). Evidence of compassion fatigue following the September 11 terrorist attacks: A study of secondary trauma among social workers in New York. *International Journal of Emergency Mental Health, 6,* 98–108.

Bourke, L. B. (1989). *Defining rape.* Durham, NC: Duke University Press.

Bowers, K. J., Hirschfield, A., & Johnson, S. D. (1998). Victimization revisited: A case study of on-residential repeat burglary on Merseyside. *British Journal of Criminology, 38,* 429–452.

Bowleg, L., & Stoll, K. A. (1991). *More harm than help: The ramifications for rape survivors of mandatory HIV testing of rapists.* Washington, DC: Center for Women Policy Studies.

Braithwaite, J. (1989). *Crime, shame and reintegration.* Cambridge: Cambridge University Press.

Braithwaite, J. (1999). Restorative justice: Assessing optimistic and pessimistic accounts. In M. Tonry (Ed.), *Crime and justice: A review of research: Vol. 25.* Chicago: University of Chicago Press.

Braithwaite, J. (2002). *Restorative justice and responsive regulation.* New York: Oxford University Press.

Braithwaite, J. (2003). Restorative justice and a better future. In E. McLaughlin, R. Fergusson, G. Hughes, & K. Westmarland (Eds.), *Restorative justice: Critical issues*. Thousand Oaks, CA: Sage.

Brancatelli, M. (2009). Facilitating children's testimony: Close circuit television. *The Prosecutor, 40*(2), 40–44.

Braverman, M. (1999). *Preventing workplace violence: A guide for employers and practitioners*. Thousand Oaks, CA: Sage.

Brecklin, L. E., & Ullman, S. R. (2001). The role of offender alcohol use in rape attacks: An analysis of National Crime Victimization Survey Data. *Journal of Interpersonal Violence, 16*, 3–21.

Bridenback, M. L., Imhoff, P. L., & Blanchard, J. P. (1980). *The use of mediation/arbitration in the juvenile justice process: A study of three programs*. Tallahassee, FL: Office of the State Court Administrator.

Brien, V. O. (1992). *OVC bulletin: Civil legal remedies for crime victims*. Washington, DC: U.S. Department of Justice.

Brookman, F., & Maguire, M. (2005). Reducing homicide: A review of the possibilities. *Crime, Law & Social Change, 42*, 325–403.

Brookoff, D. (1997). *Drugs, alcohol, and domestic violence in Memphis*. Washington, DC: U.S. Department of Justice.

Brooks, A. D. (1996). Megan's law: Constitutionality and policy. *Criminal Justice Ethics, 15*, 56–66.

Brooks, J. A. (1975). How well are criminal injury boards performing? *Crime and Delinquency, 21*, 50–56.

Browne, A. (1987). *When battered women kill*. New York: Free Press.

Browning, J., & Dutton, D. (1986). Assessment of wife assault with the conflict tactics scale: Using couple data to quantify the differential reporting effect. *Journal of Marriage and the Family, 48*, 375–379.

Brownmiller, S. (1975). *Against our will: Men, women and rape*. New York: Simon and Schuster.

Bruinsma, G. J. N., & Fiselier, J. P. S. (1982). The poverty of victimology. In H. J. Schneider (Ed.), *The victim in international perspective*. New York: Walter de Gruyter & Company.

Bruinsma, G., & Bernasco, W. (2004). Criminal groups and transnational illegal markets: A more detailed examination on the basis of social network theory. *Crime, Law & Social Change, 41*, 79–94.

Bureau of Justice Statistics. (1997). *Criminal victimization in the United States, 1994*. Washington, DC: U. S. Government Printing Office.

Bureau of Justice Statistics. (2003). *Criminal victimization in the United States, 2002, statistical tables*. Washington, DC: United States Government Printing Office.

Bureau of Justice Statistics. (2006a). *Criminal victimization in the United States, 2005, statistical tables*. Washington, DC: Bureau of Justice Statistics.

Bureau of Justice Statistics. (2008). *National Crime Victimization Survey: NCVS- 1 Basic Screen Questionnaire*. Washington, DC: Bureau of Justice Statistics.

Bureau of Justice Statistics. (2010a). *Criminal victimization in the United States, 2007, statistical tables*. Washington, DC: Bureau of Justice Statistics.

Bureau of Justice Statistics. (2010b). *National Crime Victimization Survey, 2008, statistical tables*. Washington, DC: Bureau of Justice Statistics.

Bureau of Labor Statistics. (2006). *Survey of workplace violence prevention 2005*. Washington, DC: Bureau of Labor Statistics.

Bureau of Labor Statistics. (2012). *National census of fatal occupational injuries in 2011 (preliminary results)*. Retrieved on June 8, 2013, from http://www.bls.gov/news.release/pdf/cfoi.pdf.

Bureau of Labor Statistics. (2013). *Workplace homicides from shootings*. Retrieved on July 17, 2013, from http://www.bls.gov/iif/oshwc/cfoi/osar0016.htm.

Burgess, A. W. (1995). Rape trauma syndrome. In P. Searles & R. J. Berger (Eds.), *Rape and society: Readings on the problem of sexual assault*. Boulder, CO: Westview Press.

Burgess, A. W., & Draper, P. (1989). The explanation of family violence: The role of biological, behavioral, and cultural selection. In L. Ohlin & N. Tonry (Eds.), *Family violence*. Chicago: University of Chicago Press.

Burgess, A. W., & Holmstrom, L. L. (1974). Rape trauma syndrome. *American Journal of Psychiatry, 131*, 981–986.

Burnett, J., Regev, T., Pickens, S., Prati, L. L., Aung, K., Moore, J., et al. (2006). Social networks: A profile of the elderly who self-neglect. *Journal of Elder Abuse & Neglect, 18*, 35–49.

Burr, R. (2003). Litigating with victim impact testimony: The serendipity that has come from *Payne v. Tennessee*. *Cornell Law Review, 88*, 517–529.

Burt, M. R., & Estep, R. E. (1981). Who is a victim? Definitional problems in sexual victimization. *Victimology, 6*, 15–28.

Burt, M. R., & Katz, B. L. (1985). Rape, robbery, and burglary: Responses to actual and feared criminal victimization, with special focus on women and elderly. *Victimology, 10*, 325–358.

Buzawa, E. S., & Buzawa, C. G. (1990). *Domestic violence: The criminal justice response*. Newbury Park, CA: Sage.

Byers, B. (1991). Death notification. In J. E. Hendricks (Ed.), *Crisis intervention in criminal justice/social service*. Springfield, IL: Charles C. Thomas.

Caffey, J. (1946). Multiple fractures in the long bones of infants suffering from chronic subdural hemotoma. *American Journal of Roentology, 56*, 163–173.

Caffey, J. (1957). Traumatic lesions in growing bones other than fractures and lesions: Clinical and radiological features. *British Journal of Radiology, 30*, 225–238.

Calcutt, P. B. (1988). The Victims' Rights Act of 1988, the Florida Constitution, and the new struggle for victims' rights. *Florida State University Law Review, 16*, 811–834.

Caldera, D., Burrell, L., Rodriguez, K., Crowne, S. S., Rohde, C., & Duggan, A. (2007). Impact of a statewide home visiting program on parenting and on child health and development. *Child Abuse & Neglect, 31*, 829–852.

Caliber Associates. (2004). *Assessment of the effects of the national victim assistance academy: Final report*. Washington, DC: U.S. Department of Justice.

Call, J. E., Nice, D., & Talarico, S. M. (1991). An analysis of state rape shield laws. *Social Science Quarterly, 72*, 774–788.

Campbell, D. T., & Stanley, D. C. (1963). *Experimental and quasi-experimental designs for research*. Chicago: Rand McNally & Company.

Campbell, J. C., Glass, N., Sharps, P. W., Laughon, K., & Bloom, T. (2007). Intimate partner homicide: Review and implications of research and policy. *Trauma, Violence, & Abuse, 8*, 246–269.

Campbell, R., Adams, A. E., Wasco, S. M., Ahrens, C. E., & Sefl, T. (2009). Training interviewers for research on sexual violence: A qualitative study of rape survivors' recommendations for interview practice. *Violence Against Women, 15*, 595–617.

Campbell, J. C., Webster, D. W., & Glass, N. (2009). The danger assessment: Validation of a lethality risk assessment instrument for intimate partner femicide. *Journal of Interpersonal Violence, 24*, 653–674.

Campbell, J. C., Webster, D., Koziol-McLain, J., Block, C. R., Campbell, D., Curry, M. A., et al. (2003). Assessing risk factors for intimate partner homicide. *NIJ Journal, 250*, 14–19. Retrieved on May 17, 2013, from https://www.ncjrs.gov/pdffiles1/jr000250e.pdf.

Campbell, R. (1995). The role of work experience and individual beliefs in police officers' perceptions of date rape: An integration of quantitative and qualitative methods. *American Journal of Community Psychology, 23*, 249–277.

Campbell, R. (2005). What really happened? A validation study of rape survivors' help-seeking experiences with the legal and medical systems. *Violence and Victims, 29*, 55–68.

Campbell, R., & Johnson, C. R. (1997). Police officers' perception of rape: Is there consistency between state law and individual beliefs? *Journal of Interpersonal Violence, 12*, 255–274.

Campbell, R., Adams, A. E., Wasco, S. M., Ahrens, C. E., & Sefl, T. (2010). What has it been like for you to talk to me today? The impact of participating in interview research on rape survivors. *Violence Against Women, 16*, 60–83.

Campbell, R., Bybee, D., Kelley, K. D., Dworkin, E. R., & Patterson, D. (2012a). The impact of sexual assault nurse examiner (SANE) program services on law enforcement investigational practices: A mediational analysis. *Criminal Justice and Behavior, 39*, 169–184.

Campbell, R., Patterson, D., & Bybee, D. (2012b). Prosecution of adult sexual assault cases: A longitudinal analysis of the impact of a sexual assault nurse examiner program. *Violence Against Women, 18*, 223–244.

Campbell, R., Patterson, D., & Lichty, L. F. (2005). The effectiveness of sexual assault nurse examiner (SANE) programs: A review of psychological, medical, legal, and community outcomes. *Trauma, Violence, & Abuse, 6*, 313–329.

Cancer Prevention Research Center. (2013). *Detailed overview of the transtheoretical model.* Kingston: University of Rhode Island. Retrieved on May 17, 2013, from http://www.uri.edu/research/cprc/transtheoretical_model/ttm_detailed.html.

Cannavale, F. J., Jr., & Falcon, W. D. (1976). *Improving witness cooperation: Summary report of the District of Columbia witness survey and a handbook for witness management.* Washington, DC: U.S. Department of Justice.

Caplan, J. M. (2010). Parole release decisions: Impact of positive and negative victim and nonvictim input on a representative sample of parole-eligible inmates. *Violence and Victims, 25*, 224–242.

Caringella-MacDonald, S. (1984). Sexual assault prosecution: An examination of model rape legislation in Michigan. *Women and Politics, 4*, 65–82.

Carmody, D. C., & Washington, L. M. (2001). Rape myth acceptance among college women: The impact of race and prior victimization. *Journal of Interpersonal Violence, 16*, 424–436.

Carrington, F. (1981). Victims' rights litigation: A wave of the future? In B. Galaway & J. Hudson (Eds.), *Perspectives on crime victims.* St. Louis, MO: C.V. Mosby.

Carrow, D. M. (1980). *Rape: Guidelines for a community response.* Washington, DC: U.S. Department of Justice.

Casaday, T. (2009). A police chief's viewpoint: Geographic aspects of sex offender residency restrictions. *Criminal Justice Policy Review, 20*, 16–20.

Cassell, P. G. (1997). *Statement before the committee on the judiciary, United States Senate, concerning a constitutional amendment protecting the rights of crime victims on April 16, 1997.*

Cassell, P. G. (2009). In defense of victim impact statements. *Ohio State Journal of Criminal Law*, *6*, 611–648.

Castillo, R., Dressler, T. W., Foglia, R., & Faber, M. J. (1979). The use of civil liability to aid crime victims. *Journal of Criminal Law & Criminology*, *70*, 57–62.

Catalano, S. (2007). *Intimate partner violence in the United States*. Washington, DC: Bureau of Justice. Retrieved on May 17, 2013, from http://www.bjs.gov/content/pub/pdf/ipvus.pdf.

Catalano, S. (2012a). *Intimate partner violence, 1993—2010*. Washington, DC: Bureau of Justice Statistics.

Catalano, S. (2012b). *Stalking victims in the United States–Revised*. Washington, DC: Bureau of Justice Statistics.

Cattaneo, L. B., Dunn, J. L., & Chapman, A. R. (2013). The court impact scale: A tool for evaluating IPV victims' experience in court. *Journal of Interpersonal Violence*, *28*, 1088–1108.

Center for Effective Discipline. (2013). *Corporal punishment and paddling statistics by state and race*. Canal Winchester, OH: The Center for Effective Discipline. Retrieved on May 20, 2013, from http://www.stophitting.com/index.php?page=statesbanning.

Center for Family Safety and Healing. (2013). *Shaken baby syndrome prevention*. Columbus, OH: Nationwide Children's Hospital. Retrieved on May 22, 2013, from http://www.nationwidechildrens.org/shaken-baby-syndrome-prevention.

Centers for Disease Control and Prevention. (2006). Sexually transmitted diseases treatment guidelines, 2006. *Morbidity and Mortality Weekly Report*, *55*(RR-11), 80–83.

Centers for Disease Control and Prevention. (2012). *CDC fact sheet: New HIV infections in the United States*. Atlanta: National Center for HIV/AIDS, Viral Hepatitis, STD, and TB Prevention. Retrieved on April 27, 2013, from http://www.cdc.gov/nchhstp/newsroom/docs/2012/HIV-Infections-2007-2010.pdf.

Centers for Disease Control and Prevention. (2013). *National violent death reporting system*. Retrieved on May 22, 2013, from http://www.cdc.gov/violenceprevention/nvdrs/.

Chaffin, M., & Bard, D. (2006). Impact of intervention surveillance bias on analyses of child welfare report outcomes. *Child Maltreatment*, *11*, 301–312.

Challeen, D. A., & Heinlen, J. H. (1978). The win-onus restitution program. In B. Galaway & J. Hudson (Eds.), *Offender restitution in theory and action*. Lexington, MA: D.C. Heath.

Champlin, L. (1986). The battered elderly. *Geriatrics*, *37*, 115–116, 121.

Chan, W. (2005). Crime, deportation and the regulation of immigrants in Canada. *Crime, Law, and Social Change*, *44*, 153–180.

Chandler, N. (2000). *Best practices for establishing a children's advocacy center program* (3rd ed.). Washington, DC: National Children's Alliance. Retrieved on June 2, 2013, from http://www.fncac.org/file.php/2129/BEST+PRACTICES.pdf.

Chappell, D., & DiMartino, V. (1998). *Violence at work*. Geneva: International Labor Office.

Chelimsky, E. (1981). Serving victims: Agency incentives and individual needs. In S. R. Salasin (Ed.), *Evaluating victim services*. Beverly Hills, CA: Sage.

Chen, Y., & Ullman, S. E. (2010). Women's reporting of sexual and physical assaults to police in the National Violence Against Women Survey. *Violence Against Women*, *16*, 262–279.

Child Welfare Information Gateway. (2007). *Recognizing child abuse and neglect: Signs and symptoms*. Washington, DC: U.S. Department of Health & Human Services, Children's Bureau. Retrieved on May 21, 2013, from http://www.childwelfare.gov/pubs/factsheets/signs.cfm.

Child Welfare Information Gateway. (2008). *What are the major types of child abuse and neglect?* Washington, DC: U.S. Department of Health and Human Services, Children's Bureau. Retrieved on May 20, 2013, from http://www.childwelfare.gov/pubs/factsheets/whatiscan.cfm.

Child Welfare Information Gateway. (2010). *Infant safe haven laws: Summary of state laws.* Washington, DC: U.S. Department of Health and Human Services, Children's Bureau. Retrieved on May 21, 2013, from www.childwelfare.gov/systemwide/laws_policies/statutes/safehaven.cfm.

Child Welfare Information Gateway. (2012a). *Mandatory reporters of child abuse and neglect.* Washington, DC: U.S. Department of Health and Human Services, Children's Bureau. Retrieved on May 21, 2013, from https://www.childwelfare.gov/systemwide/laws_policies/statutes/manda.cfm.

Child Welfare Information Gateway. (2012b). *Child maltreatment 2011.* Washington, DC: U.S. Department of Health and Human Services, Children's Bureau. Retrieved on May 21, 2013, from http://www.acf.hhs.gov/sites/default/files/cb/cm11.pdf.

Child Welfare Information Gateway. (2013a). *How the child welfare system works.* Washington, DC: U.S. Department of Health and Human Services, Children's Bureau. Retrieved on May 21, 2013, from https://www.childwelfare.gov/pubs/factsheets/cpswork.pdf.

Child Welfare Information Gateway. (2013b). *Child maltreatment 2011: Summary of key findings.* Washington, DC: U.S. Department of Health and Human Services. Children's Bureau. Retrieved on May 21, 2013, from https://www.childwelfare.gov/pubs/factsheets/canstats.pdf.

Child Welfare Information Gateway. (2013c). *Child abuse and neglect fatalities 2011: Statistics and interventions.* Washington, DC: U.S. Department of Health and Human Services. Children's Bureau. Retrieved on May 21, 2013, from https://www.childwelfare.gov/pubs/factsheets/fatality.pdf.

Chilton, R. (2010). Uniform Crime Reporting (UCR) Program. In B. S. Fisher & S. P. Lab (Eds.), *Encyclopedia of victimology and crime prevention.* Los Angeles: Sage.

Cicirelli, V. G. (1986). The helping relationship and family neglect in later life. In K. A. Pillemer & R. S. Wolf (Eds.), *Elder abuse: Conflict in the family.* Dover, MA: Auburn House.

Clay-Warner, J., & Burt, C. H. (2005). Rape reporting after reforms: Have times really changed? *Violence Against Women, 11,* 150–176.

Coates, R. B., & Gehm, J. (1989). An empirical assessment. In M. Wright & B. Galaway (Eds.), *Mediation and criminal justice: Victims, offenders and community.* Newbury Park, CA: Sage.

Cohen, A. K. (1955). *Delinquent boys: The culture of the gang.* Glencoe, IL: Free Press.

Cohen, F. (1995). Sex offender registration laws: Constitutional and policy issues. *Criminal Law Bulletin, 31,* 151–160.

Cohen, L. E., & Felson, M. (1979). Social changes and crime rate trends: A routine activities approach. *American Sociological Review, 44,* 588–608.

Collins, J. J. (1989). Alcohol and interpersonal violence: Less than meets the eye. In N. A. Weiner & M. E. Wolfgang (Eds.), *Pathways to criminal violence.* Newbury Park, CA: Sage.

Colomb, W., & Damphousse, K. (2004). Examination of newspaper coverage of hate crimes: A moral panic perspective. *American Journal of Criminal Justice, 28,* 147–163.

Congressional Record. (2007). *Senate resolution 396, 110th Congress, 1st session, 13 December.* Washington, DC: Government Printing Office. Retrieved on July 5, 2013, from http://www.gpo.gov/fdsys/pkg/BILLS-110sres396ats/pdf/BILLS-110sres396ats.pdf.

Cook, R. F., Roehl, J. A., & Sheppard, D. I. (1980). *Neighborhood justice centers field test, executive summary.* Washington, DC: National Institute of Justice.

Cook, S. L., Gidycz, C. A., Koss, M. P., & Murphy, M. (2011). Emerging issues in the measurement of rape victimization. *Violence Against Women, 17,* 201–218.

Cooper, A., & Smith, E. L. (2011). *Homicide trends in the United States, 1980–2008.* Washington, DC: Bureau of Justice Statistics. Retrieved on May 17, 2013, from http://www.bjs.gov/content/pub/pdf/htus8008.pdf.

Corbin, W. R., Bernat, J. A., Calhoun, K. S., McNair, L. D., & Seals, K. L. (2001). The role of alcohol expectancies and alcohol consumption among sexually victimized and nonvictimized college women. *Journal of Interpersonal Violence, 16,* 297–311.

Corrado, R. R., Cohen, I. M., & Odgers, C. (2003). Multi-problem violent youths: A challenge for the restorative justice paradigm. In E. G. M. Weitekamp & H. Kerner (Eds.), *Restorative justice in context: International practice and directions.* Portland, OR: Willan.

Corso, P. S., Mercy, J. A., Simon, T. R., Finkelstein, E. A., & Miller, T. R. (2007). Medical costs and productivity losses due to interpersonal and self-directed violence in the United States. *American Journal of Preventive Medicine, 32,* 474–484.

Costa, J. J. (1984). *Abuse of women: Legislation, reporting, and prevention.* Lexington, MA: Lexington Books.

Costin, F., & Schwarz, N. (1987). Beliefs about rape and women's social roles: A four-nation study. *Journal of Interpersonal Violence, 2,* 46–56.

Crawford, A., & Newburn, T. (2003). *Youth offending and restorative justice: Implementing reform in youth justice.* Portland, OR: Willan.

Crenshaw, W. B., Crenshaw, L. M., & Lichtenberg, J. W. (1995). When educators confront child abuse: An analysis of the decision to report. *Child Abuse & Neglect, 19,* 1095–1113.

Cronk, T. M. (2013, April 10). *New approach helps sexual assault victims recall details. American Forces Press Service.* Washington, DC: U.S. Department of Defense. Retrieved on April 20, 2013, from http://www.defense.gov/news/newsarticle.aspx?id=119738.

Cross, T. P., & Casanueva, C. (2009). Caseworker judgments and substantiation. *Child Maltreatment, 14,* 38–52.

Cross, T. P., Finkelhor, D., & Ormrod, R. (2005). Police involvement in child protective services investigations: Literature review and secondary data analysis. *Child Maltreatment, 10,* 224–244.

Cross, T. P., Jones, L. M., Walsh, W. A., Simone, M., Kolko, D. J., Szczepanski, J., et al. (2008). *Evaluating children's advocacy centers' response to child sexual abuse.* Washington, DC: U.S. Department of Justice, Office of Juvenile Justice and Delinquency Prevention. Retrieved on June 2, 2013, from https://www.ncjrs.gov/pdffiles1/ojjdp/218530.pdf.

Crume, T. L., DiGuiseppi, C., Byers, T., Sirotnak, A. P., & Garrett, C. J. (2002). Underascertainment of child maltreatment fatalities by death certificates, 1990–1998. *Pediatrics, 110,* 18.

Crystal, S. (1986). Social policy and elder abuse. In K. A. Pillemer & R. S. Wolf (Eds.), *Elder abuse: Conflict in the family.* Dover, MA: Auburn House.

Curtis, L. A. (1974). *Criminal violence: National patterns and behavior.* Lexington, MA: D.C. Heath and Company.

Daly, K. (2002). Restorative justice: The real story. *Punishment and Society, 4,* 5–79.

Daly, K. (2003). Making variation a virtue: Evaluating the potential and limits of restorative justice. In E. G. M. Weitekamp & H. Kerner (Eds.), *Restorative justice in context: International practices and directions.* Portland, OR: Willan.

Davis, K. C., Norris, J., George, W. H., Martell, J., & Heiman, J. R. (2006). Rape-myth congruent beliefs in women resulting from exposure to pornography: Effects of alcohol and sexual arousal. *Journal of Interpersonal Violence, 21,* 1208–1223.

Davis, P. W., Chandler, J. L., & LaRossa, R. (2004). I've tried the switch but he laughs through the tears: The use and conceptualization of corporal punishment during the Machine Age, 1924–1939. *Child Abuse & Neglect, 28,* 1291–1310.

Davis, R. C. (1982). Mediation: The Brooklyn experiment. In R. Tomasic & M. M. Feeley (Eds.), *Neighborhood justice: Assessment of an emerging idea.* New York: Longman.

Davis, R. C. (1983). Victim/witness noncooperation: A second look at a persistent phenomenon. *Journal of Criminal Justice, 11,* 287–299.

Davis, R. C., & Smith, B. E. (1994). Victim impact statements and victim satisfaction: An unfulfilled promise? *Journal of Criminal Justice, 22,* 1–12.

Davis, R. C., & Smith, B. E. (1995). Domestic violence reforms: Empty promises or fulfilled expectations? *Crime & Delinquency, 41,* 541–552.

Davis, R. C., & Taylor, B. G. (1997). A proactive response to family violence: The results of a randomized experiment. *Criminology, 35,* 307–334.

Davis, R. C., Henley, M., & Smith, B. (1990). *Victim impact statements: Their effects on court outcomes and victim satisfaction.* Washington, DC: National Institute of Justice.

Davis, R. C., Smith, B. E., & Taylor, B. (2003). Increasing the proportion of domestic violence arrests that are prosecuted: A natural experiment in Milwaukee. *Criminology & Public Policy, 2,* 263–282.

Davis, R. C., Tishane, M., & Grayson, D. (1980). *Mediation and arbitration as alternatives to criminal prosecution in felony arrest cases: An evaluation of the Brooklyn Dispute Resolution Center (first year).* New York: Vera Institute.

Davis, R. C., O'Sullivan, C. S., Farole, D. J., Jr., & Rempel, M. (2008). A comparison of two prosecution policies in cases of intimate partner violence: Mandatory case filing versus following the victim's lead. *Criminology & Public Policy, 7,* 633–662.

Dawson, M., & Dinovitzer, R. (2001). Victim cooperation and the prosecution of domestic violence in a specialized court. *Justice Quarterly, 18,* 593–622.

Dawson, R. K. (1989). Civil suits for sexual assault victims: The up side. *Journal of Interpersonal Violence, 4,* 114–115.

Day, L. E., & Vandiver, M. (2000). Criminology and genocide studies: Notes on what might have been and what still could be. *Crime, Law and Social Change, 34,* 43–59.

DeFrances, C. J., Smith, S. K., & Does, L. V. D. (1996). *Prosecutors in state courts, 1994.* Washington, DC: U.S. Department of Justice.

DeHart, D. D. (2003). *National victim assistance standards consortium: Standards for victim assistance programs and providers.* Columbia: Center for Child and Family Studies, University of South Carolina. Retrieved on July 5, 2010, from http://www.sc.edu/ccfs/training/victimstandards.pdf.

DeHart, D., Webb, J., & Cornman, C. (2009). Prevention of elder mistreatment in nursing homes: Competencies for direct-care staff. *Journal of Elder Abuse & Neglect, 21,* 360–378.

Deisz, R., Doueck, J. H., & George, N. (1996). Reasonable cause: A qualitative study of mandated reporting. *Child Abuse & Neglect, 20,* 275–287.

DeJong, W. (1993). *Building the peace: The Resolving Conflict Creatively Program (RCCP). NIJ Program Focus.* Washington, DC: U.S. Department of Justice.

DeKeseredy, W. S., & Kelly, K. (1995). Sexual abuse in Canadian University and college dating relationships: The contribution of male peer support. *Journal of Family Violence, 10,* 41–53.

DeKeseredy, W. S., Schwartz, M. D., Fagen, D., & Hall, M. (2006). Separation/divorce sexual assault: The contribution of male support. *Feminist Criminology, 1,* 228–250.

deMause, L. (1974). *The history of childhood.* New York: Psycho-History Press.

DePanfilis, D., Dubowitz, H., & Kunz, J. (2008). Assessing the cost-effectiveness of family connections. *Child Abuse & Neglect, 32*, 335–351.

Derene, S. (2005). *Crime victims fund report: Past, present, and future.* Washington, DC: National Association of VOCA Assistance Administrators.

Detmer, C. M., & Lamberti, J. W. (1991). Family grief. *Death Studies, 15*, 363–374.

Dexheimer, E. (2012). Texas hate crime law has little effect. *American-Statesman.* 24 January. Retrieved on July 20, 2013, from http://www.statesman.com/news/news/special-reports/texas-hate-crime-law-has-little-effect/nRjsf/.

Dey, E. L., Korn, J. S., & Sax, L. J. (1996). Betrayed by the academy: The sexual harassment of women college faculty. *Journal of Higher Education, 67*, 149–173.

Deyo, G., Skybo, T., & Carroll, A. (2008). Secondary analysis of the "Love me... never shake me" SBS education program. *Child Abuse & Neglect, 32*, 1017–1025.

Dible, D. A., & Teske, R. H. C. (1993). An analysis of the prosecutory effects of a child sexual abuse victim-witness program. *Journal of Criminal Justice, 21*, 79–85.

Dichter, M. E., Marcus, S. C., Morabito, M. S., & Rhodes, K. V. (2011). Explaining the IPV arrest decision: Incident, agency, and community factors. *Criminal Justice Review, 36*, 22–39.

Dinkes, R., Kemp, J., Baum, K., & Snyder, T. D. (2009). *Indicators of school crime and safety: 2009.* Washington, DC: Bureau of Justice Statistics.

Disha, I., Cavendish, J. C., & King, R. D. (2011). Historical events and spaces of hate: Hate crimes against Arabs and Muslims in post-9/11 America. *Social Problems, 58*, 21–46.

Dissell, R., & Atassi, L. (2010). Cuyahoga juvenile court judge Alison Floyd orders sex assault victims to take polygraph tests. *The Plain Dealer.* March 19. Retrieved on April 5, 2013, from http://blog.cleveland.com/metro/2010/03/juvenile_court_judge_alison_fl.html.

Diviney, C. L., Parekh, A., & Olson, L. M. (2009). Outcomes of civil protective orders: Results from one state. *Journal of Interpersonal Violence, 24*, 1209–1221.

Dobash, R. E., & Dobash, R. P. (1977–78). Wives: The "appropriate" victims of marital violence. *Victimology, 2*, 426–442.

Dobash, R. E., & Dobash, R. P. (1979). *Violence against wives: A case against the patriarchy.* New York: Free Press.

Dobash, R. E., Dobash, R. P., Wilson, M., & Daly, M. (1992). The myth of sexual symmetry in marital violence. *Social Problems, 39*, 71–91.

Dodge, R. W. (1985). *Bureau of justice statistics technical report: Response to screening questions in the National Crime Survey.* Washington, DC: U.S. Government Printing Office.

Doerner, W. G. (1977). State victim compensation programs in action. *Victimology, 2*, 106–109.

Doerner, W. G. (1978a). A quasi-experimental analysis of selected Canadian victim compensation programs. *Canadian Journal of Criminology, 20*, 239–251.

Doerner, W. G. (1978b). An examination of the alleged latent effects of victim compensation programs upon crime reporting. *LAE Journal, 41*, 71–76.

Doerner, W. G. (1979). The violent world of Johnny Reb: An attitudinal analysis of the "regional culture of violence" thesis. *Sociological Forum, 2*, 61–71.

Doerner, W. G. (1980). Trends in Southern homicide: Is the South a "regional culture of violence?" *Journal of Crime and Justice, 3*, 83–94.

Doerner, W. G. (1983). Why does Johnny Reb die when shot? The impact of medical resources upon lethality. *Sociological Inquiry, 53*, 1–15.

Doerner, W. G. (1987). Child maltreatment seriousness and juvenile delinquency. *Youth & Society, 19*, 197–244.

Doerner, W. G. (1988). The impact of medical resources on criminally induced lethality: A further examination. *Criminology, 26,* 171–179.

Doerner, W. G. (2012). *Introduction to law enforcement: An insider's view* (4th ed.). Dubuque, IA: Kendall/Hunt Publishing Company.

Doerner, W. G., & Lab, S. P. (1980). The impact of crimes compensation upon victim attitudes toward the criminal justice system. *Victimology, 5,* 61–67.

Doerner, W. G., & Speir, J. C. (1986). Stitch and sew: The impact of medical resources upon criminally induced lethality. *Criminology, 24,* 319–330.

Doerner, W. G., & Tsai, T. (1990). Child maltreatment and juvenile delinquency in Taiwan. *International Journal of Comparative and Applied Criminal Justice, 14,* 225–238.

Doerner, W. G., Knudten, M. S., Knudten, R. D., & Meade, A. C. (1976). Correspondence between crime victim needs and available public services. *Social Service Review, 50,* 482–490.

Dolliver, J. M. (1987). Victims' Rights Constitutional Amendment: A bad idea whose time should not come. *The Wayne Law Review, 34,* 87–93.

Dolon, R., & Hendricks, J. E. (1989). An exploratory study comparing attitudes and practices of police officers and social service providers in elder abuse and neglect cases. *Journal of Elder Abuse & Neglect, 1,* 75–90.

Dolon, R., & Blakely, B. (1989). Elder abuse and neglect: A study of adult protective service workers in the United States. *Journal of Elder Abuse and Neglect, 1,* 31–49.

Domestic Abuse Intervention Programs (n.d.). *The power and control wheel.* Duluth, MN: Domestic Abuse Intervention Programs. Retrieved on May 14, 2013, from http://www.theduluthmodel.org/pdf/PowerandControl.pdf.

Domestic Violence Prosecution Committee. (2004). *Guidelines for prosecution of domestic violence cases.* Montgomery: Alabama Coalition Against Domestic Violence. Retrieved on May 16, 2013, from http://www.acadv.org/Prosecutionguidelines.pdf.

Dominick, J. R. (1978). Crime and law enforcement in the mass media. In C. Winick (Ed.), *Deviance and mass media.* Beverly Hills: Sage.

Donnerstein, E. (1980). Aggressive erotica and violence against women. *Journal of Personality and Social Psychology, 39,* 269–277.

Donnerstein, E., & Hallam, J. (1978). Effects of erotic stimuli on male aggression toward females. *Journal of Personality and Social Psychology, 32,* 237–244.

Doty, P., & Sullivan, E. W. (1983). Community involvement in combating abuse, neglect and mistreatment in nursing homes. *Milbank Memorial Fund Quarterly/Health and Society, 37,* 115–121.

Douglas, E. M., & Cunningham, J. M. (2008). Recommendations from child fatality review teams: Results of a U.S. nationwide exploratory study concerning maltreatment fatalities and social service delivery. *Child Abuse Review, 17,* 331–351.

Dressler, J. (2006). Battered women and sleeping abusers: Some reflections. *Ohio State Journal of Criminal Law, 3,* 457–471.

Dugan, L. (2003). Domestic violence legislation: Exploring its impact on the likelihood of domestic violence, police involvement, and arrest. *Criminology & Public Policy, 2,* 283–312.

Duggan, A., Caldera, D., Rodriguez, K., Burrell, L., Rohde, C., & Crowne, S. S. (2007). Impact of a statewide home visiting program to prevent child abuse. *Child Abuse & Neglect, 31,* 801–827.

Duggan, A., Fuddy, L., Burrell, L., Higman, S. M., McFarlane, E., Windham, A., et al. (2004a). Randomized trial of a statewide home visiting program: Impact in reducing parental risk factors. *Child Abuse & Neglect, 28,* 623–643.

Duggan, A., McFarlane, E., Fuddy, L., Burrell, L., Higman, S. M., Windham, A., et al. (2004b). Randomized trial of a statewide home visiting program: Impact in preventing child abuse and neglect. *Child Abuse & Neglect, 28*, 597–622.

Duhart, D. T. (2001). *Violence in the workplace, 1993–99.* Bureau of Justice Statistics Special Report. Washington, DC: Bureau of Justice Statistics.

DuMont, K., Mitchell-Herzfeld, S., Greene, R., Lee, E., Lowenfels, A., Rodriguez, M., et al. (2008). Healthy Families New York (HFNY) randomized trial: Effects on early child abuse and neglect. *Child Abuse & Neglect, 32*, 295–315.

Dunford, F. D. (1990). System initiated warrants for suspects of misdemeanor domestic assault: A pilot study. *Justice Quarterly, 7*, 631–653.

Dunford, F. D., Huizinga, D., & Elliott, D. S. (1989). *The Omaha domestic violence police experiments: Final report.* Washington, DC: National Institute of Justice.

Durfee, A. (2009). Victim narratives, legal representation, and domestic violence civil protection orders. *Feminist Criminology, 4*, 7–31.

Durkheim, E. (1933). *The division of labor in society (G. Simpson, Trans.).* New York: Free Press.

Dutton, D. G., & Starzomski, A. J. (1994). Psychological differences between court-referred and self-referred wife assaulters. *Criminal Justice and Behavior, 21*, 203–221.

Edelhertz, H., & Geis, G. (1974). *Public compensation to victims of crime.* New York: Praeger.

Edwards, S. S. M. (1989). *Policing "domestic" violence: Women, the law and the state.* Newbury Park, CA: Sage.

Ehrhardt, C. W., Hubbart, P. A., Levinson, L. H., Smiley, W. M., & Wills, T. A. (1973). The aftermath of *Furman*: The Florida experience. *Journal of Criminal Law and Criminology, 64*, 2–21.

Ehrhart, J. K., & Sandler, B. R. (1985). *Myths and realities about rape.* Washington, DC: Project on the Status and Education of Women.

Eigenberg, H. M. (1990). The National Crime Survey and rape: The case of the missing question. *Justice Quarterly, 7*, 655–671.

Eigenberg, H. M., McGuffee, K., Berry, P., & Hall, W. H. (2003). Protective order legislation: Trends in state statutes. *Journal of Criminal Justice, 31*, 411–422.

Eikenberry, K. (1987). Victims of crime/victims of justice. *The Wayne Law Review, 34*, 29–49.

Eisikovits, Z. (1996). The aftermath of wife beating: Strategies of bounding violent events. *Journal of Interpersonal Violence, 11*, 459–474.

Eisikovits, Z., & Buchbinder, E. (1996). Pathways to disenchantment: Battered women's views of their social workers. *Journal of Interpersonal Violence, 11*, 425–440.

Elias, R. (1990). Which victim movement? The politics of victim policy. In A. J. Lurigio, W. G. Skogan & R. C. Davis (Eds.), *Victims of crime: Problems, policies and programs.* Newbury Park, CA: Sage.

Ellingworth, D., Farrell, G., & Pease, K. (1995). Victim is a victim is a victim? Chronic victimization in four sweeps of the British Crime Survey. *British Journal of Criminology, 35*, 360–365.

Elliott, D. S. (1989). Criminal justice procedures in family violence crimes. In L. Ohlin & M. Tonry (Eds.), *Family violence.* Chicago: University of Chicago.

Ellis, D. (1992). Toward a consistent recognition of the forbidden inference: The Illinois rape shield statute. *Journal of Criminal Law & Criminology, 83*, 395–436.

Employment Law Alliance. (2007). *Abusive boss charts.* Retrieved from http://www.millercanfield.com/media/news/200036_ELA%20Abusive%20Boss%20Charts%20D2%20031907.pdf.

Ennis, P. (1967). *Criminal victimization in the United States: A report of a national survey.* Chicago: National Opinion Research Center.

Equal Employment Opportunity Commission. (1999). *Enforcement guidance: Vicarious employer liability for unlawful harassment by supervisors.* Retrieved on June 18, 2013, from http://www.eeoc.gov/docs/harassment.html.

Equal Employment Opportunity Commission. (2013). *Sexual harassment charges EEOC & FEPAs combined: FY 1997-FY 2011.* Retrieved on June 18, 2013, from http://www.eeoc.gov/eeoc/statistics/enforcement/sexual_harassment.cfm.

Erez, E. (1990). Victim participation in sentencing: Rhetoric and reality. *Journal of Criminal Justice, 18,* 19–31.

Erez, E., & Roeger, L. (1995). The effect of victim impact statements on sentencing patterns and outcomes: The Australian experience. *Journal of Criminal Justice, 23,* 363–375.

Erez, E., & Tontodonato, P. (1990). The effect of victim participation in sentencing on sentence outcome. *Criminology, 28,* 451–474.

Erez, E., & Tontodonato, P. (1992). Victim participation in sentencing and satisfaction with justice. *Justice Quarterly, 9,* 393–417.

Erlanger, H. S. (1974). The empirical status of the subculture of violence thesis. *Social Problems, 20,* 280–292.

Erlanger, H. S. (1975). Is there a "subculture of violence" in the South? *Journal of Criminal Law and Criminology, 66,* 483–490.

Ervin, L., & Schneider, A. (1990). Explaining the effects of restitution on offenders: Results from a national experiment in juvenile courts. In B. Galaway & J. Hudson (Eds.), *Criminal justice, restitution, and reconciliation.* Monsey, NY: Criminal Justice Press.

Everson, M. D., Boat, B. W., Bourg, S., & Robertson, K. R. (1996). Beliefs among professionals about rates of false allegations of child sexual abuse. *Journal of Interpersonal Violence, 11,* 541–553.

Ewing, D. (2007). Prosecuting batters in the wake of *Davis* and *Hammon. American Journal of Criminal Law, 35,* 91–106.

Eyles, J., & Woods, K. J. (1983). *The social geography of medicine and health.* New York: St. Martin's Press.

Fagan, A. A. (2005). The relationship between adolescent physical abuse and criminal offending: Support for an enduring and generalized cycle of violence. *Journal of Family Violence, 20,* 279–290.

Fang, X., Brown, D. S., Florence, C. S., & Mercy, J. A. (2012). The economic burden of child maltreatment in the United States and implications for prevention. *Child Abuse & Neglect, 36,* 156–165.

Farrell, A. D., & Meyer, A. L. (1997). The effectiveness of a school-based curriculum for reducing violence among urban sixth-grade students. *American Journal of Public Health, 87,* 979–988.

Farrell, G. (2005). Progress and prospects in the prevention of repeat victimization. In N. Tilley (Ed.), *Handbook of crime prevention and community safety.* Portland, OR: Willan.

Farrell, G. (2010). Repeat victimization: Theories of. In B. S. Fisher & S. P. Lab (Eds.), *Encyclopedia of victimology and crime prevention.* Los Angeles: Sage.

Farrell, G., & Bouloukos, A. C. (2001). International overview: A cross-national comparison of rates of repeat victimization. In G. Farrell & K. Pease (Eds.), *Repeat victimization.* Monsey, NY: Criminal Justice Press.

Farrell, G., & Pease, K. (2003). Measuring repeat victimization using police data: An analysis of burglary data and policy for Charlotte, North Carolina. In M. J. Smith & D. B. Cornish (Eds.), *Theory for practice in situational crime prevention.* Monsey, NY: Criminal Justice Press.

Farrell, G., Phillips, C., & Pease, K. (1995). Like taking candy: Why does repeat victimization occur? *British Journal of Criminology, 35,* 384–399.

Farrell, G., Tseloni, A., & Pease, K. (2005). Repeat victimization in the ICVS and the NCVS. *Crime Prevention and Community Safety, 7*(3), 7–18.

Fattah, E. A., & Sacco, V. F. (1989). *Crime and victimization of the elderly*. New York: Springer-Verlag.

Feder, L., & Dugan, L. (2002). A test of the efficacy of court-mandated counseling for domestic violence offenders: The Broward Experiment. *Justice Quarterly, 19*, 343–375.

Federal Bureau of Investigation. (1997). *Hate crime statistics 1996*. Washington, DC: U.S. Government Printing Office. Retrieved on July 5, 2013, from http://www.fbi.gov/about-us/cjis/ucr/hate-crime/1996/hatecrime96.pdf.

Federal Bureau of Investigation. (2000). *National incident-based reporting system. Data collection guidelines* (Vol. 1). Washington, DC: FBI.

Federal Bureau of Investigation. (2010a). *Crime in the United States 2009*. Washington, DC: U.S. Government Printing Office. Retrieved on September 14, 2010, from http://www.fbi.gov/ucr/cius2009/index.html.

Federal Bureau of Investigation. (2010b). *National incident-based reporting system (NIBRS) Categories*. Retrieved on January 26, 2011, from http://www.fbi.gov/about-us/cjis/ucr/nibrs/nibrscategories.pdf.

Federal Bureau of Investigation. (2012a). *Crime in the United States 2011*. Washington, DC: U.S. Department of Justice. Retrieved on April 17, 2013, from http://www.fbi.gov/about-us/cjis/ucr/crime-in-the-u.s/2011/crime-in-the-u.s.-2011.

Federal Bureau of Investigation. (2012b). *Expanded homicide data 2011*. Washington, DC: U.S. Department of Justice. Retrieved on May 13, 2013, from http://www.fbi.gov/about-us/cjis/ucr/crime-in-the-u.s/2011/crime-in-the-u.s.-2011/offenses-known-to-law-enforcement/expanded/expanded-homicide-data.

Federal Bureau of Investigation. (2012c). *Hate crime statistics 2011*. Washington, DC: U.S. Government Printing Office. Retrieved on July 5, 2013, from http://www.fbi.gov/about-us/cjis/ucr/hate-crime/2011/resources/about-hate-crime-statistics.

Federal Bureau of Investigation. (2012d). *UCR reporting forms: Hate crime incident report*. Washington, DC: U.S. Government Printing Office. Retrieved on July 6, 2013, from http://www.fbi.gov/about-us/cjis/ucr/reporting-forms/hate-crime-incident-report-pdf.

Federal Bureau of Investigation. (2013). *Crime in the United States 2011*. Washington, DC: U.S. Government Printing Office. Retrieved on June 5, 2013, from http://www.fbi.gov/about-us/cjis/ucr/crime-in-the-u.s/2011/crime-in-the-u.s.-2011.

Federal Interagency Forum on Aging-Related Statistics. (2012). *Older Americans 2012: Key indicators of well-being*. Washington, DC: U.S. Government Printing Office. Retrieved on June 13, 2013, from http://www.agingstats.gov/agingstatsdotnet/Main_Site/Data/2012_Documents/Docs/EntireChartbook.pdf.

Fehler-Cabral, G., Campbell, R., & Patterson, D. (2011). Adult sexual assault survivors' experiences with sexual assault nurse examiners (SANEs). *Journal of Interpersonal Violence, 26*, 3618–3639.

Feinstein, D. (2004, April 22). Scott Campbell, Stephanie Roper, Wendy Preston, Louarna Gillis, and Nila Lynn Crime Victims' Rights Act. *Congressional Record, 150*, S4260–S4265.

Feld, B. C. (1999). Rehabilitation, retribution and restorative justice: Alternative conceptions of juvenile justice. In G. Bazemore & L. Walgrave (Eds.), *Restorative juvenile justice: Repairing the harm of youth crime*. Monsey, NY: Criminal Justice Press.

Feld, L. S., & Straus, M. A. (1989). Escalation and desistance of wife assault in marriage. *Criminology, 27*, 141–161.

Felstiner, W. L. F., & Williams, L. A. (1979). *Community mediation in Dorchester, Massachusetts. Final Report*. Los Angeles, CA: University of Southern California.

Felstiner, W. L. F., & Williams, L. A. (1982). Community mediation in Dorchester, Massachusetts. In R. Tomasic & M. M. Feeley (Eds.), *Neighborhood justice: Assessment of an emerging idea*. New York: Longman.

Ferguson, C. J. (2007a). Video games: The latest scapegoat for violence. *The Chronicle of Higher Education* (June 22), B20.

Ferguson, C. J. (2007b). Evidence for publication bias in video game violence effects literature: A meta-analytic review. *Aggression and Violent Behavior, 12*, 470–482.

Ferraro, K. F. (1995). *Fear of crime: Interpreting victimization risk*. Albany, NY: SUNY Press.

Ferraro, K. F., & LaGrange, R. L. (1988). Are older people afraid of crime? *Journal of Aging Studies, 2*, 277–287.

Ferro, C., Cermele, J., & Saltzman, A. (2008). Current perceptions of marital rape: Some good and not-so-good news. *Journal of Interpersonal Violence, 23*, 764–779.

Fiegener, J. J., Fiegener, M., & Meszaros, J. (1989). Policy implications of a statewide survey on elder abuse. *Journal of Elder Abuse & Neglect, 1*, 39–58.

Fields, M. D., & Kirchner, R. M. (1978). Battered women are still in need: A reply to Steinmetz. *Victimology, 3*, 216–226.

Figley, C. R. (1995). *Compassion fatigue: Coping with secondary traumatic stress disorder in those who treat the traumatized*. New York: Brunner/Mazel.

File, T. (2013). *The diversifying electorate—Voting rates by race and Hispanic origin in 2012 (and other recent elections). Current Population Survey*. Washington, D.C: U.S. Census Bureau. Retrieved on June 13, 2013, from http://www.census.gov/prod/2013pubs/p20-568.pdf.

File, T., & Crissey, S. (2013). *Voting and registration in the election of November 2008. Current Population Reports*. Washington, D.C: U.S. Census Bureau. Retrieved on June 13, 2013, from http://www.census.gov/prod/2010pubs/p20-562.pdf.

Finkelhor, D., & Yllo, K. (1983). Common features of family abuse. In D. Finkelhor, R. J. Gelles, G. T. Hotaling & M. A. Straus (Eds.), *The dark side of families: Family violence research*. Beverly Hills: Sage.

Finkelhor, D., Ormrod, R. K., & Turner, H. A. (2007). Poly-victimization: A neglected component in child victimization. *Child Abuse & Neglect, 31*, 7–26.

Finkelhor, D., Ormrod, R. K., Turner, H. A., & Hamby, S. L. (2005). Measuring poly-victimization using the juvenile victimization questionnaire. *Child Abuse & Neglect, 29*, 1297–1312.

Finn, P., & Lee, B. N. W. (1987). *Serving crime victims and witnesses*. Washington, DC: U.S. Department of Justice.

Finneran, C., & Stephenson, R. (2012). Intimate partner violence among men who have sex with men: A systematic review. *Trauma, Violence, & Abuse, 13*, 138–185.

Fischer, K., & Rose, M. (1995). When "enough is enough:" Battered women's decision making around court orders of protection. *Crime & Delinquency, 41*, 414–429.

Fisher, B. S. (2009). The effects of survey question wording on rape estimates: Evidence from a quasi-experimental design. *Violence Against Women, 15*, 133–147.

Fisher, B. S., Daigle, L. E., Cullen, F. T., & Turner, M. G. (2003a). Reporting sexual victimization to the police and others: Results from a national-level study of college women. *Criminal Justice and Behavior, 30*, 6–38.

Fisher, B. S., Daigle, L. E., Cullen, F. T., & Turner, M. G. (2003b). Acknowledging sexual victimization as rape: Results from a national-level study. *Justice Quarterly, 20*, 535–574.

Flaherty, E. G., Jones, R., & Sege, R. (2004). Telling their stories: Primary care practitioners' experience evaluating and reporting injuries caused by child abuse. *Child Abuse & Neglect, 28*, 939–945.

Flaherty, E. G., Sege, R., Price, L. L., Christoffel, K. K., Norton, D. P., & O'Connor, K. G. (2006). Pediatrician characteristics associated with child abuse identification and reporting: Results from a national survey of pediatricians. *Child Maltreatment, 11*, 361–369.

Flavin, J. (2000). (Mis)representing risk: Headline accounts of HIV-related assaults. *American Journal of Criminal Justice, 25*, 119–136.

Flemming, B. (2003). Equal protection for victims of domestic violence. *Journal of Interpersonal Violence, 18*, 685–692.

Florida Abuse Hotline. (2004). *Florida abuse hotline fax transmittal form to report abuse/abandonment/ neglect/exploitation*. Tallahassee: Department of Children and Families. Retrieved on May 20, 2013, from http://www.dcf.state.fl.us/programs/abuse/docs/faxreport.pdf.

Florida Commission on Human Relations. (2009). *A snapshot of hate crimes/incidents in Florida*. Tallahassee: Florida Commission on Human Relations. Retrieved on July 8, 2013, from http://fchr.state.fl.us/fchr/content/download/6130/32779/file/Hate%20Crimes%20 Summit%20stat%20document-FINAL.pdf.

Florida Criminal Justice Standards and Training Commission. (2013). *Florida basic recruit training program: Law enforcement, Volume 1*. Tallahassee: Florida Department of Law Enforcement. Retrieved on July 28, 2013, from http://www.fdle.state.fl.us/Content/getdoc/ c660f6f7-0304-4ff9-a7fb-e9d554384f84/2013-07_LE_Text.aspx.

Florida Domestic Violence Fatality Review Team. (2007). *2006 annual report executive summary*. Tallahassee: Florida Department of Law Enforcement. Retrieved on May 18, 2013, from http://www.dcf.state.fl.us/programs/domesticviolence/publications/docs/Fatality Review2006.pdf.

Florida Statutes. (2012). *Official internet site of the Florida legislature*. http://www.leg.state.fl.us/ statutes/index.cfm?.

Florida's Long-Term Care Ombudsman Program. (2010). *Resident's rights*. Tallahassee: Florida Department of Elder Affairs. Retrieved on June 27, 2013, from http://ombudsman.myflorida. com/ResidentsRights.php.

Ford, D. A. (2003). Coercing victim participation in domestic violence prosecutions. *Journal of Interpersonal Violence, 18*, 669–684.

Ford, D. A. (2009). The substance, scholarship, and science of research on violence against women: A comment. *Violence Against Women, 15*, 420–424.

Fowler, T. K. (2003). *Report of the panel to review sexual misconduct allegations at the United States Air Force Academy*. Arlington, VA: Department of Air Force.

Fox, B. (2009). *Crawford* at its limits: Hearsay and forfeiture in child abuse cases. *American Criminal Law Review, 46*, 1245–1265.

Franklin, C. W., II, & Franklin, A. P. (1976). Victimology revisited: A critique and suggestions for future direction. *Criminology, 14*, 177–214.

Frazier, P. A., & Borgida, E. (1992). Rape trauma syndrome: A review of case law and psychological research. *Law and Human Behavior, 16*, 293–311.

Freeman, N. J., & Sandler, J. C. (2010). The Adam Walsh Act: A false sense of security or an effective public policy initiative? *Criminal Justice Policy Review, 21*, 31–49.

Freilich, J. D., & Rivera, C. J. (1999). Mercy, death, and politics. *American Journal of Criminal Justice, 24*, 15–29.

Frenzen, P. D. (1991). The increasing supply of physicians in U.S. urban and rural areas, 1975 to 1988. *American Journal of Public Health, 81*, 1141–1147.

Frese, B., Moya, M., & Megias, J. L. (2004). Social perception of rape: How rape myth acceptance modulates the influence of situational factors. *Journal of Interpersonal Violence, 19*, 143–161.

Friedman, J. J. (1973). Structural constraints on community action: The case of infant mortality rates. *Social Problems, 21,* 230–245.

Friedrichs, D. O. (2000). The crime of the century? The case for the Holocaust. *Crime, Law and Social Change, 23,* 21–41.

Frieze, I. H., & Browne, A. (1989). Violence in marriage. In L. Ohlin & M. Tonry (Eds.), *Family violence.* Chicago: University of Chicago Press.

Fujiwara, T., Yamada, F., Okuyama, M., Kamimaki, I., Shikoro, N., & Barr, R. G. (2012). Effectiveness of educational materials designed to change knowledge and behavior about crying and shaken baby syndrome: A replication of a randomized controlled trial in Japan. *Child Abuse & Neglect, 36,* 613–620.

Gage, E. A. (2008). Gender attitudes and sexual behaviors: Comparing center and marginal athletes and nonathletes in a collegiate setting. *Violence Against Women, 14,* 1014–1032.

Gagné, P. (1996). Identity, strategy, and feminist politics: Clemency for battered women who kill. *Social Problems, 43,* 77–93.

Galaway, B. (1981). The use of restitution. In B. Galaway & J. Hudson (Eds.), *Perspectives on crime victims.* St. Louis, MO: C.V. Mosby.

Galbraith, M. W. (1989). A critical examination of the definitional, methodological and theoretical problems of elder abuse. In R. Filinson & S. R. Ingman (Eds.), *Elder abuse: Practice and policy.* New York: Human Sciences Press.

Gallup. (2009). *The Gallup Poll.* Available at http://www.gallup.com/poll/topics.aspx.

Gallup, G., Jr. (1992). *The Gallup Poll monthly, no. 318.* Princeton, NJ: The Gallup Poll.

Galvin, J., & Polk, K. (1983). Attrition in case processing: Is rape unique? *Journal of Research in Crime & Delinquency, 20,* 126–154.

Gandy, J. T. (1978). Attitudes toward the use of restitution. In B. Galaway & J. Hudson (Eds.), *Offender restitution in theory and action.* Lexington, MA: D.C. Heath.

Gandy, J. T., & Galaway, B. (1980). Restitution as a sanction for offenders: A public's view. In J. Hudson & B. Galaway (Eds.), *Victims, offenders, and alternative sanctions.* Lexington, MA: D.C. Heath.

Garbarino, J., & Gilliam, G. (1980). *Understanding abusive families.* Lexington, MA: Lexington Books.

Garcia, C. A. (2003). Digital photographic evidence and the adjudication of domestic violence cases. *Journal of Criminal Justice, 31,* 579–587.

Garner, B. A. (2009). *Black's law dictionary* (9th ed.). St. Paul, MN: West Publishing Company.

Garner, J., & Clemmer, E. (1986). *Danger to police in domestic disturbances–New look.* Washington, DC: U.S. Department of Justice.

Garner, J., Fagan, J., & Maxwell, C. (1995). Published findings from the spouse assault replication program: A critical review. *Journal of Quantitative Criminology, 11,* 3–28.

Garofalo, J., & Connelly, K. J. (1980a). Dispute resolution centers, part I: Major features and processes. *Criminal Justice Abstracts, 12,* 416–436.

Garofalo, J., & Connelly, K. J. (1980b). Dispute resolution centers, part II: Outcomes, issues, and future directions. *Criminal Justice Abstracts, 12,* 576–611.

Gartin, P. R. (1995a). Examining differential officer effects in the Minneapolis Domestic Violence Experiment. *American Journal of Police, 14,* 93–110.

Gartin, P. R. (1995b). Dealing with design failures in randomized field experiments: Analytic issues regarding the evaluation of treatment effects. *Journal of Research in Crime & Delinquency, 32,* 425–445.

Gastil, R. D. (1971). Homicide and a regional culture of violence. *American Sociological Review, 36*, 412–427.

Gelles, R. J. (1973). Child abuse as psychopathology: A sociological critique and reformulation. *American Journal of Orthopsychiatry, 43*, 611–621.

Gelles, R. J. (1975). The social construction of child abuse. *American Journal of Orthopsychiatry, 45*, 363–371.

Gelles, R. J. (1980). Violence in the family: A review of research in the 70's. *Journal of Marriage and the Family, 42*, 873–885.

Gelles, R. J. (2000). Estimating the incidence and prevalence of violence against women: National data systems and sources. *Violence Against Women, 6*, 784–804.

Gelles, R. J., & Cornell, C. P. (1990). *Intimate violence in families* (2nd ed.). Beverly Hills: Sage.

Gelles, R. J., & Perlman, S. (2012). *Estimate annual cost of child abuse and neglect*. Chicago: Prevent Child Abuse American. Retrieved on June 3, 2013, from http://www.preventchildabuse.org/images/research/pcaa_cost_report_2012_gelles_perlman.pdf.

Gelles, R. J., & Straus, M. A. (1979). Determinants of violence in the family: A theoretical integration. In W. Burr (Ed.), *Contemporary theories about the family*. New York: Free Press.

Gelles, R. J., & Straus, M. A. (1988). *Intimate violence*. New York: Simon and Schuster.

George, L. K. (1986). Caregiver burden: Conflict between norms of reciprocity and solidarity. In K. A. Pillemer & R. S. Wolf (Eds.), *Elder abuse: Conflict in the family*. Dover, MA: Auburn House.

Gerbner, G., Gross, L., Jackson-Beeck, M., Jeffries-Fox, S., & Signorielle, N. (1978). Cultural indicators: Violence profile no. 9. *Journal of Communication, 29*, 177–196.

Gerbner, G., Gross, L., Signorielle, N., & Morgan, M. (1980). Television violence, victimization, and power. *American Behavioral Scientist, 23*, 705–716.

Gessner, B. (2008). The effect of Alaska's home visitation program for high-risk families on trends in abuse and neglect. *Child Abuse & Neglect, 32*, 317–333.

Giacopassi, D. J., & Sparger, J. R. (1992). The effects of emergency medical care on the homicide rate: Some additional evidence. *Journal of Criminal Justice, 20*, 249–259.

Giannelli, P. (1997). Rape trauma syndrome. *Criminal Law Bulletin, 33*, 270–279.

Gil, D. (1971). *Violence against children: Physical child abuse in the United States*. Cambridge, MA: Harvard University Press.

Gilbert, N. (1993). Examining the facts: Advocacy research overstates the incidence of date and acquaintance rape. In R. J. Gelles & D. R. Loseke (Eds.), *Current controversies on family violence*. Newbury Park, CA: Sage.

Giles, R. H. (2009). Difficult economic times prove value of multidisciplinary approaches to resolve child abuse. *The Prosecutor, 42*(3), 42–45.

Gill, M., & Pease, K. (1998). Repeat robbers: Are they different? In M. Gill (Ed.), *Crime at work: Increasing the risk for offenders*. Leicester: Perpetuity Press.

Gillis, B. (2013). Understanding hate crime statutes and building towards a better system in Texas. *American Journal of Criminal Law, 40*, 197–226.

Giovannoni, J. M., & Becerra, R. M. (1979). *Defining child abuse*. New York: Free Press.

Gironda, M. W., Lefever, K., Delagrammatikas, L., Nerenberg, L., Roth, R., Chen, E. A., et al. (2010). Education and training of mandated reporters: Innovative models, overcoming challenges, and lessons learned. *Journal of Elder Abuse & Neglect, 22*, 340–364.

Glaser, D. (1956). Criminality theories and behavioral images. *American Journal of Sociology, 61,* 433–444.

Gomby, D. S. (2007). The promise and limitations of home visiting: Implementing effective programs. *Child Abuse & Neglect, 31,* 793–799.

Gondolf, E. W. (2008). Implementation of case management for batterer program participants. *Violence Against Women, 14,* 208–225.

Gondolf, E. W. (2009). Implementing mental health treatment for batterer program participants: Interagency breakdowns and underlying issues. *Violence Against Women, 15,* 638–655.

Gondolf, E. W., McWilliams, J., Hart, B., & Stuehling, J. (1994). Court response to petitions for civil protection orders. *Journal of Interpersonal Violence, 9,* 503–517.

Goodman, L. A., Dutton, M. A., & Bennett, L. (2000). Predicting repeat abuse among arrested batterers: Use of the danger assessment scale in the criminal justice system. *Journal of Interpersonal Violence, 15,* 63–74.

Gordon, J. A., & Moriarty, L. J. (2003). The effects of domestic violence batterer treatment on domestic violence recidivism: The Chesterfield County experience. *Criminal Justice and Behavior, 30,* 118–134.

Gordon, M. (2000). Definitional issues in violence against women: Surveillance and research from a violence research perspective. *Violence Against Women, 6,* 747–783.

Gotsch, K. E., Annest, J. L., Mercy, J. A., & Ryan, G. W. (2001). Surveillance for fatal and nonfatal firearm-related injuries—United States, 1993–1998. *Morbidity and Mortality Weekly Report, 50*(April 13), 1–32.

Gover, A. R., Paul, D. P., & Dodge, M. (2011). Law enforcement officers' attitudes about domestic violence. *Violence Against Women, 17,* 619–636.

Government Accountability Office. (2002). *Identity theft: Prevalence and cost appear to be growing.* Washington, DC: Report to Senate Subcommittee on Technology, Terrorism, and Government Information.

Graber, D. (1977). *Ideological components in the perceptions of crime and crime news.* Paper presented to the meeting of the Society for the Study of Social Problems, .

Graber, D. (1980). *Crime news and the public.* New York: Praeger.

Graham, K., Bernards, S., Wilsnack, S. C., & Gmel, G. (2011). Alcohol may not cause partner violence but it seems to make it worse: A cross-national comparison of the relationship between alcohol and severity of partner violence. *Journal of Interpersonal Violence, 26,* 1503–1523.

Grattet, R., Jenness, V., & Curry, T. R. (1998). The homogenization and differentiation of hate crime law in the United States, 1978 to 1995: Innovation and diffusion in the criminalization of bigotry. *American Sociological Review, 63,* 286–307.

Greenberg, J., & Alge, B. J. (1998). Aggressive reactions to workplace injustice. In R. W. Griffin, A. O'Leary-Kelly & J. M. Collins (Eds.), *Dysfunctional behavior in organizations: Violence and deviant behavior.* Stamford, CT: JAI Press.

Greer, D. S. (1994). A transatlantic perspective on the compensation of crime victims in the United States. *Journal of Criminal Law and Criminology, 85,* 333–401.

Greeson, M. R., & Campbell, R. (2013). Sexual assault response teams (SARTs): An empirical review of their effectiveness and challenges to successful implementation. *Trauma, Violence, & Abuse, 14,* 83–95.

Griffin, T. (2010). An empirical examination of AMBER Alert "successes." *Journal of Criminal Justice, 38,* 1053–1062.

Griffin, T., & Miller, M. K. (2008). Child abduction, AMBER Alert, and crime control theater. *Criminal Justice Review, 33,* 159–176.

Griffin, T., Miller, M. K., Hoppe, J., Rebideaux, A., & Hammack, R. (2007). A preliminary examination of AMBER Alert's effects. *Criminal Justice Policy Review, 18*, 378–394.

Gross, M., Cramer, E. P., Forte, J., Gordon, J. A., Kunkel, T., & Moriarty, L. J. (2000). The impact of sentencing options on recidivism among domestic violence offenders: A case study. *American Journal of Criminal Justice, 24*, 301–312.

Gutek, B. (1985). *Sex and the workplace*. San Francisco: Jossey-Bass.

Hamberger, L. K. (1993). Comments on Pagelow's myth of psychopathology in woman battering. *Journal of Interpersonal Violence, 8*, 132–136.

Hammond, M., Miller, M. K., & Griffin, T. (2010). Safe haven laws as crime control theater. *Child Abuse & Neglect, 34*, 545–552.

Handelman, D. (1979). The interpretation of child abuse: Bureaucratic relevance in urban Newfoundland. *Journal of Sociology and Social Welfare, 6*, 70–88.

Hanke, P. J., & Gundlach, J. H. (1995). Damned on arrival: A preliminary study of the relationship between homicide, emergency medical care, and race. *Journal of Criminal Justice, 23*, 313–323.

Harland, A. T., & Rosen, C. J. (1990). Impediments to the recovery of restitution by crime victims. *Violence and Victims, 5*, 127–140.

Harrell, A., Castro, J., Newmark, L., & Vishers, C. (2007). *Final report on the evaluation of the judicial oversight demonstration: Executive summary*. Washington, DC: U.S. Department of Justice.

Harrington, N. T., & Leitenberg, H. (1994). Relationship between alcohol consumption and victim behaviors immediately preceding sexual aggression by an acquaintance. *Violence and Victims, 9*, 315–324.

Harris, A. J., & Lobanov-Rostovsky, C. (2010). Implementing the Adam Walsh Act's sex offender registration and notification provisions: A survey of the states. *Criminal Justice Policy Review, 21*, 202–222.

Harris, A. J., Lobanov-Rostovsky, C., & Levenson, J. S. (2010). Widening the net: The effects of transitioning to the Adam Walsh Act's federally mandated sex offender classification system. *Criminal Justice and Behavior, 37*, 503–519.

Harris, A. R., Thomas, S. H., Fisher, G. A., & Hirsch, D. J. (2002). Murder and medicine: The lethality of criminal assault 1960–1999. *Homicide Studies, 6*, 128–166.

Harris, D. K. (1999). Elder abuse in nursing homes: The theft of patients' possessions. *Journal of Elder Abuse & Neglect, 10*, 141–151.

Harris, D. K., & Benson, M. L. (1996). Theft in nursing homes: An overlooked form of elder abuse. *Advances in Bioethics, 1*, 171–188.

Harris, N. (2003). Evaluating the practice of restorative justice: The case of family group conferencing. In L. Walgrave (Ed.), *Repositioning restorative justice*. Portland, OR: Willan.

Hart, T. C. (2003). *Violent victimization of college students*. Washington, DC: U.S. Government Printing Office.

Hassler, R., Johnson, B., Town, M., & Websdale, N. (1999). *Lethality assessments as integral parts of providing full faith and credit guarantees*. Retrieved on May 18, 2013, from http://www.mincava.umn.edu/documents/ffc/chapter9/chapter9.pdf.

Hawes, C. (2003). Elder abuse in residential long-term care settings: What is known and what information is needed? In National Research Council (Ed.), *Elder mistreatment: Abuse, neglect, and exploitation in an aging America*. Washington, DC: National Academies Press.

Hayes, H., & Daly, K. (2004). Conferencing and re-offending in Queensland. *Australian and New Zealand Journal of Criminology, 37*, 167–191.

Healey, K. M. (1995). Victim and witness intimidation: New developments and emerging responses. *National Institute of Justice: Research in Action*. Washington, DC: U.S. Department of Justice.

Healey, K. M., Smith, C., & O'Sullivan, C. (1998). *Batterer intervention: Program approaches and criminal justice strategies*. Washington, DC: U.S. Department of Justice, National Institute of Justice.

Healthy Families Florida. (2011). *Frequently asked questions*. Tallahassee: Florida Chapter of Prevent Child Abuse America. Retrieved on August 10, 2010 May 22, 2013, from http://www.healthyfamiliesfla.org/faqs.html.

Heck, C., & Walsh, A. (2000). The effects of maltreatment and family structure on minor and serious delinquency. *International Journal of Offender Therapy and Comparative Criminology, 44*, 178–193.

Heffernan, C. J. (2001). *Hate crime: A prosecutor's guide*. Chicago: Governor's Commission on Discrimination & Hate Crimes. Retrieved on July 9, 2013, from http://www.google.com/url?sa=t&rct=j&q=&esrc=s&source=web&cd=6&ved=0CEYQFjAF&url=http%3A%2F%2Fileeta.org%2FTrainers_resources%2FHate%2520Crime%2520Pros%2520Guide_ashley.ppt&ei=OureUsDwJZOekAff24CgBQ&usg=AFQjCNGZm9AmGaq_ywtdxXw_dripbpgqxw&sig2=v1dn7TtOxVYJRDNMQpPVCQ&bvm=bv.59568121,d.eW0.

Hendricks, J. E. (1984). Death notification: The theory and practice of informing survivors. *Journal of Police Science and Administration, 12*, 109–116.

Henning, K., Renauer, B., & Holdford, R. (2006). Victim or offender?: Heterogeneity among women arrested for intimate partner violence. *Journal of Family Violence, 21*, 351–368.

Herman-Giddens, M. E., Brown, G., Verbiest, S., Carlson, P. J., Hooten, E. G., Howell, E., et al. (1999). Underascertainment of child abuse mortality in the United States. *Journal of the American Medical Association, 282*, 463–467.

Herrenkohl, T. I., Sousa, C., Tajima, A. A., Herrenkohl, R. C., & Moylan, C. A. (2008). Intersection of child abuse and children's exposure to domestic violence. *Trauma, Violence, & Abuse, 9*, 84–99.

Hershkowitz, I. (2001). A case study of child sexual false allegation. *Child Abuse & Neglect, 25*, 1397–1411.

Hickey, E. W. (2012). *Serial murderers and their victims* (6th ed.). Belmont, CA: Wadsworth Cenage Learning.

Hilberman, E. (1976). *The rape victim*. New York: Basic Books, Inc.

Hillenbrand, S. (1990). Restitution and victims rights in the 1980s. In A. J. Lurigio, W. G. Skogan & R. C. Davis (Eds.), *Victims of crime: Problems, policies, and programs*. Newbury Park, CA: Sage.

Hindelang, M. J. (1976). *Criminal victimization in eight American cities: A descriptive analysis of common theft and assault*. Cambridge, MA: Ballinger Publishing Company.

Hindelang, M. J., Gottfredson, M. R., & Garofalo, J. (1978). *Victims of personal crime: An empirical foundation for a theory of personal victimization*. Cambridge, MA: Ballinger.

Hirschel, J. D., Dean, C. W., & Lumb, R. C. (1994). The relative contribution of domestic violence to assault and injury of police officers. *Justice Quarterly, 11*, 99–117.

Hirschel, J. D., Buzawa, E., Pattavina, A., & Faggiani, D. (2008). Domestic violence and mandatory arrest laws: To what extent do they influence police arrest decisions? *Journal of Criminal Law & Criminology, 98*, 255–298.

Hirschel, J. D., Hutchinson, I. W., Dean, C. W., Kelley, J. J., & Pesackis, C. E. (1991). *Charlotte spouse assault replication project: Final report*. Washington, DC: National Institute of Justice.

Hirschel, J. D., Hutchison, I. W., III, & Dean, C. W. (1992). The failure of arrest to deter spouse abuse. *Journal of Research in Crime & Delinquency, 29*, 7–33.

Ho, T. (2000). Domestic violence in a southern city: The effects of a mandatory arrest policy on male-versus-female aggravated assault incidents. *American Journal of Criminal Justice, 25*, 107–118.

Hoffman, J. L. (2003). Revenge or mercy? Some thoughts about survivor opinion evidence in death penalty cases. *Cornell Law Review, 88*, 530–542.

Hoffman, M. H. (2000). Emerging combatants, war crimes and the future of international humanitarian law. *Crime, Law and Social Change, 34*, 99–110.

Hofrichter, R. (1980). Techniques of victim involvement in restitution. In J. Hudson & B. Galaway (Eds.), *Victims, offenders, and alternative sanctions*. Lexington, MA: D.C. Heath and Co.

Hofstetter, E. (1976). *Bias in the news*. Columbus, OH: Ohio State University Press.

Holder, E. (2012). *Attorney General Eric Holder announces revisions to the Uniform Crime Report's definition of rape*. Washington, DC: U.S. Department of Justice. Retrieved on April 16, 2013, from http://www.justice.gov/opa/pr/2012/January/12-ag-018.html.

Holmstrom, L. L., & Burgess, A. W. (1978). *The victim of rape: Institutional reactions*. New York: Wiley Interscience.

Holt, S., Buckley, H., & Whelan, S. (2008). The impact of exposure to domestic violence on children and young people: A review of the literature. *Child Abuse & Neglect, 32*, 797–810.

Holtfreter, K. (2004). Fraud in American organizations: An examination of control mechanisms. *Journal of Financial Crime, 12*, 88–95.

Holtfreter, K., Van Slyke, S., & Blomberg, T. G. (2005). Sociolegal change in consumer fraud: From victim-offender interactions to global networks. *Crime, Law and Social Change, 44*, 251–275.

Horne, C. (2003). Families of homicide victims: Service utilization patterns of extra- and intrafamilial homicide survivors. *Journal of Family Violence, 18*, 75–82.

Horney, J., & Spohn, C. (1991). Rape law reform and instrumental change in six urban jurisdictions. *Law & Society Review, 25*, 117–153.

Hotaling, G. T., & Sugarman, D. B. (1986). An analysis of risk markers in husband to wife violence: The current state of the evidence. *Violence and Victims, 1*, 101–124.

Hotaling, G. T., & Straus, M. A. (1989). Intrafamily violence and crime and violence outside the family. In L. Ohlin & dN. Tonry (Eds.), *Family violence*. Chicago: Univ. of Chicago Press.

Houser, K. (2007). Analysis and implications of the omission of offenders in the DoD care for victims of sexual assault task force report. *Violence Against Women, 13*, 961–970.

Howeing, G. L., & Rumburg, D. (2005). *The defense task force on sexual harassment & violence at the military service academies*. Washington, DC: Department of Defense.

Howlett, D. (1997). Oklahoma families expand victims' rights. *USA Today. March, 21*, 11A.

Hudson, J. E. (1988). Elder abuse: An overview. In B. Schlesinger & R. Schlesinger (Eds.), *Abuse of the elderly: Issues and annotated bibliography*. Toronto: University of Toronto Press.

Hudson, J., & Galaway, B. (1980). A review of the restitution and community-service sanctioning research. In J. Hudson & B. Galaway (Eds.), *Victims, offenders, and alternative sanctions*. Lexington, MA: D.C. Heath.

Huesmann, L. E., & Malamuth, N. M. (1986). Media violence and antisocial behavior: An overview. *Journal of Social Issues, 42*, 1–6.

Humphrey, S. R., & Kahn, A. S. (2000). Fraternities, athletic teams, and rape: Importance of Identification with a risky group. *Journal of Interpersonal Violence, 15*, 1313–1322.

Humphries, D. (2002). No easy answers: Public policy, criminal justice, and domestic violence. *Criminology & Public Policy, 2*, 91–96.

Hunnicutt, G. (2009). Varieties of patriarchy and violence against women: Resurrecting "patriarchy" as a theoretical tool. *Violence Against Women, 15*, 553–573.

Hurd, H. H. (2008). Death to rapists: A comment on *Kennedy v. Louisiana*. *Ohio State Journal of Criminal Law, 6*, 351–365.

Huss, M. T., & Ralston, A. (2008). Do batterer subtypes actually matter? Treatment completion, treatment response, and recidivism across a batterer typology. *Criminal Justice and Behavior, 35*, 710–724.

Hussain, A. (2009). Reviving hope for domestic violence prosecutions: *Giles v. California*. *American Criminal Law Review, 46*, 1301–1321.

Illinois Compiled Statutes. (2012). Chapter 720, 5/12–17. Retrieved on August 29, 2013, from http://www.ilga.gov/legislation/ilcs/ilcs.asp.

International Association of Chiefs of Police. (2001). *Responding to hate crimes: A police officer's guide to investigation and prevention*. Alexandria, VA: International Association of Chiefs of Police. Retrieved on July 9, 2013, from http://www.theiacp.org/tabid/299/Default.aspx?id=120&v=1.

International Association of Chiefs of Police. (2000). *Guide for preventing and responding to school violence*. Washington, DC: International Association of Chiefs of Police.

Internet Crime Complaint Center. (2013). *2012 internet crime report*. Retrieved on December 15, 2013, from http://www.ic3.gov/media/annualreport/2012_ic3report.pdf.

Jacob, B. (1976). The concept of restitution: An historical overview. In J. Hudson (Ed.), *Restitution in criminal justice*. St. Paul: Minnesota Department of Corrections.

Jenness, V., & Grattet, R. (1996). The criminalization of hate: A comparison of structural and polity influences on the passage of "bias-crime" legislation in the United States. *Sociological Perspectives, 39*, 129–154.

Jensen, G. F., & Karpos, M. A. (1993). Managing rape: Exploratory research on the behavior of rape statistics. *Criminology, 31*, 363–385.

Johnson, N. C., & Young, S. D. (1992). Survivors' response to gang violence. In R. C. Cervantes (Ed.), *Substance abuse and gang violence*. Newbury Park, CA: Sage.

Johnson, S. D., & Bowers, K. J. (2005). Domestic burglary repeats and space-time clusters: The dimensions of risk. *European Journal of Criminology, 2*, 67–92.

Johnson, S. D., Bowers, K., & Hirschfield, A. (1997). New insights into the spatial and temporal distribution of repeat victimization. *British Journal of Criminology, 37*, 224–241.

Jones, A. S. (2000). The cost of batterer programs: How much and who pays? *Journal of Interpersonal Violence, 15*, 566–586.

Jones, L. M., Cross, T. P., Walsh, W. A., & Simone, M. (2005). Criminal investigations of child abuse: The research behind "best practices." *Trauma, Violence, & Abuse, 6*, 254–268.

Jordan, C. E. (2009). Advancing the study of violence against women: Evolving research agendas into science. *Violence Against Women, 15*, 393–419.

Jurkovich, G. J., Rivara, F. P., Gurney, H. G., Fligner, C., Ries, R., Mueller, B. A., et al. (1993). The effect of acute alcohol intoxication and chronic alcohol abuse on outcome from trauma. *Journal of the American Medical Association, 270*, 51–56.

Kalichman, S. C., Craig, M. E., & Follingstad, D. R. (1990). Professionals' adherence to mandatory child abuse reporting laws: Effects of responsibility attribution, confidence ratings, and situational factors. *Child Abuse & Neglect, 14*, 69–77.

Kantor, G. K., & Straus, M. A. (1987). The "drunken bum" theory of wife beating. *Social Problems, 34*, 213–230.

Karch, D. L., Logan, J., McDaniel, D., Parks, S., & Patel, N. (2012). *Surveillance for violent deaths — national violent death reporting system, 16 states, 2009*. Retrieved on May 19, 2013, from http://www.cdc.gov/mmwr/preview/mmwrhtml/ss6106a1.htm?s_cid=ss6106a1_w#tab7.

Karp, D. R. (2001). The offender/community encounter: Stakeholder involvement in the vermont reparative boards. In D. R. Karp & T. Clear (Eds.), *What is community justice? Case studies of restorative justice and community supervision*. Thousand Oaks, CA: Sage.

Karp, D. R., & Warshaw, J. B. (2009). Their day in court: The role of murder victims' families in capital juror decision making. *Criminal Law Bulletin, 45*, 99–120.

Katz, J., Tirone, V., & Schukrafft, M. (2012). Breaking up is hard to do: Psychological entrapment and women's commitment to violent dating relationships. *Violence and Victims, 27*, 455–469.

Keldgord, R. (1978). Community restitution comes to Arizona. In B. Galaway & J. Hudson (Eds.), *Offender restitution in theory and action*. Lexington, MA: D.C. Heath.

Kellerman, A. L. (1994). Editorial: Firearm-related violence—What we don't know is killing us. *American Journal of Public Health, 84*, 541–542.

Kelley, B. T., Thornberry, T. P., & Smith, C. A. (1997). *In the wake of childhood maltreatment*. Washington, DC: Office of Juvenile Justice and Delinquency Prevention.

Kelly, D. P. (1984). Delivering legal services to victims: An evaluation and prescription. *The Justice System Journal, 9*, 62–86.

Kelly, D. P. (1987). How can we help the victim without hurting the defendant? *Criminal Justice, 2*, 14–18, 38–39.

Kelly, D. P. (1991). Have victim reforms gone too far—or not far enough? *Criminal Justice, 6*, 22–28, 38.

Kempe, C. H., Silverman, F. N., Steele, B. F., Droegemuller, W., & Silver, H. K. (1962). The battered-child syndrome. *Journal of the American Medical Association, 181*, 105–112.

Key, L. J. (1992). A working typology of grief among homicide survivors. In R. C. Cervantes (Ed.), *Substance abuse and gang violence*. Newbury Park, CA: Sage.

Kigin, R., & Novack, S. (1980). A rural restitution program for juvenile offenders and victims. In J. Hudson & B. Galaway (Eds.), *Victims, offenders, and alternative sanctions*. Lexington, MA: D.C. Heath.

Killias, M. (2010). International Crime Victimization Survey (ICVS). In B. S. Fisher & S. P. Lab (Eds.), *Encyclopedia of victimology and crime prevention*. Los Angeles: Sage.

Kindermann, C., Lynch, J., & Cantor, D. (1997). *Effects of the redesign on victimization estimates*. Washington, DC: U.S. Government Printing Office.

Kinney, L. M., Bruns, E. J., Bradley, P., Dantzler, J., & Weist, M. D. (2007). Sexual assault training of law enforcement officers: Results of a statewide survey. *Women & Criminal Justice, 18*, 81–100.

Kitson, G. C., Clark, R. D., DeGarmo, D. S., Dyches, H., & Rao, N. (1991). *Bereavement in natural and violent death*. Paper presented at the Theory Construction and Research Methodology Workshop, National Council on Family Relations Annual Meeting.

Klanwatch Project. (2011). *Ku Klux Klan: A history of racism and violence* (6th ed.). Montgomery, AL: Southern Poverty Law Center. Retrieved on July 5, 2013, from http://www.splcenter.org/sites/default/files/downloads/publication/Ku-Klux-Klan-A-History-of-Racism.pdf.

Kleemans, E. R. (2001). Repeat burglary victimization: Results of empirical research in the Netherlands. In G. Farrell & K. Pease (Eds.), *Repeat victimization*. Monsey, NY: Criminal Justice Press.

Klein, A. R., & Crowe, A. (2008). Findings from an outcome examination of Rhode Island's specialized domestic violence probation supervision program: Do specialized supervision programs of batterers reduce reabuse? *Violence Against Women, 14,* 226–246.

Klein, A. R., & Tobin, T. (2008). A longitudinal study of arrested batterers, 1995–2005: Career criminals. *Violence Against Women, 14,* 136–157.

Klevens, J., & Leeb, R. T. (2010). Child maltreatment fatalities in children under 5: Findings from the National Violence Death Reporting System. *Child Abuse & Neglect, 34,* 262–266.

Knudten, M. S., & Knudten, R. D. (1981). What happens to crime victims and witnesses in the justice system? In B. Galaway & J. Hudson (Eds.), *Perspectives on crime victims.* St. Louis: Mosby.

Knudten, R. D., Meade, A. C., Knudten, M. S., & Doerner, W. G. (1976). The victim in the administration of criminal justice: Problems and perceptions. In W. F. McDonald (Ed.), *Criminal justice and the victim.* Beverly Hills, CA: Sage.

Knudten, R. D., Meade, A. C., Knudten, M. S., & Doerner, W. G. (1977). *Victims and witnesses: Their experiences with crime and the criminal justice system: Executive summary.* Washington, DC: National Institute of Law Enforcement and Criminal Justice.

Knudten, R. D., Meade, A. C., Knudten, M. S., & Doerner, W. G. (1981). What happens to crime victims and witnesses in the justice system? In B. Galaway & J. Hudson (Eds.), *Perspectives on crime victims.* St. Louis, MO: C.V. Mosby Company.

Kohn, N. A. (2012). Keynote address: Elder rights: The next civil rights movement. *Temple Political & Civil Rights Law Review, 21,* 321–328.

Kolbos, J. R., Blakely, E. H., & Engleman, D. (1996). Children who witness domestic violence: A review of empirical literature. *Journal of Interpersonal Violence, 11,* 281–293.

Konradi, A. (1996). Preparing to testify: Rape survivors negotiating the criminal justice process. *Gender & Society, 10,* 404–432.

Kosberg, J. I. (1988). Preventing elder abuse: Identification of high risk factors prior to placement decisions. *The Gerontologist, 28,* 43–50.

Koss, M. P., & Cleveland, H. H. (1997). Stepping on toes: Social roots of date rape lead to intractability and politicization. In M. D. Schwartz (Ed.), *Researching sexual violence against women: Methodological and personal perspectives.* Thousand Oaks, CA: Sage.

Koss, M. P., & Gaines, J. A. (1993). The prediction of sexual aggression by alcohol use, athletic participation, and fraternity affiliation. *Journal of Interpersonal Violence, 8,* 94–108.

Koss, M. P., & Leonard, K. E. (1984). Sexually aggressive men: Empirical findings and theoretical implications. In N. Malamuth & E. Donnerstein (Eds.), *Pornography and sexual aggression.* New York: Academic Press.

Kothari, C. L., Rhodes, K. V., Wiley, J. A., Fink, J., Overholt, S., Dichter, M. E., et al. (2012). Protection orders protect against assault and injury: A longitudinal study of police-involved women victims of intimate partner violence. *Journal of Interpersonal Violence, 27,* 2845–2868.

Krebs, C. P., Lindquist, C. H., Warner, T. D., Fisher, B. S., Martin, S. L., & Childers, J. M. (2011). Comparing sexual assault prevalence estimates obtained with direct and indirect questioning techniques. *Violence Against Women, 17,* 219–235.

Kruzich, J. M., Clinton, J. F., & Kelber, S. T. (1992). Personal and environmental influences of nursing home satisfaction. *The Gerontologist, 32,* 342–350.

Kübler-Ross, E. (1969). *On death and dying.* New York: Macmillan.

Kuehnle, K., & Sullivan, A. (2003). Gay and lesbian victimization: Reporting factors in domestic violence and bias incidents. *Criminal Justice and Behavior, 30,* 85–96.

Kurki, L. (2000). Restorative and community justice in the United States. In M. Tonry (Ed.), *Crime and justice: A review of research (Vol. 27)*. Chicago: University of Chicago Press.

Lab, S. P., & Clark, R. D. (1996). *Discipline, control and school crime: Identifying effective intervention strategies. Final report*. Washington, DC: National Institute of Justice.

Lab, S. P., & Whitehead, J. T. (1994). Avoidance behavior as a response to in-school victimization. *Journal of Security Administration, 17*(2), 32–45.

Labriola, M., Rempel, M., O'Sullivan, C. S., Frank, P. B., McDowell, J., & Finkelstein, R. (2007). *Court responses to batterer program noncompliance: A national perspective*. New York: Center for Court Innovation. Retrieved on May 18, 2013, from http://www.courtinnovation.org/sites/default/files/Court_Responses_March2007.pdf.

Lachs, M., Psaty, I. F., Psaty, R., & Berman, J. (2011). *Under the radar: New York state elder abuse prevalence study: Self-reported prevalence and documented case surveys, final report*. New York: Lifespan of Greater Rochester, Inc., Weill Cornell Medical Center of Cornell University, & New York City Department for the Aging. Retrieved on June 15, 2013, from http://ocfs.ny.gov/main/reports/Under%20the%20Radar%2005%2012%2011%20final%20report.pdf.

Lamb, M. E., Orbach, Y., Hershkowitz, I., Esplin, P. W., & Horowitz, D. (2007). A structured forensic interview protocol improves the quality and informativeness of investigative interviews with children: A review of research using the NICHD investigative interview protocol. *Child Abuse & Neglect, 31*, 1201–1231.

Lamborn, L. L. (1987). Victim participation in the criminal justice process: The proposals for a constitutional amendment. *The Wayne Law Review, 34*, 125–220.

Lamond, D. A. P. (1989). The impact of mandatory reporting legislation on reporting behavior. *Child Abuse & Neglect, 13*, 471–480.

Langhinrichsen-Rohling, J. (2005). Top 10 greatest "hits:" Important findings and future directions for intimate partner violence research. *Journal of Interpersonal Violence, 20*, 108–118.

Langton, L. (2011). *Identity theft reported by households, 2005–2010*. Crime Data Brief NCJ 236245. Washington, DC: U.S. Department of Justice.

Langton, L., & Baum, K. (2010). *Identity theft reported by households, 2007—Statistical tables*. Washington, DC: Bureau of Justice Statistics.

Lansford, J. E., Miller-Johnson, S., Berlin, L. J., Dodge, K. A., Bates, J. E., & Pettit, G. S. (2007). Early physical abuse and later violent delinquency: A prospective longitudinal study. *Child Maltreatment, 12*, 233–245.

Latimer, J., Dowden, C., & Muise, D. (2005). The effectiveness of restorative justice practices: a meta-analysis. Ottawa, Canada: Canada department of justice. Cited in N. Rodriguez (2007). "Restorative justice at work: Examining the impact of restorative justice resolutions on juvenile recidivism." *Crime & Delinquency, 53*, 355–379.

Lawrence, R. (1990). Restitution as a cost-effective alternative to incarceration. In B. Galaway & J. Hudson (Eds.), *Criminal justice, restitution, and reconciliation*. Monsey, NY: Criminal Justice Press.

LeDoux, J. C., & Hazelwood, R. R. (1985). Police attitudes and beliefs toward rape. *Journal of Police Science and Administration, 13*, 211–220.

Ledray, L. E. (1999). *SANE: Sexual assault nurse examiner: Development and operation guide*. Washington, DC: Office for Victims of Crime. Accessed on April 27, 2013, from http://www.ojp.usdoj.gov/ovc/publications/infores/sane/saneguide.pdf.

Lempert, R. O. (1989). Humility is a virtue: On the publicization of policy-relevant research. *Law & Society Review, 23*, 145–161.

Lerner, M. J. (1980). The desire for justice and reactions to victims. In M. Walker & S. Brodsky (Eds.), *Altruism and helping behavior*. New York: Academic Press.

Levenson, J. S., & Cotter, L. P. (2005). The effect of Megan's law on sex offender reintegration. *Journal of Contemporary Criminal Justice, 21*, 49–66.

Leventhal, J. M. (1999). The challenges of recognizing child abuse. *Journal of the American Medical Association, 281*, 657–659.

Leventhal, J. M. (2001). The prevention of child abuse and neglect: Successfully out of the blocks. *Child Abuse & Neglect, 25*, 431–439.

Levi, B. H., Brown, G., & Erb, C. (2006). Reasonable suspicion: A pilot study of pediatric residents. *Child Abuse & Neglect, 30*, 345–356.

Levine, B. J. (1997). Campaign finance reform legislation in the United States Congress: A critique. *Crime, Law and Social Change, 28*, 1–25.

Levine, K. (1978). Empiricism in victimological research: A critique. *Victimology, 3*, 77–90.

Levitt, C. J., Owen, G., & Truchsess, J. (1991). Families after sexual abuse: What helps? In M. Q. Patton (Ed.), *Family sexual abuse: Frontline research and evaluation*. Newbury Park, CA: Sage.

Levrant, S., Cullen, F. T., Fulton, B., & Wozniak, J. F. (1999). Reconsidering restorative justice: The corruption of benevolence revisited? *Crime and Delinquency, 45*, 3–27.

Lewis, A. (1996). Mr. Clinton's victims. *New York Times*, June 28, A15.

Liberty Mutual. (2012). *2012 Workplace Safety Index*. Retrieved on June 7, 2013, from http://www.libertymutualgroup.com/omapps/ContentServer?c=cms_document&pagename=LMGResearchInstitute%2Fcms_document%2FShowDoc&cid=1138365240689.

Liddick, D. R., Jr. (2000). Campaign fund-raising abuses and money laundering in recent U.S. elections: Criminal networks in action. *Crime, Law and Social Change, 34*, 111–157.

Light, R. J. (1973). Abused and neglected in America: A study of alternative policies. *Harvard Educational Review, 43*, 556–598.

Lloyd, S., Farrell, G., & Pease, K. (1994). *Preventing repeated domestic violence: A demonstration project on Merseyside*. Home Office Crime Prevention Unit Paper #49. London: Home Office.

Lockhart, L. L., White, B. W., Causby, V., & Isaac, A. (1994). Letting out the secret: Violence in lesbian relationships. *Journal of Interpersonal Violence, 9*, 469–492.

Loftin, C., & Hill, R. H. (1974). Regional subculture and homicide: An examination of the Gastil-Hackney thesis. *American Sociological Review, 39*, 714–724.

Logan, T. K., & Walker, R. (2009a). Civil protective order outcomes: Violations and perceptions of effectiveness. *Journal of Interpersonal Violence, 24*, 675–692.

Logan, T. K., & Walker, R. (2009b). Partner stalking: Psychological dominance or "business as usual?" *Trauma, Violence, & Abuse, 10*, 247–270.

Logan, T. K., & Walker, R. (2010a). Toward a deeper understanding of the harms caused by partner stalking. *Violence and Victims, 25*, 440–455.

Logan, T. K., & Walker, R. (2010b). Civil protective order effectiveness: Justice or just a piece of paper? *Violence and Victims, 25*, 332–348.

Logan, T. K., Shannon, L., & Walker, R. (2005). Protective orders in rural and urban areas: A multiple perspective study. *Violence Against Women, 11*, 876–911.

Logan, T. K., Walker, R., & Hoyt, W. (2012). The economic costs of partner violence and the cost-benefit of civil protective orders. *Journal of Interpersonal Violence, 27*, 1137–1154.

Logan, T. K., Shannon, L., Walker, R., & Faragher, T. M. (2006). Protective orders: Questions and conundrums. *Trauma, Violence, & Abuse, 7*, 175–205.

Long, J. G. (2008). Prosecuting intimate partner sexual assault. *The Prosecutor, 42*(2), 20–26.

Lottes, I. L. (1988). Sexual socialization and attitudes toward rape. In A. W. Burgess (Ed.), *Rape and sexual assault, II*. New York: Garland.

Lovett, I. (2013). Neighborhoods seek to banish sex offenders by building parks. *New York Times*, March 10, 20.

Lowenstein, S. R., Weissberg, M. P., & Terry, D. (1990). Alcohol intoxication, injuries, and dangerous behaviors—and the revolving emergency department door. *Journal of Trauma, 30,* 1252–1258.

Luckenbill, D. F. (1977). Criminal homicide as a situated transaction. *Social Problems, 25,* 176–186.

Luginbuhl, J., & Burkhead, M. (1995). Victim impact evidence in a capital trial: Encouraging votes for death. *American Journal of Criminal Justice, 20,* 1–16.

Lundberg-Love, P., & Geffner, R. (1989). Date rape: Prevalence, risk factors, and a proposed model. In M. A. Pirog-Good & J. E. Stets (Eds.), *Violence in dating relationships: Emerging social issues*. New York: Praeger.

Lyon, M. R. (2004). No means no? Withdrawal of consent during intercourse and the continuing evolution of the definition of rape. *Journal of Criminal Law & Criminology, 95,* 277–314.

Maas, C., Herrenkohl, T. I., & Sousa, C. (2008). Review of research on child maltreatment and violence in youth. *Trauma, Violence, & Abuse, 9,* 56–67.

MacDonald, P. (2002). *Make a difference: Abuse/neglect pilot project*. Danvers, MA: North Shore Elder Services.

Macolini, R. M. (1995). Elder abuse policy: Considerations in research and legislation. *Behavioral Sciences and the Law, 13,* 349–363.

Maddock, J. W., Larson, P. R., & Lally, C. F. (1991). An evaluation protocol for incest family functioning. In M. Q. Patton (Ed.), *Family sexual abuse: Frontline research and evaluation*. Newbury Park, CA: Sage.

Maddox, G. L., & Wiley, J. (1976). Scope, concepts and methods in the study of aging. In R. G. Binstock & E. Shanas (Eds.), *Handbook of aging and the social sciences*. New York: Van Nostrand Reinhold.

Maguire, K. (2010). *Sourcebook of criminal justice statistics [Online]*. Retrieved on August 4, 2010, from http://www.albany.edu/sourcebook.

Maguire, K. (Ed.), (2013). *Sourcebook of criminal justice statistics*. Albany, NY: Hindelang Criminal Justice Research Center. Retrieved on June 13, 2013, from http://www.albany.edu/sourcebook.

Maguire, K., & Pastore, A. L. (1996). *Sourcebook of criminal justice statistics 1995*. Washington, DC: U.S. Department of Justice.

Maguire, K., & Pastore, A. L. (2006). *Sourcebook of criminal justice statistics 2005*. Washington, DC: U.S. Department of Justice.

Mameli, P. A. (2002). Stopping the illegal trafficking of human beings. *Crime, Law and Social Change, 38,* 67–80.

Marden, P. G. (1966). A demographic and ecological analysis of the distribution of physicians in metropolitan America. *American Journal of Sociology, 72,* 290–300.

Marquart, J. W. (2005). Editorial introduction: Bringing victims in, but how far? *Criminology & Public Policy, 4,* 329–332.

Marquez, A., & Scalora, M. J. (2011). Problematic approach of legislators: Differentiating stalking from isolated incidents. *Criminal Justice and Behavior, 38,* 1115–1126.

Marsh, J. C., Geist, A., & Caplan, N. (1982). *Rape and the limits of law reform*. Boston, MA: Auburn House.

Martin, P. Y., & Hummer, R. (1989). Fraternities and rape on campus. *Gender & Society, 3,* 357–373.

Martin, P. Y., & Powell, R. M. (1994). Accounting for the "second assault:" Legal organizations' framing of rape victims. *Law & Social Inquiry, 19,* 853–890.

Mawby, R. I., & Walklate, S. (1994). *Critical victimology.* Thousand Oaks, CA: Sage.

Maxwell, C. D., Garner, J. H., & Fagan, J. A. (2001). *Research in brief: The effects of arrest on intimate partner violence: New violence from the spouse assault reduction program.* Washington, DC: U.S. Department of Justice, National Institute of Justice.

Maxwell, C. D., Garner, J. H., & Fagan, J. A. (2002). The preventive effects of arrest on intimate partner violence: Research, policy and theory. *Criminology & Public Policy, 2,* 51–80.

Mayhew, P. (2010). British Crime Survey (BCS). In B. S. Fisher & S. P. Lab (Eds.), *Encyclopedia of victimology and crime prevention.* Los Angeles: Sage.

McCarroll, J. E., Ursano, R. J., Wright, K. M., & Fullerton, C. S. (1993). Handling bodies after violent death: Strategies for coping. *American Journal of Orthopsychiatry, 63,* 209–214.

McClennen, J. C. (2005). Domestic violence between same-sex partners: Recent findings and future research. *Journal of Interpersonal Violence, 20,* 149–154.

McCold, P. (2003). A survey of assessment research on mediation and conferencing. In L. Walgrave (Ed.), *Repositioning restorative justice.* Portland, OR: Willan.

McCold, P., & Wachtel, T. (1998). *Restorative policing experiment: The Bethlehem, Pennsylvania, police family group conferencing project.* Pipersville, PA: Community Service Foundation.

McCold, P., & Wachtel, T. (2002). Restorative justice theory validation. In E. G. M. Weitekamp & H. Kernere (Eds.), *Restorative justice: Theoretical foundations.* Portland, OR: Willan.

McCollister, K. E., French, M. T., & Fang, H. (2010). The cost of crime to society: New crime-specific estimates for policy and program evaluation. *Drug and Alcohol Dependence, 108,* 98–109.

McCormack, R. J. (1991). Compensating victims of violent crime. *Justice Quarterly, 8,* 329–346.

McCoy, H. V., Wooldredge, J. D., Cullen, F. T., Dubeck, P. J., & Browning, S. L. (1996). Lifestyles of the old and not so fearful: Life situation and older persons' fear of crime. *Journal of Criminal Justice, 24,* 191–205.

McDevitt, J., Balboni, J. M., Bennett, S., Weiss, J., Orchowsky, S., & Walbot, L. (2000). *Accuracy of bias crime statistics nationally: An assessment of the first ten years of bias crime data collection: Final report.* Boston: Northeastern University. Retrieved on July 6, 2013, from http://www.jrsa.org/pubs/reports/bjs_bias_crime_data.pdf.

McGarrell, E. F., Olivares, K., Crawford, K., & Kroovand, N. (2000). *Returning justice to the community: The Indianapolis juvenile restorative justice experiment.* Indianapolis: Hudson Institute.

McGillis, D., & Mullen, J. (1977). *Neighborhood justice centers: An analysis of potential models.* Washington, DC: Law Enforcement Assistance Administration.

McGuire, K. A. (1991). AIDS and the sexual offender: The epidemic now poses new threats to the victim and the criminal justice system. *Dickinson Law Review, 96,* 95–123.

McKinney, J. C. (1950). The role of constructive typology in scientific sociological analysis. *Social Forces, 28,* 235–240.

McKinney, J. C. (1969). Typifcation, typologies, and sociological theory. *Social Forces, 48,* 1–12.

McKinney, K. (1990). Sexual harassment of university faculty by colleagues and students. *Sex Roles, 23,* 421–438.

McLaren, J. A., Henson, V., & Stone, W. E. (2010). The sexual assault nurse examiner and the successful sexual assault prosecution. *Women & Criminal Justice, 19,* 137–152.

McLaughlin, E., Fergusson, R., Hughes, G., & Westmarland, L. (2003). Introduction: Justice in the round—Contextualizing restorative justice. In E. McLaughlin, R. Fergusson, G. Hughes & L. Westmarland (Eds.), *Restorative justice: Critical issues*. Thousand Oaks, CA: Sage.

McLeod, M. (1987). An examination of the victim's role at sentencing: Results of a survey of probation administrators. *Judicature, 71*, 162–168.

McMahon, M., & Pence, E. (1996). Replying to Dan O'Leary. *Journal of Interpersonal Violence, 11*, 452–455.

McNally, M. M., & Newman, G. R. (2008). Editor's introduction. In M. M. McNally & G. R. Newman (Eds.), *Perspectives on identity theft*. Monsey, NY: Criminal Justice Press.

McPhail, B., & Jenness, V. (2005). To charge or not to charge?—That is the question: The pursuit of strategic advantage in prosecutorial decision-making surrounding hate crime. *Journal of Hate Studies, 4*, 89–119.

McShane, M. D., & Williams, F. P., III (1992). Radical victimology: A critique of the concept of victim in traditional victimology. *Crime & Delinquency, 38*, 258–271.

Mead, G. H. (1934). *Mind, self and society*. Chicago: Univ. of Chicago Press.

Meeker, J. W., & Binder, A. (1990). Experiments as reforms: The impact of the "Minneapolis Experiment" on police policy. *Journal of Police Science and Administration, 17*, 147–153.

Meiners, R. E. (1978). *Victim compensation: Economic, legal, and political aspects*. Lexington, MA: Lexington Books.

Melton, G. B. (1980). Psycholegal issues in child victims' interaction with the legal system. *Victimology, 5*, 274–284.

Melton, G. B. (2005). Mandated reporting: A policy without reason. *Child Abuse & Neglect, 29*, 9–18.

Melton, H. C. (2007a). Stalking in the context of intimate partner abuse: In the victims' words. *Feminist Criminology, 2*, 347–363.

Melton, H. C. (2007b). Predicting the occurrence of stalking in relationships characterized by domestic violence. *Journal of Interpersonal Violence, 22*, 3–25.

Mendelsohn, B. (1956). The victimology. *Etudes Internationale de Psycho-sociologie Criminelle, July*, 23–26.

Mendelsohn, B. (1976). Victimology and contemporary society's trends. *Victimology, 1*, 8–28.

Mendelsohn, B. (1982). Socio-analytic introduction to research in a general victimological and criminological perspective. In H. J. Schneider (Ed.), *The victim in international perspective*. New York: Walter de Gruyter & Company.

Messinger, A. M. (2011). Invisible victims: Same-sex IPV in the National Violence Against Women Survey. *Journal of Interpersonal Violence, 26*, 2228–2243.

Metropolitan Life. (1993). *Violence in America's public schools*. New York: Louis Harris and Associates.

Meyer, T. P. (1972). The effects of sexually arousing and violent films on aggressive behavior. *Journal of Sex Research, 8*, 324–331.

Mignon, S. I., & Holmes, W. M. (1995). Police response to mandatory arrest laws. *Crime & Delinquency, 41*, 430–442.

Miller, J. (2006). A specification of the types of intimate partner violence experienced by women in the general population. *Violence Against Women, 12*, 1105–1131.

Miller, T. R., Cohen, M. A., & Wiersema, B. (1996). *Victim costs and consequences: A new look.* Washington, DC: National Institute of Justice.

Miller, W. B. (1958). Lower class culture as a generating milieu of gang delinquency. *Journal of Social Issues, 15,* 5–19.

Minot, D. (2012). Silenced stories: How victim impact evidence in capital trials prevents the jury from hearing the constitutionally required story of the defendant. *Journal of Criminal Law & Criminology, 102,* 227–251.

Minow, J. C., & Einolf, C. J. (2009). Sorority participation and sexual assault risk. *Violence Against Women, 15,* 835–851.

Moore, D., & O'Connell, T. (1994). Family conferencing in Wagga Wagga: A communitarian model of justice. In C. Adler & J. Wundersitz (Eds.), *Family conferencing and juvenile justice: The way forward or misplaced optimism?* Canberra, Australia: Australian Institute of Criminology.

Morgan, K., & Smith, B. L. (2005). Victims, punishment, and parole: The effect of victim participation on parole hearings. *Criminology & Public Policy, 4,* 333–360.

Murphy, C. M., & Baxter, V. A. (1997). Motivating batterers to change in the treatment context. *Journal of Interpersonal Violence, 12,* 607–619.

Myers, R. K. (1997). Victim Rights Clarification Act of 1997 affects Victim Bill of Rights Act, Violent Crime Control Act, and rule of evidence. *The Crime Victims Report, 1,* 17–29.

Namie, G. (2007). *U.S. workplace bullying survey, September, 2007.* Workplace Bullying Institute. Retrieved on July 7, 2013, from http://workplacebullying.org/multi/pdf/WBIsurvey2007.pdf.

Namie, G. (2013). *The WBI U.S. workplace bullying survey.* Retrieved on May 15, 2013, from http://workplacebullying.org/multi/pdf/WBI_2010_Natl_Survey.pdf.

Nathan, A. J. (2000). At the intersection of domestic violence and guns: The public interest exception and the Lautenberg Amendment. *Cornell Law Review, 85,* 822–858.

National Archives (n.d.). *Constitution of the United States.* Washington, DC: National Archives. Retrieved on May 13, 2013, from http://www.archives.gov/exhibits/charters/constitution_amendments_11-27.html.

National Association of Crime Victim Compensation Boards. (2007). *Crime victim compensation manager's guidebook.* Alexandria, VA: National Association of Crime Victim Compensation Boards.

National Center for Health Statistics. (2012). *Health, United States, 2012: With special feature on emergency care.* Hyattsville, MD: U.S. Department of Health and Human Services. Retrieved on June 14, 2013, from http://www.cdc.gov/nchs/data/hus/hus12.pdf.

National Center for Health Statistics. (2006). Age-adjusted death rates for leading causes of injury death by year, United States, 1979–2004. *Morbidity and Mortality Weekly Report, 55* (December 22): 1363.

National Center for Missing & Exploited Children. (2012). *2011 Amber Alert report.* Washington, DC: U.S. Department of Justice. Retrieved on May 27, 2013, from http://www.amberalert.gov/pdfs/11_amber_report.pdf.

National Center for Missing & Exploited Children. (2013). *Registered sex offenders in the United States per 100,000 population.* Alexandria, VA: National Center for Missing & Exploited Children. Retrieved on April 26, 2013, from http://www.missingkids.com/en_US/documents/Sex_Offenders_Map.pdf.

National Center for Victims of Crime. (1999). *HIV/AIDS legislation.* Washington, DC: National Center for Victims of Crime. Retrieved on April 26, 2013, from http://www.ncdsv.org/images/HIV-AIDSLegislation.pdf.

National Center for Victims of Crime. (2001). *Civil justice for victims of crime.* Washington, DC: National Center for Victims of Crime.

National Center for Victims of Crime. (2008). *Trauma of victimization.* Retrieved on October 1, 2010, from http://www.ncvc.org/ncvc/main.aspx?dbName=Document Viewer&DocumentID=32371.

National Center for Victims of Crime. (2013). *Landmarks in victims' rights & services. 2013 national crime victims' rights week resource guide.* Washington, DC: U.S. Department of Justice. Retrieved on May 9, 2013, from http://ovc.ncjrs.gov/ncvrw2013/pdf/2013ResourceGuide-Full.pdf.

National Center on Elder Abuse. (2013a). *What is abuse?* Orange, CA: Administration on Aging, Department of Health and Human Services. Retrieved on June 14, 2013, from http://www.ncea.aoa.gov/faq/index.aspx.

National Center on Elder Abuse. (2013b). *Warning signs of elder abuse.* Orange, CA: Administration on Aging, Department of Health and Human Services. Retrieved on June 28, 2013, from http://www.aoa.gov/AoA_Programs/Elder_Rights/YEAP/docs/Fact%20Sheets/AoA-119%20YEAP%20InfoFact%20Sheets_WarningSigns%28nm%291.4c.508.pdf.

National Children's Advocacy Center. (2011). *Forensic interview structure.* Huntsville, AL: National Children's Advocacy Center. Retrieved on June 2, 2013, from http://www.nationalcac.org/images/pdfs/CALiO/2a%202013-fi-structure-sheet.pdf.

National Children's Alliance. (2013). *History of national children's alliance.* Washington, DC: National Children's Alliance. Retrieved on May 22, 2013, from http://www.nationalchildrensalliance.org/index.php?s=35.

National Council on Crime and Delinquency. (2007). *Outcome evaluation of Parents Anonymous: Final report submitted to the Office of Juvenile Justice and Delinquency Prevention.* Oakland, CA: National Council on Crime and Delinquency. Retrieved on June 2, 2013, from http://www.nccdglobal.org/sites/default/files/publication_pdf/outcome-parents-anonymous.pdf.

National Council on Crime and Delinquency. (2008). *Parents Anonymous® outcome evaluation: Promising findings for child maltreatment reduction.* Oakland, CA: National Council on Crime and Delinquency. Retrieved on June 2, 2013, from http://www.nccdglobal.org/sites/default/files/publication_pdf/special-report-parents-anonymous.pdf.

National Domestic Violence Hotline. (2013a). *Am I being abused?* Austin, TX: National Domestic Violence Hotline. Retrieved on October 22, 2013, from http://www.thehotline.org/is-this-abuse/.

National Domestic Violence Hotline. (2013b). *About the hotline.* Austin, TX: National Domestic Violence Hotline. Retrieved on May 17, 2013, from http://www.thehotline.org/about-support/.

National Institute of Neurological Disorders and Stroke. (2010). *NINDS shaken baby syndrome information page.* Bethesda, MD: National Institutes of Health. Retrieved on May 21, 2013, from http://www.ninds.nih.gov/disorders/shakenbaby/shakenbaby.htm.

National Research Council. (2003). *Elder mistreatment: Abuse, neglect, and exploitation in an aging America.* Washington, DC: National Academies Press.

National Sheriffs' Association. (2010). *First response to victims of crime: A guidebook for law enforcement officers.* Washington, DC: Office for Victims of Crime. Retrieved on April 27, 2013, from http://www.ojp.usdoj.gov/ovc/publications/infores/pdftxt/2010FirstResponse-Guidebook.pdf.

National Victims' Constitutional Amendment Passage. (2012a). *State victim rights amendments.* Denver: National Victims' Constitutional Amendment Passage. Retrieved on May 9, 2013, from http://www.nvcap.org/states/stvras.html.

National Victims' Constitututional Amendment Passage. (2012b). *Victims' rights education project "Miranda card."* Denver: National Victims' Constitutional Amendment Passage. Retrieved on May 9, 2013, from http://www.nvcap.org/vrep/NVCANVREPMirandaCard.pdf.

National Violent Injury Statistics System. (2005). *Getting a handle on suicide.* Boston, MA: Harvard Injury Control Research Center, Harvard School of Public Health. Retrieved on September 21, 2010, from http://www.preventviolence.net/pdf/FinalNVDRSUpdate2005.pdf.

Naylor, R. T. (2004). The underworld of ivory. *Crime, Law and Social Change, 42,* 261–295.

Naylor, R. T. (2007). The alchemy of fraud: Investment cams in the precious-metals mining business. *Crime, Law and Social Change, 47,* 89–120.

Neff, J. L., Patterson, M. M., & Johnson, S. (2012). Meeting the training needs of those who meet the needs of victims: Assessing service providers. *Violence and Victims, 27,* 609–632.

Nelson, J. L. (1999). The Lautenberg Amendment: An essential tool for combating domestic violence. *North Dakota Law Review, 75,* 365–390.

Newman, G. R. (2010). Cybercrime: Prevention of. In B. S. Fisher & S. P. Lab (Eds.), *Encyclopedia of victimology and crime prevention.* Los Angeles: Sage.

Newman, G. R. (2008). Identity theft and opportunity. In M. M. McNally & G. R. Newman (Eds.), *Perspectives on identity theft.* Monsey, NY: Criminal Justice Press.

Newmark, L., Bonderman, J., Smith, B., & Liner, B. (2003). *National evaluation of state victims of crime act assistance and compensation programs: Trends and strategies for the future.* Washington, DC: National Institute of Justice.

Nicholl, C. G. (1999). *Community policing, community justice, and restorative justice: Exploring the links for the delivery of a balanced approach to public safety.* Washington, DC: Office of Community Oriented Policing Services.

NIOSH. (2006). *Workplace violence prevention strategies and research needs. NIOSH publication No. 2006–144.* Atlanta: Centers for Disease Control and Prevention. Retrieved on July 21, 2013, from http://www.cdc.gov/niosh/docs/2006-144.

No Author. (1964). Editorial. *Journal of the American Medical Association, 188*(April 27), 386.

No Author. (2009). *Overcoming compassion fatigue.* Retrieved on January 28, 2011, from http://www.pspinformation.com/caregiving/thecaregiver/compassion.shtml.

No Author. (2010). *National crime victimization survey crime trends, 1973–2008.* Washington, DC: Bureau of Justice Statistics. Retrieved on July 12, 2010, from http://bjs.ojp.usdoj.gov/content/glance/rape.cfm.

Norris, S. M., Huss, M. T., & Palarea, R. E. (2011). A pattern of violence: Analyzing the relationship between intimate partner violence and stalking. *Violence and Victims, 26,* 103–115.

Norton, L. (1983). Witness involvement in the criminal justice system and intention to cooperate in future prosecutions. *Journal of Criminal Justice, 11,* 143–152.

Novack, S., Galaway, B., & Hudson, J. (1980). Victim and offender perceptions of the fairness of restitution and community-service sanctions. In J. Hudson & B. Galaway (Eds.), *Victims, offenders, and alternative sanctions.* Lexington, MA: D.C. Heath.

Nugent, W. R., Umbreit, M. S., Wiinamaki, L., & Paddock, J. (1999). Participation in victim-offender mediation and severity of subsequent delinquent behavior: Successful replications? *Journal of Research in Social Work Practice, 11,* 5–23.

O'Brien, R. M. (1985). *Crime and victimization.* Beverly Hills: Sage.

O'Grady, K., Waldon, J., Carlson, W., Street, S., & Cannizzaro, C. (1992). The importance of victim satisfaction: A commentary. *The Justice System Journal, 15,* 759–764.

O'Leary, K. A. (1996). Physical aggression in intimate relationships can be treated within a marital context under certain circumstances. *Journal of Interpersonal Violence, 11,* 450–452.

O'Malley, T. A., Everitt, D. F., O'Malley, H., & Campion, E. (1983). Identifying and preventing family-mediated abuse and neglect of elderly persons. *Annals of Internal Medicine, 98,* 998–1004.

Oberman, M. (2008). Comment: Infant abandonment in Texas. *Child Maltreatment, 13,* 94–95.

Occupational Safety and Health Administration. (2002). *Workplace violence.* OSHA Fact Sheet. Washington, DC: Occupational Safety and Health Administration. Retrieved on January 22, 2014, from https://www.osha.gov/OshDoc/data_General_Facts/factsheet-workplace-violence.pdf.

Office for Victims of Crime. (1997). *Civil legal remedies for crime victims* (2nd ed.). Washington, DC: U.S. Department of Justice. Retrieved on January 22, 2014, from https://www.ncjrs.gov/txtfiles/clr.txt.

Office for Victims of Crime. (1998a). *Providing services to victims of fraud: Resources for victim/witness coordinators.* Washington, DC: Office for Victims of Crime.

Office for Victims of Crime. (1998b). *New directions from the field: Victims' rights and services for the 21st century.* Washington, DC: U.S. Department of Justice.

Office for Victims of Crime. (2002a). *Ordering restitution to the crime victim. Legal Series Bulletin #6.* Washington, DC: Office for Victims of Crime. Retrieved on January 22, 2014, from https://www.ncjrs.gov/ovc_archives/bulletins/legalseries/bulletin6/ncj189189.pdf.

Office for Victims of Crime. (2002b). *Restitution: Making it work. Legal Series Bulletin #5.* Washington, DC: Office for Victims of Crime. Retrieved on January 22, 2014, from https://www.ncjrs.gov/ovc_archives/bulletins/legalseries/bulletin5/welcome.html.

Office for Victims of Crime. (2002c). *Privacy of victims' counseling communications. Legal Series Bulletin #8.* Washington, DC: U.S. Department of Justice. Retrieved on June 3, 2013, from https://www.ncjrs.gov/ovc_archives/bulletins/legalseries/bulletin8/ncj192264.pdf.

Office for Victims of Crime. (2011). *Rising to the challenge: A new ear in victim services.* Washington, DC: U.S. Department of Justice. Retrieved on July 4, 2013, from www.ovc.gov/pubs/reporttonation2011/index.html.

Office for Victims of Crime. (2013). *State victim assistance academies.* Washington, DC: U.S. Department of Justice. Retrieved on May 9, 2013, from http://www.ovc.gov/training/svaa.html.

Office of Justice Programs. (2011). *OJP fact sheet: Hate crimes.* Washington, DC: U.S. Department of Justice. Retrieved on July 7, 2013, from http://www.ojp.usdoj.gov/newsroom/factsheets/ojpfs_hatecrimes.html.

Office of Juvenile Justice and Delinquency Prevention. (1999). *Violence after school, 1999.* Washington, DC: Office of Juvenile Justice and Delinquency Prevention. Retrieved on January 22, 2014, from https://www.ncjrs.gov/pdffiles1/ojjdp/178992.pdf.

Office of the Florida Attorney General. (2010). *Adult/adolescent forensic sexual assault examination.* Tallahassee: State of Florida. Retrieved on April 27, 2013, from http://www.fdle.state.fl.us/Content/getdoc/95f78ee8-12f4-4661-a451-d2803857f66e/A--Z-Site-Index.aspx.

Office of the Florida Attorney General. (2013). *Victim services practitioner designation requirements.* Tallahassee: Victim Services Professional Development Program. Retrieved on May 10, 2013, from http://www.fcpti.com/fcpti.nsf/pics/CFA429865A4BF438852579D70058A8D4/$file/ATT7J2TQ.pdf.

Office of the Press Secretary. (2013a). *Presidential proclamation – National Child Abuse Prevention Month, 2013, March 29.* Washington DC: The White House. Retrieved on May 20, 2013, from http://www.whitehouse.gov/the-press-office/2013/03/29/presidential-proclamation-national-child-abuse-prevention-month-2013.

Office of the Press Secretary. (2013b). *Presidential proclamation — National Crime Victims' Week, 2013, April 20.* Washington, DC: The White House. Retrieved on May 9, 2013, from http://www.whitehouse.gov/the-press-office/2013/04/20/presidential-proclamation-national-crime-victims-rights-week-2013.

Office of the U.S. Attorney General. (2012). *Attorney General guidelines for victim and witness assistance*. Washington, DC: U.S. Department of Justice. Retrieved on May 10, 2013, from http://www.justice.gov/olp/pdf/ag_guidelines2012.pdf.

Office on Violence Against Women. (2013). *What is domestic violence?* Washington, DC: U.S. Department of Justice. Retrieved on May 13, 2013, from http://www.ovw.usdoj.gov/domviolence.htm.

Ohio Revised Code. (2013). http://codes.ohio.gov/orc/2903.34.

Olweus, D. (1994). Bullying at school: Basic facts and effects of a school-based intervention program. *Journal of Child Psychology and Psychiatry and Allied Disciplines, 35*, 1171–1190.

Olweus, D. (1995). Bullying or peer abuse at school: Facts and intervention. *Current Directions in Psychological Science, 4*, 196–200.

Orcutt, J. D., & Faison, R. (1988). Sex-role attitude change and reporting of rape victimization, 1973–1985. *Sociological Quarterly, 2*, 589–604.

Orr, D. A. (2000). *Weiand v. State* and battered spouse syndrome: The toothless tigress can now roar. *Florida Bar Journal, 74*, 14–20.

Owen, G., & Steele, N. M. (1991). Incest offenders after treatment. In M. Q. Patton (Ed.), *Family sexual abuse: Frontline research and evaluation*. Newbury Park, CA: Sage.

Pagelow, M. D. (1984). *Family violence*. New York: Greenwood Press.

Pagelow, M. D. (1992). Adult victims of domestic violence: Battered women. *Journal of Interpersonal Violence, 7*, 87–120.

Pagelow, M. D. (1993). Response to Hamberger's comments. *Journal of Interpersonal Violence, 8*, 137–139.

Pallone, N. J. (2003). Without plea bargaining Megan Kanka would be alive today. *Criminology & Public Policy, 3*, 83–96.

Palusci, V. J., Yager, S., & Covington, T. M. (2010). Effects of a citizens review panel in preventing child maltreatment fatalities. *Child Abuse & Neglect, 34*, 324–331.

Parent, D. G., Auerbach, B., & Carlson, K. E. (1992). *Compensating crime victims: A summary of policies and practices*. Washington, DC: U.S. Department of Justice.

Parents Anonymous® Inc. (2013). *Adult group*. Claremont, CA: Parents Anonymous® Inc. Retrieved on May 22, 2013, from http://parentsanonymous.org/programs/parents-anonymous-groups/adult-group/.

Parker, R. N. (1989). Poverty, subculture of violence, and type of homicide. *Social Forces, 67*, 983–1007.

Parker, R. N., & Smith, M. D. (1979). Deterrence, poverty, and type of homicide. *American Journal of Sociology, 85*, 614–624.

Parnas, R. I. (1967). The police response to the domestic disturbance. *Wisconsin Law Review, 31*, 914–960.

Parry, J. K., & Thornwall, J. (1992). Death of a father. *Death Studies, 16*, 173–181.

Parsonage, W. H., Bernat, F. P., & Helfgott, J. (1994). Victim impact testimony and Pennsylvania's parole decision making process: A pilot study. *Criminal Justice Policy Review, 6*, 187–206.

Paternoster, R., & Deise, J. (2011). A heavy thumb on the scale: The effect of victim impact evidence on capital decision making. *Criminology, 49*, 129–161.

Patterson, D. (2011a). The linkage between secondary victimization by law enforcement and rape case outcomes. *Journal of Interpersonal Violence, 26*, 327–347.

Patterson, D. (2011b). The impact of detectives' manner of questioning on rape victims' disclosure. *Violence Against Women, 17*, 1349–1373.

Paulsen, D. J. (2003). Murder in black and white: The newspaper coverage of homicide in Houston. *Homicide Studies, 7*, 289–317.

Payne, B. K. (2010). Understanding elder sexual abuse and the criminal justice system's response: Comparisons to elder physical abuse. *Justice Quarterly, 27,* 206–224.

Payne, B. K. (2011). *Crime and elder abuse: An integrated perspective* (3rd ed.). Springfield, IL: Charles C. Thomas Publisher, Ltd.

Payne, B. K., & Fletcher, L. B. (2005). Elder abuse in nursing homes: Prevention and resolution strategies and barriers. *Journal of Criminal Justice, 33,* 119–125.

Payne, B. K., & Gainey, R. R. (2005). Differentiating self-neglect as a type of elder mistreatment: How do these cases compare to traditional types of elder mistreatment? *Journal of Elder Abuse & Neglect, 17,* 21–36.

Pearlman, L. A., & Saakvitne, K. W. (1995). *Trauma and the therapist: Countertransference and vicarious traumatization in psychotherapy with incest survivors.* New York: W. W. Norton.

Pease, K. (1998). *Repeat victimization: Taking stock.* Crime Detection and Prevention Series, Paper 90. London: Home Office.

Penick, B. K., & Owens, M. B., III (1976). *Surveying crime: Panel for evaluation of crime surveys.* Washington, DC: National Academy of Sciences.

Pertman, A., & Deoudes, G. (2008). Comment: Evan B. Donaldson Adoption Institute response. *Child Maltreatment, 13,* 98–100.

Peterson, R. R., & Dixon, J. (2005). Court oversight and conviction under mandatory and non-mandatory domestic violence case filing policies. *Criminology & Public Policy, 4,* 535–558.

Pfohl, S. J. (1977). The "discovery" of child abuse. *Social Problems, 24,* 310–323.

Phillip, D. J. (2011). Texas executes white supremacist for 1998 dragging death of James Byrd Jr. in Jasper. *The Dallas Morning News,* September 22. Retrieved on July 8, 2013, from http://www.dallasnews.com/news/state/headlines/20110921-white-supremacist-executed-for-dragging-death-of-james-byrd-jr..ece.

Phillips, A. (2005). Child forensic interviews after *Crawford v. Washington*: Testimonial or not? *Half A Nation,* (Fall), 1–8.

Phillips, D. P. (1982). The impact of fictional television stories on U.S. adult fatalities: New evidence on the effect of mass media on violence. *American Journal of Sociology, 87,* 1340–1359.

Phillips, D. P. (1983). The impact of mass media violence on U.S. homicides. *American Sociological Review, 48,* 560–568.

Phillips, L. E. (1986). Theoretical explanations of elder abuse: Competing hypotheses and unresolved issues. In K. A. Pillemer & R. S. Wolf (Eds.), *Elder abuse: Conflict in the family.* Dover, MA: Auburn House.

Phillips, N. D. (2009). The prosecution of hate crimes: The limitations of the hate crime typology. *Journal of Interpersonal Violence, 24,* 883–905.

Phillips, S. W., & Sobol, J. J. (2010). Twenty years of mandatory arrest: Police decision making in the face of legal requirements. *Criminal Justice Policy Review, 21,* 98–118.

Phythian, M. (2000). The illicit arms trade: Cold War and post-Cold War. *Crime, Law and Social Change, 33,* 1–52.

Pillemer, K. A. (1986). Risk factors in elder abuse: Results from a case-control study. In K. A. Pillemer & R. S. Wolf (Eds.), *Elder abuse: Conflict in the family.* Dover, MA: Auburn House.

Pillemer, K. A. (1988). Maltreatment of patients in nursing homes: Overview and research agenda. *Journal of Health and Social Behavior, 29,* 227–238.

Pillemer, K. A., & Finkelhor, D. (1988). The prevalence of elder abuse: A random sample survey. *The Gerontologist, 28,* 51–57.

Pillemer, K. A., & Moore, D. W. (1989). Abuse of patients in nursing homes: Findings from a survey of staff. *The Gerontologist, 29,* 314–320.

Planty, M., Langton, L., Krebs, C., Berzofsky, M., & Smiley-McDonald, H. (2013). *Female victims of sexual violence, 1994–2010*. Washington, DC: U.S. Bureau of Justice Statistics.

Platania, J., & Berman, G. L. (2006). The moderating effect of judge's instructions on victim impact testimony in capital cases. *Applied Psychology in Criminal Justice, 2*, 84–101.

Pleck, E. (1979). Wife beating in nineteenth-century America. *Victimology, 4*, 60–74.

Pleck, E. (1989). Criminal approaches to family violence, 1640–1980. In L. Ohlin & M. Tonry (Eds.), *Family violence*. Chicago: University of Chicago Press.

Police Chief's Association of Miami-Dade County. (2009). *Domestic violence protocol for law enforcement 2009*. Miami: Police Chief's Association of Miami-Dade County. Retrieved on May 14, 2013, from http://www.dvsacmiami.org/Committees/LERC/DV%20Protocol%20 for%20Law%20Enforcement%202009.pdf.

Police Executive Research Forum. (2012). *Improving the police response to sexual assault*. Washington, DC: Police Executive Research Forum. Retrieved on April 30, 2013, from http://policeforum. org/library/critical-issues-in-policing-series/SexualAssaulttext_web.pdf.

Pollak, J., & Levy, S. (1988). Countertransference and failure to report child abuse and neglect. *Child Abuse & Neglect, 13*, 515–522.

Polvi, N., Looman, T., Humphries, C., & Pease, K. (1990). Repeat break and enter victimization: Time course and crime prevention opportunity. *Journal of Police Science and Administration, 17*, 8–11.

Pontell, H. N. (2005). White-collar crime or just risky business? The role of fraud in major financial debacles. *Crime, Law and Social Change, 42*, 309–324.

Post, L., Page, C., Conner, T., Prokhorov, A., Fang, Y., & Biroscak, B. J. (2010). Elder abuse in long-term care: Types, patterns, and risk factors. *Research on Aging, 32*, 323–348.

Poythress, E. L., Burnett, J., Naik, A. D., Pickens, S., & Dyer, C. B. (2006). Severe self-neglect: An epidemiological and historical perspective. *Journal of Elder Abuse & Neglect, 18*, 5–12.

President's Task Force on Victims of Crime. (1982). *Final report*. Washington, DC: U.S. Government Printing Office.

Prevent Child Abuse America. (2003). *Resolution 11.14.02 resolution on home visitation*. Chicago: Prevent Child Abuse America. Retrieved on May 22, 2013, from http://www. preventchildabuse.org/advocacy/downloads/PCAA_RES_HOME_VISITATION.pdf.

Prevent Child Abuse America. (2013). *Home*. Chicago: Prevent Child Abuse America. Retrieved on May 22, 2013, from http://www.preventchildabuse.org/index.php.

Price, B. J., & Rosenbaum, A. (2009). Batterer intervention programs: A report from the field. *Violence and Victims, 24*, 757–770.

Pridemore, W. A. (2000). An empirical examination of commutations and executions in post-*Furman* capital cases. *Justice Quarterly, 17*, 159–183.

Pruitt, S. L. (2008). The number of illegally abandoned and legally surrendered newborns in the state of Texas, estimated from news stories, 1996–2006. *Child Maltreatment, 13*, 89–93.

Pumphrey-Gordon, J. E., & Gross, A. M. (2007). Alcohol consumption and females' recognition in response to date rape risk: The role of sex-related alcohol expectancies. *Journal of Family Violence, 22*, 475–485.

Quinn, M. J. (1990). Elder abuse and neglect: Treatment issues. In S. M. Stith, M. B. Williams & K. Rosen (Eds.), *Violence hits home*. New York: Springer.

Quinn, M. J., & Tomita, S. K. (1986). *Elder abuse and neglect: Causes, diagnosis and intervention strategies*. New York: Springer.

Quinn, M. J., & Tomita, S. K. (1997). *Elder abuse and neglect: Causes, diagnosis and intervention strategies* (2nd ed.). New York: Springer.

Rand, M. R. (2009). *Criminal victimization, 2008*. Washington, DC: Bureau of Justice Statistics.

Rand, M. R. (2010). National crime victimization survey, supplements. In B. S. Fisher & S. P. Lab (Eds.), *Encyclopedia of victimology and crime prevention*. Los Angeles: Sage.

Rand, M. R., Lynch, J. P., & Cantor, D. (1997). *Criminal victimization, 1973–95*. Washington, DC: U.S. Bureau of Justice Statistics.

Range, L. M., & Niss, N. M. (1990). Long-term bereavement from suicide, homicide, accidents, and natural deaths. *Death Studies, 14*, 423–433.

Ranish, D. R., & Shichor, D. (1985). The victim's role in the penal process: Recent developments in California. *Federal Probation, 49*, 50–57.

Rantala, R. R. (2008). *Cybercrime against businesses, 2005*. Washington, DC: Bureau of Justice Statistics.

Regehr, C., Hill, J., Goldberg, G., & Hughes, J. (2003). Postmortem inquiries and trauma responses in paramedics and firefighters. *Journal of Interpersonal Violence, 18*, 607–622.

Reichel, P., & Seyfrit, C. (1984). A peer jury in juvenile court. *Crime and Delinquency, 30*, 423–438.

Rennison, C. M. (2010). National Crime Victimization Survey (NCVS). In B. S. Fisher & S. P. Lab (Eds.), *Encyclopedia of victimology and crime prevention*. Los Angeles: Sage.

Resick, P. A. (1990). Victims of sexual assault. In A. J. Lurigio, W. G. Skogan & R. C. Davis (Eds.), *Victims of crime: Problems, policies, and programs*. Newbury Park, CA: Sage.

Reskin, B., & Campbell, F. (1976). Physician distribution across metropolitan areas. *American Journal of Sociology, 79*, 981–988.

Rich, J. A., & Grey, C. M. (2005). Pathways to recurrent trauma among young black men: Traumatic stress, substance use, and the code of the street. *American Journal of Public Health, 95*, 816–824.

Riedel, M., Zahn, M. A., & Mock, L. F. (1985). *The nature and patterns of American homicide*. Washington, DC: U.S. Department of Justice.

Riger, S., & Staggs, S. L. (2011). A nationwide survey of state-mandated evaluation practices for domestic violence agencies. *Journal of Interpersonal Violence, 26*, 50–70.

Ringwalt, C. L., Messerschmidt, P., Graham, L., & Collins, J. (1992). *Youth's victimization experiences, fear of attack or harm, and school avoidance behaviors. Final report*. Washington, DC: National Institute of Justice.

Rinkle, V. (1989). Federal initiatives. In R. Filinson & S. R. Ingman (Eds.), *Elder abuse: Practice and policy*. New York: Human Sciences Press.

Rivara, F. P., Mueller, B. A., Somes, G., Mendoza, C. T., Rushforth, H. B., & Kellerman, A. L. (1997). Alcohol and illicit drug abuse and the risk of violent death in the home. *Journal of the American Medical Association, 278*, 569–575.

Robers, S., Kemp, J., & Truman, J. (2013). *Indicators of school crime and safety: 2012*. Retrieved on May 16, 2013, from http://nces.ed.gov/pubsearch/pubsinfo.asp?pubid=2013036.

Roberts, K. A. (2005). Women's experience of violence during stalking by former romantic partners: Factors predictive of stalking violence. *Violence Against Women, 11*, 89–114.

Roberts, S., Weaver, A. J., Flannelly, K. J., & Figley, C. R. (2003). Compassion fatigue among chaplains and other clergy after September 11th. *Journal of Nervous and Mental Disease, 191*, 756–758.

Robinson, M. (1998). Burglary revictimization: The time period of heightened risk. *British Journal of Criminology, 38*, 78–87.

Rodriguez, N. (2005). Restorative justice, communities, and delinquency: Whom do we reintegrate? *Criminology & Public Policy, 4*, 103–130.

Rodriquez, M. A., Wallace, S. P., Woolf, N. H., & Mangione, C. M. (2006). Mandatory reporting of elder abuse: Between a rock and a hard place. *The Annals of Family Medicine, 4,* 403–409.

Roehl, J. A., & Cook, R. F. (1982). The neighborhood justice centers field test. In R. Tomasic & M. M. Feeley (Eds.), *Neighborhood justice: Assessment of an emerging idea.* New York: Longman.

Roger, K. S., & Ursel, J. (2009). Public opinion on mandatory reporting of abuse and/or neglect of older adults in Manitoba, Canada. *Journal of Elder Abuse & Neglect, 21,* 115–140.

Rosenfeld, R., & Fornango, R. (2007). The impact of economic conditions on robbery and property crime: The role of consumer sentiment. *Criminology, 45,* 735–769.

Rounsaville, B. J. (1978). Theories in marital violence: Evidence from a study of battered women. *Victimology, 3,* 11–31.

Rosenmerkel, S., Durose, M., & Farole, D. (2009). *Felony sentences in state courts, 2006–statistical tables.* Retrieved on December 16, 2013, from http://bjs.ojp.usdoj.gov/content/pub/pdf/fssc06st.pdf.

Rowley, M. S. (1990). Recidivism of juvenile offenders in a diversion restitution program. In B. Galaway & J. Hudson (Eds.), *Criminal justice, restitution, and reconciliation.* Monsey, NY: Criminal Justice Press.

Ruane, K. A., & Doyle, C. (2007). *Burning crosses, hangman's nooses, and the like: State statutes that proscribe the use of symbols of fear and violence with the intent to threaten.* Washington, DC: Library of Congress, Congressional Research Service. Retrieved on July 5, 2013, from http://www.fas.org/sgp/crs/misc/RL34200.pdf.

Ruback, R. B., & Shaffer, J. N. (2005). The role of victim-related factors in victim restitution: A multi-method analysis of restitution in Pennsylvania. *Law and Human Behavior, 29,* 657–681.

Ruback, R. B., Ruth, G. R., & Shaffer, J. N. (2005). Assessing the impact of statutory change: A statewide multilevel analysis of restitution orders in Pennsylvania. *Crime and Delinquency, 51,* 318–342.

Ruback, R. B., Shaffer, J. N., & Logue, M. A. (2004). The imposition and effects of restitution in four Pennsylvania counties: Effects of size of county and specialized collection units. *Crime and Delinquency, 50,* 168–188.

Rubin, P. N. (1995). *Civil rights and criminal justice: Primer on sexual harassment. National Institute of Justice: Research in Action.* Washington, DC: National Institute of Justice.

Rushing, W. A. (1975). *Community, physicians and inequality.* Lexington, MA: Lexington.

Rushing, W. A., & Wade, G. I. (1973). Community-structure constraints on the distribution of physicians. *Health Services Research, 8,* 283–297.

Russell, D. E. H. (1982). *Rape in marriage.* New York: MacMillan.

Ryan, R. M. (1995). The sex right: A legal history of the marital rape exemption. *Law & Social Inquiry, 20,* 941–1001.

Saltzman, L. E., Mercy, J. A., O'Caroll, P. W., Rosenberg, M. L., & Rhodes, P. H. (1992). Weapon involvement and injury outcomes in family and intimate assaults. *Journal of the American Medical Association, 267,* 3043–3047.

Sample, L. L., & Bray, T. M. (2003). Are sex offenders dangerous? *Criminology & Public Policy, 3,* 59–82.

Sanders, W. B. (1980). *Rape and woman's sexual identity.* Beverly Hills: Sage.

Sandholtz, N., Langton, L., & Planty, M. (2013). *Hate crime victimization, 2003–2011.* Washington, DC: Bureau of Justice Statistics. Retrieved on July 6, 2013, from http://www.bjs.gov/content/pub/pdf/hcv0311.pdf.

Sarri, R., & Bradley, P. W. (1980). Juvenile aid panels: An alternative to juvenile court processing in South Australia. *Crime and Delinquency, 26,* 42–62.

Saunders, E. J. (1988). A comparative study of attitudes toward child sexual abuse among social work and judicial system professionals. *Child Abuse & Neglect, 17*, 83–90.

Scalzo, T. P. (2007). *Prosecuting alcohol-facilitated sexual assault.* Alexandria, VA: National District Attorneys Association. Retrieved on April 29, 2010, from http://ndaa.org/pdf/pub_prosecuting_alcohol_facilitated_sexual_assault.pdf.

Schafer, J. (1996). Measuring spousal violence with the conflict tactics scale: Notes on reliability and validity issues. *Journal of Interpersonal Violence, 11*, 572–585.

Schafer, S. (1968). *The victim and his criminal: A study in functional responsibility.* New York: Random House.

Schafer, S. (1970). *Compensation and restitution to victims of crime.* Montclair, NJ: Patterson Smith.

Schaie, K. W. (1988). Methodological issues in aging research: An introduction. In K. W. Schaie, R. T. Campbell, W. Meredith & S. C. Rawlings (Eds.), *Methodological issues in aging research.* New York: Springer.

Schiff, A. (1999). The impact of restorative interventions on juvenile offenders. In G. Bazemore & L. Walgrave (Eds.), *Restorative juvenile justice: Repairing the harm of youth crime.* Monsey, NY: Criminal Justice Press.

Schissel, B. (1996). Law reform and social change: A time-series analysis of sexual assault in Canada. *Journal of Criminal Justice, 24*, 123–138.

Schlesinger, R. A. (1988). Grannybashing. In B. Schlesinger & R. Schlesinger (Eds.), *Abuse of the elderly: Issues and annotated bibliography.* Toronto: University of Toronto Press.

Schloenhardt, A. (1999). Organized crime and the business of migrant trafficking. *Crime, Law and Social Change, 32*, 203–233.

Schmidt, J., & Steury, E. H. (1989). Prosecutorial discretion in filing charges in domestic violence cases. *Criminology, 27*, 487–510.

Schneid, T. D. (1999). *Occupational health guide to violence in the workplace.* Boca Raton, FL: Lewis Publishing.

Schneider, A. L. (1986). Restitution and recidivism rates of juvenile offenders: Results from four experimental studies. *Criminology, 24*, 533–552.

Schneider, A. L., & Schneider, P. R. (1984). A comparison of programmatic and "ad hoc" restitution in juvenile courts. *Justice Quarterly, 1*, 529–548.

Schneider, A. L., Burcart, J. M., & Wilson, L. A. (1976). The role of attitudes in the decision to report crimes to the police. In W. F. McDonald (Ed.), *Criminal justice and the victim.* Beverly Hills, CA: Sage.

Schneider, A. L., Griffith, W. R., Sumi, D. H., & Burcart, J. M. (1978). *Portland forward records check of crime victims.* Washington, DC: National Institute of Law Enforcement and Criminal Justice.

Schwartz, J., & Gertseva, A. (2010). Supplementary Homicide Report (SHR). In B. S. Fisher & S. P. Lab (Eds.), *Encyclopedia of victimology and crime prevention.* Los Angeles: Sage.

Schwartz, M. D. (2000). Methodological issues in the use of survey data for measuring and characterizing violence against women. *Violence against Women, 6*, 815–838.

Shapiro, C. (1990). Is restitution legislation the chameleon of the victims' movement? In B. Galaway & J. Hudson (Eds.), *Criminal justice, restitution, and reconciliation.* Monsey, NY: Criminal Justice Press.

Shapland, J. (1983). Victim-Witness services and the needs of the victim. *Victimology, 8*, 233–237.

Sheeran, M., & Meyer, E. (2010). *Civil protection orders: A guide for improving practice.* Reno, NV: National Council of Juvenile and Family Court Judges. Retrieved on May 16, 2013, from http://www.ncjfcj.org/sites/default/files/cpo_guide_0.pdf.

Sheley, J. F., McGee, Z. T., & Wright, J. D. (1995). *Weapon-related victimization in selected inner-city high school samples*. Washington, DC: National Institute of Justice.

Shell, D. J. (1982). *Protection of the elderly: A study of elderly abuse*. Winnipeg, MAN: Manitoba Council on Aging.

Shelley, L. (2003). The trade in people in and from the former Soviet Union. *Crime, Law and Social Change, 40*, 231–250.

Sheridan, L., Davies, G. M., & Boon, J. C. W. (2001). Stalking: Perceptions and prevalence. *Journal of Interpersonal Violence, 16*, 151–167.

Sherman, L. W. (1992). *Policing domestic violence: Experiments and dilemmas*. New York: The Free Press.

Sherman, L. W. (1995). Hot spots of crime and criminal careers of places. In J. E. Eck & D. Weisburd (Eds.), *Crime and place*. Monsey, NY: Criminal Justice Press.

Sherman, L. W., & Berk, R. A. (1984). The specific deterrent effects of arrest for domestic assault. *American Sociological Review, 49*, 261–272.

Sherman, L. W., Garten, P. R., & Buerger, M. E. (1989). Hot spots of predatory crime: Routine Activities and the criminology of place. *Criminology, 27*, 27–56.

Shope, J. H. (2004). When words are not enough: The search for the effect of pornography on abused women. *Violence Against Women, 10*, 56–72.

Shulman, L. P., Muran, D., & Speck, P. M. (1992). Counseling sexual assault victims who become pregnant after the assault: Benefits and limitations for first-trimester paternity determination. *Journal of Interpersonal Violence, 7*, 205–210.

Sigler, R. T., & Shook, C. L. (1997). Judicial acceptance of the battered woman syndrome. *Criminal Justice Policy Review, 8*, 365–382.

Sigler, R. T., Crowley, J. M., & Johnson, I. (1990). Judicial and prosecutorial endorsement of innovative techniques in the trial of domestic abuse cases. *Journal of Crime and Justice, 18*, 443–454.

Sikes, A., Walley, C., & Hays, D. G. (2012). A qualitative examination of ethical and legal considerations regarding dating violence. *Journal of Interpersonal Violence, 27*, 1474–1488.

Silverman, S. S., & Doerner, W. G. (1979). The effect of victim compensation programs upon conviction rates. *Sociological Symposium, 25*, 40–60.

Simone, D. (2010). The letter that launched Amber Alert. *The Amber Advocate, 4*(1), 5. Retrieved on May 27, 2013, from http://www.amberalert.gov/newsroom/pdfs/advocate_1004.pdf.

Simpson, S. S., Bouffard, L. A., Garner, J., & Hickman, L. (2006). The influence of legal reform on the probability of arrest in domestic violence cases. *Justice Quarterly, 23*, 297–316.

Skogan, W. G. (1981). *Issues in the measurement of victimization*. Washington, DC: U.S. Department of Justice.

Skogan, W. G. (1990). The National Crime Survey redesign. *Public Opinion Quarterly, 54*, 256–272.

Skogan, W. G., & Maxfield, M. G. (1981). *Coping with crime: Individual and neighborhood reactions*. Beverly Hills: Sage.

Smith, A. (2000). It's my decision, isn't it? A research note on battered women's perceptions of mandatory intervention laws. *Violence Against Women, 6*, 1384–1402.

Smith, A. M., & Foley, C. L. (2010). *State statutes governing hate crimes*. Washington, DC: Congressional Research Service, Library of Congress. Retrieved on July 7, 2013, from http://www.fas.org/sgp/crs/misc/RL33099.pdf.

Smith, C., & Thornberry, T. P. (1995). The relationship between childhood maltreatment and adolescent involvement in delinquency. *Criminology, 33*, 451–477.

Smith, D. L., & Weis, K. (1976). Toward an open-system approach to studies in the field of victimology. In E. C. Viano (Ed.), *Victims & Society*. Washington, DC: Visage Press Inc.

Smith, M. D., & Parker, R. N. (1980). Types of homicide and variation in regional rates. *Social Forces, 59*, 136–147.

Smith, R., & Smith, T. (1979). *An evaluation of the Akron 4-A Project*. Paper presented to the Subcommittee on Courts, Civil Liberties, and the Administration of Justice, U.S. House of Representatives.

Smithey, M. (1997). Infant homicide at the hands of mothers: Toward a sociological perspective. *Deviant Behavior, 18*, 255–272.

Smotas, L. (1991). In search of a balance: AIDS, rape, and the special needs doctrine. *New York University Law Review, 66*, 1881–1928.

Snyder, J. A., Fisher, B. S., Scherer, H. L., & Daigle, L. E. (2012). Unsafe in the camouflage tower: Sexual victimization and perceptions of military academy leadership. *Journal of Interpersonal Violence, 27*, 3171–3194.

Society for Human Resource Management and the Ethics Resource Center. (2008). *Ethics landscape in American business survey report*. Retrieved on June 22, 2013, from http://www.shrm.org/Research/SurveyFindings/Articles/Pages/EthicslandscapeinAmerica.aspx.

Soderstrom, C. A., & Smith, G. S. (1993). Alcohol's effect on trauma outcomes: A reappraisal of conventional wisdom. *Journal of the American Medical Association, 270*, 93–94.

Sohn, E. F. (1994). Antistalking laws: Do they actually protect victims? *Criminal Law Bulletin, 30*, 203–241.

Sorenson, S. B., & Shen, H. (2005). Restraining orders in California: A look at statewide data. *Violence Against Women, 11*, 912–933.

South Carolina Attorney General. (2013). *Victim impact statement*. Columbia: South Carolina Attorney General's Office. Retrieved on May 9, 2013, from http://www.scag.gov/wp-content/uploads/2011/03/VictimsImpactStatement.pdf.

Southern Poverty Law Center. (2001). How hate crimes like the killing of Sasezley Ricahrdson are never counted. *Intelligence Report, 104*. Montgomery, AL: Southern Poverty Law Center. Retrieved on July 29, 2013, from http://www.splcenter.org/get-informed/intelligence-report/browse-all-issues/2001/winter/discounting-hate.

Southworth, C., Finn, J., Dawson, S., Fraser, C., & Tucker, S. (2007). Intimate partner violence, technology, and stalking. *Violence Against Women, 13*, 842–856.

Spears, J. W., & Spohn, C. C. (1996). The genuine victim and prosecutor's charging decisions in sexual assault cases. *American Journal of Criminal Justice, 29*, 183–205.

Spelman, W. (1995). Criminal careers of public places. In J. E. Eck & D. Weisburd (Eds.), *Crime and place*. Monsey, NY: Criminal Justice Press.

Spence-Diehl, E., & Potocky-Tripodi, M. (2001). Victims of stalking: A study of service needs as perceived by victim services practitioners. *Journal of Interpersonal Violence, 16*, 86–94.

Spencer, B. J. (1987). A crime victim's views on a constitutional amendment for victims. *The Wayne Law Review, 34*, 1–6.

Spinetta, J. J., & Rigler, D. (1972). The child-abusing parent: A psychological review. *Psychological Bulletin, 77*, 296–304.

Spohn, C., & Horney, J. (1990). A case of unrealistic expectations: The impact of rape reform legislation in Illinois. *Criminal Justice Policy Review, 4*, 1–18.

Spohn, C., & Spears, J. (1996). The effect of offender and victim characteristics on sexual assault case processing decisions. *Justice Quarterly, 13*, 649–680.

Sproles, E. T., III (1985). *The evaluation and management of rape and sexual abuse: A physician's guide*. Rockville, MD: U.S. National Center for Prevention and Control of Rape.

Stafford, M., & Galle, O. R. (1984). Victimization rates, exposure to risk, and fear of crime. *Criminology, 22*, 173–185.

Stalans, L. J., & Lurigio, A. J. (1995). Responding to domestic violence against women. *Crime & Delinquency, 41*, 387–398.

Stanford, R. M., & Mowry, B. L. (1990). Domestic disturbance danger rate. *Journal of Police Science and Administration, 17*, 244–249.

Stanley, J. L., Bartholomew, K., Taylor, T., Oram, D., & Landolt, M. (2006). Intimate violence in male same-sex relationships. *Journal of Family Violence, 21*, 31–41.

State of Nevada Advisory Council for Prosecuting Attorneys. (2006). *Nevada domestic violence prosecution best practice guidelines*. Reno: State of Nevada Advisory Council for Prosecuting Attorneys. Retrieved on May 16, 2013, from http://nvpac.nv.gov/uploadedFiles/nvpacnvgov/Content/Resources/DV_Best_Practice_Guidelines.pdf.

Stearns, P. J. (1986). Old age family conflict: The perspective of the past. In K. A. Pillemer & R. S. Wolf (Eds.), *Elder abuse: Conflict in the family*. Dover, MA: Auburn House.

Steele, B. F., & Pollock, C. B. (1974). A psychiatric study of parents who abuse infants and small children. In R. E. Helfer & C. H. Kempe (Eds.), *The battered child* (2nd ed.). Chicago: University of Chicago Press.

Steinman, M. (1988). Anticipating rank and file police reactions to arrest policies regarding spouse abuse. *Criminal Justice Research Bulletin, 4*, 1–5.

Steinmetz, S. K. (1977–78). The battered husband syndrome. *Victimology, 2*, 499–509.

Steinmetz, S. K. (1978a). Services to battered women: Our greatest need. A reply to Field and Kirchner. *Victimology, 3*, 222–226.

Steinmetz, S. K. (1978b). Battered parents. *Society, (July/August)*, 54–55.

Steinmetz, S. K. (1983). Dependency, stress and violence between middle-aged caregivers and their elderly parents. In J. I. Kosberg (Ed.), *Abuse and maltreatment of the elderly*. Boston: John Wright.

Steinmetz, S. K. (1988). *Duty bound: Elder abuse and family care*. Newbury Park, CA: Sage.

Stitt, B. G., & Lentz, S. A. (1996). Consent and its meaning to the sexual victimization of women. *American Journal of Criminal Justice, 20*, 237–257.

Stombler, M. (1994). "Buddies" or "slutties:" The collective sexual reputation of fraternity little sisters. *Gender & Society, 8*, 297–323.

Stovall, C. J. (1997). *Statement before the Committee on the Judiciary, United States Senate, Concerning a Constitutional Amendment Protecting the Rights of Crime Victims, on April 16, 1997*.

Straus, M. A. (1978). Wife-beating: How common and why. *Victimology, 2*, 443–458.

Straus, M. A., & Douglas, E. M. (2004). A short form of the revised conflict tactics scales, and typologies for severity and mutuality. *Violence and Victims, 19*, 507–520.

Straus, M. A., Gelles, R., & Steinmetz, S. (1980). *Behind closed doors: Violence in the American family*. Garden City, NY: Anchor Press.

Straus, M. A., Hamby, S. L., Boney-McCoy, & Sugarman, D. B. (1996). The revised conflict tactics scales (CTS2): Development and preliminary psychometric data. *Journal of Family Issues, 17*, 283–316.

Strickland, R. A. (2004). *Restorative justice*. New York: Peter Lang Publishing, Inc.

Stuart, B. (1996). Circle sentencing: Turning swords into ploughshares. In B. Galaway & J. Hudson (Eds.), *Restorative justice: International perspectives*. Monsey, NY: Criminal Justice Press.

Stuart, G. L., Moore, T. M., Gordon, K. C., Ramsey, S. E., & Kahler, C. W. (2006). Psychopathology in women arrested for domestic violence. *Journal of Interpersonal Violence, 21*, 376–389.

Supreme Court of Florida. (2003). *Probate, guardianship, & mental/medical health functional requirements document*. Tallahassee, FL: Office of the State Courts Administrator. Retrieved on June 27, 2013, from http://www.floridasupremecourt.org/clerk/adminorders/2003/forms/Probate%20FRD%20final%202-03.pdf.

Surette, R. (2011). *Media, crime, and criminal justice: Images and realities* (4th ed.). Belmont, CA: Wadsworth.

Suris, A., & Lind, L. (2008). Military sexual trauma: A review of prevalence and associated health consequences in veterans. *Trauma, Violence, & Abuse, 9*, 250–269.

Sutherland, E. M. (1939). *Principles of criminology* (3rd ed.). Philadelphia: Lippincott.

Sutocky, J. W., Shultz, J. M., & Kizer, K. W. (1993). Alcohol-related mortality in California, 1980 to 1989. *American Journal of Public Health, 83*, 817–823.

Swatt, M. L., & He, N. P. (2006). Exploring the difference between male and female intimate partner homicides: Revisiting the concept of situated transactions. *Homicide Studies, 10*, 279–292.

Swisher, K. (1995). Businesses should clearly define sexual harassment. In K. L. Swisher (Ed.), *What is sexual harassment?*. San Diego, CA: Greenhaven Press.

Synovate. (2007). *Federal Trade Commission—2006 identity theft survey report*. McLean, VA: Synovate.

Task Force on Ohio College Campus Safety and Security. (2007). *Report to Governor Ted Strickland*. Columbus: Ohio Board of Regents. Retrieved on July 21, 2013, from http://www.uc.edu/content/dam/uc/publicsafety/docs/TaskForceon CampusSecurityFinalReport.pdf.

Tatara, T., & Cyphers, G. (1998). *The national elder abuse incidence study: Final report*. Washington, DC: The National Center on Elder Abuse. Retrieved on June 15, 2013, from http://aoa.gov/AoARoot/AoA_Programs/Elder_Rights/Elder_Abuse/docs/ABuseReport_Full.pdf.

Taylor, B. G., Davis, R. C., & Maxwell, C. D. (2001). The effects of a group batterer treatment program: A randomized experiment in Brooklyn. *Justice Quarterly, 18*, 171–201.

Taylor, I., & Jamieson, R. (1999). Sex trafficking and the mainstream of market culture. *Crime, Law and Social Change, 32*, 257–278.

Taylor, L. (2000). Patterns of electoral corruption in Peru: The April 2000 general election. *Crime, Law and Social Change, 34*, 391–415.

Teaster, P. B., Dugar, T. A., Mendiondo, M. S., Abner, E. L., & Cecil, K. A. (2007). *The 2004 survey of state adult protective services: Abuse of vulnerable adults 18 years of age and older*. Washington, D.C.: National Center on Elder Abuse. Retrieved on June 15, 2013, from http://www.ncea.aoa.gov/Resources/Publication/docs/APS_2004NCEASurvey.pdf.

Temkin, J. (1996). Doctors, rape and criminal justice. *The Howard Journal, 35*, 1–20.

Tewksbury, R. (2005). Collateral consequences of sex offender registration. *Journal of Contemporary Criminal Justice, 21*, 67–81.

Tewksbury, R., & Lees, M. B. (2007). Perceptions of punishment: How registered sex offenders view registries. *Crime & Delinquency, 53*, 380–407.

Texas Department of Criminal Justice. (2013). *Fiscal year 2012 annual report*. Austin: Victim Services Division. Retrieved on May 10, 2013, from http://www.tdcj.state.tx.us/documents/VSD_Annual_Report_2012.pdf.

The President's Commission on Law Enforcement and Administration of Justice. (1967). *Task Force report: Crime and its impact—An assessment*. Washington, DC: U.S. Government Printing Office.

The President's Task Force on Victims of Crime. (1982). *Final report*. Washington, DC: U.S. Government Printing Office.

Thobaben, M. (1989). State elder/adult abuse and protection laws. In R. Filinson & S. R. Ingman (Eds.), *Elder abuse: Practice and policy*. New York: Human Sciences Press.

Thomas, K. R. (1997). How to stop the stalker: State antistalking laws. *Criminal Law Bulletin, 29*, 124–136.

Thomas, M. P., Jr. (1972). Child abuse and neglect, part I: Historical overview, legal matrix, and social perspectives. *North Carolina Law Review, 50*, 293–349.

Thompson, K. M., Wonderlich, S. A., Crosby, R. D., Ammerman, F. F., Mitchell, R. D., & Brownfield, D. (2001). An assessment of the recidivism rates of substantiated and unsubstantiated maltreatment cases. *Child Abuse & Neglect, 25*, 1207–1218.

Thoresen, S., & Overlien, C. (2009). Trauma victim: Yes or no? Why it may be difficult to answer questions regarding violence, sexual abuse, and other traumatic events. *Violence Against Women, 15*, 699–719.

Thorvaldson, A. (1990). Restitution and victim participation in sentencing: A comparison of two models. In B. Galaway & J. Hudson (Eds.), *Criminal justice, restitution, and reconciliation*. Monsey, NY: Criminal Justice Press.

Tittle, C. (1978). Restitution and deterrence: An evaluation of compatibility. In B. Galaway & J. Hudson (Eds.), *Offender restitution in theory and practice*. Lexington, MA: Lexington Books.

Titus, R. M., Heinzelmann, F., & Boyle, J. M. (1995). Victimization of persons by fraud. *Crime and Delinquency, 41*, 54–72.

Tjaden, P., & Thoennes, N. (2000). *Full report of the prevalence, incidence, and consequences of violence against women: Findings from the National Violence Against Women Survey*. Washington, DC: U.S. Department of Justice.

Toennies, F. (1957). *Community and society (C. P. Loomis, Trans.)*. East Lansing: Michigan State University.

Tolman, R. M., & Weisz, A. (1995). Coordinated community intervention for domestic violence: The effects of arrest and prosecution on recidivism of woman abuse perpetrators. *Crime & Delinquency, 41*, 481–495.

Tomz, J. E., & McGillis, D. (1997). *Serving crime victims and witnesses* (2nd ed). Washington, DC: U.S. Department of Justice.

Toseland, R. W. (1982). Fear of crime: Who is most vulnerable? *Journal of Criminal Justice, 10*, 199–210.

Truman, J. L. (2011). *Criminal victimization, 2010*. Washington, DC: Bureau of Justice Statistics.

Truman, J. L., & Planty, M. (2012). *Criminal victimization, 2011*. Washington, DC: Bureau of Justice Statistics.

U.K. Office of Fair Trading. (2006). *Research on impact of mass marketed scams: A summary of research into the impact of scams on UK consumers*. London: Office of Fair Trading.

U.S. Attorney General's Commission on Pornography. (1986). *Final report*. Washington, DC: U.S. Government Printing Office.

U.S. Attorney General's Task Force. (1984). *Family violence*. Washington, DC: U.S. Government Printing Office.

U.S. Attorneys Office, Northern District of Illinois. (2013). *Victim witness unit: Crime victims' bill of rights*. Chicago: U.S. Department of Justice. Retrieved on May 9, 2013, from http://www.justice.gov/usao/iln/rights.html.

U.S. Census Bureau. (2010). *Statistical abstract of the United States 2009*. Washington, DC: U.S. Census Bureau. Retrieved on June 13, 2013, from http://www.census.gov/prod/2008pubs/09statab/pop.pdf.

U.S. Department of Education. (2013). *Campus security: Data on campus crime*. Retrieved on June 1, 2013, from http://www2.ed.gov/admins/lead/safety/campus.html#data.

U.S. Department of Justice. (2010b). *Criminal victimization in the United States, 2007—Statistical tables*. Washington, DC: Bureau of Justice Statistics. Retrieved on June 13, 2013, from http://www.bjs.gov/content/pub/pdf/cvus0701.pdf.

U.S. Department of Justice. (1986). *Four years later: A report on the President's Task Force on Victims of Crime*. Washington, DC: U.S. Government Printing Office.

U.S. Department of Justice. (2002). *Enforcement of protective orders*. Washington, DC: Office for Victims of Crime.

U.S. Department of Justice. (2010a). *Mass-marketing fraud*. Retrieved on December 6, 2013, from http://www.justice.gov/criminal/fraud/internet/.

U.S. Department of Justice. (2013a). *Guidelines on criteria for issuing AMBER Alerts*. Washington, DC: Office of Justice Programs. Retrieved on May 27, 2013, from http://www.amberalert.gov/guidelines.htm.

U.S. Department of Justice. (2013b). *A national protocol for sexual assault medical forensic examinations: Adults/adolescents* (2nd ed.). Washington, DC: Office on Violence Against Women. Retrieved on April 30, 2013, from https://www.ncjrs.gov/pdffiles1/ovw/241903.pdf.

U.S. Department of Justice. (2013c). *National crime victims' rights week resource guide: New challenges, new solutions*. Washington, DC: National Center for Victims of Crime. Retrieved on July 4, 2013, from http://ovc.gov/ncvrw2013/index.htm.

U.S. Department of Justice. (2013d). *Jurisdictions that have substantially implemented SORNA*. Washington, DC: Office of Sex Offender Sentencing, Monitoring, Apprehending, Registering, and Tracking (SMART). Retrieved on October 23, 2013, from http://www.ojp.usdoj.gov/smart/newsroom_jurisdictions_sorna.htm.

U.S. Government Accountability Office. (2002). *Nursing homes: More can be done to protect residents from abuse*. Washington, DC: U.S. General Accounting Office. Retrieved on June 28, 2013, from http://www.gao.gov/products/GAO-02-312.

U.S. Government Accountability Office. (2010). *Poorly performing nursing homes: Special focus facilities are often improving, but CMS's program could be strengthened*. Washington, DC: U.S. General Accounting Office. Retrieved on June 28, 2013, from http://www.gao.gov/products/GAO-10-197.

U.S. Government Accountability Office. (2011a). *Nursing home quality: Implementation of the quality indicator survey*. Washington, DC: U.S. General Accounting Office. Retrieved on June 28, 2013, from http://www.gao.gov/products/GAO-11-403R.

U.S. Government Accountability Office. (2011b). *Nursing homes: Private investment homes sometimes differed from others in deficiencies, staffing, and financial performance*. Washington, DC: U.S. Government Accountability Office. Retrieved on June 28, 2013, from http://gao.gov/products/GAO-11-571.

U.S. Government Accountability Office. (2012). *Elder justice: National strategy needed to effectively combat elder financial exploitation*. Washington, DC: U.S. Government Accountability Office. Retrieved on June 28, 2013, from http://www.gao.gov/products/GAO-13-110.

Ullman, S. R., Karabatsos, G., & Koss, M. P. (1999). Alcohol and sexual assault in a national sample of college women. *Journal of Interpersonal Violence, 14*, 603–625.

Umbreit, M. S. (1997). Victim-offender dialogue: From the margins to the mainstream throughout the world. *The Crime Victims Report, 1*, 35–36, 48.

Umbreit, M. S. (1999). Avoiding the marginalization and "McDonaldization" of victim offender mediation: A case study in moving toward the mainstream. In G. Bazemore & L. Walgrave (Eds.), *Restorative juvenile justice*. Monsey, NY: Criminal Justice Press.

Umbreit, M. S., & Coates, R. B. (1993). Cross-site analysis of victim-offender mediation in four states. *Crime & Delinquency, 39*, 565–585.

Umbreit, M. S., Coates, R. B., & Vos, B. (2001). *Juvenile offender mediation in six Oregon counties.* Salem, OR: Oregon Dispute Resolution Commission.

Umbreit, M. S., Vos, B., Coates, R. B., & Brown, K. A. (2003). *Facing violence: The path of restorative justice and dialogue.* Monsey, NY: Criminal Justice Press.

United Nations Committee on the Rights of the Child. (2013). *Ending corporal punishment of children.* Geneva: Switzerland. United Nations Human Rights. Retrieved on May 20, 2013, from http://www.ohchr.org/EN/NewsEvents/Pages/CorporalPunishment.aspx.

Uzzell, D. (2012). *AMBER Alert best practices.* Washington, DC: U.S. Department of Justice, Office of Juvenile Justice and Delinquency Prevention. Retrieved on May 27, 2013, from http://www.ojjdp.gov/pubs/232271.pdf.

van Duyne, P. C. (2003). Organizing cigarette smuggling and policy making, ending up in smoke. *Crime, Law and Social Change, 39,* 285–317.

Vandervort, F. E. (2006). Videotaping investigative interviews of children in cases of child sexual abuse: One community's approach. *Journal of Criminal Law & Criminology, 96,* 1353–1416.

Vandiver, D. M., Dial, K. C., & Worley, R. M. (2008). A qualitative assessment of registered female sex offenders: Judicial processing experiences and perceived effects of a public registry. *Criminal Justice Review, 33,* 177–198.

Van Ness, D. W., & Strong, K. H. (2002). *Restoring justice: An introduction to restorative justice* (2nd ed.). Cincinnati, OH: Anderson Publishing.

Van Ness, D. W., & Strong, K. H. (2006). *Restoring justice: An introduction to restorative justice* (3rd ed.). Cincinnati, OH: Anderson Publishing.

Van Ness, D. W., & Strong, K. H. (2010). *Restoring justice: An introduction to restorative justice* (4th ed.). New Providence, NJ: LexisNexis Matthew Bender (Anderson Publishing).

Veevers, J. (1989). Pre-court diversion for juvenile offenders. In M. Wright & B. Galaway (Eds.), *Mediation and criminal justice: Victims, offenders and community.* Newbury Park, CA: Sage.

Viano, E. C. (1979). *Victim/witness services: A review of the model.* Washington, DC: U.S. Department of Justice.

Viano, E. C. (1987). Victims' rights and the Constitution: Reflections on a bicentennial. *Crime & Delinquency, 33,* 438–451.

Villmoare, E., & Neto, V. V. (1987). *Victim appearances at sentencing under California's victims' bill of rights.* Washington, DC: National Institute of Justice.

Visher, C. A., Harrell, A. V., & Newmark, L. C. (2007). *Pretrial innovations for domestic violence offenders and victims: Lessons from the judicial oversight demonstration initiative.* Washington, DC: National Institute of Justice. Retrieved on May 18, 2013, from https://www.ncjrs.gov/pdffiles1/nij/216041.pdf.

von Hentig, H. (1941). Remarks on the interaction of perpetrator and victim. *Journal of Criminal Law, Criminology and Police Science, 31,* 303–309.

von Hentig, H. (1948). *The criminal and his victim: Studies in the sociobiology of crime.* New Haven: Yale University Press.

Vorenberg, E. W. (1981). *A state of the art survey of dispute resolution programs involving juveniles.* Chicago, IL: National Center for the Assessment of Alternatives to Juvenile Justice Processing, University of Chicago.

Wachtel, T. (1995). Family group conferencing: Restorative justice in practice. *Juvenile Justice Update, 1*(4), 1–2, 13–14.

Walker, G. (1990). Crisis-care in critical incident debriefing. *Death Studies, 14,* 121–133.

Walker, L. E. (1979). *The battered woman.* New York: Harper & Row.

Wallace, H., & Kelty, K. (1995). Stalking and restraining orders: A legal and psychological perspective. *Journal of Crime and Justice, 18,* 99–111.

Walsh, A. (1986). Placebo justice: Victim recommendations and offender sentences in sexual assault cases. *Journal of Criminal Law & Criminology, 77,* 1126–1141.

Walters, S., Holmes, L., Bauer, G., & Vieth, Victor (2003). *Finding words: Interviewing children and preparing for court.* Alexandria, VA: American Prosecutors Research Institute. Retrieved on June 2, 2013, from http://www.gacdl.org/zoomdocs/misc/finding_words_2003.pdf.

Wan, A. M. (2000). Battered women in the restraining order process: Observations on a court advocacy program. *Social Science Quarterly, 65,* 681–702.

Ward, R. A., LaGory, M., & Sherman, S. R. (1986). Fear of crime among the elderly as person/environment interaction. *Sociological Quarterly, 27,* 327–341.

Wardell, L., Gillespie, D. L., & Leffler, A. (1983). Science and violence against wives. In D. Finkelhor, R. J. Gelles, G. T. Hotaling & M. A. Straus (Eds.), *The dark side of families: Current family violence research.* Beverly Hills: Sage.

Warner, J. E., & Hansen, D. J. (1994). The identification and reporting of physical abuse by physicians: A review and implications for research. *Child Abuse & Neglect, 18,* 11–25.

Warr, M. (1984). Fear of victimization: Why are some women and the elderly more afraid? *Social Science Quarterly, 65,* 681–702.

Way, I., VanDeusen, K. M., Martin, G., Applegate, B., & Jandle, D. (2004). Vicarious trauma: A comparison of clinicians who treat survivors of sexual abuse and sexual offenders. *Journal of Interpersonal Violence, 19,* 49–71.

Weaver, G. S., Wittekind, J. E. C., Huff-Corzine, L., Corzine, J., Petee, T. A., & Jarvis, J. P. (2004). Violent encounters: A criminal event analysis of lethal and nonlethal outcomes. *Journal of Contemporary Criminal Justice, 20,* 348–368.

Webster, B. (1988). *Victim assistance programs report increased workloads. National Institute of Justice: Research in Action.* Washington, DC: U.S. Department of Justice.

Webster, S. W., O'Toole, R., O'Toole, A. W., & Lucal, B. (2005). Overreporting and underreporting of child abuse: Teachers' use of professional discretion. *Child Abuse & Neglect, 29,* 1281–1296.

Weigend, T. (1983). Problems of victim/witness assistance programs. *Victimology, 8,* 91–101.

Weis, K. (1976). Rape as a crime without victims and offenders? A methodological critique. In E. C. Viano (Ed.), *Victims & society.* Washington, DC: Visage Press Inc.

Weis, K., & Borges, S. S. (1973). Victimology and rape: The case of the legitimate victim. *Issues in Criminology, 8,* 71–115.

Weisel, D. L. (2005). *Analyzing repeat victimization. Problem oriented guides for police.* Washington, DC: U.S. Department of Justice, Office of Community Oriented Policing Services.

Weiss, A., & Boruch, R. F. (1996). On the use of police officers in randomized field experiments: Some lessons from the Milwaukee domestic violence experiment. *Police Studies, 19,* 45–52.

Weisz, A. N., Tolman, R. M., & Saunders, D. G. (2000). Assessing the risk of severe domestic violence: The importance of survivors' predictions. *Journal of Interpersonal Violence, 15,* 75–90.

Weitekamp, E. G. M. (2010). Restorative justice. In B. S. Fisher & S. P. Lab (Eds.), *Encyclopedia of victimology and crime prevention.* Los Angeles: Sage.

Wessler, S., & Moss, M. (2001). *Hate crimes on campus: The problem and efforts to confront it.* Washington, DC: Bureau of Justice Statistics. Retrieved on July 10, 2013, from https://www.ncjrs.gov/pdffiles1/bja/187249.pdf.

Whitaker, C. J. (1989). *Bureau of justice statistics special report: The redesigned National Crime Survey: Selected new data.* Washington, DC: U.S. Government Printing Office.

Whitaker, D. J., Lutzker, J. R., & Shelley, G. A. (2005). Child maltreatment prevention priorities at the Centers for Disease Control and Prevention. *Child Maltreatment, 10,* 245–259.

Whitby, D. (2001). Conspiracy and cover-up. *Crime, Law and Social Change, 35,* 21–41.

Whitehead, J. T., & Lab, S. P. (2009). *Juvenile justice: An introduction* (5th ed.). Newark, NJ: Lexis-Nexis Matthew Bender (Anderson Publishing).

Whitehead, J. T., & Lab, S. P. (2013). *Juvenile justice: An introduction* (7th ed.). Burlington, MA: Elsevier (Anderson Publishing).

Widom, C. S. (1989). Child abuse, neglect, and violent criminal behavior. *Criminology, 27*, 251–271.

Widom, C. S., & Maxfield, M. G. (2001). *An update on the cycle of violence*. Washington, DC: U.S. Department of Justice, National Institute of Justice.

Wieczorek, K. (2010). A forensic nursing protocol for initiating human immunodeficiency virus postexposure prophylaxis following sexual assault. *Journal of Forensic Nursing, 6*, 29–39.

Wilbanks, W. (1984). *Murder in Miami: An analysis of homicide patterns and trends in Dade County (Miami), Florida 1917–1983*. Lanham, MD: University Press of America.

Willis, C. L., & Wells, R. H. (1988). The police and child abuse: An analysis of police decisions to report illegal behavior. *Criminology, 26*, 695–715.

Winslett, A. H., & Gross, A. M. (2008). Sexual boundaries: An examination of the importance of talking before touching. *Violence Against Women, 14*, 542–562.

Wisconsin Coalition Against Sexual Assault. (2011). *Wisconsin adult sexual assault response team protocol*. Madison: Wisconsin Office of Justice Assistance. Retrieved on April 5, 2013, from http://www.wcasa.org/file_open.php?id=203.

Wisconsin Office of Justice Assistance. (2009). *Prosecutor's sexual assault reference book*. Madison: Wisconsin Office of Justice Assistance. Retrieved on April 27, 2013, from http://www.wcasa.org/file_open.php?id=3.

Wolf, R. S., & Pillemer, K. A. (1989). *Helping elderly victims: The reality of elder abuse*. New York: Columbia University Press.

Wolfgang, M. E. (1958). *Patterns in criminal homicide*. Montclair, NJ: Patterson Smith.

Wolfgang, M. E., & Ferracuti, F. (1967). *The subculture of violence: Towards an integrated theory of criminology*. London: Tavistock Publications.

Women Against Violence Against Women. (2013). *Rape myths*. Vancouver, British Columbia, Canada: WAVAW Rape Crisis Centre. Retrieved on April 30, 2013, from http://www.wavaw.ca/mythbusting/rape-myths.

Woodworth, D. L. (1991). Evaluation of a multiple-family incest treatment program. In M. Q. Patton (Ed.), *Family sexual abuse: Frontline research and evaluation*. Newbury Park, CA: Sage.

Woolf, P. D., Cox, C., McDonald, J. V., Kelly, M., Nichols, D., Hamill, T., et al. (1991). Effects of intoxication on the catecholamine response to multisystem injury. *Journal of Trauma, 31*, 1271–1276.

Workplace Bullying Institute. (2010). *Definition of workplace bullying*. Retrieved on July 15, 2013, from http://www.workplacebullying.org/targets/problem/definition.html.

Wright, J. A., Burgess, A. G., Burgess, A. W., Laszlo, A. T., McCrary, G. O., & Douglas, J. E. (1997). A typology of interpersonal stalking. *Journal of Interpersonal Violence, 11*, 487–502.

Wright, J. L. (2012). *Department of Defense annual report on sexual harassment and violence at the military service academies: Academic program year 2011–2012*. Washington, DC: U.S. Department of Defense. Retrieved on April 20, 2013, from http://www.sapr.mil/media/pdf/reports/FINAL_APY_11-12_MSA_Report.pdf.

Wright, L. (1976). The "sick but slick" syndrome as a personality component of parents of battered children. *Journal of Clinical Psychology, 32*, 41–45.

Wright, M. (1991). *Justice for victims and offenders: A restorative response to crime*. Philadelphia: Open University Press.

Wright, R. G. (2003). Sex offender registration and notification: Public attention, political emphasis, and fear. *Criminology & Public Policy, 3*, 97–104.

Wyatt, G. E., & Riederle, M. (1995). The prevalence and contact of sexual harassment among African American and white American women. *Journal of Interpersonal Violence, 10,* 309–321.

Yacoubian, G. S., Jr. (2000). The (in)significance of genocidal behavior to the discipline of criminology. *Crime, Law and Social Change, 34,* 7–19.

Yllo, K. (1999). Wife rape: A social problem for the 21st century. *Violence Against Women, 5,* 1059–1063.

Young, M. A. (1987). A constitutional amendment for victims of crime: The victim's perspective. *The Wayne Law Review, 34,* 51–68.

Younglove, J. A., Kerr, M. G., & Vitello, C. J. (2002). Law enforcement officers' perceptions of same sex domestic violence: Reason for cautious optimism. *Criminal Justice and Behavior, 17,* 760–772.

Younglove, J. A., Nelligan, P. J., & Reisner, R. L. (2009). Victim character evidence in death penalty cases: How many songs is too many? *Criminal Justice Review, 34,* 536–552.

Yun, I., Johnson, M., & Kercher, G. (2005). *Victim impact statements: What victims have to say.* Huntsville, TX: Crime Victims' Institute, Criminal Justice Center of Sam Houston State University. Retrieved on June 25, 2010, from http://www.crimevictimsinstitute.org/documents/vis.pdf.

Zandbergen, P. A., & Hart, T. C. (2009). Geocoding accuracy considerations in determining residency restrictions for sex offenders. *Criminal Justice Policy Review, 20,* 62–90.

Zandbergen, P. A., Levenson, J. S., & Hart, T. C. (2010). Residential proximity to schools and daycares: An empirical analysis of sex offense recidivism. *Criminal Justice and Behavior, 37,* 482–502.

Zaykowski, H. (2010). Racial disparities in hate crime reporting. *Violence and Victims, 25,* 378–394.

Zehr, H., & Mika, H. (2003). Fundamental concepts of restorative justice. In E. McLaughlin, R. Fergusson, G. Hughes & L. Westmarland (Eds.), *Restorative justice: Critical issues.* Thousand Oaks, CA: Sage.

Zellman, G. L. (1990a). Child abuse reporting and failure to report among mandated reporters: Prevalence, incidence, and reasons. *Journal of Interpersonal Violence, 5,* 3–22.

Zellman, G. L. (1990b). Report decision-making patterns among mandated child abuse reporters. *Child Abuse & Neglect, 14,* 325–336.

Zeoli, A. M., Norris, A., & Brenner, H. (2011). A summary and analysis of warrantless arrest statutes for domestic violence in the United States. *Journal of Interpersonal Violence, 26,* 2811–2833.

Zgoba, K. (2004). The Amber Alert: The appropriate solution to preventing child abduction? *The Journal of Psychiatry & Law, 32,* 71–88.

Zgoba, K., Levenson, J., & McKee, T. (2009). Examining the impact of sex offender residence restrictions on housing availability. *Criminal Justice Policy Review, 20,* 91–110.

Zillman, G. L., Bryant, J., & Carveth, R. A. (1981). The effects of erotica featuring sadomasochism and bestiality on motivated intermale aggression. *Personality and Social Psychology Bulletin, 7,* 153–159.

Zingraff, M. T., Leiter, J., Myers, K. A., & Johnson, M. C. (1993). Child maltreatment and youthful problem behavior. *Criminology, 31,* 173–202.

Zoellner, L. A., Feeny, N. C., Alvarez, J., Watlington, C., O'Neill, M. L., Zager, R., et al. (2000). Factors associated with completion of the restraining order process in female victims of partner violence. *Journal of Interpersonal Violence, 15,* 1081–1099.

Zolotor, A. J., & Puzia, M. E. (2010). Bans against corporal punishment: A systematic review of the laws, changes in attitudes and behaviours. *Child Abuse Review, 19,* 229–247.

Index